BASIL HALL

Basil Hall was Professor of Ecclesiastical History at the University of Manchester and then Fellow and Dean of St John's College, Cambridge until his retirement in 1979. He has since been lecturing at the University of Exeter, of which he is an Honorary Fellow.

HUMANISTS
AND
PROTESTANTS

HUMANISTS

AND

PROTESTANTS

1500–1900

Basil Hall

T&T CLARK
EDINBURGH

T & T CLARK
59 GEORGE STREET
EDINBURGH EH2 2LQ
SCOTLAND

First published 1990

British Library Cataloguing in Publication Data
Hall, Basil
Humanists and Protestants
1. Christian doctrine. Influence of humanism, history
I. Title
230'.09

ISBN 0 567 09531 2

Typeset by C R Barber & Partners (Highlands) Ltd, Fort William
Printed and bound in Great Britain by Billing & Sons Ltd, Worcester

Contents

Preface   vii

1   Cardinal Jiménez de Cisneros and the
    Complutensian Bible   1
2   Erasmus: Biblical Scholar and Catholic Reformer   52
3   The Reformation City   86
4   Diakonia in Martin Bucer   127
5   The Colloquies between Catholics and Protestants,
    1539–41   142
6   John a Lasco: The Humanist Turned Protestant,
    1499–1560   171
7   The Early Rise and Gradual Decline of Lutheranism
    in England, 1520–1600   208
8   Puritanism: The Problem of Definition   237
9   Defoe: The Protestant Flail   255
10 'An Inverted Hypocrite': Swift the Churchman   280
11 Alessandro Gavazzi: A Barnabite Friar and the
    Risorgimento   313

For Valerie

Preface

The well-informed will know that the word humanists in the title does not refer to the modern identification of humanism with a belief in human effort and ingenuity rather than religion. This volume is an attempt to examine in depth what the humanist culture of the early sixteenth century could achieve in the two specific instances of the careers of Cardinal Jiménez de Cisneros and of Erasmus, followed by studies which show in varying degrees the influence of this biblical humanism upon Protestantism, for many, if not all, of the earlier converts to Protestantism had shared in the methods and purposes of Erasmus and his supporters. Most of the Reformation cities showed the influence of the humanists; the young Martin Bucer found Erasmus as well as Luther to be the grounds of hope for the future of the Christian Church; the Colloquies urged by Charles V to try to heal the schism which was breaking the unity of the Empire were inspired by the humanist outlook; and the youthful years of that intransigent Protestant Jan Laski were wholly given to admiration of Erasmus which led him to purchase the library of Erasmus at Basel. In turning next to England and the state-ridden Reformation of its Church, Archbishop Cranmer's association with the Erasmian themes in the Henrician court is set within the context of Lutheranism and the English Church.

On moving into the following century of English church history

Puritanism is found to be even stronger than it could become under Elizabeth I, as well as uninterested in Cranmer's intentions and models – this is a Protestant theme needing clarification. In the next century English Protestantism turned to different goals: Jonathan Swift is an example – too rarely thought of in this context by historians – of an Anglican Protestantism that rejected both Puritanism (and the incipient evangelicalism which was its heir) and High-Church Non-Jurors; Daniel Defoe provides an example of what happened in the religion of those who broke from the established Church after 1662 – again a name too rarely thought of in this context by ecclesiastical historians. Both these men share the undeserved dismissal of their claims to religious belief and practice as being insincere or irrelevant to their life's work; and both it can be proposed shared, though indirectly, in the 'reverent scepticism' to be found in Erasmus. The final Protestant variation in this volume is that represented by Alessandro Gavazzi: here is a form of Protestantism which was newly invented without reference to either humanism or the Reformation, by an Italian Catholic priest disillusioned with the Papacy and zealous for what he regarded as his country's freedom (these grounds, however, had also been in part the origins of Protestantism in the sixteenth century). He sought a new form of Christianity, in which he wished to avoid what he thought of as the narrow dogmas of the Protestant missions in Italy, worked out within the movement of the Risorgimento in Italy. This study includes an examination of the religious problems of the Risorgimento, and also looks at what could arise in English-speaking Protestantism when the moderation of biblical humanism had long been lost and anti-Papalism had become the dogma of the ill-informed crowd.

Cardinal Cisneros and the Complutensian Polyglot Bible is wholly new, though it covers the ground of the first two of four Birkbeck Lectures in Ecclesiastical History delivered at Cambridge in 1975. Ill-health prevented these lectures appearing in the form of a book. I hope that this fresh study will go some way now to express my thanks to the Master and Fellows of Trinity College, Cambridge, for inviting me to be their Birkbeck Lecturer that year. *Jan Laski: a Humanist turned Protestant* is a thorough revision and expansion of a lecture given at the Dr. William's Library in 1971. (It would be courteous to the Polish people to state that the L of Laski is the anglicised form of the Polish letter, here represented as an L, with a diagonal stroke running down through the upright from right to left, and pronounced as if it were 'w'.) The subject of the Reformation city seemed in 1953 to call for investigation and I began research on it, but three years later another scholar claimed priority and I abandoned the project. When that scholar produced his book as late as 1969 it proved to be on totally different lines from those I had been pursuing: Bernd Moeller's admirable monograph had appeared in 1962 though it did not follow all the lines I had intended. It seemed to me therefore to be permissible to resume these studies and summarise them in two lectures given at the John Rylands Library in Manchester. These lectures have now been updated and revised. Three of the other studies published here were originally commissioned: *Diakonia in Martin Bucer* for a symposium *Service in Christ* for Karl Barth (this paper was translated and published in a German Journal); the essays on *Swift* and *Erasmus* appeared in collections on those authors. *Lutheranism in England* appeared first in the *Concordia Theological Monthly* St. Louis, Missouri, 1967 and was revised for *Studies in Church History*; the paper on *Gavazzi* was published in *Studies in Church History*, and formed the Presidential address to the Society for the Study of Church History. All the reprinted materials have received additions, corrections and updating, and some have been enlarged or partly rewritten.

I am grateful to the librarians and staff of the following libraries: Cambridge University Library and St. John's College Library; The John Rylands University Library of Manchester; Dr. Williams's Library; The Polish Library, London; The National Library of Wales; The University Library, Aberystwyth; The National Library of Spain, Madrid; the Library of the Complutensian University of Madrid; the Library of the Monastery of El Escorial; the Cathedral Library, Seville; the Municipal Library of Barcelona; the Library of the Waldensian Faculty of Theology, Rome; the Vatican Library and the Archivio Segreto, Rome; the Library of Exeter University.

Acknowledgments are due for permission to republish to the following: Associated Book Publishers Ltd. for *Erasmus: Biblical Scholar and Reformer* from *Erasmus*, ed. T. A. Dorey, Routledge and Kegan Paul, 1970. *The Bulletin of The John Rylands University Library, Manchester* for *The Reformation City*, 1971. Basil Blackwell, Oxford, for '*An Inverted Hypocrite'*: Swift the Churchman, in *The World of Jonathan Swift*, ed. Brian Vickers, 1968; and also for the papers originally published in *Studies in Church History*, *The Early Rise and Gradual Decline of Lutheranism in England (1520–1600)*, 1979; *Puritanism: the Problem of Definition*, 1965; *The Colloquies between Catholics and Protestants, 1539–1541*, 1971; *Alessandro Gavazzi: A Barnabite Friar in the Risorgimento*, 1975. The Epworth Press for *Diakonia in Martin Bucer* from *Service in Christ*, Essays presented to Karl Barth, ed. J. I. McCord and T. H. L. Parker, 1966; and for *Daniel Defoe and Scotland* in *Reformation, Conformity and Dissent*, Essays in Honour of Geoffrey Nuttall, ed. R. B. Knox, 1977. The Friends of the Dr. William's Library for *John à Lasco: A Pole in Reformation England*, 1971.

1

Cardinal Jiménez de Cisneros and the Complutensian Bible

The collection of 'testimonies, memorials, letters and diverse tractates' relating to Cardinal Jiménez de Cisneros in the manuscript section of the Law Library of the Complutensian University of Madrid has the title: 'La historia del Illustrissimo D. F. Francisco Ximenez de Cisneros, Arcobispo de Toledo, Cardenal de Sancta Balbina, Chanciller major de Castilla, Reformador de las Religiones, Inquisidor general, Capitan general de toda el Africa, Conquistador de Orán, Confesor de la Reyna nuestra senora, Gobernador dos veces de España, Fundador del Collegio major de S. Ilephonso, Universidad de Alcalá, y otras obras pios . . .'[1] This is a splendid carillon of titles of achievement, and even so it is not complete, since under 'other pious works' should be included his reform of the moral life and administrative functions of the secular clergy of the Church in Spain, as well as the reform of the regular Orders of clergy, the founding of the University of Alcalá de Henares (Complutum) and the preparation

---

[1] The title page (in the original orthography) is from the collection of materials by the Spanish humanist and historian Alvar Gomez de Castro (who published the life of Cisneros in 1569); it includes a Latin manuscript life of the Cardinal which has additional, or differently presented, matter from that in the published Latin text. There are also many manuscript pieces in Spanish concerning the Cardinal. These materials are in the Law Library of the Complutensian University of Madrid.

there of the first printed Polyglot Bible. This Complutensian Bible
together with the work of the grammarian, biblical scholar and jurist,
Antonio de Nebrija, who was concerned with both that University
and Bible, represent the first flowering in Spain of that humanism
associated with biblical studies usually, but inaccurately, identified
almost exclusively as originating in the career of Erasmus. That an
aging friar, in a country only recently politically united after centuries
of internal war, with a court and nobility more concerned with the
soldier's art than with the arts of life, with universities which were
still immersed in medieval Scholastic methods and indifferent to
linguistic achievements, should have established that Complutensian
University which Erasmus praised as 'flourishing in all kinds of
studies', and worthy to be called 'πάμπλυτον' [rich in all things],[2] and
that Complutensian Bible which Menéndez Pelayo described as
'*monumento de eterna gloria para España*',[3] are not just matters for
rhetorical flourishes from the past or the present, but pose the
historian's question: 'What stirred this extraordinary Cardinal to these
particular achievements?'

This Castilian, born in 1436 and baptised González at Torrelaguna
north of Madrid, had graduated in both civil and canon law after the
usual studies in arts, with some theology, at the University of
Salamanca, and then moved to the curia at Rome as an advocate, and
was ordained to the priesthood there. On the death of his father he
returned to Spain where he opposed the Archbishop of Toledo who
had refused to convey to him the office of Archpriest of Uceda
which had been conferred on him by papal requirement in 1471.
Because of this opposition he was confined first at Uceda then in the
castle of Santorcaz.[4] His stubborn will to hold to his right is
characteristic of the man who held out for several years against the
Archbishop and primate of Spain, using his period of imprisonment
to further his biblical studies and meditation, until eventually he was
released and appointed to be Archpriest at Uceda which he soon
exchanged for a canonry at Sigüenza. However, a career in the
hierarchy of the Church no longer appealed to him after the years of
enforced retreat passing daily hours in prayer and meditation, and
after the period at Sigüenza in which, among other studies, he had
learned Hebrew and Aramaic with a rabbi, Cisneros decided to

[2] P. S. Allen, *Opus Epistolarum Des. Erasmi Roterodami*: 1928, VII, 169, (To Francisco Vergara): Epis. 1876.
[3] Marcelino Menéndez Pelayo. *Historia de los Heterodoxos Españoles* (Biblioteca de Autores Cristianos), Madrid, 1956, I, 777.
[4] Bernardino Llorca, S.J., *Historia de la Iglesia Católica*, (*Biblioteca de Autores Cristianos*), Madrid, 1967, III, 617.

withdraw from the world and become a member of the Order of Friars Minor of the Observance in 1484, and changed his name in religion to Francisco. This did not mean a change in his complex and in some ways contradictory character; he still remained a man of great tenacity of purpose though flexible in attaining his goals; he was severe but could be paternal; he was humble in accepting the standards of St. Francis but indomitable, and he could be as warlike as a crusading hidalgo but knew the value of being pacific when occasion required it; he was suspicious, a product of his training in law, but like a faithful friar he could be trustful. In appearance he was tall and commanding, austere and taciturn, with a sombre gaze; in his presence men felt his great energy and were impressed by his air of courage, something like that of an idealistic soldier.

Such a man could not be left in his quiet retreat and when the Nasrid kingdom of Granada capitulated in 1491 to the Catholic Kings, Isabella and Ferdinand, the Queen on advice called Cisneros to Valladolid to be her confessor, though he refused to live at the court. The Franciscans elected him two years later to the office of Provincial of Castile, which covered most of Spain – no doubt they hoped that this would give them a voice at court. In a sense they were right for, at the request of the Catholic Kings, Pope Alexander VI in 1493 provided a brief and then a bull for the visitation by Cisneros of all the convents of the Franciscans, and, later, of the houses of other Orders to make sure that they were living according to their rules and statutes.[5] This was not a sudden decision, since in 1485 the Catholic Kings made a public declaration that: 'In our kingdoms there are many monasteries and houses of religion, both of men and of women, which are very dissolute and disordered in their life and in their administration . . . from which are born many scandals . . . and evil examples.'[6] They proposed reforms following lines laid down in the earlier 1415 reform by the Franciscan Pedro de Villacreces.[7] The first Archbishop of Granada, Hernando de Talavera, had already begun reforms in monastic life before Cisneros took up this task. There were numbers who resisted since they preferred the disorderly life of the religious houses at this time. An armed riot of friars took place at Salamanca, and about four hundred friars from southern Spain fled to Morocco preferring Islam to having to endure the restoration of the life of poverty, chastity and discipline in Christian

[5] Bernardino Llorca, op. cit., 619, 620. José García Oro, O.F.M., *Cisneros y la Reforma del Clero Español en tiempo de los Reyes Católicos*, Madrid, 1971, 46–7, 185–6, 192–237.

[6] Pedro Sainz Rodríguez. *La Siembra mística del Cardenal Cisneros y las Reformas en la Iglesia*, Madrid, 1979, 21.

[7] García Oro, op. cit., 27–28. Bernardino Llorca, 542.

Spain.[8] In this considerable task Cisneros, who at the request of the Catholic Kings had been made the papal commissioner for these duties, and his delegates, were supported by Ferdinand and Isabella. It was Isabella who in 1495 persuaded Alexander VI to accept Cisneros as Archbishop of Toledo and primate of all Spain and, also by this office, chancellor of Castile. His loyalty to Franciscan simplicity and poverty was maintained in his private life and led him to challenge the luxury and lack of piety of the canons of the cathedral. In spite of their attempt to protest against him at Rome, which he adroitly prevented, he sought to persuade them to return to the Augustinian rule by reasoning with them rather than by applying that peremptory force whcih he had on occasion used in reforming the Orders – he could be a man of peace when occasion required it.[9] Also at the cathedral he provided resources for priests to serve daily for the divine office and the celebration of mass in the chapel of Corpus Christi where the Mozarabic liturgy which had almost disappeared from Spain could be renewed, with the Isadorian Breviary and Missal restored and reprinted. From the wealth of his see churches and hospitals were built by him.

The next stage of his programme of church renewal, closely supported by Isabella, came with the reform of the Church's administration and of the lives of the secular clergy which now engaged his full energy. He established throughout Spain annual synods where a more disciplined piety for both priests and people could be provided for and watched over. The principles of this reform were established by nineteen Constitutions together with a short catechism all aimed at enforcing concern for pastoral care in the priesthood as well as abolishing non-residence; maintaining baptismal registers; providing for the effective and spiritual conduct of public worship and making clear to the people what were the bases of the faith and a moral life. It is strange how little effective work was done in providing priests with manuals of instruction for simple teaching of the laity in view of the numerous conversions of Moors and Jews occurring after the fall of Granada in 1491 – this was to be the cause of numbers of the uninstructed baptised being drawn into the prisons of the Inquisition since they were unaware of what was required of them by their new faith.[10] During the absence of Ferdinand in Italy Cisneros was regent of Spain from 1506 to 1507 (he was also made

[8] For Hernando de Talavera, García Oro, op. cit., 85, 232. For the friars' opposition, Bernardino Llorca, op. cit., 620–1.
[9] García Oro, op. cit., 281 ff. Bernardino Llorca, op. cit., 623.
[10] For this study amid a considerable literature of varying merit the following have been useful: Henry Kamen, *The Spanish Inquisition*, 1968; H. C. Lea, *A History of the Inquisition of*

Inquisitor General in May 1507), and he was again to be chosen regent by the nobles who in spite of their resentment at his restriction of their political activities saw him as the only hope for efficient rule after the death of Ferdinand in 1516. But Charles of Ghent, who came to his kingdom in November 1517 as Charles I, and was to become the Emperor Charles V, coldly postponed a meeting.[11] As the indomitable eighty-one year old Cardinal drew near to death he received the last volume of the Complutensian Bible, now fresh from the press and more important to him than the will of princes, and turning to his close circle of friends said: 'I have done many difficult and costly things up to today for the benefit of the republic but none of these things can compare to this for which you should congratulate me most warmly since today this Bible has set forth all the sources of our religion from which one can drink theological knowledge more purely.'[12]

Cisneros was not only an effective ruler and founder of the Spain of the new age, he also tried to renew the old crusading activity of his countrymen. In 1497 Cisneros visited the monastery of Cardeña near Burgos to see the tomb of the hammer of the Moors, 'El Cid,' Rodrigo Díaz de Vivar, who had conquered Valencia. He ordered the cover of the sarcophagus to be raised while he kissed the bones within for he saw El Cid as not only the representative of Spanish chivalry and the inspiration of a poem from the heroic age, but as one who fought for the faith against Islam.[13] The time came in 1509 when Cisneros raised a Crusade from southern Spain against the wealthy north African Moorish city of Orán which protected the pirates who raided the commerce, and attacked the coastal towns, of Spain. Cisneros wished to attend the army into battle, but he was persuaded by his officers to pray for victory and this he did 'en profunda oración'. That a third of the Moorish population was massacred was no doubt not his fault, though he was soon to introduce the Inquisition there. He urged the army in vain to go on to conquer the strongholds of the Moors up to the Pillars of Hercules (indeed, he dreamed of opposing Islam until the recapture of Jerusalem). In this he was more far-sighted

Spain, New York, 1906–8, 4 vols.; For the *conversos*, Yitzhak Baer, *A History of the Jews in Christian Spain*, Philadelphia, 1966, 2 vols.; Antonio Domínguez Ortiz, *Los Conversos de origen judío despúes de la expulsión*, Madrid, 1957; Miguel de la Pinto Llorente, *La Inquisición Española y las problemas de la Cultura y de la Intolerancia*, Madrid, 1953.

[11] *The Cambridge Modern History*, Cambridge, 1902, I, 370.

[12] Alvar Gomez de Castro, *De Rebus Gestis a Francisco Ximenio Cisnerio*, Alcalá de Henares, 1569, lib. II, 38.

[13] Juan de Vallejo, *Memorial de la vida de Fray Francisco Jiménez Cisneros*, ed. A. de la Torre, Madrid, 1913, 20.

than the king or the army: Ferdinand wanted to follow the Aragonese tradition of war in Italy, and the army wanted to enjoy their spoils at home.[14] This meant that for the next century Spain suffered severely from this failure to follow up the victory of Orán by conquering the Moors of north Africa. Cisneros as in most matters concerning the Church's task had agreed with and urged forward Isabella, and after her death in 1504, he readily followed her policy of compelling Jews and Moors to conformity with Catholic Spain. He rejected the policy of persuasion held by the first Archbishop of Granada, Hernando de Talavera, who sought by understanding and by interest in Arabic studies to win the Moors to accept the Christian faith. For Cisneros the missionary method was to offer baptism or expulsion from Spain, and he who was to become the patron of learning on a vast scale enforced a holocaust of Islamic writings at Granada, although later he protected those *conversos* who had inherited the fulness of rabbinic learning which he needed for the Complutensian Bible while supporting the Inquisition in rooting out heresy.[15]

However, this complex man should not be seen only as a hard ruler and harsh Inquisitor, he was also a man of deep spirituality who, if he had not been called to the service of the state and to the administration of the Church which the Catholic Kings had urged upon him, could have been know to history as one of the company of contemplatives of Spain's new age of saints and a more distinguished writer on the spiritual life with no doubt a strong biblical base than his relative and contemporary, Garciá Ximénez de Cisneros, who unlike the Cardinal, has some columns of approval in the *Dictionnaire de Spiritualité*.[16] This energetic career of church

[14] Carl Joseph Hefele, *Der Cardinal Ximenes*, 2 ed., Tübingen, 1851, 380 ff. follows Gomez closely in the description of the Cardinal before Oran. Baltasar Porreño, *Dos tratados históricos tocantes al Cardenal Ximenez de Cisneros*, Madrid, 1918. (*Vida del Cardenal Don Fray Francisco Ximenez de Cisneros*) the prayer of Cisneros at Orán, 158. This life dates approximately a hundred years later in which considerable reliance is placed on previous writers, Porreño had access to documents and memories during his student years at Alcalá, 'mi madre'. For the wish to pursue 'the Crusade' further, v. A. C. Hess, *The Forgotten Frontier: A History of the Sixteenth Century Ibero-African Frontier*, Chicago, 1978, 38–9.

[15] However, Lea commented that 'we may feel assured that he showed no mercy to those who sought to coin into money the blood of the *conversos*'. Kamen, op. cit., 60. Tarsicio de Azcona, O.F.M., *La Eleccion y Reforma del Episcopado Español en tiempo de los Reyes Catolicos*, Madrid, 1960, 261–2, shows that many, especially the Dominicans, objected strongly to Cisneros becoming Grand Inquisitor. In a letter by Diego de Deza to Ferdinand, Jan., 1507, he complains that Cisneros had been opposing the Inquisition for some years. The letter is bitterly hostile to Cisneros as a man whose attitude was 'gran ofensa de Dios y para la destruccion de la Inquisición' and thereby he would be helping to destroy 'nuestra sagrada fe'. It is to be noted that a while before this Diego de Deza had sequestrated the papers of Antonio de Nebrija, a man so much admired by Cisneros.

[16] For García Ximénez de Cisneros, Sainz Rodríguez, op. cit., 35. Porreño, 4. Porreño described the Cardinal as 'Aficionado a la Sagrada Escritura', and his works '... ansi mismo

reform, of political shrewdness in administration by a leading founder of Spain's power in the sixteenth century, her *Siglo de Oro*, was accompanied by his personal life of deep piety, frugality and indifference to worldly glory. From his passion to make the clergy aware of their proper concern for the people in their charge, and from his hours of meditation and Bible study, from his zeal to compel Islam and Judaism in Spain to submit their Scriptures to the supreme Scriptures of the Catholic Church, from his desire to ensure that the Church's learning was inspiring and irrefutable, came the wish to focus his powerful will on a newly-invigorated training for the priesthood by founding a university in which biblical studies were essential and undertaken in the original languages.[17] To this end he determined to call together learned men in a new kind of academic environment to teach future generations of priests how to confute Judaism from its own sacred language, and in addition to demonstrate that Catholicism understood and accepted the original Greek version of the New Testament as essential to the faith, and did not intend to leave the writings of the Apostles in Greek to the exclusive possession of the Orthodox Church.[18]

Cisneros chose the small town of Alcalá de Henares where there were an archiepiscopal residence for the diocese of Toledo, and a Franciscan convent with a college incorporated in it – perhaps memories of his school days in the town called him as well.[19] Moreover, a predecessor as Archbishop of Toledo, Alonso Carrillo, had obtained in 1459 a bull from Pius II in order to transfer the incomes from certain benefices in the diocese to establish three regents of the *artes liberales* at the college in the Franciscan convent at Alcalá. '... cupiens ut in vinea Domini pullularent plantulae, quae suo tempore amabiles fructus redderent, in oppido de Alcalá de Henares Toletanae Diocesis ...'[20] A close friend of Cisneros had founded the

compuso un tratado muy docto de diversas materias theológicas, como son *De Natura Angelica, De Peccatis* y otras semejantes, cuio original se conserva oy dia, escrito de su propria mano, en el monasterio de nuestra señora de la Salceda, donde fué Guardián'.

[17] Bernardino Llorca, op. cit., 628. Porreño, op. cit., 231 ff. Juan de Vallejo, op. cit., 68, reported that Alonso de Toro, 'learned in sacred theology' who had returned to Spain in 1504 from the university of Paris, gave Cisneros information on the patterns of teaching, organisation and religious life there. His own early biblical studies, the writings of Nebrija, and his student days at the college of San Bartolomé, Salamanca also influenced Cisneros in emphasising the centrality of biblical scholarship.

[18] It should be noted that trilingual professors were appointed and had begun teaching at San Ildefonso before any trilingual college was founded elsewhere.

[19] C. M. Ajo G. y Sainz de Zúñiga, *Historia de las universidades hispanicos*, Avila, 1958, II, (*El siglo de Oro universitario*), 379.

[20] Sainz de Zuñiga, op. cit., 378; the text of the Bull, 584–6.

University of Sigüenza, and perhaps also the Archbishop had remembered the particular qualities of the Colegio de San Bartolomé from his early years as a student at Salamanca. At those synods which he had inaugurated for the reform of the Spanish Church Cisneros had denounced on several occasions the *ignorantia damnosa* of the priesthood: he now went beyond criticism to action and set about founding, 'unum Collegium scholarum in quo theologiae, et juris canonici, ac liberalium artium facultes legi possint', and obtained the necessary bull from Alexander VI in April 1499.[21] Bataillon rightly drew attention to a frequent misunderstanding of Cisneros's purpose, that of assuming that he intended his new University at Alcalá de Henares to be founded as a triumph of humanism.[22] For, to follow the rising star of Italianate humanism which was about to appear in Spain was not his purpose, since his intention was still medieval in principle in continuing the traditional lines on the close religious discipline of theological study and student life. There were changes and new developments but Cisneros would have had no desire to adopt what many Erasmians were to promote which could lead to opposing Church authority. The development of Spanish humanism was bound up with the traditional life of the Church in Spain as this was being repristinated in the reforms of Cisneros.[23] Spain was not Italy, Nebrija was no sceptical Pomponazzi.

The energetic Cisneros, impatient to begin, laid the foundation stone on 14 March 1499 of the Colegio Mayor dedicated to San Ildefonso the monk, doctor of the Spanish Church and former Archbishop of Toledo (607-669), though the building was not to be completed in its plateresque Renaissance style by a later architect until 1543.[24] It was on 13 April 1499 that Alexander VI issued the necessary bull and eventually approved the first set of statutes drawn up by Cisneros when they were prepared in 1510. On the 26 July 1508, after the first students had arrived, the inaugural Mass in the parish Church of Santiago was held, and courses began in October of that year. In 1512 Julius II, upon the urging of Cisneros, agreed that the new university should be granted the privileges of Paris and

---

[21] D. Vicente de la Fuente, *Historia de las universidades, colegios y demás establecimientos de enseñanza en España*, Madrid, 1885, 4 vols., II appendix 13.

[22] Marcel Bataillon, *Erasme et l'Espagne*, Paris, 1937, II. (There is a 'corrected and enlarged' Spanish translation, second edition, Mexico, 1966, but in no passage from Bataillon cited here is any difference shown from the French edition, therefore this is used in these notes.)

[23] V. Beltrán de Heredia, *La Teologiá en la Universidad de Alcalá, Revista Española de Teología*, 1945, V, 168.

[24] Benito Hernando y Espinosa, *Cisneros y la fundación de la Universidad de Alcalá, Boletín de la Institución libre de Enseñanza*, Madrid, (Dec. 1898) XXII, 334–5, 358.

Salamanca which allowed masters and scholars to be exempt from episcopal interference. Cisneros, with variations, based his statutes upon those of Paris where many Spanish scholars were already teaching.[25] Some of these who had studied and taught at Paris were called to teach at Alcalá, for example, Pedro de Lerma who began a course in 1512 on the Ethics of Aristotle, the philosopher most favoured by Cisneros; Gonzalo Gil who taught nominalist theology; and Pedro Ciruelo who though he had taught nominalism at Paris was appointed at Alcalá to the chair of Thomism.[26] The statutes, in memory of the thirty-three years of Christ's incarnation, provided for thirty-three poor students already graduates (bachillers) with bursaries at San Ildefonso. These were to be governed by a rector and three councillors elected annually from among the college members. There were to be twelve chaplains, in memory of the twelve apostles, two were to work at parish churches in the town and ten were of lesser status on a four-yearly basis.[27] The patrons of the College were the King of Castile, the Archbishop of Toledo, the Duque del Infantado and the Conde de la Coruña. The visitor for oversight of good order at the College was chosen by the chapter of the collegiate church of San Just at Alcalá from among their canons, and hospices were to be provided for sick students.[28] The University was based upon the Colegio Mayor of San Ildefonso which took priority over the conventual houses of friars which were soon to be built for members of their Orders to study there, and also over the seven minor colleges which were developed by Cisneros after the university had commenced work – one college of theology, two of philosophy, two for grammar, Greek and Latin, one for medicine, and a hospital college – that these colleges were all for poor students was a special provision made by him. Two citations from the Statutes underline the aims of Cisneros: 'Grammar and Rhetoric are fundamental and the science of all other sciences, and if there are not sufficient preceptors and intensive study herein those students who pass to other studies will do so on a defective foundation'; and trilingual learning is essential because by it 'comes the dissemination of the Word of God by the preaching of the Sacred Scriptures, which must be the principal end of theologians'.[29] An excellent library was

[25] Sainz de Zúñiga, op. cit., 381, for the Papal Privilege. Ricardo Garciá Villoslada, *La Universidad de París durante los Estudios de Francisco de Vitoria 1507–1522*, Rome, 1938.

[26] *Revista de Archivos, Bibliotecas y Museos* (abbrev., RABM) Madrid, A. de la Torre y del Cerro, *La Universidad de Alcalá, Datos para su estudio, cátedras y catedráticos*, 1909, (xx) 416 ff., (xxi), 48–71.

[27] Hernando y Espinosa, op. cit., (*Boletín*, XXII) 357.

[28] Op. cit., 357.

[29] Bernardino Llorca, 632. The insight of the Cardinal on 'the word of God' was not to be

established which eventually, according to Vicente de la Fuente, 'neither the university of Salamanca, nor any other in Spain could rival' and was the most impressive building in the new university.[30] When Francis I, held captive in Spain by Charles V after the battle of Pavia in 1525, visited Alcalá and inquired about the organisation of the university, he said: 'Your Jimenez de Cisneros conceived and carried out that which I never would have the boldness to undertake for fear of failure. The university of Paris, the pride of my kingdom is the work of many kings whilst all this is exclusively that of Cisneros.' At least so Alvar Gómez gracefully renders the no doubt cautiously polished phrases of the captive royal guest.[31] The founding of the trilingual college of St. Jerome in 1528 showed the full impact of biblical humanism in Alcalá, though the university chairs of Hebrew, Greek and Latin had been established long before, with professors who contributed greatly to the Complutensian Bible.[32] The bursaries at St. Jerome provided for twelve students in Latin, twelve in Greek and seven in Hebrew. There was one outstanding omission in the statutes of Alcalá, there was no faculty of civil law. Cisneros was determined to protect his university from the consequences of such studies. His own earlier years had been dominated by them in both the civil and canon laws, and he is reported by Alvar Gómez as detesting the laws and wishing that 'he could disgorge all that he had acquired in this study'.[33] He apparently regarded law students as being too numerous, too ambitious and too concerned with the lust for riches: as has been seen, he provided for attendance by poor students whose only ambitions he hoped would be piety and sound learning in preparation for a dedicated priestly life. He had, of course, to allow canon law to be taught since it was essential to the training of a priest at a university by papal command based on ancient custom. Finally, it is worth remembering that the most solemn festivals of the university were those of the saints' days of the Latin doctors of the Church, St. Jerome, St. Augustine, St. Ambrose and St. Gregory, showing no doubt a desire for the

fully realized until the encyclical of Pope Pius XII, *Divino afflante Spiritu*, and the Constitution *Dei Verbum* of the Second Vatican Council.

[30] Fuente, *Formación y vicisitudes de la Biblioteca Complutense*, *Boletín-Revista de la Universidad de Madrid*, 1870, 25 April.

[31] Eusebio Martínez de Velasco, *El Cardenal Ximénes de Cisneros*, Madrid, 1883, 164.

[32] Hernando y Espinosa, op. cit., *Boletín*, 361; Zúñiga, op. cit., I, 304.

[33] Beltrán de Heredia, op. cit., 169 refers to Gómez, op. cit., fol. 89V., '... neminem ad Ildephonsi admittunt, nisi probe in theologia versatum, aut qui publice aliquam ejus disciplinae peritjam exhibuerit.' Bataillon, op. cit., 14, cites Gomez, fol. 3, V⁰, 'Nam a civilibus et forensibus studiis adeo natura sua abhorrebat, ut multi serio affirmantem audiverint, quicquid illius disciplinae pectore concepisset, se si fieri posset libenter evomiturum.'

recollection of the patristic age with its positive theology rather than the period of Scholasticism and its more recent saints.[34] This brief narrative of what occurred at Alcalá de Henares in the development of the university from 1498 to 1528 provides a frame of reference – it is useful in showing the purposes of Cisneros and in avoiding misleading generalisations.

A greater insight would be provided by focusing attention on the remarkable group of professors who were associated with the Complutensian Bible to show what was happening at Alcalá which made it unique in Spain at that time. A context for these men can be given in an onomasticon of the university teachers who were their colleagues, which will indicate the elements of traditionalism in the university. In addition to the scholars mentioned above as having been trained at Paris and now appointed to Alcalá, there were Miguel Pardo who taught nominalist logic; Agustín Pérez de Oliván who taught physical philosophy; Sancho Carranza de Miranda who taught arts and theology from 1512, and was to become a supporter of Erasmus in the controversy that arose about Erasmianism later;[35] there were three professors for grammar and rhetoric, Juan de Angulo, Juan Jiménez, Hernando Alonso de Herrera; for dialectic there was Luis Pérez de Castelar and for metaphysics, Antonio de Morales; for medicine, Doctors Tarragona, Antonio Cartagena and Bernaldino, these taught in alternate courses from Avicenna and then from Hippocrates and Galen; for canon law Villar del Say y Loranca; for Scotism, the Franciscan Clemente Ramirez. These are mostly forgotten men though some of them occur in discussions of their subject, especially Alonso de Herrera who disliked the terminist logic of Paris and wrote against the stultification of the liberal arts by 'the Aristotelians' – this was a sign of things to come.[36]

The most remarkable names (which will be discussed later) in the first years of the Complutensian university included the first humanist of Spain, Antonio de Nebrija; the hellenist, Hernán Núñez de Guzmán, and the *conversos* Pablo Coronel and Alfonso de Zamora. These were men skilled in the biblical languages who took part in the Cardinal's great work, (*la obra del Cardenal* as the Book of the Treasurer of Alcalá called it) who showed a markedly new direction from the traditionalism of the subjects taught by their colleagues, and

[34] Bernardino Llorca, 630.
[35] RABM (A de la Torre), 1909, 48 ff. For Carranza and Erasmus, v. Bataillon, 131 ff. The University of Salamanca viewed with alarm the establishment of these chairs in theology as well as the linguistic claims; resentment of Alcalá continued there.
[36] A. Bonilla, *Un Antiaristotélico del Renacimiento, Hernando Alonso de Herrera . . .* , *Revue Hispanique*, 1920, 62 ff.

yet without antagonism leading to disruption. This can be contrasted with that university which needed a succession of French kings to establish it, and which would have refused with contumely the admission of the *Lecteurs Royaux*, to its faculties and privileges – the scholars who formed the trilingual college which was to be known later as the *Collège de France*, created by Francis I at Paris in 1530 to satisfy the French hellenist Guillaume Budé and win the approval of Erasmus.[37]

When did Cisneros decide on publishing this Bible in six folio volumes? The record is far from clear and some of the confident assertions of Juan de Vallejo, who pushed confused recollections of a later period at Alcalá to an early date, probably should be set aside. However, Alvar Gómez, took from Vallejo the assumption that it was during the days of rejoicing for a royal marriage during the presence of the Court at Toledo in the summer of 1502 that Cisneros retired to his private apartments in his palace there and began to prepare plans for this Bible, considering the names of scholars to gather about him, and where to obtain sufficiently authentic manuscripts and codices of the biblical texts.[38] Some writers have assumed that it was Nebrija who proposed this enterprise to him, at least in the form of publishing a Bible with corrected texts in the original languages – here Nebrija's fame as a trilingual scholar is carrying more weight than it deserves. Nebrija himself wrote later on the subject as if it were the Cardinal's proposal rather than his own, and Nebrija was not a man to give way to modesty, stating that he was called to Alcalá together with 'Hebrews and Greeks' so that, he for the Latin, and they for their languages, could undertake the emendations of the texts in order to prepare a trilingual edition of the Bible.[39] Among the documents at the Complutensian university of Madrid, concerning the affairs of the Cardinal, there is one entitled *Apuntamientos de Roderigo de Monsalves tocantes a la Biblia Complutense, año 1511*, which shows that Ferdinand was in Salamanca from October 1505 to March 1506.[40] Cisneros for reasons of state would have been with the king at least part of this period, and in view of his concern with editing this Bible he would almost certainly have discussed it

---

[37] A. Lefranc, *Histoire du Collège de France*, 1873.

[38] Hefele, op. cit., 116 ff. citing Gomez, op. cit., 965, 36 ff.

[39] *Tertia Quinquagena*, v. vol. VIII, Part II, 91 ff. *Critici Sacri sive Annotata . . . in Vetus ac Novum Testamentum quibus accedunt Tractatus Varii*, Amsterdam, 1698.

[40] No. 3, leg. 11, cited Angel Saénz-Badillos, *La Filologiá Bíblica en los Helenistas de Alcalá*, 39. (Tesis doctoral presentada en la Universidad complutense de Madrid bajo la direccion del Catedratico, Dr. Luis Gil, Madrid, 1972. I am indebted to Professor Saenz-Badillos of the Complutensian University of Madrid for allowing me to consult his thesis and cite it in 1977, and to Professor Luis Gil for arranging for me to consult it).

with Nebrija who was professor of grammar at Salamanca. In the *Tertia Quinquagena* Nebrija refers to a discussion with the Cardinal: 'Eramus tunc in aula perquam reverendi atque proinde clementissimi Domini Francisci Ximenez Archiepiscopi Toletani et Hispaniarum Protomystae, cui jampridem investigandae antiquitatis S. literarum cura vel praecipua incumbit, et conquirendorum voluminum ad eam rem non minor diligentia.'[41] Here it is not a Polyglot Bible but arriving at the best bases for biblical study, and the codices for this, which are referred to, and in the preface Nebrija mentions the Court as meeting at Salamanca. Bataillon dates this book in 1507 or 1508. Again in his *Apologia earum rerum quae illi objiciuntur* written in 1505 and with slight re-editing published in 1507, addressed to Cisneros, he refers to the period when the Court resided at Salamanca when he showed Cisneros a manuscript and asked for his support. This relates to a discussion of problems concerning the source of corrections to the biblical text on which Nebrija had been challenged by the Inquisitor General, Diego de Deza.[42] If Pablo de Coronel was working with Cisneros in 1502, as seems to be certain, then the work on these textual studies began to be organised that year. A further reference from Nebrija in the *Tertia Quinquagena* shows that he had talked to Coronel in the period not long after 1502: 'Consulto itaque magistro Paulo, viro utriusque linguae, Arameam dico atque Hebraicum, erudito, et qui Hebraeis codicibus perquam reverendi Patris Protomystae Toletani praeest . . .'[43]

Cisneros, therefore, from 1502 had begun to gather scholars about him at his palace at Alcalá, and to organise these biblical textual studies which by 1505 were well under way. The next stage of publishing a Polyglot Bible, a great undertaking, arose out of these studies in the texts, and presumably began after 1508. For this the first need was to obtain the most ancient codices in order to establish a purer text, a search that continued up to 1512 at least. In the prologue to the Bible addressed to Leo X, Cisneros described this as 'the greatest part of the labour' – and proved to be a heavy expense.[44] Even after the expulsion of those many Jews who refused to accept baptism in 1492, who had taken their ancient and treasured texts with them, there were still codices in Spain, but the most desirable were rare and only to be obtained for large sums. Some of these codices purchased by Cisneros remarkably survive with other biblical

[41] *Tertia Quinquagena*, ch. XVIII, v. *Critici Sacri*, VIII, II, col. 106.
[42] Bataillon, op. cit., 31, n. 5.
[43] *Tertia Quinquagena*, v. *Critici Sacri*, vol. VIII, II, ch. XLV, col. 128.
[44] Bataillon, op. cit., 41, n. 2. Porreño, op. cit., 273, states that seven Hebrew manuscripts alone cost 4,000 ducats.

manuscripts in Madrid.[45] The Greek texts for the New Testament
have not survived, or were returned to their original owners and
since lost, and to the Vatican Library to which was sent back a copy
of a large portion of the Septuagint.[46] Another copy of the Septuagint
was corrected from one belonging to Cardinal Bessarion at Venice:
this survived the wars of Spain until the Civil War of 1936–39
when it was thrown by a mob from the Law College of San Bernardo
in Madrid into the street and burned with other books and documents
– against its number and title in the catalogue of that collection, now
in the Complutensian University of Madrid, is written the grim
word *quemada* (burned).[47] Three Latin codices of the Vulgate also
survived – Nebrija in the *Quinquagena* writes of matters 'in cod.
vetustis, Longobardis et Goticis inter Poenas et Latinis'.[48] The Hebrew
codices which were used in the preparation of the Old Testament
text cost a considerable amount. A more detailed account of the
codices used in the editing of the Complutensian Bible will be given
at a later stage.

The editors of these texts were not looking in the same direction as
the Cardinal who, while seeking to use the grammatical and lexical
aids to establish the most reliable text of Scripture, its 'verity', was
looking back to the work of restoration in the life of the Church in
Spain which he had already achieved, so that he could use the restored
Scriptures together with theological renewal to support, as part of
the repristination of the priesthood, the still somewhat medieval goal
of the spirituality of the *beata* Angela de Foligno, St. Catherine of
Siena, St. Vincent Ferrer and even Savonarola and Raymond Llull
whose writings or selections from them he caused to be printed at
Alcalá de Henares or Toledo, while the Bible was being edited and
printed at Alcalá.[49] On the other hand his editors for the Bible were
not professional theologians (with perhaps the exception of Diego de
Zúñiga), nor were they committed to the spirituality which so deeply
attracted Cisneros, they were grammarians, textual critics not

[45] In the Law Library of the Complutensian University of Madrid.
[46] Preface to vol. I of the Polyglot Bible: 'Atque ex ipsis [exemplaribus] quidem graeca.
Sanctitati Tuae debemus; qui ex ista apostolica Biblioteca antiquissimos tum Veteris tum Novi
Testamenti codices perquam humane ad nos misisti.'
[47] Villa-Amil y Castro: *Catálogo de los manuscritos existentes en la Biblioteca del Noviciado de la
Universidad Central Madrid*, 1878, 5, No. 22. These are now in the Law Library of the
Complutensian University of Madrid, newly catalogued. (This codex contains the historical
books, Proverbs, Ecclesiastes, Canticles, and some of the Deutero-canonical books).
[48] *Tertia Quinquagena*, v. *Critici Sacri*, ch. XV, vol. VIII, II, col. 103. Old Catalogue,
No. 31, Vulgate. One of the 'ancient Gothic codices' mentioned in the Preface of the Polyglot
Bible.
[49] Sainz Rodríguez, op. cit., 36, 47. Brocar printed these works for the Cardinal. Pages 94–
111 provide the bibliography.

concerned with exegesis; trilingual learning was their method and their goal — though this does not mean that they were ignorant of theology and the problems of expounding the Bible. It was a tragedy for Spain, a deep wound in her cultural development, that the Crown, from the time of the Catholic Kings, saw the need for conformity based on rigid traditional Christian orthodoxy as a political necessity for the stability of the state, which was to be strictly enforced by the Inquisition seen as an instrument of the state, functioning as one of the Councils of the kingdom, the *Consejo de la Suprema y General Inquisición*. Inevitably it challenged the work undertaken not by theologians to whom this study should be confined but grammarians, apparently undermining the traditional assumptions about the Bible and this by men of whom many were *conversos*, and not *cristianos viejos* (old Christians) who possessed that *limpieza de sangre* (purity of blood) which meant they were untainted by Jewish or Moorish descent.[50] Alcalá was not alone in possessing young students eager to take up trilingual learning, it was a movement which could arise throughout the universities of Spain though it varied from place to place, was thin on the ground, and was within two decades to face an Inquisition in full pursuit of *conversos* and of those humanist scholars whose themes were disapproved of as potentially Erasmians, Lutherans, the Illuminated or simply judaisers.[51] Spain alone in Europe was prevented from a full development of that flowering of what is called Renaissance humanism in Italy, France, Germany, the Low Countries, England and elsewhere. To survive, those scholars, priests and writers who turned to it had to hold contradictions together in a manner that established a uniquely Spanish character. Only Spain could have produced *Don Quijote* and the ironies of Cervantes; the picaresque tradition of Quevedo's rogue *El Buscón* who lives precariously within the labyrinth of social and religious formalism of Spanish society; and the intensity of controlled religious feeling in St. Teresa of Avila, St. John of the Cross and St. Ignatius Loyola — all these were well aware of, and some were entangled with, the power of the Inquisition.[52]

---

[50] Albert Sicroff, *Les Controverses des statuts de 'pureté de sang' en Espagne du XVe au XVIIe siecle*, Paris, 1960. The Inquisition insisted that the statutes for colleges, cathedral chapters, university chairs, the military Orders, even of cities, should contain a provision for excluding *conversos* from office, this applied gradually to the religious Orders also. Americo Castro, *De la Edad Conflictiva*, Madrid, 1961, shows the relation of the concept of 'honour', a powerful force in Spain, to 'purity of blood', 64 ff.

[51] The Inquisition was in pursuit not only of *conversos* as actual or potential 'judaisers' but also attacked 'Erasmianism' thereby severely damaging the spiritual and intellectual life of Spain. e.g. Bernardino Llorca, *Sefarad*, 1942, 125 ff.

[52] When St. Ignatius Loyola studied at Alcalá his religious zeal in 1527 led him to be suspected on three occasions at Alcalá and one at Salamanca, when he was before diocesan

Regrettably, the history of Spanish biblical humanism is a progress from coming under suspicion to accepting ultimate defeat. However, the Inquisition alone cannot be blamed for everything in this struggle for survival. There was no wide support in Spain for the aspirations of a Nebrija or a Luis de León compared with that available to such men in the free cities of the Empire, the Italian city states, and the courts of France or England. The Spanish nobility had fought the long war of the *Reconquista* and were making new conquests in South America – this, in their view, called for the warrior's virtues rather than good latinity. Those Spaniards who wished to study preferred theology or law as the means to a certain livelihood, and saw no need for trilingual studies, or even the new way of studying Latin, and would avoid anything that could attract the attention of the familiars of the Inquisition. Nebrija had written in 1492 in the preface to his *Vocabulario español-latino* that he had a mission 'to root out the barbarism of the men of our nation',[53] and also in a letter to Cisneros in 1514/1515 wrote of certain Dominicans, theologians at Salamanca university, one of whom:

> preaching in the Schools on Saint Jerome's day, turning part of the Gospel from Latin into Spanish 'non transibit unum iota neque unus apex' said that from the Law should not be removed one 'i' which was the smallest letter of the alphabet, nor one bee which was so small a creature. All those present, Doctors and Masters and other persons . . . of the profession of letters received this as if St. Jerome or St. Augustine had spoken it, no one laughed . . . they sat like stones or trunks of trees . . . I alone laughed, and gave my elbow to those sitting listening beside me. . . .
> Another, translating into Spanish a phrase from the Gospel 'qui ambulat in tenebris offendet', not understanding the significance of the verb 'offendet' which is to stumble, thinking that it meant 'to do harm to another', said that he who walks by night will snatch a cloak, or stab or break a head.[54]

That this is not an exaggeration by Nebrija can be seen in the comment of the Sicilian humanist Lucio Marineo Siculo (and this

---

tribunals accused of 'Illuminism' (as a suspect *alumbrado*). *Boletín de la Real Academia Historica*, 1898, (33), 431 ff. For St. Teresa of Avila and the Inquisition, v. *Autobiography*, ch. 25, (*Obras de Santa Teresa*, ed. La Fuente). For St. John of the Cross, Bernardino Llorca, *San Juan de la Cruz y la Inquisición*, 103 ff.

[53] Antonio de Nebrija, *Vocabularii Anthonii Nebrissensis, ex sermone latino in hispaniensem*, Seville, 1503, aiii, r. He several times refers to 'barbarians', e.g. 'Sic ego in erradicanda ex nostris hominibus barbaria non aliunde quam a Salmanticense academia sum auspicatus: qua velut arce quadam expugnata.'

[54] *Epístola del Maestro de Lebrija al Cardinal, quando aviso que en la interpretación de las Dicciones de la Biblia no mandarse seguir al Remigio sin que primero viessen su obra*, ed. Roque Chabas, RABM VIII, 1903, 495. This is one of several examples of the ignorance of scholars given by Nebrija.

was during the time that Nebrija was at Salamanca) that among the thirty professors of different subjects and the seven thousand students, none, in his opinion, had 'savoured the sweet and mellow fruit of the Latin language' or at least could speak it becomingly in an accurate grammatical fashion.[55] Juan de Lucena wrote of a man 'who asked me who were *Santoficeto* [sanctificetur] and *Dona Bisodia* [da nobis hodie] in the Paternoster? I told him that *Dona Bisodia* was the name of the she ass who carried Christ and *Santoficeto* was the foal of the ass.'[56]

These citations should not be dismissed as the contemptuous arrogance of scholars, for they point to the widespread ignorance of even the Latin of the Bible not only among students and parish priests but professors also. The editors of the Complutensian Bible faced not only danger from frowning Inquisitors through their emphasis on the Hebrew and Greek texts, but they also faced apathy and indifference from those who should have welcomed this enterprise. The most renowned of these editors, Antonio de Nebrija, who left Salamanca and was appointed to the chair of rhetoric at Alcalá in 1513, was a greater trilingual scholar than Erasmus since he knew Hebrew, and was also the man who claimed with reason to be the first of his nation to bring the light of humanist studies to Spain.[57] Demetrios Ducas of Crete was brought by Cisneros to the chair of Greek at Alcalá from Venice where he had been working for the Aldine Press in that splendid centre of humanism.[58] The date of his arrival is not certain, but he was receiving what he complained of as a small salary in 1513.[59] Presumably his function was to see through

[55] As Luis Gil states 'exageración sin duda', since Siculo was at Salamanca at the same time as Nebrija taught there. Nevertheless, so many humanist scholars make the same complaint, that the criticism stands. Cited by Luis Gil in *El Humanismo Español del siglo XVI*, 218, for the third Spanish Congress for Classical Studies, 1966.

[56] Juan de Lucena, *Epístola exhortatoria de las letras*, in *Opúsculos literarios de las siglos XIV a XVI*, Madrid, 1892, 212.

[57] Pedro Lemus y Rubio, *El Maestro Elio Antonio de Lebrixa, Revue Hispanique*, 1910, 459 ff. Felix G. Olmedo, S.J. *Nebrija (1441–1522), Debelador de la barbarie . . .* Madrid, 1942; Julio Fernández-Sevilla, *Un maestro preterido: Elio Antonio de Nebrija, Thesaurus*, XXIX, 1974; Antonio Odriozola: *Aljunos problemas bibliográficos que plantean las obras de Nebrija, Bibliograpica Hispánica*, IV, Madrid, 1945, 213 ff.; V. Beltrán de Heredia, O.P., *Nebrija y los téologos de San Esteban principios del siglo XVI, Ciencia Tomista* LXI, 40 (this shows resentment at the 'inmodesta de este escritor', and quotes Menéndez y Pelayo on a 'carácter mordaz y vanidoso', *Historia de Heterodoxos Españoles*).

[58] For the Aldine Press at Venice he had published *Rhetores Graeci*, 1508–9, and *Moralia* of Plutarch, 1509.

[59] He arrived at Alcalá between 1510 and 1515, but there is no evidence when he began work there. A. de la Torre, RABM, II, 1909, 262 quotes a manuscript showing his fees. He left Alcalá for Rome where he taught Greek from 1518. Saénz-Badillos believes that he was the chief editor of the New Testament Greek text.

the press the Greek text of the New Testament and to assist in ensuring that this was a scholarly version edited from early codices. At the end of the edition of the Greek grammar of Chrysolaras, the *Erotemata*, which he published at the same press at Alcalá (and using the same Greek type fount) he wrote:

> Called into Spain for the Greek language by the most reverend Cardinal of Spain, and having found a great poverty or rather a total absence of Greek books, I have published according to the measure of my strength some grammatical and poetical texts with the characters I had under my hand, and I offer them to you. Without assistance from anyone, neither for the heavy expenses of printing, nor for the labours of correction, alone, and burdened also with daily teaching, copying and correcting, I have had difficulty in completing the work.[60]

Soon after the completion of the Complutensian Bible he left Alcalá and returned to Italy. About the time Ducas arrived in Alcalá, Hernán Núñez de Guzmán, a proud man of noble family known as *El Comendador Griego* (he was Commander of the military Order of Santiago and wished this title to be observed) who had become a pupil of Nebrija at Salamanca, was listed as having a house at Alcalá in 1513, but he was not appointed to the chair of Greek until 1519, after it had been vacated for some time by Ducas.[61] Hernán Núñez (also called *El Pinciano* from his birthplace) was a splendid trilingual scholar who worked on the Bible at Alcalá from 1513 until the *comuneros* troubles there in 1521–1522, when, after participating in them, he departed to a chair at Salamanca.[62] Even more than Nebrija he was a man of independent spirit, boldly claiming a freedom of judgement in his fields of study which was nearer to Italy than traditionalist Spain. This can be seen in an extract from his commentary on the work of the poet Juan de Mena, in which also he gives graceful recognition to Nebrija his master. Writing of a meteorological phenomenon and its colours and exercising, as he said, his own judgement:

> The truth is that Aristotle and Pliny were manifestly in error in what

---

[60] *Erotemata Chrysolarae*, 1514, Guillén de Brocar, Alcalá. Norton *A Descriptive Catalogue of Printing in Spain and Portugal: 1501–1520*, Cambridge, 1978, 30, provides the Greek original.

[61] The significance of membership of, and the statutes of, a Military Order can be found in the romanticised, *A Brief Account of the Military Orders in Spain*, G. G. King, New York, 1921. L. P. Wright, *The Military Orders in Sixteenth and Seventeenth Century Spanish Society, Past and Present*, No. 43, 34 ff., is thorough.

[62] He was a native of Valladolid (Lat.: Pintia) He had fought in the conquest of Granada, became a pupil of Nebrija at Salamanca and, like Nebrija before him, he studied Greek at Bologna. For the dates concerning his work at Alcalá, Jose Lopez Rueda, *Helenistas Españoles del siglo XV*, Madrid, 1973, 24 ff.

they say . . . I am an eyewitness . . . I will add another witness who is the venerable and most learned man Antonio de Nebrija our most erudite preceptor in all kinds of learning whose powerful and melodious lute more felicitous than that of the Thracian Orpheus which brought faithful Eurydice from the underworld – I mean he revived among us the Latin language and humane learning which for so many years were extinguished in Spain. Nebrija and I, travelling from Alcantara to Villanueva de la Serena, journeying one showery evening saw this arc of light which was caused by lunar rays which cast light on a facing cloud.[63]

He added that they were pleased to see this since Aristotle was misleading on the phenomenon.

El Comendador Griego was involved with the preparation of the first volume of the Bible to be printed, the New Testament, to which his name is attached, particularly with the Vulgate text accompanying the Greek. Ms 117–Z–1 at the University of Madrid is one of the surviving Complutensian materials; it shows the comparison of the Greek with the Vulgate in his method and was probably used for this edition of the New Testament.[64] He also almost certainly shared in the interlinear Latin version provided for the Septuagint. Cisneros had hoped that Erasmus could be brought to Alcalá, either for one of the chairs of liberal arts or for work on the New Testament Greek, but at the time of this invitation the Cardinal had not seen in him those developments which were to cause the Spanish Inquisition to declare what it called Erasmianism to be a heresy and begin to root out its supporters over a decade later. Erasmus, however, wanted nothing to do with Spain, for he wrote to Beatus Rhenanus in 1517 that in spite of the invitation from Cisneros, 'I have no mind to Hispanize'.[65] To Capito the hebraist of Strasbourg, he wrote warning him against studying the Talmud and the Kabbala, 'I would prefer to see Christ poisoned by Duns Scotus than by that kind of nonsense; in Spain there are so many Jews that there are hardly any Christians'.[66] Instead, Cisneros looked to two other scholars. The name of Bartolomé de Castro is given in vol. V

---

[63] The first published work by Nuñez was, *Los ccc del famosissimo poeta Juā de Mena . . . Glosa sobre las trēziētas del famoso poeta . . .: Cōpuesta por Fernan Nuñez comendador de la ordē de Sātiago*, Seville, 1512, f.59, v. He is discussing 'iris cō todas sus bivas colores'.

[64] Helen Nader, '"The Greek Commander" Hernán Núñez de Toledo, Spanish Humanist and Civic Leader', *Renaissance Quarterly*, 1978, 463 ff. is the most recent account. Saénz-Badillos, 688 ff., stated that Núñez was concerned with Greek and humanist learning rather than with theological preoccupations. That Núñez worked in some capacity on the New Testament Greek is shown in the Latin verses at the end of the Apocalypse. Saénz-Badillos drew attention to the resemblance between the marginal notes in MS. 117–Z–1 (Codex 41) in the Law Library of Madrid to those in the *Oratio ad Pueros* of Nuñez.

[65] Allen, op. cit., III, Ep. 628 'verum non est animus' ἱσπανίζειν'

[66] Allen, op. cit., II, Ep. 541.

of this Bible and he apparently collaborated in the preparation of the Greek text since he compiled the manuscript *Vocabularius verborum gracecorum editus a magistro barthol. Castrensi*, dated 1516.[67] Almost nothing is known of him save that he stated in a book on logic which he published at Alcalá in 1512 that he taught philosophy there for four years, and also published a book on the Predicaments of Aristotle which concluded with a tract on numbers in which he followed Lefèvre d'Etaples with approval.[68] The appearance of his name in connection with the Bible and his knowledge of Greek imply collaboration on the text of the Septuagint, or that of the New Testament – nothing more has yet been discovered.

Diego López de Zúñiga was an excellent if truculent theologian and trilingual scholar who had a notably bitter controversy from 1520 onwards with Erasmus, and is known to have collaborated in the preparation of the Bible.[69] He was well acquainted with the diversities which occurred in the Greek texts, but he tended to choose the reading nearest to that found in the Vulgate. Through years of study he knew well the problems of translation from Hebrew and Greek, and had good command of the grammatical and lexical problems in the New Testament, as his controversial writings show, but his stance was conservative in seeking to defend the Vulgate even where this was indefensible.[70] Little is known of his contribution to the work though he refers once, '. . . hortatu ac iussu patris Reverendissimi Francisci Cisneri Cardinalis Toletani' to collating the Latin and Greek codices.[71] Juan de Vergara was an able young graduate of Alcalá, a pupil of Hernán Núñez though not so well grounded in Greek.[72] We know by his testimony to the Inquisitors

---

[67] Saénz-Badillos, 608 citing MS. 7.1.10, Colombina Library, Seville.

[68] Bartolomé de Castro published *Termini logicales*, 1512, but no copy appears to have survived (Norton, op. cit., 8), and *Questiones* at Salamanca, 1518, (Norton, 214) dedicated to Cisneros. This shows that he left for Salamanca after the Cardinal's death. His humanism is demonstrated by his adding a little treatise *Canones triumphi numerorum* which follows the ideas of Jacques Lefèvre d'Etaples, the French humanist and biblical scholar, in 'seeking knowledge by mathematics and experience'. This is discussed in Muñoz Delgado, *La lógica nominalista*, 1964, 163–73 (cited in *El Erasmismo en España*, Colloquy, Santánder, 1986, 152).

[69] He was a pupil of the Portuguese Arias Barbosa at Salamanca who had studied in Italy. (Zuñiga's *Annotationes adversus Erasmi Roterodami*, Romans 15:24. He praised Nebrija at Mark 5:41). Otherwise nothing is known of him before he went to Alcalá.

[70] Saénz-Badillos considers him as 'excesivamente conservador' and as having an 'actitud excesivamente tradicional'.

[71] In his *Annotationes Jacobi Lopidis Stunicae contra Jacobum Fabrum Stapulensem*, A. 3. (Mariano Revilla Rico, O.S.A., *La Poliglota de Alcalá*, in *Ciudad de Dios* 1917, 170).

[72] He admired Erasmus, see his letter, Ep. 1814, from Valladolid, 1527, Allen, op. cit., V, 40 ff. The extent of his work on the New Testament is not known. His younger brother Francisco produced an admirable Greek grammar which for the first time discussed biblical Greek. He died young. (Jerry H. Bentley, *Humanists and Holy Writ*, Princeton, 1983, confuses Juan and Francisco Vergara in writing of Juan's early death who in fact died in 1557).

after his arrest in 1532 (he was of Jewish descent, *cristiano nuevo*) that he provided some of the interlinear Latin versions of the Old Testament, including some of the Wisdom books from the Septuagint.[73] In any case his name appears in some verses in praise of Cisneros at the end of the New Testament volume. He is significant as a member of the next generation of trilingual scholars of Spain for he shows the powerful influence which Alcalá was making in Spain, deeply concerned as it was with these studies and less dedicated to traditional theology.

To these men Cisneros added two hebraists, both *conversos*; Pablo Coronel of Segovia who was claimed by Nebrija and later by Joseph de Sigüenza to be the chief editor of the Hebrew text of the Complutensian Polyglot Bible, but he remains a shadowy figure who came into the group Cisneros gathered about him from 1502;[74] and *el gran converso*, Alfonso de Zamora, who came from Salamanca to the chair of Hebrew at Alcalá in 1512 and represented the great tradition of medieval Sephardic Judaism in Spain.[75] Alfonso de Alcalá de Real, who had graduated in medicine at Salamanca and then renounced Judaism presumably in or soon after 1492, and thereafter studied theology and the Scriptures at Salamanca, is said to have worked for Cisneros on the Latin version of certain Hebrew texts for his Bible – but the attribution is vague and almost nothing is known of him further save that he was in Salamanca in 1540.[76]

---

[73] Archivo Historico Nacional, Madrid, Inquisition of Toledo, leg. 223, esp. 4º 7, 1º, f 141v, 274v. (Saénz-Badillos, 513).

[74] In the El Escorial Library there is an apparently unique copy of a book by Coronel, *Additiones ad librum N. Lyrani de differentiis translationum* (c. 1526?) The librarian José de Sigüenza (a pupil of Benito Arias Montano who had studied at Alcalá) has written in this book at three places. On the blank at the end of the 'Annotatio' to Malachi, facing page ¶.1, he wrote describing the burial place of Coronel at Segovia, adding: '... et ego Fr. Joseph de Sigüenza audivi ab ipso ore Doctoris Coronel nepotis eiusdem Magistri Pauli cum ipse avunculus haec dictus et literis ipse excipiebat et ob maximam suam humilitatem proprium ocultavit nomen quod et fecit vir eruditissimus in opere illo illustrissimo et eruditissimo bibliae complutensis ut ex apendice supra inmediate posito post conclusionem Nicolai conieci potest siquidem de complutensi bibliotheca fit mentio. Futurae memoriae tanti viri haec dicta sint.' On page ¶.1 at the top he has written, 'Per magrum Paulum Coronel Bibliae Complutensis solertissimus auctor.' I have not seen this evidence noted before. J. Rodríguez de Castro, *Biblioteca española ... los escritores rabinos españoles*, Madrid, 2 vols. 1781–6, vol. 1, 398, provides information on Coronel. Federico Pérez Castro, *El manuscrito apologético de Alfonso de Zamora*, Madrid, 1950, LVII, translates from Hebrew the end of MS. 1229 of the Bibliothèque Nationale, Paris, written by Zamora in 1527 'por consejo del sabio perfecto, maestro Pablo Núñez Coronel, hombre integro y recto, temeroso de Dios y apartado de mal, de fama en toda la tierra'.

[75] Pérez Castro, op. cit., XI–CI., *Semblanza bio-bibliografica de Alfonso de Zamora*.

[76] Rodríguez de Castro, op. cit., vol. I, 398. This claims he was a trilingual scholar and shared with Alfonso de Zamora the translation into Latin of 'books of the Old Testament' – this is unclear and no evidence is given.

It is certain that Cisneros brought all these scholars to Alcalá not
only to assist the fame of the College of San Ildefonso, but also to
undertake the fulfilment of his second ambition for the
Complutensian University, that is to make it the home of the first
Bible to appear in print in the earliest languages of Scripture –
Hebrew, Aramaic, Greek and Latin – together with a considerable
apparatus of grammars, lexicons, the Targum of Onkelos, interlinear
Latin translations and powerful prologues arguing that the basis of
both sound learning and the life of piety must be biblical study. In
view of the great problems its editors faced and the vast expense
incurred, this was an enterprise of extraordinary courage and
achievement. Of these editors Nebrija was the eldest (1441–1522) a
scholar who knew the world of medieval learning including its
methods of biblical interpretation, but also he had studied in Italy at
the College of St. Clement at Bologna at least for part of the time
from 1460 to 1470, taking courses in the usual subjects of theology,
law and medicine though he did not graduate in them, for his chief
aim when in Italy was to become a trilingual scholar.[77] Under Marcio
Galeoto at Bologna he learned Greek and Hebrew, and also he
perfected his Latin studies in this period in order, as he said, to restore
to his native land 'those Latin authors banished from it'.[78]

On his return to Spain he was in the service of Alonso de Fonseca,
Archbishop of Seville, a patron of men of letters, then he moved to
the university of Salamanca, which he saw as a traditionalist 'fortress
he took by assault'.[79] He gave extra-curricular courses there on
points of grammar until he was appointed to one of the chairs of
grammar, and published one of his great contributions to humanist
learning, the *Grammatica sey Introductiones Latinae* which appeared in
its definitive form in 1485. Soon the Queen Isabella came to regard
Nebrija as 'one of the most precious ornaments of her crown'.[80] In
1486 he entered the service of Juan de Zúñiga, Grand Master of the
Order of Alcántara, a rich patron of scholars and poets. Here at

[77] Juan Gil Fernández, *Nebrija en el Colegio de los Españoles en Bolonia. Emérita*, 1965,
347–9.
[78] Nebrija's Preface addressed to Juan de Zúñiga of his *Dictionarium ex hispaniensis in Latinum
sermonem.* Salamanca 1492, a ii, v 'autores del latin . . . desterrados de españa.'
[79] Nebrija, op. cit., a iii, '. . . como una fortaleza tomado por cóbate'.
[80] Olmedo, op. cit., 25. This book should be used with caution, for here as elsewhere
Olmedo blurs an important matter. What is sufficiently clear is that Nebrija wrote in the
preface to his *Arte de la lengua Castellana* of 1492, that 'language is always the companion of
Empire' a point of which Queen Isabella was reminded when she asked what was the use of a
Spanish grammar when it was presented to her – at a time when Columbus was voyaging
westward. A new state required a new linguistic policy. (Eugenio Asensio, *La lengua companera
del Imperio, Revista de Filología Española*, Madrid, XLIII, 1960, 399–413 who describes the source
of the phrase).

Zalamea he met the younger man Hernán Núñez de Guzmán, a future collaborator with him on the Complutensian Bible who has already been discussed. At this period Nebrija began to give himself wholly to studying biblical philology, the accents, the transcription of Hebrew and Greek names, questions of textual transmission and biblical coinage and chronology.[81] In his biblical studies he admired, frequently cited and criticised, St. Jerome, somewhat as Erasmus was to do, and showed in his writings the influence of the methods of interpretation and critical acumen associated with Lorenzo Valla which he had learned in Italy.

His major activity as a biblical scholar lay in his use of his considerable grammatical and lexical skills in the clarification of obscurities in the Hebrew or Greek text. His methods were, to seek as did St. Jerome the *hebracia veritas*, (though this led him to confine himself to correcting the Vulgate text for unlike Erasmus he saw no need for a new Latin translation), and the search for the earliest codices. His weakness lay in his being held at times by his theological and legal studies to maintain the medieval concept of authority and so set aside what may be the earlier text.[82] Moreover, his Hebrew learning though adequate was less than his ability in Greek: it was in latinity that he excelled. In the exposition of difficult passages he was sensible, and like trilingual scholars elsewhere he sought out the literal sense. In his *Apologia*, prepared in 1506–07 when attacked by the Inquisition, he wrote that like St. Augustine he desired the best corrected text, therefore, referring to book II of that Father's *De Doctrina Christiana*, he wished to compare various codices since one of the first duties in studying the Scriptures is to emend their texts carefully – or else how do we know what is or is not of faith? He added that St. Jerome in all his prologues, epistles and commentaries showed that where there is a discrepancy in the Latin then the original Greek should be consulted, and for the Old Testament the Hebrew text should be used. He repeated what he had discussed in the *Tertia Quinquagena* (1516): it is better to say with Christ *Talitha cumi* than to say with the ignorant *Tabitha cumi* as though this were the girl's name – an error that Erasmus was to maintain since he had not understood the Aramaic of *Talitha*.[83]

Nebrija claimed proudly that he was a professor of Grammar at the University with power to dispute, and to judge those things

[81] Sáenz-Badillos, 105 ff.
[82] Sáenz-Badillos, 224.
[83] *Tertia Quinquagena*, v. *Critici Sacri* ch. XLV, cols. 127–8. Diego de Zúñiga (Stunica) praised Nebrija for his contribution on Tabitha/Talitha in his *Annotationes adversus Er. Rot.* on Mark 5:41.

belonging to his profession. What do people now know of the plants and animals of the Bible, what were the *onocrotalus* the *porphyrio* and the *git*: what did they know of metals, coins, clothing and the names of places or where they were now to be found, and the meaning of personal names?[84] All these studies, said Nebrija, he wished to undertake and promote for in this he was better employed that in disputing in the Schools, 'utrum quidditates Scoti transeuntes per latera puncti possint implere ventrem chimerae'. He crowned his discourse with a peroration to Cisneros:

> Thou best of fathers, mainstay of the republic of Spain . . . divine providence gave me in you . . . a witness and a judge. I beseech you hasten to my aid, bring succour to the declining world of letters, undertake its patronage before it perishes utterly . . . bring back those two extinct lights of our religion the Greek and Hebrew languages, offer rewards to those who labour in this matter, drive those who seek to prevent this, beyond the Sarmatians and the Garamantes the remotest of men.[85]

The Cardinal's response had already begun in the preparations of the Bible by then under way, but he was able to give Nebrija a kind welcome to Alcalá when trouble arose at Salamanca. The election to chairs there was by popular vote of the university members and Nebrija, through overlong absences which he thought justified, at a disputed election lost his chair early in 1513. Alvar Gómez in the Latin manuscript life of Cisneros describes what followed:

> [Nebrija] took such exception to this that a short while afterwards in the porch [of the university] taking off his shoes, according to the injunction in the gospel and brushing the dust off his feet, threw the dust into the air, absolved himself from his contract to this ungrateful university. He came to Cisneros to ask for a post, . . . and was given a high salary by him . . . in recognition of the services by which he had made the whole of Spain beholden to him by delivering it from being judged to be barbarian. Thereafter Cisneros held him in such regard . . . that he received him with a touch to the hat which he used in walking in the street in order to honour him when he came to him . . . this was from a man who was chary in other respects about this kind of thing . . . . Whenever he came from his Palace to the College he deliberately turned aside to the printer's workshop near which Nebrija had his residence and summoned him to the window of the lower room which overhung the public way . . . and discussed certain problems with him concerning his readings and meditations . . .[86]

---

[84] *Tertia Quinquagena*, op. cit. ch. XX, col. 108, ch. XXXIII, col. 117, ch. XXXVI. col. 120.
[85] Olmedo, op. cit., 135 gives the Latin text.
[86] Gómez, MS. Latin life of Cisneros, f184v. f185r.

In the working notes or first draft in Spanish of the work, Gómez gives more details on this which he must have decided to omit as too indiscreet: 'The Cardinal stood in the street and Nebrija at the window grating . . . The Cardinal . . . was invited inside and urged [Nebrija's] wife to persuade him to drink less wine' – this was perhaps as good as any other way of dealing with textual problems in the Complutensian Bible.[87] Certainly Cisneros regarded Nebrija's judgement as of great importance and Nebrija collaborated closely on the project from 1513 possibly into 1515. His task was the provision of the best text of the Vulgate, on which he wrote in the letter to the Cardinal: 'I came to Alcalá to take part in the correction of the Latin which is commonly corrupted in all the Latin Bibles, by comparing it with the Hebrew, Aramaic and Greek.'[88] But he found this was not to be so, the Cardinal wished to arrive at a better Vulgate text by using the earliest codices to obtain better readings (this is also the method of modern editing of the Latin text since it is an independent textual source). Nebrija on the other hand wished to correct the Vulgate from the original languages.

A further point of difference was the method of editing the lexicons of Hebrew, Aramaic and Greek names for the New Testament and that for the Old Testament (in volumes V and VI of the Polyglot Bible). For centuries the lexical basis for these names had been that attributed to Remigius (Remi of Auxerre d.908). Nebrija believed this source was so unscholarly as to be at times absurd – he had already written on the subject.[89] He was not ignored for whoever edited the lexicon of volume VI corrected many of the traditional interpretations by Nebrija's own conclusions, but Nebrija would not bow even to the Cardinal's authority on the way to correct the Vulgate text and withdrew from the work on the Bible. It is not disproportionate to give an account of Nebrija at this length in spite of the short period he was at work on this Bible, for the Cardinal and posterity regarded him as of the first rank as a trilingual scholar and as an inspiration to the scholarship of succeeding generations in Spain.

The other editor who deserves extended treatment is Alfonso de Zamora, the ablest Christian Spanish hebraist of his time, for he

---

[87] Gómez, MS in Spanish draft. 'Estava concertado el cardinal con su muger que entre dia no le dexase bever vino'.

[88] Epístola del maestro de Lebrija al Cardenal . . . Chabas, RABM, 1903, 493.

[89] Apparently he had criticised Remigius in a Repetition now lost. In Cod. Vatican Borg. 148, fols. 91–180 Lexicon Primum (published as Nebrissensis Biblica, ed. Paschalis Galindo et Aloysius Ortiz, Madrid, 1950), Nebrija showed how he dealt with Hebrew names in literal, historical and lexical methods.

represented the flower of Hebrew studies deriving from the rabbinical traditions in which Spain had been rich before 1492. He was born about 1474 the son of the rabbi Juan de Zamora, probably at Los Arcos, and was soon moved to Zamora by his father where there was a large community of Jews most of whom had been expelled from Portugal. When he became a *converso* is not known (possibly his father had become a *converso* in view of his name Juan).[90] As a customary part of rabbinical training Alfonso acquired a trade, that of shoemaker like his father before him, while attending the Hebrew school at Zamora – though this school is perhaps not sufficient to explain his great mastery of Hebrew learning, even if we allow that Talmudic studies were prominent in a town with two synagogues. Almost nothing is known of him beyond these few facts and assumptions until his candidature for the chair of Hebrew, Aramaic and Arabic at Salamanca. His predecessors had failed to fulfil their obligations and there had been a gap in this teaching 'since there was no one sufficient' for the post. In February 1511 it was decided that 'Alonso de Arcos', *zapatero*, could teach these languages for no one else was available, but the councillors and rectors hesitated for some months, and then turned to Hernán Núñez, since 'the Comendador was endowed with the grammar of Greek, Arabic, Hebrew and Aramaic and had expertise in teaching'. There was a long discussion to which Antonio de Nebrija contributed the predictable opinion that a person learned in Latin was essential for the chair so that he could expound his subject matter in that language. However, another professor stated that 'Alonso de Zamora' could both read and speak Hebrew and Aramaic whereas there was no evidence that the Comendador could do both. A newly elected rector, who had apparently hoped to appoint the Comendador but failing in this waited until no further opportunity was available for discussion and then appointed a nonentity to the chair in 1512. The watchful Cisneros, no doubt well-informed about the frustrating academic intrigues at Salamanca, immediately recruited both the original candidates there for San Ildefonso. The Comendador was of noble stock, and had the status with which powerful academic and ecclesiastical connections together with membership of the Order of Santiago endowed him; therefore, he could ignore what had happened, but Zamora would find this affair to be one more of a number of occasions of isolation and humiliation. He wrote on two widely separated occasions of the insecurity and fear of the *converso*, before his death, sometime after 1544 when he was seventy. In 1520 he wrote in Hebrew in the colophon of MS 118–Z–21.

⁹⁰ Pérez Castro, op. cit., XII–XIX for the little that is known of the life of Zamora.

I Alfonso de Zamora, on the first of the month of March of the year 1520 from now henceforth deprived of my strength, grown weak in spirit, my eyes wearied, strayed out of my paths, forgotten and hated by all my friends, my enemies entwined about me, without finding repose neither for my mind nor for the soles of my feet, my days are consumed and my spirit blotted out from God . . .

The manuscript lacks the ending at this point and the occasion of this lament is not shown, but it is evident that trouble had arisen at Alcalá after the death of Cisneros in 1517 since a royal provision of 15 November, 1520, signed by the regent, Cardinal Adrian, in the absence of Charles, required the Dominican, Miguel Ramírez, to conduct an inquiry and undertake reform. It is clear that discipline in maintaining the constitutions, and even good moral behaviour, had been undermined. Moreover, the Andalusians strongly opposed both the rector and this inquiry since there were active political divisions in the university, and the revolt of the *comuneros* supported by the *Comendador griego* brought about a severe crisis.[91] It could have been ominous for Zamora that the Court had been informed that in Castile the root cause of the revolt had been the *conversos*.

Apart from his writings on Hebraica only two letters by Zamora survive and show the sadness of his life, one addressed to Pope Paul III, and the other to the Cardinal of Sancta Balbina, Pedro Pablo Parisio, to convey a petition to the Pope, both written in 1544. They were intended to seek help for the university of Alcalá because the Archbishop of Toledo, Juan Tavera, who was also Inquisitor General, was causing considerable difficulties there by infringing the privileges of the university, in particular by attacking Hebrew studies there – in whose eyes wrote Zamora the regents of Alcalá were but as 'beasts for the slaughterhouse'. Both letters were composed in, or translated into Hebrew, by the hand of Zamora and contain a firm defence of biblical studies in the original languages to which he added at the end of the first letter that it was completed on 31 March 1544, '. . . by the hand of Alfonso de Zamora who teaches the Hebrew language in this university to all who desire to learn it, and although I am now seventy years old I do not remember any joyful day'.[92]

Jews had responded to occasional risings against them involving massacre, by changing their religion, large numbers did so after the slaughters of 1391 and 1449, so that in the second half of the fifteenth century *conversos* could be numbered in tens of thousands. Conversion

[91] Joseph Pérez. *L'Université d'Alcalá de Henares en 1520–1521*, 214 ff. J. A. Maravall, *Historia de las comunidades [comuneros] estudios sobre el pensamiento español*.
[92] Pérez Castro, op. cit., XXV.

improved the social and financial position of Jews and all honours of office were open to the *conversos*, since baptism cleansed the past and made them new men taking away all blame; but this brought upon them the envy of the less successful *cristianos viejos* and the suspicion of the Inquisition.[93] For many Jews the translation from Judaism was eased by their having lapsed from orthodoxy under Islam into something near to rationalistic Averroism; for these the book of Ecclesiastes constituted all you could hope for in religion.[94] This insincerity in conversation was to be one cause of the activity of the Inquisition against *conversos*, though there were numbers of Jews who were genuine converts who were attracted by Paulinism and sought for the inner force of religious experience rather than mere conformity to external formalism – this also would cause trouble with the Inquisition. Since many *conversos* were men of wealth and standing there had for long been intermarriage and assimilation with the various ranks of the nobility, even Ferdinand himself is believed to have had a Jewish ancestor. The Spaniards who could effectively claim that they possessed *limpieza de sangre* were the *cristianos viejos*, the peasants of Castile and the underprivileged in the towns. Their hatred of tax-farmers and financiers, so often *conversos*, brought out the mobs who watched the rich and powerful suffer in being burned at an *auto da fé*. The fear this created led frightened men to speak fiercely against their fellow *conversos*, and even to betray them to the familiars of the Inquisition, for they were the product of a society where failure to conform to social pressures brought not toleration but total condemnation.[95] Paradoxically, as Americo Castro pointed out, *conversos*, only partially aware of the implications of the Christian faith, urged strongly the theme of a state enforced religion, already seen on a smaller scale in their theocratic and conformist *aljamas*.[96] The only relaxation of his position for a *converso* lay in the fact that one aspect of the *Siglo de Oro* was its expanding and obsessive bureaucracy which involved bureaucrats who could be idle, corrupt and incompetent, and who failed to follow up efficiently the pursuit of *conversos*.[97]

[93] A. Domínguez Ortiz, *Los conversos de origen judió de la expulsión*, Madrid, 1956, is a useful study of the *converso* situation.

[94] Yitzhak Baer, op. cit., II, 255, 258, 274, 282, wrote of this decline of faith among Jewish intellectuals in the fifteenth century and its continuing consequences into the next century.

[95] It should be understood that the Inquisition was not condemning *conversos* because they were Jews by race, there was no crude racial anti-semitism in the trials, it was condemning what it believed to be insufficient obedience to Christian orthodoxy. The conformism this produced led to that degree of intellectual stagnation challenged in the ironies of Golden Age writers like Cervantes.

[96] Americo Castro, *The Structure of Spanish History*, trans. E. L. King, Princeton, 1954, 533–4. *Aljamas* were the Jewish headquarters.

[97] This comment on bureaucratic indifference does not imply a general rule: it depended on the place and the time.

Felipe de la Torre in his *Institución de un rey christiano* dedicated to Philip II, in criticising the attitude to *conversos*, wrote that it was hypocrisy under the pretext of religion to defame one's neighbour and rob his goods; and for the Christian to seek death for someone to whom Christ gave life.[98] Here it is not so much physical death that is referred to, but that special sorrow for the *converso*, which is spiritual death, since he cannot fulfil himself properly as a Christian.

The well-intentioned *converso* found his tragedy lay not so much in his sense of his own jewishness in living among gentiles, but that he had become suspect and treated with injustice by the Church and society to which he believed he now belonged but found these to be unaware of the essential meaning of the faith into which they had baptised him. In the light of these attitudes the distress expressed by Zamora in the passages cited from him is painfully understandable.

Some account of Zamora's surviving manuscripts will show the range of his powers. There is a major group which provides edited Hebrew texts of the greater part of the Old Testament accompanied by his own Latin version together with marginal notes of lexical, grammatical and expository importance including the manuscript of Genesis addressed to Fonseca, Archbishop of Toledo, with a significant Preface (MS G.1.4) in the library of the monastery of the El Escorial[99] He may have hoped originally that a new Latin version of the Hebrew Old Testament with such useful notes would be made available in the Complutensian Polyglot Bible. But as will be shown more fully later Cisneros was unwilling to appear to compromise the authority of the Vulgate text by producing a new Latin version. Further it was hoped that Zamora's enterprise, in which Professor Pedro Ciruelo of Alcalá assisted him, would have been freed from suspicion by the publication of the literal Latin version of the Old Testament by the Italian Dominican *converso* Santi Pagnini in his Latin version of the Bible of 1528 published with Papal Privileges, but their work was never printed.[100] Inquisitorial suspicion of hebraists was mounting in the period in which the translating was done. Zamora translated,

[98] J. A. Maravall, *La oposición político religiosa del siglo XVI. El erasmismo tardio de Felipe de la Torre* in *La oposicion politica bajo los Austrias*, Barcelona, 1972, 55 ff., 89.

[99] Perez Castro, op. cit., XXXIV ff.

[100] Ciruelo combined the best in Graeco-Latin and medieval culture, and was the first to publish a treatise on mathematics in Spain. Zamora refers to his oversight of these Latin translations with respect. (Ciruelo as a theologian would be maintaining orthodoxy on behalf of Cisneros). He gave the long-lost university oration on the death of Cisneros. For Pagnini, *Cambridge History of the Bible*, II, 69–70. For the interlinear Latin version of Zamora, v. José Llamas, O.S.A., *Biblia latina interlineal inedita*, La Cindad de Dios 1951, vol. CLXIII, 257 ff.

presumably also for inclusion in the Polyglot, a number of Targums into Latin, originally at the request of Cisneros, but only that of Onkelos was printed. A Spanish translation by him of David Kimhi's commentary on Isaiah survives in part as well as his Latin translation of David Kimhi's Hebrew grammar.[101] It should be made clear that, in spite of suggestions sometimes made that he was, not sound in Latin, Zamora was an excellent Latinist. It is also clear that he was a thoroughly competent Talmudic scholar as his *Sefer Hokmat Elohim* in Latin and Hebrew shows.[102] While this is obviously based on the previous apologetic work defending the Christian faith against Jewish criticism, the *Pugio Fidei* of Raimundo Martín, it also shows Zamora using the Haggadah and midrashic methods by which he was bringing the best of the rabbinical tradition into that biblical humanism which was developing strongly at Alcalá.

Two works of his were published; an expanded version of the Hebrew grammar he had prepared for the Polyglot Bible, 1526, and a little book, *Loor de virtudes nuevamente impresso . . . por el maestro Alonso de Çamora: regēte en la universidad de Alcala*, Alcalá de Henares, 1525.[103] This consists of a number of verses based on passages from Ecclesiastes, Wisdom and Job. There are no citations from the New Testament nor references to it, though there are some classical references including Seneca. It is curious that there is little if anything that can be seen as specifically Christian in doctrine or the terminology of Christian piety here – it reflects no more than the spirit of the Wisdom literature in showing virtues and contrasted vices. Perhaps it would be out of place to speculate on whether this little book implies that Zamora was a *converso* who was essentially a moralist on familiar liberal Jewish lines, rather than a wholly committed Christian, not

---

[101] Pérez Castro, op. cit., XLII ff. for the Targums, XLIX, LI.

[102] Pérez Castro, op. cit., LXI ff. (*The Book of the Wisdom of God* is the apologetic manuscript edited here.)

[103] Zamora's was the first thorough and competent Hebrew grammar in Latin, a marked improvement on that of Reuchlin, in which the traditional methods of Jewish grammarians especially of the Kimhis are presented in the systematic manner of humanist scholarship. I have found no other copy of the *Loor de virtudes*, save that in the Biblioteca Nacional at Madrid. This small book contains simply expressed precepts for a moral life. There is a reference to 'al glorioso redemptor', and one to 'dios trino y verdadero' supported by a quotation from Deuteronomy, but the following are not significantly Christian in tone.

> En juventud no sabemos
> y en mediedad no ay querer
> ni en senectud el poder
>
> y por esto nos perdimos
> son las pōpas de esta vida
> como sueño
> que se aparta de su dueño
> de corrida.

least since Cisneros accepted him, and Zamora's book against the Jews strongly defends the messiahship of Jesus, His divinity, and the Trinity. Nevertheless, his very existence at Alcalá and the nature of his writings there would help to bring about, as did the work of other *conversos* (and not only *conversos*) in universities elsewhere, the desire to study the Bible in Greek and Hebrew, instead of confining this study to the Vulgate; all this leads to that difficulty in sustaining these studies after 1550 and the near quenching of them under the repression of the Inquisition.

A paraphrase of some observations by Zamora will be necessary, in order to understand more fully what the Polyglot Bible was intended to achieve, followed by the Cardinal's definitive statements on this subject. Although it was dated in 1526, MS G.1.4., the Genesis in Hebrew and Latin referred to above, clearly relates to the Cardinal's hopes for biblical studies and was intended for publication with a dedication to the Archbishop of Toledo, Alfonso de Fonseca, in which Zamora and Ciruelo trust that it will not be made an occasion of calumny and will help to support the 'verity' of the Vulgate.[104] The preface to this manuscript has historical significance though its aspirations were ignored. It may be summarily paraphrased as follows. St. Jerome as translator is treated with deep respect while it is shown that he did not give a literal word for word translation but accommodated the Hebrew to Latin idiom – sometimes he added to or omitted from the original, and covered the discrepancies in meaning in the original to arrive at a consistent and flowing Latin. He advised in case of difficulty of interpretation that the prudent man should go to the Hebrew and Greek originals. Cardinal Cisneros well aware of this therefore provided the interpretations of biblical names, the vocabulary of the original languages and the annotations on the differences in the Old Testament of Nicholas of Lyra. This, however, Zamora wrote, still leaves the problem for the reader of searching through these different aids to find the meaning of a particular passage which is a cumbersome task. Moreover, the Jews state that St. Jerome corrupted Scripture, for if the Vulgate is compared with the Hebrew false renderings are clearly seen. Therefore, Ciruelo and Zamora have decided for these reasons to translate the Old Testament word by word in such a way that each Hebrew word should be rendered by a Latin word written underneath it, thus saving the reader considerable labour and incidentally show against Jewish criticism how close to the 'verity' of the original St. Jerome was – and overcome

---

[104] Pérez Castro, op. cit., fol. 5r begins the Prologue, of which some passages are reproduced, XXXV ff., translated by J. Llamas, *Sefarad*, 1946, 293–4.

the difficulty created by the fact that the copying from manuscript to manuscript through the centuries has led to many corruptions occurring which were not in St. Jerome's original text of long ago. Erasmus for years had been complaining strongly of the corruptions in the copies of the Vulgate which prevented a proper understanding of Scripture and increased the danger of false theological assumptions being made. Here we see at Alcalá the full flowering of what biblical humanism desired, the uninhibited return to the original texts of Scripture, the provision (as Zamora in particular did with these translations) of interpretative and grammatical notes to these texts, accompanied by a new literal version of the originals – some theologically more radical humanists would prefer a contemporary, more literary, Latin version, for example, Castellio in Basle.[105]

However, as was stated earlier, the younger men looked forward to the humanist future whereas Cardinal Cisneros, who kept a firm hand on the editing of this Bible, was still held by the medieval tradition of biblical interpretation. His intentions were in part a compromise between the need for maintaining the primary authority of the Vulgate and the need for the purpose of study by the linguistic student of a closer relation of the Latin version to the Hebrew and Greek originals, while allowing the humanists their own way with the Septuagint, the Targum and the literal Latin versions of these texts. Cisneros provided the definitive statement of his purposes in the letter addressed to Pope Leo X by way of a Prologue to the first volume of the Polyglot. Here he states that there were several reasons which compelled him to print the original text of Scripture, and gives three of them. No version can translate faithfully all the force and the peculiarities of the original words. The letter of Scripture is dead and needs quickening by the Spirit to bring it alive so that we may learn 'the inner mysteries of God's word', which can only be effectively known from the original language in which Scripture was written. The Latin codices show variations which suggests that the text has been corrupted due to the ignorance and neglect of copyists, so we must go to the original source and correct the books of the Old Testament according to the Hebrew text and those of the New Testament according to the Greek – as St. Jerome and St. Augustine and others warned us to do. This seems to be ambiguous for this Polyglot Bible did not maintain the policy of correcting the Vulgate to bring it into line with the Hebrew and Greek texts it established, rather the editors, as has been indicated above, sought out the earliest

[105] *Cambridge History of the Bible*, II, 71–2, (Basil Hall, *Biblical Scholarship: editions and commentaries*) Cambridge 1963.

manuscripts of the Vulgate from which to arrive at a sound text. However, the passage could be read to suggest that the Latin version, and the Hebrew and Greek originals, should be corrected from the earliest manuscripts of each text. What is not potentially ambiguous but a reversion to medieval tradition is that Cisneros included the interpretation of the proper names in the Scriptures, since 'these contain hidden mysteries'.[106] The humanist purpose is to be maintained, however, by Cisneros including dictionaries of Hebrew and Greek, a Hebrew grammar, a summary of Greek grammar, and a revised and corrected version of the annotations on the divergences in the Old Testament by Nicholas of Lyra. The six volumes have been printed, he writes, and are now being sent to Pope Leo for approval so that, 'the study of divine letters will be revived which up to this time has been as though dead'. It is clear from this Prologue as well as from the Prologue to the Reader which follows it that Cisneros was not merely providing the financial support for this Bible, but also he was in control of the texts which were to be printed and of their scholarly editors.

The second Prologue, whose themes follow immediately on the concluding words of the first, is addressed to 'Studiose Lector' and concerns the method of editing the Old Testament which, it is stated, has three languages, Hebrew, Aramaic and Greek which are published here each with its Latin version – the Vulgate for the 'Hebrew verity', new interlinear literal versions in Latin for the Aramaic of the Targum of the Pentateuch, and for the Septuagint. Other Targums, since 'they are corrupt in places and contain tales and trifles from the Talmud and are therefore unworthy to be published with the sacred text' are omitted, but because of their being clear in some places they have been closely translated into Latin and placed in the Library of the University of Alcalá.[107] The extra-canonical books which survive only in the Greek of the Septuagint have been given a literal interlinear Latin translation as well as that of the Vulgate. Cisneros added an assertion, not acceptable to the Council of Trent later in the century, that the Church 'receives these books only for the edification of the people rather than for confirming the authority of the Church's teaching'. In the outer margin of the Old Testament pages is the

---

[106] Several Christian Hebraists including Reuchlin were attracted to the study of the Jewish mystical tradition in the *Kabbala* and sought occult meanings in Hebrew names – for the Rabbis the very letters of the Hebrew alphabet and of the Hebrew biblical text held mystical power. *Interpretations hebraicorum: chaldeorum: grecorum nominum* . . . are at 174 ff. of volume VI of the Polyglot.

[107] For the manuscripts (their library and catalogue numbers) of the Aramaic and Latin texts written and annotated by Zamora, v. Pérez Castro, XLII–XLVIII.

Hebrew text and in the inner margin is the Greek Septuagint with the Vulgate in the central column, 'as though between the Synagogue and the Eastern Church like the two thieves on either side of Jesus, that is the Roman or Latin Church'; for this alone is founded on firm rock since the others deviate from the true understanding of Scripture. This has been frequently misunderstood as meaning that the Vulgate is the only true text from which the Hebrew and Greek deviate, whereas it is the Latin Church which is shown as alone founded on the rock but the churches of the Jews and Greeks are not, and do not rightly interpret the Scriptures. Cisneros then explains that small Latin letters are printed above Hebrew words and a similar letter is placed above Latin words in the Vulgate so that a reader can see which word of the translation relates to a Hebrew word. Sometimes a point is placed beneath a small letter to indicate that the particular Hebrew word has two different meanings ('hides a secret knowledge of mysteries'); the dictionary appended should then be consulted for the meanings. Certain letters are used as vowels י ו ה א and if an Aramaic word to which nothing in the margins corresponds is not found in the dictionary these letters should be removed in order to establish the consonants which can lead to the root.

It is stated that the accents are omitted since they make no difference to the meaning or pronunciation of a word: they were used only in chanting the text. However, where rarely a Hebrew word is not accented on the last syllable, the sign ˆ is placed on the accented syllable. Reference is made to the manuscripts used in the making of the Bible, and where they have not been returned to the original owners, but belonged to the Cardinal, they have been deposited in the library of the University of Alcalá. The variations of spelling of personal names ('vitio scriptorum') in the different texts have been left as they were written. In the Psalms the Latin Vulgate has been printed interlinearly above the Septuagint line since it is translated almost verbatim. Useful guidance reprinted from the Hebrew grammar is then provided in finding the root of a Hebrew word.

There is a preface to the New Testament which explains that the early Greeks did not use accents, as their ancient manuscripts and monuments show, and the writers of the New Testament omitted them together with the breathings. Attention is drawn to the device of placing identical small letters over Latin and Greek words to help the beginner to identify which word translated what. The Preface insisted on the great age of the manuscripts used which, it was claimed, 'are therefore wholly reliable' but none have survived and no positive evidences have been found yet for the source of the

Greek text published here. No variant readings were provided, and only on four occasions was a note given which dealt with what could be called textual criticism, otherwise only slight and unimportant observations also occur, none of which assist in establishing the manuscripts used. It should be added that the division of this Bible was by chapters in the manner used by Hugh of St. Clair in the thirteenth century, and not by verses – an improvement which was to come with Robert Estienne over thirty years later.[108]

The texts published in this Bible have not received the attention they deserve until the last two or three decades; though some pioneer work appeared in the past it is only recently that extended analysis has been undertaken. No more than a summary account can be given. The Hebrew text was, of course, not the first printed Hebrew Bible since several editions had appeared in Italy under Jewish editorship but it is the first edition of it issued by the authority of the Catholic Church under the direction of a member of its hierarchy.[109] No Jewish editor would have printed the Hebrew text beginning at the front of the volume and paged from left to right, nor would a Jew have reduced I and II Samuel, I and II Kings, Ezra–Nehemiah and I and II Chronicles into two books respectively as well as changing the order of other books; omitted the Kere, altered radically the vocalisation and almost totally omitted, or put to different use, the accents. By modern standards of editing these actions weaken the value of the text, but Cisneros was not concerned with those standards nor did this prevent his text from having considerable interest and value in its consonantal form for modern scholars, in spite of Paul Kahle's assertion that 'the Hebrew text of the Complutensis as such had no future'.[110] The consonantal text is important because of its provenance in the famed codices of Sephardic Spain which were highly regarded by the rabbis in the Jewish world from the later middle ages onwards – for example, the scriptoria of Toledo produced admirable examples based on the tenth century Ben Asher text[111]

Among the manuscripts which Cisneros said had been placed in the Library of the University of Alcalá some of the Hebrew codices still survive now in the Library of the Complutensian University at Madrid of which two in particular are notable, MS 118–Z–42 (now cited as M 1) and MS 118–Z–21 (now cited as M 2), as well as MS

---

[108] Elizabeth Armstrong, *Robert Estienne*, (revised edition, 1986), 301.

[109] The Soncino Press (a town near Mantua) published the first printed complete Hebrew Bible in 1488, another edition was printed at Brescia 1492, 1494.

[110] Paul Kahle, *The Cairo Geniza*, 1959, 129.

[111] C. D. Ginsburg, *Introduction to the Massoretico-Critical Edition of the Hebrew Bible*, 1897. For the consonantal text, 917.

G–1–5 in the library of E1 Escorial. M 1 written on parchment in three columns may be of the twelfth century and has a colophon in which its owners rabbi Isaak and rabbi Abraham, 'physicians and sons of rabbi Maimonides' give the date 1280 as that of its purchase at Toledo. It is complete save for a fragment of Exodus; it has the large and small Massorahs and at certain sections has Masoretic additions. The 33 leaves are magnificently presented with occasional loops of the Massorah in gold and blue colours and the text in splendid quadrate characters. M 2 was written in two columns, with Massorahs (and a Masoretic appendix, in 1482), to which Zamora added the sad colophon of 1520 already cited, for he had carefully read all three codices before the printing began. To follow Zamora through these codices reveals his editorial hand in the indications of chapters and numbers marked in red ink; the 'llamada' in Psalm 113, at folio 66 in G.1.5, and the occasional marginal word, in Hester (for example, folio 116) with that name, as with the other book titles, latinised and in red; above all in seeing his red ink *ojo* where he had found a word omitted in Esdras at folio 139 r.[112] In M 1, again, his red markings and chapter numbers are to be found. His careful work can be seen in a codex of the Pentateuch in two columns on parchment with missing leaves of text supplied on paper by Zamora which he described in a note at the end, 'llevo 8 pligos [*sic*] de faltas con lo que aclare in el cap. 10 de gene. y en el cap. 21 y 22 del libro de numero. y el ultimo cap. de deutero'. These Hebrew codices alone of the few manuscripts surviving from those originally deposited by the Cardinal in the Library of the University of Alcalá, show an editorial hand and signature. A recent study shows that the Hebrew text of the Polyglot follows primarily M 2, M 1 follows next and finally occurs G.1.5.[113]

The Targum of Onkelos was the only Targum published in the Polyglot for the reason already shown from the Prologue. This was somewhat more than a close paraphrase since it contained both Halakic and Haggadic material of that Talmudic origin disapproved by Cisneros. Two manuscripts of this Targum survive, MS 117–Z–15 at the University of Madrid and G–111–3 at El Escorial. Another manuscript which contained most of the Pentateuch and parts of other books, elaborately decorated with gold and other colours and containing the Massorah and the Targum, may have been used which

---

[112] These manuscripts are described in some detail, J. Llamas, *Los manuscritos hebreos de la Universidad de Madrid, Sefarad,* 1945, 261–284. The matters cited here are from my own observation.

[113] Teresa Ortega Monasterio, *Más sobre la relación entre los manuscritos bíblicos hebreos complutenses y la Poliglota de Alcalá, Sefarad,* 1977, 215. (This judgement is based on a few passages but the methodology and the results are sufficient to justify it.)

was incomplete and dated from the twelfth century. A recent collation finds evidence of another source beside the first two, and it may have been this third manuscript.[114] All three were overseen by Zamora; he added a note at the end of 117–Z–15, 'llevo tres pligos [sic] de emiendas'.[115] Paul Kahle has suggested that he rehandled the Targum text himself by his own emendations, which may account for the variations in the text which differ from the first two manuscripts. The Latin translation of the Targum is almost certainly that of Zamora himself.

Cisneros claimed in the Prologue great antiquity for the Septuagint codices used in the Polyglot. Until recently this was seen as an exaggeration not uncommon among the humanists, whose enthusiasm for antiquity in texts was not matched by their skill in palaeography.[116] Vercellone discovered an inventory of the library of Leo X made in 1518 which describes two codices lent to Cisneros, these are known as Vatican Greek 330 (the Rahlfs catalogue numbered this text 108) and Vatican Greek 346 (Rahlfs 248) – the first covers Genesis to Tobit the other the Wisdom books to Judith.[117] Two further manuscripts were used which were numbers 22 and 23 (Rahlfs 442 and 1670) in the Complutensian University of Madrid and originally at Alcalá. One was a copy of part of the Septuagint codex belonging to Cardinal Bessarion at Venice, Judges to third Maccabees, this is no doubt that which the Prologue to the Reader refers to, 'partem ex Bessarionis castigatissimo codice summa diligentia transcriptam Illustris Venetorum Senatus ad nos misit'. The word quemada is placed beside it in the catalogue now in Madrid showing its destruction during the Civil War. The other manuscript survives and is a Psalter lacking the beginning and end leaves, together with some canticles, dating perhaps from the early fourteenth century. It has recently been established that in the Twelve Prophets the Polyglot editors used a text of great antiquity (here Cisneros can be justified), and the variations from the accepted norm of the Septuagint which were formerly thought to be recensions by the editors are in fact original and can be seen in the Washington Codex (W) dating from the third century. These variations can also be found in the Hebrew

---

[114] This third manuscript described here is No. 3 of the Villa-Amil Catalogue of 1878 of the Complutensian manuscripts: it has either been destroyed, like some of the others in the Civil War, or is untraceable. In the original San Bernardo copy it is marked *Falta*.
[115] L. Diéz Merino (*La Biblia aramea . . ., Cuadernos Biblicos*, 1981) collated Genesis I, and discusses the relation of these manuscripts to the Polyglot text of the Targum.
[116] Bishop Brian Walton in the *Prolegomena* to the London *Polyglot Bible*, 1657, described this text as *consarcinata*, 64.
[117] C. Vercellone, *Dissertazioni accademiche*, Roma, 1864, 409.

fragments recently recovered at Nahal Hever showing these readings as early as Qumran.[118] Further, Angel Sáenz-Badillos wrote on 1 Kings, 1–8, that the Polyglot Greek readings were not adjusted by the editors to accommodate to the Vulgate or Hebrew texts save in the proper names, and this accommodation was intended to help the reader in consulting the index of those names – his conclusion is that manuscripts not now extant were the source of these readings.[119] However, for the first ten chapters of Job the editor or editors followed manuscript 248 (Rahlfs), as for the rest of this book, but they also used for these chapters readings from Theodotion, Aquila and Symmachus which they found in the margins of this manuscript so that they might conform to the original Hebrew. Therefore, the editing of this biblical text as with others in the Polyglot was not remarkable for consistency by modern critical standards, nevertheless it is sufficiently clear that the severe strictures on the Septuagint text from the seventeenth century onwards were not justified. Here as elsewhere in the Polyglot this text contains surprises that call for the extended attention of modern scholarship.

It has already been stated above that the manuscripts used for the New Testament have not survived. Zúñiga wrote of the 'Codex Rhodiensis' for the Epistles but it cannot be traced.[120] It might be assumed that modern scholarship could find the sources for the printed text from the large range of manuscripts available, but so far this has not been achieved. Wettstein in the eighteenth century claimed that the Greek text had been adapted to conform to the Vulgate and was therefore unreliable. This theme has been taken up again recently where the annotations in manuscript to the Greek New Testament (bound up with a printed copy of Lorenzo Valla's *Annotationes* edited by Erasmus in 1505; and with twelve printed leaves of interpretation of Hebrew, Aramaic and Greek names) have been used to demonstrate this adjusting of the Greek text to conform to the Vulgate, and for good measure to show that the editing of the Polyglot Vulgate text 'was a haphazard not to say a sloppy affair'.[121] These strongly worded judgements ignore the conditions laid down for his editors by Cisneros, as well as the difficulties created by the Spanish ecclesiastical and theological environment; also, they set aside the accepted view of modern textual scholarship that the

[118] Natalio Fernández Marcos, *El texto Griego de la Complutense en Doce Profetas, Sefarad,* 1979, 1–25.
   [119] Saénz-Badillos, op. cit., 654 ff.
   [120] Diego López Zúñiga (Stunica) *Annotationes contra Erasmum Roterodamum in defensionem tralationis novi testamenti.* Alcala, 1520, GII, Ki, Kii.
   [121] Jerry H. Bentley, *Humanists and Holy Writ,* Princeton, 1983, 108.

Complutensian text of the New Testament is of value and superior to that of Erasmus. At the same time the methods of the modern textual scholar are used to castigate severely the Complutensian editors, but this severity is not applied to the text of Erasmus.[122] Moreover, these judgements are preceded by the statement that their author is the first to give a full study of this manuscript since the superficial treatment of it by Revilla.[123] This is incorrect, a thorough account of its contents with a careful analysis suggesting its possible author, as well as a thorough examination of its usefulness in relation to the editing of the Greek and Vulgate texts concerned were provided by Angel Sáenz-Badillos in his *La Filología Bíblica en los helenistas de Alcalá*, Madrid, 1972.[124] Here we are shown a more mature judgement on the complexities of relating the citations from Greek in the manuscript to the Complutensian text and of the treatment of the Vulgate text; also the interesting suggestion is made that the Complutensian Greek text can be associated with the variants which modern scholarship has provided, which at least shows that the editors had a wide range of now unknown uncial texts from which to make their – in their circumstances inevitably – conservative choices.

There had been a number of editions of the Vulgate text from the Gutenberg Bible (1455) to that of Venice (1511) but none had shown interest in an effectively critical edition of the text: it was Cisneros who first attempted the collecting of early codices so that his editors could seek to arrive at a corrected edition. In the Prologue to the Reader the editors wrote that they had collated, 'the Latin version of St. Jerome with numerous manuscripts of venerable antiquity, especially those kept in the public library of our university'. Three of these manuscripts from the Library at Alcalá survive today in Madrid. 115–Z–7 is a splendid codex of the ninth century, damaged in the

---

[122] Bentley writes extensively and informatively on Erasmus seen as a critic of the text of the Greek New Testament in successive editions of the Annotations, but he has not set aside the long-held conclusion that Erasmus provided an inadequate text which was inferior to that of the Complutensian Bible. For Bentley 'the Polyglot editions of the Greek and Latin New Testament did not result from careful, professional editorial scholarship.' He should have added that the failure of Erasmus in this respect was even greater, apart from 'hundreds of typographical errors', parts of his text of *Revelation* and of some other places, are self-made translations into Greek from the Vulgate readings unknown to any Greek manuscript, which he left uncorrected in his final edition. B. M. Metzger, *The Text of the New Testament*, Oxford, 1964, 98 ff.

[123] Bentley, op. cit., 98. '. . . it is now possible to resort to a hitherto unused source that provides the sort of information needed.' This provision is an assumption, and, further, one that is not adequately demonstrated since the manuscript need have been no more than one editor's work which was used occasionally along with uncial manuscripts by other editors.

[124] n. 40 supra. and op. cit., 686 ff.

pillage of the college of San Bernardo during the Civil War, which contains most of the Vulgate text of both Testaments including variants for the New Testament, though certain of the Old Testament books are in Old Latin. 115–Z–6 of the ninth or tenth century contains some of the Old Testament but the New Testament is complete save for much of Revelation. 115–Z–4 is of the thirteenth century or earlier where many of the Old Testament books are lacking, and the musical markings and lection divisions show that it had been used for liturgical purposes. The first two of these codices have the 'gothic characters' mentioned by Nebrija in the *Tertia Quinquagena* and are considered to be those used for the Polyglot text – the second codex in particular is proposed as the basis for the New Testament Vulgate text of this edition. The Old Testament readings of the Vulgate of the Polyglot show a tendency to choose a variant reading which is nearer to the Hebrew, but in the New Testament a more conservative attitude prevailed, the traditional Vulgate text is largely evident and variants which were in line with the Greek are frequently rejected. This suggests that more than one editor was concerned with the Vulgate text, and that different views were held which led to contradictions in method in the New Testament. It is plain that there was an overriding intention to protect the traditional Vulgate in the interests of maintaining the text behind traditional Church teaching on faith, morals and liturgical practice. The episcopal office of the Cardinal hindered him from following the more critical attitude of Nebrija and his pupil Juan Vergara: the long-standing essential words of dogmatic definition had to be preserved. There is an improvement on previous editions of the Vulgate text but much more might have been achieved in the New Testament if the dogmatic and liturgical tradition had not been preserved with such close care. Its weaknesses, however, did not prevent this text being reprinted several times even as late as the Paris Polyglot (1628–1645), some time after the Clementine edition of the Vulgate of 1592 had been declared to be the final official text at Rome.

The Latin translations of the Septuagint and of the Targum of Onkelos were intended to be literal though the translation by Zamora of the Targum was freer and in accord with that good latinity which shows in his use of *que* copulative. The translation of the Septuagint, however, was often extremely literal and word for word, ignoring the structure of Latin syntax. The intention here is clearly pedagogic in keeping so close to the Greek so that those learning the language could find their way through the text. The translators were Zúñiga, the Comendador Núñez and Ducas with some participation by Juan Vergara who gave this information about himself to the Inquisitors at his trial after 1532. The Psalter published in volume three, as the translation of the Septuagint, is not, however, new since they used the Psalter Gallicanum which had been made from the Greek, the central column continues with the Vulgate version of St. Jerome from the Hebrew. Cisneros no doubt thought it desirable to have both traditional versions known through liturgical use for this Bible.[125]

The great achievement of the Complutensian Bible lies not only in the energy of Cisneros and the work of his scholars, but also in the splendour of the typography which puts this Bible in the first rank in the history of printing. Cisneros was fortunate in choosing the most suitable printer available to him in Spain for this work, the Franco-Navarrese Guillén de Brocar. His first known work was a liturgical text printed at Pamplona in 1490 and he continued in this lucrative field of liturgical printing for the rest of his career, though his publications were not confined to this field for among other things he printed literary works in Spanish. When political troubles arose in Pamplona he moved his press to Logroño in 1502 where he began the use of the Gothic type-fount originally cut in Paris which became popular in Spain. He printed Nebrija's *Introductiones Latinae* in 1503, and in 1507 he issued anonymously Nebrija's *Apologia* and from then he printed almost all Nebrija's works, an association which showed that Brocar wished to be concerned with the humanist circles coming into being in Spain.[126] It is reasonable to suppose that it was Nebrija who suggested Brocar to Cisneros as the most suitable printer for the Polyglot Bible and in 1511 his press was established at Alcalá, where many of his books carry the arms of the Cardinal on their title-pages. Through the generous payments made by Cisneros Brocar provided the remarkable new fount for the Greek of the New Testament with the more customary and less attractive smaller Greek type used for the Septuagint; a new Roman type for the Latin together with his older but attractive Gothic types; three new type founts of Hebrew consisting of some large initial letters, the main text fount, and the smaller fount for the Hebrew roots in the margins, and for the Targum.[127] In one of the prologues to the Bible, possibly by Brocar, it is stated that the Greek type was cut on the pattern of the letters in

---

[125] For these Latin manuscripts see F. J. Fernández Vallina and L. Vegas Montaner, *Lengua y literatura en las Biblias Políglotas Españolas. Sefarad*, 42, 1982, 129 ff. F. Perez Castro, *El manuscrito apologético de Alfonso de Zamora*, Madrid, 1950; H. Quentin, *Mémoire sur l'établissement du texte de la Vulgate*, I, Rome, 1922; J. Villa-Amil y Castro, *Catálogo de los manuscritos existentes en la Biblioteca del Noviciado de la Universidad Central*, Madrid, 1878.
[126] F. J. Norton, *Printing in Spain; 1501–1520*. Cambridge, 1966, 36.
[127] Ibid, 40 n.2., 41.

the Greek manuscripts lent to Cisneros by Leo X, but it is more likely to have been influenced by a similar type fount used by Nicolas Jensen at Venice in the fifteenth century.[128] The type face is larger than that of Jensen and all the ligatures and contractions are omitted (the absence of breathings and accents has already been mentioned). Scholderer, an authority on early Greek printing, describes this fount as 'the last and most beautiful of the Jensonian class of type carrying it to the limit of its possibilities . . . and is the king of all Greek founts . . . the only original contribution of Spain to Hellenic typography, taking the form of a vindication of old and fine standards . . .'

The care of the printer is seen in the fact that there are comparatively few printers' errors in the text of the Greek New Testament. The splendour of this Greek fount should not detract from that of the Hebrew, especially that of the first column in the first four volumes, for the vowel points are clear and neat, though the technical problems of printing these articulated with the consonantal text were formidable. The result was an elegant proportion in the printed line that had not been equalled by previous printers of Hebrew. A detailed typographical description of the six volumes was provided by F. J. Norton.[129] It is sufficient to add here that the Hebrew roots were printed in the margin of the Hebrew first column; St. Jerome's prefaces were added throughout including his letter to Damasus which accompanied the New Testament; the Acts of the Apostles was printed after the Pauline epistles; and volume six contained aids to biblical study including a dictionary of Hebrew, and Aramaic words, the admirable Hebrew grammar by Alfonso de Zamora and a lexicon for the interpretation of Hebrew and Greek names. Volume five, containing the Greek text and the Vulgate version of the New Testament, alone provides the very few critical notes in this Bible; it also adds a summary of Greek grammar.

The last page of the first gathering in volume one (a convenient blank) was used to published the letter of Leo X of 22 March, 1520, providing a privilege of seven years for this Bible and referring to the sudden death of Cisneros which had caused the delay in obtaining papal approval for publishing this Bible already printed by 1517. The complete Bible was presented to the Pope and was placed in the Vatican Library on 5 December 1521 which could therefore be taken to be the approved date of publication. Possible causes for the delay

[128] Victor Scholderer, *Greek Printing Types, 1465–1927*, 1927, 10. F. J. Norton, *A Descriptive Catalogue of Printing in Spain and Portugal 1501–1520*, Cambridge 1978. For an account of Brocar, v. 159.
[129] F. J. Norton *A Descriptive Catalogue*, 11–15. A. F. Johnson, *Selected Essays on Books and Printing.* ed. P. H. Muir, Amsterdam, 1971, 73–6.

in obtaining the papal privilege include jealousy from a Spanish lobby at Rome, and the disquiet of an Italian lobby in licensing a Bible not yet thoroughly examined at Rome, but these speculations are not profitable in the absence of evidence. An obvious cause of the delay was that Erasmus had gained papal sanction for his edition of the New Testament of 1516, and also a privilege lasting for four years from the Emperor Maximilian I: these sanctions would have caused Leo X to wait until march 1520 before granting his privilege.[130] However, it is a reasonable assumption that copies of this Bible were in use before that date, for example, that sent to the Cardinal and that given to the University of Alcalá.

After the Cardinal's death the Flemish court, newly arrived in Spain, claimed the Cardinal's books and papers for the Crown in spite of the efforts of the University of Alcalá to retain them. The court profited from the sale of copies of the Bible before 1523 when the College of San Ildefonso managed to regain the remainder after the King's regent, Cardinal Adrian of Utrecht, acting in the absence of Charles, allowed the return of the Cardinal's books and papers.[131] From the papal letter of 1520 it appears that about six hundred copies of this Bible were printed. A letter of Philip II reported that many sets were lost in a Spanish ship sailing to Italy: this, together with the considerable increase in price after 1523, limited its wide dispersal.[132] Perhaps about one hundred and fifty to two hundred sets (or partial sets) survive today as a visible symbol of the first great flowering of the typography and trilingual learning of Spain – cette merveille wrote Bataillon of the Polyglot Bible of Alcalá.[133]

What could have been the second flowering, the Polyglot Bible of Antwerp of 1572, was, however, not so much a renewal as a conclusion since it was the autumnal and last harvest of Spanish humanism and biblical learning. This second Polyglot Bible was undertaken because of the scarcity of the first, by one who admired its makers, used its surviving manuscripts and repristinated its textual traditions, the royal chaplain Benito Arias Montano, a distinguished scholar; and by a printer more renowned than Brocar, the Frenchman Christophe Plantin who had proposed this enterprise and produced it at his press at Antwerp in the Spanish Netherlands, 1568–1572.[134] It

---

[130] T. H. Darlow and H. F. Moule, *Historical Catalogue of the Printed Editions of Holy Scripture in the Library of the British and Foreign Bible Society*, 1903, Part II, Division I, Polyglots, 3.

[131] Bataillon. op. cit., 46 and n.2 gives extracts from the University records on this affair.

[132] T. González Carvajal, *Elogio histórico del Doctor Benito Arias Montano*, in *Memorias de la Real Academia de la Historia*, Madrid 1832, 144.

[133] F. J. Norton, *A Descriptive Catalogue*, 14.

[134] C. Clair, *Christopher Plantin*, 1960 and L. Voet *The Golden Compasses*, Amsterdam, 1969. Plantin was made *prototypographe du Roy*. He decided to publish a Bible in four languages

needed considerable pressure from Philip II to achieve the publication in Spain of this *Biblia Regia* in eight volumes after a long delay caused by the Spanish Inquisition and suspicion at Rome.[135] What Cisneros had held in check until his death, the power of the Inquisition, and what Nebrija had tried to overcome, 'the power of ignorant and unworthy men', as Rodríguez Manríquez described them in 1533, were to break forth and defeat these studies. 'Our country is a land of envy, pride and barbarism' wrote Manríquez, son of the Inquisitor General, 'no one can cultivate good letters in Spain with moderation without there being discovered in them an accumulation of errors, heresies, and judaising. In this way silence is imposed upon the learned; those who have recourse to erudition are overwhelmed by a great terror . . . In Alcalá an attempt is being made to eradicate the study of Greek when at this same time they seek to establish it at Paris.'[136]

Brocar withdrew from Alcalá and apparently his large Hebrew and Greek type founts disappeared; most of the scholars gathered there by Cisneros soon departed. Alfonso de Zamora within a decade was under suspicion from the Inquisition as a *converso*, and by 1530 it began to include among its targets not only *conversos* but what it regarded as the errors of Erasmianism, Illuminism and Lutheranism – which were in fact largely variants of Erasmian themes.[137] Spain was to become a society closed to foreign books, whose students were to be forbidden to study abroad and in which foreign travellers would be regarded with suspicion.

(eventually five) in 1565; to secure this, amid the political dangers at Antwerp, he wrote to Philip II 'our Catholic King' to accept patronage of the work. M. Rooses and J. Dénuce, *Correspondence de Plantin*, 8 vols. Antwerp 1883–1914; I, no. 20 Philip II wrote in March, 1568 to the Duke of Alba in the Spanish Netherlands concerning 'la biblia quadrilingue que el cardenal fray Francisco Ximénez imprimió en Alcalá de Henares': 'one of the most noble and useful works for the universal Church to have seen the light of day . . . but since a great number of these bibles was lost at sea . . . Christopher Plantin . . . seeking to renew this Bible and print it with excellent types in all languages under our name and authority . . . we have accepted'. Arias Montano was sent to oversee the publication.

[135] For a brief account of the *Royal Polyglot Bible of Antwerp*, v. Basil Hall, *The Great Polyglot Bibles*, The Book Club of California, San Francisco, 1966. A more detailed account is in B.Rekers, *Benito Arias Montano*, London and Leiden, 1972, ch.III.

[136] De Vocht, *Monumenta Humanistica Lovaniensia*, Louvain, 1934, 427 ff. Manríquez was writing from Paris, when trouble had arisen temporarily for the *Lecteurs Royaux*, to Luis Vives one of Spain's greatest humanists.

[137] The *Alumbrados* (Illuminists), maintained a mystical challenge to excessive formalism in religion which relied on subjective experience in passive surrender in order to communicate with God – this was seen by Inquisitors as setting aside grace, sacraments and good works. Since Luther (and Erasmus) had offered, from differing standpoints, criticism of contemporary orthodoxy on these matters their writings could be seen simplistically, with the activity of the *Alumbrados*, as one heresy with various ramifications. A. Márquez, *Los Alumbrados*, Madrid, 1972. Alvaro Huerga, *Erasmismo y Alumbradismo* in *El Erasmismo en Espana*, 338–356, questions Bataillon's close association of Erasmianism and Illuminism.

Alfonso Garciá Matamoros wrote of Juan de Vergara, who had been one of the Cardinal's scholars: 'My companion and friend Alvar Gomez said that possibly some equalled him [Vergara] but none excelled him.'[138] Vergara, however, had been the admired correspondent of Erasmus, and Erasmus was now regarded as heretical by traditionalist Spanish Dominicans, and those who feared and disliked the study of Hebrew and Greek – and Vergara was of *converso* stock. The *beata* Francisca Hernández of Valladolid under examination by the Inquisition for participating in the spiritual exaltation of Illuminism denounced Vergara and others as 'Lutherans'.[139] In 1532 he was arrested but he was not cowed, rather he made a vigorous defence of scriptural study in the original languages, since St. Jerome and other Fathers had urged this and since St. Augustine and others had recommended the correction of the Latin versions by the original.[140] It is curious to note the ambivalence that could arise for Spanish humanists since the Benedictine Alonso de Virues, a theologian and orientalist, an admirer of Erasmus, who after being imprisoned by the Inquisition at Seville as a 'Lutheran', and released by the urging of Charles V who admired his sermons, went to the Inquisition at Toledo and denounced Vergara as one who did not believe in the sacramental *ex opere operato*.[141] Vergara made an agile defence against this attack citing recent debates on sacramental grace and pointing to the generalised nature of the accusation. He complained of the wearisome slowness of the trial procedures which, he hinted, reflected the dull minds of the Inquisitors, and defended his orthodoxy with vigour and theologial energy. His honour was offended that the accusations of an 'illuminated' *beata*, and of an obtuse scholar who had treated his casual conversation as if it were a formal statement of belief, should be regarded so seriously as to require his imprisonment and prolonged interrogations. Nevertheless, Vergara had to endure in December 1535 the humiliation of abjuring on the scaffold, paying a large fine, and being sent to a monastery in January, 1536, for a year of enforced penitence.

---

[138] José López de Toro, *Alfonso García Matamoros; Apologia 'Pro Adserenda Hispanorum Eruditione.'* [1555], Madrid, 1943, 214 (par. 116). Matamoros was a professor of Rhetoric at Alcalá 1542, later a canon at Seville, a great admirer of Erasmus.

[139] Manuel Serrano y Sanz, *Juan de Vergara y la Inquisición de Toledo*, RABM, 1901, 896 ff., 1902, 29 ff., gave an overall and documented view of this trial. Bataillon, 473–508, provides a full account based on the trial records. Among other accusations was that which stated that Vergara denied (with Erasmus) that auricular confession was *de jure divino*.

[140] Bataillon, 498. Vergara pointed out that Cardinal Cajetan for correcting the Vulgate according to the Greek, and also St. Jerome and St. Augustine, should be declared heretics.

[141] Miguel de la Pinta Llorente, *Una testificación del Erasmista Alonso Virues contra el Dr. Juan de Vergara, Ciudad de Dios*, vol. 153, 345 ff. It is interesting that Virues could be described as: 'Erasmi usque ad invidiam percupidus.' 348.

He was more fortunate than others. Juan de Castillo, a humanist whose patron was the Duke of Infantado, had supported Illuminist piety similar in some ways to that piety promulgated by Cisneros, and having affinities with Erasmus' 'Philosophia Christi' which to Inquisitors could be seen as 'Lutheranism'. He had thought it safer to go to Italy but he was captured at Bologna, brought to Spain for trial, and confessed under torture to the uselessness of good works and free will for salvation, and that Church laws on fasting, and other matters were not obligatory.[142] Fine distinctions about similarities between some of these ideas and those of Cardinal Contarini or the Cologne doctors, were not made by the Inquisition and Castillo was burned.[143] A former rector of the college of San Ildefonso at Alcalá was indicted for heresy and after release from prison he passed the remainder of his life at Rome. Pedro de Lerma, Chancellor of the University of Alcalá, was required to retract publicly 'scandalous and heretical propositions', after which he went to Paris where he became Dean of the Faculty of Theology there, which was regarded throughout Europe as the defender of Catholic orthodoxy.[144]

Opposition to trilingual studies grew: the *Procesos inquisitoriales contra los catedráticos hebraístas de Salamanca*, according to the irony of Miguel de la Pinta Llorente, 'constitute an immortal page in Spanish culture in the sixteenth century'. These professors of Hebrew were Gaspar de Grajal, Martín Martínez de Cantalapiedra, and associated with them was the theologian and trilingual scholar, Fray Luis de León an Augustinian who was also a poet (*refinado y maravilloso*) and one of the makers of Spain's *Siglo de Oro*.[145] The Dominicans, though admired for their theological learning in Scholasticism as well as in canon law and moral theology, were weak in the biblical languages and resented those whom they dismissed as grammarians, since they saw them as deviating from their Scholastic and traditional

---

[142] The power of the Inquisition can be seen in its covert search for him in Italy. The Consejo wrote to the royal secretary at Rome, 'seria bien que V. M. Muy secretamente se informe donde puede estar', Inquisition register: cited Bataillon, 518.

[143] v. Infra, 160. Contarini had described justification by faith by 1512, the Cologne theologian Gropper taught a double justification, moderating works.

[144] His sermons were thought to be Erasmian; presumably he preached energetically from Scripture. He had to abjure eleven propositions 'offensive to pious ears', drawn from them. His nephew, also Chancellor of Alcalá, wary of the Inquisiton, left for Paris in 1551.

[145] Miguel de la Pinta Llorente, *Proceso Criminal contra el hebraista Salmantino Martín Martínez de Cantalapiedra*, Madrid, 1946. The Introduction (*Estudio*) XIII–CXLVII is useful for all three trials; 3–400 contains Inquisition records. For the trial of Luis de León, *Collection de Documentos inéditos para la historia de España*, X–XI, Madrid, 1847. M. de la Pinta Llorente, *La Inquisición Española y los problemas de la Cultura y de la Intolerancia*, Madrid, 1953, is valuable for this episode.

terminology which by now had been largely reinforced at the Council of Trent, where the priority and authority of the Vulgate text had been affirmed as *de fide*. The earlier glory of Dominican theology founded by Francisco de Vitoria at Salamanca (where he renewed Thomism within the framework of the Scriptures and the Fathers, whose pupils and successors in the chair of theology, Dominic Soto and Melchor Cano, helped to make Spain's powerful contribution to the Council of Trent) was declining from the lingering theme of humanism into a narrower and harsher orthodoxy.[146]

Among the Dominican epigones of Salamanca was Bartolomé de Medina *letor de theulugia* [*sic*] as he is described in the Inquisitorial interrogation of Martínez de Cantalapiedra whom he accused in his testimony of stating, '. . . erat carmen amatorium Salomonis in laudem filiae Pharonis, et contrarium asserere est futile'. He further deposed that the hebraists of Salamanca commonly followed the propositions of the Jews and rabbis rather than those of the holy Fathers, and that these professors challenged the reliability of the Vulgate and contended that a better Latin translation could be made, for this reason preferring the Latin version of Pagnini.[147] However, well before this trial of the hebraists the professor of Greek at Salamanca, León de Castro, had worked himself into a state of paranoia about them. He urged his scholarship in Greek with vainglorious pedantry, demanded high fees from his pupils, and was jealous of his younger and abler linguistic colleagues whom he saw as machiavellian rivals enmeshing him with intrigue. He opposed in vain the founding of a trilingual college at Salamanca (proposed because of the admired example of that of Alcalá) which was begun in 1555, and was for him a source of rivalry with other faculties, including the attracting of students from them and a potential source of heresy. He charged double fees for lectures which he required students to attend at his house over and above his university courses: when challenged by the university council who asked why he broke the regulations when he was relentless in claiming that others did so, he angrily claimed that his enemies had caused the students to complain.[148] He wrote a vast commentary on Isaiah, though he was

---

[146] C. Pozo, *Fuentes para la historia del método teológico en la escuela de Salamanca*, (on Vitoria, De Soto and Melchor Cano), *Biblioteca Teológica Granadina*, 6. Granada, 1962.

[147] Llorente, op. cit., 5, 6. He claimed that all three hebraists 'quitan alguna autoridad a la edición Bulgata, diziendo que se puede hazer otra mejor, y que tiene artas falsedades; esto de la edicion Bulgata es público e notorio.'

[148] Rekers, op. cit., 49–66 writes on Castro's attitude to Arias Montano. Montano was in danger of being enmeshed in the trial of his friend and correspondent Luis de León. However, both in citation of records, and in judgements on them, Rekers is liable on occasion to mislead. My review of Rekers in *The Journal of Ecclesiastical History*, vol. XXVI, 1975, 318–20.

ignorant of Hebrew, in which he claimed that the Septuagint text was free of the corrupt alterations made by the Jews in the Hebrew text: when the book was delayed for three years by the Inquisition until 1570 he blamed the Hebrew professors. León de Castro at the same period wished to ban the writings of the French logician Pierre de la Ramée (Ramus) which the Inquisition were inquiring into, and he resented objection to this by the linguistic scholars who saw that Ramus had restored the original Greek of Aristotle against the corrupted Latin version used in logical treatises.[149] The culmination of his anger came when he proposed the condemnation of the annotations of Vatable in a proposed new edition of the Pagnini version (which he also disliked), and Luis de León at the meeting of the university council which discussed the matter remarked that it would be better to ban Castro's commentary on Isaiah. To this Castro replied bitterly that neither he nor his book were in danger of fire, in contrast with those whose lineage should be examined – Luis de León had Jewish ancestry. When his book failed to sell and his printer demanded compensation, he saw again an intrigue of the three hebraists, and he denounced them to the Inquisition.

At the trial, in 1571, he made the same accusations against them which the Dominican Medina made, and in this sour story of jealousy and ignorant denunciation it is difficult to discover whether Castro's paranoia led him to be used as an instrument by the Dominicans, or whether two varieties of fear and dislike of trilingual scholarship came together, the fear that traditional Scholastic theology (defended at Trent by Dominicans) could be undermined by Augustinians (who had sought to modify and update that learning at Trent) and the fear that grammarians were eroding the authority of the Vulgate.[150] Cisneros had held such fears at bay – but now the Inquisition and those willing to denounce distinguished scholars to its tribunals were in power. The Augustinian Luis de León, a man outstanding as a poet, as a theologian and as a biblical scholar, passed almost five years

[149] Pierre de la Ramée challenged Aristotelianism in two books in 1543 at Paris, and taught at the Collège de France 1551–1559. In his *Remonstrance au conseil privé* he wrote in defence '. . . toute cette logigue ne m'avait rendu plus savant dans l'histoire et la connaissance de l'antiquité, ni plus habite dans l'art de la parole . . . ni plus sage . . .' he moved like Calvin before him from Catholic humanism into Protestantism (1562). His work (in linking dialectic with rhetoric) pursued more thoroughly similar themes developed by earlier humanists, for example, in the use of *topoi*. He dismissed the *scholasticus morbus* dear to Castro and traditionalist Aristotelians. He had a considerable influence even reaching to Milton's *Logica*.

[150] The Council of Trent had to find a middle road between the conflicting views of the Scholastic theologians. The General of the Augustinian Order, Seripando, and some others including Sanfelice, bishop of Cava, sought to moderate the terms of defining the relation of Scripture and tradition, and the doctrines of sin and grace. H. Jedin, *The Council of Trent*. Spanish theologians gradually came to dominate at the Council.

(like his two colleagues, one of whom died) in the prisons of the Inquisition.

León de Castro was still not satisfied: he also denounced Spain's most renowned biblical scholar of that time, Benito Arias Montano, who sought to maintain Catholic spirituality, and to reject Protestant teaching on its own ground, without recourse to the traditional envelope of Scholastic method or patristic allegorising. He was a priest of the Order of Santiago and had been a theological adviser with the Spanish delegation at the last session of the Council of Trent; he was skilled in semitic languages as well as humanist learning – his fellow students at Alcalá named him the Spanish Jerome – and for the Latin verse of his *Rhetorica* he received the title at Alcalá of Poet Laureate.[151] While he reluctantly accepted the demand of the censors of Louvain and the Council of the Inquisition that the Vulgate should be printed in volumes I to IV alongside the Hebrew text of the Complutensian Polyglot now corrected (the *Biblia Regia* of Antwerp was based upon the revised texts of that of Alcalá with additional targums, and for the New Testament the recently published Syriac version transliterated into Hebrew characters was added to the Greek and Latin texts), but he got his way by printing the version of Pagnini, aslo corrected, in volume VII. Volumes VI (the New Testament), and VII and VIII of this Polyglot showed Arias Montano, assisted by French and Flemish scholars, boldly challenging the narrow traditionalist resentment of linguistic learning by putting passages of the Vulgate into the margin of the New Testament, and replacing them with a more accurate Latin version, and by writing treatises of wide range and depth in which Jewish and Protestant scholars were cited with approval, in spite of warnings from Alaclá and elsewhere that he should be careful.[152] The insistent support of Philip II, and the presence of Arias Montano at Rome with a copy of the Bible, obtained a privilege for it from the hesitant Gregory XIII in 1572. From early in 1570 León de Castro began to attack this Polyglot,

---

[151] A. .F. G. Bell, *Benito Arias Montano*, Oxford, 1922. His biblical learning was derived from his years at Alcalá, 1548 onwards. He held a certificate of *limpieza de sangre* which could (ironically) suggest a *converso* ancestry, but this accusation was not made in his lifetime. He had advised on divorce and on communicating in both kinds at Trent, and became chaplain to Philip II, 1566. D. Tomás González Carvajal, *Elogio Historico del Doctor Benito Arias Montano, Memorias de la Real Academia de la Historia*, Madrid, 1832, 1–99, is still the most reliable basis for his biography.
[152] Vol. VII, contained the various lexicons of the biblical languages; Vol. VIII, contained a number of treatises by Arias Montano on measures, the twelve tribes and the partition of Palestine, on the temple and the Ark, on the Mazoreth and other matters. Andreas Masius, the Flemish hebraist, warned Arias Montano to be careful in a letter, October, 1568, cited Rekers, 143.

hitherto unpublished as judaising, and tried to influence the court, but failed.

He tried again in 1574 by denouncing this Bible to the court at Madrid, on the grounds that the Hebrew text should be altered to conform to the Vulgate, the Pagnini version could well be omitted, and the treatises contained heresy. Again the court suppressed the matter.

Castro now turned to the Tribunal of the Inquisition but once again Arias Montano was fortunate in not only having support at court, including that of the king's secretary Gabriel de Zayas, but also that of powerfully placed university men. Castro was more successful in influencing theologians at Rome for, while the *Congregatio Concili* there gave reluctant approval to the *Biblia Regia*, it withdrew the *Apparatus* from the papal privilege; Gregory XIII, unwilling to challenge Philip II, referred the matter to the Spanish Inquisition which also was wary of royal anger and asked the Jesuit Juan de Mariana, the historian of Spain, to examine the Polyglot of Antwerp. He was a man who sympathised with this humanistic approach to biblical studies as well as being competent in the languages they involved.[153] Mariana gave his report to the Tribunal of the Inqusition in August, 1577, in which he demonstrated that there were textual and other errors through haste in the preparation of this Bible, and that too much weight had been given to Jewish scholarship, but that, nevertheless, doctrinal orthodoxy had not been endangered. To Mariana it was obvious that Spain could not simply abolish Hebrew studies because Castro and others disapproved of them, and he agreed in principle with Arias Montano in the view that it was not improper to use the scholarly work even of Jews and some Protestants, since a man might err on dogma but know how to understand the text. For Mariana it was clear that 'since Christ came the Church has never doubted that the works of the Jews may be used'. Mariana disliked Castro whose character and intriguing bigotry he found distasteful. How could one take seriously Castro's complaint that Arias Montano had printed in Hebrew after the sections of the Hebrew biblical text the statement, above his signature, that the text was correctly given, and placed underneath in cursive Arabic the word 'tilmidh' (disciple) which, since it was read ignorantly by Castro from left to right to whom it looked like 'rabi', he declared this proved that Montano was secretly a rabbi, a judaiser, a potent danger to the faithful?

Benito Arias Montano, who died in 1598, and whose works were put on the papal Index of Prohibited Books in 1607, was the last of

---

[153] G. Cirot, *Mariana Historien*, Paris, 1905. Mariana took two years to prepare his report. Cirot, 399 ff. reproduces Mariana's letters to the Inquisition.

that school of scholarship which looked to the biblical studies and trilingual learning, begun at Alcalá de Henares by Cardinal Cisneros, as the way to quicken and renew the theology and spirituality of Spain as well as to stimulate humane learning and 'bonae litterae.'

This study closes by showing Arias Montano as the conclusion of the methods of biblical study begun at Alcalá de Henares. However, Biblical scholars and exegetes continued to write in Spain, for example, Alfonso Salmeron, a leading theologian at Trent, the Jesuits Francisco Ribera and Nicolas de Lorena, among others, but now Spanish scholars were using a Tridentine framework and setting aside the former tradition of biblical humanism.

2

Erasmus: Biblical Scholar and Catholic Reformer

Mark Pattison wrote that Erasmus 'in whom the Humanist and Reformer were pretty equally mixed perceived what a powerful weapon the Greek original [of the New Testament] might be made'.[1] In fact this was to be the chief of several powerful weapons which Erasmus used to advance his programme of religious reform. The theme of the Erasmian humanistic reform was summed up in his own phrase *philosophia Christi*. Here we are shown the centrality of Christ found through the Bible, especially the Gospels, without reference to the dogmatic definitions of Scholasticism or to many of the popular forms of piety which had developed in Catholicism, to both of which, Erasmus claimed, the learning and piety of the age of the Fathers of the first centuries of the Church were to be preferred. The anti-dogmatic, anti-speculative and anti-Scholastic attitude of Erasmus led him to insist on that simplicity of faith in Christ which he proclaimed and supported with eloquent latinity, characteristic of the Erasmian movement of religious reform. This movement was a powerful influence on many Catholics including those who were to become Protestants concerned about the moral, social and religious

[1] *Essays by the late Mark Pattison*, ed. H. Nettleship, Oxford, 1889, vol. I, 79.

52

problems of the time who recognised the need for a new moral and intellectual motivation to bring improvement. Thomas More wrote to Erasmus in December 1516 nearly nine months after the publication of Erasmus' Greek and Latin New Testament: 'The Bishop of Winchester, who is, as you are aware, a man of very sound judgement, was present at a large gathering of distinguished people when the conversation turned upon you and your lucubrations; he testified, to everyone's approval, that your version of the New Testament was better to him than ten commentaries, since it brought so much light to bear upon it.'[2] This Bishop of Winchester was Richard Foxe who in the following year was to found Corpus Christi College, Oxford, where he wished to promote those new studies which Erasmus had so strongly emphasised, at the same time as Erasmus himself was preparing the way for the founding of the Trilingual College at Louvain which he hoped would become the international centre of this renewal.

There can be no doubt that the inspiration of this trilingual 'new learning' lay in the work of that saint whom Erasmus most admired, St. Jerome, who had been *Hebraeus, Graecus, Latinis trilinguis*, with all that this implied: and the influence of Jerome on Erasmus was fundamental since he adopted something of Jerome's style and more of his methods as a scholar. Nevertheless as he progressed through his editions of the Annotations he shows at times severe criticism of Jerome's translation, even questioning his ability in Greek and the correctness of his latinity from which, wrote Erasmus, no doubt arose Jerome's errors in translation. In the *Ratio* he pointed out that Jerome was but a man who, though pious and learned, could err. From his youth in the monastery at Steyn to his closing years in the new world of the transformed *Respublica Litterarum* which he had helped to create, Erasmus was never to be far from Jerome. Jerome has recorded that he had known a deep struggle between his love for the pagan classical writers and his love for the Scriptures: for Erasmus these were not so much opposed as transmuted. Towards the end of his career in his *Ciceronianus* he challenged the pedantic Ciceronianism of some humanists, showing it to be a lifeless antiquarianism, and affirmed yet once again the importance of the intimate association of the best in Classical culture with Christian values.

> BULEPHORUS: He who will bring to the study of Christian philosophy the zeal which Cicero brought to that of profane philosophy; he who will draw into himself the Psalms and the Prophets as Cicero did with the

---

[2] *Opus Epistolarum Des. Erasmi Roterodami*, ed. P. S. Allen, Oxford, vol. II, 420.

pagan poets; he who will employ his nights in learning the decrees of
Apostles, the rites of the Church, the birth, the progress and the fall of
the Christian republic, as Cicero searched the institutions and the laws
of Roman provinces, municipalities and of allied nations; and through
all these studies has prepared himself for the present time – that man
will have the right to pretend to the name of Ciceronian.

NOSOPONUS: But all the studies which you have enumerated will make us
speak as Christians not as Ciceronians.

BULEPHORUS: What then? . . .[3]

Here Erasmus demonstrates the need for what he called a 'Christian
philosophy' which would gradually transform the life of the
contemporary Church and society through the study of the Bible,
the Church Fathers, and Christian origins, and through taking
warning from the Church's past weaknesses – for Erasmus, major
weaknesses lay in much of the thought and many of the practices of
the later medieval Church. It is characteristic of Erasmus, though he
had begun his ecclesiastical career as an Augustinian canon, that he
chose Jerome from his early days as the symbol of this renewal rather
than St. Augustine, since Augustine was so much the master of the
medieval mind and had set the vocabulary and patterns of so many
areas of dogmatic development for 'he brought Scholastic theology
from his mind as Jupiter did Minerva'.[4] Moreover, Augustine had
himself confessed his inability in the biblical languages. In contrast to
this Jerome was *primus Christianae religionis doctor*.[5] In his letter to
John Eck Erasmus showed his preference for Jerome over Augustine
in 1518.[6] To appeal to Jerome was to go back to what he conceived
to be a golden age, the first Christian centuries which lay behind the
middle ages, since the latter was the period when, for Erasmus, the
'barbarians' (that is, the Scholastic theologians) triumphed.

When Erasmus began his lifelong and increasing devotion to
Jerome is not easily determined, but the influence of the Brethren of
the Common Life on his youth was more marked than he was
afterwards ready to admit. The house of the Brethren at Deventer
where he had studied was dedicated to Jerome; and from among the
earlier of his surviving letters we know of his friendship with the
Augustinian canon Cornelius Gerard, probably his teacher, who was
made laureate by the Emperor Maximilian (this at least suggests that

---

[3] *Desiderii Erasmi Roterodami Opera Omnia*, Leyden, 1703, [Abbrev. LB] I, 1001E 19.
[4] *Opera Omnia, Hyperaspistes* LB, II, 1495. D. Cardinal Bembo could warn Sadoleto to
beware lest his style be corrupted by reading the Epistles of St. Paul. *Ciceronianus*, trans. I.
Scott, New York, 1908. Preface, 8.
[5] Allen, op. cit., I, 34.
[6] Allen, op. cit.

he was a skilful latinist), and who in 1516 was known to be working on a life of Jerome based on preparatory studies he had made while he was at the University of Paris in 1497. While still in the convent at Steyn, Erasmus wrote to Gerard in 1489 with approval of Jerome. He also told Gerard that he had copied out all the letters of Jerome and found in them weapons against 'the barbarians', and that from these letters he had learned that ignorant barbarism (rusticitatem) is not holiness, and sound latinity (disertitudinem) is not identical with impiety.[7] It is certain that by 1500 he had committed himself to editing the works of Jerome for he wrote in December of that year to another correspondent, Greverade:

> My mind has long burned with incredible ardour to illustrate with a commentary the letters of Jerome. In daring to conceive so great a design which no one has hitherto attempted, I feel that some god inflames and directs my heart. I am moved by the piety of that heavenly man of all Christians beyond question the most learned and most eloquent; whose writings though they deserve to be read and learned everywhere and by all, are read by few, admired by fewer still, and understood by scarcely any.... What a task it will be in the first place to clear away the errors which during so many ages have become established in the text.... What a style, what a mastery of language....[8]

And to James Batt he wrote in the same month that he wished, 'to restore the whole work of Jerome greatly as it is corrupted, mutilated and confused by the ignorance of the theologians'.[9] It was from Jerome that Erasmus learned that he could live a life of usefulness and honour in combining the best of literary culture with Christian piety. It was from Jerome that he first evolved the *philosophia Christi* with which he opposed both the logic of the Scholastic theologians and certain debased forms of popular piety. For Erasmus, Jerome was the ideal of the true theologian unlike Augustine who had disturbed the simplicity of the Gospels and Epistles of the first days of the Church with his philosophic subtleties on sin and grace. Erasmus could accuse Augustine of stating that God works in us both good and bad, and rewards his own good works in us and punishes the bad; this, he argued, is a paradox which it is better not to announce publicly.[10] In

---

[7] Allen, op. cit., I, 103.

[8] Allen, op. cit., I, 332.

[9] Allen, op. cit., I, 328.

[10] Erasmus, *De Libero Arbitrio*, διάτριβη. Charles Béné, *Erasme et Saint Augustin, ou l'influence de Saint Augustin sur l'humanisme d'Erasme*, Geneva, 1969, has sought, among other matters, to show the considerable influence of *De Doctrina Christiana* in the works of Erasmus. However, where Erasmus invokes the writings of Augustine, including the work named, he is concerned with the linguistic learning necessary to a grammarian rather than theology. Béné has not

the preface to volume II of the edition of Jerome's works in which he shared as editor he stated plainly that Jerome is the best of theologians, and not even the Greek Fathers produced a better: 'Jerome is a river of gold, he who has Jerome alone needs no more ample library.' He was to echo again in 1515 what he had written to Greverade in 1500: 'The work of correcting and commenting on Jerome interests my mind so warmly, that I feel as if I had been inspired by some god'.[11]

There was, however, another major influence on the young Erasmus, which would continue with him for some time and one which led him to produce that work, his edition of the Greek New Testament with Latin translation and notes, which was to prove to be so revolutionary. At eighteen Erasmus had already epitomised the *Elegantiae* of Lorenzo Valla and from that time his mind was gripped by the brilliance of style, the subtle and attractive latinity which clothed the writings of Valla, who grounded them on an erudition applied to their content with cool realism and clear judgement. In 1489 he wrote to Cornelius Gerard defending Valla, saying that the greatest praise is due to Valla who had, 'with great industry, zeal and labour repelled the absurdities of the barbarians, rescued buried literature from destruction and restored to Italy the splendour of her former eloquence'.[12] He found another side to Valla's work when he discovered, in the summer of 1504, in the library of the Premonstratensian Abbey of Parc at Louvain, a manuscript of Valla's annotations on the Greek New Testament, which showed Erasmus what possibilities lay in Valla's grammatical exegesis: here too he saw no doubt the practical application of part of Jerome's methods in handling Scripture. It was Valla who showed Erasmus that Scholasticism was based on formulas in the Vulgate, in itself an inaccurate version of the Greek, from which Augustine and Boethius had begun that corruption of Christian truth based on a corrupt text of Scripture which was to be developed in Scholasticism.

From now on Erasmus was determined to work on the Greek New Testament at the same time as his labours on Jerome. He foresaw trouble from conservative theologians in going directly to the Greek and leaving aside the Vulgate version, and probably one reason for his publishing Valla's annotations was to prepare the way for his own fuller and more revolutionary work. His preface to Valla's book,

demonstrated that Augustine lies closely behind the theology of Erasmus on the doctrine of grace. For Erasmus' opposition to Augustine on free will, see Charles Trinkaus, *Erasmus, Augustine and the Nominalists*. *Archiv für Reformationsgeschichte* 67, 1976, 5 ff.

[11] *Hieronymi Opera Omnia*, Chevallon, Paris, 1533. Prefatory letter to Archbishop Warham, 1524. Allen, op. cit., II, 220.

[12] Allen, op. cit., I, 115.

published in 1505, was addressed to an Englishman Christopher Fisher, papal protonotary in Paris. Here he asks,

> What crime is it in Laurentius if after collating some ancient and correct Greek copies he has noted in the New Testament, which is derived from the Greek, some passages which either differ from our version or seem to be inaptly rendered owing to a passing want of vigilance in the translator, or are expressed more significantly in the Greek; or, finally, if it appears that something in our text is corrupt?[13]

Typically he cites Jerome's authority for understanding and translating, 'by erudition and command of language'. And how ominous to traditional theologians would be the proud claim of Erasmus: 'I had rather see with my own eyes than with those of others, and in the next place, much as they have said [that is, the old interpreters] they have left much to be said by posterity.'[14] In this preface Erasmus is using Valla as a weapon against the forces of mere traditionalism; here he shows the need for going to the sources, and correcting the Vulgate by the Greek original, even to providing a new translation more correct and more appropriate to the present time. To us this seems the reasonable and desirable activity of sound scholarship, but in 1505 these proposals were revolutionary. The Greek original was regarded as the biased authority of schismatical, if not heterodox, Greeks: to use their Greek original was to favour their dangerous opinions. Again it was assumed that the making of the Vulgate Latin version had been guided by the inspiration of the Holy Spirit; it had been sanctified by eleven hundred years of use in the Latin Church; and it was most intimately related to the most sacred traditions of worship, piety and doctrine. Many thought that to turn aside to the Greek was not only unnecessary, it would begin the dissolution of Catholic authority. The full weight of this traditionalist attack would fall on Erasmus from 1516 after his edition of the New Testament appeared. In that year, however, Froben, the same printer, published the works of Jerome for which Erasmus had been the chief among the editors. Erasmus could now face the challenge, which he knew was coming, with the formidable support of Jerome.

Erasmus showed both courage and integrity in carrying through to fulfilment, in these labours, his years of devotion to Jerome and to the principles of Valla, and in thus challenging Scholasticism, obscurantism and the superstitions of popular piety. He stubbornly maintained his position on the New Testament, and on his annotations

---

[13] Allen, op. cit., I, 410.
[14] Allen, op. cit., I, 412. He was opposing: 'Illud audio quosdam dicere, veteres interpretes, trium linguarum peritos satis explicuisse sicubi fuit opus'.

to it, until his death a year after the fifth edition of the work amid serious hostility and amid increasing difficulties. If some degree of mild persecution mania suggests itself, it is not altogether surprising in view of these problems – for instance, he seems to have had a rule that when in doubt of the source of an attack he should blame Cardinal Aleandro.[15] Alongside of his scholar's courage, however, there was a certain deviousness, or, less pejoratively, a certain skill in manoeuvre in seeking to disarm his enemies and to explain away acerbities by sheltering behind great or respected names, for example, the Bishop of Cambrai, Archbishop Warham, and Pope Leo X; John Colet who would impress the English; and Sir Thomas More who had both an English and a European reputation. Like the English Fabians of the 1890s he wrote manifestos announcing a new way of life, and like them he was unwilling by temperament, and because of his chosen method, to see this way introduced by violent means. But he certainly produced the manifestos though he later showed the uncommitted intellectual's shock when men used them in a revolutionary way as, for example, von Hutten did in Germany. Two of his most significant writings of this challenging kind were the introduction to the New Testament, the *Paraclesis*, and his life of Jerome used as an introduction to Froben's edition of the collected works of Jerome. This life of Jerome shows Erasmus as the cunctative revolutionary challenging the dying middle ages in religion, learning, piety and social order, in the name of the saint whom he admired more than any other of the Fathers and Doctors of the Church. He may have thought of writing it to provide a protective shield for his own work, but his pen moulded it into a weapon of attack.

The *Life of Jerome* is a powerful attempt to establish the facts while at the same time ignoring the traditional envelope of hagiography. It is hardly a product of his earlier studies in Jerome, for it is the result of mature work on and deep knowledge of the writings of Jerome. On his second visit to England in 1509 he had lectured on the letters of Jerome, and three years later Badius at Paris wrote to Erasmus asking if he could publish Erasmus' edition of these letters. But by the end of 1513 he was attracted to the presses of Amerbach and Froben at Basel who planned to publish the whole of Jerome's works. Froben persuaded Erasmus to guide the editorial team and to be himself responsible for the letters. In the event Erasmus achieved more than this since he added notes to the text and provided the *Life* as an introduction. In the *Life of Jerome* Erasmus introduced a different method in writing the life of a saint, and the characteristic accretions

[15] Allen, op. cit. IX, 370.

of legend in hagiography were firmly set aside. The new departure here was that Erasmus used nothing save the earliest and best records: 'I think there is nothing fairer than to describe saints of the kind of which they themselves were, as men in whose lives even the discovery of anything wrong can be turned into an example of goodness. . . . But who could endure those who with ravings worse than those of old women, children, illiterates, and fools do not exalt the saints but rather drag them down?'[16] Erasmus then states that he will use only the most trustworthy sources written by Jerome's contemporaries Prosper, Severus, Orosius, Rufinus and that even more diligence would be given to tracing out the life of Jerome from his own writings. In scorn, for example, of the pious stories in the Golden Legend, he added that those who wished to find miracles in Jerome's life would do better to read his works which are themselves as it were miraculous. It is unfortunate, though perhaps inevitable in view of the state of exact learning at the time, that Erasmus began the *Life* with an error of his own in stating that Jerome was born under the Emperor Constantine instead of Constantius, and produced some other minor misunderstandings on times, persons and places.

Erasmus found an opportunity in the *Life* to point more than one contemporary moral, thus underlining its quality of being a manifesto. This soon appears when he wrote that it was to Jerome's youthful training in 'good letters' that we owe an incomparable Doctor of the Church, 'non loquacium sophistarum scholis'.[17] In the vocabulary of Erasmus sophist was an alternative word for barbarian to describe a Scholastic theologian. Erasmus points another moral when he contrasts contemporary monasticism with that of Jerome's time: '. . . quod ne quis in hoc erret, id temporis longe diversum erat ac hoc quod hodie videmus caerimoniis obstrictum . . .'[18] Again Jerome was, of course, not a cardinal though iconography showed him in a cardinal's hat and the tradition of his being a cardinal–priest is echoed in the Golden Legend, but Erasmus is quick both to point out the error and to make the comment that the splendour and dignity of cardinals in the sixteenth century were unknown in Jerome's time, just as he showed that Jerome was a 'true monk' which enabled him to follow Christ freely, something which is impossible now, he added ironically, since this kind of monk is no longer to be found. In describing Jerome as receiving by night the Jew Bar Hanina to teach Jerome Hebrew, like another Nicodemus coming secretly to avoid

---

[16] *Erasmi Opuscula*, ed. W. K. Ferguson, The Hague, 1933, 136.
[17] Ferguson, op. cit., 141.
[18] Ferguson, op. cit., 145.

the hatred of the Jews, Erasmus would touch many a contemporary scholar, for this expensive procedure was still employed by Christians seeking to learn Hebrew – he himself had possibly used it. It was this continuous suggestion of contemporaneity with the past which gave the living quality to the *Life*. For fifteenth-century writers the men of the fourth century had been clothed in forms appropriate to medieval culture: Erasmus toiled to place Jerome exactly in his true period, using the scholarship available to him with the greatest skill, and in doing so he made Jerome more alive and more contemporary because he made him appropriate to an age of humanism and not of medievalism. That Erasmus wrote in favour of biblical humanism and the priority of trilingual learning can be seen in his taking for granted what was in fact not true, that Augustine must have consistently disliked Jerome; for Erasmus saw Augustine, while respecting him for his greatness, as the father of that dogmatic theology which he himself distrusted. Erasmus is equally committed, as though it were in his own quarrel, when he attacked Rufinus, whom he unjustly saw as being wholly wrong in his opposition to Jerome: but no doubt he saw in Rufinus Jerome's Aleandro. The *Life of Jerome* gradually moved to a climax by becoming more and more a contemporary document. Erasmus indignantly attacked the Scholastics for denying that Jerome was a theologian and demoting him to being a mere grammarian, 'because he does not crackle with majors and minors' like the followers of Scotus.[19] He paused to exclaim:

> Who could have guessed that this kind of theology would develop among Christians? . . . Who would guess that there would be those who would refashion the whole of theology from head to heel, as they say, and make out of what had been a heavenly subject something Sophistic, Thomistic, or Scotist, or Occamist? . . . What a calamity for Christendom, which had managed for more than a thousand years without theologians![20]

The *Life* concludes with a vigorous defence of good letters grounded on trilingual learning and on scriptural piety against Scholastic divinity, and against half-pagan Ciceronianism. Here Erasmus aims his blows at contemporary Italian humanists (generally somewhat suspect to the more sober biblical humanism of northern Europe) whose names crackle through these sentences like abusive expletives –

[19] Ferguson, op. cit., 178.
[20] Ferguson, op. cit., 179. In the Annotations to the New Testament at 1 Cor. 1:10. Paul's precept is set beside '. . . mordicus tenet Scotisticam sectam, alius Thomisticam, alius Occamisticam, alius Albertisticam'. The *Antibarborum liber* of 1520 had for its adversaries from twenty years before, the intellectual methods of the Scholastic theologians, 'the barbarians'.

one example is his tart rebuke of Filippo Beroaldo for criticising Jerome's taste in using the words 'pexa tunica'. For good measure he added the lyrical statement that Bethlehem was twice happy since there Christ was born for the world and Jerome was born for heaven. 'There was no kind of teaching which here cannot be aided, no foundation of life which cannot be embellished by his precepts', and Erasmus dourly concluded, 'Jerome hated and abhorred heretics, those alone he had for his bitterest enemies',[21] to show that he aligned himself with ancient orthodoxy and implied a warning that criticism of biblical humanism might in turn be challenged as heresy.

This *Life* and the edition of Jerome's Works, while they were a powerful demonstration of the status and significance of biblical humanism, could not be in themselves a justification of Erasmus as a trilingual scholar. We have to go elsewhere to examine his competence in Greek and Hebrew. It would not have been obvious to those who knew him that in 1499 he would turn from concentrating on classical studies to the biblical languages. We must allow for the hidden and slow gestation of genius, and not look for a lightning flash of decision by which to determine precisely where, when and why Erasmus made this change of direction. It should not be forgotten, moreover, that Erasmus never lost touch with the piety of his youthful environment, and was always a moralist. But it was probably in 1499, on his first visit to England, that he made up his mind to take up these new studies. There is no proof of it, but it was most probably his friendship with the single-minded and devout John Colet that helped him towards this change. Colet himself knew Greek imperfectly and no Hebrew, yet he lectured on the Bible urging that from this starting point alone could new insights into the Christian faith begin. Colet's concentration on biblically grounded Christian values, his contempt for popular superstitions, and his scorn for Scholastic theologians (not excluding Aquinas whom Erasmus had thought it expedient to praise) impressed the less committed Erasmus. He left England for Paris determined to master Greek, for he was now fully convinced that through this language the mind would be enlarged, that men could break free from the iron bands of Scholastic latinity with more assurance by its means. The task before him, and so many other younger aspirants to trilingual learning at that time, was formidable. Teachers were few, expensive and educationally incompetent: the university faculties ignored and distrusted these studies; and grammars and dictionaries barely existed. Aldus Manutius had published the Greek grammar of the Byzantine refugee Lascaris in 1495 but there was little else of use. Men would have to wait until 1520 for the thorough though complex *Commentarii Linguae Graecae* of Guillaume Budé at Paris, and a useful dictionary did not appear until the *Lexicon Graeco-Latinum* published at Paris in 1530. Only the intensely dedicated could track their way through the forest of difficulties in studying Greek outside Italy in 1500. Lack of resources and the pressure of patronage allowed Erasmus to go no further than Paris.

In April 1500 he wrote to Batt that he was applying his whole mind to learning Greek, spending what little money he had first on Greek books, with clothing coming a late second.[22] To another friend from whom he had borrowed a copy of Homer he wrote that year saying he burned with love for the author but was unable to understand him effectively.[23] There must be a touch of modesty here, for an admiring pupil records that Erasmus produced some excellent Latin translations from the Odyssey at that time. In any case Erasmus had very probably acquired the elements of Greek in his youth; his problem in 1499 had been that he knew he had no real grip on the language. At Paris he found a teacher in George Hermonymus of Sparta, as we learn from his autobiographical letter to Botzheim over twenty years later, where he adds that when he began there were hardly any books in Greek available, and even fewer teachers of it. Of this master he could say no more than that he stammered the language and was twice a Greek in being always greedy and charging a high salary: this no doubt means that while Hermonymus spoke Greek he was inadequate in teaching method and grammatical exposition.[24] But in 1501 Erasmus was deep in Lascaris' Greek grammar, and also worked through that of the Italian master in Greek of Leo X, the Franciscan Bolzani. With the excitement of discovery he showed a friend that year how in Psalm 50 a knowledge of Greek could transform meaningfully a passage of Scripture otherwise misleading and obscure in Latin. (His weakness in Hebrew shows why he used the Septuagint Greek for the Old Testament):

> Who could understand the sentence in the Psalm, 'Et peccatum meum contra me est semper', unless he has read the Greek? This runs as follows, καὶ ἡ ἁμαρτία μου ἐνώπιόν μου ἐστὶδιαπαντός. At this point some theologian will spin a long story of how the flesh is perpetually in

[22] Allen, op. cit., I, 288.
[23] Allen, op. cit., I, 305.
[24] Allen, op. cit., I, 7. '... Hermonymus Graece balbutiebat, sed talis ut neque potuisset docere, si valuisset, neque voluisset, si potuisset.'

conflict with the spirit, having been misled by the double meaning of the preposition, that is, *contra*, when the word ἐνώπιον refers not to 'conflict' but to 'position', as if you were to say 'opposite', that is, 'in sight': so that the prophet's meaning was that his fault was so hateful to him that the memory of it never left him, but floated always before his mind as if it were present.[25]

The following year his tense concentration is shown in the words 'in Graecis litteris sum totus'.[26] By 1506 he had published Valla's annotations on the Greek New Testament, and he was publishing his own Latin version of certain plays by Euripides.

That Erasmus widened and deepened his Greek learning in his visits to Italy and to England in the sixteen years up to 1516 should not overshadow his achievement in the period 1499–1505 which is a record of intense devotion to his conception of his life's work. Those sixteen years of labour show that he had learned to use Greek with something of that familiarity with which he had previously learned to use Latin as a living language. This sense of the past as if it were restored to life in the present enabled Erasmus to give contemporaneity to the Greek writings of what he believed to be the golden age of the Church.

He held also to the Greek pagan writers of the Empire, Lucian – whom he warmly recommended to the students of the trilingual college of Busleiden at Louvain – and Plutarch, preferring them to Aristotle and to a less degree to Plato. Just as he showed little interest in Christian mysticism so he was unattracted by the Italian enthusiasm for reading Plato through the haze of neo-Platonism, a fashion which captured Jacques Lefèvre and even affected Colet's pragmatic mind. Erasmus delighted in Lucian's irony, and his genius for social criticism in dramatic dialogue; and Plutarch attracted his interest through his handling of men's histories within the frame of moral criticism. The great philosophical tradition of Greece was for him too speculative and too dialectical. These attitudes to Greek learning can be seen too in his lack of the profound philological concern of Guillaume Budé, and of the paedagogic zeal of the young Melanchthon.

He also attempted to learn Hebrew in pursuit of his ideal of being like Jerome a trilingual scholar. Possibly he had tried it earlier, but by 1503 he sadly concedes that he had undertaken too much at his age. 'I began also to look into Hebrew, but I was put off by the strangeness of the language, and also because neither my age nor my ability can

---

[25] Allen, op. cit., I, 352, (The Vulgate number of this Psalm is 50.)
[26] Allen, op. cit., I, 381.

handle several things at once, I gave up.'[27] The difficulty here was even more formidable than with Greek, as no satisfactory grammars or dictionaries yet existed in forms suitable for non-Jewish beginners. A small volume had been produced by Pellican at Strasbourg in 1503, and while the German biblical humanist Reuchlin could claim to be the first who opened the way for non-Jews to learn Hebrew in his *De Rudimentis Linguae Hebraicae* in 1506, it was no wonder of scholarship, for it contained some errors and obscurities. A good dictionary was also lacking for some years to come. When he was working on the text of Jerome's Works in 1515 for Froben, Erasmus found a number of Hebrew words and phrases in the biblical commentaries of Jerome, and he confessed, 'these letters I had barely more than tasted and scarcely touched upon'.[28] In the Preface to Jerome's Works he stated that he had had to find help from the three sons of Amerbach: 'Quorum equidem auxilio libenter sum usus, quod Hebraeorum literas degustassem verius quam dedicissem.'[29] Again he had to rely on Froben's proof-reader, Oecolampadius, who was later to become the Protestant reformer at Basel, for similar help where necessary with those Hebrew words he desired to consider in his notes to the Greek-Latin New Testament he published in Basel in 1516. In 1517 Erasmus has a vague reference to his taking some Hebrew lessons at Louvain, probably from Cellarius, but this effort soon faded, and we hear no more of his Hebrew studies. In *De Recta Pronuntiatone Dialogus* he observed of the study of Hebrew, 'Judaeis ac Theologis relinquerem'.[30]

In Hebrew studies, in contrast with the competence he achieved in Greek, he got no further than the basic paradigms: almost certainly he could not have accurately provided with the vowel-points a consonantal text, nor could he have followed the intricacies of the Hebrew verbs. In his exegesis of passages from the Old Testament, where one would have expected him to refer to the Hebrew text, he almost wholly ignores it, and relies on the Septuagint Greek. More boldly in his commentary, or *enarratio*, on certain Psalms, Erasmus cautiously introduces a comment on the Hebrew original in some such phrase as, 'qui fontes Hebraicarum litterarum excutere studuerunt . . .' (Ps. 33) or, 'quidam admonet apud Hebraeos hic aliam esse vocem' (Ps. 38). In his annotations of the New Testament and in helping to edit Jerome's exegetical works, where Hebrew words were cited, he had assistance as shown above from scholars working for Froben's press.

[27] Allen, op. cit., I, 405.
[28] Allen, op. cit., II, 77.
[29] *Hieronymi Opera Omnia*, vol. I, 3v. Allen, op. cit., II, 218.
[30] LB, I, 923, Allen, op. cit., III, 96 for the Hebrew lessons.

Inside so many of the humanists of his own and of the succeeding generation a pedant was struggling, sometimes successfully, to get out. Erasmus, however, achieved 'humanitas' as a style of living as well as of writing: for him pursuing scholarship into pedantry was a deviation from a reasonable norm. This is part of his attraction as a writer but it had the regrettable consequence that he lacked the perfectionism of the pure scholar; while he had insight and originality, he was careless about precision in a reading, the collation of texts and painstaking care in interpreting them. At Rome he was called *Errasmus* for his not infrequent errors. Even the young Calvin in his commentary on Seneca's *De Clementia* could write 'errat tamen Erasmus'. The scholar's perfectionism in detail was for Erasmus a rare achievement – he was not a Housman. With his literary flair rather than scholarly precision in handling Greek texts, and with the weakness in Hebrew, which he himself acknowledged, he was not the most suitable editor of a biblical text. The editors of the text of the New Testament in the Complutensian Polyglot Bible, printed though not published in 1514, produced more careful and significant work, and Simon de Colines, either through his own skills or more probably through the work of a scholar otherwise unknown to us, printed what was a better version of the text of the Greek New Testament at Paris in 1535 than Erasmus had achieved in five editions by that year. But where Erasmus gained all Europe's attention was in the boldness and vigour of his Latin translation from the Greek and his annotations, especially since these were written by the author of the *Enchiridion* and the *Moriae Encomium*. A generation of converts to the 'New Learning' grew up with Erasmus' editions of the New Testament. But some of this generation came to wonder whether all the skill of Erasmus in writing, his freedom from anachronisms and from the Scholastic manifold meanings of even the literal sense of Scripture, had sufficiently covered his lack of theological depth and energy in his interpretations, and his casual methods of emending the Greek text – scholars of his own generation publicly expressed their doubts, including the powerful names of Luther and Stunica. Moreover, the toils of Browning's Grammarian were not for Erasmus: he had mocked the consequences of such labours in his *Moriae Encomium*. His gifts lay in creating new insights, and in the art of literary allusion (in which he was almost as wide-ranging as the Deipnosophists of Athenaeus), and not in the technical scholarship necessary for the editing of texts.

Frequently the excuse is made for him that this skill was unknown in his time, but someone used it in preparing the text of de Colines' Greek New Testament; and the Christian Hebraists of Alcalá de

Henares prepared after some years of effort the Hebrew text of the Old Testament in the Complutensian Polyglot Bible, which is still of interest to scholars.[31] Erasmus might have created a thirst for better scholarship through the potent attraction of his name and of his edition of the New Testament, so that younger men could have done better what he had done imperfectly, if it had not been for the fact that both Catholics and Protestants, locked in an exhausting and inconclusive struggle to demonstrate each other's errors, ended by mid-century in that theological authoritarianism which Erasmus feared would develop from Luther's protest. In this situation there could be little scholarly advance; what was achieved was greater precision but with narrowed insights. The excessive caution shown by Beza in his edition of the text of the Greek New Testament (when he had the Western text before him to show him new possibilities) demonstrates this in the second half of the century.

It is probable that Erasmus first thought of preparing annotations to the Greek New Testament when he prepared those of Lorenzo Valla for the press in 1505, and it is even more probable that in the same period he began to consider preparing his own Latin version of the Greek New Testament, but it was not until 1512–13, while he was in England, that he decided to prepare an edition of the Greek text.[32] It is very difficult to disentangle his allusions to the preparation of his annotations but they seem to have been put together in a desultory manner (though he was busy with them in August 1514 as

[31] The severely critical view of Erasmus as a textual scholar in editing the Greek of the New Testament, has been challenged by C. C. Tarelli, *Erasmus' Manuscripts of the Gospels*, J.T.S., 1943, Bo Reicke, *Erasmus und die neutestamentliche Textgeschichte*, *Thelogische Zeitschrift*, 1966. 254–265 and J. Hadot, *La critique textuelle dans l'edition du Nouveau Testament, Colloquia Erasmiana Turonensia*, Toronto, 1972, II. While these writers could persuade critics to be less harsh, they, (particularly M. Hadot) have not set aside the accepted view of Erasmus' shortcomings in textual scholarship – Erasmus seems to have preferred writing annotations to the labour of finding and collating manuscripts, 'this hateful mill'. J. H. Bentley, *Humanists and Holy Writ*, Princeton, 1983 112–122 provides a brief account of this work by Erasmus on the New Testament. His account of Erasmus as a biblical critic, 123–193, is thorough, especially in his use of the Annotations which accompanied the Greek and Latin versions. Its value is weakened, however, by not identifying his discussion and findings on Erasmus with the relevant edition of the Annotations, and, by avoiding mention of Erasmus' weaknesses, he thereby exaggerates his virtues. Further his treatment of Stunica (as with the Complutensian scholars generally) is depreciatory and selective; for example, the points where Stunica's scholarship compelled Erasmus to modify his Greek text are dismissed by Bentley as minor, and he altogether ignores Stunica's justifiable attack on Erasmus for pretentiousness in Hebrew based on ignorance of Hebrew and Aramaic and of the significance of semitic idiom and vocabulary for New Testament Greek. The edition of the Greek New Testament published by Simon Colines and the third edition of that of Robert Estienne, both improved on Erasmus by reading widely in manuscripts, while using his text.
[32] Allen, op. cit., III, 182–183, Allen describes Erasmus' preprarations for his New Testament.

a letter to Reuchlin shows)[33] probably to accompany his proposed new Latin version, though they were made upon the Vulgate text, and in the event a considerable number of them were prepared while the first edition of the New Testament was in the press at Basel in 1515: 'Then they induced me to add much more copious annotations.'[34] But there is clear evidence concerning his preparation of a new Latin version, for a magnificent copy of it exists containing the gospels and epistles made by the scribe Peter Meghen, on Colet's orders, during 1506–9.

Another manuscript of this version exists which is interlined with the Vulgate, and is less magnificent though probably dating from the same period.[35] Undoubtedly Colet persuaded Erasmus to begin translating the Greek New Testament in 1505 and most probably the task was completed by 1506: these statements do not require the view that Erasmus intended to publish this version at that period; it was not until 1514 that he began to consider issuing this version with his edition of the Greek New Testament and accompanying annotations. His preparation of the Greek text is less easy to determine, but there are occasional references to his working on it and it is probable that he had begun collating Greek manuscripts by 1512–13 if not earlier, for he wrote from London in September 1512 to Peter Gilles, 'absolvam castigationes Novi Testamenti . . .' Again in July 1514 he wrote to Servatius Rogerius: 'Ex Graecorum et antiquorum codicum collatione castigavi totum Novum Testamentum . . . commentarios in Epistolas Pauli incepi, quos absolvam ubi haec edidero.'[36]

From July 1514 to March 1515 Erasmus was at Basel but no evidence is available that he thought of publishing there his Latin New Testament with annotations during this period. Possibly he had been thinking of an Italian publisher, perhaps Aldus Manutius who had been the first printer of his *Adagia* and to whom he had written in October 1507 wondering why he did not publish the New Testament. But a sense of urgency developed when Froben, it is conjectured, heard of the completion of the printing of the Greek New Testament at Alcalá de Henares in 1514 (left unbound in sheets awaiting the publication of the whole work) and that the editors were pressing on with the Old Testament of the Polyglot Bible. Beatus Rhenanus wrote to Erasmus twice in April 1515 to say that Froben would like to publish the edition of the New Testament

---

[33] Allen, op. cit., II, 4.
[34] Allen, op. cit., II, 253.
[35] Allen, op. cit., II, 182.
[36] Allen, op. cit., I: to Gilles 517, to Rogerius 570.

which Erasmus was known to be preparing, on the first occasion adding that Froben would offer a price equal to that of any other printer. It is not explicit that both the Greek text and the new Latin version of Erasmus were intended in these brief sentences, but since Erasmus wrote to Wimpfeling in September 1514: 'Superest Novum Testamentum a me versum et e regione Graecum . . .'; and again to Cardinal Grimani in May 1515[37] that he had in mind to publish commentaries on the Pauline epistles following in the steps of Valla and Lefèvre d'Etaples, he was now probably considering the preparation of a Greek text to accompany the Latin version and the commentary. What emerges from these tantalising and inexplicit surviving references to his preparing to publish the New Testament, is that Erasmus for some time intended to prepare no more than his new Latin version with annotations in the method of Valla, and that the decision to publish the Greek text to accompany these was taken much later and probably at Froben's suggestion. In the event he had less than a year, at a time when he was also pressed with other work, to prepare the Greek text for publication.

Erasmus claimed on the title page of the work, again in a declaration at the end, and more fully and confidently still in the dedicatory letter to Leo X, that he had used many old and correct manuscripts of the Greek text as well as citations of the New Testament text made by the Greek Fathers. This is disingenuous. He could claim from the generously disposed that he meant that he had consulted some old manuscripts when he had been preparing his notes, but the implications of the language he used in the passages mentioned was that he had edited the printed Greek text by the careful collation of a number of ancient manuscripts – and this was not true, or at best it was no more than a half-truth. In the short time he allowed himself for the preparation of the whole work for the printers, together with his seeing through the press his Jerome and other writings, he had little opportunity to collate and refine. He did no more than to deliver in the first place to the printers two manuscripts, one of the gospels, and one of the epistles, which he found to his hand at Basel, and which are still preserved in that city. The general consensus of scholars has considered these to be of late origin possibly as late as the fifteenth century. He himself recognised that they were defective in textual value, and complained to Budé that he had had to make corrections in them before sending them to Froben's compositors after a hasty comparison with a few other manuscripts at Basel. Since the book of Revelation was lacking in the

[37] Allen, op. cit., II, 23. Allen, op. cit., II, 78.

second manuscript he gave to the printers, he used another manuscript lent to him by Reuchlin, which also still survives. Because the biblical text was connected with a commentary in Greek in this manuscript, Erasmus had to make a copy himself of the actual text of Revelation contained in the manuscript, but he did not do this with the necessary care since he failed to correct some false readings. Further the manuscript lacked the last five verses of Revelation and he translated these verses into his own Greek from the Vulgate text (he also added at Acts 8:37 and Acts 9:5–6 Greek not to be found in the manuscripts). He admitted this in the Annotations but, again disingenuously, or possibly ignorantly, suggested that he is translating some words which do not appear in the Greek. Also in the Annotations he cited readings from manuscripts he had consulted in different cities in the years in which he had been preparing his Latin version. Since a few of these readings have not been found in any manuscripts since, it may be possible that he made some independent readings of his own, or else he was relying on defective memory.

Not only was the text hastily prepared but also the printers were careless in their work. That twelve pages, a ternion, were printed daily shows the haste of the compositors, and the pressure on the proof-readers, Nicholas Gerbel and Oecolampadius, whom Erasmus blamed in the following year somewhat ungenerously since both were competent in Greek and zealous for the good of the work.[38] Printing had begun in October 1515 and the whole work was completed and published in March 1516. But this important and influential edition was half-hidden under a cloud of typographical and other errors: 501 itacisms have been counted which were taken over from the manuscripts into the printed text. The perfectionism of later textual criticism looked on this Greek text – which formed part of the foundation of the 'textus receptus' for four centuries – with dubiety. And Scrivener wrote of its typographical errors, 'the first edition is the most faulty book I know'.[39] This is applying too harshly later standards of typographical and scholarly precision to the early sixteenth century, but Erasmus was also challenged for his casualness in his own time. Erasmus was not exaggerating when he admitted that this work, which was to have so great an influence on his time, nevertheless, 'praecipitatum est verius quam aeditum'; but he could also write to a friend: 'Aeditum est pro temporis angustia satis accurate',[40] which

---

[38] Allen, op. cit., II, 253.
[39] F. H. A. Scrivener, *A Plain Introduction to the Criticism of the New Testament*, 4th edition, 1894, vol. II, 185.
[40] Allen, op. cit., II, 226 and 248.

does not suggest that he was much perturbed by its precipitate appearance.

The new Latin translation which Erasmus provided to accompany the Greek text showed that greater care had been given to this text, which he had been working on at different periods for longer than he worked at the editing of the Greek text. It should not be overlooked that the excitement caused by this edition of the New Testament was also occasioned by the Latin version made by Erasmus, and the accompanying annotations. Not only was the publication of the Greek text a new departure, but also it was new boldly to set aside the Vulgate, the authoritative version, hallowed by tradition for Christian thought, worship, and piety, in favour of this product of contemporary latinity. The impact of this version can be seen in the tragedy of Thomas Bilney, Fellow of Trinity Hall, Cambridge, burned for heresy at Norwich in 1531, who was set on the road leading him to death by fire as a Protestant martyr through his admiration for this Latin version of Erasmus which led him into deeper theological waters than he had known of before. He probably would have benefited little from the Greek text because of the weakness of Greek studies in England at that time. Bilney wrote to Cuthbert Tunstall, Bishop of London, in 1527 giving an account of the change thus made in him years before: '. . . At last I heard speak of Jesus, even then when the New Testament was set forth by Erasmus; which when I understood to be eloquently done by him, being allured rather by the Latin than by the word of God, for at that time I knew not what it meant, I bought it even by the providence of God . . .'[41] In this he was one of a large company of young men whose lives were set on different courses (not only towards Protestantism, but also towards Catholic reformist ideals) by this Greek-Latin New Testament of Erasmus: a whole generation of young scholars was roused by it. That Bilney was 'allured by the Latin' would have pleased Erasmus – though Bilney's Protestantism would not – for he claimed that he had prepared his Latin version not for common use but as a help to those who were professionally students of theology: 'non ita scribuntur multitudine sed eruditis et praecipiis Theologiae candidatis'. This was no doubt an attempt to anticipate the attack on his boldness in setting aside the Vulgate in favour of his own version, just as he sought to play down potential hostility to his Annotations by stating that they were not theological commentaries.

His new Latin version, however, not only expressed his concern for contemporary standards of latinity, but also his genuine principles

[41] John Foxe, *Actes and Monuments*, ed. J. Pratt, 4th edit. n.d. vol. IV, 635.

in setting aside the Vulgate. Erasmus had written years before to Archbishop Warham in a letter published as a preface to his translation of two plays by Euripides: 'The mere task of putting real Greek into real Latin is such that it requires an extraordinary artist, and not only a man with a rich store of scholarship in both languages at his fingertips, but one exceedingly alert and observant'.[42] He wished to make the Greek as clear as possible, it was not enough to give a bare literal version for this can obscure the meaning, and he defended his recent Latin Paraphrases of the New Testament as clarifying the difficulties of New Testament idiom for the inexpert reader. In a letter of August 1518 to Antony Pucci, at the time papal nuncio in Switzerland, he wrote:

> We placed our translation by the side of the Greek text, so that the reader might readily compare the two, the translation being so made, that it was our first study to preserve, as far as was permissible, the integrity of the Latin tongue without injury to the simplicity of the apostolic language. Our next care was to provide that any sentences which had before given trouble to the reader, either by ambiguity or obscurity of language, or by faulty or unsuitable expressions, should be explained and made clear with as little deviation as possible from the words of the original, and none from the sense.[43]

In the Annotations he showed the problems created by the Vulgate rendering, and gave reasons for his own translation where it differed from the Vulgate: as he noted in his *Apologia* (one of the four preliminary portions, Dedication to Leo X, *Paraclesis, Ratio seu Methodus,* and *Apologia,* set before these editions) his purpose was not to replace the official wording – essential to the authoritative transactions of the Church – but to send his own version forth as a help to understanding better the Vulgate. But in spite of his ingenuous hope he was, in the eyes of his critics, undermining by his methods in translation and annotation the authority of the Vulgate.

His version, he insisted, for he did not wish it to be misconceived as consciously literary, was to be seen rather as clear and plain, 'non tam elegantius, quam dilucidus ac fidelius'.[44] A version nearer to showing the Bible 'designed to be read as literature', in twentieth-century phrase, was not to come until that of Sebastian Castellio forty years later. Nevertheless, for Bilney it was the allurement of the Latin which provided the first attraction; and no one who glances through three consecutive pages of the Latin version and the

[42] Allen, op. cit., I, 418.
[43] Allen, op. cit., III, 381.
[44] LB VI, *In Annotationes Novi Testamenti Praefatio.*

accompanying notes could miss the Erasmian *suavitas* and the conscious pleasure in classical allusions – in a word style. Perhaps Erasmus did not realise how revolutionary could be the effect of his style and method: his version of the New Testament made it seem like a new discovery, new threads of unsuspected meanings could be unwound with increasing excitement. For the most famous of German jurists, the humanist scholar Zazius, this version of Erasmus gave clearer sense and better Latin than the Vulgate. He seemed to have created a new biblical language, for in his version the inhibiting traces of Hebrew and Greek idiom almost disappeared; and his short preparatory treatises were read as manifestos challenging the language, methods, and even the principles of a traditionalism grounded on an increasingly barren Scholasticism. John Watson, Fellow of Peterhouse and soon to be Vice-Chancellor of Cambridge University, represents one of a great number of enthusiastic greetings fired by this freshness of insight obtained on the publication of the work: 'By your correction of the New Testament accompanied by your annotations you have thrown a marvellous light on Christ, and deserved well of all his zealous followers.'[45]

These Annotations were both part of the fascination of the work, and also the ground for some of the bitterest attacks upon it. Here Erasmus demonstrated what was no more than implicit in his new Latin version, that there were errors and obscurities in the Vulgate. Erasmus pointed out that no Council had approved the Vulgate (later the Council of Trent did) and even if a Council had done so this would not prevent the correction of the current text by a better version of the original. Would a Council approve the corruptions in errors in the text – and what of the variations in texts of the Vulgate? But also something of the style and manner of the notes to his *Adagia*, so attractive to his contemporaries, with their illuminating digressions and complete mastery of classical learning, could be found in the Annotations. For those who attacked him there was more of literature than theological exegesis in them. However, in the preface to his readers Erasmus had provided a defence in advance by describing them as, 'annotatiunculas ... non commentarios'. The method of Erasmus in annotating the New Testament differs little from that he used in editing, for example, Jerome's letters, but he emphasised that to comment at all on the New Testament it was essential to know Greek and to have a thorough acquaintance with Gospels and Epistles, for learning and piety go together. Moreover, he emphasised in the *Ratio* simple directness, *verum opinor ... Christum*

[45] Allen, op. cit., IV, 310.

simpliciter sensisse. Yet in spite of this insistence on simplicity he had to face the fact that Scripture shows a strange presentation of language for it is wrapped in allegories, or tropes, and is frequently oblique in statement. He saw this in terms of contemporary humanist scholars, as the 'art of rhetoric', so that rhetorical analysis after the manner of, for example, Quintilian is necessary to describe the scriptural allegories as synecdoche, hyperbole, and the rest. Also the Old Testament must be christianised through the use of allegory. The *rhetorici et grammatici scriptores*, therefore, are of more use than the attempts to apply the medieval fourfold sense which St. Thomas Aquinas and others sought to use.[46] The favour long given to the New Testament commentary of Aquinas would be shaken, in the eyes of many rudely challenged, by a mere grammarian when Erasmus wrote, 'Thomas hoc loco se torquet', and the phrases, 'Thomas frustra philosophans in loco depravato, Thomas lapsus, Thomas lapsus miserandus, Thomae annotatio ridicula' appear in marginal references and index; whereas only once 'Thomas laudatus' appears. He thought Thomas was too Aristotelian and possessed, 'insignitae cuiusdam impudentiae' in writing on the New Testament with authority when he had not used the Greek text.[47] On that most controverted topic of the time, the Pauline doctrine of Predestination, about which he wrestled with Luther in his *De Libero Arbitrio*, Erasmus can say little more in a note on Romans 8 than, 'Nor am I ignorant that there are certain persons, who on this passage seek a field for exercising their ingenuity and philosophise on the foreknowledge and predestination of God', and added with irony, 'of their diligence I do not disapprove'. Those who took for granted the plain authority of the word of God were alarmed at his note on Romans 9:5, where he showed that the obscurity of the Greek offers no clear rejection of Arianism since the words, 'benedictus in secula' may refer not to Christ, as was usually understood, but to God the Father. Even more serious was his omission of 1 John 5:7 in the first two editions of his Greek version, for the soundest of critical reasons that it was not in the early manuscripts: the note on the text in the later editions was not considered helpful any more than his long note on John 1:1, justifying his use of 'sermo' for 'verbum', in the edition of 1519. Again, he replaced the angelic greeting to Mary *Ave gratia plena* by *Ave gratiosa* since the Greek could mean 'greet' but did not mean 'full of grace' – the effect of this proposed change may be imagined.[48] Equally serious

---

[46] LB VI, 623 F.
[47] LB VI, 77E, 998D.
[48] In the Annotation at Luke 1:28, in the second edition of 1519, he wrote; 'Unde nil

in the eyes of many were his digressive comments, sometimes ironical, more often Erasmus at his most serious, on what he regarded as scandals in the lives of the Christians of his own time: on the vestments and ceremonies of the Church, on marriage, divorce and the possible modification of clerical celibacy, on penance and the use of relics, and on various aspects of monasticism and the making of vows. There were those outside of the sodalities of 'good letters', which accepted Erasmus gladly, who could be seriously offended at his scornful listing of, 'Mary's milk exhibited in our churches for money; Francis' hood shown at one altar and the Virgin Mary's shift at another; in one Church Anna's comb, in another Joseph's boot,' and so on.[49] Further, the comment, removed from later editions, on Peter lodging with Simon the tanner (Acts 9:43): 'the chief of the Apostles to lodge with so humble a host; in our time three royal palaces barely suffice to receive Peter's vicar', would challenge customary deference as did other similar ironies on the Papacy.

More serious occasions for alarm were given when Erasmus was found to have proposed corrections to the Vulgate text; and, worse, suggested that certain passages in the gospels were of doubtful authenticity; and equally dangerously questioned whether texts traditionally used in support of long-held dogmas could be read in this way. He corrected the latinity of the Vulgate when he rejected its version of John 16:13, 'docebit vos omnem veritatem' to read, 'ducet (ὁδηγήσει) vos in omnem veritatem'. He drew attention to the probability that the last twelve verses of the gospel of Mark were inauthentic, and also argued the same on the passage John 7:53–8:11, the story of the woman taken in adultery, since it was absent from the early patristic references to John's gospel, and from the best manuscripts: both his critical acumen and his courage are equally praiseworthy in maintaining in later editions that these passages might well be interpolations. He undermined traditional dogmatic proof-texts when he translated μετανοεῖτε, in the annotations as 'resipiscite' or 'ad mentem redite' thereby drawing attention to the ambiguity in the Vulgate rendering 'penitentiam agite', since the noun means both 'repentance' and 'penance' – an ambiguity essential to the then current Catholic interpretation of the Sacrament of Penance. Erasmus wished confession to awaken the sleeping soul and quicken it into maturity in the practice of piety, rather than to mortify the will by making isolated acts of penance. At several other places Erasmus indicated

referebat, salve vertisset in ave reddat? Nec est 'gratia plena' sed ut ad verbum reddam Gratificata. . . . Proinde ne quis ad eundem impingat lapidem nos vertimus Gratiosa.'
    [49] *Novi Testamenti Annotationes*, ed. 1519, Matthew 23:5.

that the Vulgate text did not provide those proofs of dogmas for which it was frequently adduced. At Romans 5:12, he gave a lengthy note of six and a half pages challenging the traditional doctrine of original sin and its derivation from the sin of Adam. At Romans 9:5, Philippians 2:6, Colossians 11:9 he undermined the value of their use against Arianism; and at 1 Timothy 3:16, he argued θεός had been added later to make the text explicit against the Arians. He curtly challenged the current view of merit when he wrote under Titus 2:11, 'non merito nostro salvati simus' in discussing briefly the saving grace of God.

Under Matthew 2, Erasmus stated that the writers of the gospels might have erred in not examining the books they quoted or paraphrased, and trusted too much to memory. After this it would appear less startling to learn that he thought Mark was merely a compendium of Matthew, that Luke was not an eye-witness, that the epistle of James lacked apostolic majesty and probably apostolic authority, that Hebrews was not by Paul (could it have been written by Clement of Rome he asked?), and, why should it be in the canon?, and lastly, did the heretic Cerinthus write Revelation, for John surely could not have done so? Amid these heady themes it was a relief to his opponents that his own work as an annotator was not impeccable and they gladly pointed out his occasional geographical errors (for example, his assumption on Acts 16:11, that the port of Neapolis was a town in Caria, in Asia instead of Macedonia), and his weakness in Hebrew was noted, for example, when he introduced a curious lady called Tabitha in misreading the Aramaic 'Talitha cumi' at Mark 5:41 – almost as curious as his invention of a non-existent Church Father unfortunately named Vulgarius by Erasmus, who had apparently misread βουλγαρίας as βουλγαρίον and read θεοφυλακτοῦ as a descriptive adjective in the title in a manuscript copy of a commentary on Matthew by the Byzantine Theophylact of Bulgaria. Among these sharp critics of his work on the New Testament were first in the field two Englishmen; a Franciscan, Henry Standish, who was promoted bishop of St Asaph (a fact which gave Erasmus the opportunity of describing him as 'episcopus de St Asino'), and Edward Lee, later Archbishop of York. Dr Standish, preaching at Paul's Cross, usually a sounding board for official views in Church and State, informed the mildly surprised Lord Mayor and Corporation that the total extinction of Christianity was at hand, and wept like Tweedledee's Walrus, to relate that Erasmus could alter John 1:1, to 'in principio erat sermo'.[50] Dr Lee was much more formidable. He

---

[50] Allen, op. cit., IV, 310. '. . . testatus immenere Christianae religionis τιανολε θριαν, nisi

produced a book of criticisms in spite of threats from Erasmus, who had learned of the forthcoming work beforehand, that he would be supported by his German friends, 'who still retained their native ferocity'.[51] Lee rightly complained of the casual haste with which Erasmus had edited the text, introduced unusual views in his Annotations, and occasionally translated what was absent from the Greek in his own Latin version – and expressed outrage not least at Erasmus providing some Greek of his own to conclude Revelation.[52] Even more formidable was the Spaniard, Diego Lopez de Zúñiga (Stunica), an able editor of the Greek New Testament printed for the magnificent Polyglot Bible at Alcalá de Henares (Complutum) in 1514, though unpublished until eight years later. Stunica must have taken it hard that what he rightly knew was a better text, better prepared and edited by himself and his colleagues, already printed in sheets in 1514, failed to achieve priority in publication through the delay of Leo X in licensing their Bible, and instead saw the renown and popularity which Erasmus had achieved by his hastily issued edition. Stunica, from the high chair of his own undoubted trilingual learning, attacked Erasmus at the lowest level for being a typical Dutchman soaked in beer and butter, who had won some renown in literature particularly, he wrote ominously, for his studies in proverbs and the works of Lucian; and at the higher level drew attention to the deficiencies of Erasmus' editing of the Greek text. For example, Stunica criticised the annotation by Erasmus to Luke 7:22 where, in commenting on *Pauperes evangelizantur*, Erasmus wrote:

> Porro pauperes vocat mites, sive mansuetos Hebraeorum more, quibus עני ab Hieronymo vertitur pauper, a Septuaginta mansuetus . . .

Stunica challenged this, writing that עני does not mean *mansuetus* for that should be ענו: the Septuagint sometimes confuses י with ו. Erasmus replied that the Hebrew in Jerome sometimes meant *pauper*, and *mansuetus* in the Septuagint. But Erasmus is concealing ignorance here since in no passage in the Septuagint is עני translated by a term which could mean *mansuetus*. Stunica's challenge, and knowledge of Hebrew, were valid – he was pointing to a

novae translationes omnes subito de medio tollerentur', '. . . suspicans fore ut hac tam flebili querimonia lachrymas excuteret populo.' For the Annotations in general v. E. Rummel, *Erasmus' Annotations on the New Testament*, Toronto, 1986.

[51] Allen, IV, 11. Letter to Edward Lee from Louvain, 15 July 1519. Allen refers to the 'trickery' employed by Erasmus to get hold of Lee's notes.

[52] *Annotationū Libri duo alter in annotatiōes prioris aeditionis novi testamenti Desiderii Erasmi alter in annotatiōes posteriopis aeditiois eiusdē*, Louvain, 1520. On the lack of basis in the Greek text for the Latin translation, sig. DDiii. For the verses at the end of Revelation provided by Erasmus, Fo. LXXXVII. 'Nam si graeca bene habent; cur emendatur? sin male: cur tantopere tibi placet: secundum ea: nostra mutare: reijicere: damnare?'

Hebraism.[53] It was some tribute to Stunica's critical acumen (in spite of his unwarrantable defence of a number of places in the Vulgate against what he thought of as the Arianising of Erasmus) that Erasmus silently corrected a number of errors pointed out by Stunica in later editions of his New Testament.

Erasmus was not done with his labours on the New Testament after 1516 when, in that year, he wrote to Pirckheimer, 'in the labour house at Basel' he had done the work of six years in eight months. From June 1517 he began to reflect upon the second edition in the event not wholly overseen by himself, and by the end of the year he wrote to another friend: 'Here I am once more in this hateful mill'. This edition was published in 1519 and was, however, really a corrected reprint of the former edition for which only one new Greek manuscript was used, with some revised notes; moreover new faults are found among the corrected old ones. Now appeared, without any modifications to accommodate with the Vulgate in the gospels, as he did in the first edition, the original wholly Erasmian Latin version which has been considered above; and there appeared also the more traditional title *Novum Testamentum* instead of the unusual *Novum Instrumentum* of his first edition. The famous short treatise 'Ratio seu Compendium verae Theologiae' was now set before the second edition with a reply to his detractors, 'Capita argumentorum contra morosos quosdam ac indoctos', considerably expanded in the fourth and fifth editions. Another edition appeared in 1522 which included the *Comma Joanneum* (1 John 5:7) after Stunica's fierce attack, on the weak admission that he had found it in one Greek manuscript (miniscule 61) at last – now long since known to be a late interpolation there – with some corrections too from the Complutensian Polyglot and the addition of the Vulgate version alongside his own. The fourth edition came in 1527 and the fifth and last edition in Erasmus' lifetime came in the year before his death, 1535, with a few minor alterations to the fourth, of little importance. As well as the edition of the Greek and Latin New Testament Erasmus published commentaries in the form of Paraphrases in Latin to give a wider currency to his understanding of the New Testament.

---

[53] Angel Saenz-Badillos, *La Filologia Biblica en los Helenistas de Alcalá*, 1972, 370, 392. Again at Romans 8:15. on the meaning of *Abba* Erasmus derived this from Hebrew, but Zúñiga rightly showed it was Aramaic and is a vocative not a nominative. The reply of Erasmus here, as in many other instances, is bland, evasive and basically unsatisfactory. A. Bludau, *Die beiden ersten Erasmus-Ausgaben des NT* (*Biblische Studien*, Band, VII, Heft 5), Freiburg im Breisgau, 1902, discussed the controversies which arose. Bentley, op. cit., 195 ff. provides a recent and useful account. Also v. introduction to the text of Erasmus' first Apologia in the ASD, IX, 2, Amsterdam, 1983 by H. J. de Jonghe. This includes an account of the controversy with Stunica.

The leading criticisms of his opponents were that the Greeks had tampered with the Greek manuscripts of the New Testament after the Schism, and that Erasmus had not received authority to make this edition. Erasmus tried to forestall the developing attack on him, which he learned of from various friends in England and elsewhere, by writing in the *Contra Morosos ac Indoctos* published in the 1519 edition, that he had never wished to depart by a finger or nail's breadth from the judgement of the Catholic Church. But an opponent of long-standing, the Carmelite Nicholas Egmond, who according to Erasmus had turned Cardinal Aleandro against him, an impassioned antagonist of trilingual learning, asserted that Erasmus' New Testament foreshadowed the coming of Anti-Christ; though he took care to keep himself from contamination by saying that he had never looked into the book nor would he do so.[54] From a friar of opposite views, Luther, who had at first approved the publication of the work, soon came appreciation qualified by doubts about the competence and validity of his interpretation of Scripture: 'Erasmus has performed the task to which he was called, he has reinstated the ancient languages and recalled them from pagan studies. Perhaps like Moses he will die in the land of Moab, for he is powerless to guide men to those higher studies which lead to divine blessedness. I should very much like him to stop expounding the Scriptures for he is not equal to the task.'[55] Here Luther plainly does not consider that Erasmus has provided an effective theological exposition of the New Testament in his Annotations: as was shown above, Erasmus produced them in the form and style of his commentary in his *Adagia* and had affirmed that they were not intended as theological exegesis. However, he did emphasise that the Holy Spirit alone is able to lead us to the inner meaning of Scripture: we must submit through purity of heart to the Spirit if we are to understand Scripture effectively, while it is still necessary to be acquainted with languages and the techniques of Rhetoric. Nevertheless, later, in his *Hyperaspites*, he stated that an emphasis on the Holy Spirit could cause difficulties since this would lead to us having to give credence, 'to all the fanatics who claim to possess the Spirit with more obstinacy than those who have a better claim to this exceptional gift'. Eventually he fell back on the position he had begun with in the life of Jerome, 'good letters and scriptural piety' should be the rule. This distinguishing of

---

[54] Allen, op. cit., IV, 556.

[55] *D. Martin Luthers Werke: Kritische Gesamtausgabe; Briefwechsel*, Weimar, 1933, Band III, 96. Luther could also say: 'Erasmus est anguilla. Niemand kan yhn ergreiffen sondern Christus allein. Est vir duplex.'

emphasis and purpose between himself and Luther marks the watershed between Erasmus on the one hand and developing Protestantism and the theological counter-attack by reforming Catholicism on the other. Erasmus deliberately intended to limit theological controversy: he would accept that the new theology written by the Lutherans was better written than that of the Scholastics and less swaddled in syllogisms, but nevertheless he saw it as a dogmatic theology, though now wholly grounded on the Scriptures and the Fathers; and dogmatic theology on any basis, Scholastic or biblical, Erasmus believed to be a turning away from the simplicity of the teaching of Christ and His apostles, he preferred to say: 'ego sum christianus'.[56] That Erasmus, like the Protestant Luther and like the Catholic Contarini, was a religious reformer who deeply desired newness of life in the Church should not need to be emphasised – it is the major reason for his editing, translating and annotating the Greek New Testament.[57]

Erasmus the Reformer turned away from the institutional aspects of the Church and the secularised nature of its curial control which was diffused throughout the hierarchy and based upon the complexities of canon law, a legal system loathed by the humanist jurisconsults who admired Erasmus. He instinctively responded to the sympathy of so many of the best informed laymen of his time as well as of those clergy sympathetic to the new trilingual studies, who desired the renewal of a piety (*in puram ac simplicem Christianisimus*) which did not rely on mere sacramentalism, so formalised by this time; or on preaching farced with irrelevant if entertaining stories from the legends of saints; or on theologians who were the swordsmen of dialectics rather than guides to Christ's people. He tried to turn men away from these false directions to another path which he described in a phrase which could be understood today, 'philosophia Christi', for it did not mean an elaborate intellectual structure but a living relationship with Christ not in the mystical sense but in the sense of the moral life of Christ. Here he showed his debt (not readily acknowledged by him) to the spirit of the *Devotio moderna*, seen at its noblest in the *De Imitatione Christi* of Thomas à Kempis, and the environment of his youth among the Brethren of the Common Life; to the insistence of Colet on the freshness of the new biblical studies of the New Testament in Greek; and to his

---

[56] Annotation to 1 Corinthians 1:12. Also: 'Quid diceret si hoc saeculo audiret confusas hominum linguas: ego sum theologus transalpinus, ego cisalpinus, ego scotista, ego thomista, ego occamista, ego realis, ego nominalis, ego parisiensis, ego lutheranus, ego carolstadianus, ego evangelicus, ego papista. Pudet me referre caetera.'

[57] In his Colloquy entitled *Peregrinatio religionis ergo*, 1526, there are foreshadowed many changes about to take place in England on the subject of images, relics and pilgrimages.

reading of Origen who showed him how piety and learning could expound the Scriptures without the wearisome distinctions of Scholastic exegesis, or the earnest but narrow efforts of the greatest of medieval exegetes, Nicolas of Lyra. Erasmus knew better than Luther the courts of princes and the households of prelates, the secularised intrigues of the Curia and the ramifications of that spirit throughout the hierarchy in Christendom. He knew that formalised sacramentalism could not be a substitute for an inward piety transforming life; he knew that Scripture must be the source and goal of all sound theology, and that faith was trust in God and not merely the things to be believed in order to avoid heresy. But he saw no advantage in rending the visible Church asunder nor, in order to reform it, in insisting on the centrality and concentrated force of the Augustinian doctrine of grace with its emphasis on man's depravity, loss of freewill to do good in God's sight, the consequent irrelevance of good works as conducing to salvation, and its impassioned assertion of prevenient grace. That his own alternative was possible in the situation of the times; that Luther was right in the end because he went to the root of the matter; and that Erasmus was too donnish and literary, will always be arguable: but that Erasmus had a consistent position as a Reformer and as an advocate of renewed Christian faith and life, that he was not merely an ambitious literary man who used these themes to attract notice, beat down his enemies, and find the favour of the fashionable and powerful, can be demonstrated.

With undeniable integrity and often real courage in face of positive danger, Erasmus expounded, allusively in ironies like *Moriae Encomium*; directly in serious writings on religion like the *Enchiridion Militis Christianae*; more discursively in his *Adagia*, *Colloquia*, and *Querela Pacis*; and supremely concentrated in the prefaces, as well as to a less degree in the Annotations to his edition of the New Testament, and his *Paraphrases* (summing up in themselves the Erasmian style of religion and piety) a way of religious renewal which he hoped would indirectly affect the administration, worship and theology of the Church and more directly influence the daily lives of Christian men and women. He did not explicitly call for alteration in the institutions of the Church, in the papacy and the hierarchy, nor did he call for radical changes in the sacramental system so important for the institutional Church, but he did undermine some of these walls of largely medieval construction although he thought of himself as proposing no more than themes of renewal. In Spain, Italy and England especially, and also in France and Germany, the Erasmians were prominent men and most of them conceived of Church reform along lines indicated by Erasmus. It would be difficult to define the range and quality of the influence of Erasmus on so many men in the first half of the sixteenth century in matters of religious reform, though the task is not impossible as the example of *Erasme et l'Espagne* by M. Bataillon showed in a thorough examination of this influence in one country. That this influence was not only literary can be seen in the possibility that the Henrician Reformation in England was not merely an arbitrary rejection of the papacy in favour of a brutal Royal Supremacy as many saw the changes under Henry VIII (including Luther and Calvin as well as Catholic observers), but as capable of description on Erasmian lines, although Erasmus himself would have disapproved of the schism. The main decisions could be paralleled in his writings: the turning to the Christian Prince (Charles V, Francis I, Henry VIII) for initiative in Church reform when the papacy seemed powerless or unwilling to do more; the abolition of the religious life in monasteries and nunneries would seem little loss to Erasmus the detractor of monks; nor would the cutting down of too many Saints' Days which led the people into idleness and, worse, half-secularised religion, have lacked his approval; the abolition of centres of superstitious concern for relics at the shrines would find support from Erasmus' ironically contemptuous account of the visit of Colet and himself to the shrine of St Thomas of Canterbury; the publishing of the Bible in English had the backing of his assertions on the value of vernacular versions of the Scriptures; the support by Henry for a trilingual college at Oxford and his appointing of professorships in the biblical languages shows his approval of that New Learning which Erasmus made it a great part of his life's work to promote. It is equally significant that Henry, whose accession had delighted the humanists of Europe, was an admirer of men of the New Learning, praised Erasmus to Charles V and Leo X and gave him other excuses for boasting of this royal flattery. It was tragic for his hopes that Erasmus lived to hear of Henry's judicial murder of St. Thomas More whom he regarded as an exemplar of the *philosophia Christi*, and whose desire for Church reform (which did not weaken his rejection of schism) he would have preferred to the confident Protestantism of Ulrich Zwingli or the sectarianism of Hans Denck, though both were strongly Erasmian in their beginnings.

The essential theme of the *philosophia Christi*, as has been seen above, was marked by the anti-Scholastic, anti-dogmatic and anti-speculative habit of mind and by a marked distrust of, if not positive rejection of, much of the theology of the Schools whether Thomist, Scotist or Occamist. It meant concentrating not upon the wide range of dogmas and the philosophical analysis and defence of them, but upon the limitation of the number of dogmas and upon them being clearly shown to be scriptural in origin; and turning away from over-emphasis on the sacramental system as well as from the debate on grace involving the grim labyrinth of antinomies on predestination and freewill, foreknowledge and meritorious works.[58] Here Erasmus showed his aversion to the way the debates of late Scholasticism on the doctrines of the sacraments and of grace helped to evolve the divisions between Catholics and Protestants. Against formalism and rigidity, Erasmus insisted on those things which made for Christian freedom in the gospel. For him the method of Church reform lay not in vigorous attacks on merit, on clerical abuses, and on the papacy, but on a slow process of self-knowledge and self-improvement by members of the Church led by gentle persuasion. Its foundation was the Bible, more especially the New Testament with its teachings made as practicable and intelligible as would be consistent with loyalty to the text; and to achieve this end, more would be gained by studying classical authors and the patristic biblical exegetes like Jerome and Origen than from becoming entangled in the nets of Scholastic interpretations of the fourfold sense of Scripture. All was to be focused on piety of mind and heart through the personal conviction and effort of the believer, who should not rely alone on the external rites of a judically conceived Church since these were by comparison with Scripture poor conductors of spiritual insight. The life of virtue should be the product of the *philosophia Christi* shown especially in loving kindness: the traditionalist assertors of dogmatic rectitude seemed to Erasmus to be men of worldly power rather than followers of Christ. Again and again Erasmus returned to the theme of Christian love which was also the drive behind his passionate detestation of war with its hatreds, its cruelties, and its mindless destruction. The *Querela Pacis* is only one instance of his writings on this theme, and it was his love for peace and charity which drew him away from schism or Protestantism in Christendom.

Erasmus set forth plainly the meaning of the *philosophia Christi* in the *Paraclesis* placed before his edition of the New Testament[59] and

---

[58] Gordon Rupp introduced his edition of Erasmus on Freewill in English with the sub-title *The Erasmian Enigma* in which he asked, 'How seriously must we take Erasmus as a theologian?' Trinkaus, op. cit., answered, 'Very'. M. O'R. Boyle, *Erasmus on Theological Method*, Toronto, 1977, also provided an affirmative answer to Rupp's question. Lowell C. Green, *Doctrine of Justification, Church History* 1974, briefly and usefully defined the terms and showed Erasmus preceding Luther in rejecting *gratia infusa*. J. B. Payne, in *Erasmus and Lefèvre d'Étaples as Interpreters of Paul*, ARG, 1974, also indicated the qualities of Erasmus as a theologian. Perhaps Rupp's question should be rephrased to read: 'Can it be said that Erasmus' theological affirmations were adequate to the serious theological crisis of his time?'

[59] 'Quid autem aliud est Christi philosophia, quam ipse renascent iam vocat, quam instauratio bene condite naturae?'

less directly in its companion little treatise the *Ratio seu Methodus compendio perveniendi ad veram theologiam*. The sub-heading of the *Paraclesis* is 'Exhortation to the study of the Christian Philosophy' and the phrase occurs fourteen times set out in the pattern of rhetorical exhortation renewed by the humanists of the time, for 'eloquence' was one of the driving forces of the early sixteenth century and Erasmus used it to call men of good-will concerned for this ideal of the Christian life to seek a nobler eloquence than Cicero because more effective if not so elegant. (Erasmus disliked Ciceronianism not only because of its tendency to artificiality but also because of its use as a papal instrument of diplomacy.) The preconditions of this philosophy of Christ are the spirit of piety and gentleness, and a pure and simple faith in the Word of God; and these can be found not only among the great ones of the world and the educated, but also among simple folk and it is found in manner of life rather than in argument and debate.

> I am not at all in agreement with those who wish to prevent the Holy Scripture being read by the unlearned and translated into popular speech, as if Christ had taught things so complicated that scarcely a handful of theologians could understand them, or as if the Christian religion had no other defence than ignorance ... This kind of philosophy rests upon the feelings more than upon syllogisms, it is rather life than discussion, rather inspiration than erudition and rather conversion than reasoning. ... If it is reserved for some to become learned men it is not forbidden to anyone to be Christian, to nobody to have faith, I would even boldly say, to no one to become a theologian. ... The philosophy of Christ, which calls itself a rebirth, is it in fact any other thing than the restoration of a nature which had been created good? ... The goal is to follow the pattern of Jesus Christ: the rules of religious orders or teachings of theological Schools are not necessary to understanding the simplicity of the teaching of Christ and His apostles: Christ is the way of life, the goal of mankind's endeavour and he is found uniquely in the New Testament. He said: 'If you love me, keep my word'.[60]

That Erasmus was a forerunner of both textual and historical criticism of the Bible is true but subsidiary to his ultimate purpose of the transformation of European society by men of good-will following the teaching of Christ and His apostles.[61] Since ,this by-passed so

---

[60] LB VI.

[61] Within the terms of reference provided for this study there was no space to deal with Erasmus' other writings on Scriptural subjects: his expositions of the Psalms, his Paraphrases, and his writings on the principles of hermeneutics, nor to draw attention to his views on the Old Testament and his use, of and methods in, allegorising.

much of what the medieval Church had built up to provide salvation for men, was Erasmus proposing an alternative version of the Church, a spiritual society? Catholic historians like Joseph Lortz and Hubert Jedin saw him as undermining and betraying Catholicism: for Lortz he was as serious a danger as Luther. In his own time he was accused of heresy by ardent traditionalists at the faculties of theology at Paris and Louvain, but these judgements were and are excessive. The position of Lortz and Jedin rests upon a view of Catholicism repristinated at the Council of Trent and which was not clearly expressed in Erasmus' lifetime, and is now under serious challenge in the theological situation arising from the Council of the Vatican II. Those of his Catholic contemporaries who opposed him were narrow and uninspired in outlook, nor did their judgement commend itself to men like More and Contarini whose loyalty to the Catholic Church should be beyond dispute. The admiration of Bucer, Zwingli and Oecolampadius and that of the Edwardine Protestants who caused the English version of Erasmus' *Paraphrases* to be set up in the parish churches of England, did not mean that he was a Protestant in all but name. But men would not forget that he died at Basel in a city brought into Protestantism by his disciple Oecolampadius.

He certainly had in common with the Protestant Reformers their principles of appeal to the Scriptures as the source of theological truth and Christian life, of insisting on the Church being seen as the congregation of faithful men and women, the Corpus Mysticum, and turning away from the juridical and legalistic aspects of the Church's institutions; of turning away from the view of the sacraments as being of themselves the instruments of salvation, to emphasise two or three of them, especially baptism, and this with intense concern for their spiritual reality. Baptism is the essential element of this restored Christianity, it is the sign of a new life in Christ, a life in the spirit, delivered from sin – 'Ergo curate ut perfecti sitis'. This is, however, certainly not Lutheran. He could even write of justification by faith as in his Paraphrase of Romans 1:13, 'Evangelium autem voco justificationem per fidem in Jesum Christum filium Dei quem lex promisit et praefiguravit': although he saw no need for the revolutionary force which Luther put into the concept. Erasmus had no use for religion that struck like a thunderclap, and Calvin's insistence on all things being brought in subjection to the sovereignty of God would have seemed to him as a potential distortion of the simplicities of faith. It is true that observers of insight deeply involved in the spiritual crisis of the time like Albrecht Dürer saw in Erasmus in 1521, on a false rumour of Luther's death, Luther's successor in the struggle against the abuses of the Roman Church. But that was in

1521; Erasmus had not then finally committed himself against Luther: that was to come three years later in his *De Libero Arbitrio*. Did the Protestants feel like Browning on Wordsworth:

> 'Just for a handful of silver he left us,
> Just for a ribbon to stick in his coat?'

From the outsider's viewpoint, Erasmus died rich and there was a persistent rumour that the Pope had offered him high status if he remained a Catholic (though Erasmus did not in fact allow himself to be compromised in this way). But Erasmus never really shared the Protestant experience of grace; the agony of Luther's struggle like the 'subita conversio' of Calvin were not for him. His energies were dying when the Protestants began to flourish, and their insistence on schism deeply disturbed him. Whatever the Sorbonne or other centres of orthodoxy said against him, he remained a Catholic.

Erasmus belonged to an earlier generation, to the men of the golden age of Northern Christian humanism 1490–1530, who believed in amelioration and never dreamed of schism or of rival orthodoxies vying in bitterness with the diatribes in that Scholasticism which they thought they had overcome. By the Diet of Worms, 1521, Luther's revolution was under way, and Europe was going to be rent asunder after the Diet of Augsburg in 1530. Erasmus' reform failed in his hopes for it in his lifetime through forces which he had not foreseen though its inspiration was never lost: the followers of Melanchthon shared many of his principles, Erasmus' fellow-countryman Hugo Grotius was a new Erasmus for his time, and the Church of England has never forgotten wholly its Erasmian beginnings – for did not the Laudians face Puritanism with certain weapons used by Erasmus? How many of the interests of reform Catholicism in our time, after Vatican II, revive, even if unconsciously, his aspirations for his Church?

3

The Reformation City

It would be well for us to take up Hamlet's purpose to go back to
school in Wittenberg, and set aside 'the truant disposition' of his
fellow-student Horatio who left Wittenberg behind him. For to think
of Luther without his city is a not infrequent fallacy. He who talks
about the Reformation must begin with Wittenberg since it was
there that Luther began and maintained the Reformation. All
subtleties of definition on what we mean by the Reformation, on the
historical importance of the earlier beginnings and later deviations of
other men besides Luther who were inspired by the need for reform
in the Church, cannot set aside that fact. The Protestant Reformation,
which began and developed in the German Reich, showed the closest
interrelation of religious movement and urban environment: for that
matter the origins of Protestantism were everywhere urban. The first
victories of Luther's theology up to 1525 were achieved as a popular
movement within towns, especially in the free cities of the Empire.
The successful rise of early Protestantism took place, for example, in
Bugenhagen's Hamburg and Lübeck, Spengler's Nürnberg,
Oecolampadius' Basel, Zwingli's Zürich, Bucer's Strasbourg – and,
later, Calvin's Geneva.[1] Anabaptism, which was regarded by the

---

[1] Geneva, before its rejection of its bishop, was a Savoyard town and to that extent was part
of the Holy Roman Empire.

Reformers as a fanatical attempt to overthrow the barely established reformed Churches by a parasitical invasion of their cities, in one of its forms won and shattered the city of Münster. But the implications of the fact of the essentially urban environment of the Reformation seem to have attracted too little attention from historians. It is significant that Koenigsberger and Mosse in their book *Europe in the Sixteenth Century* in a bibliography attached to the chapter on towns and cities wrote: 'Unlike the medieval town, on the one hand, and the modern industrial town, on the other, the Renaissance and Baroque town has never been systematically studied as an historical phenomenon. At best, we have studies of the economic or of the social and constitutional history of some of the towns of the Empire.'[2] From their bibliography there are two omissions which may be intentional, for the two studies are well-known. The first omission of note is that of the two articles contributed in 1937 by Hans Baron to the *English Historical Review*, entitled 'Religion and politics in the German Imperial Cities during the Reformation'. The other omission is that of the excellent study by Bernd Moeller, *Reichstadt und Reformation*, published in 1962.[3] The omission of those two studies is strange. The value of Baron's articles, which have been widely cited, can be seen in the fact that A. G. Dickens relied almost exclusively on them for the brief account of the Reformation cities in his *Reformation and Society* (1966),[4] and Moeller's book deserves Gordon Rupp's justifiable reference to it as a brilliant essay in his *Patterns of Reformation*.[5] This survey is offered in order to call attention to the comparative neglect of an important subject, and to suggest that neither Baron nor Moeller though admirable is entirely satisfactory.[6] Baron gave a useful discussion of the political activities of city magistrates in relation to Catholic Habsburg power and to the Protestant princes, but he gave less attention to the individual character of the various cities and to the intimate relation of the versions of Protestant theology which they adopted to the social and

---

[2] H. G. Koenigsberger and George L. Mosse, *Europe in the Sixteenth Century*, 1968, 54, under *Bibliography*.

[3] Published in *Schriften des Vereins für Reformationsgeschichte*, No. 180, 1962 (ET, Imperial Cities and the Reformation, Philadelphia, 1972).

[4] Op. cit., 76–79.

[5] E. G. Rupp, *Patterns of Reformation*, 1969, xiv.

[6] Since this study was published in 1971 Steven E. Ozment's *The Reformation in the Cities*, Yale, 1975, has appeared. It is full and useful, with emphasis on social and political rather than theological themes. He states that I share many of Moeller's views: this, however, in so far as it is true, is coincidence, and not unacknowledged borrowing. The substance of this study was based in part on research developed for my lecture course at Cambridge in 1960, entitled *Centres of Reformation*.

political concerns of the cities. Moeller shows the rôle of the cities as that of a homogeneous and passive reception of the Reformers' teachings, whereas many of them were actively and diversely engaged in political revolution seen in the overthrow of conservative patrician groups and they were aided therein to a greater or less degree by the Reformers' teachings on men's duties in society, and on the nature of 'Obrigkeit' or government.

There is another difficulty derived from the assumptions we have grown up with from our schooldays on the way we should study the past, we tend to make the economic and political history of the sixteenth century separately identifiable from the thought forms of the men who experienced that economic and political life. But in the sixteenth century religion was essential to the ways in which men expressed political ideas, social judgements, and economic practices: to separate the political, social and economic from the religious in that age is difficult and when attempted can be misleading. The religious and the secular were not divisible. Some sixteenth-century European men may have disliked the Church of Rome or the Churches of the Reformation or hated the clergy of either, but they were not therefore secular-minded or irreligious, and they clothed their political, economic and moral views in religious terms, not because they had no other language for them but because they wanted to do so. It is misleading to describe the religious views of Luther on 'Obrigkeit' in modern political terms to accommodate a Harold Laski; or to describe Calvin's religious view of banking practice at Geneva in terms appropriate to the sociological or economic viewpoints of a Max Weber or an R. H. Tawney.[7] This can lead to entanglements from which such writers seek to extricate themselves by distorting, if not weakening, the careful balance of judgement which Luther or Calvin had maintained. This should not allow us, however, to take the easier road of writing on the theologies, the liturgies, the church structures of Luther and the Lutherans, Bucer, Zwingli and Calvin, as though these were ends in themselves, without reference to the changing environment of the cities where revolutions took place which made possible the expression of those themes and which helped to mould their differing patterns. We should give more attention than is usual to examining how the theologians of the cities of the Reformation experienced limitation in the conditions of the

---

[7] R. H. Tawney was a distinguished economic historian whose book *Religion and the Rise of Capitalism* established (together with Weber's on the same subject) a central theme for study and controversy for decades. Pages 111–139 on Calvin are a record of inaccurate and misleading citations, unexamined sources and ungrounded arbitrary judgements, which helped to create the dark myth of Calvin's oppression.

environment of their cities as well as a fruitful stimulus for new developments; how they sought religious sanctions for political change; and how they made the cities into propagandist strongpoints for counter-attack on resistant Catholicism.

The very close interplay of these factors is clear from the large correspondence of all these men: it springs out vividly from their pages. Yet their correspondence is frequently neglected by those who write on the Reformers, for writers find it easier to discuss a Reformer's theological treatise uncluttered by political, social or economic limitations than to analyse the historical contingencies in his letters. It was environmental pressures which helped to divide Luther from Zwingli, as well as differences in temperament and in theology. When Luther faced Zwingli in debate at Marburg in 1529 the current of hostility could leap between them even from their differences in speech: Luther, the royalist High German of the Empire, found Zwingli's Swiss German to be speech appropriate to what he regarded as the religious fanaticism and the dubious republicanism of the Swiss Confederates. For Luther afterwards Zwingli was not just 'schweizerisch' but 'schwetzerisch'.[8] This is no excuse, of course, for falling into the trap of making religious themes the product of environmental determinism. We must maintain the independence and vitality of the thought of the Reformers, and we must not modify it in accordance with preconceived views on the social and economic structures of the period. Whatever the hesitations about the possibility, or the usefulness, of this study it should be agreed that regardless of the environment, in the last resort those powerful theologians of the great Reformation cities vigorously asserted the truth as they saw it, in spite of what princes, bishops or city magistrates might propose. Nevertheless, they did not live all their lives at the stage of 'in the last resort', but in the ongoing life of their cities, which pressed their theologies into new moulds; and it is in that context that this discussion is set.

Let us then 'go back to school in Wittenberg', which was the backdrop of the Lutheran drama, and not only to *Lutherstadt Wittenberg*, but also let us go to Lübeck, representative of the northern cities and of the dying political power of the Hanseatic League: to the golden city of Augsburg, centre of the Fuggers, where it was said a Scottish king could wish to have been housed as nobly as one of its patricians: to Nürnberg, where Dürer's eye saw life with a new religious realism yet a city cautious, conservative and always loyal to the Emperor: to Strasbourg, tolerant of many varieties of religious

---

[8] *D. Martin Luthers Werke*, Weimarer Ausgabe, Tischreden, vol. iv, 1916, No. 5005.

belief, home of the politically and religiously radical guilds, especially
the stormy guild of gardeners of which even Bucer was a guildsman:
to Basel the university city of the humanist Reformer Oecolampadius
and the chosen home of Erasmus, who died there protesting against
its Protestantism: to Zürich, where Zwingli, a prophet in arms, made
a civic community into a Church and died for his city as a good
confederate should: to Geneva, the Savoyard city, where dice-playing
swordsmen made a revolution and captured to serve them a young
and reluctant Frenchman, Calvin, who made them the not always
willing servants of his 'civitas Dei'. Also we should go to school to
Ulm, Regensburg, Hamburg, Constance and Memmingen, and to
the city of the blood-stained saints, Münster. If we did so we should
glimpse a great variety of constitutions and of city councils, political
associations, economic and social life, in a bewildering range of
patterns, in which it is dangerous to generalise from one group to
another. Each city had its particular characteristics and the contrasts
between them are sometimes extreme. There was nothing in common
between, for example, the political, cultural and economic life of
Wittenberg and of Geneva. We must distinguish between the
conservative northern imperial cities, the more intellectually and
socially lively southern imperial cities, and the cities of the Swiss
Confederation which had only a shadowy relation to the Empire.
Geneva was not even Swiss but Savoyard and therefore associated
with the Empire. Strasbourg had no tradition comparable to the
Swiss independence of Zürich, and it had no large cantonal region
from which it could draw a ready manpower like Zürich and Berne,
from whose villages, as from those of other cantons, came the
mercenaries who fought in most major European conflicts on either
side in the period up to the battle of Marignano in 1524. But
Strasbourg, because of increasingly weak episcopal control in the
fifteenth century, had won not only independence, but also through
its able statesmen, a most liberal and balanced constitution which was
much admired by Erasmus and other humanists. Basel more than any
of the other cities, not excluding Augsburg and Nüremberg famed
for the arts, was the spiritual home of many northern humanists. It
was the city where Erasmus chose to return to end his days, in spite
of its Protestantism, in doing so rejecting Oxford, Cambridge,
Louvain, and Paris, where he could have triumphed: but they lacked
free air, they were not free cities. However, the northern imperial
free cities had no universities, no humanists, no Swiss republicanism,
and they settled for a conservative Lutheranism and did not deviate
from it. The northern cities differed for the worse from the southern
in their degree of intellectual liveliness. The south German imperial

cities, on the other hand, through their political needs as well as developing intellectual trends were influenced by Zwingli's Zürich.

All these major centres are sufficiently different to make generalisations dangerous, but, allowing for the different economic and political settings, all these cities wanted greater expansion and social change and in all of them religious reform was an initiating or contributing factor in that expansion and change.[9] Nevertheless, these centres of social experiment and intellectual vitality were doomed to lose their initiative and much of their freedom by the middle of the sixteenth century. They lost their leadership and the drive behind the renewal they sought, through the increasing pressure of Charles V (relying no longer as at first on the appeal to imperial unity, but on his Spanish and Flemish resources in men and money), and through the princes of the Empire, who saw in the cities an undesirable independence of mind and political life. One by one, with the exception of the confederate cities of Basel and Zürich, though these were also constricted, they lost their effective freedom of initiative and were assimilated to the neighbouring power-structure of an Elector, prince or duke. Because of its distance from these forces in the Empire only Geneva survived in independence along with her allies the Swiss.

The upsurge and decline in the dynamic energies of the cities came in the period 1450–1550. This is equally the period of the upsurge of the northern humanist and Reformation movements and of their later loss of dynamism. By 1550 had come the full development of the national power structures of Spain, France, and, of the lesser nations, England and the rest, whereby the medieval concept of the democratic and free city as an independent political unit was lost. Even Zürich and Geneva had by that time come to resemble on their small scale the nation-state ideal of the politics of the period in which political freedom and social experiment were considerably limited. But in 1450 only the most astute of statesmen in the Empire would have grasped how great a change in the status of the free cities was to come. To understand that upsurge of energy in the cities after 1450 already mentioned we should remember the origins of the sense of corporate identity in the city. The free cities of the mid-fifteenth century had grown because *Stadtluft macht frei*: men did not build their city walls to shut in serfs. Men moved into the medieval town to win a measure of freedom, and to find variety in place of the monotony of labour in the fields, for in the town they found taverns,

---

[9] Useful material on the cities can be found in *Deutches Städtebuch*, vols. i–v, and in *Recueils de la Société Jean Bodin*, vols. vi–vii, *La Ville*.

the continually moving spectacle of street life, and the great churches with their popular preachers. In the towns men found community; not least, if they could acquire the skills, they could enter the community of brotherhood in the guilds. If a man was ambitious, or young and hopeful, he came to the towns for opportunity – though only a very few of the immigrants could become Dick Whittingtons, yet still they came. (It has been calculated that nearly 50 per cent. of the population of the Netherlands in the sixteenth century were town-dwellers.) Like Gray's frustrated peasants, the majority of citizens were poor, and 'chill Penury repressed their noble rage'. Bread riots were endemic, but this at least added stimulus to town politics.

Special opportunities had come to the towns in the early thirteenth century when many towns became almost independent states. From this period grow two kinds of towns in Germany (and the distinction is important), towns of the Empire, *Reichstädte*, which could develop into free cities; and territorial towns, *Landstädte*, which were subjected to a lay or ecclesiastical prince: it was the *Reichstädte* which became free cities which are important. By the fifteenth century the free cities of the Empire were struggling against interference from neighbouring princes, or against the resident bishop. This was because up to then they had been comparatively free from interference: until about 1350 the energies of the German princes and knights had been taken up by opposing or fighting for the Emperor, in either case to establish or extend their own territories.

In their struggles for freedom the imperial cities became the most efficient and planned political structures in the German Empire. The cities kept chronicles, records of their transactions and council decisions – this literacy meant a stimulus to education in which laymen could share, for within the city walls it had become no longer the exclusive monopoly of churchmen.[10] This literacy meant the historical awareness of precedent, and of the means of constitutional change, and of political expertise. The economy of the cities was a planned economy, subject to control, in which merchants had to proceed according to statute. But capital could and did accumulate, a fact dangerous for the survival of the democracy of the guilds in the fifteenth century, which was to be supplanted in so many cities by the oligarchy of patrician merchants. Cities developed their own laws and from the fourteenth century onwards were bringing in jurists familiar with Roman civil law, which in most cities came to be combined with the local or territorial law. This

---

[10] M. U. Chrisman, 'Lay Response to the Protestant Reformation in Germany, 1520–1528', in *Reformation Principle and Practice,* Essays in honour of A. G. Dickens, ed. P. N. Brooks, 1980.

brought a greater sophistication in the administration of the law in the cities compared with the more cumbersome procedures of the countryside and of the princely courts; and again provided a field for the educated layman. Further, the cities, through their trade, developed an international awareness; when merchants corresponded with foreign cities on the state of trade their horizons in more ways than one were enlarged. This internationalism brought with it diplomatic skills, and also, another sign of increasing political sophistication, espionage, in the watch kept on strangers at the inns. Police organisation, night watchmen, and other ways of social control were characteristic of the cities in notable contrast to the lawlessness and brutality of the countryside. Doctors and midwives were appointed and salaried by city councils. Cities had their regulations on extravagance in dress, licentious behaviour, gambling, prostitution, the punishment of insults to religion, including work on Sundays. Even the attitude to begging, regarded as an opportunity for Christian good works, changed in the cities, since townsmen thought hard work a sign of the good life. For example, Strasbourg in the later fifteenth century clamped down on its hordes of beggars, and insisted that those wholly incapable of work should be registered and made to wear a distinctive badge.[11] More efficient taxation systems were evolved to pay for and to manage all this. Military service was demanded for the protection of the city and grew to something much more significant than a mob of armed citizens. The patrician lords of Nürnberg, for example, took knightly arms for their shields and banners, raised their troops, and gave money for cannon foundries which provided the famous artillery of that city.

Cities expanded their territories, ensured that the villages in their orbit gave them food and soldiers, and provided them with protection in return; however, this expansion was restricted by the jealousy and vigour of neighbouring princes, one reason why the pattern of the Italian city-state did not develop in Germany. Another area of expansion in the life of the cities was found in that most enduring and self-governing medieval institution, the Church, which was brought in several ways under the authority of city councils.[12] Because of the influence of the clergy on political and social matters, city magistrates intervened in ecclesiastical affairs: here they followed the example of the princes in concerning themselves with the

---

[11] Otto Winckelmann. *Das Fürsorgewesen der Stadt Strassburg vor und nach der Reformation bis zum Ausgang der sechzehnten Jahrhundert's*, Leipzig, 1922, contains a wide range of source material.
[12] For example, Nürnberg, Gerald Strauss, *Protestant Dogma and City Government: the case of Nuremberg, Past and Present*, 1967, 39 ff.

appointment of abbots and, where cathedral chapters contained canons belonging to prominent patrician families, sought to influence episcopal elections. They even nominated priests for benefices. They controlled ecclesiastical building: the soaring spire of Strasbourg cathedral was begun under the care of the citizens whose magistrates controlled the fabric. The secularisation of church property in closing religious houses where this was thought to be desirable was well under way a century before the Reformation, which in this respect no more than completed a process already begun, by wholly rejecting the religious life. Moreover, in the fifteenth century anti-clericalism was marked in all imperial cities, as it was in the towns in general. The struggle for power between citizens and bishops of all episcopal towns had been a constant factor of medieval life, and in the fifteenth century many bishops temporarily or permanently left to reside outside of the city walls to avoid the frequent disturbances.[13] By the early sixteenth century only the Archbishop of Cologne succeeded in holding to his status within his city. As part of the background to these attitudes to the Church we should remember that the Church owned, it has been suggested, nearly one third of all the land in Germany.

One aspect of this city life is particularly important for our purpose, and that was the sense of a corporate identity among citizens. You belonged to your town not only visibly by residence but invisibly in a mystical sense of identity with it. When you took your vow of citizenship at moments of peril in the city, it was as serious as baptismal vows and with a similar sense of mystical identification. The German imperial city held its citizens as the Jews of old had been held by Zion. Sin or blasphemy by individuals was not only against the glory of God but could destroy a city like the invasion of disease could destroy an organism. How significant this idea could be for developments in the Reformation period should need no emphasis, especially at Zürich and Geneva, which survived the loss, or great curtailment, of political independence experienced by the German imperial cities.

The development of a city council, it is also obvious, was of fundamental importance for the self-government and sense of independence of the citizens. Where a council began to develop, it meant that there was a conscious aim of the citizens to win political control for themselves, for example, at Geneva from the prince-bishop; and the composition of a city-council reflected the power

---

[13] For example, Henri Naef, *Les Origines de la Réforme à Genève*, 2 vols., Geneva, 1936, demonstrates thoroughly the winning of the *Franchises* from the bishop.

pressures of different social groups. Many cities had a patrician class whose families were alone capable of electing members of the council, which became a self-perpetuating oligarchy. But other cities either cast out the patrician group, as for example, at Basel, won control for the guilds, or made a compromise which was effected by the admission of new members to the patrician class, at the same time appointing guildsmen to one or more of an increased number of councils. There was tension here between the pressing forward by the craft guilds and the resistance of the patrician merchants who tried to close the ring against them. This tension was further stimulated by the renewed growth of population in the fifteenth century, which in turn raised new pressures through the increased development of industry and commerce.

Behind this local political tension lay the problem of the relation of the cities to the government of the complex and unwieldy Empire. Jurists seemed to be unable to solve the question, Was the Empire a monarchy, an aristocracy, or a mixed state? The word *Obrigkeit*, which had first appeared in the thirteenth century, began to come into general use and new significance in the second half of the fifteenth century. It was a term denoting the institution and function of ruling. It became related to the explosive question of autonomy for the cities: could an imperial city exercise rule over its citizens similar to the authority of the emperor in the Empire, and independently of him? This question was brought into the foreground in the late fifteenth and early sixteenth centuries by the changes in the relation of the cities to the Empire, as well as because of movements for political reform in the Empire itself. In 1495, at a Diet at Worms under Maximilian I, two new developments of great importance occurred: a Public and Eternal Peace was decreed to be maintained to check the lawlessness and feuding which greatly disturbed trade, and the Imperial Chamber Tribunal was established as the chief legal body of the Empire. To assist this Tribunal, or Court, six Circles (*Reichskreise*) of the Empire were created. This development helped to undermine the power of the princes, and incidentally weakened the autonomy of the cities. With the election of Charles V as Emperor in 1519, his frequent and prolonged absences from the Empire while he resided in Spain were to be covered by a *Reichsregiment* or Imperial Governing Council. Through these developments the cities were losing ground at the imperial Diets.[14] They were increasingly ignored by the princes, who even tried to prevent them being

[14] H. Holborn, *A History of Modern Germany, I: The Reformation*, 1958, provides a framework for these developments.

represented at the Diets. The Imperial Chamber Tribunal, the Circles of the Empire, and the newer Imperial Governing Council, all involved greatly increased funds, and that meant increased taxation. The princes tried to push the main burden of this taxation on to the cities on the ground that their trade greatly benefited from the Public and Eternal Peace. Also á general customs duty on wool and cloth had been imposed at the frontiers, which the cities rightly claimed could put them out of the market through foreign competition. Hans Baron noted how the cities won surprisingly in 1524 from Charles V freedom from the frontier customs duties, and attained from him recognition of their constitutional claims in the Diets. Baron then most ably showed how this victory dominated the minds of the political leaders of the cities who hoped after the Reformation had entered their cities to by-pass the princes, and the provisions of the Edict of Worms against Protestantism, by direct dealings with the Emperor.[15] The collapse of this policy after 1529, at the Diet of Speyer, was to have far-reaching consequences which will be shown later.

Again it should be noted that the Swiss cities were hostile to the new political arrangements in the Empire. They refused to take part in this reorganisation of the Empire, and, though still in theory and tradition a part of it, they refused to pay any of the taxes imposed to carry out these reforms. The north German cities, wealthy and oligarchic, concentrated even more on their own affairs, the south German cities tended to be restlessly alert to new political possibilities if these should arise. Here, then, we have the situation of the free imperial cities around 1500. There was tension between the guilds and the patrician groups struggling to win political power. With the desire for greater autonomy there was a marked growth of anti-clericalism. Political and economic frustration had increased within the Empire. Over two-thirds of the cities' populations were unrepresented politically, ignored and held in contempt by those with power, and were increasingly restless with these frustrations.

Into this situation, between 1517 and 1521, Martin Luther burst forth with challenge after challenge to the structure of the Church, to the traditions of dogma and worship, to the accepted notions of the nature of society and of men's relations to each other in it, and leaving men bewildered as to where he would break out next. All this came not from a new Savonarola, a prophet of righteousness, nor from a Taborite preacher of fanaticism and war, but from a highly professional professor of biblical studies in the recently founded

[15] *The English Historical Review*, LII, 1937, 408.

university of Wittenberg, a position which he held throughout his life. Not the least part of the extraordinary quality of Luther's reformation was that it should have come from remote and shabby Wittenberg and not from a great and well-known city like Nürnberg, Lübeck or Strasbourg. Wittenberg was not a free city of the Empire, and it did not even have a German name, for it had originated with Flemish immigrants in a region which was not even ethnically German but Wendish.[16] It is true that it was the residence of the Elector of Saxony, Frederick the Wise, who, ashamed of its appearance, had undertaken a great building programme between 1490 and 1509 to improve its appearance and amenities. In that period he completely rebuilt the castle, the castle church, the town-hall or *Rathaus*, in Renaissance style, and in 1502 founded the university, and rebuilt the Augustinian house in which Luther came to live as a friar. But contemporaries were not impressed. Cochlaeus, Luther's able Catholic opponent, described Wittenberg in the twenties as 'a miserable poor dirty village in comparison with Prague'. But then he was not comparing like with like. Even Luther's friend Myconius (though he was not a native son) could describe it as more like an old village than a town. But the peak of exasperation with remote and shabby Wittenberg was achieved by Duke George of rival Ernestine and Catholic Saxony when he said, 'that a single monk out of such a hole should undertake a reformation is not to be tolerated.'[17] Wittenberg was a town far removed from the possibility of comparison with Strasbourg with its soaring cathedral tower, from the patrician splendour of Augsburg or Nürnberg, from the pomp and dignity of the Hanse cities, from the humanist culture of Basel, and from the vital energies of the guildsmen of Zürich.[18]

The creative ideas were being tested first within the house of the Augustinian Eremites and within the walls of the university, but when they moved out into the pulpit of the castle church, and in the form of the *Ninety-five Theses* on Indulgences in German translation published in the streets, the ordinary man was roused and pressed forward to hear more about this freedom of grace which cut through a tangled undergrowth of prohibitions, superstitions, and financial exactions for priestly services. When he also learned that there was no distinction between a priest and a layman and that all baptised Christians had the priest-like task of praying to God and praying for their neighbour, then he held a new political

[16] E. G. Schwiebert, *Luther and his Times*, St. Louis, Missouri, 1950, 200 ff.
[17] Ibid., 206.
[18] For the importance of humanism in many of the cities, Hans Rupprich, *Humanismus und Renaissance in den deutschen Städten und an den Universitäten*, 2 vols., Leipzig, 1935.

weapon in his hand. For the last forty years most writing, by Catholics as well as by Protestants, has been directed to the theological development of the young Luther. That this intensive study has been most fruitful and indeed has transformed not only Luther studies but also studies of the intellectual origins of the Reformation cannot be doubted. But it has not been accompanied by an equally thorough study of the social and political energies of the early Reformation years, which saw such vigorous activity stirred up by Luther's message.

Luther was like someone who dynamites an old house to clear the way to build a new one, without thinking of the effects on adjoining properties, and is then astonished to see how many more houses come tumbling down – for Luther's teaching was immensely explosive, to his own surprise, at just that period of time and in that country. Luther had never intended what occurred during his enforced absence in the Wartburg after the Diet of Worms in 1521, the sharp radical trend of Carlstadt's innovations at Wittenberg, where Melanchthon trembled before the prophets of judgement from nearby Taborite-influenced Zwickau who were stirring the citizens to new heights of excitement.[19] It was the Elector who called a halt to this millenarian trend, and Luther himself had to return to restore order, realising slowly that he must adjust the balance disturbed by his own earlier teaching on the freedom of a Christian man.[20] For it had proved to be heady teaching to ordinary townsmen to learn that all baptised Christians were as if priests.[21] What had been lacking for many a frustrated Savonarola or Hans the Drummer, from the fifteenth century up to Luther's time, was now, it seemed, available: here at last was a theological justification for change in political structures which were so intimately linked with ecclesiastical structures. Protestant historiography, especially where it has been associated with the traditions of Lutheranism in church life and practice, has drawn the picture of a cautious conservatism in the

[19] Nikolaus Müller, *Die Wittenbergerer Bewegung, 1521 und 1522: die Vorgange in und um Wittenberg wahrend Luther's Wartburg aufenthalt*, 2 ed., Leipzig, 1911; J. S. Preus, *Carlstadt's 'Ordinationes' and Luther's Liberty: A Study of the Wittenberg Movement 1521–1522*, Harvard, 1974.

[20] Wittenberg was an electoral city but the Elector co-operated with the city council, and to that extent it had autonomy in its own affairs. v. Edith Eschenhagen, *Wittenberger Studien: Beitrage zur sozial und Wirtschaftsgeschichte der Stadt Wittenberg in der Reformationszeit*, Luther Jahrbuch 9, 1927.

[21] This was easily misunderstood, Luther did not mean that laymen could be ministers of the Word and Sacraments, but that the laity had the calling as baptised to pray to God on behalf of their neighbour – only in this sense is the 'Priesthood of all believers' asserted by Luther. The phrase is not used in any Lutheran or Reformed Confession of Faith before the Second Helvetic Confession of 1566 (which did not set aside the necessity of calling certain men to the ministry of the Word and Sacraments).

Lutheran preachers and their princes who brought a gradual change
from one ecclesiastical structure into another and more effective one,
and then drawn a further picture which showed that social radicalism
was the work of the Zwinglians and the Calvinists. According to this
view, Lutheranism was essentially concerned with Scripture and grace,
and it was the Swiss who added a more radical social programme to
their theological purposes. This is, of course, true, but it leaves out
too much, and therefore it blurs the actual situation. First, the troubles
at Wittenberg in the winter of 1521–2 were a paradigm of what
could happen elsewhere, and secondly, the concentration of attention
on Luther's theology of grace is too exclusive. Luther not only 'coram
Deo' through biblical study, *Anfechtungen* or trials of faith, and his
skill in the techniques of that Scholastic theology available to him,
rediscovered the Pauline doctrine of grace but also, without his
originally intending it, let loose powerful forces opposing the
structures of the visible Church of his time. Luther had wanted to
talk about justifying grace at Leipzig and Worms in 1519 and 1521
but John Eck, and other opponents, forced him on to ground from
which he had to challenge papal authority and the totalitarian
authoritarianism of curia and hierarchy who used councils and canons
in support of that authoritarianism. Luther's new theology, in the
eyes of both intellectuals and of ordinary men, was not only setting
forth 'sola scriptura' and 'sola gratia', it was also consequently seeking
new ways of organising men's lives, in giving a new and simpler
pattern to ecclesiastical structures and in making their society more
amenable to their own control. Therefore, 'sola gratia' and 'sola
scriptura' were instruments by which men who sincerely believed in
them found release from the sense of restriction under complicated
controls which seemed antiquated and frustrating. The Reformation
ran across the Holy Roman Empire, across the German Reich, from
city to city like a sweeping flood, in this great territory lacking
centralised royal power. When it faced much better organised and
centralised monarchical states like France, Spain and England, or the
Catholic nationalism of highly sophisticated societies like those of
Northern Italy, it slowed down: its only hope was that the prince
could accept it or tolerate it, or alternatively its leaders could prepare
for a martyr's struggle. We hardly appreciate enough how intense for
so many ordinary townsfolk was their anti-clericalism, their powerful
dislike of the ecclesiastical system which touched their lives at so
many points and, they felt, too often with ill-effects.[22] Townsmen

---

[22] At Diet after Diet of the Empire complaints were frequent about lawsuits in papal courts,
concerning benefices, being prolonged and the costs raised. There were complaints about the
exploitation of clerical rights to raise taxes by tithes, annates and expectations, complaints about

felt that they must have greater freedom of social and political action to obtain improvements in economic affairs and in the administration of justice.

Sometimes their anti-clericalism was more vigorous than coherent: the following incident must have been reproduced in many places. In a letter of April 1522 from the parish priest Lucas Leder in the town of Oschatz, in the territory of Duke George of Saxony (who was vigorously Catholic), we read of an angry group of townsmen hammering on the priest's door and window-shutters. Their purpose was incoherently expressed, but it was plain they wished to be rid of him. Fr. Leder wrote that he obtained no help from the Mayor or from the town council the following day, and in fear he is writing to his ordinary the Bishop of Meissen for advice and, better still, positive aid.[23] These townsfolk were expressing a frustrated desire for change. But another example will show men who found coherence through the assistance of a capable lawyer to express their views in writing, and who found their aims through adopting the ideas of Luther on the freedom of a Christian man through the pattern of a Christian *Gemeinde* or congregation. Here the citizens of the south German town of Wendelstein address a new parish priest sent by their prince, Casimir, *c.* 1525–6:

> Honourable, dear brother! ... According to the testimony of Holy Scripture, it is the duty of a Christian congregation to ask God, the Lord, to send workers into his harvest; [a christian congregation] also has the power unanimously to seek an honourable man with good reputation from within [the congregation] who would [preach] the Word of God according to the true understanding ... A Christian congregation also has the authority to dismiss [this man] again and to appoint someone else in his stead ... Now, in these final days, this aforementioned custom has been taken from the Christian congregation through the Anti-Christ. ...[24]

This document reflects the early teaching of Luther on these themes, but it is even more revolutionary than Luther had been in 1523, for it appears to be the *Gemeinde* that decides on whether its pastor is to be dismissed or not. Since it comes from a south German town it also shows elsewhere in the document the influence of the Zwinglian view of the eucharist. Strauss, who has provided an excellent study of

the increase in the charges and taxes for dispensations, privileges and absolutions; and complaints about the arbitrary distribution of clerical benefices to privileged monasteries.

[23] Hans Eberhardt and Horst Schlecht, *Die Reformation in Dokumenten*, Weimar, 1967, No. 15, 40.

[24] Gottfried G. Krodel, *Studies in Medieval and Renaissance History*, vol. V ('State and Church in Brandenburg-Ansbach-Kulmbach, 1524–1526'), 151 ff.

Nürnberg in the sixteenth century, points out that there were nearly 3,000 cities and towns in Germany and they were a uniquely German phenomenon in their attitudes and social patterns: they were not like towns elsewhere in Europe. This is especially true of the imperial cities or *Reichstädte* – 'They were the glory of Germany and the admiration of foreign visitors.' Most of these 3,000 towns were of small size and with not more than 2,000 or 3,000 inhabitants and the significant ones amounted to no more than about fifty, and of these again only about eight or nine represented the full splendour of the German city. Machiavelli could write that the power of Germany certainly resided more in her cities than in her princes.[25] Here his political shrewdness had seen the implications of the fact that the great and influential cities were immediately subjects of the Empire itself, and not of a neighbouring prince or of the Emperor. But all to a greater or less degree were ecclesiastically subordinate to a bishop. In some cases, as with Cologne, the largest German city, he was a ruling prince.

In the period 1521–35 it was these cities which made the running in the spread of reformation, from Lübeck on the Baltic down through the centre and west to the south German cities, Augsburg, Nürnberg and Strasbourg, and across to those cities which had only a shadowy relation to the Empire since they belonged to, or became clients of, the militarily powerful and *de facto* independent Swiss Confederation, Basle, Zürich, Berne and then Berne's subordinate towns of Lausanne, Neuchâtel, and alongside of these her protegée Geneva.[26] Wherever reformation came some degree at least of social change took place; it increased the desire for freedom of action in the cities or small towns it touched, and it caused either radical or conservative revolutions, or produced in turn a counter-revolution if change had been too violent or produced too many difficulties. When the Lutheran movement rolled forward across the Reich there sprang up as it were from the ground, no one knowing precisely whence they came, groups of radical extremists frustrated and dormant for decades, lacking leaders, favourable opportunities, and an ideology. These were the heirs of the Spiritual Franciscans, the Waldensian groups, the Taborites, the author of the *Reformatio Sigismundi*, the apocalyptic writings of Joachim of Fiore and his disciples, the descendants of the Brethren of the Free Spirit, the Winckler and other groups who represented 'the poor in the land'.[27] These saw in

---

[25] Gerald Strauss, *Nuremberg in the Sixteenth Century*, New York, 1960, 4.

[26] For example, the struggle of the city of St. Gall to free itself from its Prince Abbot, and its consequences for Zürich. v. G. R. Potter, *Zwingli*, Cambridge, 1976, ch. XI.

[27] Gordon Leff, *Heresy in the Later Middle Ages*, Manchester, 1967, describes the various groups.

the Lutheran movement the dawn of a long-awaited day, the realisation of an eschatological hope, when a new world-age would begin. They bitterly hated the old ecclesiastical forms in worship, church organisation, sacraments and doctrine, and they rejected any compromise between traditional structures, for example, the conception of the parish, with secular government. These men sprang up behind the Lutheran movement, as at Wittenberg in the first days of the Reformation, and bedevilled its attempt to create an orderly transition from stable Catholicism to stable Lutheranism – in one case causing a completely successful radical extremist revolution at Münster. These groups went under the general name of Anabaptists, too general a name, since it covered a great number of people whose views were by no means capable of reconciliation one with another and as misleading in its application by historians as that other term to describe groups equally hard to define under one head, Puritanism. These Anabaptist groups refused any compromise between the churches of the saints and a corrupt social order; certainly in any way that would resemble the Church and State relations of Catholics or Lutherans. They thought of infant baptism as imprisoning people in that political ecclesiastical structure and it became for them the symbol of what was wrong with Church and society – therefore like Voltaire they could have said *écrasez l'infâme*. In south Germany Lutheranism met another check to its successful development not only from Anabaptist groups as, for example, at Augsburg, but from Zwinglianism, a less conservative and more popularly assimilable creed than Lutheranism since it greatly simplified worship, the administration of the sacraments, identified community structures and church structures more closely, and carried with it the prestige of being the first state to adopt Protestantism.[28]

This alternative creed was not confined to Zwingli's Zürich but spread rapidly to other Swiss towns and cantons like Berne, and also as far north as Augsburg where the Zwinglian view of the eucharist prevailed over that of Luther. It also strongly affected Strasbourg, Basel, and nearby Ulm. That this advance was more deliberate and purposeful than Luther's original activity as a reformer (who could say, 'Philip and Amsdorf and I sat drinking our Wittenberg beer and the Word did the work')[29] can be seen in Zwingli's letter of April 1527 to the city of Ulm, in which he justified his intervention there:

---

[28] Ulrich Gäbler, *Huldrych Zwingli: Leben und Werk*, Munich, 1983, provides an excellent demonstration of the relationship of theology and social change at Zürich.

[29] *D. Martin Luthers Werke*: Weimarer Ausgabe, vol. x, 1905, 18–19.

There are many points on which your lords and mine of Zürich are in accord because of an aristocracy, that is, a government chosen from among the best men in the town and region ... that is why I am seriously concerned to watch for all the good that shall be undertaken among you by God, and by the example of your wisdom could also be admitted amongst us and our example made available for you.[30]

Zwingli said explicitly elsewhere that magistrate and prophet should collaborate to form a true Christian town, for example, Strasbourg as well as Zürich: that was the drawing power of his appeal to the south German cities. Luther was more doubtful whether all citizens of a given area could obviously form a church; he tended to think more of truly pious groups within the large framework of a parish and to concentrate his hopes on those. Here, then, were cities of the Reich, and the Swiss Confederation still vestigially part of that Reich, open to the impact of Lutheran, Anabaptist and Zwinglian influences.

These changes in certain cities which can be seen as representing the varying influences already described will now be considered, beginning where all this began, at Wittenberg. The period 1519-25 was that of the years of innocence of the Reformation when men could move freely into a new world of grace without thought of the consequences. Although Wittenberg, during Luther's absence in the winter of 1521-2, was gripped by those disturbances referred to above, created by the Zwickau prophets, it had calmed down on his effective reappearance, and it is significant of the still comparatively conservative situation which was maintained there that not until his death-bed did Frederick the Wise receive communion under the new form. But in 1525 came the change from innocence to near anarchy: the Peasants rose in war against the Princes encouraged by the parish priest of Alstedt, Thomas Müntzer (originally influenced by Luther), who taught that God guided them to use the sword against the ungodly.[31] How Luther opposed this popular tumult is well-known: he had to show that his teaching on the 'Liberty of a Christian Man' did not mean the abolition or total transformation of ecclesiastical and social order. Luther had been profoundly disturbed by the fanaticism in religion and social order of Müntzer and to a less degree of his own former colleague, Carlstadt, and a slowly developing conservative reaction began through which much of the popular interest in Protestant reform died down. It became the activity of the governing classes, of the men who exercised *Obrigkeit*, who used it for solving social and political tensions within their boundaries or for

[30] *Corpus Reformatorum*: Zwingli, vol ix, No. 606.
[31] Rupp, op. cit. part iii.

political manoeuvre against the Emperor or Catholic princes. After 1530 Luther accepted the view of the Saxon jurists that one might defend the faith against attack by war – a remarkable and little noticed change of emphasis to which Baron rightly draws attention.[32] Wittenberg had provided a paradigm for the development of the Reformation, especially for the cities of the Empire, allowing for differences of emphasis owing to different geographical situation and political organisation and for the fact that Wittenberg was not a free imperial city. First to be considered should be the north German cities, of which Lübeck, which was rich and powerful and the leading city of the Hanseatic League, was the greatest, perhaps the only German trading city which could be mentioned in the same sentence as Venice. Here, as was universal in the north when Protestantism entered, it came in with Lutheran preachers who attracted the populace.[33] When the patricians tried to suppress this preaching they were challenged by the merchants, who were not patricians, and who saw here a lever to power not available in their struggle with the patricians before this. The patrician council reluctantly allowed the Lutheran preachers to continue, and the religious revolution proceeded rapidly until by 1531 Lübeck had become Lutheran, and also had found a social and political leader in the non-patrician Wullenwever, who had become burgomaster on the back of the Lutheran movement. However, to this temporary success for social change came the challenge of a patrician counter-offensive through the failure of Wullenwever's foreign policy for Lübeck and a naval defeat. Thereafter Lübeck returned to the political and religious conservatism of strict Lutheranism, and became no longer the city she had been before the religious revolution.[34] What had begun as a great upsurge to transform Lübeck politically as well as religiously had failed. A similar pattern emerged in several of the north German cities. Münster is the interesting exception since it showed the Lutheran Reformation being overrun by radical extremists supported by a large-scale immigration there of Frisian revolutionaries.

In the south German cities, once again, there appeared Lutheran preaching rousing, for example, the populace in Augsburg which moved soon from Lutheranism towards Zwinglianism and even Anabaptism since the tolerant council at first gave the religious reform movement its head. But once again a conservative patrician

---

[32] Baron, *English Historical Review*, LII, 423.

[33] Ozment, 209, cites Johann Schildauer, *Soziale politische und religiose Auseinandersetzungen in ... Stralsund, Rostock und Wismar in ersten Drittel des 16 Jahrhunderts*, Weimar, 1959, 26–40, 93–8, for the broadening of social status in consequence of the Reformation.

[34] A. von Brandt, *Geist und Politik in der Lübeckische Geschichte*, Lübeck, 1954.

restoration effected a religious and political counter-offensive; this time Catholicism gained most of the city which was left with only a remnant of Lutheranism. Here the weakness of Protestantism was that it was in conflict with the economic needs of the city since it was the home of great banking houses like the Imhof, Fugger, and others, and the guilds which could have forced political and social change had to rely on that capital accumulation of the Fuggers and its functions to maintain their own life. The heart of the problem lay in the fact that this finance capital was supported by investment in imperial possessions far from the city, which laid Augsburg wide open to counter-attack by Charles V, who after the Diet of Speyer in 1529 was firmly against any political compromise with Protestantism for at least a decade. In the event, the protestant-minded guilds of Augsburg were defeated by Catholic patricians aided by Charles.[35]

Nürnberg, though it became Lutheran, very soon quenched any advance beyond a very conservative form of Lutheranism and contrived to survive as a Protestant city, as Augsburg had not, by a skilful policy of always supporting the Empire and Emperor and refusing to join other Protestant cities and princes in the Schmalkaldic League. The admirable book by Gerald Strauss on Nürnberg in the sixteenth century contains a useful chapter on 'Nürnberg and the Reformation'. But the following points may still be made. There was no difficult conflict of interests between Church and State at Nürnberg since its relationship to its ecclesiastical lord, the Bishop of Bamberg, had gradually been loosened.[36] The town had gained control of its ecclesiastical affairs before the Reformation began, and it kept a firm hand on the priests and religious within its walls. It has been estimated that only about two per cent. of the population were ecclesiastics and this number included servants. From the fourteenth century it successfully claimed its rights in the appointment of the priests of the two parishes. The council set up *Kirchenpfleger* for the oversight of the churches, monasteries, convents and other ecclesiastical property; the priests had no direct responsibility for

---

[35] Baron, op. cit., 633. A full treatment is in F. Roth, *Augsburger Reformationsgeschichte*, 2 ed., Munich, 1901–11. Philip Broadhead, 'Politics and Expediency in the Augsburg Reformation' in *Reformation Principles and Practice*, ed. P. N. Brooks, 1980, gives an excellent account of the discussions before the Council by lawyers and Protestant ministers, which shows the Council trying to weigh the legal, political and economic results of becoming Protestant in 1534. As he states, 'Reform amounted to economic and political suicide, a threat which became tragic reality for the citizens of Augsburg in 1548'.

[36] L. P. Buck and J. W. Zophy, eds., *The Social History of the Reformation*, Columbus, 1972, includes papers on Nürnberg, and Wenzeslaus Linck (like Luther an Augustinian Observant) who aided the Reform there by powerful preaching of Lutheran themes and emphasising education, 17–73.

church finances. By 1514 the council had won the right of presentation of priests to the parishes of Nürnberg.

But in spite of the mastery of ecclesiastical life at Nürnberg by the council, there was anti-clericalism there as elsewhere judging by the writings of Hans Sachs, the guild poet romanticised by Wagner, whose satirical verses against the clergy and papal authority were well-received by the city.[37] In 1520 the council irritably declared itself upon the frequent complaints about its inefficient and immoral clergy not only in Nürnberg but in its countryside. It also disapproved of the practice of citing its citizens to legal tribunals at Rome: this cause of complaint was continual and widespread in Germany; the citizens of Wendelstein were emphatic against this in the document quoted above. Another sore point against the papacy at Nürnberg was the revoking by Adrian VI of a decision of Leo X who, upon payment of a large amount of money, had given the city its full rights of church patronage. Adrian demanded further large sums before he would agree. Here Nürnberg was provided with an example in high places of the late medieval complaint that the priest was the man who wanted money.[38] The reformation at Nürnberg was in part a response to this anti-clerical resentment of its citizens. But this was not a revolutionary process: there was no background of guild conflict or of lesser merchants against nobles at Nürnberg since it was effectively controlled, without hope of serious challenge, by forty-three patrician families who governed the wealthy city and its regions. But the council were not unwilling to move towards Lutheranism backed by the anti-clericalism of the people.

A number of prominent citizens had formed the *Sodalitas Staupitziana*, including Albrecht Dürer and the city secretary Lazarus Spengler, who both were to become strong Lutherans. This 'Sodalitas' had been founded as a discussion group in honour of Johann Staupitz, the superior of the Order of Augustinian Eremites in Germany, who was well-received on several occasions as a preacher at Nürnberg, and under whom Luther had graduated into a Reformer. It was significant that change was coming when the council refused to allow the preaching of the Indulgence for St. Peter's at Rome. About the same time Spengler openly said that Luther's teachings must be true since they conformed to the Gospels, Paul and the Prophets. In 1521, at the Diet of Worms, the decision was taken to make Nürnberg the

---

[37] *Weltgeschichte* ed. J von Pflugk-Hartung, Berlin, 1907, *Geschichte der Neuzeit: Das Religiöse Zeitalter 1500–1650*, 293, for Sachs '*Wittenbergisch Nachtigall*'.

[38] Hans von Schubert, *Die Reformation in Nürnberg*, Nürnberg, 1925, is valuable on these matters.

seat of the two great instruments of centralisation and political reform of the Reich, the Imperial Governing Council and the Imperial Chamber Court: this could have severely restricted the gradual movement to Lutheranism there, but in spite of this decision the council supported by the citizens guardedly but firmly refused to accept the imperial ban on Luther. In 1523 Nürnberg again refused to act upon the Worms decree against Luther. Three years earlier Dürer had declared that Luther had delivered him from great fear. For Dürer new political and religious insights derived from Luther brought invigorating new life.[39]

But from all this we cannot discover evidence for Nürnberg adopting the Reformation because of social, economic or political strains other than a restless desire to have complete and unquestioned control in all things, including ecclesiastical matters. After the Disputation of 1525, when Nürnberg adopted the conservative Lutheran type of reform (in the theological and ecclesiastical sense), its clergy became simply citizens. In this respect it was an exception among the cities: it experienced no popular outburst implying social change or radical consequences deriving from religious views, for it obtained what not even Wittenberg had achieved, a quiet change of religion: this was undoubtedly due to the tight control of the council, and the patrician spirit, over the city.[40] Its changeover was made through the moral pressure of leading intellectuals on the council, and it was initiated by the council and not through popular pressure. The mould imposed by the environment there led to one of the most conservative forms of Lutheranism.

In sharp contrast to this quiet change was the revolution at Münster, in which popular pressure and a different political framework led to an original Lutheran reform being run away with into a political and religious radicalism which destroyed itself.[41] Münster was a town of 15,000 inhabitants in which the bishop was the civil as well as the spiritual ruler, although it had gained a fair degree of self-government. Westphalia was a region of social conflict and some economic distress, and like the neighbouring towns of the Netherlands it felt these

---

[39] W. Waetzwoldt, *Dürer*, ET, 1950, 165.

[40] The impact of lawyers in the Reformation Cities should not be overlooked, Christoph Scheurl, well-read in Roman law and the relevant sections of canon law, defended the Reformation at Nürnberg against the Emperor and the papal delegate, Corregio. v. Buck and Zophy, op. cit.

[41] *Die Geschichtsquellen des Bisthums Münster*, vol 2. (C. A. Cornelius, *Berichte der Augenzeugen über das Münsterische Wiedertäuferreich* Münster, 1853) provides contemporary accounts of the proceedings. Also, C. A. Cornelius, *Geschichte des Münsterische Aufruhrs* I, 1855, II, 1860. A useful introduction is R. Stupperich, *Das Münsterische Taufertum, Ergebrisse und Probleme der neuren Forschung*, Schriften der historischen Kommissich für Westfalen, 2, 1950.

pressures badly. There had been large price increases and heavy taxes at Münster. This had led to a serious revolt in the city in 1525. There were seventeen craft and merchant guilds which were very strong there and a corporation had been formed with two representatives from each guild. These guilds were well-represented on the council: no important decision could be made without the co-operation of the guilds. At the time when Lutheranism was vigorously gaining control in other cities, the guilds of Münster had become dissatisfied with the patrician city government and were certainly hostile to the wealth of the religious Orders there. Thirty-six Articles were drawn up in 1525 to meet the demands of the guilds, but the bishop was able to prevent the acceptance of these Articles. He felt it to be safer to reside outside of the city and in 1531 he left to live some miles away (he had some spiritual jurisdiction in the Netherlands as well as in Westphalia). In June 1532, a new bishop, Franz von Waldeck, was elected – who at this stage (1532) tried to enforce the imperial edicts against heresy but failed to persuade the council to act.

There were three fateful figures in the origins of the Reformation at Münster against whose influence the bishop perhaps moved too late, although the social tensions and political structure there would most probably have hindered efforts to check any Protestant influence entering the city. First, Melchior Hofmann, a furrier from south Germany, who began his Protestant career as a lay preacher of the early themes of Lutheranism in Livonia in 1523; he even received a certificate of approval from Luther at Wittenberg for the Articles he drew up in Livonia. Luther, hostile to religious fanaticism, had unknowingly backed a man who was to become one of the most dangerous of fanatics, not least because of his influence on others. Hofmann began to emphasise the second coming of Christ in his preaching and to spiritualise the meaning of the sacraments. He became a Lutheran pastor at Stockholm and began to be strongly influenced by the wayward theology of Luther's former professorial colleague Carlstadt.[42] He was found unacceptable to the Swedish authorities and moved on to various towns. He preached that the city of God would come by divine intervention and, though it was not to be brought in by force, believers should be formed into covenanted groups (*Bundesgenossen*) to prepare for it, and he began to baptise believers. He expected a new Elijah to bring in the city of God which was to appear at Strasbourg in 1533. On making a second visit there to await the event he was imprisoned and eventually died there.

Hofmann was responsible for the development of what became

---

[42] For Carlstadt see Rupp, op. cit., Part ii.

known as Melchiorite themes in the Anabaptist movement. That is, the sharp distinction between believer and unbeliever, the identification of believers (who had covenanted together) with a limited number of elect saints who would be received with approval by the Lord at his second coming, not only to share with him in bliss but also to take revenge upon unbelievers. These Melchiorite ideas flourished among the dispossessed who felt that the future before them was without hope because of the very bad economic situation of the Dutch towns at that time. These men, who began to think of bringing in the city of God by violence, first thought of Amsterdam and next Münster after the failure of Hofmann's prophecy that Strasbourg would be the centre of this eschatological hope.[43] His heady, chiliastic preaching left among his followers two attitudes to the future expected event: one group followed Hofmann's refusal to advocate violence, another more vigorous group was led by two of his converts in the Netherlands, Jan Matthys and Jan of Leiden, who decided that the saints must act to bring in the city of God. Matthys had been baptised by Hofmann in 1531 after he had heard him preaching of the approaching kingdom of bliss to be given to the elect who would form a priesthood of believers. Matthys began to preach these new doctrines in the Netherlands at this time.

The second figure of fateful importance for Münster was Bernhard Rothmann who, after an education among the Brethren of the Common Life and further studies at the University of Mainz, became a priest, and was appointed as preacher at St. Mauritz in Münster. Lutheranism had already made some impact at Münster and the neighbouring region, though it had received a setback after a significant attempt by the guilds to suppress economic competition by the monastery of Niesing in the city's jurisdiction, and bring in social and religious reforms, had failed. Lutheran themes had been interpreted by the guildsmen in a social and political sense. By 1531 Rothmann's vigorous preaching attracted the citizens of Münster, and by mob violence he was given a pulpit outside of his church in which to preach without intervention by higher ecclesiastical authority. Rothmann sought support by visiting Wittenberg, Strasbourg, and other centres of Reformation, but on his return the bishop compelled him to leave in 1532. Nevertheless, Rothmann's supporters took over the church of St. Lambert and found Lutheran preachers for themselves. The new bishop of that year, von Waldeck, decided to challenge the guilds and their mob support by suppressive

---

[43] Cornelius Krahn, *Dutch Anabaptism, 1450–1600*, The Hague, 1968, provides an account of the Melchiorites.

action. The citizens who supported Rothmann, a considerable number, formed a league and appointed a committee of thirty-six to care for the continuance of Lutheran preaching in the city. After the refusal of the Catholic clergy to hold a Disputation, the league took over the churches of the city except the cathedral. Event followed event rapidly; Rothmann returned and introduced a Zwinglian form of holy communion, for he was already moving away from strict Lutheranism and even taking up some Anabaptist ideas. By early in 1533 Rothmann and his followers dominated the religious life of Münster, supported by the guilds and the majority of the citizens.

A crucial influence to a more radical trend had been the appearance of Sacramentarian preachers from nearby Wassenberg who gave impulse in an iconoclastic anti-Lutheran direction.[44] Rothmann now turned away from the council-supported Lutheran party and led what became a majority party, supported by the guilds and the townsmen, of near-Anabaptist enthusiasm. The Lutheran group on the council joined ranks with the returning Catholics and the bishop, and this produced a lull. But in the second half of 1533 numbers of strangers, including Melchiorites, followers of Hofmann, flowed into the city, and in January 1534 came two disciples of Jan Matthys, a baker from Haarlem, and later Matthys himself accompanied by Jan of Leiden (Jan Beukels or Bockelszoon), and within a short time nearly 1,500 persons had been baptised. The visionary Matthys regarded himself as the new Enoch, the fore-runner of the new age and a fanatical advocate of Hofmann's view of forming a convenanted people and preparing for the city of God. Bernard Knipperdolling, a cloth merchant and a councillor, may be taken as representative of the social radicalism which accompanied religious change at Münster: he had begun by supporting Rothmann against his fellow-councillors. It was he who led the meeting of all the guilds in July 1532 to form a covenant to protect Rothmann and his teachings. Rothmann's rapid development as a revolutionary was supported by his appeal to the rights of the ordinary citizens to make decisions binding upon the city. Knipperdolling became an impassioned advocate of this principle of the rights of the people which, when combined with his eventual fanatical devotion to the new leader Jan of Leiden, made him a formidable instrument of revolution.

The third fateful figure for Münster was this Jan of Leiden or Jan Bockelszoon who was to become the Davidic king of Münster.[45] Handsome, and with a compelling personality, but lacking the manic

[44] Krahn, op. cit. 119–35.
[45] Ibid., 124 ff., 133–49.

fanaticism of Matthys, he had come from a varied career in the half-world of social unease in the Netherlands, as tradesman, poet and actor – he was the illegitimate son of a village woman from the Münster region. He had belonged to one of those curious institutions of that country and period, the Chambers of Rhetoric – these promoted the arts at the level of popular culture and undertook the writing and producing of plays of a religious and sometimes secular nature which by the eve of the Reformation had emphasised criticism of the conditions in the Church.[46] By the year 1530 the Chambers had largely become centres of somewhat confused Reformation propaganda through these new-style Morality or Mystery plays. Jan of Leiden had moved on from this career to becoming a strong advocate of violent action in support of Melchior Hofmann's dream of a new city of God, after being baptised by him. He and Matthys saw Münster as the centre for realising the New Age. But it is an open question how far Jan of Leiden retained some purely political shrewdness in the events which now took place, as distinct from being swept away by apocalyptic imagery as Matthys was. Certainly there was a complicating degree of ambivalence between religious fanaticism and worldly ambition on the part of Jan of Leiden.

By December 1533 the council had become powerless before the guilds, not least the aggressive Smiths' guild, and was faced now with a new and positive ideology of revolution preached by Matthys and Jan of Leiden, with Rothmann taking second place as the pamphleteer of the movement, expounding in biblical terms each new development. The Articles of Münster were prepared which attacked 'pagan' authority (that is, all traditional conceptions of *Obrigkeit*) and demanded obedience to the laws of God alone. Freedom of faith was next proclaimed, which meant in the circumstances control by the peculiar form of Anabaptism now established. Most of the convinced Lutherans and Catholics left the city. Knipperdolling was made burgomaster, or chief magistrate; community of goods was introduced, and seven deacons were set up to look after the riches collected together from the churches, religious houses, and the homes of those who had left, or been expelled as 'godless'. Then all books found in the city were ordered to be burned, since only the Bible was regarded as the authentic book for the new Israel. The preachers, originally Rothmann's followers, who had now been baptised by Matthys, stood ready in the central square to baptise all who wished to remain in Münster and take an oath and covenant together. In this city of the new saints there could be no room for

[46] Ibid., 66–8.

doubters: a blacksmith, Hubert Ruescher, who called Matthys a deceiver, was killed where he stood.[47] By this time Münster was under siege conducted by troops of the bishop, von Waldeck, assisted by soldiers from the neighbouring Protestant states. Both Catholics and Protestants saw the changes at Münster as wholly intolerable to order. Matthys in obedience to a vision walked out of the city prophesying against the besiegers and was killed. This made the way clear for Jan of Leiden to take complete control of the city.

It would be possible and easy to describe the events which follow as an orgy of irrational fanaticism deprived of all sense and reality. But beneath the extravagance there lie certain patterns of direction. Once the revolutionary has destroyed the existing framework of a society he is often uncertain about how to proceed. Given the utterly unprecedented nature of the situation, and granted that baptising ignorant and fanatical guildsmen amid ecstatic apocalyptic preaching could not bring the supernatural event of the second coming expected by these believers with such simplemindedness, Jan of Leiden showed very considerable organising ability and created a consistent pattern of order on the basis of an attempt, however eccentric in practice, to recreate the old Jerusalem of king David at Münster – this was his substitute for the New Jerusalem of the vision of John the Divine. We should remember how Bibles of the period, Latin and vernacular, were illustrated: the woodcuts of the court of David and the city of Jerusalem and its inhabitants all resembled, almost to minor details, contemporary courts, cities and citizens. Israelite soldiers were clad in contemporary armour and with the kind of weapons men of the time themselves used: Jewish peasant women and great ladies were shown in sixteenth-century dress; houses, furniture, castles and fortifications reflected contemporary Nürnberg and Augsburg. For unsophisticated guildsmen and labourers and their wives, the court and city of king David were not buried in a remote past, they were recent in the imagination and could, therefore, given the opportunity, be recreated.

Jan of Leiden did precisely this. In May 1534, the council of Münster was dissolved and twelve elders representing the twelve tribes of Israel were now to govern the new Israel, with Jan of Leiden as its prophet. As in Jerusalem of old no pollution should be allowed by sin, so in this new Jerusalem all sin was to be punished – with none of the humane safe-guards left by the old Jewish legal system. The obviously acted sins such as theft and adultery were to be punished by death, but also such ill-defined sins as envy and wrath were given the death penalty. At least this implied strict discipline. Certainly Jan of Leiden achieved for the besieged a better military discipline than that of the besiegers. Special areas were set apart for making gun powder: the twelve elders and Jan met daily: armed groups made quick sallies from the gates and brought in supplies (it is very strange how ineffective the encirclement of the walls by the besiegers was for some time yet). In May an attempt to scale the walls and take the city by the encircling troops failed, and this was taken as a sign of the proof of Jan's prophecy that the city could not be taken by the godless. Messengers were more than once sent out to bring in the 'saints' from across Europe to Münster, but nearly all such groups which gathered together with arms to go to the defence of the city were broken up. There were several formed haphazardly in the Netherlands. Still Jan held the besieged together by strength of will and the power of prophecy: he seemed able to go into a prophetic trance almost at will.

At this stage occurred a social change of great magnitude which caused much of the horror in which Münster's new Zion came to be held, as happened much later with the early development of Mormonism in Utah. Either through seeking to fulfil literally the accounts of polygamy in the Old Testament, or through the curious idea which was not unknown elsewhere in other circumstances that women could only have full access to the blessings of the new order through the bond of marriage, or quite simply because the number of women exceeded the number of men there (many had come in as refugees with men who had since died in defence of the city) – or because, as one sour eye-witness who survived suggested, Jan, already married, wished to marry Divara the beautiful widow of Matthys – whatever the reason or mixture of reasons, Jan proclaimed as the result of a vision that polygamy was to be introduced at Münster.[48] This was too much for the hitherto compliant Rothmann and others and an embittered debate of eight days took place. But eventually Jan imposed his will, Rothmann wrote a pamphlet defending the new way of life on the first two grounds suggested above, and those few who protested, women or men, against this reversal of all hitherto accepted sound order, were instantly killed. Knipperdolling with a great two-handed sword had become the executioner of justice, and he did not hesitate to use it – there was no room for self-doubt or any other kind of doubt in the new Zion. Rothmann wrote that there were three world ages (as Joachim of Fiore, whose subtle dreams occur frequently in the radical religious circles of the period, had

[48] Cornelius, op. cit., 59–79.

once taught of three world ages) from Adam to Noah, from Noah to the coming of Christ, and then from Christ to the preparation for Christ's coming again through the setting up of the kingdom of Münster.

In August 1534, Jan was declared to be the Davidic king of these new chosen people, and Divara the queen, Rothmann was to be court preacher and various other offices were filled. Court ceremonial was introduced with rich, specially designed robes; Jan could only be approached by kneeling; special banquets were held in the square before the cathedral, which was the new Temple; and elaborate dances were performed. When all was over and Jan was examined under torture, he confessed that he had not received a vision to become king, he had deceived the people because he thought the situation in Münster required these changes to help the people to endure the siege.

An example of the biblical literalism that ruled imaginations at Münster can be seen in the action of the young woman Hille Feyken who, seeing herself as a new Judith, tried to penetrate through the besieging army to reach the bishop and destroy him, but was captured and killed. Not all of Jan's expedients could stave off famine and the horrors of a siege: the hoped-for aid from the Netherlands and elsewhere, as has been noted, failed to arrive. But it was not until June 1535 (after numbers in the city had been greatly reduced by secret flight, the expulsion of the old and children to the besieging army, which was by now greatly increased), and then only by betrayal to a large force of the besiegers by the opening of one of the gates, that the city was finally captured. The slaughter was thorough. Rothmann's body was not found. Knipperdolling and Jan of Leiden were imprisoned, examined and then tortured to death with red hot pincers in January 1536.[49] Münster inevitably reverted to the most strict Catholicism, and a closely restricted social and political life.

The grounds for this account at greater length than for other cities are to make explicit how the idea of the city dominated men's minds in that period – the city as a place of potential freedom of social experiment – and also to show how originally Lutheran teaching in a city where grave social and political unease existed could, for lack of strong central government, become so far changed to radicalism in religion and social organisation as to be self-destructive. If the kingdom of Jan of Leiden had occurred in 1525 how much more difficult would the changes in many cities have been. Men saw it not, as we tend to do, as eccentric religious fantasy but as political

[49] Krahn, op. cit., 163.

revolution of the most dangerous kind. This experiment should remind us once again that the Reformation was an urban movement and that it cannot be divorced from its contemporary social and political setting.

Two other cities can be adduced to show the variety of patterns which occurred: these are Strasbourg and Geneva. Strasbourg had achieved in the thirteenth century what some citizens of Münster achieved only fleetingly in 1533–6, freedom from the civil jurisdiction of a bishop.[50] It became a free town of the empire so that its only political external authority lay in the Diets of the Empire at which it was represented. After the expulsion of the bishop as civil lord his connections with Strasbourg were remote: the episcopal election of 1506 was the first time in a century that the citizens saw their bishop or heard him preach in the city. The political structure which operated at Strasbourg from a new constitution in 1482, which was greatly admired by Erasmus because of its balance between powers, marked a more democratic order than that of Nürnberg. The chief Magistrate was the *Ammeister*, elected each year from the ranks of the burghers, who was aided by four *Stettmeister* from the patrician families, on a rotation of one for each quarter of the year: together with these were several councils, the Thirteen for foreign affairs and defence, the Fifteen for finance and justice, these two together with the addition of four men elected for life (the other council members were subject to re-election) formed the council of Twenty-one (the name has no relation to the actual number of members). The social structure of the city lay in the patrician families, many of whom lived outside the walls on their estates; the merchants or landowners who belonged to the burgher groups; and the craftsmen who were organised in twenty guilds: each guild, or 'tribe' had fifteen *Schöffen* at its head – these three hundred *Schöffen* formed on important occasions a general assembly to decide on matters gravely affecting the city. The guilds of Strasbourg in the fifteenth-century reorganisation ceased to be purely craft guilds; for example, all the burghers who had no corporate memberships elsewhere belonged to two guilds of their own. Whoever achieved full citizenship, *Bürgerrecht*, was automatically appointed to a guild. This was the system which Erasmus praised:

> I saw a monarchy without tyranny, an aristocracy without factions, a democracy without disorder, prosperity without luxury, happiness without insolence.[51]

[50] M. V. Chrisman, *Strasbourg and the Reform*, New Haven, 1967, 35 ff. T. A. Brady, Jr., *Ruling Class, Régime and Reformation in Strasbourg 1520–1555*, Leiden, 1978, while useful and informative presents 'structural studies' as suitably replacing the effect of religion and ideas.

[51] P. S. Allen, *Opus Epistolarum Des. Erasmi Roterodami*, ii, 1514–1517, 19. Letter 305, to James Wimpfeling.

This still left the labouring and more unskilled groups of inhabitants unrepresented, a fact ignored as irrelevant by Erasmus, yet it did not lead to any noticeable degree of unrest at Strasbourg; there was no climate of sullen resentment awaiting a revolutionary leadership as at Münster. The inhabitants of Strasbourg felt that the world went as well as could be expected; their patrician leaders in external affairs kept their city secure by balancing between the rival powers of Habsburg and Valois which faced each other across the Rhine; and their merchants and craftsmen by their skills made a reasonably good life available to most who lived there. Yet there was still an area of potential change. For, unlike Nürnberg, the political control of the city, as has been seen, was not extremely close and confined to one class, and also there were various threads of religious idealism divorced from formal ecclesiastical structures there. John Geiler, preacher of moral reform, and John Tauler, the mystic, had left influences which implied the possibility of the Christian life free of some of the medieval moulds; and the memories of the Winckler movement and the teachings of Huss were not wholly forgotten.

Ecclesiastical authority in the city lay in the five chapters of the cathedral and the collegiate churches. These chapters on the eve of the Reformation were largely indifferent to the needs of the churches at Strasbourg: the canons of the cathedral were of patrician birth and were interested in little beyond accumulating rich benefices and increasing the status of their families. Strasbourg was well-provided with land-owning churches, monastic houses and nunneries: some of the last were as socially exclusive as the cathedral chapter and the chapter of St. Thomas. Many of the citizens of Strasbourg were tenants or servants of the religious houses and chapters, and there was the usual amount of exacerbation of relationships between city and church concerning clerical privileges and taxes. The position of the church was weak in that it was neither wholly acceptable in its administrative aspect to the city council nor was it acceptable to the bishops, who regarded the leading churchmen of Strasbourg as being frequently too willing to think more of their relationship to the city than of their relationship to their bishop. Throughout the fifteenth century the council had been winning increasing control of church affairs, though not to that degree to be seen at Nürnberg. Piety at Strasbourg had been aided by a movement which found its energies outside of ecclesiastical structures, Rhineland mysticism, of which one of the chief exponents had been the Strasbourg mystic John Tauler whose work Luther came to admire. John Geiler of Kaisersberg from 1480 to 1510 vigorously preached at the cathedral the need for church reform, a reform of the morals of the clergy and laity alike, and set forth the way of better piety, though still in traditional terms.[52] Strasbourg had become an important printing centre, and produced a notable quantity of Bibles, including a vernacular edition, and also the *De Imitatione Christi* of Thomas á Kempis, and volumes of sermons, including Geiler's, as well as other works of religious edification. Where there was good printing there were humanists: nearby Sélestat had a remarkable Latin school which trained a number of citizens of Strasbourg in the new methods of humanism. Famous names among the city's humanists were Sebastian Brandt, Jacob Wimpfeling, Beatus Rhenanus and Jacob Sturm, who was to become one of the great educationists of that century. Where there were humanists there came criticism of deadness in the life of the Church, though those of Strasbourg were conservative minded. That Erasmus admired Strasbourg and its intellectual life was a portent of challenge and change to come: where Erasmus had friends reform, though not necessarily Protestant reform, could be promoted.

As elsewhere the Reformation came with ardent though conservative Lutheran preaching: conservative in the sense that it was confined to Luther's teaching on grace and Scripture and did not extend to challenging traditional patterns of church organisation at that stage. It represented the impact made on young men trained in the new studies of biblical humanism (those studies of the generation of humanists younger than the more traditionally minded Wimpfeling and Brandt) by Luther's early teaching. Nicholas Gerbel, secretary of the cathedral chapter, held Lutheran views though unwilling to go beyond the early Luther, but a vigorous Lutheran reform preaching was given by Matthew Zell, a stirring preacher of a more advanced Lutheranism, who attracted great attention which led to a council decree in 1523: 'Only the holy Gospel may be preached at Strasbourg'. Wolfgang Capito, provost of the chapter of St. Thomas and a hebraist, – one of the few competent Christian Hebrew scholars of that time and its standards – was perhaps more Erasmian than Lutheran, a fact which made him open to influences alien to Lutheran orthodoxy from, for example, Zwingli's Zürich. Capito's friend, Caspar Hedio, also was Erasmian rather than Lutheran, but he was overshadowed by Capito and Bucer.

---

[52] L. Dacheux, *Un réformateur catholique à la fin du XVe siècle, Jean Geiler de Kayersberg,* Paris, 1876, is still useful. Geiler was responsible by his urgent sermons for social improvements in the case of the sick and the poor. After his death his 'reforming' sermons helped to open the way to Lutheran ideas, this led to them being placed on the *Index Librorum Prohibitorum.*

Martin Bucer was a former Dominican friar who had been educated at Sélestat and whose father had burgher rights at Strasbourg; he became a 'Martinian' while resident at Heidelberg on hearing Luther dispute in the university there. After several vicissitudes, including support for that exploded star von Sickingen and then marriage, he came as a refugee Protestant to Strasbourg in 1523. By popular demand (and the voice of the people had become loud in religious choices there in that decade) he was made a parish priest, and therefore granted citizenship.

In order to understand later developments at Strasbourg we should remember its political situation at that time. It had moved out of its fifteenth-century security into taking sides in the great change of the period; and while it could still hope to balance between Habsburg and Valois, neither had chosen Protestantism and it needed powerful allies. The strong centre of Lutheranism lay far to the north, but much nearer political support lay in the Swiss Confederation with the cities of Basel, Zürich and Berne.[53] However, they had chosen, or were to choose, a religious pattern which was more radical than that of Wittenberg and from 1530 onward Martin Bucer wanted to mediate between Lutheranism and Zwinglianism, or to form a union between them. Against the power of Charles V whose attention was long distracted elsewhere, fortunately for Strasbourg, its only hope lay in the military support of the Swiss (for it was strategically weak in wartime); this meant drawing near to Zwinglian theology and church practice. To assume that Bucer sat at his desk writing his theology without reference to this situation would be to misread his work and its purposes. Not only did he show the desire to mediate between Luther's 'Real Presence' and what has been disparagingly called Zwingli's 'Real Absence' in eucharistic theology; but also his theology is much concerned with the Church seen as the community wherein each man serves his neighbour, which in return reflects the social outlook of a city very self-conscious in matters of social welfare and the best arrangement of good and balanced living. Another development in Strasbourg, growing before the Reformation, and one which was to flourish in the hothouse atmosphere there in 1525–35, was that of heresy. This is difficult to define; inevitably it was below the surface, but Strasbourg had seen many burnings for heresy, and among ordinary folk in the city and its region were those influenced by Waldensian or Hussite ideas. When the Peasant's War reached the neighbourhood of the city in 1525 political radicalism sprang up there and the gardeners' guild demanded the distribution

[53] Baron, op. cit., 621 ff.

of the wealth of the clergy, and refused to continue to pay rent and tithe to the chapter of St. Thomas. But revolution did not develop in Strasbourg, thanks to its carefully balanced constitution, and the Peasants' War passed without further disturbance. Yet the gardeners' guild also laid the way open to religious radicalism through the preaching of a guildsman Clement Ziegler: Anabaptism came in at the back of these teachings of Ziegler about the brotherhood of all men, the need to smash the images in the churches and abolish the old sacramental ideas.[54] Prior to the collapse of Protestantism at Strasbourg in 1548, when Charles V imposed the Interim, Anabaptist leaders of various patterns of thought and behaviour came to Strasbourg because of its comparative toleration, and Capito's willingness to listen to new views; Melchior Hofmann preached and died there in prison awaiting the 'day of the Lord' when Strasbourg would become the new Jerusalem; Pilgram Marpeck, Caspar Schwenckfeld and Sebastian Franck were more peaceful but equally as strange as Hofmann in the eyes of Bucer. But Strasbourg tolerated Catholics, Lutherans, Zwinglians, Anabaptists and supported Bucer's churchmanship and theology as long as the former groups did not seek to overthrow the latter.

In a short work with the long but significant title *Everyone should live not for himself but for others, and how men may fulfil this*, Bucer revealed a lifelong preoccupation, which though it may well have grown out of his earliest reflections on the meaning of Luther's teaching, was developed and deepened through his struggle with the problems of establishing a reformed church at Strasbourg. The basis of his conception of the Church as the community which serves God through Christ and through Christ serves all men is seen in his statement: 'One must make no difference between men but have the same love and desire to procure for each all the good to which he is responsive'.[55] Church and State (and Bucer saw this intensively at Strasbourg as Church and city) have a mutual relationship for the service of the whole of society. The function of the Christian is to promote public usefulness both spiritual and secular. He struggled against the continual pressure of the varieties of Anabaptism at Strasbourg because he passionately held that one should not as a Christian withdraw from the world's need into separately organized communities of the holy. He thought of Strasbourg as the 'Christian

---

[54] Chrisman, 181 ff. For the Anabaptists, and also the general background of the Reformation at Strasbourg, v. *Strasbourg au Coeur religieux du XVIe siècle*, Strasbourg, 1977.

[55] Bucer, *Das ym selbs niemant sonder anderen leben soll und wie der mensch. dahyn kummen mög, 1523.* v. 131 infra.

Republic' in which all aspects of life, including particularly social welfare, were part of the duty of Christian citizens. Bucer in his *De Regno Christi*, written after he had regretfully left Strasbourg for Cambridge as a refugee once again, could go as far as to associate a political programme of reform with fulfilling one's eternal salvation – an overstatement but one arising from his experience of Strasbourg as the centre of a well balanced political constitution and a city concerned for the well-being of its citizens.[56] His concern for the practice of church discipline, a recurring theme in his work which was to influence Calvin during his residence at Strasbourg, is closely related to his efforts to create an effective church life which showed the fruit of faith in good works. Strasbourg had found a man worthy to present theologically her civic pride in her cultural tradition and her sense of responsibility for her citizens.

Bucer, for all his tireless energy, was not in himself an army, and Strasbourg, strategically defenceless and too exposed for help from the Swiss, capitulated before Charles V in 1548 – a symbol of the declining power of the German cities after 1530. In the Swiss imperial cities, still (though remotely) imperial, cities like Basel and in particular Zürich, the situation was different from that in north and south Germany since the major theological influence was Zwinglian and not Lutheran. There was also a difference in the scale since they were smaller: Zürich did not compare in size with, for example, Augsburg or Strasbourg. Also there was the powerful impact of the sense of being the 'Confederates' which held the Swiss, and brought a new dimension to the corporate sense of the city. The ecclesiastical revolution began at Zurich with the repudiation of the lenten fast in the name of Christian liberty: episcopal authority at Constance was repudiated in 1522 when the bishop sought to maintain the status quo. By 1526 the Council had dissolved the monasteries, the Great Minster was turned into an economic and educational institution. The 'Prophesying' was established where lectures were given on the biblical text to train the clergy in the new theology – this institution was to be influential later elsewhere including England. A commission of morals under the control of the Council was established and with difficulty the challenge to Zwingli by the Anabaptists was overcome essentially because they wished to set up holiness groups rather than a church for the whole of the citizenry. Zürich was united in a civic and ecclesiastical community since the city was seen as an Israel restored in which Zwingli was the chief prophet who taught the law

---

[56] *Martini Buceri Opera Latina*, vol xv. *De Regno Christ*, ed. F. Wendel, Paris, 1955, 71, 266, 294–5.

from Scripture in a theological method sharply contrasted with that of Luther. Zwingli was not only a theologian of Erasmian reforming origins; he was also a good Swiss confederate who associated the doctrine of grace with the concept of the local community which visibly identified itself with the reformed Church, so that Church and community were mutually energized and intimately related in a way which did not develop in the Lutheran areas of northern Germany.[57] Basel, Strasbourg, Zürich and Geneva – unlike Wittenberg – were restlessly alive with citizens aware of their powers and possibilities: Wittenberg and Saxony as elsewhere in Lutheranism formed a territorial culture of the 'Land' energised by a city culture, and under Electoral leadership.

As Moeller has shown, Luther who was not a member of an imperial city, helped to kill the city principle in Germany since he thought of the Church fundamentally as a community enclosed among the large crowd of the lukewarm.[58] However varied the description he gave of the Church from time to time, he did not think, as Zwingli could do, in terms of a people's church, the Church being the community as a whole. If Luther had done so this would have produced greater social and political change in the north. It was the city of Zürich which represented the ideal of a community church, a *Volkskirche*, and Zwingli, as Luther did not, adapted those traditional urban aspirations, referred to before, to the outward forms of the Church in its organisation and community relations.

At Geneva there was an even greater contrast than Zürich showed with the imperial free cities of Germany.[59] It had no social or religious problem left behind by the Peasants' War since that had been a wholly German phenomenon. It had no powerful guilds, indeed compared with elsewhere it had no effective guild organisations until the second half of the sixteenth century. It had no sophisticated merchant class as at Augsburg or Nürnberg with a taste for the arts: humanist culture could hardly be found there, and it had only a handful of printers confining themselves to pedestrian ecclesiastical publishing and some popular vernacular work. There was no underground activity of heresy: no echoes of Waldensianism could be heard there. It was a trading centre on the economic crossways between Italy, France and Germany, its staple needs being in corn and wine. It was at the hub of the spokes of the wheel of political pressures between French Burgundy, Savoy, Berne and Fribourg:

[57] Robert C. Walton, *Zwingli's Theocracy*, Toronto, 1967.
[58] Moeller, *Reichstadt und Reformation*, (Gütersloh, 1962), ch. iv.
[59] Henri Naef, *Les Origines de la Réforme à Genève*, vols. i and ii, Geneva, 1936.

though it was to turn this source of weakness partly by skill and partly by sheer good chance into a source of strength and independence.[60] Though the contrast with the imperial cities is marked, yet one part of the pattern is similar to that of many German towns – the struggle for independence from a prince-bishop. Geneva strove at intervals for two centuries to gain greater autonomy from its bishops, who were members of, or sponsored by, the House of Savoy, and Savoyard in their outlook and sympathies. The citizens had won the *Franchises* from the bishop, which included their right to meet in general council and to choose their own chief officers, the four Syndics who were elected annually.[61] The councils of Two Hundred, Sixty, and the Twenty-five were formed gradually. But the citizens needed a lever to gain freedom from control from Savoy and they turned gratefully to the Swiss from 1519, first to Catholic Fribourg and then to Berne which was to become Protestant in 1528. It was with the aid of Berne, the most powerful military force near to Savoy, that a political revolution was initiated in 1530 when Geneva was blockaded by the bishop from Savoy, and relieved in 1535–6. Geneva was now in danger of becoming a subject of Berne, like neighbouring Lausanne. In May 1536 Geneva showed that Protestantism had also come to stay, following upon the political changes, in affirming that the city, 'would live henceforth according to the law of the Gospel and the Word of God and . . . abolish all papal abuses.'[62] According to Geneva they had reclaimed and endorsed ancient political liberties, but in fact their enterprise was revolutionary in spite of, or because of, the fact that, as Richard Hooker said later, their bishop, 'had departed as it were by moonlight'.[63] But this change of status at Geneva was not the product of Protestant zeal. There had been little Lutheran activity at Geneva before 1535, in part because there was no intellectual milieu in which it could, as elsewhere, originate: humanists were few, unoriginal or unlikely to impress anyone beyond their walls; the canons of the cathedral chapter had the social interests of patricians and were little concerned with the arts, worship or theology. There was no native tradition of theological energy, and in the event her reformers had to be foreigners. Protestantism came in with Berne's troops billeted in Geneva during the revolution. The first promoters of Protestant preaching were ministers supported by Berne, of whom a Frenchman

[60] William Monter, *Calvin's Geneva*, New York, 1967, 19.

[61] Naef, op. cit., vol. i, p. 31 ff.

[62] *Corpus Reformatorum. Opera omnia Calvini*, vol. xx, *Les Annales*, col. 201.

[63] R. Hooker, *The Laws of Ecclesiastical Polity*, Preface, chap. ii, par. 4, in *The Works of Hooker*, ed. Keble, 3rd ed., i, Oxford, 1845, 132.

from Dauphiné, Guillaume Farel, was the chief.[64] It is significant of Geneva's violence that Protestantism could be promoted by murder when a canon of Catholic Fribourg, sword in hand, shouted to all good Christians to gather round him during a street riot in the city and was killed by Protestant zealots whom he had attacked. Of themselves the Genevan leading families and the city's councillors would not have urged Protestantism forward in their city: they were cautiously conservative and with little religious zeal Catholic or Protestant, and preferred to remain content with the revolution they had achieved. It was Berne's steady pressure, since religion meant political allegiance in that time, which brought Geneva confusedly into Protestantism.[65]

Farel, the leader of the early form of Geneva's Protestantism, had begun his career at Meaux, and then elsewhere in France before moving to Berne. His theology was much more simplistic and radical in its implications than that of Luther, and nearer to Zwingli on the sacraments (Berne itself had adopted Zwinglianism from its neighbour Zürich), without becoming wholly Zwinglian. He lacked the theological training or equipment to work out a deep and satisfactory theology, Zwinglian or otherwise. His strength lay in preaching and exhortation: he could truculently face a hostile crowd. He was a storm trooper of reformation suited to challenge the violence and indifference prevailing at Geneva. A quieter and less truculent figure was the younger man who assisted him at a major Disputation at Geneva in 1535, Pierre Viret, a native of Vaud and therefore now a subject of Berne. But the council still hesitated to act, though it suspended the Mass for the time being. Calvin's description of the religious situation at Geneva when he arrived there is pointed: 'When I first came in this church there was almost nothing. There was preaching and nothing more. They sought out the idols and burned them, but that is not reformation. Everything was in tumult.'[66]

Calvin came as a young humanist French civil lawyer, originally preparing for the priesthood, who in 1536 was passing through Geneva on his way either to Basel or to Strasbourg, cities of humanist culture as well as Reformed theology, but Farel, aware of Calvin's standing among French Protestants and the brilliance of the first edition of Calvin's *Institutio*, just published, exhorted him to stay and assist with building up the reformation at Geneva. For Calvin an

---

[64] The fullest account of Farel is in *Guillaume Farel, 1482–1565*, Paris, 1930.
[65] Naef, op. cit., I, 107. 'L'indépendence et la réformation genevoises sont deux soeurs inséparables. Quelle fut l'aînée?
[66] *Opera Omnia Calvini, Corpus Reformatorum*, vol. ix, col. 891.

unlettered city of swordsmen such as Geneva was would never have been a first choice. For him the fundamental needs of the reformed Church by 1536 were order, liturgy, well-constituted sacraments, discipline and well-balanced theology. To struggle to achieve these things with little ministerial aid, no effective native traditions of culture, theological enterprise or significant piety, was formidable and heart-breaking. The councillors were always aware of the fact that they had got rid of the bishop and brought Geneva to independence. They had no thought of putting their city into subjection to a religious order and discipline imposed by French foreigners. Freedom from the bishop, the pope's laws and the rule of Savoy meant freedom to do as you please.[67] Faced by this sullen indifference to what Calvin regarded, and by any of the ecclesiastical standards of his time (Catholic, Lutheran, Reformed, or Anabaptist) justifiably regarded, as essential to church discipline, the inevitable conflict of wills led to Calvin's ignominious dismissal. Three years later a change of heart at Geneva led to Calvin being urgently recalled there, and reluctantly he came.

One of the conditions of his return had been that the magistracy should accept the establishment of an agreed syllabus of order for church government, worship, marriage regulations and disciplinary procedure – the *Ordonnances ecclésiastiques*.[68] This did not form a code of law but principles and methods for guidance: the magistracy would not allow it to be published for many years to come; that would have been to imply they were bound by it. They always wished to retain the initiative. Discipline at Geneva was always exercised by the Church's representatives by exhortation; the council alone could give punishment to those who gravely offended by heresy or immorality. The magistracy always reserved to itself the right to punish, and it held the reins of power at all times. The image of Calvin as Geneva's dictator is a stereotype invented and developed from the eighteenth century onwards. Calvin did not suffer like a sultan from the ennui

[67] The attitude of Bonivard, himself a priest and Abbot of St. Victor (Byron's Prisoner of Chillon) is typical (Naef, vol. ii, 155 ff.). Bonivard was a Resistance hero for the Genevese. In 1529, he wrote that he was asked by citizens for advice about the Reformation: 'Vous voulez que nostre église soit reformée? Vous dictes que les prebstres, moynes et autres de l'église romaine sontz joueurs, yvrognes, gourmantz, paillardtz ... Mais vous qu'estes vous? Vous voulez chasser les prebstres et tout l'état papistique, et en leur place colloquer des prédicants de l'évangile. Je confesse que c'est un grandt bien ... mais ung grandt mal à èsgars de vous que n'estimez autre bien felicité que de jouir de vous plaisirs désordonnez. Peu de gentz de bien se sont la meslez d'avancer l'évangile en nostre cité ... Advisez que vous ferez, vous ne les haurez pas gardez deux ans que ne serez plus faschez de eux que de nous ...'
[68] B. J. Kidd, *Documents Illustrative of the Continental Reformation*, Oxford, 1911, is still an excellent collection of records, including these *Ordonnances*, 589–603, for studying the Genevan Reformation, 477–651.

of power, but from the frequent frustrations and humiliations which occasionally brought on bouts of hysteria, through the obtuseness, indifference to, or insidious attack upon, his principles shown by Geneva's citizens until the comparative calm of the last few years of his life there. Nevertheless, Calvin impressed much of his organising intellect and will on this small Savoyard city, which made it in the sixteenth century the 'city of Calvin' in a way which cannot be said of Bucer's impress on Strasbourg or even Luther's at Wittenberg or Zwingli at Zürich. This was not only because Calvin created a theological order there to defend its reformed Church but also because no one native to the city or reflecting the city's own peculiar characteristics arose who was competent in the arts of government, law, politics and international relations as well as church affairs to compare with Calvin. Without Calvin Geneva would have remained almost as culturally obscure as Neuchâtel in that time.

How did Geneva affect Calvin? It is too often assumed that the impact was one-sided, and that Calvin masterfully moulded the city to his own will. The circumstances existing and forces which came to bear on Geneva during his stay there made him more implicitly radical in his theology and church practice and in his views of economic, political and international affairs than by temperament, training or original purpose he would have been in a different place, for example, in a town of his native France. It is frequently forgotten that Calvin claimed that it took some time for him to break 'the visible unity of the Church' by becoming a Protestant: his sense of the Church, the body of Christ, an ordered sacramental society set in the world for sinful man, is more marked than in any other Reformer. The description of the Church, its sacraments and ministry, form the largest section of the *Institutio* and he wrote more elsewhere on these themes than he did on predestination;[69] indeed, in his ecclesiological discussion he ignores the predestinarian emphases which were regarded as basic to that discussion by those who were later to be called 'the Calvinists'. His first period of creative writing at the full stretch of his powers was at Strasbourg where he had no authority. Geneva compelled him to apply his ideal views to conform to a situation differing from the setting he would have wished to give them. Again, it is too often not realised that when Calvin said he admired Luther and thought that he himself was fulfilling Luther's

[69] He described probing into the subject of Predestination as 'a labyrinth', he thought it should be accepted as a mystery beyond human argument. The only occasion he preached a group of sermons on it was by order of the Council when a fierce attack on the subject had been made at Geneva. Calvin's sermons in general deal with the subject not at all or as a brief declaration of it, when the biblical passage requires it.

original teaching, he meant what he said and was not merely making a debating point. Like the young Luther, and even more like the French *légistes* among whom he had been trained, Guillaume Budé and others, he neither favoured armed resistance nor democratic political programmes: the contrary is true. His distaste for mobs of armed men at election times at Geneva is exposed over and over again in his sermons at those periods. In his economic thought, provided that justice was done between neighbours and that business men could make a modest living while remembering the golden rule (views he stated most guardedly), he showed no concern to promote 'usury'.[70] The needs of trade at Geneva constrained him here. His desperate efforts to avoid any positive concession to the Huguenots' wish to justify military action mark his insistence on avoiding overt rebellion: the nearest he came to assent are two or three riddling sentences marked by ambiguity.[71] In spite of this it has become a commonplace to refer to the Calvinist political activism of his followers or soi-disant followers. It is true that reading back towards Calvin's Geneva from later periods we pass through political radicalism, economic activism, sophisticated international politics, Presbyterianism in its varied forms, Puritanism, doctrinaire theological systems and much else – all of which at the most represent the later products of compromises he had to make with the Genevan ecclesiastical, social and political situation. That Calvin should have been associated on the wall monument of the Reformation in modern Geneva with Roger Williams, John Knox and Oliver Cromwell, for example, is an irony of history when we recollect the degrees of abhorrence to the views and actions of these men which Calvin would have held. Such men are represented on that wall because the consequences others drew later from his work at Geneva reflect the ways in which he was drawn beyond his own original hopes and aspirations.

An attempt has been made here, though all too briefly, to show how it came about that Protestant theology came to be related to efforts at political and social change which had received new impulses in the period 1520–40. The one reacted upon the other even to effecting limitation or new moulds for a Reformer's theological views, and to encouraging new social patterns because of a Reformer's theological views. The small scale of the city enables us to see the development of those relations. It is unwise, if not unhistorical, to ignore them.

---

[70] *Opera Selecta Calvini*, ed. P. Barth and D. Scheuner, ii, Munich, 1952, 392 ff.

[71] E.g., *Opera Omnia Calvini*, vol ii, col 116 (*Institutio*, bk. iv, ch. xx, f. 31). Sermons on Daniel, *Opera*, vol. xli, cols. 395, 415.

4

Diakonia in Martin Bucer

Luther, indignant at Bucer's developing talent for trying to talk theological opponents into the appearance of agreement, called him a *Klappermaul*.[1] Moreover, Calvin wrote once of Bucer that his pen could not keep pace with the fluency of his ideas and language and grace them with clarity;[2] and Bucer himself confessed as much, describing his own writing as '. . . *perplexa, indigesta, obscura omnia,* . . .'[3] But on the theme of the Church's service of mankind Bucer is clear, forceful and consistent; he has more to say to the point here than any of his contemporaries – and he wrote of this service more urgently than most theologians since his time. He could well deserve the name of 'the theologian of *diakonia*'.

Karl Barth has written what could serve as an admirable epigraph for this study of Bucer as the theologian of the ministering community: 'Diaconate means quite simply and generally the rendering of service. Hence it does not denote only a specific action

---

[1] *D. Martin Luthers Werke*, Weimar, 1883 ff. Br., 10, 618 (No. 4014).

[2] Calvin, *Calvini Opera Omnia* (C. R.) vol. X, Pars posterior, 404, Epistle no. 191. 'Bucer et prolixior est quam ut ab hominibus aliis occupationibus districtis raptem legi, et sublimior quam ut ab humilibus et non valde attentes intelligi facile queat. Nam ad cuiusque argumenti tractationem si contulit, tam multa illi ad manum suggeruntur ut incredibili qua pollet ingeni feccunditate, ut manum de tabula tollere nesciat.'

[3] Gustav Anrich, *Martin Bucer*, Strasbourg, 1914, p. 70.

of the community but the whole breadth and depth of its action.'
Then after referring to the deacons of Acts 6, he goes on to write: 'In
the rest of the New Testament the word διακονία usually indicates
quite generally the relationship of service in which especially the
apostles stand, but also all other Christians, and Jesus Christ Himself
at their head (Romans 15:8)'.[4] Nevertheless, this theme of the
ministering community has not been heavily stressed in the Church's
long history; not even during the Reformation, when the purpose of
the Church was fundamentally re-examined. It is hardly surprising
that the questions, among so many other important questions raised
during the Reformation, What is the Church of Christ, What does
He intend it to do, and How does it set about doing this? received
answers in the sixteenth century which often were unavoidably
controlled by the social and political needs of the time, and by the
dogmatic requirements of the theological controversy with Roman
Catholicism. While the Reformers, in this difficult situation, did not
overlook the theme of the Church rendering service to mankind,
Bucer alone among them gave this theme a fundamental place. From
his first appearance in print at Strasbourg in 1523 to the year of his
death in exile from that city when he completed his last important
work *De Regno Christi* at Cambridge in 1550, Bucer strove to show
how the Christian community should serve God in serving its
neighbours – 'his end was in his beginning'. He alone of all the
theologians of his time gave intense concern to putting in the
foreground of Christian faith and practice the διακονία of the
Church to mankind. His emphasis on discipline (unlike Calvin he
made it a *nota* of the Church), reflects precisely his concern that
Christians, because of their holiness in Christ the head of the Church,
must serve their neighbours in love. For this emphasis Bucer has been
called, misleadingly, the first Pietist, and this is not the only way in
which he has been misunderstood. Unless we discern his motives and
his theological principles, we shall continue to misunderstand him,
not least in failing to grasp what he intended in his discussions of
both aspects of διακονία; the ministering by Christians to their
neighbours, and the special ministry of deacons in the Church.

All his life Bucer differed from the great theologians who were his
contemporaries in avoiding definitive theological formulations
marked by a precision tending to exclusiveness. He wished to find
and emphasise the essentials in the Christian faith, setting aside non-
essential rites and ceremonies, each church in different countries could
exercise its liberty here as long as moral discipline was maintained

---

[4] Karl Barth, *Church Dogmatics*, vol. IV, Part III, pp. 889–90.

through the established ministry. But Bucer in his ecumenical zeal wished, as we say nowadays, to be 'open-ended' in church relations; he desired fluidity and not doctrinal hardness in describing the great truths of the faith, that faith which is supremely manifested in love.[5] It is not easy for the authors of *Dogmengeschichte* to give an account of Bucer's theology, not because he was incoherent, or self-contradictory or lacked theological acumen; but because he wished to turn away from formulations that might become 'Scholastic'. Bucer wished to point instead to the dynamic life of the Christian community fulfilling by faith in Christ through the Holy Spirit the works of love – and, therefore, he emphasised this fundamental theme and its Christological reference in his discussion of the Church and its ministry.

No significant theologian fails to reflect the influences which formed his mind at the onset of his own creative powers – if he did not reflect them at that period, he would not be a significant theologian. Bucer was not the only man of his generation to owe a great debt to both Luther and Erasmus, but none went to their writings with such simplicity and directness and found there two major themes which were to become rapidly fused and developed as the ground bass of a theology. He makes the source of his debt plain for us when we read his letter to Luther in 1520: 'You and Erasmus are holy'.[6] And two years earlier Bucer in hearing Luther at the Disputation at Heidelberg and talking to him used words to become characteristic of him when he described to his friend Beatus Rhenanus the joy, release and freedom he found, since, 'He who is a child of God always has love poured out in his heart by the Spirit . . . this is pious and holy [through] the indwelling Christ'; he contrasts this with 'the strengthless, wooden and obtuse Scholastic theologians'.[7] When Bucer wrote in the Preface to the first edition of his commentary on the Gospels, 1527 *sua fide justus vivit, non aliena* he shows his debt to Luther, but he owed him more than this. He heard Luther's twenty-eighth thesis at the Heidelberg Disputation in 1518: 'Man's love is aroused by what man likes, but God's love finds nothing lovable in man. God excites in man what God loves': and he also heard Luther's explanation, 'the love of the Cross, born of the

---

[5] Deutsche Schriften Band 1 (1962) 92, '. . . allein die rechtgeschaffene gute werk seind, müssen aus bruderliche liebe, den nechsten bewisen werden.'

[6] E. L. Enders, *Luther's Briefwechsel* (1884) vol. II, 301 'Nam secundum canonicas scripturas tua et Erasmi sententia nullam habeo sanctorum. (letter no. 263, 28 January 1520) Addressed to: 'Christianissimo theologo P. Martinus Lutherio Wittenbergae sacras literas multo cum fructi profetenti acro post Christum primo.'

[7] J. W. Baum, *Capito und Butzer*, Elberfeld, 1860, 99.

Cross, is this: it transfers itself not where it finds some good to be enjoyed, but there where it may confer some good to a sinner or to an unfortunate'.[8] Further, Bucer read and appropriated for his own theological creativity such themes as these from Luther's *Treatise on Christian Liberty*: that our works are to be given over to the welfare of others, and that every Christian must give himself as a Christ to his neighbour, just as Christ offered Himself for us; and that what we do in this life should be necessary, profitable and salutary to our neighbour, since through faith we have an abundance of all good things in Christ.[9] Luther also had a powerful and liberating effect on the developing theology of Bucer, the Dominican wearied, as he said, using a plodding joke of his student years, by, 'den verführerischen unchristlichen Büchern ihres Thomas von Wasserburg, den sie von Aquino nennen' in his *Verantwortung Martin Bitzers ...*' of 1523, challenging the Dominican way of life.[10]

But an earlier influence than that of Luther had also been at work, Erasmus, who was for Bucer *tantum numen*. J.-B. Pineau summed up the ethic of Erasmus as 'the double commandment of the Gospel, love of God and love of the neighbour'.[11] From the writings of Erasmus issued prior to 1520, Bucer would learn of the innocence and joy to be found in that obedience to Christ so clearly shown in the New Testament when its interpretation was shorn of dogmatic and Scholastic presuppositions. Erasmus' letter to the Archbishop of Palermo in 1523, to be printed as a preface to his own edition of the writings of St. Hilary, contains, among other matters of which Bucer would have approved, these words: 'true theological science consists in defining nothing which is not prescribed in Scripture, and these instructions should be set forth in simplicity and in good faith ... One will not be condemned for being ignorant of whether the procession of the Holy Spirit is single or double, but one will not avoid damnation if one does not try to possess the fruits of the Spirit, which are love, joy, patience, goodness, sweetness, faith, modesty, continence ...'[12] This non-doctrinaire approach to theology stayed with Bucer to the end.

[8] *D. Martin Luthers Werke, Kritische Gesammtausgabe*, Weimar, 1897, Band 7.
[9] Ibid., Band 7, 65, 66.
[10] J. W. Baum, op. cit., 95. Baum, 93, states that 'die Klosterbrüder' made this jest through 'den eigenen überdruss humoristich'.
[11] J.-B. Pineau, *Erasme, sa pensée religieuse*, Paris 1924, 248.
[12] 'Imo hoc demum est eruditionis theologicae, nihil ultra quam sacris literis proditum est, definire; verum id quod proditum est, bona fide dispensare.' *Opus Epistolarum Des. Erasmi Roteradami*, P. S. and H. M. Allen, tom. V, 178. This letter addressed by Erasmus to John Caronselet and published as the preface to the edition of the works of Hilary, which Erasmus issued at Basle in 1523, is of fundamental importance for Erasmus's views on theological renewal against traditionalist Scholasticism through biblical studies.

After his transformation from a Dominican made restless with
'Thomas von Wasserburg' by his Erasmian reading, to a 'Martinian',
a devotee of Luther, Bucer was comparatively inactive, seeking an
outlet for his considerable energies, until he appeared as a chaplain
under the patronage of Von Sickingen. Fortunately, he had no need
to follow so dubiously ruthless a representative of *obrigkeit* again.
Then briefly he was parish priest at Wissenburg until he was
excommunicated by the Archbishop of Speier for marrying a wife.
When he came thereafter to claim the protection of Strasbourg where
his father had citizen's rights, and where according to Gerbel two
years before 'our preachers are lukewarm and cold',[13] Bucer had to
defend his preaching at Wissenburg, about which malicious reports
were spreading – and the complaint was not that this preaching was
'cold'. Bucer's defence issued in 1523 shows that from the first he was
preaching on that dominant theme which stayed with him all his life:
'The whole law is fulfilled in loving thy neighbour as thyself.'[14] Here
he claims too that Christian freedom delivers men from the elaborate
laws of the Church concerning fasting, of eating and drinking; but
christlicher freyheit is also freedom for the service of others.[15]

Also in 1523 appeared at Strasbourg a much more important book
than his apology for his first sermons, this was issued with the
cumbersome but self-explanatory title *Everyone should live not for
himself but for others, and how men may fulfil this*, words which show
his simple theme and its practical application. 'One must make no
difference between men but have the same love and desire to procure
for each all the good to which he is responsive. From this it follows
that the best, the most perfect and blessed condition on earth is that
in which a man can most usefully and profitably serve his neighbour
... The ministry [of the pastors of the Church] serves not some
particular men, but the community, it deals not with material but
only spiritual things, and leads to eternal blessedness', concluding,
'gedeynt würt, das alter volkumnest ampt, beruff und dyenst ist'.[16]

---

[13] 'Unsere Prediger sind lau und kalt ...', N. Gerbel to J. Schwebel, 20 December 1521,
cited by J. W. Baum, op. cit., 199.

[14] *Martin Butzer an ein christlichen Rath und Gemeyn der statt Weissenburg Summary seiner Predig
daselbst gethon* (1523, reprinted Strasbourg, 1891, ed. A. Erichson), 20. 'Dann so alles gesatz
erfullt würt in disem einigen Wort. Hab dein nechsten also lieb als dich selb, und der Herr Mat.
VII sagt.'

[15] Again in the *Christliche Rath*: 'Bund so er vernimpt des der herr all unser thun will zu gut
und frummen geschehen unsern nechsten, so geüst er sich, und ergibt sich gantz zu dienst und
guthät des nechsten, on alles hoffen einiger vergeltung on alles ansehen einiger person.' Op.
cit., 28.

[16] *Das ym selbs niemant, sonder anderen leben soll, und wie der mensch dahyn kummen mög.* 1523,
(Deutsche Schriften, Band 1, 1960, 51).

He goes on to state that although all must show 'love' to one another, this especially is true of the ministry proper; and next to this office is that of the secular authority which has a duty and responsibility reaching out to the whole community. Here Bucer first brings forward what is going to be characteristic of his later activity, and was going to dominate his last great work *De Regno Christi*, the mutual relationship of Church and State for the service of the whole of society. Bucer then ends the first part of his little treatise: 'To conclude . . . according to the order and commandment of the Creator, no one should live for himself but each man should out of love for God live for his neighbour and by all means be of service to him in matters pertaining to both the spirit and the body; that this obligation rests above all on those who were called and established to promote public usefulness, both spiritual and secular . . .'[17] Bucer was clear from the beginning – where his colleague at Strasbourg, Capito, was not – that there should be no sympathetic collaboration with Anabaptist ideas of withdrawing from the corruptions of the world into separately organised communities of saints. In this, as in other ways, Bucer does not suit the description of being a Pietist. His whole concern is for an outgoing service within the full range of men's social existence to transform it. This transformation must not be construed as an early version of the *syllogismus practicus*: his doctrine of predestination, as he will develop it later, is not set down in terms that lead to that trap of later Puritanism. In his other works the activity of the elect in the loving service of mankind is seen by Bucer not as a proof of election but as a consequence of it;[18] and at this stage of his thought, the first theological writing, he states: '. . . Faith, finally, takes away from us love for the present life – its honours, fortunes and pleasures – love which hinders so many from exercising a true love and service to their neighbour. Faith brings . . . living wholly for others for the glory of God. . . . If faith is not such, then it is not true and legitimate faith, it is a dead faith, it is no faith at all.'[19]

Citations from several of his works at different periods of his life show the same theme recurring until its final reassertion in Bucer's last full-scale work *De Regno Christi*. In 1527 appeared Bucer's first open attack on Anabaptism in his *Getrewe Warnung gegen Jakob Kautz*

[17] Op. cit., *Deutsche Schriften* (1960), Band 1 (Das ym selbs . . .). 59.
[18] Several places, e.g. *Commentary on Ephesians* 1562, Basel 26 f. Again in his commentary on *Gospel of St John* (1553), 260. [To the elect]' . . . nihil aeque illos ad amorem Dei aeque inde ad omne opum bonum que at excitari.'
[19] Op. cit., *Deutsche Schriften*, Band 1 (1960) (Das ym selbs . . .).

(an Anabaptist preacher at Worms), and here again comes the
characteristic theme that good works must follow upon faith in
Christ, love must reach out through good works: 'that love which is
described in the first epistle to the Corinthians is the fulfilling of the
law, and the sum of all good works which derive only from faith in
our Lord Jesus Christ'.[20] Again in the sermon he preached at Bern
during the Disputation there in 1528 Bucer said: 'In all works we
must practise brotherly love unremittingly, in them all we shall . . .
please our God and father, praise His honour, and improve our
neighbour.' Further, in his characteristic German: 'Was ist läben . . . ?
das ein mensch alles güten versychert sey, müteg, frondig und zü
allen das gut ist vermöglich dasselbig zuthün? Das zytlich läben ist
des nur ein schatten. So aber Gott seinen geyst geben hätt . . . das er
uns entlich gar fromm und sälig machen werde'.[21] In his commentary
on the gospels at Matthew 5, Bucer has a long section headed *De
Proximo* where he makes it plain that our neighbour is whoever God
places us next to to help him and to aid him even if he should be an
enemy; and on Matthew 25, 1536 edition (a chapter frequently used
by Bucer), he begins: 'Nemo est piorum qui nesciat ut aegre vigilemus
in opere Domini . . . utque negligentur ipsum spectemus . . .'; and on
the two parables of the chapter he concludes by emphasising selfless
love of our neighbour.[22]

In his *Ein summarischer Vergriff der Christlichen Lehre und Religion
. . .*, 1548, which was a defence of the Strasbourg Reformers against
the charge of Anabaptism, presented to the Emperor shortly before
the Interim was declared which led to Bucer's exile, he wrote: 'Love
fulfils the divine law in such a way that a man is led to learn to do
and suffer . . . as the eternal and temporal salvation of his neighbour
requires him . . . Without this love of God and men which leads to a
constant zeal for good works, there is no true faith in Christ, and
those who lack it do not belong to Him.'[23] Two years later in
England in his *De Regno Christi* prepared for Edward VI in 1550

[20] Bucer: *Deutsche Schriften*, Band 2 (*Schriften der Jahre*, 1524–8), 251.

[21] Op. cit., *Martin Butzers Predig gethon zü Bern*. Deutsche Schrfiten, Band 2, (1962), 93.

[22] 'Duabus itaque his parabolis tota pietatis ratio tradita est; priore fides . . . qua abstracti ab
rebus aliis quibuscunque bonitate Dei addicimur, ut nostri quidem caussa, nihil aeque optemus,
quam venienti sponso abvia ire: hac vero syncera dilectio, qua nihil nostri quaerentes, toti in
hoc incumbimus ut iis quae a Deo accepimus, sive spiritalia sint, sive temporalia proximis
inserviamus: in primis tamen, hoc dantes operam, ut Deo ipsos lucremur.' 472, 473 *In sacra
quatuor Evangelia Enarrationes perpetuae*, Basel, 1536. In his *Commentary on the Psalms*, Bucer
also has the same emphasis: 'Deus praecepto dilectionis proximi summavit omnia. Nihil igitur
indecens vel dicet vel aget imo ne cogitabit quidem, dilectione semper profictura proximis, hoc
est vere sancta, Deoque grata suggerente.' Geneva, 1554, 17, 18.

[23] Reprinted with introduction and notes by F. Wendel in *Revue d'histoire et de philosophie
religieuses* 1951, No. 1, 38.

(thought it was not published until 1557, at Basel), Bucer renews the theme: 'Christ our governor and master lives and labours in all the faithful, He seeks in all by the ministry of all, those who are lost and leads them to salvation. It is necessary then that all those who are of Christ should have the care of their brothers in His name and in His authority, and exhort them by all means possible to do their duty.'[24] This general statement – which he has made so frequently before – Bucer now expands and particularises on the following lines: the Church must improve men's moral and intellectual education beginning especially through catechising the young; there must be in the 'Christian Republic' a thorough organisation of poor relief and assistance to the sick (it is here that he expands for the first time the work of 'Deacons'); for the fulfilment of these ends discipline is essential, and so there must be a thorough organisation of labour and leisure. As derivatives of these principles he showed the need for a better professional training through the improvement of schools and universities; improved technological efficiency in mining, the wool industry, and farming, all of which he found to be economically inferior to Imperial German methods. (Like Erasmus – they were both proud citizens of the empire – he also 'thought imperially' in urging on another occasion his need of one of the great tiled German stoves for central heating in cold, damp Cambridge.) At several points in these prescriptions he showed that such matters are important, not in themselves alone, but because of their consequences for one's neighbour: for example, if the rich show luxury in dress or manners, then there is lack of love for their neighbour. Again in writing of reform of the civil laws, Bucer added: 'It is necessary that all laws both divine and human should be related to these two points (the love of God and of the neighbour, citing Luke 10:27), and that those who ordain ... the laws ... should look above all to command only the things which agree with the purity and integrity of the service of God, and with charity towards the neighbour, and to forbid what does not agree with these.'[25]

How far Bucer's book represents the old humanist pedagogic weakness of treating men as though their social, economic, intellectual, and religious lives could be encompassed within the syllabus of a lecture room, is arguable; but this was the age of More's *Utopia*, and of the zealous renewal of study of Plato's *Republic*, a loved work of Bucer's humanist young manhood at Heidelberg.

[24] *Martini Buceri Opera Latini*, vol. XV, *De Regno Christi*, ed. F. Wendel Paris, 1955, 71. Bucer adds, 'a peccatlisque omnibus pro virili sua arceant, vel retrahant in ea lapsos.'
[25] Op. cit., 266.

Bucer was uneasily aware of this possible criticism when he wrote at the end of *De Regno Christi* of those, 'who consider I have proposed things strange and contrary to the usage of this age, and which one would rather dream of than practise, as if I had built a Republic as Plato did . . .' He insisted, however, that his work should not be judged, 'by the judgement of men but by the eternal and immutable Word of God, for these matters are necessary to the eternal salvation of all men'.[26] Whether Hopf is right in asserting without qualification that passages in the *De Regno Christi* were the foundation of the poor law made under Elizabeth I, is doubtful when we bear in mind that in spite of Bucer's protest about all his work being founded on the word of God, this programme of reform, financial, legal and economic, reflected ideas deriving from the English 'Commonwealth men' and their writings.[27] Or, perhaps, it may be argued that such matters can be regarded – and that Bucer believed them to be so – as legitimate extensions of the fundamental requirements of the word of God. If other Reformers did not go so far was it not because they hesitated to decide that a particular political programme of reform was necessarily tied to men's eternal salvation? Calvin, for example, did not build such activities at Geneva upon the same ground as that of men's salvation.

From this, if nothing else, it is plain that Bucer was concerned with the relations of Church and 'Commonwealth', with Church and society, and his work in England (which reflected the economic problems of the Tudors), as elsewhere, was related to the context in which he was writing. In fact his discussions of the nature of the Church, and of discipline which was in his eyes fundamental to the well-being of the Church, grew out of the changing environment of Strasbourg from 1524 onwards. Here we see that there was one danger which by that year Bucer had not foreseen, and that was the use of his characteristic theme in his treatise of 1523 by Anabaptists who sought a withdrawn society of the pure who fulfilled good works to each other. It was during the years 1524–30 that Anabaptism was most dangerous at Strasbourg, and its influence had attracted his fellow-minister Capito. This was also the period of transition from Lutheran teaching at Strasbourg to a south German or Zwinglian type of theology. From 1526 onwards Bucer led attacks on the Anabaptists, and succeeded, in 1528 and again in 1530, in persuading the magistrates to issue edicts against them. In the struggle Bucer saw

---

[26] Op. cit., 294, 295. '. . . non ex hominum iudicio, qui vel sint nostro vel fuerint superioribus saeculis, sed ex acterno et immutabili. Dei verbo diiudicare atque existimare.

[27] Op. cit., cf. Introduction by F. Wendel, 41. v. Constantin Hopf, *Martin Bucer and the English Reformation*, Oxford, 1946, 116 ff.

the need to emphasise the visible church against the sectarian principle
of the Anabaptists, and to this end he brought together election and
works within the Church which was *Corpus Christi, Sponsa Christi,*
and *Regnum Christi,* and particularly he emphasised 'Discipline' as
fundamental to the well-being of the Church. Church and discipline,
after the first almost naïve assumption on how easy it is to love God
and one's neighbour (as shown in *Das ym selbs niemant*), become very
soon for Bucer the means which God sets in the world to make this
love effective. From this emphasis on discipline derived the
Disziplinordnung of 1535 at Strasbourg.

Bucer defined the Church in *De vera animarum cura* as, 'the
congregation and society of those who in Christ Jesus our Lord
are congregated and associated together from the world so that they
may be one body . . . from which each and everyone has the office
and labour of building up the whole body and all of its
members'.[28] In his *Defensio de Christiana Reformatione* of Herman,
Archbishop of Cologne, he wrote, 'there is the visible church where
is the congregation of the faithful, who can be easily discerned . . .
who live in the world, though they are not of this world . . . by
their fruits . . . by the true confession of Christ, and communication
with all members of Christ in the Word, sacraments, and
discipline.'[29] Also in this book he explicitly makes 'discipline' a
signum of the Church. Bucer strove to make visible, incarnate
among men, the invisible church of the elect, as the setting from
within which Christ through the Holy Spirit works for the advance
of His kingdom. In his *Ein summarischer Vergriff der Christlichen
Lehre* he writes of members of the Church as being built up by
Christ: 'He fortifies them, and makes them progress by His constant
teaching and His discipline . . . He makes this building up of the
new life effective in Him through all His members without
exception'.[30] How Bucer conceived the function of the Church in
the whole of society has already been seen in discussing his *De
Regno Christi* above, where he would even go as far as saying that
idleness was anti-social and a sin against one's neighbour, supporting
himself on the Pauline injunction in 2 Thessalonians 3:10.[31] By
'discipline', which should enable the Church to fulfil its duty, Bucer
could mean much, including the discipline of life and manners,
penance, liturgy and ceremonies, fast days, special festivals as 'ways

---

[28] *Scripta Anglicana fere omnia . . .* (Basel, 1577), 267.
[29] This work was not published until 1613, at Geneva, 106.
[30] Op. cit., 44, '. . . hoffnung, liebe und heiligkeit' come through living in this faith.
[31] Op. cit., 88. Bucer cites this text with approval in three places.

of glorifying God and showing love to one's neighbour'.[32] Discipline 'consists not only in what the pastors and ministers do (who always have the principal duty here) but also everyone in particular has care for his neighbour to confirm him, to advance and exhort him by all possible means to pursue always more and more the way to heavenly life ... in the authority and name of our Lord Jesus Christ as his disciples'.[33] Discipline, as exercised by the ministers of the Church, braces the Christian and helps him to bear himself as an effective member of the Kingdom of God, and contribute to his own increase in holiness and to that of his fellow citizens. Here it will be seen that discipline involves emphasising the special ministry within the Church, as distinct from the general ministry of all Church members to each other and to their fellow men, and in particular as part of the Church's διακονία; this is seen in the ministry of 'deacons'. To understand what Bucer means by deacons we must consider his description of the Church's ministers, though here, as on other themes, he does not always write with consistent clarity.

The most convenient sources for Bucer's view of the special ministry in the Church, are his Commentary on Ephesians, *De Ordinatione, De Vera Animarum Cura, Defensio de Christiana Reformatione* and *De Regno Christi*, for here he is clearer than elsewhere in what he wrote about the ministry and especially that of 'deacons'. He more frequently stated that there are two orders or grades of the ministry: 'The ministry of the Church is of a twofold kind: according to the institution of the Holy Spirit, in one is retained the administration of the Word, sacraments, and discipline of Christ, which belongs properly to bishops and presbyters; in the other is the care of the poor, which is committed to those called deacons.'[34] Though in the same work he wrote later of 'three orders'; the primary order of bishops (*episcopus*) or superintendents (*superintendens*) and presbyters who can be divided into a second and third order, that is, of presbyters proper and those presbyters called deacons.[35] In his work on Ephesians he wrote, however, of the ministry as consisting of evangelists and doctors; pastors, who are bishops

---

[32] *De Regno Christi*, 70. Disciplina ecclesiae ... est triplex: una, vitae et morum; altera, poenitentiae, si quis gravius delequerit, tertia, sacrarum caeremoniarum.

[33] Op. cit., 70, 71.

[34] *Scripta Anglicana fere omnia. De Ordinatione*, 238. After referring to the ancient forms of ministry, *Lectores, Exorcistae*, etc., he adds, 'Nunc autem de ministerio praecipue quaeritur verbi Dei, sacramentorum et disciplinae, totiusque curae animarum.'

[35] Op. cit., 259.

[36] *Enarratio Epistolae D. Pauli Ephesios*, Basel, 1562, 'Evangelistae et doctores praedicando Evangelium Christi, et communicando doctrinam eius; pastores, episcopi et presbyteri

and presbyters; and deacons.[36] In his *De Vera Animarum Cura* he wrote in characteristic Latinity: '. . . tum iuxta communem Ecclesiae ordinationem, tum iuxta peculiare mandatum presbyterorum, ac praecipue pastoris superioris, hoc est, Episcopi: Sicuti nimirum Episcopus, tanquam Inspector super omnem Ecclesiae necessitatem supremus : et presbyteri; tanquam conspectores: quotidianam Christianorum necessitatem peregrinorum pariter et domesticorum experiuntur, iudicantque illis pro Ecclesiae facultate opem ferendam. Porro ad accepta et expensa bonorum Ecclesiasticorum quod attinet, semper Diaconi illi fidelem reddiderunt rationem: ut apud antiquos Patres et in Canonibus clare videre possumus.'[37] In his *Defensio de Christiana Reformatione* he described the pastoral origins and development of the seven orders of ministry, where he showed deacons to have been assistants to the bishops and presbyters in doctrine, sacraments and discipline. It is highly significant that he concluded that historical discussion with the statement: 'Nulla enim potestas est in Ecclesia Dei nisi ad aedificationem' – the implication of this statement will surely be clear in the context of this essay.

It will be seen that there is lacking here a clearly consistent definition of the nature and functions of the ministry of the Church; however, this is in line with Bucer's continually guarded way of avoiding too great precision which might weaken the Christian's obedience in the here and now of his life to the word of God, or his own responsibility in his moral choices. While it not the clearest of his formal statements, yet since it was addressed to the emperor in 1548 at a time of great urgency which led to conciseness and intensity of statement, *Ein summarischer Vergriff . . .* is a useful point of departure for a closer discussion of what Bucer intended deacons to be and to do. 'We teach that the Holy Spirit has instituted two distinct grades in the ministry of the Church, one which consists of the superior pastors (*Seelesorge*) whom the Holy Spirit describes as overseers (*Auffseher*) and elders (*Elteren*) to whom He entrusts the ministry of teaching, of the holy sacraments, and of Christian discipline, that is, the whole cure of souls. The other grade comprises the ministers who assist the others in the ministry of the cure of souls, and tending the flock of Christ and also zealously assisting the poor . . . We teach that these true ministers of Christ, in whatever Church . . . great or small they are, have received from the Lord the same spiritual power and

administrando etiam Christi sacramenta, et disciplinam: Diaconi, ceteris ordinibus ad huc omnia ministrando, et pauperes procurando', 117.
[37] *Scripta Anglicana fere omnia. De vera animarum cura*, 277.

authority, to exercise together ecclesiastical ministry including teaching, the sacraments, and penitential discipline, aid to the poor, in such wise as to feed the flock of Christ according to all its needs, and lead it to eternal life.'[38]

From this brief discussion of the Church and its offices of ministry, it will be seen that Bucer has less to say about the ministry of deacons, in comparison with other ministries, especially the ministering of all Christians to their fellow men, than might be expected; his only statement at length about deacons, and this is almost wholly devoted to their duties, is to be found in the *De Regno Christi*. Nevertheless, some other descriptions of the office of deacon may be useful, since he says little about the definition of a deacon in comparison with what he says about the deacon's work in that book.

'Deacons are joined to the ministry of bishops and presbyters to minister to them and especially to care for the poor', he wrote in his Commentary on Ephesians 4.[39] In *De Vera Animarum Cura* he wrote that 'the *officium et munus* of Deacons . . . is for the sustaining of the poor . . . Private men, great or small in condition, must contribute to the work of God in the Churches, both from their immovable and movable goods . . . [the Deacons are] diligently to distribute from this to all the poor in the Church, whether local people or strangers'.[40] Bucer, thereafter, having referred with approval to *pulchra iudicia* in the Epistles of St Gregory – *qui pius fuit Romanus pontifex* – on the subject of the work of deacons, added indignantly, 'this office and function are now in the Church, alas, wholly fallen in ruins through pontifical tyranny . . . so that few if any who are Deacons . . . know what their office and function should be . . . they think that their only duty is to sing the Gospel and Epistle at Mass'.[41] In his Commentary on Ephesians 4, Bucer showed that διακονία relates specifically to serving others and has nothing to do with 'otiose and vain titles of dignity' whose holders despoil the goods of the Church to ignoble ends.[42]

In the *Defensio de Reformatione Christiana* he claimed that the 'distinction of these ministries in the Churches is not an Apostolic and necessary tradition, but a free matter which any Church can order . . . and no Church is bound to another', and he added that '. . . the ministry of specially approved persons is received with the consent

[38] *Scripta Anglicana*, 47, the margin has the subtitle here 'Episcopos et Presbyteros' (*sic*), 49.
[39] *Enarratio . . . Ephesios*, 117.
[40] *Scripta Anglicana*, 277.
[41] Op. cit., 277.
[42] Op. cit., 163.
[43] Op. cit., 110.

of the faithful'.[43] Bucer, it is plain, accepts as reasonable that in different nations, and under different governments, there will be different ways of arranging for the ministry of the Church, which is not a matter for Christians to quarrel over. The significant thing about a deacon, therefore, is not so much to define his status and to show his apostolic lineage, but to show what his functions are, and these, with all other gifts (*dona varia, secundum gratiam* ...) are for *aedificationem communem totius corporis, omniumque membrorum*.[44] Corroboration of this can be seen in Bucer's order for Ordination in his *Pia Deliberatio* for Herman, Archbishop of Cologne, when there is only one ordaining formula for all three offices of ministry, bishop, presbyter, deacon: 'The hand of Almighty God, the Father, Son and Holy Spirit, be upon you and protect and govern you, that you may go and bear fruit by your ministry, and remain in you to life eternal' – 'go and bear fruit by your ministry' is the important matter for a deacon, as for all other Christians.[45]

Chapter XIV of the second book of the *De Regno Christi* is entitled *Lex Sexta de Procurandis Egenis*, that is, the sixth of fourteen laws which 'the Almighty Lord has ordained for His people, for the defence and preservation of the Christian religion'. After the King, Edward VI, has restored the Church's goods, Christ's patrimony, then holy provision and care for the needy poor must be undertaken for 'without it there can be no true communion of saints'.[46] (Did Bucer in his sickness and overwork at Cambridge not realise how utopian this hope was? Could English nobles like the Dudleys be thought of as magistrates like the Sturms of Strasbourg?) For this in all the churches there must be, 'deacons who are men of good report, full of the Holy Spirit and of wisdom', and each church shall have a sufficient number of them to fulfil this duty.[47] The first duty of the deacons is to distinguish between the deserving and undeserving poor, for the former to inquire carefully into their needs; the latter, if they lead disorderly lives at the expense of others, to expel them from the community of the faithful. Care, next is to be taken for needy widows. The second duty of deacons is to keep a written record of accounts, having sought diligently for the proper collecting of funds from all the parishioners according to their capacity. In order that deacons should have the greatest authority among the people, the ancient churches associated them with the holy ministry

[44] *Scripta Anglicana. De vera animarum cura*, 269.
[45] *Pia Deliberatio*, in *Scripta Anglicana*, 52.
[46] *De Regno Christi*, 143.
[47] Ibid., 145.

in the dispensing of doctrine and of the holy sacraments. Next, Bucer repeats the charges against the corruption of this office in papal times in similar words to those quoted above on this point; nevertheless, he has already established at the end of his paragraph on the first part of the office of deacons that, 'they must aid and serve the Bishop and the Presbyters in all the discipline of Christ'.[48] Bucer, after giving some historical account of methods of dealing with the poor with some advice to the king attached, next goes on to reject the customary view that a man has a right to make his almsgiving individually and according to his own views. Bucer is aware, however, that there are some of the poor who will be ashamed to reveal the extent of their need to the deacons, and so discreet neighbours should privately inform them of the fact. On the other hand, he insists that the deacons must be sensitive to the shames of poverty and distribute to the poor with prudence, and not behave as it were like the beadle Bumble in *Oliver Twist*.[49] In all this Bucer is again concerned to show that all Christians are members of one another and there is no place for individualism, either in the great scattering 'largesse' or the small resorting to begging. If dispute should arise in a parish concerning this poor relief then the deacons should consult with 'the Bishop and assembly of Presbyters', so that 'all things should be done by authority of the Word of God.'[50] Bucer probably thought here of the establishing of many more bishops than those provided for by the ancient dioceses of England, and of assemblies of clergy more frequent and local than Convocations, a foreshadowing of Archbishop Usher's view of a 'moderate episcopacy' and similar themes dear to some Puritans later.

On the title page of *Das ym Selbs niemant* of 1523 there are four citations from Scripture around the printer's woodcut containing the title. Two of these may form a fitting conclusion to this study of Bucer's teaching on διακονία in the Church.

ὁ γὰρ πᾶς νόμος ἐν ἑνὶ λόγῳ πεπλήρωται, ἐν τῷ ἀγαπήσεις τὸν πλησίον σοῦ ὡς σεαυτόν [Galatians 5:14].

Alles das ir wöllen das eüch die leüt thün sollen das thuend ynen auch ir, das ist das gesatz und die propheten. [Matthew 7:12].

5

The Colloquies between Catholics and Protestants, 1539–41

Ranke, whose judgements always deserve respect, said of the Colloquy of Regensburg:

> If I am not mistaken this was a period of vital importance for Germany and even for the world. For Germany . . . [came] at last the possibility of reforming the ecclesiastical constitution of the nation, and, in relation to the Pope, of giving it a freer and more independent position, exempt from his temporal encroachments. The unity of the Church, and with it that of the nation, would have been maintained, and even more immense and enduring results would have emerged. If the moderate party, by whom these attempts began and were guided, could have maintained its ascendancy in Rome and in Italy, the Catholic world must have assumed a very different aspect.[1]

While it is true that the 'might-have-beens' of history are unprofitable speculations, yet the possibility behind that Colloquy of Regensburg has been too much neglected.

---

[1] Leopold von Ranke, *Sämmtliche Werke* (3rd collected edition), vol. 37, *Die Römischen Päpste in den letzen vier Iahrhunderten*, 1900, I, 107.

Has any Catholic scholar writing with authority spoken favourably and sympathetically of the Colloquies which took place between Catholics and Protestants in Germany in the period 1539–41? From John Eck who took part in them down to Dr Hubert Jedin, author of the magisterial history of the Council of Trent, as far as I am aware, the Colloquies have been dismissed as ill-grounded and irresponsible attempts at reconciling Catholic truth with heresy by unauthorised means – a movement bound to fail because it was undertaken by the wrong people, with the wrong methods, and with wrong ends in view. It is not that the Colloquies have been unduly neglected; Sleidan, Sarpi, and Seckendorf gave some desultory account of them long ago, and in the second half of the nineteenth century a number of books were written in Germany, especially by Catholics, which gave close attention to the Colloquies.[2] But the inevitable conclusion was, as Pastor exemplifies,[3] that they were an unfortunate interlude of political manoeuvring prior to the decisive and doctrinally sound purpose of holding a General Council under the Pope's authority. After the final session of the Council of Trent it was apparently psychologically impossible for Catholics to regard the Colloquies as having been a valid means for understanding and reunion. The Council had laid down a retrospective condemnation of Protestantism and its works. Perhaps since the Council of the Vatican II there are now Catholic scholars who may take a more favourable look at that ecumenical failure at Regensburg in 1541 and what preceded it. Protestant scholars, while not so thorough in condemnation, have tended to ignore the Colloquies or to see them as offering little that is theologically fruitful and dismiss them as delusive gatherings hopeless from the beginning.[4]

But judgements that may have seemed clearly demonstrated and final in, say, 1545, 1890, or 1960, may be reconsidered, for such judgements are made from within certain historical situations, under the pressure of particular convictions and particular apologetic trends, and with the course of time the situations change. Moreover, historians have oversimplified the issues with the certainties of hindsight. But it cannot be right that historians should continue to be

---

[2] For the nineteenth-century writers in Germany see the literature at the head of the article by Kolde, 'Regensburger Religionsgespräch und Regensburger Buch 1541', *Realencyklopädie für Protestantische Theologie und Kirche*, 3rd ed. 1905, vol. 16.
[3] This is a major theme of his book: Ludwig Pastor, *Die kirchlichen Reunionsbestrebungen während der Regierung Karls V*, Freiburg, 1879.
[4] Peter Matheson; *Cardinal Contarini at Regensburg*, Oxford, 1972, gives the Colloquy a chapter heading, 'A Futile Waste of Time'. He represents (20) Bucer as deceiving Granvelle, and equal in spirit with curial diplomacy, therefore insincere from the beginning.

content with over-simplifications where contemporaries felt torturing complexities. If good men of undoubted Catholic piety, learning and integrity like Cardinals Contarini, Sadoleto, and the Cologne theologian Gropper, to name but a few, believed that it was worth while to try to reconcile Protestants on the great question of grace, and from that basis come to an understanding on the nature of the sacraments, the Church and the Papacy, why dismiss their judgement with the easy hindsight of four centuries of Tridentinism triumphant? Again, if Protestants like Melanchthon reluctantly and Bucer with greater commitment, for example, could discuss eirenically with Catholics about the great question of grace, and after agreement there, go the second mile in seeking understanding on the question of the sacraments, the authority of the Church, and the status of the Bishop of Rome, should they be dismissed as the weak instruments of Imperial Chancellor Granvelle's political manoeuvres, or as themselves seeking to manipulate the Catholics for Protestant gains? If a handful of men of good-will on both sides could agree on the very matter on which Luther had stormed out of the Church of Rome in 1521 (or as sounder commentators wish to affirm was thrust into a position which he had not originally taken, and from thence compelled to act as he did after 1521), in spite of the enormous pressures against such an agreement by 1541, is it not reasonable to look at the matter again, firmly setting aside as far as possible the simplifications of either Catholic or Protestant hindsight? The task will not be easy: it is not just a matter of considering the theological texts which the theologians of the Colloquies kept before them, or agreed upon, in 1539–41, for that would be another form of over-simplification. Those Colloquies were deeply involved in the oppositions of imperial, papal and French politics; they were heavily compromised by the intransigents who were not present, Martin Luther and the Elector at Wittenberg and Pope Paul III at Rome, who showed fervent mutual distrust; princes were changing sides during the period of the meetings, the Elector of Brandenburg came into Protestantism while continuing to attend Mass with cheerful inconsistency at Regensburg, and the Landgrave Philip of Hesse broke the Protestant alliance to support Charles V through fear of the legal consequences of his own bigamous marriage; and through all this the Catholic Bavarian dukes with blunt simplicity explained to the Emperor that the answer to all these problems of schism, heresy and political division was 'war, bloody war'.

Before entering upon an account of the Colloquies and of the political and partisan problems which were entangled with them, it would be well to ask whether the common assumption is valid that the Protestants were wholly opposed to Catholicism because of the basic principles on which they grounded their beliefs.[5] If we come forward from 1517 instead of going back through centuries of embittered antagonism we would find that the first reformers retained much of the Catholicism they are confidently assumed by Protestant controversialists to have opposed. It is significant that the Lutheran scholar, Jaroslav Pellikan, could write: 'Martin Luther was the first Protestant, and yet he was more Catholic than many of his Roman Catholic opponents.'[6] This apparent paradox contains a demonstrable and important truth which it has been possible to affirm only recently after centuries of holding Protestantism and Catholicism as self-evident terms of black and white opposition. This could lead us, of course, into a discussion of what meanings should be attached to these two words, but I do not propose to undertake this analysis, since it has for long been bound up with manoeuvring for positions suitable for defensive and offensive tactics characteristic of the controversy between Protestant and Catholic since Church History emerged as a specialist study in the sixteenth century precisely to enable both sides to demonstrate as fully as possible each other's fatal errors.[7] Let us rather look for common ground behind those two words which have been all too evocative of embattled fortresses.

Catholicism, in the form which challenged Luther to recant, can be understood as essentially consisting in the obedience of the faithful to papal and hierarchical absolutist authority, supported on the one hand by the all-embracing legal obligations of the Canon Law, and on the other by Scholasticism busily determining heresies by a computerising process of showing how new theological views might be placed in parallel with old condemnations, and then using the overpowering bludgeon of canonical authority to hammer down the proposers of such views into silence. Before all those of good-will dismiss this description of sixteenth-century Catholicism in terms of an oppressive tyranny, as an ill-drawn caricature, let them remember that on that basis John Eck challenged Luther at the public debate at Leipzig. Eck was largely indifferent to the great matter of grace raised by Luther as a faithful Catholic seeking to re-establish sound doctrine against decaying Scholastic opinions and the development of

---

[5] For example, *Dictionnaire de Théologie Catholique*, 1936, vol. 13, art. 'Réforme'.

[6] Jaroslav Pellikan, *Obedient Rebels*, 1964, II.

[7] The *Historia Ecclesiae Christi*, 1559–74, edited by Flacius Illyricus with his collaborators ('the Magdeburg Centuriators'), was intended as a demonstration of the increasing domination of an earlier purer Christianity by the 'anti-Christian' Papacy. In spite of this partisan intention it initiated the modern study of Church History by its full use of sources. It was answered by the *Annales Ecclesiastici*, 1588–1607, of Cesare Baronius.

superstitious practices; in fact Eck avoided discussion with Luther, at bottom he was possibly bored with the subject or, more probably, realised how difficult it would be to refute Luther on it, and preferred to spend his energies in demonstrating, by bludgeoning authoritarianism, that Luther was really a Hussite, who had defied the authority of the Pope and the laws of the Church, and who should forthwith recant or be condemned out of hand. Even Cardinal Cajetan, a distinguished Thomist, and competent in the new biblical learning, who could have understood Luther's concern about grace, unfortunately (for this was a crucial interview) irritably shifted the ground to that of authority with its requirement 'be silent and obey'.

Luther was bustled out of the Church under misleading labels and by noisy demonstrations of authority: his whole effort at repristinating the meaning of grace, including the initiative of God and the centrality of Christ and therefore of the sacraments, and the nature of the Church as the *corpus mysticum*, was ignored or overshadowed by insistence on papal authority and its associated legalism. The theologically grounded opposition from Latomus, Cochlaeus and Murner, among others, did not get to close grips with Luther's profound analysis of the nature of justification. Laymen of sound piety, of whom the Elector Frederick the Wise may be taken as a significant example, could not see where theologically on the basis of Scripture Luther had been refuted – this was a major reason why Eck's debating victory at Leipzig to his own surprise and irritation came to nothing. Even at the end of his life under what was tantamount to exile in an Austrian monastery Luther's former superior in religion and confessor, John Staupitz, was not convinced that Luther up to 1519 was theologically unsound on justification.[8]

Nor was Luther's position unique among those who were to become Protestants, in seeking to retain elements of Catholic substance in his theological work of renewal. Melanchthon, in the Augsburg Confession, deliberately ignored what were later to become extremist Protestant positions, and intended the Confession as a basis for healing the growing schism. Bucer was prepared to go to greater lengths than other Protestants to find grounds for agreement on Catholic substance between Catholics and Protestants. Calvin wrote explicitly of his reluctance to break with the visible unity[9] of the Catholic Church, and throughout his career as a theologian thought of himself as restoring sound Catholicism rather than as creating a

---

[8] *Luther's Werke*, Weimar Ausgabe, *Briefwechsel*, III, No. 726.
[9] *Ioannis Calvini Opera quae supersunt omnia*, ed. H. W. Baum, E. Cunitz & E. Reuss, 1866, vol. v, col. 412. 'Una praesertim res animum ab illis meum avertebat, ecclesiae reverentia.'

particular Protestant Church and society, as for example, his massive number of references to the Fathers demonstrates. Few realise, who have read little of Calvin, how very much more his writings are concerned with the Church and the sacraments than with predestination. Archbishop Cranmer has suffered, like his continental contemporaries, from English writers whose Protestant zeal roused vigorous high-church counter-attack so that the Catholic substance of his work (which excluded the Canon Law conceptions of the Church) like that in the work of the men he so much admired and used, from Melanchthon and Bucer down to Justus Jonas, has been almost ignored by his English friends and foes in the last hundred and thirty years.

With the changes in historical and especially theological perspectives which have been taking place in the last decade (for example, the decline in the appeal to authority for its own sake, the shift away from traditional Scholastic philosophy and theology; the raising again with fresh insights of the question of justification by Hans Küng) we can more easily see than could Joseph Lortz or Hubert Jedin[10] or many of their Protestant contemporaries, that there was some measure of common ground that could make it sensible to try to bring Catholics and Protestants to discuss the possibility of reunion in the mid-sixteenth century.

A basis for providing a stand against taking those reunion talks seriously (other than by the method of authoritarian dismissal), which was insisted on by both Lortz and Jedin, is that the participants in and promoters of those Colloquies were the victims of Erasmianism. In his profound account of the German Reformation Lortz showed the strongest hostility to Erasmus: 'Erasmus constituted a threat to Christianity and to the Church.'[11] For him, before Erasmus can be interpreted, the definitive presupposition is required; one must believe in the necessity of a dogmatically fixed religion.[12] On that basis Erasmus and consequently the Erasmians are condemned with barely a hearing: 'He represented the threat to dogma by relativism, to the kingdom of grace and redemption by ennobled stoic morality.'[13] Lortz also attacked Melanchthon for relativising Luther's dogmatic principles by his humanist approach in the Augsburg Confession. He could even write: 'The timid, petty, sly dishonesty of Erasmus cast its

---

[10] Joseph Lortz, *The Reformation of Germany* 1968; Eng. trans. of *Die Reformation in Deutschland*, 3rd ed., 2 vols., Freiburg im Breisgau, 1949; Hubert Jedin, *A History of the Council of Trent*, vol. I, Eng. trans. 1957, vol. II, 1961, *Geschichte des Konzils von Trient*, 1949.

[11] Joseph Lortz, *The Reformation in Germany*, I, 152.

[12] Ibid., 153.

[13] Ibid., 152–3.

shadow upon Melanchthon's image.'[14] After this it is not surprising that in his brief account of what he called 'the conciliatory theology' of the period of the Colloquies he described it as 'founded on Erasmus and his relativism'.[15]

Jedin went even further.[16] On Erasmus he makes the surprisingly pietistic statement that, 'the circumstance that the *Praise of Folly* was written while Erasmus was staying in the house of a canonised saint does not alter the fact that . . . he had exposed to ridicule persons and institutions which up till then had been held in reverence'.[17] Again, Jedin prefaces his discussion of the Erasmianism of the Colloquies by showing that Erasmus was hopelessly at fault in, 'coming to the conclusion that, given a measure of good-will, the sickness [of schism] was by no means incurable', and for adopting the attitude that 'after all both parties continued to believe in Christ!'.[18] He points to the large number of clergy, including some bishops, and also powerful laymen who were ecclesiastical politicians, influenced – apparently he only just stops at saying infected – by Erasmian ideas.[19] Then in one swingeing sentence Jedin condemns Erasmus by irrelevant association:

> The Erasmians did not form a secret society as did the freemasons of the era of Enlightenment; they were linked together by the same community of thought as were the ecclesiastical rationalists two centuries later, and just as the ideas of the latter coincided largely with those of the Jansenists – hence with a current which at least in its beginnings ran directly counter to theirs – so did the Erasmian mentality coincide with that of the 'evangelicals'.[20]

Here freemasonry, the rationalism of the Enlightenment, and Jansenism are associated with Erasmus, not because they were directly relevant but because presumably they represent standard subjects of orthodox disapproval to make our flesh creep – and the wholly misleading word 'evangelical' is brought in to add another to its confusing usages. Thus the period of the Colloquies is condemned, before it is adequately discussed, as falsely grounded. But Erasmus was not responsible for Contarini discovering from his own studies something near to Luther's doctrine of justification in 1511. Nor was he responsible for the fact that across Europe there were many men who were deeply disturbed by the implications of merit-theology,

[14] Ibid.
[15] Ibid., 245.
[16] Hubert Jedin, *A History of the Council of Trent*, I, 156 ff.
[17] Ibid., 160.
[18] Ibid., 359.
[19] Ibid., 364.
[20] Ibid., 364.

with the lack of spiritual depth in teaching about the use of the sacraments, and who were weary of those Scholastic theologians who behaved as the swordsmen of dialectics rather than as pastors of the flock. His success as a writer was due at least in part to the fact that this situation existed – he did not create it, he addressed it, and roused with real insight fresh resources of the Christian spirit through his return to the sources in Scripture and the Fathers.

Few scholars at this time, including theologians, would agree with the attitude of Lortz and Jedin to Erasmus. In the years which have passed since they wrote there has emerged a sympathetic exposition of his work as one who sought to restore ancient piety, provide the basic principles for a new theological method, and provide a framework for these activities in the labour of editing the New Testament in Greek and scholarly editions of the Fathers.[21] From this more appreciative view of Erasmus's work as containing positive good, it is possible to see, more sympathetically than did Lortz or Jedin, the men who took part in the Colloquies. The Colloquies were not just politicians' devices or attempts by one religious party to put the other in a false position (though many on either side had hoped for this unscrupulous device) any more than they were examples of misleading Erasmianism; rather they contained within them the potential for mutual understanding at least on the doctrine of grace, and even of reconciliation undertaken amid great difficulties from the opposition of extremists of both sides.

The religious condition within the German Empire was grave enough. Cardinal Aleandro after an Austrian journey wrote to the Pope in September 1538, with glum though pardonable exaggerations, that:

> divine worship and the administration of the sacraments had for the most part ceased. The secular princes, with the exception of Ferdinand I, were either entirely Lutheran or full of hatred for the priesthood and greed of Church property; the prelates lived just as extravagantly as before and merely held positions in the Church. The religious orders had dwindled down to handfuls, the secular clergy were not much more numerous, and so immoral and ignorant that the few Catholics there were shunned them.[22]

This taken together with the political situation in the German Empire

---

[21] For example W. P. Eckert, *Erasmus von Rotterdam Werk und Werkung*, 2 vols., Cologne, 1967; C. Béné, *Erasme et St Augustin*, Geneva, 1969; J.-C. Margolin, *Recherches Erasmiennes*, Geneva, 1969. The new Dutch edition of his works in Latin, and the collected works in English at Toronto, both in progress.

[22] Pastor, *The History of the Popes*, 1912, XI, 362.

and the long procrastination in the past of Clement VII – who, fearing the consequences for himself,[23] had been opposed to calling a General Council of the Church anywhere at any time, in spite of his vague promises to the contrary – and the hesitations about the timing and procedure of a Council by Paul III, who was nevertheless guardedly in favour of one being called, brought Charles V, who was sincerely concerned about the well-being of souls in his dominions, to feel that further delay in dealing with the Protestant schism would prove to be fatal. He determined to make an approach to the Protestant princes and in the Frankfurt *Standstill* of April 1539 provided that those who held to the Augsburg Confession should be free from attacks by the Catholic states for the sake of religion, and that all legal proceedings, for example, for the recovery of lands appropriated from the Church by Protestants, should be held over for a period (in the event six months). On the Protestant side no attacks should be made on Catholic states because of religion, no attempt should be made to draw hitherto Catholic or wavering princes into the Protestant defensive League of Schmalkald, and no further inroads upon church property should be made. It was further agreed that a meeting should be held at Nürnberg in August to which both sides should send moderate-minded theologians to try to heal the divisions. There was from both sides, however, opposition to the *Standstill*: even the eirenic Bucer and the Landgrave Philip of Hesse (the leading Protestant prince in the League of Schmalkald) feared a political coup; and the Bavarian dukes exemplified extremist suspicion on the Catholic side. One significant, and remarkable, step in this decision, however, was the indifference shown to the position of Paul III; the papal legate had been excluded from the decision-making process, and religious discussions appeared to be about to take place without the Curia being represented.

But even this *Standstill* was ineffective, events were dissolving this uneasy compromise. Luther's old enemy, the Catholic Duke George the Bearded of Saxony, died that year, and his brother Henry, in spite of the terms of the *Standstill*, brought his territory into Lutheranism – and Leipzig, where Eck had defended the authority of the Papacy against Luther twenty years before, became a stronghold against that authority. Further, a very conservative form of Protestantism was adopted for his territory by the Elector of Brandenburg. At the same time the Emperor's hope of peace with

---

[23] Among other problems for Clement VII was the fact of his illegitimate birth; Ranke, *Werke*, 37, I., but his major concern was that a Council might weaken his authority over the Church.

France seemed about to fade, and the temporary truce with the Turks ceased. Charles greatly needed a settlement in the Empire, which meant a religious settlement, in order to meet these political challenges.

At this point some account is necessary of the political environment of the Colloquies which Charles was about to call to establish this religious settlement. Imperial counsellors had urged upon Charles from the beginning that he was Emperor as though ordained by God himself: a ruler not acting immediately but mediately as the moral and political leader of the Christian West, one of whose functions was to challenge Islam and heresy after the tradition of the 'Catholic Kings' in Spain. Charles said at the Diet of Worms in 1521 that he was determined to hold fast the Catholic faith and defend it: he meant this and held to it all his life, and believed that his peculiar position as Emperor and, therefore, moral leader of the Christian West gave him the authority to initiate church reform, and to demand that the Pope should call a Council of the Church. These Ghibelline assumptions outraged the Curia, and an early attempt to challenge them in 1527 brought the Sack of Rome by Catholic as well as Protestant troops. Whatever steps Charles wished to take to heal the German schism were bound to produce counter-activity from the Curia, so that the Colloquies were held against the background of papal suspicion, a flurry of nuncios and the determined policy of the Pope to ensure that proposals and, even more so, decisions, concerning religious unity should be dependent on his assent. Alongside of this went the political rivalry with France. The French could not be content with the prospect of a massive power-complex from the Low Countries through to Germany, Italy and Spain on her borders, so Francis I would never let Charles rest. To Francis the healing of the religious schism in Germany could be disastrous, since it would increase enormously Charles' centralisation of power. In fact he somewhat overrated this situation, since the source of Habsburg political, military and economic power was shifting from the Empire to Spain. Francis, though 'the Most Christian King', went so far as to make an alliance with the Turks to harass Charles when Charles invaded France in 1536 (Francis allied with them again in 1544), during the decade when Charles was exerting all his strength to halt the Turkish advance in Hungary and the Mediterranean. Francis was also willing to ally with the Protestant princes of Germany when the latter formed the Schmalkaldic League of defence against the Catholic princes. Charles not only faced difficulty from the Papacy, and from political relations with France and the Turks, but also his hope of mending the religious division, disappointed in 1530 at Augsburg,

was made more difficult with the ten years' further delay which
followed. Both sides had obtained martyrs, built up strong points of
resistance on the dogmatic issues, created libraries of offence and
defence which constituted a literary arms race over twenty years.
Further, there was the determination to maintain opposition springing
from such comparatively slighter matters as simple slander: for
example, that the Protestants were not concerned with religious
matters but really wanted the Church's money, and cynically wished
to use religious conferences as loud-hailers for their propaganda; that
the Catholics were uninterested in religious truth and reform of
abuses, and only concerned with imperial or papal politics; and that
the Pope was wholly untrustworthy, and for some he was in any case
the Antichrist. A study of the range of these problems in detail leads
to surprise that the Colloquies ever took place, and achieved anything
at all.

Against this grim background and because the *Standstill* of 1539
appeared to be in danger of dissolving, Charles called for a conference
on religious affairs for the Diet at Speyer in June 1540, and brushed aside
papal indignation against laymen meeting to judge upon a discussion of
theologians not authorised by the Holy See. Before the meeting
arranged for June Charles had assumed that, like another Constantine,
he could act as arbitrator; the Protestant princes suspiciously demanded
that doctrinal decisions if made should be made on the basis of Scripture
only; and the Curia made renewed efforts to turn the Emperor's policy
aside by proposing a General Council, the only effective instrument for
unity in faith and custom. But Charles admonished the legate that an
Italian-based Council would not do, not only did the Protestants object
to a Council outside of Germany itself, but also the Catholic princes
were dubious, and three times he irritably remarked, 'His Holiness had
only to declare the Council open',[24] and concluded by stating that a
religious conference was the only solution. Faced by this the Pope
decided not to send the Cardinal Legate, Cervini, who remained with
Charles in the Low Countries, but a nuncio, Morone, who was
instructed to take no part in the forthcoming debate, and to offer no
concessions. He had already denounced the Archbishop of Lund for
proposing a gathering of laymen and theologians to deal with the
religious question at the diet of Frankfurt, in 1539.[25] Bishop Morone
was a friend of the Cardinals Pole and Contarini and sympathetic to
their viewpoint on justification, and on Christian humanist views, but
wholly committed, as they were, to the principle of papal authority.

[24] Pastor, *History of the Popes*, XI, 383.
[25] Matheson, op. cit., 11, 14–15.

Plague at Speyer, however, led to the conference being called to meet at Hagenau. Only a few princes and bishops arrived for the conference, the Elector of Saxony and the Landgrave of Hesse refused to attend because they held that the conference had not been called in terms of the Frankfurt *Standstill*, and Melanchthon, whose presence would have been of primary importance, took ill and failed to appear. King Ferdinand, on behalf of his brother Charles, was in charge of the proceedings, but because no adequate preparation had been made beforehand the meeting broke down on a discussion of procedure and of the matters to be debated. At the beginning the problem arose of the norm for the making of decisions; the Protestant theologians, of whom Bucer was the chief, together with some second-rank Wittenbergers, insisted that Scripture as interpreted by the Apostolic Church should be the standard of decision, and not the decrees of Fathers and Councils. The Catholic theologians, including Eck and Cochlaeus, suggested that the discussion should be based on the articles of compromise proposed at Augsburg in 1530 – this was supported by Ferdinand.[26] But the Protestants insisted that those compromise articles had not been agreed upon in 1530, and demanded that the Augsburg Confession itself must be the basis for discussion since it contained the doctrine of 'the one ancient, true and Apostolic Church'. When Ferdinand reminded those present that the Pope would have to be consulted about any theological decisions taken, the Protestants true to their name protested. The conference had failed to get off the ground, and Ferdinand, since nothing effective could be done in the absence of the Elector of Saxony and the Landgrave of Hesse, postponed the conference, deciding that it should be convened again at Worms in October 1540.

The failure at Hagenau was due to clearly inadequate preparations beforehand: merely bringing men to a debate in the presence of members of the Diet, and hoping that something would emerge, had been shown to be useless. Before the meeting at Worms, a greater hope of something positive being achieved was possible because the Protestant demand that discussion should be on the basis of the Augsburg Confession was accepted, no doubt with some reservations, on the Catholic side. Certainly this was disapproved of at Rome, since once again a religious conference was to take place in the presence of laymen, and on the undesirable basis of a Protestant statement. Nevertheless, Paul III recognised that he must formally be represented at the conference for, as the nuncio to Charles, Poggio, said: 'If the Pope does not decide to send a legate and learned men to

---

[26] F. Lau and E. Bizer, *A History of the Reformation in Germany to 1555*, 1969, 162.

the conference, then the whole of Germany, indeed the whole of Christendom, will think that his Holiness does not trouble himself about religion and this nation, as many have already openly declared.'[27] The Pope appointed a canonist (hardly the most fruitful form of competence for a Colloquy), Bishop Tommaso Campeggio, not a cardinal, as his special nuncio; also four theologians to represent the Holy See; the nuncios to the Emperor, Morone and Poggio, were also to attend. Also present at the Colloquy of Worms was the Bishop of Capo d'Istria, Pietro Paolo Vergerio (later to be accused of Protestant heresy at Rome, and to end his days as an anti-papal polemicist, though not acceptable as a theologically sound Protestant), one of those curious cross-bench figures of the period, who was probably secretly representing the interests of the French.

Before the Colloquy at Worms opened, the Elector of Saxony had instructed his Wittenberg theologians to reject any decisions which would recognise the primacy of the Pope and the papal right to make the final decision upon the conclusions of the Colloquy. The various theologians arrived in good time. On the Catholic side, Eck and Cochlaeus were present as well as the more eirenical Gropper and Pflug, who shared the old Erasmian hope of reunion on biblical and patristic rather than Scholastic lines. For the Protestants there were Bucer and Capito from Strasbourg (accompanying them as a representative for that city, though not commissioned as a debater, was Calvin); and there were Melanchthon, Osiander, Brenz and Amsdorf from among the Lutherans. But the Colloquy was held up for a month awaiting the arrival of Granvelle, the Imperial Chancellor, representing Charles, who opened the meetings formally on 25 November, with a speech grumbling about the seditious evils Protestantism had created in the Empire.[28] The nuncio, Campeggio, did not appear until 8 December, and was given an inferior place by Granvelle, who during Campeggio's rather flat speech about the Pope's zeal for unity did not uncover at the Pope's name, but did so when the Emperor's name was mentioned, a fact not lost on the Protestants present.[29] Granvelle also permitted Protestant preaching in certain churches during the Colloquy. It is curious to learn that while the Protestants – frequently accused by their opponents of theological divisions among themselves – held a united front, as Bucer showed in a letter to Blaurer, 'Nostri ad unum consentiunt ut nihil remittatur quod per se Christi est',[30] the Catholics on the other hand

[27] Pastor, *History of the Popes*, XI, 403.
[28] *Ioannis Calvini Opera quae supersunt omnia*, XI, col. 136.
[29] Pastor, *History of the Popes*, XI, 410–11.
[30] *Ioannis Calvini Opera quae supersunt omnia*, XI, col. 103.

were in some disarray. In this situation the nuncio Morone proposed, in what was his only positive effort at Worms, that the Catholic states should come to an understanding by presenting written statements of the viewpoint on the controverted issues. Four of these have been recovered, those from the Electors of Mainz, Trier, Cologne, the Bishops of Magdeburg, Salzburg and Strasbourg, and the representatives of the Bavarians, a document projected by Eck himself; from the representatives of the Elector of Brandenburg; from the representatives of the Elector Palatine; and from the representatives of the Dukes of Jülich and Cleves.[31] These statements are not remarkable theologically for either depth or insight, nor on the other hand do they show a narrow dogmatic intransigence. The comment of their editor that the theology does not go very deep is judicious, but we should not let it further persuade us to see weakness here through the eyes of Tridentine hindsight after the manner of Lortz and Jedin.[32]

Some comments of Calvin, whose letters from Worms provide one of our witnesses to those events, give some interesting sidelights. On worship at Worms he wrote that after Granvelle's opening of the sessions on 25 November: 'Cecinerunt igitur missam suam de spiritu sancto ut auspicato aggrederentur. Nos etiam solennes supplicationes in templo nostro habuimus.'[33] His comment, in a letter to Farel, on Eck who was the dominating figure among the Catholic theologians is interesting though mordant: 'Propone tibi imaginem barbari sophistae inter illiteratos stolide exultantis, et habetis dimidiam partem Ecki.'[34] In fairness, an epigram on Calvin should be quoted, written with many others on the Protestant and Catholic theologians present by a humanist poet who observed both sides with shrewd irony:

> Quaeso, quid indigne tot fundis inania verba?
> Doctus es, at quid tum? Sis quoque porro pius![35]

In fact the making of verses seems to have been the only alleviation to the tedium of the long procedural discussions between 21 November and 14 January at Worms. Calvin records that he, Melanchthon, Sturm and others wrote verses on the Catholics present;

---

[31] *Archiv für Reformationsgeschichte*, vol. 43, I, 1952. W. Lipgens, 'Theologischer Standort fürstlicher Räte im sechzehnten Jahrhundert. Neue Quellen zum Wormser Verglichsgspräch, 1540/41'.

[32] Ibid., 44.

[33] *Ioannis Calvini opera quae supersunt omnia*, XI, col. 137.

[34] Ibid., XI, col. 146.

[35] *Zeitschrift für Kirchengeschichte*, vol. 50, 1931, *Epigramme auf Teilnehmer am Wormser Religionsgespräch*, 1540–41. O. Clemen, 449.

Calvin's poem alone survives, *Epinicion Christo Cantatum*, a Juvenalian exercise in which Eck, Cochlaeus, Nausea and other Catholic theologians appear as captives chained to the triumph-car of Christ, victor over his enemies.[36]

The outcome of the procedural wrangling – about methods of voting, who were to debate and who were to judge – was a decision to have one speaker from each side, and after further delay until 14 January 1541, Eck and Melanchthon, the appointed representatives, began a debate on original sin, and successfully reached an agreement in four days. But the Emperor commanded Granvelle to close the Colloquy on the ground that no progress was being made, and Granvelle referred the debate to the next Diet, which was to be at Regensburg in March 1541. Sleidan, the historian and an agent of the French crown in this period, wrote in an aside on the eve of the Colloquy of Worms: 'This year was memorable for extraordinary heat and drought, however the wine was excellent.'[37] Much heat and aridity was to be felt at the Colloquy, but we should not overlook the excellent wine, since behind the official meetings there was a fruitful understanding of the first importance through secret meetings between Bucer and Gropper which led to the production of articles of agreement on many of the chief subjects of controversy between the two sides. Granvelle, shrewd in judging men and situations, saw little use in holding public discussions upon subjects to be decided on publicly with consequent delays in manoeuvring for position amid mutual suspicion. He was aware that the Protestants were afraid that the Colloquies might be a cover behind which preparations were being made for war, since the attitude of the Bavarian dukes was well known, and Wauchope (a Scot, one of the four papal theologians at Worms) advocated in private that war was the only solution, a judgement in which he was certainly not alone at Rome.[38] Therefore Granvelle was all the more anxious to promote these private

---

[36] Calvin, *Opera*, V, 427.
> Eccius hesterno ruber atque inflatus Iaccho
> Praebeat huc duris terga subacta flagris.
> Huc caput indomitum subdat, verum ante recepta,
> Qua semper caruit, fronte Cochlaeus iners.
> Nausea verbosis generans fastidia libris
> Occluso tacitus iam ferat ore iugum.

[37] *The General History of the Reformation of the Church, written in Latin by John Sleidan, and faithfully Englished, by E. Bohun*, 1689, 269.

[38] Calvin, *Opera*, XI, col. 66. Calvin here claimed that the Pope had offered 300,000 ducats to promote war. Philip of Hesse, under the ban of the Empire for bigamy came to terms with the Emperor and gave up the military leadership of the Protestant forces. Max Lenz, ed., *Briefwechel Landgraf Philipps des Grossmüthigen von Hesse mit Bucer*. 3 vols. Leipzig, 1880–91, I, 283.

discussions, for fear that the Protestant leaders might return home, or be too suspicious to agree to anything. Bucer and Capito had to inform Jacob Sturm, the able diplomatist and head of the Strasbourg delegation at the Colloquy, of the possibility of private meetings with certain Catholics; the chancellor of Hesse, Feize, was also privately consulted. These two laymen were not attracted to the idea of secret meetings, since these would by-pass the public Colloquy, and they also feared that the Lutherans would be hostile to what would be produced because their representatives were not consulted; but after reflection they consented, since without the secret meetings there appeared to be no hope of progress.[39]

Veltwyk, an Imperial secretary and a Jewish convert to Catholicism was strongly attracted to Christian humanist studies. He was a friend of his fellow-Rhinelander Gropper and they held in common the Christian humanists' teachings on justification and original sin, and their emphasis on the centrality of Christ rather than on authoritarian legalism in the Church. Bucer had already met Gropper at the first Colloquy at Hagenau, and they found that they had many religious interests in common. During the wearying delays in November and December at Worms, Veltwyk, Gropper, Bucer and Capito found opportunities to talk together privately, and to discover how much ground they had in common, since all were influenced by the principles of Christian humanism, and none of them held the extremist views of, for example, Cochlaeus on the one side and Amsdorf on the other. Gropper had published his *Enchiridion Christianae Institutionis* in 1538: its very title was typical of the Christian humanist reform movement, *Enchiridion* and *Institutio* were Erasmian words, and the young Calvin, for example, had chosen the latter for his famous book first published in 1536. As late as 1533 Erasmus had written the *Liber sarciendi ecclesiae concordia* calling for mutual forbearance and understanding between Catholic and Protestant.[40] Gropper's book set out at some length his view of justification in which he hoped to reconcile the Protestant and Catholic positions. His interpretation resembles suggestions of Erasmus and is very close to the full statement of a similar development of justification in the writings of Contarini. Also

[39] Hastings Eells, 'The Origins of the Regensburg Book', *Princeton Theological Review*, XXVI, 1928, 359. This study was based on the materials in M. Lenz, op. cit., but should be used with caution.

[40] Matheson, op. cit., however, expresses this in less positive terms: 'Veltwyck impressed Bucer with his learning and he became convinced that . . . Gropper . . . was genuinely concerned with reforming the Church.' Matheson's views of the efforts of Bucer and Gropper and of their mutual theological sympathy are almost relentlessly negative.

Gropper had begun a reform in Cologne diocese on behalf of Archbishop Hermann von Wied, and he feared that this movement might collapse through extremist Catholic reaction, or through being taken over by extremist Lutheranism. Therefore he was anxious to find a compromise between the extremes of both parties. Bucer had similar ends in view, and he had much in common theologically with Gropper, but he saw, if Sturm had not made it clear to him, that Granvelle, on behalf of the Emperor, wished to gain political advantage from a Protestant-Catholic agreement.

Early in December, Veltwyk had urged Granvelle to see Bucer privately, and Bucer called on Granvelle at 6 a.m., by request, though he was happy to accept since he was always an aggressively early riser, and had to listen to a statement from him, characteristic in its pendulum swing between threats and assurances, concluding with the promise that no harm would come to Bucer and Capito by their sharing in a secret discussion with two Catholics, and that the public Colloquy would not be destroyed by these private meetings.[41] Bucer's deep and always sincere eirenical concern rose above this dubious presentation, and he agreed to bring Capito into a discussion with Gropper, not least because he was convinced by now that the public Colloquy would not prove to be fruitful. Whether Sturm had warned him, or whether he himself saw the danger of acting independently and secretly in discussion with Catholics, Bucer saw that he might bring on himself a disastrous and discreditable rejection by the Protestant leaders. Therefore, he urged the Landgrave Philip, with whom he had good relations, to provide him with a letter authorising him by name to undertake this secret discussion beginning on 15 December, and to date it 10 December. The Landgrave said it should include the provision that Bucer was not to commit himself to anything to the detriment of the Protestant states. It is typical of the atmosphere of unease and political tension at the Colloquies that the Landgrave in turn tried to get Granvelle to send him a letter so that he would not be thought of as acting independently of the Emperor, and clear himself too with the other Protestant leaders. At the same time Philip glumly reminded Bucer of the Scylla and Charybdis of Luther and the Pope.[42] What he had seen as a starting point might be running into trouble.[43]

The secret meetings took place on several occasions in the second half of December. After various statements made by the four

---

[41] Eells, 359.
[42] Ibid., 363.
[43] Lenz, op. cit., I, 309.

participants on doctrinal matters including justification, and on those aspects of discipline particularly emphasised by Bucer throughout his career, for example, a godly and hard-working priesthood, the purification of worship from superstition or inessential ceremonial, the revision of the liturgy, and the manner of dispensing the sacraments, Gropper drew up articles based on the theological issues which had been debated. Bucer proposed some modifications of this draft prepared by Gropper, and, at the request of the Landgrave Philip, translated the articles into German, upon which Philip suggested some slight changes and sent them to the Elector of Brandenburg, asking the Elector after he had considered them to obtain Luther's opinion of them. Luther disliked the articles as too much of a compromise and because they would fail to satisfy the Lutheran theologians at a number of points. Melanchthon said cryptically of the articles, '*Politia Platonis*', and it should be remembered that he had not been aware of the secret meetings at Worms where they were prepared.[44] The articles were then sent to Granvelle, who asked Gropper and some Catholic theologians to consider them, and after various emendations were made they were sent to the Emperor.[45]

The next stage after the transfer of the Colloquy from Worms to Regensburg was the bringing of pressure to bear on Rome by Granvelle for the Pope to send a cardinal legate with considerable authority to Regensburg. Contarini was mentioned among other names because he was highly regarded in Germany; and on 10 January 1541, the Pope appointed Contarini *legatus a latere* for Germany.[46] Meanwhile, Morone told the nuncio Campeggio sourly that he could advise Paul III, when he returned to Rome, that nothing would come of the proposed Colloquy at Regensburg; and the Bavarian dukes told Charles V that an attempt at reunion was a waste of time.[47] On 28 January the Pope sent instructions to Contarini in which full power to come to an agreement with the Protestants was not allowed, but which enabled him to sound the Protestant leaders to find what Catholic principles they had retained so that on this basis an understanding might be approached, for example, on the

---

[44] Kolde, *Regensburger Religionsgespräch*, 548.

[45] Granvelle cautiously presented the book to the Colloquy as the work of learned and deceased men in Belgium. Wilhelm van Gulik, *Johannes Gropper 1503–1559*, Freiburg im Breisgau, 1906, 70–71. (Cited in H. Mackensen, *The Diplomatic Role of Gasparo Cardinal Contarini at the Colloquy of Ratisbon of 1541*, Church History, 1958, 320 and n.) but Contarini quickly saw through this.

[46] Pastor, *History of the Popes*, XI, 421.

[47] Ibid., 425.

papal primacy, the seven sacraments, and the long-authorised
traditions of the Church – 'you know what they are' ('tibi nota esse
bene scimus'). This vagueness was deliberate, and if not helpful to
Contarini it was helpful to the Pope.[48]

Cardinal Contarini is a most attractive figure among the
participants at the Colloquy: he came to it sincerely to try to achieve
religious peace, and this was recognised by Melanchthon, Bucer and
other Protestants. Contarini had come near to Luther's position on
justification as early as 1511:[49] he believed that this was the heart of
the matter, and that once this could be decided favourably other
matters, such as papal authority and the sacraments, would fall into
line. His doctrine of justification, as Ranke showed long ago, does
not derive from the Cologne theologians, Pigghe and Gropper
(though this has not prevented writers from trying to establish that it
does); it came to him through those Pauline and Augustinian studies
in Italy which were prominent in the groups around Victoria
Colonna, the Valdes brothers, and the author of that seminal work
Beneficio di Cristo.[50] Contarini had written to his friend Giustiniani in
February 1523: 'I have truly come to the firm conclusion . . . that no
one can justify himself by his works . . . one must turn to the divine
grace which can be obtained through faith in Jesus Christ as St Paul
said . . . Wherefore I conclude that every living man is a thing of
vanity and that one must justify oneself through another's
righteousness, that is, through Christ's, and when one joins oneself to
Him his righteousness becomes ours, nor must we then depend upon
ourselves, even in the slightest degree.'[51] Again, in a treatise on
Penance, Contarini wrote: 'Since therefore the foundation of the
Lutheran edifice is true, we must say nothing against it but we must
accept it as true and Catholic, indeed as the foundation of the
Christian religion.'[52] He could write passages in which he reduces
man's righteousness to almost nothing, and in which the righteousness
of Christ is alone of value for salvation – passages which the
Inquisition suppressed in the Venetian edition of his works in 1584.
Nevertheless, he left open a possible merit of good works before God
as a general principle. With the presence of such a man at the

[48] Ibid., 429. For the written instructions of the Pope see Document 32 in Ranke, *Werke*, 37,
III.

[49] *Archiv für Reformationsgeschichte*, 51, I, H. Mackensen, 'Contarini's Theological Role at
Ratisbon in 1541', 50.

[50] Ranke, *Werke*, 37, I. 91, and n. 2, and Hans Rückert, *Die Theologische Entwicklung Casparo
Contarinis*, Bonn, 1926, 103.

[51] *Archiv für Reformationsgeschichte*, 51, I, Mackensen, 55.

[52] Ibid., 41.

Colloquy the prospect of understanding if not reunion had come closer than ever before.[53]

On 23 February the Emperor came to Regensburg more than ever anxious to find religious peace for the Empire in view of the mounting threat of the renewal of war by the Turks and because he was aware of the diplomatic moves by Francis I to create an alliance with the Lutheran princes directed against himself. Contarini did not arrive until over two weeks after the Emperor, whom he told that he would aid him with all his strength to achieve religious peace in Germany. Gradually the other members of the Diet gathered together, and on 5 April 1541, the Colloquy – which was held within the setting of the Imperial Diet – was opened in the presence of the Emperor. A declaration of the Emperor's purpose was read in which the need for religious unity was strongly emphasised; it was affirmed that the debate was to be commenced on a new basis (that is, not starting from the Augsburg Confession, or from prolonged procedural discussions); and it was made known that he himself would select the theologians from both sides who should debate those matters wherein the two parties chiefly differed. On 21 April he chose Melanchthon, Bucer, and Pistorius (a theologian from the Landgrave's Church of Hesse) to represent the Protestants, and Gropper (now bishop-elect of Naumburg), Pflug, a theologian of similar interests, and Eck. The original purpose had been to keep Eck out of the debate but, on instructions from Rome, Contarini and Morone insisted on his being one of the Catholic speakers. Earlier, in January 1541, Contarini had written to Eck, who it should not be forgotten was to be the spokesman for intransigent Bavaria, 'Verum, doctissimi Ecki, etiam in causa desperata non est omnino viro christiano desperandum, quem deceat credere in spem etiam contra spem.'[54] The presidents of the Colloquy were to be the Count Palatine, and Granvelle: there were also to be six observers present; among these were Burkhardt, Chancellor of Saxony, Feize, Chancellor of Hesse, and Sturm of Strasbourg. The balance between Catholic and Protestant authorities will be seen here. Sealed copies of the Articles, the *Regensburg Book*, as it came to be called later, but without title or other description, were presented to the debaters, and taken up again each evening. It is interesting to learn that Veltwyk introduced Bucer to Cardinal Contarini on the opening of the Colloquy, and that

---

[53] The theological insights on justification of Contarini are almost passed over by Matheson, whereas, as most writers are aware, it was of real significance at the Colloquy and led to serious danger for him at Rome. Mackensen, *Role of Contarini*, 334, n. 87.

[54] Fr. Dittrich, ed., *Registen und Briefe des Cardinals Contarini*, Brausberg, Haye, 1881, cited by Mackensen n. 87.

Contarini showed his zeal for reunion in the words: 'How great will be the fruit of unity, and how profound the gratitude of all mankind.' To which Bucer replied more explicitly: 'Both sides have failed. Some of us have overemphasised unimportant points, and others have not adequately reformed obvious abuses. With God's will we shall ultimately find the truth.'[55]

At this point it would be well to examine, though inevitably too briefly, the theological content of the *Regensburg Book*.[56] The first five articles deal with the great issues relating to the doctrine of grace: 1. 'De conditione hominis et ante lapsum naturae integritate'; 2. De libero arbitrio'; 3. 'De causa peccati'; 4. 'De originali peccato'; 5. 'De restitutione regenerationis et justificatione hominis gratia et merito, fide et operibus'. After alterations had been made when the form in which Article 5 was presented to the debaters was found unsuitable, the article as finally agreed retained the characteristic marks of the mediating doctrine of justification taught by Gropper and Contarini known since as double justification because of the polarity of the terms used – *iustitia imputata* and *iustitia inhaerens*.[57] Imputed justice is obtained by faith, not only conceived of in the sense of accepting and appropriating to oneself doctrinal truths, but also in the sense Luther had urged long before, trust in the promises of God. This justification by faith is seen as the beginning of an inherent justice, since the faith which justifies is also seen as faith effective through love (*per charitatem*). Therefore, the Christian man is 'just' in a twofold way: he is reputed to be just by faith and by grace, and is actually just through his doing the works of love. However, the state of being just *per charitatem* is by nature imperfect; since it is derived from man, it cannot be said that the certainty of salvation rests in any way upon it: rather assurance of salvation always rests on being justified by faith and grace, that is, on *iustitia Christi nobis donata*.[58] Nevertheless, God does not ignore the inherent justice of those who seek diligently to fulfil the law of love: they have their reward, but

---

[55] Karl Brandi, *The Emperor Charles V*, trans. C. V. Wedgwood, 1954, 447.

[56] The Articles were published by Melanchton and Bucer, and a French version was issued by Calvin. *Philippi Melanthonis opera quae supersunt omnia*, ed. E. G. Bretschneider, IV, 1836 ff.; Martin Bucer: *Acta Colloquii in comitiis imperii Ratisponae habiti hoc est articuli de religione conciliati, et non conciliati omnes ut ab Imperatore Ordinibus Imperii ad iudicandum, et deliberandum propositi sunt.* Strasbourg 1541. Robert Stupperich, *Der Ursprung des 'Regensburger Buche' von 1541 und seine Rechtfertigungstlehre.* ARG, 1939, 88–116 is thorough.

[57] *Melanthonis opera*, IV, col. 200: 'Iustitiam, quae est in Christo, sibi gratis imputari, et quae simul pollicitationem Spiritus Sancti et charitatem accipit . . . Etsi autem is, qui iustificatur, iustitiam accipit et habet per Christum, etiam inhaerentem . . .'

[58] Ibid., col. 200: 'sed soli iustitiae Christi nobis donatae, sine qua omnino nulla est nec esse potest iustitia'.

the concept of *meritum* is not mentioned, and the dubious consequences of merit-theology which Luther had so passionately attacked are intended to be ruled out. Even the phrase which is the touchstone of Lutheran orthodoxy is commended, 'sola fide iustificamur', provided that penitence and the desire to fulfil the works of love are closely associated with it.[59]

There lie behind this concept of double justification ideas expressed by Gropper in his *Enchiridion* of 1538, which Contarini had learned from his own experience and reflection in Italy after 1511 and which the *Loci* of Melanchthon of 1533 had also set forth. Gropper began from a position originally conceived of as opposing a Protestant error, when he insisted that justification must represent an inner reality, but he challenged that weakness in contemporary Catholic theology which Luther had challenged (in his doctrine of the enslaved will and in his assertion that the whole initiative of justifying grace lay in God alone) when he wrote of the distinction between the justice of man and the justice of God, from which he deduced that none of our acts can effectively be the cause of our justification. He affirmed as strongly as Luther that all our trust must rest on Christ. Faith justifies only because it makes us able to receive divine mercy. It turns us to God, and then calls us to follow good. So the efficient cause of our salvation is God alone, and the formal cause is his own grace which renews our hearts. The instrumental cause is faith in Christ, and the justification thus brought to us fills our hearts with love which we fulfil in works. These works are imperfect, but they become acceptable to God because of Christ in whom they are performed. It is characteristic of Gropper's position to affirm that our acts are only *causae dispositivae et susceptivae*. At this point it will suffice to add that Contarini agreed with the doctrine of double justification, and his position on this can be summed up thus, 'nos iustificari fide efficaci per charitatem'.[60]

Articles 6 to 9 deal with the Church and how it is to be recognised; article 6, 'De Ecclesia, et illius signis ac autoritate', begins with the definition: 'The Church is the assembly or congregation of men of all places, and of all times, who are called in the communion of the

---

[59] Ibid., col. 201, in the last paragraph of Article 5.

[60] *Archiv für Reformationsgeschichte*, 1960, 51, I, H. Mackensen, 'Contarini's Theological Role at Ratisbon in 1541', provides an analysis of Contarini's views on Justification. For a brief account of the views of Gropper on justification see W. van Gulik, op. cit., 50 ff. Gulik cites the *Enchiridion* of Gropper, fol. 167b, 'Ob id tandum dicimus, fidem iustificare, non quia sit causa iustificationis, sed quia nulla alia re misericordiam et gratiam Dei . . . accipiamus'; fol. 171b, 'Constat enim in universum, operibus nostri causam iustificationis detrahi et recte ac vere dici nos sine operibus iustificari.' For the *causae* of justification see Gulik's citations from Gropper's *Antididagma*, fol. 13b, and his *Enchiridion*, fol. 129b; Gulik, 54.

profession of the one same faith, doctrine and sacraments, according to the Catholic, true and Apostolic doctrine.' Article 7, 'De nota verbi', describes the first 'nota' or mark of the Church, the Word of God, though it does not set forth how this is to be developed, and adds that the true Church has the anointing of the Spirit which instructs us in all things. Article 8, 'De poenitentia post lapsum', which demonstrates that in this Catholic Church alone is there remission of sins, given to the penitent not only at baptism but also afterwards. Article 9, 'De autoritate Ecclesiae in discernanda et interpretanda Scriptura', in which it is asserted that the Church has the right to judge the Scriptures, and to discern what is canonical Scripture from what is not. Against this Article the Protestant collocutors were to present a criticism in writing closer to their view of the subject at the time it was debated. Article 10, 'De Sacramentis', is a very brief statement on the sacraments in general, declaring that they are effective visible signs of the invisible grace of God – the Word is joined to the element to make the sacrament. Articles 11 to 17 take the Seven Sacraments in turn. Article 11 on the Sacrament of Order shows that Order is essential to prevent uncertainty on doctrine, and seven Orders are named. The element of this Sacrament is the imposition of hands by a bishop. Article 12, on Baptism, where the anxious mind is assured that Baptism conveys justification (Gal. 3:27), and our baptism is to be remembered and exercised during the whole of our lives. Article 14 on the Eucharist contains these words, 'post consecrationem, verum corpus et verus sanguis domini, vere et substantialiter adsint, et fidelibus sub specie panis et vini' and in the original form they were followed immediately by the words, 'distribuuntur, qui habet in hunc modum. Accipite et manducati . . . Bibite'. Even Morone could accept this *communio sub utraque*. But Eck in his later refutation in his *Apologia . . . adversus mucores et calumnias Buceri super actis comitiorum Ratisponae*, Ingolstadt, 1542, f. 27. v, attacked this concept of sacrifice as *Gottesfrevel* (impietas).[61] But the following words were inserted between the two passages cited, probably by Contarini, or at his instigation, after the Worms text was prepared and prior to the debate at Regensburg: 'illis nimirum, hoc est, pane et vino in corpus et sanguinem transmutatis et transubstantiatis' – words which occasioned a sharp reaction from the Protestants. Melanchthon added in the margin against these words in his published edition of the Articles: 'Hic collocutores protestantium exhibuerunt suum scriptum signatum B.' Calvin himself was to intervene in the debate at this point: 'Me quoque exponere latine

---

[61] E. Iserloh, *Die Eucharistie in der Darstellung des Joh. Eck*, Munster, 1950, 352–9.

oportuit quid sentirem . . . libere tamen sine timore offensionis, illam localem praesentiam damnavi: adorationem asserui mihi esse intolerabilem.' Further, alongside of Article 15, the Sacrament of Penance, the Protestants were to present at the debate two writings giving their point of view. Article 18, 'De vinculo caritatis, quae est tertia Ecclesiae nota', represents the third sign of the presence of the Church after the Word and Sacraments set forth in Articles 7 and 10. Article 19, 'De Ecclesiae hierarchico ordine et in constituenda politia autoritate', shows that hierarchical order was also reckoned a note of the Church. Alongside of this Article the Protestants were to present during the debate at Regensburg a statement on the unity of the Church, in which they do not oppose episcopacy but outline its duties while rejecting idle and ignorant prelates, and they grant primacy to the Roman see but not a final authority of jurisdiction to it. Article 20, 'Dogmata quaedam quae ecclesiae autoritate declarata, firmata sunt', discusses such matters as invocation of saints (alongside of which the Protestants were to present a writing during the debate giving their view on this matter), relics, images and prayers for the dead. Article 21, 'De usu et administratione sacramentorum, et ceremoniis quibusdam speciatim', is on the ceremonial of the Mass and associated themes. Once again the Protestants were to present a writing here on the sacrifice of the Mass, insisting that the sacrifice was offered by Christ Himself to the Father, and opposing the association of merit with it and the conception of it as an offering for the dead as well as the living. Further, they added another writing objecting to the concept of private Masses. Article 22, 'De disciplina ecclesiastica', relates to celibacy, the condemnation of priestly concubinage, and reforms among monks. The last Article, 23, 'De disciplina populi', is on excommunication, public penance, and fasting.

Eck, well prepared on the Augsburg Confession since 1530, wished rather to discuss that document, and, as Morone noted, 'sought to assume a sort of sovereign and judicial authority in the deliberations and showed himself, to the disapproval of all men, more than necessarily contentious'.[62] But he was overruled, and had to accept as the basis of debate the secretly prepared articles of Worms handed to him with the other debaters under seal. As a further check on Eck, and also to maintain a united Catholic viewpoint, Gropper, Pflug and Eck met with Contarini every morning to discuss the subjects to be debated. The debates began on 27 April and lasted for a month. Contarini soon found that Eck needed careful handling, and at one

---

[62] Pastor, *History of the Popes*, 439.

stage he began to think that Eck, true to his old approach at Leipzig in 1519, brought forward much too early and too aggressively the highly divisive topic of papal authority and supremacy, and was trying to wreck the Colloquy. The first four Articles were soon accepted – agreement had already been reached on original sin at Worms – but the fifth Article on justification, which was much longer, was unacceptable because it was thought by both sides to be imprecise. An attempt was made to revise the Article, in which Contarini himself took part. Then, on 2 May, agreement was at last reached, through a reformulation by Gropper and Melanchthon, on this hitherto most divisive subject and which led to the astonishing hope that after all agreement could be possible between the two sides. Contarini had taken a vital part in this achievement, and the Article formulated showed close affinities with his own thought. Calvin was deeply impressed that 'the adversaries' had agreed to this statement in which nothing is present, he wrote, which cannot be found in 'our writings', and concluded that 'this was a considerable achievement'.[63]

One of the most enthusiastic responses to Contarini's success over Article 5, which he himself described joyfully as miraculous, was that of his friend Cardinal Pole: 'When I observed this union of opinion I felt a delight such as no harmony of sounds could have inspired me with; not only because I see the approach of peace and concord, but because these Articles [that is, 1 to 5] are the foundation of the whole Christian faith.'[64] The reaction of Francis I, however, was predictably furious indignation in which he denounced the agreement to the papal nuncios in France, and wrote to the Protestant princes to dissuade them from supporting it: 'The advice of other princes [that is, from outside of Germany] should have been invited.'[65] Many of the German Catholic princes did not even attend the Diet, and an anonymous and indignant German wrote to the Pope about the Emperor, 'Nihil ordinabatur pro robore ecclesiae, quid timetur illi displicere.'[66] That the Colloquy was in danger was not yet immediately evident. There seems to have been little dispute on the Articles on the sacraments until Article 14, 'De sacramento eucharistiae', when the Protestants led by Melanchthon challenged the concept of transubstantiation and the veneration of the reserved sacrament. Contarini, who was not as well informed as he had

[63] A. L. Herminjard, ed., *Correspondance des réformateurs dans les pays de la langue française*, Geneva, 1886, VII, 111.

[64] Ranke, *Werke*, 37, I, 107, citing Quirini, *Epistolae Reginaldi Poli*, t. III, 25.

[65] Ranke, *Werke*, 37, I, 109 and n. 1, citing Quirini, *Epistolae Reginaldi Poli*, t. III, ep. CCLV.

[66] Ranke, *Werke*, 37, I, 110, n. 2, citing Rainaldus.

thought on Protestantism, had not expected this, and was astonished and hurt. It was difficult if not impossible for Catholics, in the temper of the time, to reject the declared dogma of the Fourth Lateran Council, however much the Protestants argued that Councils of the Church could and would err. Granvelle, however, was surprised at Contarini's indignation, since for him transubstantiation was 'una cosa sottile e pertinente solo alli dotti, non toccata al popolo'[67] – for Jedin this is characteristic of the weak and betraying Erasmianism of the Imperial Chancellor. The Emperor would have been willing to be content with a declaration that Christ is really and truly present in the Eucharist, and to leave discussion of so Scholastic a point as transubstantiation for a General Council to decide. There is no effective support for the view that the Emperor held to a purely political stance and intended war from the beginning notwithstanding that Hastings Eels thought otherwise in his *The Failure of Church Unification Efforts during the German Reformation*, (ARG, 1951).

The Colloquy had now begun to drift back into the old antagonisms. The Protestants refused to accept the necessity of Penance, though they were willing to allow its practice. Even so, Bucer and Melanchthon (since Eck was ill and absent, Pistorius withdrew) accepted a Papal primacy – though not of jurisdiction – and debated amicably enough the Canon of the Mass, private Masses, and communion in both kinds. By the end of May, Granvelle sensed that matters were reaching an impasse and he began to bring pressure on the Pope to call a General Council, and the Pope replied in June that he could tell the Emperor that a Council would be convened, since the Colloquy had broken down and no other solution remained. For all his great efforts Contarini, when he left Regensburg on 29 July, had won nothing of lasting value and he returned to Italy under the stigma of having turned Lutheran. His part in the final revision and acceptance of Article 5 on justification left him under the grave suspicion of having betrayed Catholic truth, and the last year of his life brought bitter difficulties for him in Italy, where the Inquisition was already attacking his friends and where the defence of his position at Regensburg in his last writing, *Epistola de iustificatione*, was received with hostility.

Contarini met the attacks on him with silent dignity, but the other participants in the Colloquy who were politically more vulnerable than a cardinal almost immediately began to publish explanations of their position at the Colloquy. The meeting of the Diet had barely closed before Eck was denouncing the *Regensburg Book*, as it was now being called, saying that he had not seen it beforehand, that its articles represented the views of Lutherans, that the Book was unacceptable to Catholics and that it 'Melanchthonised'.[68] Bucer published at Strasbourg promptly in 1541 the whole Book with the judgements as presented to the Diet by the Protestant and Catholic princes and cities, in which he inserted a short paragraph containing the reported view of Eck and his own comment, to which Bucer added appended material in evidence.[69] This was a letter written by Pflug and Gropper in more graceful Latinity than Bucer's own complicated sentences usually attained, in which they indignantly reject Eck's report to 'Illustrissimi Principes Bavari' that he wished to have nothing to do with the Book.[70] They go on to show that Eck had shared with them in the discussions and the judgements arrived at together, and that they had acted with integrity throughout. One consequence of the secret preparation of the *Regensburg Book* at Worms was that doubt could be cast on its authenticity, and on who had prepared it and with what intentions. Bucer was indignant when Melanchthon began to spread the rumour that Bucer had written it, and Bucer said somewhat disingenuously that he knew of the preparation of it, but had only discussed it with its authors Gropper and Veltwyk and not written it. Melanchthon conceded he had made a mistake, and privately wrote later that Gropper had prepared it.[71] It is obvious that because the Colloquy had failed to achieve agreement, and because a vigorous opposition from Luther, the Pope, the Bavarian princes, Francis I and others had appeared, the participants tried to dissociate themselves from the probable consequences of condemnation or at least loss of prestige. Eck began this process of Pilate-like repudiation, but the effect of Bucer's account of the proceedings and that of Melanchthon was to make the Protestants' position at Regensburg seem more positively Protestant than it was in fact. Eck followed up in 1542 with a little book in which he denounced what he called the calumnies of Bucer and offered a defence of Contarini as upholding the Church

[68] 'Neque placuit, neque placet, liber iste insulsus, neque placebit quo tot errores et vitia deprehendi: unde iudico, sicut semper iudicavi, eum a Catholicis nō recipiendū, qui relicto nō loquendi ecclesiae et patrū, Melanchthonizat.'

[69] 'Quā vane et impudenter haec Eccius scripserit, cognosces pie lector, ex supplicatione subiecta in qua nihil illi quod nō ita se habet, commemorarunt.' *Acta Colloquii in Comites Imperii Ratisponae habiti*, Strasbourg, 1541.

[70] 'haec febricitans [Eck had recently recovered from the fever which had prevented him debating for a time at Regensburg] forsan impetu magis animi quam certo iudicio effuderit, comperimus tamen illum, hac sua suggestione evicisse . . . ad sic, ut ille vellet sentiendum sint [the princes and others] persuasi, et non persuasi tantum quod ad se attinet, sed etiam huc adducti, ut Caesariae quoque Maiestati haec quae Eccius effutivit, quam maxime approbata velint.'

[71] *Melanthonis opera*, V, 88.

and papal authority.[72] Eck claimed that while Bucer considered the Articles to be reconciling and capable of being accepted by the Catholic princes, in fact the two Catholic debaters in the absence of Eck (he apparently wished to make it seem that he had hardly been more than present for a time, and then as a defender of Catholic truth against Protestant heresies) were 'non magni nominis in theologia', and yet, he wrote, all the 'Catholic Princes and Bishops were to cede to them!'.[73] In this climate of inglorious exculpation the impact of the Regensburg Book achieved little.

The more moderate or central group of princes, for example Brandenburg and Cologne, were willing to accept the Book at the end of the Colloquy, but the 'war party' headed by Bavaria opposed this. In the event the more extreme Catholic and Protestant positions won the day, since neither was prepared to compromise themselves by accepting the Book after the Colloquy had broken up. Contarini told the Emperor in July that he could not speak for the Pope, for the Book had to be judged by Paul III. On returning to Rome he tried to find a compromise whereby both sides could obtain a mutual toleration and find therein a better understanding, but the Curia rejected this outright – its mind could not grasp so eirenical a viewpoint. However, before leaving for Rome Contarini achieved the unique record of convoking the whole of the German episcopate before him and giving them a thorough dressing-down on their personal shortcomings and the need for effective reforms of abuses in their dioceses – this formal admonition of the legate sufficiently impressed the Emperor, if not the bishops, for he obtained a copy and sent it to the Estates of the Diet.

For Jedin the failure of the Regensburg attempt at reunion could justify the drawing of the Tridentine line of demarcation.[74] But that Tridentine line for many today would seem to have resembled the Berlin Wall, an aggressive rejection of the possibility of union with the probability of death for infringement of it, even if it could be accepted that the failure of Regensburg necessarily demanded Tridentinism. Certainly the Emperor, and many others of Catholic mind, did not envisage that development but hoped for a Council which could approach the issues in the spirit represented by the

---

[72] *Apologia pro reverendis et illustris Principibus Catholics, ac aliis ordinibus Imperii adversus mucores et calumnias Buceri, super actis Comicorum Ratisponae. Apologia pro Reverendiss. se ap. Legato et Cardinale, Caspare Contareno. Iohan. Eckio Authore.* Cologne 1542. In the preface Eck accused Bucer of slandering the Catholic princes and Contarini in his account of the proceedings at Regensburg.

[73] Ibid., sig. B (the book is unpaginated).

[74] Jedin, *History of the Council of Trent*, 408–9.

Book. For Jedin, again, the rupture at Regensburg was caused essentially by 'the irreconcilable opposition of contradictory doctrines'.[75] In the light of what Gropper and Bucer sought to achieve and came near to achieving, this judgement is unduly harsh. Further, Tridentinism was not the only possible Catholic response, if theology alone was in question. But this was precisely the intolerable complexity of the problem: it was not theology alone, it was political intransigence that proved to be so harmful. The Bavarian dukes, Francis I, the Papacy in its political aspect, the Catholic League, the Schmalkaldic League, the Elector of Saxony, and after these the varying gradations of political colouring, used the Colloquies like the night battle at Jutland for manoeuvres and counter-manoeuvres. In those troubled waters the ark which Gropper and Bucer launched sank almost without trace. Some today might consider an attempt to raise it again to be a tiresome archaeological enterprise, on the ground that a new society like our own needs new theological methods. But Christianity is most intimately associated with the idea of the Church, and the Church is an historical reality. From that basis attempts at a better understanding between 'Catholic' and 'Protestant' might well find a starting-point in the themes which lay behind the *Regensburg Book*. We can derive hope from the decision, after the meeting in 1980 of Pope John Paul II with Protestants at Mainz, to seek ecumenical co-operation which led to the establishment of a Joint Ecumenical Commission in 1982. This resolved to call upon an Ecumenical Study Group of Protestant and Catholic theologians to examine and overcome the mutual doctrinal condemnation that occurred in effect after the failure at Regensburg.[76]

[75] Ibid., 409.
[76] An example of better understanding, among others, is George Yule, ed., *Luther: Theologian for Catholics and Protestants*, Edinburgh, 1985.

6

John a Lasco: The Humanist Turned Protestant, 1499–1560

R. W. Dixon, in what is still a stimulating as well as full account of the English Reformation, in a paragraph characteristic of his Pre-Raphaelite style, grasp of essentials and personal predilections wrote of Laski, that he was:

> ... a man of the most illustrious family, the nephew of an archbishop and legate, the brother of two of the most brilliant nobles of the age, of whom the one was the kingmaker of Hungary, the other the familiar of the gallant king Francis of France; himself a bishop, [sic], the friend and patron of Erasmus, had relinquished his career, left his country, married his wife, and settled himself in a more occidental territory, where a reforming count gave him the title of Superintendent of all the churches, ten years before the reign of the Josiah of England. The fury of his reformations, for Laski became the reformer of East Friesland, swept away every trace of the old system in his adopted country: the confession of faith which he published, was so low in doctrine that it aroused the indignation of the Lutheran divines: but whilst he engaged in the bitterest controversy with them, the imitator of Zwingli held himself aloof from the Anabaptist sectaries, with whom he might have been believed to have had the most in common.

The power of his enemies and the call of Cranmer reduced on the one hand his general superintendency to a single congregation, and opened on the other the prospect of a new settlement in England. The intercourse of six months convinced him of the facility of the English Primate: he made his terms, imposed his conditions, retired, and returned with his congregation at his back. In another strange land he resumed the title of Superintendent and extended his jurisdiction over several congregations. The Alascans, as his followers were sometimes called, filled St Katherine's and Southwark, and transmitted his name: but the influence of Laski was wider still. He instigated Hooper and defied Ridley. He resumed against Bucer, on the question of the habits, his former differences with the Lutherans. He ridiculed with impunity the ceremonies and order of the Church of the land that harboured him. He exhibited before the nation, and not without effect, a foreign model of worship, by publishing in Latin the forms of prayer that he used in Dutch. As for his congregations, they were troublesome from the first: their intestine commotions required at times the attention of the Council, and may perhaps, in some interval of languor, merit that of the reader.[1]

This suggests that Laski deserves more attention than the incidental references given to him in histories of the Reformation by writers in English. This essay, therefore, attempts to set down the main periods of Laski's life and his central aims as a Reformer, not to urge approval of his career but to draw attention to it, and to his writings, since they show an unusual pattern in the early development of Protestantism.

The Polish historian Bartel challenged the view held not only by Dixon and others but by Laski's contemporaries, that Laski was a man of most illustrious family.[2] He argued from a careful genealogical account of Laski's family origins that it was not of the high nobility of Poland. He showed rather that the Laskis came from Kalisz, a branch of the not very significant Krowicki family, and that they were small landowners in the still feudal organisation of Polish society where Jan was born in the castle of Lask in 1499. In this otherwise unremarkable family appeared an onset of new power and ambition with intellectual energy in Jan Laski (1456–1531) the uncle of the Reformer, who became a priest, then secretary to the chancellor of Poland.[3] He represented Poland on several missions abroad in which he showed marked diplomatic skill; he was appointed royal secretary in 1502; in 1503 chancellor of Poland, and finally in 1512 after other

[1] R. W. Dixon, *A History of the Church of England from the Abolition of the Roman Jurisdiction*, vol. III, 234–6.
[2] O. Bartel, *Towarzystwo Badan Dziejow Reformacii W Polsce, Jan Laski*: (Zesc I, 1499–1556), Warsaw, 1955, ch. II, especially 23–30.
[3] *Polski Stownik Biograficzny* (Article on Jan Laski 1456–1531), Tom. XVIII/2, Zeszyt 77, 229–37.

ecclesiastical promotions, he was made Archbishop of Gniezno (Gnesen) and Primate of Poland. His brother Jaroslav had three sons all as intellectually alert as their uncle the Primate. All three were influential outside of Poland, Jaroslav (Jerome) the eldest who developed his uncle's diplomatic skills in France, Hungary and Turkey; Jan who became a priest and rose quickly in preferments through his uncle's aid until he chose first Erasmianism and then Protestantism, working abroad until his final few years spent in Poland; and Stanislas who became a minor diplomat.[4] It was to his uncle, and to a less degree to his elder brother, that Jan owed the great respect with which he was received abroad. It was his uncle's status that gave him immediate acceptance, first in Erasmian circles, and later among Reformers. A note made by Heinrich Bullinger of Zürich on the back of the first letter he received from Jan in 1544, shows how impressed Bullinger was by the connections of this new correspondent: 'Joannes a Lasco a most noble baron of Poland, formerly dean of Gnesen, intimate friend of Erasmus of Rotterdam, ambassador of the king of Poland – whose relative, also called John a Lasco, was Archbishop of Gnesen.'[5] That fanfare of titles and names of honour sounded out before Jan Laski in Switzerland, Hungary, France, Frisia and England, without them he might well have achieved less than he did – to be his uncle's nephew was almost a career in itself. Moreover interest in Jan Laski the Reformer should not lead to ignoring Jan Laski the politician and diplomat of the years 1528–36 when he followed his brother Jaroslav's various missions and political schemes.

When Jan was about ten years old he and his brothers left their home to live with their distinguished uncle at Cracow to pursue their education there privately under tutors in the environment of the humanist learning which flourished at Cracow, mingling with nobles, statesmen, courtiers and learned men who visited their uncle who was himself a statesman and ambassador as well as Primate.[6] The uncle had seen the advantages of humanist studies during his own travels, and would have known them during his period as canon of Cracow where Conrad Celtis the German humanist had founded the *Sodalitas Litteraria Vistulana*. In 1513 the Archbishop was sent by King Sigismund I to the Lateran Council at Rome where he represented

[4] H. Zeissberg, *Joh. Laski, Erzbischof von Gnesen und sein Testament*, Vienna, 1884. A. Hirschberg, *Hieronim Laski*, Lwow, 1888.

[5] A. Kuyper, *Joannis a Lasco opera tam edita quam inedita*, 2 vols., Amsterdam, 1860. Vol. II, 569.

[6] *The Polish Review*, New York, 1965, Konstantin Zantuan, *Erasmus and the Cracow Humanists*.

the king's cause against the Order of Teutonic Knights, and he was accompanied there by his nephews. Dalton, who wrote the most comprehensive life of Jan Laski, assumes that the youths would attend the newly founded College for Greek studies on the Esquiline Hill to which the pope sought to attract pupils, but this is no more than a possibility:[7] certainty about their studies is found in the letter, 1514, to the Archbishop from their tutor Jan Braniczki who had been required to take them to the University of Bologna, and who describes the young Jan as possessing *summa virtus*, 'never have I seen a boy like him, may he live long.'[8] Again from this period at Bologna there is a letter from Jaroslav the elder brother who writes of Jan that one is compelled to admire, 'the perseverance and gravity with which the youth is inspired, all are filled with respect and reverence for him (*eum omnes facile timemus et veneramur*).'[9] That Jan and his brother Jaroslav should study at the most famous law school of Italy would be important to the Archbishop who was himself the first to gather and publish the laws of Poland. In 1517 the Archbishop was irritated because Jan had left the University of Bologna without informing his uncle where he had gone, and in 1518 Jan was excommunicated at Rome because a cousin there had used his name on a bill and failed to honour it – the nephew of such an uncle must have been thought good for any credit.[10]

Meanwhile the Archbishop was active in preparing Jan for a career in the Church; he caused him to be made canon at the collegiate Church at Leczyca, coadjutor to the Dean of Gniezno, canon of Cracow and of Plock. In his will the Archbishop stated the sum of gold which had been required for distribution among officials at Rome to endorse these preferments of one under canonical age.[11] In 1521 Jan was ordained priest and promoted from being coadjutor at Gniezno to being dean there. Jaroslav had already commenced his diplomatic career in 1514 and, having become involved with Bishop Tomiczki's attempt to bring Erasmus to the University of Cracow in 1524 (internal troubles were endangering its future), he took Jan with

---

[7] Hermann Dalton, *John a Lasco: his earlier life and labours.* (Trans. M. J. Evans, 1886, first part of *Johannes a Lasco*, Gotha, 1881), 57.

[8] Dalton, 63.

[9] Dalton, 64. 'I became a new man on meeting him. He has augmented the stores of his mind, and his knowledge, which he has shown in discourse of prose and verse, and that far beyond the measure of other young men, during his sojourn in Germany.'

[10] Dalton, 78. The excommunication was just a police measure for the 670 gulden concerned. Jan knew nothing of his cousin's (Martin Rambiewski) act. The Archbishop paid, writing, 'Many clergy of high position have incurred this punishment without the victims being bad men.' *Acta Tomician*, VI, 8.

[11] Archbishop Laski's will, 1517, 'my marshal knows the order of distribution', Dalton, 65.

him on this mission to Basel.[12] The Cracow humanists disliked
Luther's writings and royal edicts had been issued against the heresy
of Wittenberg. Jaroslav took with him to Basel the hostile *Encomia
Lutheri* of the Cracow humanist Krzycki to test the attitude of
Erasmus to Luther, to discover if he were still orthodox, since Basel
contained many Protestant scholars, and to report to Tomiczki on
Erasmus's suitability for Cracow.[13] The brothers Laski arrived in the
spring of 1524. Erasmus described the visit of Jaroslav to his house in
a letter to Botzheim (*Catalogus Erasmi Lucubrationum*) showing that
Jaroslav tried to remove by stealth a letter from Luther to Erasmus
which was lying on a table, but being forestalled by Erasmus, he said
that the king of Poland was hostile to Luther's writings. Erasmus
gave a guarded reply – but this did not mean that he was indifferent
to Poland for he wrote at this time to Archbishop Warham, *Polonia
mea est*.[14] Jaroslav departed apparently satisfied since he gave Erasmus
a splendid silver vase.[15] The purpose behind his brother's visit was to
have its effect on Jan, which was to be reinforced later at Basel this
same year, for he was to show a lifelong distaste for Luther's theology,
and acquired from the writings of Erasmus some themes which
formed an undercurrent to his own future writings. Jan accompanied
Jaroslav to Paris who conducted secret diplomacy at the court of
Francis I. Jan moved freely in these court circles and may have met
there Lefèvre d'Étaples, one of the reforming Catholic group the
'men of Meaux', to whom he referred in a later work as if through
personal knowledge.[16]

After a brief visit to Poland Jan returned eagerly to Basel in
February 1525 and stayed for some months in the home of Erasmus.
With Polish generosity and love of the fine gesture he spent lavishly
and made generous gifts. Since Jan seems to have paid for the whole
of the cuisine of the house as well as for his own room, Erasmus,
whose penurious beginnings left their mark, must have been delighted
to have become a guest in his own house. When he departed Jan left,
as generous tokens of his style of living, a silver fork, two square
plates of silver, and a golden flask. But his supreme gesture at Basel

[12] Piotr Tomicki, Bishop of Cracow and vice-chancellor. Erasmus sent him his edition of the
works of Seneca.
[13] Andrzej Krzycki, *Encomia Lutheri*, Cracow, 1524 (The American *National Union Catalog*
rightly puts a warning '!' after *Encomia*.) Zantuan, *The Polish Review*, 21 ff. For Erasmus and
the Poles: Maria Cytowska, *Korrespondencia Erazma z Rotterdamu z Polakami*, Warszawa, 1965.
[14] *Opus Epistolarum Des. Erasmi Roterodami*, ed. P. S. Allen, V, 535. Also IX, 339; VI, 325.
[15] Allen, I, 32. On Luther's letter: Erasmus smiling said '. . . hic furtum aliquid. Arrisit ille
. . .' Jaroslav 'deposito in mensam vasculo argenteo'.
[16] *Opera*, I, 53. '. . . vir et pietate et eruditione insignis Jacobus Faber Stapulensis'. This is the
only name he comments on among several scholars cited.

was to purchase the library of Erasmus. It was not that Jan had no other books in view, for a beautifully bound edition of Erasmus' *Adagia* with the Laski arms of nobility exists, on the title page of which he was written '*Johannis a Lasco et amicorum est.*' The agreement for this library was drawn up on 20 June 1525 and stated that Erasmus had sold his library to 'the illustrious Polish Baron Jan Laski' for four hundred gulden, provided that Erasmus could have the use of it while he lived and thereafter it would belong to Laski and his heirs; an inventory of all the books would be provided for the purchaser; all books which were added should be purchased later; but the expensive manuscripts would be reserved for further discussion. Laski paid two hundred gulden and received a copy of the inventory.[17] Unfortunately, both Jan and Jaroslav lost considerable sums in the ensuing years in support of Jaroslav's political ambitions in Hungary, and this delayed further payment. After Erasmus' death in 1536 his executor the jurisconsult Bonifacius Amerbach wrote to Jan Laski that since Erasmus' own works had been added to the collection a further one hundred gulden were required. The sum owing raised with difficulty, was paid by Laski's emissary and eventually the books arrived in Cracow in April, 1539 where Laski signed the receipt.[18]

Erasmus was delighted by the society of so distinguished and generous a guest, and wrote of him in the highest praise more than once: 'While a man of no ordinary learning he is in his life as spotlessly pure as fresh-fallen snow; he is kindly and amiable, so that everyone begins to live again in his company, and all have a sense of loss at his departure; he has a golden disposition, he is a true pearl, and so unassuming and free from arrogance, although he is called some day to fill one of the highest offices in his native land.'[19] Erasmus must have hoped for much from Laski's future in Poland for he referred to him in print in the dedication to a nobleman at Cracow as one whose integrity of character showed that, 'Astraea in flying from the earth had left the last traces of her stay here, among the Polish people.'[20] To the Archbishop Erasmus had also written, 'I cannot hesitate to confess that I, an old man, became better in the company of this young man. . . . O race born for piety!'[21] Years later

[17] Zantuan, *The Polish Review*, 27. H. Dalton, *Lasciana*, Berlin, 1898, 97.
[18] K. Miaskowski, Pięć Listów A. F. Modrzewskiego, 512 (cited in Zantuan, *The Polish Review*).
[19] Allen, VI, 186, 188. Karl Utenhove (half-brother of John who was to be a refugee in England, where he became a friend of Bishop Hooper and supporter of Laski in London and later) from Ghent lodged with Erasmus at this time, but Laski was prodigal with his money.
[20] Allen, VI, 138.
[21] Allen, VII, 120.

in 1544 Laski wrote to Conrad Pellikan from Emden, whom he had known long before on his visit to Basel, where Pellikan had already established himself as a biblical humanist, not least as a hebraist, that he could never remember without great joy in his heart the fellowship they had together at Basel, and adds to this the names of Oecolampadius and Erasmus. It was under Pellikan (whom he was to describe in 1544 as, *veterem amicum meum adeaque Praeceptorem*) that Jan had begun to learn Hebrew, though he wrote at a later date how the pressures on him in later life had prevented him from continuing that study.[22]

Probably this period he spent at Basel was the happiest of his life; he was young, rich, and his mind was opened to the splendour of biblical humanist studies in one of the great centres of such studies at that time. Here he made friendships which were a powerful stimulus at his most impressionable period in seeking new ways of intellectual development. It was at Basel that he came to know Erasmus's publisher Froben and the humanist lawyer Bonifacius Amerbach, and to Oecolampadius the Reformer at Basel he owed a special debt, for traces of the writings of Oecolampadius can be found in Laski's own works. Also at Basel he became a close friend of Beatus Rhenanus, who was one of the printer Froben's efficient collaborators and who was to edit Erasmus' works. Rhenanus later dedicated a small work to Laski stating that he was not seeking a gift from a rich patron but remembering thankfully their fellowship together at Basel and his deep affection for him.[23] With Glarean, a future editor of Livy and intimate of the Erasmian circle at Basel, Laski had also formed a close friendship and for some years after his stay in Basel Laski was still receiving accounts from Glarean of his researches in ancient music and arithmetic, and the interpretation of Livy. Glarean wrote a dedication to Laski in a work on ancient geography published in 1530 in which he described him as, 'the principal honour not only of his family but of all the kingdom of Poland'. He added that there were three reasons for a dedication to Laski which were that 'the great Erasmus' gave to him the advice to do so, that Laski had deserved it, and that young men won by Laski's example would give themselves up to this learning more readily since so young and so noble a man followed it so zealously and had become so proficient in it.[24]

[22] *Opera*, II, 583.

[23] Beatus Rhenanus cited from Bertram, *Historia critica Johannis a Lasco*, Aurich, 1733, in Petrus Bartels, *Johannes a Lasco*, Elberfeld, 1860, 6.

[24] Glareanus, Preface to *De Geographica*, 1529, Allen, VII, 66.

Few men can have made so many influential and distinguished friends in so short a period: that he was a wealthy patron of humanists, may have counted for something, but that he was *nobilissimus Poloniae Baro* and the nephew of the great Archbishop and former chancellor of Poland counted for much more. But it cannot be overlooked that the Erasmian circle at Basel would not merely flatter an heir to future power; Laski had clearly shown potential ability as a humanist scholar. That ability was not in the event to attain its full fruition, since Laski's attention was to be deflected to follow the principles of a more radical reform than Erasmus himself could approve and to a more active career than that of a scholar. He retained in later life however the evidence of these early studies not through writing biblical expositions as did other Reformers of his generation, but through his grasp of the Greek New Testament which he used effectively in controversy. His copy of Erasmus' Greek New Testament, 1522, with his coat of arms and the inscription, 'Be sober minded and avoid credulity' survives in the Queens' College Library at Cambridge.

Laski was later to devote his energies not to the humanist studies of his youth, but to becoming a Reformer who opposed Catholicism and Lutheranism in favour of the radical Protestantism of Zwingli especially as it concerned the eucharist.[25] It is probable that Laski had acquired an unfavourable view of Luther from the circles he had moved in at Basel as has been seen, for Luther was now suspect to Erasmus as too doctrinaire, too revolutionary and too little concerned with the affairs of the *respublica litterarum* which for Erasmus were second only to allegiance to Christ, and he had challenged Luther in 1524 by writing *De Libero Arbitrio* against Luther's view of the enslaved will. Laski ignored this doctrine of predestination, so important in Reformed theology, for the rest of his life, Peter Martyr wrote of him later, *Praedestinationis doctrinam sincere non admittit.*[26] Also the reform party led by Oecolampadius disassociated itself positively from Luther's eucharistic doctrine of the Real Presence and the accompying conservatism in eucharistic worship, as well as in some other matters. But if Laski had committed himself in his heart to Oecolampadius's position, or had begun to move towards Zwinglianism he gave no evidence of it. He may have taken careful note of Erasmus' prudence in concealing one's thoughts from too close inspection by others. He was still a Catholic though now a Catholic imbued with the tenets of the Erasmian programme of Church reform.

[25] He acknowledged his debt to Zwingli in 1560 in his *Responsio* to Westphal, *Opera*, I, 282. 'De Zwinglio . . . meque per virum illum ad Evangelii lectionem primum omnium inductum esse ante annos quatuor et triginta aut eo amplius . . .'

[26] *Calvini Opera*, XV, 493. *Opera*, II, 625.

The development of this young Erasmian Dean of Gniezno from reforming Catholicism to Protestantism was as yet no more than a possibility and it was not to be fulfilled for fifteen years. After he left Basel in 1525 it was intended by his uncle the Archbishop that he should study further for a short time at Padua and Venice, and then return to his duties in Poland strengthened by these studies abroad. Laski was accompanied from Basel on his journey to Italy by a young man from Ghent, an amanuensis of Erasmus, Charles Utenhove, whose half-brother John was to become an ardent Zwinglian and to share more than once in Laski's later career. Italy held Laski only briefly.[27] Venice was no compensation for his longing to return to his friends at Basel. He first thought of going to Spain, to Francis I held captive at Madrid, where his younger brother Stanislas was already with the French court about its captive king, so that he might renew his former intimacy with that court. However, no doubt at his uncle's insistence he went back to Poland in 1526 first pausing at Poznan then going to Cracow. 'Here are only battles, dreadful battles, nothing else,' he wrote to Amerbach at Basel in 1527 of the political situation in Hungary and Bohemia and the prospect of Poland's involvement.[28] It should never be overlooked in examining Laski's career that he was always aware of, and often involved in, diplomacy in which he followed the example of his uncle and his brothers especially the elder, Jaroslav. In the period 1526–1538 he does not show himself merely as a church administrator and scholar, since in his correspondence he demonstrated his talent for diplomacy in his frequent addresses to kings, statesmen and politically active nobles, and in his occasional journeys to centres of political activity and his involvement in them.

Little information survives on the nature of Laski's activities during the years 1526–1536, though it is known that for part of the period he aided the political aims of his brother Jaroslav in Hungary. Jaroslav, who had been prepared for a career in international politics by his uncle the Archbishop, undertook to support the Transylvanian nobleman John Zapolya, as king of Hungary against Ferdinand of Austria, brother of the Emperor Charles V, in that divided and distressed kingdom. This eventually won him honours, for he could write of himself, 'Hieronymus de Lasco, Palatinus Sieradiensis,

---

[27] Dalton, E.T., 35. He wrote from Venice to Amerbach, 'Jamque vale amicorum amicissime et me ut coepisti ama et Erasmo meo subinde commende, Glareano nunc profecto scribere non narravit . . . eum tamen et Beatam ac etiam Pellicanum meum ex me cupio diligenter salutari.'

[28] Letter to Amerbach at Basel, 1527, *Lasciana*, 103. War was being prepared by the King of Bohemia against the Hungarians. Laski preferred Basel, 'quam in primo huc reditu meo, aulam fugiens, susceperam'.

sacratiss. et christianis. francisci regis eques ordinibus S. Michaelis, et consiliarius, dominus in Kyesmark et Dunajecz.' In a letter to Antonio Rinçon, councillor of Francis I, Jan Laski gives a detailed account of the complicated political situation in Hungary in 1528 which provides a setting for his brother's actions.[29] It is not clear, however, on whose behalf Jaroslav was acting, perhaps he was part of the complicated network of anti-Habsburg activity established by Francis I, since he was not acting openly for the Polish King Sigismund – but Poland supported Hungarian national aspirations against Habsburg imperialism. Jan Laski followed him in his Hungarian adventure for a time, and as a reward for his aid to Zapolya he was nominated by him to the see of Veszprim in 1529 and was supported strongly in this proposed advancement by his uncle the Archbishop.[30] This nomination has been misunderstood by writers who created the legend that Laski had been bishop of an ancient and distinguished see. The offer of the see of Cujavia (Wladislavia) to him in 1538 by the Polish king no doubt assisted the legend – but Laski withdrew from this nomination. Records, however, do not show his name for any see in Hungary or elsewhere. Some vague, and unsubstantiated, assertions in contemporary writings that he was Bishop of Veszprim include the letter of Erasmus to Amerbach in 1529, which states that Laski had been made (*esse factum*) bishop in Hungary, and Erasmus adds, 'I deplore his fate'.[31] Laski himself never claimed to have been consecrated a bishop and Bullinger's description of his titles of honour in May 1544, says nothing of his episcopacy.

When Zapolya turned against Jaroslav Laski and imprisoned him, his brother Jan made vigorous efforts to have him released which eventually succeeded.[32] After Jan Laski returned from Hungary to Poland he took up his studies again. A contemporary, Bishop Stanislas Hosius, wrote of him at that time, 'Erudition and probity are intermingled in him . . . He is taken with great love of quiet and

[29] *Opera*, II, 548. Rinçon or Rynkon was a captain in the Spanish army, and acted as ambassador to Francis I. He also visited Zapolya in 1526 on an embassy.

[30] Lewis L. Kropf, *John á Lasco's Church Preferments, The English Historical Review*, vol. XI, 1896, 103–12. P. B. Gams, *Series episcoporum Ecclesiae Catholicae Beato Petri Apostolo*, Ratisbon, 1873–1886. A letter, 1530, in *Acta Tomiciana* states that 'the Archbishop would gladly resign his archbishopric if he were able to promote, as he ardently desires to do, the interests of his nephew Jan.'

[31] Allen, VIII, 369. The correspondence of Erasmus with Laski declines after this date, save for matters concerning the library. Jaroslav was now 'Palatinus Sieradiensis, dominus in Kyesmark et Dunajecz.' – these were in Hungary.

[32] *Acta Tomiciana, Sumptibus Bibliothecae Kornicensis*, Poznan, 1852 ff., Tom. XVII, March 1535, 217, Laski's letter to the vice-chancellor of the King of Bohemia on behalf of his brother. *Lasciana*, 154, letter to the King of Hungary, 'meum fratrem neglectis amicis omnibus, patria, uxore, liberis, neglecto suo principe . . .'

time for study'; though he did not neglect his administrative duties for he became Archdeacon of Warsaw in 1538.[33]

Among other matters on which we have too little knowledge about Laski is information on when, why and how he turned to Protestantism. It is known that he visited Melanchthon at Leipzig in 1539 but the Cracow humanists had seen Melanchthon not as a Lutheran but as a humanist.[34] Was Laski's spiritual pilgrimage a gradual change from Erasmian biblical humanism, through the Protestantism of Oecolampadius to the more aggressive theology of Zürich culminating in 1541, or in 1542? At the end of 1539 he asked permission from King Sigismund to leave Poland for a time and then travelled to various towns including Frankfurt and Louvain. Whether this move was made necessary by the rising pressure of his late uncle's enemies against himself and his family, or whether he was moving nearer to Protestantism is not known – he was not out of favour with the king since he was offered the bishopric of Cujavia (Wladislavia) by him. At Frankfurt he became a close friend of Albert Hardenberg from the Netherlands who had been educated by the Brethren of the Common Life and had then become a monk. Hardenberg was moving away from strict orthodoxy and may have adopted Erasmian views. Laski was present at Hardenberg's promotion as doctor of theology at the university of Mainz and seems to have passed a year there.[35] In the summer of 1540 he wrote that he was staying briefly in Antwerp, and there he was visited by the Margrave of Brandenburg who was in the city; also offers were made by both the Emperor and King Ferdinand of Hungary.[36] He added that Melanchthon's book contrasting Protestant and Catholic teachings shows him to be not merely equal, but superior, to Luther. The same year he was at Louvain the home of a college of biblical humanist studies promoted by Erasmus. At Louvain he lodged in the

---

[33] G. Pascal, *Jean de Lasco, baron de Pologne*, Paris, 1894, III, cites Stanislas Hosius (Hozjusz, Bishop of Worms), letter to Lazarus Bonamino, 'One cannot imagine anyone more holy than he is . . . even innocence itself.' *Stanislaí Hosii . . . epistolae . . . orationes . . .*, ed. F. Hipler and V. Zakrzewski, 2 vols. Cracow, 1879–88. Hosius turned against Laski when he became a Protestant.

[34] *Lasciana*, 145, Letter of March, 1533. Laski had read Melanchthon's *Commentary on the Epistle to the Romans* of 1532, he saw this in humanist rather than Protestant terms. Melanchthon was invited to Cracow by Kazycki when Erasmus refused to go. Zantuan, *The Polish Review*, 25. E. J. Jørgensen, *Ökumenische Bestrebungen unter den Polnischen Protestanten bis zum Jahre 1645*, Copenhagen, 89 ff. where Laski is shown as finding modesty and moderation in Melanchthon.

[35] Laski gave Hardenberg Reuchlin's *De Rudimentis Hebraicis*, 1506, which had once belonged to Erasmus. 'Sum Erasmi nec mutuo dominum.'

[36] *Opera*, II, 552. 'nunc etiam Antwerpiae plurima et magni viri me officii causa inviserent . . .'

house of a widow, Antoinette van Rosners, where a small company
of people gathered to study the Bible in the vernacular, though
without the intention of schism from the Catholic Church. Such
meetings, however, implied Protestant leanings and some members
of this secret gathering were later tried and condemned.
It is significant that all the Protestant leaders of standing who had
formerly been priests, undertook marriage as if it were a public
declaration of their allegiance to Protestantism, and from this group
at Louvain Laski found a wife – though for him this does not seem
to have meant final commitment to Protestantism. This, no doubt,
roused attention in Poland since it was a decisive step for a priest to
take who held those distinguished church appointments which he had
recently administered, and still held. Clearly, as he was to call to
Hardenberg to do later, he was approaching the time when he would
come out from among 'the Pharisees'.[37] He moved to Emden in
Frisia in December in 1540, with his young wife, because it was
dangerous to remain at Louvain as one suspected of Protestantism.
Frisia under its Count Enno had chosen Protestantism, but not
exclusively Lutheranism, and many of the people of Emden welcomed
the Anabaptists who found a base here under the court's policy of
toleration for all who did not cause social disturbance, including
Catholics.[38] Laski continued his reading in Protestant theology,
Melanchthon as well as Reformed theologians, although the climate
and local diet did not suit him and he was frequently unwell. In
September, 1541, he visited Leipzig again and from there he wrote to
Lukas de Gorca recently appointed as Bishop of Cujavia stating that
Christ is the only source of salvation and commented on the joy of
leaving Babylonian captivity for the liberty of the Gospel.[39]
In pursuit of his diplomatic career in Hungary and Turkey Jaroslav
Laski, who had changed sides and now supported the Habsburgs,
after returning from a dangerous diplomatic mission to

[37] *Opera*, II, 555–7.
[38] K. A. R. Kruske, *Johanne a Lasco und der Sacramentsstreit*, Leipzig, 1901, 24–53. J. V. Pollet,
O.P., *Martin Bucer*, Études sur les relations de Bucer avec les pays-bas . . . Leiden, 1985, Tome
I, 280 ff. discusses Laski. Pollet considers K. Hein, *Die Sakramentslehre des Johannes a Lasco*,
(Diss.), Berlin, 1904, corrects Kruske's views. This means, however, that Hein defends Laski's
Zwinglianism, claiming that Laski deepened Zwingli through emphasizing 'une consignation
objective operé par le St. Esprit'. This is a defensive overstatement by Hein.
[39] *Lasciana*, 283 ff. 'Certe omnes fatentur plurimoque abusus exstare in ecclesia quos corrigi
oporteat.' But what was he now to do? 'Et quidem grave mihi fuisse ingenue fateor patriam
mihi carissimam, amicos delectissimos mea insuper omnia relinquere . . .', 286. However, the
letter concluded, 'Joannis a Lasco multis olim titulis insignis nunc autem nudus nudi Jesu Christi
crucifixi servus . . .' Jørgensen, 28, states that Laski informed Gorca that he was married but the
letter refers to abuses including celibacy 'permissum esse omnibus usum conjugii qui non
possunt continere': there is no reference to his own marriage.

Constantinople arrived ill and dying at Cracow towards the end of 1541. He wrote to his brother Jan to come to him and there he persuaded him that if ever he should be called back to Poland under conditions which would allow him to live there without unduly compromising himself with Catholic orthodoxy he should do so. In a casual sentence in a letter from Emden in May 1542 to Hardenberg, now in Bremen, Laski refers contemptuously to some affair (what he does not say) with the bishops in Poland, 'You would laugh if you heard what I have been doing with our Bishops in my country'.[40] It must have been in February 1542 that he signed the Oath, in the presence of the Archbishop of Gniezno and the Bishop of Cracow, which has caused much debate among historians. If those words cast aside to Hardenberg had been expanded we could perhaps have learned what lay behind this strange episode. In the royal archives at Königsberg there survives a copy of an *Iuramentum* sworn and signed by Laski. This document is without date and is inscribed: 'This oath written in his own hand Joannes à Lasco presented to the Archbishop of Gniezno and the Bishop of Cracow when he returned from Germany and affirmed that he had not taken a wife nor adhered to Evangelical doctrine'.[41] The essential parts of the document read:

> I profess that I never adhered to any opinion . . . nor that I embraced any dogma . . . voluntarily and knowingly which I knew specifically to be repugnant to the Holy Catholic and Apostolic Roman Church . . .
> I confess that I do not wish to follow any sects or doctrine which might in any way depart from the unity of the Holy Catholic and Apostolic Roman Church and I shall be obedient . . . to the ordinaries my bishops . . . in all things permitted and honourable, and so I swear, may God help me in this matter, and the holy gospels of God.

This comprehensive and thorough declaration which the weight of the evidence would date 6 February 1542, undermines the reputation for integrity asserted of Laski by his contemporaries throughout his life from Erasmus onwards, if he had identified himself with Protestantism earlier. Writers, including the hagiographical Dalton, followed Kuyper who asserted that the date of the oath should be 1526 when Laski had returned to Poland from Basel strongly influenced by Erasmus and Oecolampadius but still a Catholic as he was to be for some years to come as his correspondence shows.[42] Pascal, accepting 1526, for example, sought to save Laski's integrity at the expense of credibility and other documentary evidence by the

---

[40] *Opera*, II, 556.
[41] D. G. Kawerau, *Der Reiniggungseid des Johannes Laski, Neue Kirchliche Zeitschrift*, vol. X, 1899, 430–41. This is the definitive statement on this difficult episode.
[42] *Opera*, II, 547 – for date 1526, and the oath.

device of declaring this evidence of an oath to be, 'fraudes pieuses et utiles ... dans les moeurs de l'Eglise depuis les Fausses Decretales'.[43] However, Kawerau presented the formidable case for 1542 by showing, among several other matters, that Laski wanted to hold a canonry at Cracow and obtain its income since he had recently married and had been in financial distress from 1538 at least, when he and his brother had lost considerable sums in the Hungarian enterprise – he had found difficulty in paying the remaining sum for Erasmus' library to Amerbach and soon after 1542 he had to sell a part of this library at Emden.[44] The episode is mysterious: perhaps his career in assisting his brother's diplomacy had led him to think of compromise and mental reservation as reasonable devices. However, the Polish historian Bartel suggests that after taking this oath and deeply disturbed by his brother's death, Laski felt that he could no longer hesitate and finally decided for Protestantism.[45]

In 1542 he wrote from Emden urging Hardenberg to 'become separated from the Pharisees' and leave his monastery – though Hardenberg delayed a further few months. Laski also sought to win from a Beguine House Truytje Syssinghe (*in't eerste Baghynenhoff te Groningen*) to honour the merits and glory of Christ and not dishonour them by continuing in conventual life.[46] At Emden the Countess Anna of Opdenburg, the widow of Count Enno, ruled as regent during the minority of her young sons, and willingly supported Protestantism. Lutheran teaching had earlier penetrated into Frisia and became acceptable to many, but Zwinglianism began to appear in 1525 and in 1529 Karlstadt and Melchior Hofmann propagated their more extreme views among supporters of Anabaptism. Nevertheless Lutheran pastors had gained ground and won the support of Count Enno, although 'variis homnibus aures dabat', who established the Lutheran Luneburg Church Order and decided to appoint a Superintendent who could hold the various parties under control. Count Enno in his dealings with the religious groups offered toleration to all. Now his widow in view of the influx from the Netherlands of Anabaptists escaping persecution felt the need of strong control and early in 1543 she appointed Laski as Superintendent to the oversight of all the churches in her territory. Laski signed the Luneberg Order but in view of his attack on it later he did so with mental reservation, and he began his successful work

[43] Pascal, 143.
[44] S. A. Gabbema, *Epistolarum ab illustribus et claris viris scriptarum centuriae tres: quas passim ex autographis collegit ac edidit S.A.G.*, Harlingae Frisiorum, 1669, Epis. 6.
[45] Bartel, 126 ff.
[46] *Opera*, II, 578–80.

of creating an ordered and disciplined church life in Frisia. It is evident that he regarded himself, and was regarded by others, as having a special fitness for church administration, and he was to prove that he was particularly competent at organisation and discipline on lines similar to, though at times significantly different from, those of Oecolampadius and Zwingli. Further, he had one remarkable gift that wherever he settled it was not long before he found a circle of the most influential people to support him. Laski's major activity in Poland had been given to ecclesiastical administration: he now turned that ability into Protestant channels.

The situation in Frisia created a number of problems of organisation and procedure for Laski. Franciscans and Anabaptist preachers as well as a number of Lutherans stood their ground. When he took up his superintendency the common form of service in the churches of Emden was a sermon followed by mass with communion in both kinds, together with the traditional ceremonial, vestments and retention of images. Laski soon challenged all this. No doubt this is what Dixon meant by 'the fury of his reformations', which 'swept away every trace of the old system in his adopted country'. Laski forbade the Franciscans to preach or to celebrate baptism, and required the removal of the images. The Franciscans relying on Count John the Countess's brother-in-law, who considered that he should be regent, and who was supported in his Catholic opposition to Anna's proceedings by Charles V, hoped that Laski would be dismissed. Laski gradually overcame their resistance, by urging the Countess to command the removal of the images from the churches on the ground that the word of God must be made the foundation of all worship and administration in the churches, and not human traditions and ordinances. She agrees to the removal of the images though requiring that it be done discreetly and by night so that no disturbance should be caused.[47] It is interesting however to note that toleration still prevailed to the extent that the Franciscans were left in their conventual house undisturbed.

At Emden, as happened frequently elsewhere, men thought that Reformation meant rejection of the papacy and its laws, the setting up of preaching, and little else. There was hardly any discipline introduced into the churches of Emden, and no clear pattern of teaching to mark a distinctive theological focus. This was an open door for sectarianism, and the Anabaptists had passed through it. Whatever divisions there were among them, they all could claim that they practised a strict congregational discipline. Laski was well aware

[47] *Opera*, II, 597.

that Anabaptism could undermine the churches of Emden unless a coherent theological pattern was provided based on an organisation using effective methods of discipline. In 1544 Laski set up four laymen to assist the ministers of the chief parish of Emden in oversight of the lives of the parishioners, with power jointly to excommunicate the unworthy.[48] A general visitation of the churches by Laski and his fellow ministers was undertaken through the region, with the aim of establishing an ordered and moral ministry throughout the land obedient to rules he drew up for that good order. As the chief instrument of this order he set up the *Coetus* consisting of all the clergy of the region, which was to meet each Monday in Emden, from Easter to Michaelmas, assisted by its President and secretary. Like the meetings of the Venerable Company of Pastors at Geneva it was concerned with the moral life and valid teaching of the individual ministers; also it took up the duty of examining and accepting candidates for the ministry; and finally, it undertook regular discussion of leading points of belief based on Scripture.

Laski could not have claimed originality for this body; something like it had been instituted elsewhere, for example, at Zürich and at Geneva. Perhaps the real difference between his practice and that of these other Reformed centres was that Laski was a kind of Reformed bishop, he was the Superintendent of all the churches of Emden and its region. It is characteristic of him and his sense of his office, that throughout most of his career he held to this function and its duties and status, in Frisia, in England and wherever he found a reasonable settlement. Laski never quite forgot, nor did those who appointed him that he had more than once been offered a bishopric: he never lost the indomitable sense of the great Archbishop his uncle and of his elder brother the kingmaker, that the Laskis were born to rule. Together with this went an unbending sense of the rightness of his own judgements in doctrine and church administration; he did not think it possible to yield diplomatically in the needs of changing situations. This was to cause considerable exasperation to other Reformation leaders as well as to powerful statesmen, Farel's comment, in 1556, to Calvin is typical: 'I do not know how it may be but the more a Lasco exerts himself the more peace declines.'[49]

This does not mean that he became intolerant – apart from his frequent attacks until his death on the Lutheran doctrine of the eucharistic presence. His dealings with Anabaptism at Emden show a surprising degree of tolerance when we remember how sharply

[48] *Opera*, II, 575.
[49] *Calvini Opera*, (*Corpus Reformatorum*) XVI, 259.

negative many Reformers elsewhere had been to the Anabaptists. Unlike Luther or Calvin or Zwingli, Laski was prepared to see some good in certain Anabaptist teachings. Like Martin Bucer in the early days at Strasbourg, or Francis Lambert, he felt one could reason with the Anabaptists to persuade them, through some degree of common ground, for example, the centrality of Scripture and the need for church discipline, to accept the broad principles of the Reformed pattern of doctrine, worship and discipline. But he could argue decisively against those more distinctively sectarian Anabaptists like David Joris who had been associated with the Melchiorites, followers of Melchior Hofmann the inspirer of the wild men of Münster; or with Menno Simons, a native of Frisia whose christology like Joris (also associated with the Melchiorite christology) he found to be wholly unbiblical and destructive of the principle of the Incarnation.[50] Menno was in Emden at the same time as Laski, and they discussed their views together in the presence of leading ministers particularly on the Incarnation, the nature of Baptism, and the method of calling men to the ministry, and failed to agree. Laski took the trouble to write at some length against Menno's Melchiorite christology (that is, the view that Christ though born of her did not take human flesh from the Virgin Mary, but came into the world in a heavenly flesh), a teaching strange and unbiblical in itself and opposed to the Christian doctrine of the Incarnation.[51] This tract was lengthy though clear and full in argument, but neither Calvin nor Luther would have treated these opinions so fully and tolerantly. Nevertheless, Melanchthon liked the book and told others of it. Yet Laski was unwilling to initiate or support a general persecution of Anabaptist sectaries at Emden. He regarded the great majority of them as simple, unlearned and inoffensive folk who could be tolerated in the hope that they might be brought to join with the Reformed.

Alongside of his treatise against Menno, Laski also wrote a tractate, 1546, on the need for people of Protestant leanings to give up attendance at Catholic services, and in spite of hardship and persecution to stand by their convictions.[52] That many were in the

---

[50] *Defensio verae semperque in Ecclesia receptae doctrinae de Christi Domini. Adversus Mennonē Simonis, Anabaptistarū Doctorem, per Ioannem à Lasco, Poloniae Baronē, Ministrum Ecclesiarum Phrisiae Orientalis.* Kuyper, *Opera,* I, 1–62.

[51] Menno refused to use the term 'Trinity'. Cornelius Krahn, *Menno Simons (1496–1561), Ein Beitrag zur Geschichte und Theologie der Taufgeninnten,* 1936. For Laski's tolerant attitude to Anabaptists, *Opera,* II, 597.

[52] *Het Ghevoelen Joannis a Lasco, Baroens en Polen, Superintendents der Ghemeynte der vremdelinghen te London. Of het den Christenen nadien zy het word Godes ende de godlooszheit des Pauwstdoms bekent hebben, eenighszins ver is zy in den Pauwstlichen godsdiensten, ende in zonderheit in der Misse vinden laten,* 1557. There was a French version printed at Geneva, 1556. The Latin original does not appear to have survived if it was printed.

troubled state of liking the old services and ceremonies, though convinced of what the Reformers conceived to be biblical truth must have been a familiar fact in all places where the Reformation was being introduced. Calvin had written forcefully on this theme in 1543 calling such people Nicodemites, for resembling the Nicodemus of St John's Gospel. Mention has already been given of Laski's efforts to persuade Hardenberg and his future wife, the Beguine Truytje, to give up this stumbling between two ways. The treatise is clear, painstaking and perhaps too full, lacking the incisiveness of Calvin, whom Laski cites, or the vigour which Luther would have put into this theme.[53] But Laski's most significant treatise at Emden was his account of the doctrine of the churches of East Frisia the *Epitome*.[54] This is his first full statement of his doctrinal views, though it was not printed but dispersed to Reformed centres in manuscript. The opening sections demonstrate what we are required to know concerning God as Lord, justice, truth and mercy, and shows the Reformed emphasis on the glory of God and the consequent requirement of obedience from men who of themselves can do nothing to save themselves because of the consequences of sin, and who have no other source but Scripture for their knowledge of God's requirements. Sin is expounded curiously enough under the Catholic terms, for original sin, actual sin, venial sin and mortal sin are given as headings; the promises of God are analysed with frequent use of Greek terms; and faith is defined not as intellectual assent but as an affection of the soul – it is the heart that believes we are justified, not the intellect. It is interesting that there are no distinctive headings for predestination, for the law, or for justification. It is curious that he describes Baptism at disproportionate length (perhaps influenced here by Erasmus who had given strong emphasis to this sacrament) but gives less space to the discussion of the Lord's Supper. He immediately attacks the association of the body and blood of Christ with the elements of bread and wine and states that transubstantiation is simply idolatry. We must emphasise Christ's saying, 'Do this in remembrance of me', and Laski frequently uses the word symbols to apply to the elements and also the word sealing – the Supper seals Christ's promises. Here we lack the sense of mystery and awe which both Luther and Calvin had found in the holy communion; there is missing here Luther's association of this sacrament with the forgiveness of sins, and Calvin's sense of this sacrament as the food of eternal life. In a letter by Laski on the

---

[53] Kuyper, *Opera*, I, 89. 'dien andworde ick mit Jo. Calvini . . .'
[54] *Epitome Doctrinae Ecclesiarum Phrisiae Orientalis*, (1544), Kuyper, *Opera*, I, 481–557.

subject which Kuyper has appended to the *Epitome*, he particularly makes use of the 83rd homily of Chrysostom on St Matthew, annotated by Erasmus in his edition of Chrysostom's works, in opposing the doctrine of the Real Presence – although in so doing he was ignoring what could be found elsewhere in Chrysostom and other Fathers in a direction contrary to his own.[55] Laski affirms that he did not obtain his doctrine of the Lord's Supper from Karlstadt nor from Zwingli: he agrees with them in principle, he says, though he does not follow them in the interpretation of the words used by Christ at the last supper.[56]

Copies of this manuscript *Epitome* were received by Melanchthon at Wittenberg and by Bullinger at Zürich but it was not approved at either centre, and Melanchthon objected particularly to the section on baptism.[57] Laski accepted these doubts of Bullinger and Melanchthon and did not publish the book in print.

Since the *Epitome* had not been printed and since the churches at Emden needed a clear instruction in the new faith for common use, Laski compiled a *Catechism* in 1546, (published nearly a decade later in a reduced form) prepared in the name of the ministers of Emden, though the chief work must have been done by Laski as Kuyper ably demonstrated.[58] It begins, after a brief preliminary questioning, with the Decalogue and what may be learned from the precepts of the law, and shows that the law is necessary, *utilitatem assiduo studio occupantur*. This tends to bring in legalistic morality, a concern with works, *nova obedientia bonorum operum*, which was to be a theological preoccupation in English Puritanism. It is true that Laski is using the catechetical division: decalogue, creed or articles of faith, and prayer based on the Lord's prayer, but Luther and others used these divisions to a different and less legalistic purpose. The definition of the Church also goes beyond that of Luther and Calvin, in describing the visible signs of the Church, in adding ecclesiastical discipline to the other two of the preaching of the word of God, and the right use of the sacraments. On participation in the Lord's Supper certain phrases occur which were to be echoed in the Scottish *Confession of Faith* of 1560.[59] The warmth, the theological originality

---

[55] Kuyper, *Opera*, I, 557–72. On certain passages in the Pauline epistles. This is a rare instance of Laski's use of the Fathers, and of his citing contemporary scholars.

[56] Kuyper, *Opera*, I, 564.

[57] Kuyper, *Opera*, I, XLIX. Melanchthon: 'Es sind böse opiniones von dem Tauffe in des Laski Schrift.' Bullinger: 'lapsi ac restituti rursum hominis' was ill-expressed.

[58] Kuyper, *Opera*, I, LXXXI–XCVIII.

[59] Kuyper, *Opera*, II, 531. 'Dewyle wy synes Lyves unde Blodes deelhafftich syn, fleisch van synen fleische, unde knaken van synem knakenem . . .' but this is through our faith, 'dorch den geloven . . .'

and depth of those famous catechisms of the Reformation, of Luther, of Geneva, of Heidelberg, even the spiritual energy of those puritanical documents the catechisms of the Westminster Assembly of Divines in the following century, are lacking. It must have been also a burden for the young and those of poor memory, since only those who could intelligibly answer its questions could become church members or attend the Lord's Supper – it was not so much an aid to piety as an instrument of discipline.

It is not surprising in the light of these theological views to see that trouble began to stir against Laski at Emden particularly on the Lord's Supper. Lutheranism was still tolerated there and some of the Lutheran clergy refused to join the *Coetus* at Emden, and attacked Laski's views as being Sacramentarian (i.e. Zwinglian). Further, many of the clergy in the *Coetus* were indifferent to Laski's zeal for the practice of discipline, and would not follow his doctrinal requirements. Finally he resigned diplomatically as Superintendent early in 1546, and became a parish minister briefly – he took up the office of Superintendent again later. But his reformation was becoming known: Calvin dedicated a new catechism for Geneva to the ministers of East Frisia. Laski had been at the Diet of Worms in May 1545 where he foresaw grave troubles ahead for Protestantism in view of the determination of Charles V to crush it. This attitude of Charles was made plain when after the Diet of Augsburg in 1547, the Interim was to be enforced throughout the Empire in 1548. Stanislas Laski, Jan's younger and surviving brother, was at Augsburg on behalf of Poland and wrote to Jan of what was coming. Charles brought pressure to get rid of Laski.

However unfortunate the Interim was for those Protestants who suffered through their inability to accept it, Archbishop Cranmer found its enforcement useful in obtaining distinguished foreign Reformers for aid in the work of reform in the Church of England.[60] He persuaded Peter Martyr, Martin Bucer and others to come to England, and also thought of Laski. Cranmer had written to Laski at the time of the Interim in July, 1548, stating that, 'We are desirous of setting forth in our churches the true doctrine of God . . .' and added that the English intended to invite various learned men from abroad to help in this, 'and as they have come over to us without any reluctance, so that we scarcely have to regret the absence of any of

---

[60] Laski has published only two treatises, on 'Menno Simons', and 'On leaving Popery', which could not place him in the same rank as the other distinguished foreign Reformers who were invited. The letters of Erasmus, which had been published in 1544, included those to Laski and this would have helped his reputation.

them, with the exception of yourself and Melanchthon, we earnestly request you, both to come yourself, and if possible to bring Melanchthon with you'.[61] Why was Cranmer eager to invite Laski, for he had published nothing of note by that date, unlike Bucer, Martyr, and the others who came, nor could he compare in theological standing with Melanchthon? Presumably once again it was his fame as a 'Baron of Poland', as his uncle's nephew and as the friend of Erasmus, but also Cranmer would be aware of Laski's status as a diplomat. William Turner, a physician and later Dean of Wells had urged Cranmer to bring Laski, for he had passed some time at Emden a few years before. Somerset wrote to the Countess Anna asking her to release Laski to serve in England. The journey for Laski was perilous; imperial officials were looking for him, but he passed through the Netherlands in disguise and so to Calais and England by September 1548, where he stayed in the Archbishop's Palace at Lambeth.[62] On the exaggerated evidence of the Swiss ab Ulmis and Traheron it has frequently been accepted that Laski prodded Cranmer away from his early Lutheran influences into a positive alignment with the theology of Zürich.[63] But both ab Ulmis and Traheron were convinced supporters of Bullinger and no other evidence for their assertion survives, whereas there is evidence that Bishop Ridley was urging Cranmer forward though not on the basis of Zwingli. Laski made powerfully placed friends, for example William Cecil, newly appointed secretary to the Lord Protector, and also Sir John Cheke a tutor of Edward VI.

Then in March 1549 Laski, whose permission to leave Emden, received from the Countess, had run out, left for Emden again. On board ship he heard from Count Mansfeld of the formation of a league against Charles V and the enforcement of the Interim, consisting of states containing Brandenburg, Prussia, England and Poland among others, and he therefore travelled in north Germany and to Danzig in diplomatic activity for the affair.[64] There was the possibility either of his moving to Prussia, or, if Poland decided to challenge its enemy Charles V, of moving there if changes should begin. However, the Interim was rigorously imposed at Emden in

[61] *Works of Thomas Cranmer*, Parker Society, Cambridge, 1846, II, 420, 421. Peter Martyr also encouraged Cranmer to write to Laski. Dalton, E.T., 362. Laski himself thought it important to persuade Melanchthon to go to England, according to Dalton he tried to persuade him, Dalton, E.T., 361.
[62] Dalton, E.T., 365. *Calendar of State Paper*, Domestic Series, 1856, Edward VI, 1550, No. 253: for Laski's journey in disguise, and these diplomatic efforts against the Emperor.
[63] *Zurich Letters, Original Letters*, Parker Society, Cambridge, 1847, IV, 383 (Nov. 1548).
[64] *Acts of the Privy Council*, N.S., 1550–1552, vol. III. Nov. 1551.

1549 though Laski returned there to help the *Coetus* if he could, and then found he must leave for as long as the Interim ruled since the Court of Brabant was determined to be rid of him.[65] He went to Bremen where he stayed with Hardenberg in October, 1549, then to Hamburg where he talked with the Lutheran Westphal with whom later he was to have a severe controversy. Then in May, 1550, through invitations from English friends, he decided to move to England with his family.

The most important period of Laski's life as a Protestant now began, not that we can underestimate his work at Emden or influence in the Netherlands and elsewhere, but because the most significant writings of Laski were produced in England, and his most effective administration was conducted here since he had largely a free hand, and he could exercise close control. In June, 1550, Edward VI granted him and his family right of residence and in effect English citizenship.[66] In July, 1550, he was granted by Letters Patent the Church of the Austin Friars for the use of the Germans (this included Dutch and Belgians) and the French 'Strangers' and refugees in London. He was given, as Superintendent of the Churches of the Strangers, a free hand in preaching, teaching, worship and discipline, without reference even to the Bishop of London. The ministers chosen by the congregations, and the Superintendent, were approved by the king in person.[67] This was a unique concession: where else at that time was such complete liberty available to set up a different worship and church organisation from that supported by the state, and with direct backing by the state? But the bishops disapproved, not least Ridley who was Bishop of London, and disliked this challenge to the form which the Church of England was taking, made by the Strangers whose worship could attract discontented Englishmen and thereby encourage a rival alternative. Laski himself published his view explicitly to the king of Poland later that he intended that the Church of the Strangers would show England the example of a pure and apostolic reformed church.[68] Ridley and other ecclesiastical officers

[65] Kruske, 67, who cites Eggerik Beninga, *Chronyk van Ostfrieslant Met Rand . . . door E. F. Harkenroht*, Emden, 1723. 'Welck alles geschehen, dewyle Keys. Maj. so hart up dat Interim to underholden drengede.' This undermined the Countess's support for 'den Hochgeleerden und Hochberoemden Johanni a Lasco den Superintendent.'

[66] *Calendar of Patent Rolls*, Edward VI (1549–51), vol. III, 316, 317. Rymer, *Foedera Conventiones*, 1713, XV, 238.

[67] F. de Schickler, *Les Églises du Réfuge en Angleterre*, 3 vols., Paris, 1892, III, 5. The Royal Diploma is in *Opera*, II, 278–83, especially see 281.

[68] *Opera*, II, 10, 11. The use of the word 'puritatem' is ominous for the future in England – '. . . ut Anglicae quoque Ecclesiae ad puritatem Apostolicam amplectandum unanimi omnium regni ordinum consensu excitarentur.'

tried to impose at least the ceremonies of the *Book of Common Prayer* on Laski's congregations but this was disallowed by the Council.[69]

At the end of 1550 Laski wrote his longest treatise, 'All the form and manner of the ecclesiastical ministry in the Church of the Strangers formed at London', the *Forma ac Ratio*.[70] This contained a treatise on his teaching by way of a preface, to the king of Poland, in its printed form of 1556; the preface to Edward VI of 1550; an account of the election of the ministers, of the elders, the deacons, the superintendent and of their duties. It also contained the liturgy or public prayers of the congregations, and of the administration of the sacraments, a form of catechising for those to be admitted to the Lord's Supper, and a long discussion of the nature of the Lord's Supper. This was followed by a full account of the ecclesiastical discipline of these churches, public and private, including excommunication; forms of marriage, the visitation of the sick, and burial. This provides one of the lengthiest of such documents from the Reformation period: the collection of all these materials into one book was unique. Laski must have found the long days while he was at Lambeth profitable for preparing this work, built upon his previous experience at Emden. Even this lengthy work was not all. There were also prepared a *Confession* and a *Catechism* in 1551, the year after Laski had completed this lengthy treatise, and these were sizeable works which, though better organised and wider ranging, showed now marked theological differences from the *Epitome*.[71]

A detailed account of Laski's theology and church order is desirable at this stage. For Laski it was a fundamental principle to harmonise doctrine and life so that moral rectitude, through effective

---

[69] *Opera*, II, 672, Laski to Cecil complaining of his church members being threatened with prison by the bishop's officers, Nov. 1552. (Also see *Acts of the Privy Council*, 1552). Martin Micronius, one of Laski's aides, in letters to Bullinger, Oct. 1550, Aug. 1551, Nov. 1551, describes these pressures from 'these enemies of Christ, the hypocritical and heretical bishops'. A serious part of the problem for Ridley was that a variety of heresies arose in the Flemish congregation of the Strangers' Church, of Anabaptist and anti-Trinitarian origin, in part due to Laski's unwillingness to test too closely the beliefs of his Church members. The minister of the Italian congregation was deprived for fornication in January 1553, and tried to damage Laski in revenge by accusing him of not holding the orthodox view of Predestination, but failed in this attack.

[70] *Forma ac Ratio tota ecclesiastici Ministerii, in peregrinorum, potissimum vero Germanorum Ecclesia: instituta Londini in Anglia, per Pientissimum Principem Angliae etc. Regem Eduardum, eius nominis Sextū . . . 1550 Addito ad calcem libelli Privilegio suae Maiestatis.*

[71] To this was appended: *Forma Precum Publicarum quae pro concionibus in Ecclesiis Peregrinorum habentur*. London 1551. *Compendium Doctrinae de vera unicaque Dei et Christi Ecclesia, eiusque fide et confessione pura: in qua Peregrinorum Ecclesia Londini instituta est. De Catechismus oft Kinder leere, diemen te Londen, inde Duytsche ghemeynte, is ghebruyekende*, 1551. *Consensus Tigurinus* was added to this, with the hitherto unpublished tractate by Bullinger on the Lord's Supper appended.

organisation and discipline, was to take priority over systematic theological exposition. Laski was not so much a theologian as a pragmatic writer on moral discipline who saw the sacraments as moral exercises and church worship as moral exhortation. Laski's doctrinal statement in the *Epitome* was remarkable for how much he omitted theologically and for the pragmatic viewpoint in which doctrine must lead to moral life if it is to be worthy of attention. This differs from the method of the confessional statements or catechisms of other Reformers for whom right doctrine comes first, church order comes next and then, in varying ways discipline for the maintenance of morals is described where this subject was considered to be relevant. Discipline is a *nota* of the church for Laski, as it was for John Knox, whereas for Calvin it was not, however fruitful it was in his eyes as the 'sinews of the christian life'.[72]

This leads to some investigation of the possible sources of Laski's doctrinal views. In his young manhood his great admiration for Erasmus and his writings lies behind certain aspects of his thought. In March, 1544, he wrote to Bullinger: 'Erasmus was the first who began to establish me in true religion.'[73] Laski's unwillingness to commit himself to more than what he regarded as the essentials of Christian doctrine and his desire for flexibility within the practice of discipline were intended to be eirenical in the manner of Erasmus' *Enchiridion Militis Christiani*. In a letter of June, 1534, he wrote that all men should follow the teachings of Erasmus, reject the spirit of disagreement and treat one another with kindness, but by 1538 Laski had moved beyond Erasmus to the influence of Melanchthon whom he called an object of 'pride for our age' and superior to Luther. For Poles the rejection of Luther with contumely accompanied, paradoxically, admiration for Melanchthon who was seen as 'Erasmian'.[74] Laski in a letter to Melanchthon in 1543 on the question, is Baptism necessary for membership of the Church puts the extreme case of the children of Christian parents in slavery among the Turks, where they had no Scripture, no word of God and no sacraments, yet declares they are not separated from Christ nor from the Church though unbaptised. While this does not represent his considered view of the Church and sacraments, and was unacceptable to Melanchthon, yet compared with other Protestant leaders it shows ecclesiological

---

[72] On discipline, *Opera*, II, 177, 348.

[73] *Opera*, II, 569. March, 1544, to Bullinger: 'Jam si scire cupias, quisnam sim, facile id ex Erasmi Roterodami scriptis cognosces – extant enim aliquot illius ad me epistolae – qui etiam mihi autor fuit, ut animum ad sacra adiicerem, imo vero ille primus me in vera religione instituere coepit.'

[74] Jørgensen, 89.

weakness in which moral principle comes before theological rectitude. Laski's conception of the Church, as will be shown, was wholly different from Calvin in almost every particular: to call him a Calvinist in doctrine, Church order or discipline is to misrepresent Laski. For him the Church is a community of free choice in which individual freedom is still important and charity and good life are essential characteristics of the Church. This implies a humanistic anthropology divorced from Calvin's Augustinian anthropology. This explains why Laski wanted Bullinger to persuade (if others from Zürich were unavailable) Castellio to come to England and join the other continental scholars teaching at the English universities – no doubt to Bullinger's surprise for Castellio while cautiously accepted at Basel had become unacceptable at Geneva and Zürich.[75] Castellio was to become remarkable as foreshadowing the Protestant liberalism which arose in the nineteenth century. This attitude of Laski further helps to explain why Lutherans like Westphal saw him as theologically simplistic to the point of heresy, whereas Laski saw these Lutherans as truculent obscurantist promoters of 'αρτολατρεία who wilfully opposed the obvious rightness of his straightforward views on doctrine and discipline – as Kuyper wrote of him, *dogmatizavit polemicis de causis*. Two other influences may also be detected on Laski, first the disciplined biblical piety of the Brethren of the Common Life of which Hardenberg was an example and Erasmus an echo, and secondly, the writings of Oecolampadius whose biblical commentaries are reflected occasionally in Laski's works and whose *catena* of Patristic statements believed to be in opposition to the Real Presence, helped Laski in his own controversies on the subject.

That Laski had diplomatic skills was clear to German, Polish and English statesmen, but his competence as a theologian is less clear. His terminology changes, and he is unsystematic. His most significant contribution to theological writing is in the doctrine of the Church – his eucharistic theology is based on simplistic variations on Zwinglian themes presented cogently and thoroughly within an envelope of repudiation of the views of others – but he has changes of emphasis which are not resolved into an effective pattern. His ability lay in moulding the administration of the Church to meet the social and political environment of the different countries in which he resided so that ecclesiology tends to fit administrative needs. Laski, unlike

[75] F. Buisson, *Sebastien Castellion* (1515–1563) . . . *Etude sur les origines du protestantisme libéral français*, 2 vols. Paris, 1892. Stefan Zweig's study of Castellio, (in its English form, *The Right to Heresy* 1936) demonstrates the point.

some other Reformers, tended to sweep aside all that came from the
past, in spite of his unexpanded occasional references to 'the Councils'
dismissing such matters as being the doctrines of Antichrist – though
he kept reasonably close to Chalcedonian christology – in order to
start anew from the Scriptures. He claimed, as did other Reformers,
to follow the purity of the apostolic Church, but unlike them, he
gave no clear pattern based on, for example, the Pauline writings.
The Holy Spirit dwelt within the Apostles and guided them in all
truth and this we must follow. Our reason in divine matters is useless,
neither our philosophy nor our learning will help us to find the
meaning of the Church, we need the 'indwelling Spirit' to enlighten
us.[76] On a number of occasions he disapproved of the arrogance of
theologians in rationalising theology, and their pride in their biblical
erudition.

The foundation of the Church lies in Peter's confession revealed to
him by God (not in the man Peter and certainly not the Pope), *omnes
intelligant non aliam ullam . . . Ecclesiam . . . quam quae Catholicam illam
Apostolorum omnium fidem, ore Petri prolatam, publice profiteatur.. . .*[77]
The Church, however, did not begin with Peter's confession, since
Christ is co-eternal with the Father he has established the Church
from the beginning soon after the fall of Adam; because Adam and
Eve believed in God's promise they began the existence of the Church
in the world.[78] Throughout the Old Testament Christ has guided
His Church so that the Church of the old covenant is identical with
the Church of the new covenant: they are one because they have one
faith and one mediator and this Church has always enjoyed
communion in the body and blood of Christ in various signs
including the Passover. This simple affirmation which occurs with
variations in his different writings calls out for exposition and
qualification, but Laski leaves it undeveloped beyond showing that
the Church under Israel was limited to the Jews whereas under the
Apostles the Church is limitless and for all peoples. The primary
meaning of church is that it is an assembly (which can mean the
church of a nation and also the church consisting of people of all
nations) because it is derived from *evocando* (in Greek 'Ἐκκαλέω)
since God calls into it members from all mankind. It forms a *coetus*
and differs from other human institutions because through God's
promise it has the forgiveness of sins, the communion of saints, the
resurrection of the flesh and eternal life.[79] (However, elsewhere in his

[76] *Opera*, I, 510 (*Epitome*).
[77] *Opera*, II, 290, also *Opera*, I, 459.
[78] *Opera*, II, 298.
[79] *Opera*, II, 434, 436, 520.

writings and practice *coetus* refers to the assembly of ministers and elders, and meetings for discipline.)

His strong pragmatic purpose leads Laski away from analysis of the spiritual significance of the Church to the Church described as a visible reality. He rejected, or at least ignored, the Reformation distinction between the visible and invisible Church, in order to emphasise the visible *coetus* consisting of wheat and tares but seeking to become more effectively the Church of saints. His Erasmian concern for virtuous living did not allow him to dwell on the Protestant emphasis on man as a sinner lost without God's initiative of grace: he did not deny this but passed it by in order to concentrate on bringing the members of his congregation to acquiring perfection so that they should become the people of God clearly discernible in the world. This Church, the *coetus fidelium*, is seen where there are the ministry of the word, the sacraments of Baptism and the Lord's Supper and the exercise of discipline. There are further emphases which Laski made: he was concerned that the ministry should not have special status in itself above the laity, but the ministers were to be heard as prophets, the voice of God could be heard through their prophetic calling. Also the Church can claim antiquity not as Catholics or, for example, Melanchthon saw it, since it goes back to Adam and has always professed, as did Peter, the incarnate Christ who is seen as Prophet, Priest and King. Laski argued frequently and positively for the doctrine of the Word made flesh which he had sharpened in early controversy with the Melchiorite christology of the Anabaptists.

Again, the Church is free, it is not a rigid construction. There will be variations on how the Church is to be defined by those who seek to follow the Gospel but these are unimportant and should be resolved by peaceful discussion based on the Scriptures. He made this attitude plain in his letter to Edward VI in 1552, 'What ought to be sought out and desired in the Church of Christ . . . [is that] . . . all of us in mutual love and concord should unitedly testify we are indeed members of one body under our head Christ our Lord.'[80] Unlike Calvin, (and this qualification could cover many of Laski's statements on doctrine) salvation for Laski does not depend on membership of the Church. There is a great company outside of the Church but it is absurd to think that they are condemned to eternal punishment: once again the humanist liberal theme occurs. This irritated Melanchthon which caused Laski to reply to him that he meant that the great company outside consisted of those who believe or wished to believe

---

[80] *Opera*, I, 106.

in their hearts and he was not referring to those who blasphemously scorned Christ. For him, the Church is a company of believers in which his emphasis lies on the people themselves and not on the Church seen objectively as our mother who nourishes us in God's grace as Calvin taught following Cyprian. Laski very rarely cites the Fathers, and further, here as elsewhere he set aside the doctrine of predestination, and ignored the Augustinian theme of the Church founded on the elect. Laski also ignored classical Greek and Roman writers, there are very few literary or historical allusions, surprisingly in a disciple of Erasmus. He ignores the Scholastic theologians and rarely cites his Protestant contemporaries except on the doctrine of the Lord's Supper; this is neither arrogance nor presumably ignorance: rather it affirms that in all matters of theology, Church order and discipline it is the Bible and the Holy Spirit which alone are to be the guides. It is worth noting that in spite of his early respect for Zwingli and his close relationship with Bullinger, Laski did not associate himself with the theology of covenant or covenanting which was to be developed at Zürich and other Reformed centres.[81]

The Church has four activities, the ministry of the word, the administration of the two sacraments, public worship and the exercise of discipline as we learn from his fullest description of the Church in his *Forma ac Ratio* which he prepared in England. The ministry exists for the church members, it has no independent authority and no lingering remnant of sacral status. It is the members who are essentially the Church and they do not receive passively what the ministers preach, since this is open to discussion. There is liberty not only of prophesying but also of the discussion of its validity. This is seen in the *examinatio ministrorum* which is under the guidance of the elders and deacons.[82] Here is Laski's variation on the 'Prophesying' established at Zürich by which he sought to keep ministers alert, to enable members to have a voice in their own religious instruction and to exercise in the Scriptures the elders, to whom had been given moral oversight. This positive participation of the laity would have been frowned upon elsewhere in Protestantism as leading to what has been disparagingly called 'ochlochracy'. This democratic element could lead to a change of ceremony in public worship by popular discussion and vote. It can be no matter of surprise that Bishop Ridley and others were seriously concerned about this Trojan horse which Cranmer had unwittingly drawn into London.

---

[81] Laski uses the word 'foedus' where it is relevant from scriptural usage, but there is no development of the covenant theme.

[82] *Opera*, I, 388; II, 103. 'Deinde ministris verbi excutetur torpor atque otium.'

For Laski the sacraments are useful to us because they quicken our faith but they do not save and they have no virtue in themselves, they are no more than a means for renewing our faith in Christ's promises. Baptism is a seal of our acceptance into God's grace, it does not provide grace of itself, by it we are united in the public assembly of Christians and children rightly receive it following the example of circumcision. The significance of the Lord's Supper is in the action of distributing the bread and wine, which in themselves have no importance there is no relationship between the bread and the wine and the body and the blood of Christ, (*discrimen loci*) since the elements are *vilissima pars sacramenti*. The Lord's Supper has been instituted, *Quam ob causam potissimum ut esset sui apud nos reminiscentia sive recordatio*, this is a remembering not only of the death of Christ but also of his merits and virtues as our Saviour.[83] Laski believed that he was in agreement with the *Consensus Tigurinus* but he must have interpreted it in the Zwinglian sense and not in the modification of Zwingli accepted by Bullinger and urged by Calvin. For Laski Christ's words 'Hoc facite' relate to the act of breaking the bread and that act is the sign of his body, and the whole rite is dependent on the faith of the believers. This position he defended, with minor variations of phrasing, consistently and vigorously against the Lutherans and by implication anyone else who disagreed with it, including Bucer on the eve of his death at Cambridge.[84] Fifteen days prior to the administration of the Lord's Supper there is to be a service of preparation for it, consisting of exhortation to a process of self-examination lasting during two weeks of reflection. During this period of preparation the elders learn the names of those who will participate, after some have been excluded by failing to give a good account of themselves to the minister or an elder. This brings the Lord's Supper into being an aspect of moral discipline wherein exhortation, worthiness and the repelling of the unworthy are emphasised.

The discipline in Laski's congregations was an essential part of the life of the Church, undertaken with continuous exhortations, and included the reporting by individuals in public assembly on the

---

[83] *Opera*, I, 550; II, 115. Reception at the Lord's Supper was by sitting at the table. 'Huic accumbunt et ministri et convivae Coenae suas vices omnes atque accumbenti mensae e ministri accumbentis manibus coenam Domini sumunt.'

[84] D. F. Wright, *Commonplaces of Martin Bucer*, 1972, 384. For Bucer's reply to Laski, J. V. Pollet, *Martin Bucer: Etudes sur la correspondance* . . ., Paris, 1958, I, 285 ff. In Laski's letter to Bullinger of January 7 1551, he wrote, 'We [of the Strangers' Church] follow it [the *Consensus Tigurinus*] although we sometimes express it in different words.' This was a crucial modification. *Opera*, II, 646.

unworthiness of other members – mere denigration, however, would lead to public rebuke.[85] The declaration of the full penalty was not reserved to the ministry or eldership, for before excommunication could take place the whole membership of a congregation must consent: those who were blameworthy could pray for pardon before the decision was taken and after excommunication the blameworthy could be received again after showing valid signs of repentance. A special discipline existed for ministers, elders and deacons who were to meet together with the Superintendent on stated occasions for 'Censures': this is reciprocal and members of the congregation can come to present complaints against one or more of these officers concerning their doctrine or conduct.[86] Even the Superintendent should receive admonishment if necessary. All this constant exhortation in public worship and discussion in meetings for discipline, in which all members as well as the church's officers were involved, must have proved to be a strain. The relation of Church and State for Laski was simplified: the Church is governed by God through Christ and it does not belong to the State to interfere in its worship, doctrine or discipline. Laski granted that in England Edward VI was the chief minister of God for the Church, but this did not extend to officers of the Crown, besides, by Letters Patent Edward had made the Churches of the Strangers virtually free from all interference.

In Frisia there had been one minister and four elders to form a church council or consistory, but no number was specified for the London councils. Ministers and elders were one in office though with different functions, whereas for Calvin the elders were laymen and had no share in the functions of the ministry of the word and sacraments.[87] It has been frequently asserted that Laski's Churches of the Strangers were the first appearance of Presbyterianism in England; but there was no *classis* with the authority which Presbyterians gave to it, nor General Assembly as a court of final authority, and the extensive congregational democracy which Laski encouraged was more appropriate to Congregationalism than to Presbyterianism. Finally the office of Superintendent, however mitigated, was more episcopal than presbyterian, an office (*Inspector ministerium*) which he did not consider to be merely an administrative convenience, for he claimed it to be a divine institution (*esse Divinam ordinationem in Christi Ecclesia*), established by Christ in giving to Peter the charge of the brethren (an authority also given to James and John) an office

---

[85] *Opera*, II, 170 ff.

[86] *Opera*, II, 227.

[87] The imposition of hands, 'ministri et seniores ecclesiae omnes et capitibus illorum manus.' *Opera*, II, 72.

essential to the Church since it is better for one man to decide on certain questions. It is clear from his practice that the office of Superintendent which Laski himself held was not to be confined to attending, and offering occasional judgements to, monthly meetings or annual gatherings for discipline or debate. By background, temperament and personal weight of experience and authority Laski could not be contained within the confines of the *Forma ac Ratio*, for he addressed kings with confidence and powerful statesmen as an equal, and challenged the leaders of other churches with authority. Laski's church order was unique but it established no denomination to continue its distinctive characteristics, for the better established Presbyterian order of the Reformed churches set aside Laski's mingling of congregationalism and episcopacy. Laski's unique form of churchmanship suffered several changes at Emden while he was in England: even his former friend Hardenberg came to oppose some of his methods and doctrines. At Frankfurt the remnant of his Church of Strangers was to disintegrate after his leaving it for Poland where his arrangements were modified in the Reformed Church.[88] No one effectively undertook to follow that model of lengthy description of church order, of intensive almost claustrophobic disciplinary self-examination and mutual criticism. His form of church worship is sensible in its pattern but contains an excessive amount of exhortation, – for example, seventeen closely printed pages about the service of matrimony must be the longest recorded.[89]

It is difficult to determine what influence the writings of Laski produced in England or who followed the example of his church practices there. That Laski vigorously supported Bishop Hooper, the solitary disciple of Zürich among the English bishops, in opposing the use of vestments and certain of the ceremonies of *The Book of Common Prayer* is well known, as is the fact that he was the only foreign Protestant to do this, but in spite of his energetic interference in writing to Archbishop Cranmer, to Bucer and to Bullinger, Laski failed in his attack and Hooper had to capitulate.[90] He received a gift of money from the Privy Council for his work for the commission on the *Reformatio Legum Ecclesiasticarum*, and he may well have been one of those, like John Knox, who were behind the insertion of what came to be called the Black Rubric in the second *Book of Common*

---

[88] Cf. the concluding section on Poland in *Lasciana*, 397 ff.

[89] *Opera*, II, 249–67.

[90] For Laski's zeal here, *Lasciana*, 60–62. *Opera*, II, 646–647. Laski describes Hooper as having 'candorem, simplicitatem, eruditionem et pietatem'. To Cranmer, Aug. 1551, Laski was aggressively positive (*vehementer optarim*) on what the Archbishop should do. II, 658, 659.

Prayer.[91] What Laski's writings did provide was an example to later developments in English Puritanism; a legalistic morality based on close analysis of the Decalogue; one possible origin of the Elizabethan Puritan demand for elders or seniors; an example of one kind of Prophesying; and for those Englishmen who were attracted to the worship of the Churches of the Strangers was the view in practice of certain aspects of Zürich simplicity in the theology and administrations of the sacraments with the addition of sitting at the table – and they would see churches organised which were accepted by the state, supported by the Crown, but outside of the jurisdiction of the bishops. No doubt by 1552 Cranmer was wondering whether it would not be opportune if Laski were to take up his Superintendency elsewhere and remove his congregations with him – certainly if he did so he would not have been the first to feel that Laski's reputation and influence exceeded the quality of his activities.

Laski's first wife died towards the end of 1552 and some months later he married an English girl to look after his children and care for his own declining health.[92] In July, 1553, the death of Edward VI and the coming of Catholic Mary urged Laski, now fifty-four, to go on his travels again accompanied not only by his family but now also by the majority of the members of his congregations from England. A partisan account of their difficult journeys and their hostile reception in Denmark and Germany was written by his secretary John Utenhove whose talent for exaggeration and one-sided interpretation of the views of others had made difficulties for Cranmer through Utenhove's correspondence with Zürich and elsewhere.[93] This manuscript was sent to Calvin in 1558 since its publication at Geneva would be a propaganda triumph for Utenhove and Laski against the Lutherans but Calvin refused to allow it to be printed there. Calvin had also ignored Laski's request that Calvin should write a preface to his attack on the Lutheran Westphal in 1554. Calvin was becoming weary of Laski's talent for stubbornness and controversy.[94]

---

[91] *Acts of the Privy Council, 1550–1552*, 420, for the gift of money. Words from his Order of Worship can be found in the Confession and Absolution in the Book of Common Prayer, 1552. F. Procter, W. H. Frere, *The Book of Common Prayer*, 1965, 89. C. W. Dugmore, *The English Prayer Book, 1548–1662*, 1963, 25, on the Black Rubric and Laski.

[92] Laski to Bullinger, June, 1553. *Opera*, II, 674–8.

[93] *Simplex et fidelis narratio de instituta ac demum dissipata Belgarum aliorumque peregrinorum in Angliae Ecclesiae . . . per Joan. Utenhovium Gandavum*, 1560, Basel. Calvin wrote to Bullinger on Utenhove, 'tam prolixe scribere'. *Calvini Opera*, XVII, 298.

[94] Calvin and Martyr disagreed with Laski, *Calvini Opera*, XV, 493, 723. Kruske, 71 ff., describes Laski's bitter controversy with the Lutheran Joachim Westphal. Calvin later commented on Laski's attack '. . . sed vulnera renovare quae odia semisepulta iterum accendant'. *Calvini Opera*, XVII, 379. Kruske's judgement on the affair is terse, 'Keiner der Streiter hat einen neuen Gedanken produziert.'

The presence of two Danish ships moored in the Thames provided for the flight of Laski and a number of his people who arrived, after near shipwreck, in Denmark in October – but Denmark had become a Lutheran land. The leading Lutheran pastor Noviomagus preached before the King when Laski, Utenhove and Micronius were present, on the sacrament of the altar 'impudentissime' according to Utenhove, who with his colleagues believed the choice of subject, and the rejection of those who denied the Real Presence as heretics, were a deliberate challenge, though in fact the Lord's Supper had been the lectionary subject for that day.[95] The King, though he wished to be welcoming to these religious refugees, was troubled about the possibility of disturbances in religion at a time when the Reformation had not yet obtained a thorough hold on Denmark. Laski and his associates resolutely refused to compromise their doctrine and practice in any way and at a colloquy held between the Lutheran clergy and Laski before the royal council, Laski attacked Lutheran teaching as being opposed to the word of God. Reluctantly King Christian asked them to depart and gave Laski a hundred golden thalers to assist the refugees. Laski and his people indignantly sailed for Emden since the Hanse cities also refused to receive them. Utenhove's one-sided account of King Christian and the Danish Lutherans as unfeeling bigots was offset by his condemning their 'absurd toleration of the monks, those wolves and enemies of religion', in Denmark. Laski included a brief but vigorously antagonistic account of the Danish episode, showing the unscriptural worthlessness of the half-way house of Lutheranism, in his prefatory address to King Sigismund II of Poland accompanying a gift of his Forma ac Ratio.[96] Once again he and his congregations returned to Emden where he took up again his Superintendency and expressed his gratitude, 'benevolentiam ... munificentiam satis praedicare non possem', but the situation had changed there; Lutheranism had become stronger and even his friend Hardenberg compromised with Lutheran doctrine and practice to Laski's indignant sense of betrayal. Laski renewed his intransigent attack on Lutheranism, and among other targets of criticism described church organs as 'the devil's whistles'. Emden could no longer endure this hostility and was uneasy also about the increasing numbers of refugees from the Netherlands and elsewhere who joined Laski's

---

[95] R. Mönckeberg, *Johannes a Lasco und seiner Fremdegemeinde Aufnahme in Dänemark und Norddeutschland.* (*Zeitschrift für Kirchliche Wissenschaft*, 1883, 590 ff.) Kruske, 84 ff. *Opera*, II, 680–4. Letter from the King of Denmark to Laski and Micronius, with two more letters from Laski to the King.

[96] For Laski the Lutherans represented no more than modified Catholicism: they were 'Lutheranopapists', 'Syncretistarum Parasitomini perfidia', *Opera*, II, 31.

church. Once again it was time for Laski and his church to move and in April, 1955, he departed for Frankfurt with a section of his church and joined the English and French refugee congregation there, and became officially a Superintendent again.

He was becoming weary of these wanderings, and longed for Poland: earlier, in December 1552, he had written to the Palatine of Wilna, Nicholas Radziwill, who was to urge him to return, that no one knew how long he had felt a great desire to serve his country.[97] It was becoming inevitable that he would have to move again since renewed conflict arose with the Lutherans, and the magistrates wished him and his church members to sign the Augsburg Confession, which he regarded as wrong in principle since Scripture alone could bind the conscience. Calvin tried to alter Laski's viewpoint stating that he himself had willingly and freely signed the Confession and approved of Melanchthon's interpretation of it.[98] Laski brushed this aside and tried to persuade Calvin to isolate Melanchthon – this was ignored by Calvin. Bullinger, not surprisingly, wrote to Calvin wishing that Laski would have prudence and that he would not commit himself to a course of action he would regret all his life.[99] Laski never seems to have understood Luther's writings, even if he had studied them, for his collected works and letters give no adequate evidence of this: to Bullinger once he wrote Luther off as 'insolent, impudent, and full of vanity.' For him the Lutheran teaching on the Lord's Supper was simply idolatry to be dismissed by his own more rational view of it. Since Frankfurt an imperial city was legally bound to the Augsburg Confession it could not accept Laski's assertion that God's word bound his conscience and compelled him to challenge the 'Lutheropapists'. He felt offended by Lutheran intransigence, oppressed by the magistrates who feared divisions among the Protestants which could destroy political stability, and stirred by a deep nostalgia for his homeland. Encouraged by a letter from the king, he left Frankfurt and his church, and after a brief stay in Stuttgart, returned to Poland with his family in April 1556. He had already sent letters to King Sigismund II and to influential nobles urging the reformation of the Church by a national synod to seek unity among the Protestant groups – but he must have realised there were serious problems.[100]

[97] *Opera*, II, 674. (Dec. 1552).

[98] *Calvini Opera*, XVI, 430. (April 1556) 'nec vero Augustanam confessionem repudio ... volens ac libens subscripsi.'

[99] *Calvini Opera*, XVI, 121, 687.

[100] *Opera*, II, 738. For a recent discussion of the Zwinglian and Lutheran doctrines of the Eucharist, cf. Basil Hall, *Hoc est corpus meum: The centrality of the Real Presence for Luther.*

At this period Poland was a powerful kingdom with an elective
monarchy working together with the Diets, or national assemblies, of
noblemen of independent views, in which Catholicism still was strong
but challenged by various Protestant groups including the Reformed
and Antitrinatarians. From Prussia which was a vassal territory of
Poland Lutheranism had infiltrated the kingdom, and through the
close political association with Bohemia religious refugees had been
received from there and settled by some of the nobles on their estates.
These were the Bohemian Brethren (the *Unitas Fratrum*), of Hussite
origin, who maintained the Real Presence, a strict discipline including
private confession, and more traditional ceremonies. When Laski
arrived to face this complex religious situation he was greeted
incautiously with enthusiasm as the man who could help to resolve
it. As one indignant observer commented, his arrival was welcomed
in Poland 'as if St Peter had dropped from heaven', and a year later a
bishop complained, *Laski in Pinczow papam agere dicitur*.[101]

Laski's undoctrinaire form of churchmanship enabled him to seek
union among the rival Protestant groups, but doctrinally committed
Lutherans, Reformed and Bohemian Brethren were unwilling to
accept Laski's ecclesiologically informal *coetus*. Moreover, Laski's view
of the Lord's Supper offended not only Lutherans but the Bohemian
Brethren, whose confession of faith and ceremonies he had sharply
attacked. Since he urged the King to undertake reform in order to
have a united kingdom, and appealed to the nobles, dissatisfied with
the Catholic Church's political control in Poland, to support
Protestantism which would give them more freedom of action, Laski's
efforts for Protestant union were suspect to the Protestants as having
primarily a political rather than a religious purpose. In spite of years
of friendly correspondence with Albrecht of Prussia, and a visit to
Königsberg in 1558, Laski felt betrayed by Prussian insistence on
making the Augsburg Confession the basis of Polish Protestantism.[102]
Again, he felt unsupported by the King who agreed that a national
council should be called to reform religion but never called it for
fear of the political consequences of religious schism.

However, Laski was able to carry through the re-modelling of the
Reformed congregations largely on his own pattern of church order
and moral discipline set forth in the *Forma ac Ratio* though with some
modification to meet the Polish situation. The *coetus* and meetings for
discipline differed somewhat from the practice used in London which

Luther: Theologian for Catholics and Protestants, ed. George Yule, T. & T. Clark, Edinburgh,
1985.
[101] Kruske, 160.
[102] *Opera*, 755 ff.

had been the one period of his Protestant career when Laski had total control of a close-knit organisation and when he had no need to compromise with previous arrangements or political support. The offices of superintendent (now enlarged in scope) and minister were established as before but the elders and deacons were to be elected from the nobility, no doubt to ensure political support, though in effect he was subordinating the Reformed Church to their control which was something he had sought to avoid as recently as his residence in Frankfurt. The Polish situation was clearly different from that of London, or even Emden, where he had found strong support by the central authority without interference in the church's affairs. Since the King seemed unwilling to give positive commitment to church reform Laski had turned to the nobles. He was not made superintendent for one had already been established before his arrival, Felix Cruciger, but he was treated with great respect at the annual synodical assemblies attended by church members, as well as by the monthly synods concerned with church discipline when increasing ill-health allowed him to attend them.[103] His high standing with kings, princes and magnates would alone have ensured this apart from his undoubted administrative ability and moral authority.

In Reformed centres elsewhere a confession of faith was thought to be essential to the well-being of the Church, but Laski was unwilling to accept the urging from Zürich and Geneva to prepare one since he feared that a confession would hinder Protestant unity in Poland; moreover, as has been seen, both by temperament and conviction, he was unwilling to commit the church to a closely organised system of doctrine. It was only some years after his death that the Reformed Church in Poland conformed to the general Reformed pattern, in this and in other ways, and produced a confession of faith which was based on the *Confessio Helveticum Posterior* thereby demonstrating the more powerful influence of Zürich than of Geneva in line with Laski's own preference. The Polish Reformed Church was faced by heavy financial burdens, the maintenance of a college at Pinczow (where Laski chiefly resided), the preparation for, and the printing of a Polish translation of the Bible, the building of churches and schools, and funding the establishing of presses for the provision of Protestant literature in the vernacular. Laski, ill and overburdened at his age died on 8 January 1560, his last months embittered by the controversy begun by Franciszek Stankar to promote that antitrinitarianism which was later to divide the Reformed Church in Poland into orthodox and Arian

---

[103] *Lasciana*, 426 ff.

bodies. The synodical report of his funeral included these words: 'As soon as he had heard that the light of evangelical doctrine was arising in his country, although old, not so much through years as through his labours for the Church of God, he left England and came back to Poland so that he could energetically promote the glory of God a service he performed in the presence of kings and nobles – *feliciter in Domino translatus est ex morte in vitam.*'[104]

<hr/>

[104] *Lasciana*, 492. A canon of Cracow noted, 'Nova huc nulla sunt hoc tempore praeter hoc unum quod Lasci hereticus vel iam potius mahometicus moratur hic, quandoque in Arce Ribsia.' (Schloss Ribstein.). *Lasciana*, 35.

7

The Early Rise and Gradual Decline of Lutheranism in England 1520–1600

Bishop Gardiner, whom the polemical John Bale described as 'the great Caiaphas of Winchester', sharply drew the attention of the lord protector, Seymour, to 'two seditious books' not long after the death of Henry VIII in 1547, showing his anxiety to oppose the advance of Protestantism which he saw as leading to civil as well as religious rebellion; both books were by Bale, at this time in exile abroad.

> I have perceived by books written without authority, as by Master Bale, Joy and others, and especially as Bale useth now, that Scripture doth, by abuse, service to the right hand and the left at once, insomuch as at one time Bale praiseth Luther, and setteth his death forth in English, with commendation as of a saint; which Luther (whatsoever he was otherwise) stoutly approved the presence really of Christ's natural body in the sacrament of the altar. And yet Bale, the noble clerk, would have Anne Askew, blasphemously denying the presence of Christ's natural body, to be taken for a saint also.[1]

Gardiner was showing the characteristic Catholic opposition to

[1] J. Foxe, *Acts and Monuments*, ed Josiah Pratt, London, 1870, 6, 30 ff. The two books by

Protestantism by pointing to its divisions, and to the contradictions among English Protestants who were drawing theological aid from opposed sources, Lutheran on the one hand and south German and Swiss on the other. From the beginning, English Protestants, including William Tyndale, one of the earliest able theologians among them, were willing to accept gladly Luther's theological aid in attacking Catholicism while on the whole discarding his sacramental teaching and eventually failing to give central place to his concept of law and the dialectic of law and gospel. Lutheranism won easy victories in Germany and Scandinavia, but in England it faced a native biblical tradition hostile to its theological subtlety; a political situation wholly different not least because the English king had early committed himself to opposing Luther; and the increasing influence of theologians at Basel, Strasbourg and Zürich. That Lutheranism achieved the degree of influence which will be briefly described in this essay shows both the intellectual energy of Lutheran theologians and liturgical writers, and the eclecticism of their English counterparts who were restricted by the pressure of political changes and by the need to find a balance between contending theological views.

The subject of Lutheran influences in the English Reformation is not new. Books which were wholly committed to claiming it were H. E. Jacobs, *The Lutheran Movement in England during the Reigns of Henry VIII and Edward VI and its Literary Monuments* (1890); Carl Meyer, *Elizabeth and the Religious Settlement of 1559* (1960); N. S. Tjernagel, *Henry VIII and the Lutherans* (1965). These writers were American Lutherans zealous to show the Lutheran base of the English Reformation and of Anglicanism; and provided a useful corrective to those complacent defenders of the English Reformation as an achievement little influenced by foreigners, of whom Gairdner and Maynard Smith were typical.[2] But they tend to overstate their case: to describe as does Tjernagel the Thirty-Nine Articles, and therefore, as he assumes, Anglicanism, to be fundamentally Lutheran is to ignore the powerful influence which can also be documented of other theological definitions and purposes. To say that, 'At Henry's death England was quite prepared to accept the Lutheran faith in its totality'

Bale were: *The true hystorie of the Christen departynge of the reverende man D. Martyne Luther*, 1546, and *The Lattre Examinacyon of Anne Askewe*, 1547. While Bale corresponded with Lutherans and was a friend of Robert Barnes, he did not adopt Lutheranism. In 1544 he published an account of the 'examination and death of the blessed Martir Sir John Oldcastle', a lollard, and published the treatise on the Lord's supper by the Zwinglian John Lambert.

[2] Erwin Doernberg, *Henry VIII and Luther*, London, 1961, ably covers similar ground to that more thoroughly analysed by Tjernagel, with less emphasis on the Lutheran commitment in the English reformation. J. Gairdner, *Lollardy and the Reformation*, 4 vols, London 1908. H. M. Smith, *Henry VIII and the Reformation*, London, 1948.

is a demonstration of enthusiasm overcoming facts to the contrary.[3] This, however, does not detract from the value of Tjernagel's thorough analysis of the diplomatic and theological relations of England and Germany 1536–9. For Meyer the dominant theme in the Elizabethan settlement of religion is Melanchthonian, a view he reinforced with his article on Melanchthon's influence on English thought: again the purpose is useful and provides new perspectives but ignores the complex problems of how other forces compelling eclecticism in ideas were at work.[4] A shorter, better balanced account of Lutheranism and the English was *Studies in the Making of the English Protestant Tradition* by E. G. Rupp (1947), which among other matters dealt with Tyndale, Barnes, the Articles and the 'Bishops' and 'King's' books; again Luther is the central theme, following the description of surviving lollardy and its biblicism. Rupp curiously saw no conflict between this English biblicism and the developing influence of Lutheranism. A corrective to his Protestant federalism is found in *England's Earliest Protestants, 1520–1535*, by W. A. Clebsch, who demonstrated that the corrosive influence of south German and Swiss theology was already at work on Lutheranism in England. In 1966 Rupp sought to brush aside Clebsch's findings by associating him with Trinterud's study of the origins of covenant theology and thus fathering on Tyndale the future development of covenant theology in America – a view Clebsch was not seeking to promote.[5] On this basis Rupp wrote that Clebsch overstated and mis-stated his case for Tyndale's change to an ethical emphasis on law and the covenant: but this will not do, even when Rupp's point that Tyndale understood well and did not depart from Luther's insights on justification by faith is accepted, for the evidence adduced by Clebsch is clear and full.

The Lutheran overstatement may be corrected by pointing to the other factors at work in the English Reformation, not only theological but political, even when the areas of Lutheran influence are described and related to their complex content. By the reign of Elizabeth Lutheranism had effectively lost ground. The vigorous Protestantism of Elizabeth's bishops, theologians and lay religious leaders did not see the settlement as conservative Lutheranism but as an Erastian device, temporary perhaps, at best expedient at worst 'popish' – Luther and his immediate disciples had given England a lead once but

[3] Tjernagel, 253.
[4] C. S. Meyer, 'Melanchthon's influence on English thought in the sixteenth century', *Miscellanea Historiae Ecclesiasticae*, 2, Louvain, 1967.
[5] E. G. Rupp. *Patterns of Salvation in the First Age of the Reformation*, ARG (1967) Heft 1/2, 64.

the world was changed. Hooker's defence of the settlement provided no Lutheran renewal, and used no Lutheran props to support it.[6]

For example, in a new calendar associated with the *Book of Common Prayer* in 1578 there are four days of some interest to those concerned with English attitudes to Lutheranism in the sixteenth century:

February 16	the learned clerk Philip Melanchthon as upon this day was born.
February 18	Martin Luther the servant of God died as upon this day.
February 22	Martin Luther his body as upon this day was translated to Witemberg and buried in the chapel of the Castle there.
October 31	This day in the yeere of our Lord God 1517 and 101 yeere after ye death of John Hus, Martin Luther gave his propositions in ye universitie of Witemberg against ye Pope's pardons.[7]

But this calendar was an unofficial enterprise intended to oppose the names of 'Protestant saints' to those of 'popish saints' in the traditional calendars in Elizabethan use, and it cannot be taken to mean that a deep or ready sympathy existed for Lutheran doctrine and religious practices at that time. In fact it would be difficult to find an Elizabethan writer approving of Lutheran teachings and methods of worship and advocating them apart from those subjects which had become common to Protestantism, including justification by faith.

For example, in the controversy between the Puritan Thomas Cartwright and Archbishop Whitgift, Cartwright, in seeking support for his criticism of the state of the Church of England, cited Peter Martyr:

> who upon the tenth chapter of II Book of Kings saith: The Lutherans must take heed lest whilst they cut off many popish errors, they follow Jehu by retaining also many popish things. For they defend still the real presence in the bread of the Supper, and images and vestments, and saith that religion must be wholly reformed to the quick.

Archbishop Whitgift replied:

---

[6] Meyer suggested, in his article on Melanchthon's influence (p. 183), that Hooker may have derived his concept of natural law in part from Melanchthon and cites the *Loci Communes*, 1521 without precise reference. Given the period in which Hooker was writing and the wide range of his reading in Scholastic writers and contemporary legal theorists this is improbable.

[7] *Liturgies and occasional forms of Prayer set forth in the reign of Queen Elizabeth*, PS (1847), 445, 453.

M. Martyr nameth the popish things which the Lutherans observe to be the real presence, images, all the popish apparel which they used in their mass (for so doth he mean) and this Church [the Church of England] hath refused.[8]

Again, it is surprising to find Richard Hooker the carefully eirenic apologist of the *Ecclesia Anglicana* writing in his *Second Sermon on Justification, Works and how the Foundation of Faith is Overthrown* in 1585, that the Church of Rome in its teachings 'in spite of their confessing remission of sins through Christ overthrew the very foundation of faith by consequent: doth not that so likewise which the Lutheran churches do at this day so stiffly and so fiercely maintain?' He then adds: 'For mine own part, I dare not hereupon deny the possibility of their salvation, which have been the chiefest instruments of ours albeit they carried to their grave a persuasion so greatly repugnant to the truth.'[9] The Elizabethan attitude to Lutheranism can also be seen at the popular level in a doggerel rhyme against a Romanist:

> Till Luther's time you say that we
> Heard not of Christ: but you shall see
> That we, not you, have heard of him,
> As only pardoner of our sinne
> Thrise happy Luther, and the rest,
> (Except some faults which we detest).[10]

In sum the majority of Elizabethan Protestant Englishmen, almost without exception, were willing to admire Martin Luther for his stand against the Pope, and for his great insight in rediscovering the truth of justification by faith alone, but they believed that he and his followers allowed in the Lutheran churches the development of dangerous doctrines and the continuation of certain 'popish' practices which must be totally rejected.

But would an observer of the religious changes among Englishmen in the reign of Henry VIII have been able to predict the probability of this rejection of Lutheranism in the reign of Elizabeth I? Dickens can go so far as to write, in the epilogue to his excellent study *The English Reformation*, 'If Henry had foreseen the ultimate political dangers of Calvinist Protestantism, he might have been prompted to thrust aside his scruples and adopt as his State Religion a fully-fledged

---

[8] *The Works of John Whitgift*, PS (1853), 3, 549–50.

[9] *The Works of Richard Hooker*, ed J. Keble (3 ed 1845) 3, 503. Hooker is positive in statement but allusive (and elusive) in what he is intending to attack.

[10] *Select Poetry, chiefly devotional, of the reign of Queen Elizabeth*, PS (1845) 2, 288. *An Answere to a Romish Rime lately printed*, 1602.

Lutheranism, with its veneration for the godly prince. Yet whether this step would have exorcised more radical creeds or merely paved the way for their advent, we can only conjecture.'[11] Nevertheless, the more one reflects upon Henry's attitude to Luther himself and his ill-informed dislike of Lutheran doctrines; upon his hostility to foreign influences in England; and upon his obtaining all that the doctrine of the godly prince could convey both in fact through his own political action, and in theory through the strong advocacy on the one hand of Archbishop Cranmer who profoundly believed in it, and on the other, through the cautious but powerful support of Bishop Gardiner's authoritarian legalism in his *De vera obedientia*, the more one doubts that Henry would have allowed the Church of England to become Lutheran.[12] It is true that Henry chose Latimer and Cranmer for bishops and that both of these men were influenced by Lutheran doctrines, especially Cranmer who had been closely associated at first hand with German Lutheranism; but neither of them was a wholehearted Lutheran, in the sense of accepting the full range of Lutheran theology. Cranmer moved eventually from the Lutheran doctrine of the Real Presence to that of the Spiritual Presence. Latimer in a sermon before Edward VI in 1549 said: 'Oh Luther when he came into the world first and disputed against the Decretals and the Canon Law, what ado had he! But ye will say peradventure he was deceived in some things. I will not take it upon me to defend him in all points. I will not stand to it that all that he wrote was true.'[13] When Latimer went to his death at the stake in 1553 he was to be burned, as was his younger friend Cranmer who saw his death agony from the roof of the Oxford prison? Bocardo, for denying the Real Presence *transubstantialiter*, and their own belief on the eucharistic presence could not be described in terms acceptable to their Lutheran contemporaries. In fact it would be difficult to determine who maintained in England consistently through his Protestant career and in writing from Tyndale onwards, the Lutheran doctrine of the sacrament of the Lord's supper.

This was indeed to be the chief hindrance to the advance of Lutheranism in England. Bishop Hooper wrote to Martin Bucer in June 1548, while Hooper was at Zürich: 'Although I readily acknowledge with thankfulness the gifts of God in him who is now no more, yet he was not without his faults. After the dispute with

[11] A. G. Dickens, *The English Reformation*, London, 1964, 328–9.

[12] P. Janelle, *Obedience in Church and State*, gives a reprint of bishop Gardiner's *De Vera Obedientia*. Gardiner's book was printed at Hamburg for presentation to Lutheran princes and divines.

[13] *The Works of Hugh Latimer*, PS (1844), 212. From a sermon before Edward VI, 1549.

Zwingli and Oecolampadius about the Supper grew warm, he did violence to many passages of Scripture.'[14] Hooper himself was on this point as on others an adherent of Zürich theology. The Marian martyr John Bradford before he was burned at Smithfield market in 1555 said under examination in prison: 'My faith is not builded on Luther, Zwingli or Oecolampadius on this point [the Real Presence], and indeed to tell you truly, I never read any of their works in this matter.'[15] While from the beginning of the Reformation in England most English Protestants accepted Luther's teaching on justification, some to the extent of almost slavishly repeating his words, yet his doctrine of the Lord's Supper made almost all of them uneasy and even hostile. This hesitation about, and in fact rejection of, Luther's doctrine of the sacraments taken together with those factors referred to at the beginning, namely, the powerful influence of a south German and Zürich centred biblicism containing a moral legalism based on the covenant principle so alien to Luther's doctrinal method, and taken together with Henry's refusal to accept Lutheran formularies and the Lutheran agenda for cleansing abuses in the Church, prevented decisively England from becoming a Lutheran land.

The unwillingness of Englishmen to accept Luther's sacramental theology no doubt was due to influences opposed to it both from within England and from abroad. It had long been fashionable to ignore the continuing effect of lollardy in England in the sixteenth century (an attitude more recently rejected): this anti-sacerdotal and anti-sacramental movement was dismissed as negligible or irrelevant, whereas in fact it provided a widespread underground of anti-papalism before and after Protestantism entered England from Germany. It was centred on a literalistic and unscholarly biblicism affirming obedience to the precepts of the law and of the gospel, which was almost inevitable given the conditions through which it survived. Here was a continuity between the Old and New Testaments in the law of God which Luther deliberately set aside since this emphasis on precepts for obedience would bring in works again by another door. It could be, and surely was the breeding ground for 'covenant' ideas, since a covenant or federal theology soon attracted early English Protestantism – and a covenant theology of this federal type (for example, in the Scot Samuel Rutherford in the next century) is always inimical to an effective sacramental theology. This tendency towards a legalistic biblicism which could so

[14] *Original Letters relative to the English Reformation*, PS (1846) 1 series, 46.
[15] *The Writings of John Bradford*, PS (1848) 1, 525.

readily move into covenant theology, with its relation of obedience to being elect and 'foreknown', was very tenacious in England, like lollardy 'native of the soil', surviving in English nonconformity until well into the nineteenth century. It is significant that England's 'first Lutheran', William Tyndale, was unwilling to adopt Luther's sacramental teaching: almost from the first Tyndale was attracted by the principle of the covenant, a requirement of obedience in the contract between God and His people, which Zwingli had set forth at Zürich and which his successors there, especially Bullinger, were to develop.[16] Like Zwingli Tyndale affirmed the continuity between law and gospel, against Luther who firmly set them in opposition. If English Puritanism which developed later in the century may be regarded in its theology as Pietism grounded on moral legalism, then its ultimate ancestor is Tyndale. It was through Tyndale's emphasis on the covenant principle that the theology of Zürich would be developed in England. Again, one of the earliest of English Lutherans, Dr Robert Barnes the Cambridge Franciscan, whom Luther referred to after his martyrdom as 'Saint Robert', while he was wholeheartedly Lutheran during his residence at Wittenberg yet, during the last ten years of his life, he may well have increasingly accommodated his theology to the English situation which was opposing the influence of Lutheran teaching on the Real Presence.[17]

The third reason, already suggested, for Lutheranism failing to become the accepted religion of the English nation was the opposition to it shown by Henry VIII. (A comparison of the ecclesiastical situation in England with that of Sweden would be interesting: there was much in common between the aims and methods of reformation adopted in the two countries, the point of contrast is that king

[16] *Exposition and Notes of Sundry Portions of the Holy Scriptures*, William Tyndale, PS (1849). See also the prologues to various biblical books in his *Doctrinal Treatises*, PS (1848). Tyndale's positive contribution of Lutheran theology to England will be shown later.

[17] W. A. Clebsch, *England's Earliest Protestants, 1520–1535*, London, 1964, 68. 'Between 1531 and 1534 Barnes' theology exchanged its conception of autocratic magistracy for one of covenanted society, and traded its insistence on justification by faith alone for an acknowledgment of justification before the world by works.' However, Clebsch's next sentence is unacceptable which asserts that Bucer and Calvin drifted from 'the religious theocentrism of the early Luther toward the socially and ecclesiastically concerned covenant theology' – that drift is much more marked in the Zürich theologians, and to describe Calvin as drifting from theocentrism at any time is indeed a remarkable assertion. For Barnes see the modernised reprint of the major part of the *Supplication* with helpful introduction and notes by N. S. Tjernagel, *The Reformation Essays of Dr. Robert Barnes*, London, 1963. Clebsch points also to later manipulation of texts in the interests of the later theology, for example, he shows (pp. 81–5) how *Patrick's Places* by the Scot Patrick Hamilton, an early statement of Lutheran teaching in English in 1529, was modified in the interests of later protestantism by John Foxe in the *Acts and Monuments* and by John Knox in his *History of the Reformation in Scotland*. See also R. L. Greaves, *John Knox and the Covenant Tradition*, JEH (1973).

Gustavus Vasa accepted the major Lutheran doctrines for the Church
of Sweden whereas Henry rejected them for England.) Henry's view
of this kingdom, his kingship, his supreme headship of the Church,
combined with his theological conservatism, his refusal to put himself
in spiritual or intellectual tutelage to a German friar in Saxony, and
his interest in an Erasmian type of church reform, led him to oppose
the development of a Lutheran Church of England. If this is thought
to be over-emphatic then it may be well to consider here the shrewd
insight of Luther himself, for he had got the measure of Henry when
he wrote, after Robert Barnes was burned in 1540:

> When this holy martyr, St. Robert understood at last that his king (by
> your leave) Harry of England had become an enemy of the Pope, he
> returned to England with the hope that he might plant the Gospel in his
> fatherland; and at last he was successful in entering upon this ... But
> when we had deliberated, at great length, and at a great expense to our
> noble Prince Elector of Saxony, we found in the end that Harry of
> England had sent his embassy, not because he wanted to become
> evangelical, but in order that we at Wittenberg would agree to his
> divorce ... Harry is Pope, and the Pope is Henry in England. Dr.
> Robert Barnes himself often told me: *Rex meus non curat religionem.* Yet
> he so loved his king and his country, that he was ready to endure
> everything, and always he was striving how to help England ... Hope
> deceived him. For he always hoped that his king would become good.
> Among other things, we often disputed why the king should love that
> abominable title: *Defensor Fidei et in terris caput supremum et immediatum
> post Christum Ecclesiae Anglicanae.* But as this many times was the answer:
> *Sic volo, sic jubeo, sit pro ratione voluntas,* so one could see very well by
> this time that Squire Harry wished to be God and to do what he
> pleased.[18]

Henry never understood the essential themes of Luther: the doctrine
of justification by faith passed him by like words down the wind.
Henry had received some theological training alongside his other
more liberal and diversified studies, but it was theology in a traditional
Scholastic mould, producing those limitations which can be seen in
his *Assertion of the Seven Sacraments* against Luther wherein he did not
come to grips with the essential argument of Luther, although it won
for him that titular recognition from the Pope as *Defensor Fidei* which
he desired as a minor weapon in his diplomatic activities. Moreover,
Henry had been educated by men interested in the new learning, and
he had many about him at court who were influenced by humanist
writings especially those of Erasmus. Henry's friendship for men as

[18] *WA,* 51, 449–50.

diverse as Thomas More and Thomas Cranmer reflects his and their
common interest in the new learning. Some have argued that there
was no guiding principles in Henry's pattern of reformation in the
Church of England,[19] but this is to reduce one of the most powerful
and astute of princes to being a cipher. Rather, a good case could be
made for the view that the Henrician reformation of the Church
shows a very close relationship with the Erasmian principles of
ecclesiastical reform: the abolition of the jurisdiction of the Pope in
favour of the direct initiative for reform resting with the Christian
prince; the closing of religious houses; the translation of the Bible
from the original tongues into the vernacular; the cleansing of certain
abuses, for example, the excessive number of saints days and holidays
and superstitious customs associated with pilgrimages to shrines
and other old but unfruitful practices; the promotion of Hebrew and
Greek studies and good classical Latinity leading to a new biblical
theology to displace Scholasticism. These and other themes of church
reform dear to the Erasmians can all be seen at work in producing
the pattern of Henrician Catholicism.[20]

It was due to there being a measure of common ground between
Erasmians and Lutherans in biblical theology that a certain amount of
Lutheran teaching infiltrated the devotional and theological literature
of the Henrician Church. Henry, in part through ignorance of the
sources, and in part through recognising the value of the new
biblically grounded theology, did not realise how much Lutheran
influence was at work. His sharp criticisms of the 'Bishops' Book'
(*The godly and pious Institution of a Christian Man*, 1537), and his
restoration of a more conservative and traditional theology in the
'King's Book' (*The Necessary Doctrine and Erudition of a Christian
Man*, 1543) may reflect if not a suspicion of the presence of Lutheran

---

[19] For example, compare *NCModH* (1958) 2, 241.

[20] Many of these themes of church reform can be seen in Erasmus' *Enchiridion milites Christiani*,
and are implied behind the mockery of his *Moriae Encomium*. In 1522 Erasmus complacently
stated to John Glapion that *Rex* [Henry VIII] *adhuc puer nihil diligentius legit quam meas
lucubrationes, e quibus fortasse contraxit nonnihil meae phraseos, si quid tamen habet meum*. J. K.
McConica, *English Humanists and Reformation Politics under Henry VIII and Edward VI*, London,
1965, provides a full statement of this major influence. (This paragraph has been left as it stands
since it was written before McConica's work appeared. The words used are intended to draw
attention to curious parallels rather than to demonstrate that this is the major interpretation of
the Henrician reformation.) G. R. Elton, *Reform and Renewal*, London, 1973 4–5, 16–17, attacks
McConica with justice as showing 'an excessive addiction to pattern-making ... McConica's
pursuit of Erasmus really distorts ... to order all that was written – worse, all that was done –
under that single device is to obscure the history of events by hiding it behind a misleadingly
comprehensive generalisation'. This must be allowed, but Elton himself gives too little place in
his writings to this theme which until McConica's book appeared might well have not existed
as far as Elton's writings are concerned.

influence in the former then a determination to maintain orthodox
fences around the new learning he had known and admired in his
youth. Yet, in spite of Henry and in spite of the suspicion and
hostility of the men of the old learning led by Bishop Gardiner,
Lutheran influences both doctrinal and liturgical were at work in
England. Already in 1521 Archbishop Warham had become
increasingly alarmed about the number of Lutheran books circulating
in England, and he wrote to Wolsey:

> Please it your grace to understand that now lately I receyvid letters from
> the Universitie of Oxford and in those same certayne newes which I am
> very sorry to here. For I am enformyd that diverse of that Universitie be
> infectyd with the heresyes of Luther and of others of that sorte having
> among theym a grete nombre of books of the saide perverse doctrine
> which wer forboden by your graces auctoritie as Legate de latere of the
> See apostolique, and also by me as Chauncellor of the saide Universitie
> . . . But it is a sorrowful thing to see how gredyly inconstaunt men and
> specyally inexpert youthe, falleth to new doctrynes be they never so
> pestilent.[21]

There was a bonfire of Lutheran books in London 12 May 1521.
When we reflect that Lutheran influence could attain a pulpit in
Cambridge in December 1525, through Robert Barnes preaching a
sermon which wholeheartedly expounded Lutheran doctrines, then it
is not surprising that this together with other examples of the spread
of these heresies made in Germany should lead to the issuing by 1531,
or a little later, of a second list of books forbidden in England.
Among its eighty-five titles there were twenty-two by Luther.[22]

Latin works from overseas would be confined to scholars like that
group of Cambridge men, including Robert Barnes, who met in the
White Horse tavern (which in those days was in a long vanished side-
street near Queens' College), where they read and discussed Luther's
writings. Tyndale's Preface to his New Testament would bring
Lutheran teaching to many. But a wider influence for Lutheran views
could be found in the books of private devotion in English, called
primers, published for the use of laymen. When George Joye issued
the *Ortulus anime* (*Hortulus animae*) in English 1530 he used Lutheran
sources for some of the prayers, as Butterworth has shown, for
example, the morning prayer and the graces before and after dinner

[21] Henry Ellis, *Original letters, illustrative of English History* 1 series, London, 1824, 1, 239 ff.
[22] *The Acts and Monuments* of John Foxe, ed J. Pratt and J. Stoughton, London, nd, 4, 667.
Foxe gives the title of this catalogue *Libri Sectae sive Factionis Lutherianae importati ad Civitatem
London per fautores ejusdem sectae, quorum Nomina et Auctores sequuntur*, and the date as 1529, but
this is probably at least two years too early.

are taken from Luther's *Betbüchlein* and *Kleiner Katechismus* in their Latin version.[23] Also it is plain what lies behind the following extract:

> The question.
> For as the myche then as god is the spirite and may not be ymagined of other wittes: howe shall we knowe hym?
>
> The answere
> Faithe and truste fynde hym when we are in perel and shewe hym unto us and yet this faythe to fynde hym must he geve us: for if we gete us a faithe of owre owne fasshoninge whereby we beleve and truste in eny wother thinge then god, then make we us an idole: for it is the faithe and truste only in owre hartes that maketh other [either] god or ydole . . .[24]

In 1534 appeared another English primer edited by William Marshall (the first book to be printed in England containing fairly large portions of the Bible in English) which reprinted over half of Joye's version of the *Hortulus*; most of the remainder of the work was a reproduction of writings by Luther without mentioning his name, for example, the preface is adapted from the *Betbüchlein* of 1522, and later there appear free translations of sermons by Luther on prayer and on the passion.[25] Another primer of Marshall – who was bold enough to add at the foot of the title page of his little treatise against the worshipping of images, 'I dout not but some popish doctor or pevish proctor wyl grunt at this treatise' – the *Goodly Primer* of 1535, contained 'Thoffice of all estates' which showed the characteristic Lutheran theme of *beruf* as demonstrated by Tyndale.[26]

But more important, not least because of its fundamental authority and because of its having the widest dissemination was the Bible in English, beginning with William Tyndale's New Testament (1526) which had been indebted, among other versions, to Luther's translation, and included prefaces and notes reflecting Luther's theology, notably the preface to Romans which was almost a direct translation from Luther. The whole Bible, revised and completed on the basis of Tyndale's work, was prepared for publication by Miles Coverdale and the title declared it to be 'faithfully translated out of Douche and Latyn into Englishe' in 1535. 'Douche' here refers particularly to the Zürich German translation which owed much to the Swiss scholars Leo Jud and Pellikan, but also something to Luther's

---

[23] C. C. Butterworth, *The English Primers (1529–1545)* London, 1953, 33. Once again, however, it should be remembered that Joye was not a wholehearted favourer of Lutheranism, he was Zwinglian in his eucharistic doctrine like Tyndale.

[24] Ibid., 36.

[25] Ibid., 61.

[26] Ibid., 108. (Butterworth cites the colophon of the 'Treatise against Images', p. 57).

version. The 'Matthew' Bible (edited in fact by John Rogers 1537) contained Lutheran themes in some of its many notes and prologues. Coverdale not only gave much of his energy to the work of revising and editing an English version of the Bible, he also, among other literary activities translated Luther's *Der 23st Psalm auf einen Abend über Tisch nach dem Gratias ausgelegt* (*1536*) in 1537 and issued a little later his *Goostly Psalmes and Spirituale Songs drawn out of the holy Scripture* which markedly reflect the impact made on him by Luther's own metrical German versions of psalms and other biblical passages.[27] This book of *Goostly Psalmes* was listed among a large number proscribed on Henry's order, in 1539, that showed the rising tide of Lutheran literature coming into England in translation as well as in the original, which had been flowing into England from the time of the public appearance of Luther as reformer.

The influence of Lutheranism is even more marked in the doctrinal and liturgical documents of the Church of England under Henry and even under Edward, although it is being challenged and out-distanced by the increasingly dominating Swiss theology of Zürich – more marked because these were official documents almost all issued with the full authority of the crown and of the Church. The formal doctrinal statements under Henry begin with the *Ten Articles* of 1536 (the first stage in the journey to the *Thirty-Nine Articles* issued under Elizabeth I and still in use), which were described as, 'Articles devised by the King's Highest Maiestie to stablyshe Christen quietnes and Unitie amonge us and to avoyde contentious opinions'. These articles represent a curious mixture of certain characteristic themes of Lutheranism with traditional Catholicism: they are in two parts, the first doctrinal, concerning relation to the creeds, the sacraments and justification, the second ceremonial, and in the former show traces of the *Augsburg Confession* and possibly the *Apology of the Confession* by Melanchthon. To Melanchthon they could be written off, not surprisingly, as *confusissime compositum* (confusingly put together).[28] But not even the English love of compromise which these articles display in its most tortuous form could continue to satisfy Archbishop Cranmer. The next step in interpreting the belief of a church which had cast off the papacy but left the English layman puzzled about what doctrinal requirements were laid on him, was that book prepared by Archbishop Cranmer and a commission of bishops, *The Institution of a Christian Man* (popularly known as the 'Bishops' Book'), which was the nearest approach to full Protantism in an

---

[27] H. E. Jacobs, *The Lutheran Movement in England* London, 1891, 118–24.
[28] Melanchthon, *Opera quae supersunt omnia, CR* 3, col. 1490.

official publication of the reign of Henry. Here the Melanchthonian definitions which appeared, rather heavily disguised, in the *Ten Articles*, are incorporated and expanded, but more than this, both the small and large catechisms of Luther are used, close parallels occurring in several places. For example, compare the 'Bishops' Book':

> I acknowledge and confess that he suffereth and causeth the sun, the moon, the stars, the day, the night, the air, the fire, the water, the fowls, the fishes, the beasts and all the fruits of the earth, to serve me for my profit and my necessity.

with Luther's: *Der Grosse Katechismus*:

> He causes all creatures to serve for the necessities and uses of life – sun, moon and stars in the firmament, day and night, air, fire, water, earth and whatever it bears and produces, bird and fish, beasts, grain and all kinds of produce.

Again, Article 5 of the Augsburg Confession must surely lie behind the following words in the 'Bishops' Book' ('verbum et Sacramenta . . . per instrumenta . . . ut hanc fidem consequamur'):

> To the attaining of which faith, it is also to be noted, that Christ hath instituted and ordained in the world but only two means and instruments, whereof the one is the ministration of his word, and the other is the administration of his sacraments instituted by him; so that it is not possible to attain this faith, but by one, or both of these two means.[29]

The degree to which Cranmer had become committed to the doctrine of justification by faith, even to the extent of flatly opposing Henry, who never really grasped what it was about, can be seen in the annotation he made to one of several proposed additions or corrections written by Henry in the margin of the 'Bishops' Book':

> And I believe also and profess, that he is my very God, my Lord, and my Father, and that I am his servant and his own son by adoption and grace, and ★ the right inheritor of his kingdom . . .

Henry wished to add between the 'and' and 'the' (at the asterisk) the words, 'As long as I persevere in his precepts and laws, one of the right inheritors of his kingdom.' Cranmer disallows this addition, which showed Henry's Catholic legalism relying upon works, by his annotation:

> This book speaketh of the pure Christian faith unfeigned, which is without colour, as well in heart as in mouth. He that hath this faith,

---

[29] Jacobs, 109.

converteth from his sin, repenteth him . . . This is the very pure Christian faith and hope, which every good Christian man ought to profess, believe and trust . . . And as far as the other faith . . . that those which 'persevere in God's laws and precepts, so long as they so do, they be the right inheritors of his kingdom', this is not the commendation of a Christian man's faith, but a most certain proposition, which also the devils believe most certainly, and yet they shall never have their sins forgiven by this faith, nor be inheritors of God's kingdom, because they lack the very christian faith, not trusting to the goodness and mercy of God for their own offences . . .

Cranmer extends himself much further on this theme, because he recognised that Henry's proposed emendation undercut the whole doctrine of saving faith. He is more terse and pointed when Henry wished to add 'I doing my duty' to the words, 'And I believe that by this passion and death of our Saviour Jesus Christ . . .'; for he states flatly:

We may not say that we do our duty. Nevertheless he hath not the right faith in his heart, that hath not a good heart and will do his duty [and refers to the former annotation above]. But no man doth do all his duty, for then he needeth not to have any faith for the remission of his sins.[30]

Henry's need for good diplomatic relations with the Lutheran princes, at a period when he felt threatened by a Catholic alliance, led to prolonged consultations between German and English theologians which it was hoped would produce a theological formulation both sides could agree upon and which would therefore meet the demand of the Lutheran princes that they could satisfy their conscience in forming political alliances only if these reflected the confessing of the faith. The result of these discussions was the *Thirteen Articles* which, although they were set aside after the breakdown of the negotiations between Henry and the Lutheran princes in 1538 and therefore were never published or sanctioned for use, represent clearly the second stage on the road to the *Forty-Two Articles* under Edward VI and the *Thirty-Nine Articles* under Elizabeth I. Hardwick has shown not only that the *Thirteen Articles* follow closely the pattern of the Augsburg Confession, including extensive verbal agreement, but also that they formed the basis for the later development of the articles of religion where the same subject matter was required.[31] Article 7 however was not going to reappear later for it set forth the Lutheran teaching on the eucharist close to the Augsburg definition and very

---

[30] *Remains of Archbishop Cranmer*, PS (1846) 2, 84, 89.
[31] C. Hardwick, *A History of the Articles of Religion*, London, 1904, appendix 2.

close to the article on the eucharist in the conference in Wittenberg in 1536 (the *Repetitio* of Melanchthon brought back by the English commissioners?)

> On the Eucharist we constantly believe and teach that in the sacrament of the body and blood of the Lord, the body and blood of Christ are truly, substantially, and really present under the species of bread and wine: and that under the same species they are truly and really exhibited [presented] and distributed to those who receive the sacrament whether they are good or evil.[32]

Henry, however, could still bewilder and finally exasperate the Lutherans by accepting gladly and praising a work for the instruction of clergymen by the able Lutheran theologian Erasmus Sarcerius translated by Richard Taverner in 1538 as *Comon places of Scripture ordrely set forth*, and then in 1539 issuing the Six Articles ('The Whip with Six Strings') all except possibly the first attacking those who denied traditional Catholic practices already described and rejected by the Lutherans as notorious 'abuses' during the discussions in 1538. Melanchthon with unusually vigorous condemnation attacked these articles at length in a letter to Henry though crediting the bishops, especially Gardiner, with writing them – Luther more bluntly declared that he and his were 'glad to be rid of the blasphemer'.[33]

After the death of Henry Protestantism took a leap forward under his infant son Edward VI and his council. More radical, and more Swiss, theological trends developed although Archbishop Cranmer remained loyal to a more conservative Protestantism continuing to use Lutheran sources in both his doctrinal teaching in catechism, homilies and articles, and also in his remarkable though brief career as a liturgist. In 1548 appeared *Catechismus that is to say a short Instruction into Christian Religion for the synguler commoditie and profyte of childre and yong people, set forth by the moost reverende father in God Thomas Archbyshop of Canterbury, Primate of all England and Metropolitane.*

It is difficult to determine whether Cranmer was personally and wholly responsible for the work of translating the Latin catechism of Justas Jonas, senior, who had been at the diet of Augsburg in 1530 in company with Melanchthon. The translation may have been made in

---

[32] Hardwick, 266. Jacobs, 139, cites the article on the eucharist from the *Repetitio* from Seckendorf.

[33] Melanchthon, *CR* 3, col. 806. G. R. Elton shows well that Thomas Cromwell supported Lutheranism, at least on political grounds, *England under the Tudors*, London 1956, 152–6. See also the useful article by C. S. Meyer, 'Melanchthon, theologian of Ecumenism', *JEH* (October 1966), 185–207.

part by one of his chaplains set to this task by Cranmer, but it is certain that it was overseen by him and approved for publication under his authority as the title before the preface of the English edition shows, and in replying later to an attack by Bishop Gardiner he wrote on 'the Catechisme of Germany by me translated into English'. There are some minor alterations together with a few additions and deletions, and one major addition of some length attacking 'idolatry', that is, worship associated with popular English 'famouse and notoriouse' images such as those of the Virgin at Walsingham and Ipswich and of St Anne of Buxton. Two points of considerable interest arise, however, concerning the sermons on the three sacraments which are attached to Jonas's catechism and given here in English without addition or deletion: *Baptism; The Authoritie of the Kayes; The Communion or the Lord's Supper.* Here Cranmer is giving to England Lutheran teaching on absolution as it was held in the 1530s, but also he is authorising Lutheran doctrine on the communion, a fact which Bishop Gardiner, in Edward's reign, used to embarrass Cranmer by claiming that Cranmer had then taught the Real Presence.[34] In replying to Gardiner's claim that the Real Presence had been set forth in this catechism Cranmer stated that in speaking of receiving with the mouth the body and blood of Christ he was assuming acquaintance with 'olde auncient authors' and their 'phrase and manner of speech'. He added that the presence was to be understood spiritually, and that in any case nothing was said, in the sermon translated, of reserving the sacramental elements. But Cranmer must have been embarrassed by the consequences arising from the publication of the catechism for Burcher wrote to Bullinger in October, 1548, '. . . the Archbishop of Canterbury has caused a catechism of some Lutheran opinions to be translated and published in our language. This little book has occasioned no little discord, so that fightings have frequently taken place among the common people, on account of their variety of opinions, even during the sermons.'[35] This was not to be the only occasion in which Cranmer's eirenical, biblically-grounded and non-doctrinaire theology would be misrepresented by the obtuse or the partisan.

This catechism is now virtually forgotten as are doctrinal statements like the *Ten Articles* and the formerly unpublished *Thirteen Articles*, but one sourcebook for Lutheran influences in England in Cranmer's

---

[34] Burton, *Cranmer's Catechism*, London, 1829, 5, 6. Cranmer held for a period the Lutheran doctrine of the Real Presence, with other major Lutheran themes. Cranmer's early commitment to Erasmianism may have led Henry to assume that he was Erasmian rather than Lutheran.

[35] Ellis 2, 643.

time, *The Book of Common Prayer*, still survives with increasing difficulty in the worship of the Church of England in spite of episcopal pressure to conformity (as heavy as that under Elizabeth I) to its theologically weak successor, *The Alternative Service Book 1980*. This Lutheran influence, partly ignored or underestimated by certain Anglican liturgical scholars of the later nineteenth century who were unwilling to accept influences other than Catholic on the English liturgy, needs reappraisal in the light of more recent liturgical studies.[36] As long ago as 1891, the American Lutheran scholar, H. E. Jacobs, in his useful book *The Lutheran Movement in England* provided much material, but it is time that this matter should receive a new and thorough investigation, for Jacobs sometimes adduced evidence of a Lutheran influence on the English prayer book which could in fact derive from a pre-reformation source.[37]

First in time came Cranmer's English litany of 1544. Versions of this ancient form of processional prayer used for special occasions of danger, dire need, and penance, as well as during Lent had appeared already in English in the fourteenth century and also in Henry's reign, in the Sarum primer and in Marshall's 'Goodly Primer'. Marshall's version of 1535 already showed some influence of the litany which Luther had prepared for use at Wittenberg after March 1529 first in Latin and then in German. Then Cranmer issued in May 1544 an English litany under the following description: 'An exhortation unto prayer, thought mete by the kinges maiestie and his clergy, to be read to the people in every church afore processyons. Also a Letanie with suffrages to be said or song in the time of the said processyone'. In this Cranmer, editing and rewording, wove together strands from the English version set out in Marshall's primer, after excising the *Kyrie eleison* and the long list of saints' names, and from Luther's litany in both of its versions, Latin and German.[38]

The Lutheran sources are more marked in the order for holy communion in *The First Book of Common Prayer* of 1549, though these sources are almost ignored in Proctor and Frere, *A New History of the Book of Common Prayer*, where one vague parallel to a Lutheran source is mentioned in a footnote. The exhortation is modelled on that in the *Simplex et Pia Deliberatio* prepared for Archbishop Hermann of Cologne by Melanchthon and Bucer, which in turn derives from the exhortation in the order of Cassel of 1539. The third

---

[36] Older histories of *The Book of Common Prayer* which reflect the tendency observed are those of F. Procter and W. H. Frere, and of J. H. Blunt. G. J. Cuming, *A History of Anglican Liturgy*, 1969, provides summary views of Lutheran influence, but with insufficient detail.
[37] J. Dowden, *Further Studies in the Prayer Book*, London, 1908, 34.
[38] Dowden, *The Workmanship of the Prayer Book*, 2 ed, London, 1902, 152 ff.

exhortation of the order in the *Book of Common Prayer* is derived
from the second in the *Pia Deliberatio* which followed here the order
of Nürnberg by Volprecht in 1524. The language of the prayer of
confession and of the absolution in the new order of holy communion
also closely resembles that of the confession and absolution in the *Pia
Deliberatio*. The phrase 'Hear what comfortable words . . .' surely
reflect the German *Höret den evangelischen tröst* . . . also in the *Pia
Deliberatio*. Again, the words of administration very probably reflect
Luther's insistence in his *Der kleine Katechismus* and elsewhere, that
the words 'given for you' and 'shed for you' 'for the remission of
sins', were fundamental to the right observance of this sacrament.
The words of administration of the English order closely resemble
those in the order of Schwäbische-Hall prepared by Brentz in 1547.
While a similar formula can be found in the manuals, though not the
missals, of pre-reformation England, yet the vital clue for Lutheran
influence lies in the words 'given . . . shed . . . for thee', a fact ignored
or overlooked by Proctor and Frere.[39] That Cranmer was familiar
with the Lutheran words of administration can be seen from the fact
that the catechism of Justus Jonas, described above, has a brief section
on the importance of the words 'given for you' and 'shed for you'.
In the communion of the sick the rubric requiring some others to
communicate with the sick person is taken either from the *Pia
Deliberatio* or from another Lutheran order for the requirement is
almost universal in the German orders.

This is not to say that Cranmer followed any order closely, for the
originality of his liturgical genius can be seen in his additions to, and
contractions of, his various sources. He was resolute, moreover, in
suppressing from his order of holy communion the elevation, which
was retained in several Lutheran orders including that of the Palatinate
introduced by Osiander, Cranmer's wife's uncle. Nevertheless, it is
not surprising that Hilles wrote to Bullinger in June 1549 on the new
order of holy communion: 'We have a uniform communion of the
eucharist throughout the entire realm, yet after the manner of the
Nuremberg books and some of the Saxons. The bishops and
magistrates present no obstruction to the Lutherans.'[40] This statement
is not to be understood as approving of the Lutheran influence,
rather it deplores it, and within less than three years the powerful
pressure group which it represents won the removal of Lutheran
elements from the order of holy communion in *The Second Book of
Common Prayer* (1552). Here the prayer for the departed is removed

[39] Dowden, *Further Studies in the Prayer Book*, London, 1908, 236.
[40] Ellis, cxxi.

from the prayer of consecration and the words of administration are radically altered to something nearer to the position of Bullinger. Largely because of this change the Lutheran influences on the order of holy communion have been almost entirely absent from that printed in the *Book of the Common Prayer* of 1662.[41]

The order of baptism of 1549, which remained largely unaltered in the *Book of Common Prayer*, shows a much more marked influence of the Lutheran orders, for three-quarters of this rite are derived from Lutheran sources, especially from the German translation of the *Pia Deliberatio*. The exhortation is largely derived from that of Luther in 1523 in his *Taufbüchlein* which was followed in many of the German church orders. The first prayer at baptism is taken from Luther, and the collect 'Almighty and everlasting God, heavenly Father . . .' is almost wholly a direct translation from the Lutheran prayer. In the order for private baptism the questions asked follow closely those in the *Pia Deliberatio*. Other orders and forms in the *Book of Common Prayer* indicate a Lutheran background: the order of confirmation follows the *Pia Deliberatio* very probably in the use of a brief catechism, and the insistence on the creed, Lord's prayer and ten commandments in the preparation of the communicant. It is interesting that signing with the sign of the cross which was retained at baptism (though omitted at confirmation) together with the words declared at that point, are found in the *Pia Deliberatio*, and were to be one of the fundamental grounds of attack on the prayer book by the Puritans in the time of Elizabeth I as an unreformed popish ceremony.[42]

Since in the services of matins and evensong Cranmer undertook a markedly new approach to Sunday parochial worship we might expect Lutheran influence here, for there had been a similar development in Protestant Germany. Yet though well aware of the radical revision of breviary hours by Quinones and of the patterns provided by the German orders, Cranmer showed his originality and his liturgical touch at its best in the two offices, and borrowed little from other sources. There are traces, however, of the order of Kalenberg and Göttingen, of 1542, in the order of the matins in *The First Book of Common Prayer* where the arrangement of the service follows a very similar pattern.[43] The form of solemnisation of

---

[41] However, *The Communion of the Sick*, which survived in 1662, shows the influence of Lutheran orders. Dowden, *Further Studies*, 248 ff.

[42] Ibid., 271. Also, part of the general confession is derived from the *Pia Deliberatio*, F. Procter and W. H. Frere, *A New History of the Book of Common Prayer*, London, 1925, 488. Also C. Hopf, *Lutheran Influences on the Baptismal Services of the Anglican Prayer Book of 1549*, in *And Other Pastors of thy Flock*, ed. F. Hildebrandt, Cambridge, 1942.

[43] Dowden, *Further Studies*, 79.

matrimony in the *Book of Common Prayer* shows plainly the influence of Luther's *Traubüchlien für die einfältigen Pfarrherrn*, for example, the words 'Those whom God hath joined together . . .' derive from *Was Gott zusammen gefüget hat, sol kein Mensch scheiden.* Again the words: 'After God's ordinance in the holy estate of matrimony . . .' derive from *nach göttlicher Ordenung zum heilige Stande der Ehe.* Moreover, the words 'this company' so often taken to mean no more than those individually present at the ceremony reflect in fact the German *Germeinde*, meaning the Church, thereby conveying a profounder significance to the statement. The opening address on the nature of Christian marriage (which follows much that is in the Sarum order) contains several phrases echoing the Lutheran orders especially that of Schwäbische-Hall. Lastly, the words '. . . else hereafter forever hold his peace . . .' reflect words used in several Lutheran orders beginning with that of Brandenburg-Nürnberg by Osiander in 1533.[44] Finally, the order of the visitation of the sick reflects in its exhortation the Saxon order of 1539 either directly or as mediated through the *Pia Deliberatio*; and the anthem in the order for the burial of the dead, *Media Vita*, 'In the midst of life . . .' contains the words 'Suffer us not at our last hour . . .' which have no place in the original Latin sequence and derive (through Coverdale's translation of Luther's version of the sequence *Mitten wir im liben sein*) from Luther's own beautiful addition:

> Du ewiger Gott
> Lass uns nicht entfallen
> Von des rechten Glaubens Trost.[45]

'*A Catechism*', which is set in the prayer book between the baptismal and confirmation services, follow a pattern which had been established by Brentz beginning with what was given to the child in baptism and continuing through the creed, ten commandments and Lord's prayer, and in some of the explanations on the commandments appears to echo Luther's catechism. There is also an influence of Lutheranism in the provision of religious instruction for the people and this lies in the first *Book of Homilies*, issued in July 1547, containing twelve homilies. Cranmer himself was responsible for four if not five of these twelve, the third of which 'Of the Salvation of Mankind by only Christ our Saviour' is emphasised as being especially important for its teaching on justification by faith in Article II of the *Thirty-Nine Articles*. Jacobs cites among other less obvious instances the

---

44 Ibid., 283, 284.
45 Dowden, *The Workmanship of the Prayer Book* 2 ed, London, 1902, 162.

parallelism between Melanchthon's *Loci Communes: De Evangelio*: 'Justification is given fully, that is, not on account of our worth, yet there must be a ransom for us', and the words of the homily: 'Although this justification be free unto us, yet it cometh not so freely unto us, that there is no ransom paid therefore at all'.[46] While verbal similarities, in spite of Jacobs, are much more rare than this citation might suggest, yet this homily as well as those on 'Of the true and lively faith' and 'On Good Works' certainly reflect how far Cranmer was working from within the same pattern of theology as that created by Luther's great insights on the doctrine of grace.

The *Book of Homilies* is no longer meaningful in the life of the Church of England but assent to the Thirty-Nine Articles is still required of clergy upon their institution to benefices though in a formula which removes their theological significance. The preliminary drafting of the articles of religion began in 1551 and was undertaken by Cranmer himself and after some revision they were issued numbering forty-two in 1553. Archbishop Parker revised these to some extent, omitting some articles and adding others, and they were issued in their final form in 1571. Articles 1–4 reflect, sometimes verbatim, similar statements in the Augsburg Confession. Article 5 is very close to the third article of the Würtemberg Confession (this had been prepared by Brentz in 1551). Articles 9, 11, 16, 19, 20, 26, 37 and 38 all show the Augsburg Confession, and other articles have words and phrases reflecting its influence, either directly or as it was mediated through the Würtemberg Confession. (It is worth noting that what many Anglicans believe to be the moderation and traditionalism of the articles in comparison with continental confessions can be seen also in Lutheran articles, and are not therefore peculiarly distinctive of Anglicanism other than in the sense that Archbishop Parker sympathised with that kind of pattern rather than with a more radical one.) Also the *Apology of the Confession* and the Smalcald articles may be traced here and there in the Thirty-Nine Articles. But it should not be overlooked, on the other hand, that four or five of the articles show the rising influence of the Swiss theology before which from Edward's reign onwards Lutheranism was very largely retreating in England, and these few articles represent also more the specific impact of Reformed theology than those articles which reflect a Lutheran source since often enough that source may well have been common ground in Protestantism in general.[47]

[46] Jacobs, 337.
[47] Ibid., 341, 342.

The amount of Lutheran literature coming into England during Henry's reign has already been referred to above,[48] but this deserves more detailed attention. The extent of the influence of a Lutheran book imported from Germany, or translated and published in England, is imponderable – how can one tell how many readers a given book would reach? Humphry Monmouth, a London draper and alderman 'noted as well for his piety as his wealth', had 'articles mynystered against him' in November 1537: '. . . thow hast had or bought divers and many Books, Treatises, and Works of the said Martyn Luther, and other of his detestable Sect . . . thou art named and reputed to be Avancer and a Favourer of the said Martyn Luther, his Heresies and detestable Opinions, and one of the same Sect.'[49] How many came to read Luther for the first time through visiting Monmouth's house? The number of occasions on which Lutheran books are quoted or named in correspondence, heresy trials, sermons, and other English theological literature, lists of condemned books, would be a complicated study in itself. No more can be done here than to draw attention to book titles from Germany, and to the English translations of some of these during the years in which these books were prominent and indicate their characteristic subject matter. A list of prohibited books, one of several after 1526, was entitled *Libri sectae sive factionis Lutherianae importati ad civitatem London per fautores ejusdem sectae* . . . (probably dating from 1531 or a little later), and included Luther's Latin catechism, *De libertate Christiana, De Bonis Operibus, De votis monasticis*, the commentary on Galatians, and other works with some of his letters. On this list also were works by Bugenhagen, Urbanus Rhegius, Melanchthon, Agricola, and Brentz, but Zwinglian and South German writers are also found in it, Oecolampadius, Pellikan, Bucer, Francis Lambert, and Zwingli himself.[50] English translations of Lutheran literature had begun with Tyndale from 1528 and earlier in *The Parable of a Wicked Mammon*, and the prologue to the epistle to the Romans issued in Tyndale's New Testament and taken from Luther's own prologue; and by 1536 the Augsburg Confession had been translated with the apology of the confession by Richard Taverner. *The dysclosyng of the canon of the popysh Masse, with a sermon annexed unto it, of ye famous clerk of worthy memory D. Marten Luther, by me Hans Hitprycke*, (1548?), shows Luther being used as a propellant for an English rocket against 'popery'.

[48] v. supra, p. 218.
[49] Strype, *Memorials* (1721) 1, 317, 318. Also the German merchants in London would have easy means of bringing Lutheran books into England.
[50] Foxe, *Acts* 4, 667.

It is interesting that Luther's sacramental theology is avoided in English versions of his works and that in the reign of Elizabeth I the translations from Luther are from his biblical expositions (and even these are modified by the omission of passages where his sacramental teaching appears),[51] and ignore his earlier explosive treatises which would by then be considered as old weapons unsuited to post-Tridentine controversial needs. Melanchthon's confessional writings in English have been mentioned already, and also some of his minor treatises were translated including *A godlye treatyse of prayer* (1553?), Englished by John Bradford who was soon to be burned under Mary. Moreover a list of translations from other Lutheran authors could be compiled including Brentz, Osiander, Sarcerius, Rhegius, but these mostly appeared in Henry's time: hardly any Lutheran author is translated under Elizabeth I save Luther and Melanchthon, and these titles begin to disappear after 1585.

A question that is almost wholly ignored by those who write on English ecclesiastical history under the first two Stuarts is the degree to which Lutheranism, after the pattern of Melanchthon's disciples, resembled certain emphases made by the Laudians. Was this resemblance fortuitous, did like causes produce like effects in parts of Germany as in England, or was there an influence of the followers of Melanchthon even though indirectly? Arminianism in Holland, especially as seen in Grotius, represented the revival of certain emphases made by Erasmus long before, which were not far from the hearts of Melanchthon and some of his later followers, even as they were attractive to the Laudians. The note so often sounded by Erasmus and Melanchthon and others of that generation can be heard again in Richard Mountague, who in his *Apello Caesarem* (1626), written three years before he became bishop of Chichester, wrote: '[forsaking Protestant scholastic divinity] . . . I betooke myself to Scripture, the Rule of Faith, interpreted by Antiquity, the best Expositor of Faith and applyer of that Rule: holding it a point of discretion, to draw water, as neere as I could, to the wellhead, and to spare labour in vaine, in running further off to cisternes and lakes.'[52] Calixt in Germany, an admiring disciple of Melanchthon's teachings, held views similar to this principle of Mountague and opposed the orthododxy of Calov with an appeal to the Melanchthonian ideal of the *Consensus quinquesaecularis* which was also so attractive to the

---

[51] For example, see P. S. Watson, *Commentary on St. Paul's Epistle to the Galatians by Martin Luther*, London, 1953, 3, 4, 473 where he shows the deletions and adjustments made in Luther's text.

[52] Richard Mountagu, *Apello Caesarem*, London, 1625, 11, 12.

Laudians. How often one is reminded of Melanchthon's 'synergism', his eirenic attitude to Roman Catholic liturgical ceremonial an things which could be described as 'adiaphora', his emphasis on patristic studies and the consensus of the Fathers with the concurrent appeal to the first five centuries of the Church, as guiding principles for the Church, when reading the works of many of the 'Laudian divines' of the Stuart Church of England. Nevertheless, these matters are not sufficient to suggest the direct though delayed influences of Melanchthon: the Laudians could well arrive at similar conclusions by an independent though parallel route, and, moreover, they gave less heed to the Melanchthonian insistence on the *Sensus proprium* of Scripture as the norm by which all else is to be assessed. In any case the revival of Lutheranism in the Stuart Church of England was already long an impossibility: by Laud's time Lutheranism was a dead issue. The Anglican insistence on episcopalianism would not appeal to the many Lutherans (and, indeed, to none if it were to be understood as meaning that orthodoxy depended on historical succession) and much less still would Lutheran Scholasticism appeal to either Laudians or Puritans who recoiled from and rejected it with indifference or dislike.

But had there been no chance, before Puritanism arose and Laudianism developed later in opposition to it, that England might have looked again with sympathy towards the Lutherans, when Elizabeth I began to reign? It is worth remembering that Elizabeth as a girl had read Melanchthon's *Loci Communes* (the edition of 1538 was dedicated to her father). It is sometimes suggested that Elizabeth differed from her subjects in having Lutheran sympathies. This suggestion derives largely, if not exclusively from her statement to the Spanish ambassador in 1559, at the time of the Elizabethan settlement of religion that she wished 'the Augustanean Confession' to be maintained in her realm, and then added 'it would not be the Augustanean Confession but something else like it, and that she differed very little from us [that is, the Roman Catholics] as she believed that God was in the Sacrament of the Eucharist and she only dissented from three or four things in the Mass'.[53] He was not the only Spanish ambassador to be obtuse in matters of Protestant religion, many of their statements on religious matters under the Tudors are misleading or ill-stated. Did he not realise too that many Protestants could say as much as the queen did on the mass? Her statement is sometimes dismissed as diplomatic double-talk, but why should it not be taken as a simple statement of fact? Her words reflect

[53] M. A. S. Hume, *CSP Spanish, Elizabeth* (1892) 1, 61, 62.

the moderate reform views of her youth when she had translated at the age of eleven *The Mirror of a Sinful Soul* by the French princess Marguerite of Angoulême, whereas all her life she was uninfluenced by the Swiss and Genevan theology of the great majority of her subjects – in fact she detested it since she recognised in it, with an insight lacking in most of her bishops, a potential hostility to her royal prerogative in religion, incipient republicanism and consequent rebellion. The Lutheran authority of the godly prince was fundamental to her conception of her duty and her calling.

Moreover, in spite of her saying that she would have preferred something like the conservative theology of the Augsburg Confession, and in spite of her liking for that more elaborate ceremonial of church worship which Lutherans also approved, Elizabeth had no intention whatever of bringing forward Lutheran doctrine and practices in such a way that the Church of England would be associated in men's minds with Lutheran Scandinavia or north Germany. Elizabeth, like her father, put first her sovereignty which included her status as supreme governor of the Church of England. She was never troubled in conscience like the Elector John of Saxony who in Luther's time feared, under the gospel, to exercise princely rule both in Church and State.[54] It has been well-stated that:

> Elizabeth's bishops learnt very early in the reign the extent to which they depended upon the royal will, discovering that not only in matters of discipline but also of doctrine they had little power to act without at least implicit authorisation from the Queen.[55]

Her firm control – no one at home or abroad failed to see that 'she intended princely to rule' – Elizabeth exercised over all her subjects, including the clergy, as an Englishwoman over Englishmen, a nation then more given to xenophobia than nowadays. She wanted no alliances with foreign powers who could entangle her political initiative; nor would she tolerate her subjects seeking to foster such alliances even on the grounds of religion. She clearly wanted, what anti-Knox Dr Cox desired in the congregation of English refugees at Frankfurt in Mary's reign, 'the face of an English Church'. This meant that Elizabeth not only opposed the influence of Rome, Zürich or Geneva, but also that of Wittenberg. Political alliances went with confessional relations. Because of this fundamental fact Lutheranism could never hope to achieve in England what it achieved, for example, in Sweden. A well-grounded paper by W. Brown

---

[54] Article: 'Johann der Beständige', *RE* (3 ed) 9, 240–1.
[55] Claire Cross, *Church and People 1450–1660*, London, 1967, 136.

Patterson, *The Anglican Reaction to the Formula of Concord* (1577), shows Elizabeth, in seeking support for Dutch and French Reformed resistance, proposing an understanding to this end with Lutheran princes while claiming the Formula would be divisive. Elizabeth's convoluted foreign policy was never allowed, however, to bring her to accepting any alterations or new emphases in the doctrine and worship of the Church of England. None of the Tudors from the time of Henry VIII would accept putting the state of England and this included the Church of England, under the authority or guiding influence of a continental power and continental church, save Mary whose alliance with Spain and reintroduction of papal authority were detested in England by Protestants and made even Catholics uneasy because she was making England an entail of Spanish politics. The attempt by presbyterianising Puritans from 1575 onwards to bring the Church of England into line with the Reformed churches of Switzerland, France and the Palatinate, however much it was favoured by many in the Church, the Commons and even in the privy council, was rudely shattered by Elizabeth, supported by the bishops, whom she regarded as her right arm in governing the Church, not merely because she disliked anything to do with Geneva, but also because it would have weakened her policy of religious non-committment in international affairs.[56] Edmund Grindal in 1566 wrote that he was glad that England had not become a prey to Lutherans. And Robert Horne wrote to the Swiss, Gualter, in 1576 that Elizabeth 'has always abominated popery from her infancy, so also will she never admit Lutheranism, which is a greater disturber ...'.[57] Elizabeth feared its political consequences, as she feared those of Calvinism.

Would it be an inaccurate generalisation to say that Luther's theological insights, other than those associated with the dotrine of grace, were left without a witness in England under Elizabeth and afterwards? Not really: but some may wish to point to the curious case of Richard Cheney, bishop of Gloucester from 1562, cited by the Catholic historian Philip Hughes, as 'the solitary Lutheran' among the Elizabethan bishops.[58] The basis for his statement lies in Camden's description of Cheney, mediated through Strype, as 'most addicted to

---

[56] It was from Geneva that John Knox had attacked 'the monstrous regiment of women', the rule of Mary Stuart and Mary Tudor. He led a revolution in arms against his sovereign in Scotland. Elizabeth neither forgave nor forgot this fact. For her view of the political dangers inherent in presbyterianising Puritanism see her letter to James VI of Scotland, *Letters of Queen Elizabeth and King James VI of Scotland*, ed John Bruce, Camden Society (1849), 63.

[57] *Zurich Letters*, I, 169, 321.

[58] P. Hughes, *The Reformation in England* London, 1960, 3, 46.

Luther both in respect, I suppose, of the doctrine of the presence, as also for the retaining of old customs as crucifixes and pictures of saints in the churches, and such like.'[59] But this could well mean that Cheney was conservative in religion following the pattern implicit in 'The First Book of Common Prayer of 1549. Also it is known that he disliked the views and proceedings of Bishop Hooper his predecessor at Gloucester, who was certainly a Zwinglian, and Strype affirms that Cheney held 'that no doctrine could be shewn that had universally deceived an Ecumenical Council. And on this he built his Real Presence in the Sacrament: because this was the ancient faith, and the Christian World and the Company of Bishops who were the Keepers of that which was committed to the Church [Custodes Depositi] held this Doctrine'.[60] This makes a cautious conservative of Cheney and shows little ground for assuming a Lutheran theology of the presence as being attractive to him. That he was not a secret upholder of Catholicism may be seen by the fact that he risked dissenting from the articles concerning transubstantiation agreed on by convocation in 1553, at the opening of Mary's reign.[61]

Perhaps other more positive and tangible evidence of Lutheran influences could be found in Elizabeth's reign, for example, in the work of the martyrologist John Foxe, who not only wrote a commendatory preface to an English translation of one of Luther's sermons (A Commentary upon the Fifteenth Psalm, 1577) but also, and this fact is too little realised, was indebted to Luther's apocalyptic view of Christian history and also the periodisation characteristic of Melanchthonian historiography, in the earlier sections of his Acts and Monuments. Nevertheless, Foxe was markedly Swiss in his theology as a whole: in any case a few allusive swallows do not make a Lutheran summer. After Elizabeth's reign Englishmen regarded Lutheranism as part of the perspective of history and not as a living influence presenting a valid option in religious belief and practice. It is known that captain Henry Bell endured imprisonment with more ease through translating Luther's Table-Talk, and that John Wesley was profoundly moved at hearing Luther's Preface to Romans at a meeting in Aldersgate Street in London, and that Julius Hare wrote vigorously The Vindication of Luther against his recent English Assailants in 1855; but even if one were to include the great affection for 'A safe stronghold our God is still', these facts present no revival of

[59] Strype, Annals (2 ed 1725) 1, 281.
[60] ibid., 282, 283.
[61] P. Heylyn, Ecclesia Restaurata, or the History of the Reformation of the Church of England, ed. G. C. Robinson, London, 1849, 2, 387.

Lutheranism in England conceived of as a pattern of worship, a system of doctrine, and a church order. That a revival is possible would not be denied for there are today a number of Lutheran congregations in England, but these largely consist of Lutherans from abroad. That they can build on old foundations is doubtful for those foundations are long buried or built over by other more enduring structures of English design. It will be understood that while English scholars have expounded with approval several themes of Luther's theology, this likewise does not form a basis for English churches in adopting Lutheran doctrine or liturgical practice.

8

Puritanism: The Problem of Definition

There are those ready to admire the Puritans almost for the very name (as did Spurgeon), and there are others who like Sir Andrew Aguecheek when confronted with 'a kind of Puritan' are ready 'to beat him like a dog' (as did Macaulay): but may we not with Sir Toby say to both these groups, 'For being a Puritan? Thine exquisite reason?' – for Sir Toby, even in his cups, saw the need apparently to distinguish and define.

The problem of Puritanism is to define what it was and who the Puritans were – a fact often recognised but leading to little change in the treatment of the subject which is nearly always regarded as a comprehensive but homogeneous entity. One purpose of this paper is to point to the dangers in the assumption that it is homogeneous. Some examples may suffice to show what difficulties may arise for those who, seeking instruction, go to the most respected authors. First, A. S. P. Woodhouse, in *Puritanism and Liberty*, writes that 'Puritanism is an entity' capable of being extended to cover 'the varied forces generated by the Protestant Reformation and given their opportunity by the revolt against the Crown and the Church in the first half of the seventeenth century.' However, it is also possible to describe the Puritans as 'the more conservative,' 'the strictly calvinistic,' who 'followed the Genevan pattern in Church and State' and were 'synonymous with Presbyterians.' But, 'the cleavage between the Presbyterians and sectaries is marked,' yet this division leaves 'the problem of the centre party, the Independents.' Following Troeltsch, he continued, one can speak of, 'a Puritan church type and a Puritan sect type, the ideal of the holy community is true of all the Puritan groups.' Finally, 'it is not necessary to posit a unity but there is continuity in Puritan thought.'[1] Here, as elsewhere, as soon as a statement is made a qualification of it, if not a contradiction of it, becomes necessary.

G. M. Trevelyan, in *English Social History*, begins by stating that the Puritans were 'not yet dissenters but parish clergymen' who held conferences 'dangerously like Presbyterian Synods'; then, still speaking of Puritans, he writes of 'those outside like the "Brownists",' and of those 'more extreme Puritans' who were hanged. Again, he describes Bunyan's 'lonely figure with the Bible' and 'the burden of sin' as 'the representative Puritan of the English Puritan epoch,' and adds 'this was the force by which Oliver Cromwell and George Fox and John Wesley wrought their wonders.'[2] Unfortunately, contemporary records do not describe those hanged men (who had denied the royal supremacy) as Puritans, but as Brownists or Separatists, and Puritans were scorned by radicals for accepting the royal supremacy. The passage about 'the lonely figure with the Bible' is fine writing but it has no definable content, for on that basis where does one begin to describe a Puritan (with Luther?), or end (with General Booth?).

Until recently those who wrote on Puritanism resorted to generalised fine writing when seeking to define or explain it – this is a symptom of insecurity in understanding the subject. Christopher Hill, in *The Century of Revolution, 1603–1714*, 1967, 74, perhaps prolonged the life of R. H. Tawney's Christian Socialist tract *Religion and the Rise of Capitalism* by writing, 'every student of the period should read it.' Tawney introduced Puritanism in his over-praised book by writing that 'three streams descended from the teaching of Calvin', the Presbyterians, the Congregationalists and 'a doctrine of the nature of God and man [what is this doctrine?] pervasive and potent which was Puritanism.' The fine writing continues from, 'Like an iceberg which can awe the traveller by its lowering majesty only because sustained by a vaster mass which escapes his eye . . .', through phrases like 'the revolution in men's souls, the watchwords it thundered, wrestling Jacob' to the inevitable names of Fox and Bunyan ('mysticism') Cromwell ('glowing energy') and Milton ('victorious

---

[1] A. S. P. Woodhouse, *Puritanism and Liberty*, London, 1938, 35–7.
[2] G. M. Trevelyan, *Illustrated English Social History*, London, 1950, II, 37–8, 93.

tranquillity') to the climax, 'there are depths of light and darkness which posterity can observe with reverence or with horror but which its small fathom-line cannot plumb.' Ten more pages of generalisation follow where the only recognisable data are to be found in the disparate quotations set in an undefined time-scale ranging up and down between, apparently, 1645 and 1689. This material is then associated with Puritanism and the rise of capitalism in a diffused manner supported by citations taken without time sequence from anywhere between about 1640 to 1730. This is followed by some pages on the Tudor period not hitherto mentioned (focusing usefully on the controversy about 'usury') for which this earlier section of confusing generalization about the Stuart period provides no suitable assistance. This is not economic history, it is tract writing.

Christopher Hill's study *Society and Puritanism in Pre-Revolutionary England* carries a dominant tendency to be seen in the words from the Preface: 'The present work ... tries to suggest that there might be non-theological reasons for supporting the Puritans, or for being a Puritan.' The first chapter of the book is called *The Definition of a Puritan*: the most immediately striking thing about this chapter is that it refers to almost none of the reasonably accessible quotations concerning the definition of Puritanism which are given below, and provides instead quotations which are often unnecessarily ambiguous because they do not give proper place to their authors' purpose, and sometimes mislead because their context is not provided. Christopher Hill's intention seems to have been to find some support for the view that Puritanism can be seen, when divorced from its confusing religiousness, as consciously concerned with those political, economic, and social matters so important for understanding the Civil War and its consequences. His second paragraph opens in words which suggest the non-religious significance of Puritanism before Hill has demonstrated it, 'Like most political nicknames it was a "reproachfull name"' – it was certainly a 'reproachful' name, but it carried in that age no greater political implications than other names like 'Protestant' (Anglican), 'Papist,' 'Anabaptist,' and it is possibly arguable that it could carry less political implications than these. Hill cites King James[3] to show the name of Puritan to be ambiguous since he could apply it, in 1603, to the Family of Love and the Brownists; but he does not point out that James is almost alone in the contemporary literature in doing so, and that in any case James came to England as a foreigner who picked up this term of abuse, and then misconceived its true application and the extent of its pejorativeness. Again, Hill writes:

[3] C. Hill, *Society and Puritanism in Pre-Revolutionary England*, London, 1964, 17. v. infra, 241, 248.

'The shrewd Henry Parker insisted that it was necessary to distinguish at least four types of Puritan – Puritans in church policy, Puritans in religion, Puritans in State, and Puritans in morality',[4] and Parker is cited six more times in this chapter; but nowhere in these citations does Hill make it plain that in fact Parker wrote his pamphlet precisely to deny that Puritanism should be divorced from its religious content, and thus be shown to have political implications, and that the four types are Parker's description of how the varieties of abuse of Puritans could be subdivided. Moreover, the quotation from Parker (*Discourse*, 13–14) made by Hill, beginning, 'All the Commons . . .' and concluding '. . . all these are Puritans', should have been continued to add Parker's conclusion, 'But this suggestion is utterly false and impossible.'

Two further quotations from the pamphlet should suffice to demonstrate that Hill's treatment of it can be misleading, and that the 'four types' are not Parker's view of Puritanism:

> Dissent in Ecclesiasticall Policie about Ceremonies and other smaller matters, being not of the substance of Religion, first gave occasion to raise this reproachfull word Puritan in the Church . . . and peace being more firmly settled about those indifferent things, the more few Puritans remayned, and the more moderately those few inclined, the more furiously their enemies raged against them . . .

> Those whom we ordinarily call Puritans are men of strict life, and precise opinion, which cannot be hated for anything but their singularity in zeale and piety, and certainly the number of such men is too small and their condition too low, and dejected; but they which are the Devils chiefe Artificers in abusing this word, when they please can so stretch and extend the same that scarce any civill honest Protestant which is hearty and true to his Religion can avoid the aspersion of it, and when they list again, they can so shrink it into a narrow sense, that it shall seem to be aimed at none but monstrous abominable Hereticks and Miscreants. Then by its latitude it strikes generally, by its contraction it pierces deeply, by its confused application it deceives invisibly.[5]

The last word of Parker on the subject is that, 'the most ordinary badge of Puritans is their more religious and conscionable conversation [manner of life].'[6] Since this pamphlet appeared in 1641 it is interesting to see how it runs parallel in its sentiments with those sources to be cited below.

There are a few books of introduction to the varieties of Puritanism

---

[4] Op. cit., 20.

[5] (Henry Parker?) *A Discourse Concerning Puritans. A vindication of those who unjustly suffer by the mistake, abuse, and misapplication of that name*, (London?) 1641, 7, 8, 9.

[6] Op. cit., 53.

accompanied by documents; that by L. J. Trinterud, *Elizabethan Puritanism*, 1971, is useful, not least in pointing to the Catholic origins, for controversial use, of the word Puritan, though it is restricted in its contents mainly to the Presbyterianisers. Among these books is that of H. C. Porter, *Puritanism in Tudor England*, 1971, which gives with other things what is to be hoped is a unique description of Puritan origins derived from a strange quotation from Sir Francis Hastings in a speech in 1601 wherein he claimed that Laurence Humphrey, President of Magdalen College, Oxford, told him in his youth that there were four sorts of Puritans; the Catholic, the Papist, the Brownists or Family of Love, and the Evangelical Puritans, 'who insist wholly upon Scriptures as upon a sure ground'. The unreliability of that aging memory (since the able scholar Humphrey cannot be blamed surely for this eccentric description though he may have undertaken the sarcasm of *tu quoque* by dragging Catholics into sharing the contemptuous description of Puritan) is clear from the confusion between Brownists and Familists, and to describe one group of Puritans as being distinctive by their insistence on Scripture alone is useless since all called Puritans held to this attitude – though Hastings may have been trying to restrict that notion to the main body of non-separating Puritans to which he belonged. Porter provides his own four main divisions of Tudor Puritanism. First, 'the tradition of the Separatists', secondly, Hastings's Evangelical Puritans, thirdly, 'the English tradition of rhetorical and radical indignation and dissent seen in abuse for example Marprelate' – but this generic writer was fighting for specific and definable ends though his style was trenchant. To establish 'abusiveness' as in itself a division of Puritanism is fortunately a unique proposal. Fourthly, continued Porter, there was the Presbyterian movement. However, this attempt to distinguish divisions two and four will not work since many whom Porter wishes to confine to division two were ecclesiologically Presbyterian, and how does one distinguish the evangelical theology of division two from the theology of division four? Their only differentiation was that many were moderates and some were extremists. Further, Porter is unwise in describing Elizabethan intellectuals as regarding Puritans as 'curious, silly and hypocritical' since the greatest poet of that age after Shakespeare, Edmund Spenser, sympathised with the Puritans in his writings. Most writers of the time, including Shakespeare, described the foibles of the eccentric people and not the attitude of the powerful Puritans in Parliament and about the Court.

In the light of these examples there can be no hesitation in agreeing with Kitson Clark who did well to write: 'Though Puritanism plays a very important part in the development of the English heritage it is extremely difficult to give a precise meaning to the word itself . . . It is applied [by historians] to a very large number of different people and it is difficult to find a common denominator.'[7] Patrick Collinson writing in mandarin style defending historians (JEH, 1980) cites Giles Widdowes' Laudian sermon, *The Schysmaticall Puritan*, 1630, which attacks Puritanism by caricatures describing it as 'ambiguous' and therefore 'fallacious': Collinson argues that in spite of ambiguity the term (thereby shifting Widdowes' intention from subject to term) is not fallacious for historians, concluding with a graceful gesture to Parker – this leaves the matter where it was before. Plainly, many writers use the term arbitrarily and confusingly.

What has led to this position? There seem to be three driving forces behind the historiography of Puritanism which help to create the kind of difficulty shown already. First, from the early eighteenth century (at least as early as Daniel Neal's *History of the Puritans*, 1737) English dissenters have looked back to those who struggled against Anglicanism in the sixteenth and seventeenth centuries as a homogeneous group irrespective of whether they were in their own time described as Puritans or not: Puritanism became an ancestral banner under which a dissenter, after the death of Queen Anne, could sink party feelings and find an ancestry in his struggle against the established Church. More recently has come the complication that Free Church historians, unwilling to think of most of their spiritual ancestors as sectaries, list Separatists, Baptists, Presbyterians, Quakers, and others as Puritans, in spite of the evidence of contemporary sources, forming a homogeneous group upon the basis of which one could erect such themes as the Puritan doctrine of the Church, or of the Ministry, thereby confusing the issues for those secular historians who seek enlightenment from them. Secondly, from the time of Cotton Mather's *Magnalia Christi Americana*, 1702, many American historians have suffered from what amounts to being an historical fixation on Puritanism. Since modern America, from this point of view, began with Puritanism, therefore anyone who can be regarded as even potentially contributing, as an uneasy Anglican or truculent Separatist, to that national pageant moving from *The Mayflower Compact* to *The Saybrook Platform* is enhaloed as a potential Miles Standish awaiting his Longfellow.[8] This foible, however, must

---

[7] G. Kitson Clark, *The English Inheritance*, London, 1950, 103. C. H. George, *Puritanism in History and Historiography*, Past and Present, 1968, also demonstrates this point.

[8] Perry Miller in his *Orthodoxy in Massachusetts* and *The New England Mind* was an example of this foible. Later historians have made some necessary corrections. Patrick Collinson, *Godly People*, 1983, 530 ff. has some judicial words on Miller. Collinson's title here presumably represents his conclusion on how best to describe Puritans, but this means that we have to be careful in defining who were thus to be described as 'the Godly' – a very elastic usage.

not be allowed to lessen our admiration for the erudition and insight of those American scholars who, more than most writers, have contributed to the study of Puritanism by the publication, and patient examination, of the sources. Thirdly, those ecclesiastical historians who after 1662, whether writing from the point of view of Roman Catholicism, of Anglicanism, or of nineteenth-century liberalism, have accepted the principle of herding into one pound all those of Protestant convictions who troubled, or strayed from, the fold established by the Act of Uniformity of 1559, and calling it Puritanism have thus masked the emphases of Puritanism, indicated its incoherence, and regarded it with sorrow if not anger as a byword for negations and moral repressions occasionally illumined by genuine piety and moral integrity. Other historians writing from the point of view of sociology, regard 'Puritanism', however diverse, as a useful springboard for economic and political discussion without regard to its primarily and intensely religious significance, since they see religious language as a cover for the politically inarticulate to write on politics.

Briefly, the word Puritan suffers from inflation. When it can be applied to those who, however vaguely, may be called calvinistic and to those who strongly opposed calvinistic theology; to those who refused to be content with the terms of the Elizabethan Settlement of Religion and with the Jacobean and Caroline interpretations of it although they stayed in the Church of England, and nevertheless to those who fled to Holland or New England; to those who walked alone in search for truth like Milton or Cromwell – when the word means all these then it ceases to define. Puritanism originally a useful coin of some value has become overminted and ended in headlong inflation.

It is surely reasonable for historians to use a word as it was used by those who made it. The contemporary sources of the sixteenth and seventeenth centuries show that the word Puritan was used in a more limited sense than that which we give to it. Whether or not ideas which were to be prominent among Puritans can be found in writers prior to the Act of Uniformity of 1559 is open to discussion, but we should be careful how we set about such speculations lest we should be introducing an arbitrary standard of reference. The word Puritan was not apparently used before 1563. Stow has a reference to there being 'many congregations of Anabaptysts in London who cawlyd themselves Puritans or unspotted Lambs of the Lord.'[9] There is no corroborating evidence for Anabaptists calling themselves, or being

---

[9] Quoted in *The Century Dictionary*, London, 1914, VII, under *Puritan*. The quotation from Grafton is from the *DNB*, XIX, 4, *Stow*. It is regrettable that in using this quotation from Stow, Collinson, *The Elizabethan Puritan Movement*, 1967, 86, omits the words 'many congregations of Anabaptysts . . .' thus failing to show the unreliability of Stow as a witness.

called by others, Puritans. Stow, sympathetic to Catholicism, is applying vaguely a new contemporary term of abuse for religious non-conformists about whom his indifference is only emphasised by his religious conservatism − a conservatism mocked in a pun by the rival chronicler Grafton who in 1566 referred to Stow's work as 'memories of superstitious foundations, fables and lyes foolishly Stowed together.' Thomas Fuller provides a more satisfactory account of the origin of Puritanism, the name and thing, and no one (not even his astringent editor Brewer) has bettered or disproved his statement. Writing under the year 1564 he says:

> The English bishops, conceiving themselves empowered by their canons, began to shew their authority in urging the clergy of their diocese to subscribe to the liturgy, ceremonies, and discipline of the Church; and such as refused the same were branded with the odious name of puritans. A name which in this notion first began in this year, and the grief had not been great if it had ended in the same. The philosopher banisheth the term (which is *polysaemon*) that is subject to several senses out of the predicaments, as affording too much covert for cavil by the latitude thereof. On the same account could I wish that the word *puritan* were banished common discourse, because so various in the acceptions thereof. We need not speak of the ancient *cathari* or primitive puritans, sufficiently known by their heritical opinions. *Puritan* here was taken for the opposers of the hierarchy and church-service, as resenting of superstition. But profane mouths quickly improved this nickname, therewith on every occasion to abuse pious people, some of them so far from opposing the liturgy that they endeavoured (according to the instructions thereof in the preparative to the confession) to accompany the minister with a *pure* heart, and laboured (as it is in the absolution) for a life *pure* and holy. We will therefore decline the word, to prevent exceptions, which, if casually slipping from our pen, the reader knoweth that only nonconformists are thereby intended. These in this age, were divided into two ranks: some mild and moderate, contented only to enjoy their own conscience; others fierce and fiery, to the disturbance of church and state.[10]

Fuller writes of a new development in the use of the word which was begun in 1622 by De Dominis, Archbishop of Spalato, who after arriving at the view that the Pope was Nimrod became briefly Dean of Windsor:

> We must not forget that Spalato (I am confident I am not mistaken therein) was the first who, professing himself a Protestant, used the word Puritan, to signify the defenders of matters doctrinal in the English church. Formerly the word was only taken to denote such as dissented from the hierarchy in discipline and church government, which now was extended

[10] Thomas Fuller, *The Church History of Britain*, Oxford, 1845, ed. J. S. Brewer, IV, 327.

to brand such as were anti-Arminians in their judgements. As Spalato first abused the word in this sense, so we could wish he had carried it away with him in his return to Rome; whereas now leaving the word behind him in this extensive signification thereof, it hath since by others been improved to asperse the most orthodox in doctrine and religious in conversation.[11]

If Fuller shows the *terminus a quo* for the use of the word Puritan by contemporaries in 1564 then the *terminus ad quem* is shown by Baxter to be the beginning of the Civil War.[12]

When the war was beginning the parties set names of contempt upon each other, and also took such titles to themselves and their own cause as might be the fittest means for that which they designed. The old names of Puritans and Formalists were not now broad enough nor of sufficient force ... The generality of people through the land (I say not all or everyone) who were then [that is, 1642] called Puritans, precisians, religious persons that used to talk of God, and heaven, and Scripture, and holiness both preachers and people ... adhered to the parliament.[13]

Again, writing of the discussions which took place on the eve of the Restoration Baxter says:

Any man that was for a spiritual serious way of worship (though he were for moderate episcopacy and liturgy) and that lived according to his Profession, was called commonly a Presbyterian as formerly he was called a Puritan, unless he joined himself to the Independents, Anabaptists, or some other sect which might afford him a more odious name.[14]

The historian Clarendon who had lived through the period bears out Baxter's judgement: in his *History of the Rebellion* the Index has two insignificant references to 'Puritan' but Clarendon himself does not use the word, rather he uses extensively Presbyterians, Independents, Anabaptists and Quakers.

The point is the same: before 1642 the 'serious' people in the Church of England those who followed 'exact walking' and who desired some modifications in Church government and worship were called Puritans; after 1640 party names came increasingly into use of Presbyterian, Independent, and Baptist. Baxter is corroborated in

---

[11] Fuller, op. cit., v, 529.

[12] It is advisable if not essential to distinguish between the Puritanism and Separatism (with their special patterns) of 1563–1628 and the Puritanism of 1642–1660. (1628 was the year Laud became bishop of London and the promotion of Arminianism and the identifying of royal arbitrariness and religion began to develop as a focus of concentration for Puritans up to 1641).

[13] *The Reliquiae Baxterianae*, 1696, 34, 31.

[14] *The Autobiography of Richard Baxter*, ed. J. Lloyd Thomas (abridged from *The Reliquiae*, 1696), 1931, 154.

several places from which I cite one: *The Case of the Kingdom Stated*, 1647, refers to 'the Presbyterians who reckon themselves for the old Puritans of England.'[15] Moreover neither Baxter nor Bunyan, usually thought of as distinguished representatives of Puritanism, thought of themselves as Puritans. Baxter says that people so described his father, and Bunyan, in *The Life and Death of Mr Badman*, writes of a man as: 'a godly old Puritan, for so the godly were called in time past.' On the authority of Fuller and Baxter contemporary usage of the word Puritan was confined to the period 1564–1640 and applied to restlessly critical and occasionally rebellious members of the Church of England who desired some modifications in Church government and worship, but not to those who deliberately removed themselves from that Church who were given the names appropriate to their particular views of Brownists, Separatists, Barrowists, and Anabaptists.

But Fuller and Baxter are far from standing alone in this; all the contemporary evidence that I have been able to consult supports them and I now give some extracts in chronological order to show this. It is usually accepted without qualification that *The Marprelate Tracts* were written by Puritans to win a popular platform for Puritan opinions, but Martin Marprelate knew better for he wrote: 'The ministers maintenance by tithe no Puritan denieth to be unlawful [that is, the Puritan ministers held to an established Church receiving tithes]. For Martin you must understand doth account no Brownist to be a Puritan.'[16] Martin knew this well enough, for linking together in one condemnation the Puritans and his adversaries he wrote: 'The Puritans are angry with me,' and, 'After this, I had a fling at these Puritans, concerning whom my desire is that wherein I am faulty the Puritans would set me down the particulars . . . there have been some jars of unkindness betwixt us . . . the report goeth that some of you have preached against me . . . I may happen to be even with you in this manner . . .' Again, he writes: 'The Puritans craft seeks to procure me to be confuted, I know. I'll be even with them too.' And 'The Bishops mislike my manner of writing. Those whom men foolishly call Puritans like the matter I have handled, but the form they cannot brook so that herein I have them both for my adversaries.'[17]

One of the papers collected in *A parte of a register* is entitled *The complaint presented to the . . . privie Counsell by the godly Ministers*, and contains these words: 'It pleaseth them [that is, papists and sectaries] to use this name to Ministers, to Magistrates, and others, especiallie to

[15] Quoted in *OED*, under *Puritan*.
[16] W. Pierce, *The Marprelate Tracts*, London, 1911, 252.
[17] Pierce, op. cit., 118, 413, 215, 304.

such as have an eye to their iuglings, and the name being odious, many times with the ignorant sort it maketh the person odious: A shreude devise.'[18] At the trial of Barrow, Greenwood, and Penry nothing was said of their being Puritans. This is not surprising for Barrow had written in his *Brief Discovery of the False Churches*: 'All the precise Puritans who refuse the ceremonies of the Church strain at a gnat and swallow a camel. They walk in left-handed policy as Master Cartwright, Wigginton, etc.'[19]

William Bradshaw in his *English Puritanisme* (printed in 1605) cites Roman Catholic views of Puritanism which show that they did not associate it with Separatism:

> For doe not the Papistes esteeme the Puritans to be their chiefest opposites, both for will and power? Whereas they call Protestants, [i.e. Anglicans] Calvin Papists, as having their church government from them, and maintaining ceremonies retained only by their grounds. And Doleman deciding the question whether Papist, Protestant, or Puritan were more likely to prevaile in disposing of the Crowne, if (according to their plotting) there had bene shuffling for it, esteemeth the Protestant a weak partie, as consisting chiefly of Bishops and such as depends upon ecclesiastical promotions. Whereas (in his opinion) most noble men, and gentlemen of spirit, action and religion, London (heretofore swaying the state in like case) and all cities and good townes, where is diligent preaching, bee Puritans, or incline that way, because their religion seemeth most perfect. And therefore Bristow saith that all sound Protestants be Puritans in heart.[20]

Thomas Helwys puts the opposition between Puritans and the extremist groups plainly in his *The Mystery of Iniquity*, 1612, where, speaking of false professions of Christ, he wrote:

> The so much applauded profession of Puritanisme is a false profession, yea and such a false profession as wee know not the like upon the earthe ... in your manie bookes ... you cry out ... that there is a way of reformation wherein you would be, if you might have leave or licence to enter thereinto: which seeing you cannot obteyne, you justify it lawfull to walke in an unreformed profession of Religion, upon this ground because you may not have leave by act of Parliament to reforme ... You are all most unholy, and false Prophetts, the prophetts of the Beast, and

---

[18] *A parte of a register, contayninge sundrie memorable matters, written by divers godly and learned in our time, which stande for, and desire the reformation of our Church, in Discipline and Ceremonies, according to the pure worde of God, and the Lawe of our Lande.* n.p., n.d., (Middleburg?) 1593, 130.

[19] Quoted in B. Hanbury, *Historical Memorials relating to the Independents*, London, 1839, I, 36.

[20] W. Bradshaw, *English Puritanisme containeing the maine opinions of the rigidest sort of those that are called Puritanes in the Realme of England*, (Amsterdam?) 1605, with which is bound *A Survey of the Booke of Common Prayer*, dated 1606. The quotation is from the latter, 10.

not of Christ in that you are not Elected, and Ordeyned by the rules of Christ and have not the word of God nor testimony of your flocks for your true entrance . . .

And since he was a Baptist for good measure he turned on the Separatists:

The next false profession of Christ, and false prophets amongst you that we will (by God's assistance) speake of, is that false profession, and those false prophets which are usually called Brownists, you are they that say you are Jewes: but are none and have made yourselves a name to bee the Seperation, and are falsely so called.[21]

John Geree in a pamphlet entitled *The Character of an old English Puritane or Nonconformist*, printed in 1646, plainly holds that Puritanism belongs to England before 1640:

The Old English Puritane was such an one, that honoured God above all, and under God gave every one his due . . . he did not account set forms unlawfull. Therefore in that circumstance of the Church he did not wholly reject the Liturgy, but the corruption of it . . . He thought God had left a rule in his word for discipline, and that aristocratically by Elders, [i.e. Presbyters, or ministers?] not monarchicall by Bishops, not Democraticall by the people . . . Therefore hee esteemed those churches most pure where the government is by Elders, [ministers?] yet unchurched not those where it was otherwayes.[22]

In *The Harleian Miscellany* (Osborne's edition) vol. V, *A Word for the Army*, 1647, 'The army never hindered the State from a State-Religion, having only wished to enjoy now what the Puritans begged under the Prelates,' vol. II, *Tom Tell-Troath or a Free Discourse touching the Manners of the time* (1622?) '. . . your Majestie may say what you heare of Puritans, and by the Authority of your knowne Disfavour make that good Word to be taken in an ill Sense.' This shows what value should be put on James' view of Puritanism. A number of other citations in a similar usage can be found in the pamphlets of the Miscellany.

Pepys in his *Diary*, vol. I, ed. R. C. Latham, writes of an Oxford Fellow 'who spoke against the New/Old clergy', who was a Presbyterian, the editor in a footnote describes the man as a Puritan though Pepys did not. In vol. II, Pepys writes of 'Crofton the great Presbyterian minister', again there is a footnote describing Crofton as

[21] Thomas Helwys, *The Mystery of Iniquitie*, reproduced, London, 1935, from the copy presented by Helwys to King James, now in the Bodleian Library, 86–7, 93.
[22] Reprinted in the *Church Quarterly Review*, CXLVII, London, 1949, 65–71, and edited by M. Hussey.

a Puritan when Pepys did not: this is not infrequent in the editorial notes. Once again a modern historian apparently knows better than a sixteenth or seventeenth century author what that author meant. Most briefly and explicitly of all is the following quotation from John Robinson given in the O.E.D. under *Puritan* and dated there as about 1625:

> The papists plant the ruling power of Christ in the Pope, the Protestants in the bishop, the Puritans in the Presbytery, we in the body of the congregation of the multitude called the Church.

Since Robinson was the pastor of the congregation which provided the passengers for the *Mayflower*, it would be reasonable to assume on this, apart from other evidence, that no Puritan sailed to America in that ship unless he was a stowaway.

Leaving aside the religious writers and turning to the secular literature of the age, it is interesting to see that 'Puritan' is used with sufficiently clear definition, for example, by the unknown author of the play *The Puritane or the widdow of Watling streete*, 1607, where the widow refers to her dead Puritan husband as 'a man that would keep Church so duly . . . and e'en for Religious haste, go ungarter'd, unbotton'd . . . to Morning Prayer . . . Dine quickly upon Highdays . . . and rise from the Table, to get a good Seat at an Afternoon's Sermon.' Another character says, aside, 'Ay he seem'd all Church, and his Conscience was as hard as the Pulpit.'[23] Again, Ben Jonson, who sought precision in style and content to the point of pedantry (a foible mocked by some of his fellow playwrights and which led him to tell Drummond of Hawthornden that 'Shakespeare wanted art') ridiculed certain characters in his *The Alchemist*, acted in 1610, as the Saints though he does not describe them as Puritans anywhere in the play. He used phrases like the following: 'Pray God it be my Anabaptist,' and 'The holy brethren of Amsterdam, the exiled saints that hope to raise their discipline.' When he makes Ananias say: 'The motion's good and of the Spirit'[24] Jonson had caught the tone of these sectaries for the private 'motion of the Spirit' was not a Puritan theme – whereas the Separatists of Amsterdam had set out on a road the continental Anabaptists had trod before them which would lead their followers to the Inner Light of George Fox, but not via Puritanism of the sixteenth century.

An example of the use of the theme of 'special illumination' as a

---

[23] Tonson's edition, London, 1734 (where it is erroneously attributed to 'Mr. Will. Shakespeare'), 23.

[24] Jonson, *Works*, ed. C. H. Herford and P. & E. M. Simpson, Oxford, 1937, V, 333, 342.

point of description of Puritanism is found in the paper by Richard Greaves on *The Nature of the Puritan Tradition* in *Reformation, Nonconformity and Dissent*, 1977, where he states that the essence of Puritanism is not to be found in matters of polity, theological dogma, principles of authority or class orientation, 'but as Geoffrey Nuttall has shown us,in the deeply spiritual experience which Puritans and many sectaries recognized in others'. 'At the core . . . is an emotional searching for a spiritual communion with God made possible by the inner working of the Holy Spirit'. This approach is only possible if we use the writings of Puritans selectively and omit authors of the mainstream from Cartwright and Perkins to Baxter, who disliked individuals and groups whom they thought of as sectaries and eccentrics – men who 'followed the distempers of a disaffected brain'. This can lead to the well-intentioned but misleading use of an author thereby distorting that author's intentions. Francis Rous, (1579–1659), for example, is referred to by Greaves twice, using *The Heavenlie Academie* (1638) in the third edition of 1702 entitled *The Heavenly University*, to assert that the sectary did not need to study theology at one of the universities and that there was a possibility of conflicting knowledge, which was a radical extension of the sectarian belief in continuing revelation. On the contrary, Rous was not opposing an alternative 'university' to Oxford and Cambridge, but setting up an ideal of spiritual training through 'the new writing of regeneration' from which 'a new discovery of truth not known before could arise', but this was in addition to the study of Scripture and divinity. Rous was not opposing, but adding a stimulus to, the accepted divinity of Presbyterians and Independents. Since Greaves gives no context for his use of Rous save sectarianism would the reader realise that Rous was an Oxford graduate, a Spenserian poet in his youth, who became a self-taught lay theologian of considerable learning with a tendency to occasional mystical utterances and a member of Parliament, was appointed Provost of Eton in 1644, wrote that he was 'of the Presbyterian communion', but through his later disapproval of Scottish Presbyterian pressure against Toleration turned to the Independents, became a Lord of Parliament under Cromwell and a Speaker of the Nominated Parliament, where detesting its sectarianism he broke it up, and, finally left money in his will to provide for two scholars at Pembroke College, Oxford, to ensure that divinity should be carefully studied there before these scholars could graduate? This man clearly cannot be cited to support, as Greaves does, Quaker ideas or the radicalism and anti-intellectualism of the sectaries and self-appointed lay preachers.

However, even though more and yet more evidence from

contemporary sources were to be adduced, it is almost impossible today to confine the use of the word Puritan to those alone who were called Puritans by their contemporaries. An attempt so to confine it would be regarded as an intolerable pedantry and would win little acceptance: the inflation of meaning in the use of the word cannot like the inflation of the French franc be disguised by shifting a decimal point, for inflation in language is final. Perhaps nothing can now prevent most writers from describing Browne, Penry, Robinson, Milton, Cromwell, Bunyan as Puritans alongside of Cartwright, Travers, Perkins, and Preston who were Puritans in fact. Nevertheless, it may still be possible to appeal to historians to avoid unnecessary generalisations, and also to avoid the danger of setting traps for themselves by being too inclusive in their use of the word and then having to tread warily among qualifications and parenthetical disclaimers when they write of the developments of Protestantism in England – and of its social and political implications – in the period 1560–1700.

Above all, writers on this theme should realise that the word 'Puritan' is not like the word 'Methodist' which from being originally a mockery was accepted by its recipients as a term of definition, for 'Puritan' is always liable to be regarded too seriously by historians as a legitimate definition instead of used warily as a sometimes casually applied slogan of abuse not acceptable to its recipients. Parker's *Discourse*, particularly its opening and closing pages, should be read carefully as a cautionary record.

For the years 1570 to 1640 surely the position is clear enough: Puritan is the regular word even though sometimes used loosely by lay opponents for those clergymen and laymen of the established, Church of England whose attitude ranged from the tolerably comfortable to the downright obstreperous, and to those who sought to presbyterianise that Church from within. Whereas Brownist, Separatist, Barrowist, and Anabaptist are the appropriate terms (each, it will be remembered, carrying a point of differentiation) for those who refused to accept the principle that Christ's Church could be conterminous with the Tudor or Stuart state. Thereafter why should we not use for the years 1640 to 1662, as Baxter and others said men did, the party names of Presbyterian, Independent, Anabaptist (or more courteously, Baptist), and, if we wish to go further, we could add Quaker, Leveller, Ranter, Digger and others? Each of these names carries greater precision of meaning to the informed than the generalising use of the word Puritan, for each had in view a religious – and many a social – programme capable of clear description. It is, of course, true that we must not oversimplify by relating the modern use of these party names, seen as denominations, to those groups in the seventeenth century. The question usefully discussed by George Yule, Who were the Independents?[25] is not answered by assuming them to have been the same as the modern Congregationalists, any more than it is answered by placing the Independents under the heading of Puritanism.

But is it not possible that this attempt to confine the use of the word to the period prior to 1640 and to reluctant and imperfectly conforming 'Anglicans'[26] is made useless by the fact that the colonists of Congregationalist New England had been Puritans in this stricter sense in old England? But Puritanism was largely a protest, in the name of a more biblically grounded Christianity, against the Act of Uniformity and episcopal enforcement of it. Its ecclesiology, for example, tended to be conditioned by that protest: once removed, as in Massachusetts Bay, from the Laudian situation: when a new generation had found it possible to go with a clear conscience, they now believed they were 'not making a separation like Robinson, but a legitimate withdrawal'; not Puritans but Congregationalists organised in Churches in the closest relation with the civil order – in voyaging to the Wilderness, 'Puritan,' like other old-world concepts, had suffered an Atlantic sea-change.[27] Besides, it has been basic to the argument to show that once a Puritan withdrew from the Church of England to set up a Church with a distinct ecclesiology of its own, he forthwith ceased to be clearly a Puritan.

The dictum, almost a truism, *Entia non sunt multiplicanda praeter necessitatem*, like the truisms of Kipling's 'Gods of the Copybook Headings,' it is perilous to ignore. But even if writers in this field could be persuaded that Puritan is a name to use carefully yet the conviction will still be strong that there is a common factor, a common spirit or attitude, in that entity called Puritanism whether it be biblicism, or the desire and pursuit of the Holy Community, or some other theme. But when Presbyterian and Baptist held opposing views about the nature of, and the means to arrive at, the Holy Community there is not much gained by saying they had the notion

[25] George Yule, *The Independents in the English Civil War*, Cambridge University Press and Melbourne University Press, 1958. Yule, it should be understood, assumes neither of the alternatives which I have suggested are erroneous.

[26] 'Anglican', of course, derives from a later period but 'Protestants' would be now too general a term though that is what members of the Church of England called themselves. Archbishop Laud said on the scaffold, 'I have always lived in the Protestant religion.', Peter Heylyn, *Cyprianus Anglicus*, 1668, 527.

[27] K. L. Sprunger indicated this in his *William Ames and the Settlement of Massachusetts Bay*, New England Quarterly, XXXIX, 1966, 66–79. Collinson believes this change is due to William Ames whom he cites *A Second Manuduction* (Ames/Bradshaw), 1615, 33–34, Collinson, *The Religion of Protestants*, 1982, 278.

in common as Puritans. Again, it is usual to say that under the blanket of Puritanism most were Calvinists. It may be possible for those who never read through Calvin's *Institutio*, nor examine what in fact was the ecclesiastical constitution in Calvin's Geneva, to be content with this. Much could be said on this point including, for example, pointing out the curious consequences of assuming that Calvinism consisted almost exclusively of extreme views on total depravity and the eternal decrees of predestination; but the shortest comment is to state that the Puritans rightly so called rarely refer to Calvin and then selectively; the sectaries rarely, and then sometimes abusively; while those who cite Calvin more extensively and with approval are the Anglicans from Whitgift through Field to Davenant, and those other Jacobean bishops whom Baxter called the old episcopal divines in distinction from the new prelatical divines, that is, the Laudians.[28] Moreover, the Geneva of Beza made important changes from that of Calvin. For, example, Presbyterianism became *de jure divino*. In any case the English 'Calvinist' divines placed their own not inconsiderable variations on either form of Genevan Calvinism.

This leads into what may well lie at the heart of the difficulties in so much discussion of Puritanism, namely, that many of those who work on the literature and history of the sixteenth and seventeenth centuries in England do not always have the time or the interest to study the theology of these Protestants, whereas it is here largely that the distinctions and lines of development can be determined without falling back on the practice of generalisations and qualifications so often resorted to. Patrick Collinson in *The Elizabethan Puritan Movement* ignores the main weight of published works by these Puritans. He could, for example, have added purpose and depth to his discussion of Sabbatarianism by providing the essential themes of Greenham one of the earliest, most able and moderate writers on this subject. Collinson's books tell us almost everything about the Puritans except the structure and force of their published writings on religion – which they themselves thought were the heart of the matter. Theology is a discipline: it requires patience and careful study like other disciplines. It is particularly in their doctrine of the Church (including ministry, ordination, discipline of morals, and the sacraments) that the differences among those commonly called Puritans can be determined. On these points, for example, what had Bunyan in common with Baxter, or Perkins with Helwys? If we wish to discuss the aims and activities of an English Protestant of the second half of the seventeenth century, we can do so effectively only if we avoid the blanketing generalisation of 'Puritan' used as the basis of *a priori* deductions and use the names the different groups gave themselves, or others gave to them, at the time, as Baxter did.

To elucidate the aims and activities of that Englishman we should examine his writings and actions, to that degree necessary to establish his standpoint, along the lines of his views on ecclesiology;[29] the sacraments; the nature and extent of covenants and covenanting; the nature and influence of the Holy Spirit; the relations of Crown, Parliament, and Church; the ecclesiastical parish and tithes; civil polity; method of scriptural exegesis; and manner of worshipping – not just one of these but several together – on this basis 'Anglican' (awaiting a better day), 'Presbyterian,' 'Independent,' 'Baptist,' 'Fifth Monarchist,' 'Seekers,' and 'Quaker' provide more precise information than 'Puritan.'

Finally, a frequently overlooked dimension in Stuart and Commonwealth Puritanism – as I have sought to confine the term – is its profound concern with 'casuistry,' that is the study of 'cases of conscience,' including the preaching of sermons upon these 'cases.' If we must have a common denominator in the variations in 'Puritanism' then the driving force behind Puritan 'casuistry' would represent this more usefully than others which have been proposed, not least because it demonstrates the fact that Puritanism was in some ways the earlier and English form of that mutation from the Protestantism of the Reformation which on the Continent became Pietism and was influenced by English Puritans, for example, Lewis Bayley's, *Practice of Piety*, 1613 onwards. 'Casuistry' was the surviving factor passed on into Nonconformity later through *The Cripplegate Lectures* and Baxter's *Christian Directory* into the writings of, for example, Defoe.

---

[29] Baxter, *Reliquiae*, 139, 'In the time of the late unhappy wars in these kingdoms the Controversies about Church Government were in most men's mouths, and made the greatest Noise, being hotly agitated by States-men and Divines, by words and writings.' The hopes of the Long Parliament that Scripture released from trammels could provide a model for Church and Commonwealth proved to be illusory because Presbyterian polity and discipline were rejected by Independency and Toleration – and Erastianism was opposed by the sectaries. The Commonwealth foundered on the state of mind reflected in Colonel Henry Cromwell's words to General Fleetwood in October, 1658, 'Remember what has always befallen imposing spirits. Will not the loins of an imposing Independent or Anabaptist be as heavy as the loins of a imposing Prelate or presbyter? And is it a dangerous error that dominion is founded in grace when it is held by the Church of Rome, and a sound principle when it is held by the Fifth Monarchy?'

In conclusion it is worth noting that when writing on seventeenth century 'Puritanism' and its setting we should all be reminded that the most thorough, well-balanced and closely-knit work ever written which dealt with this subject was that by S. R. Gardiner in his great *History of England*, 1603–1660. There is, unfortunately, no work of equivalent weight for Elizabethan England.

9

Defoe: The Protestant Flail

Defoe and Swift had little in common save that they were the ablest writers of English prose in the opening decades of the eighteenth century. Between them, in their incomparable styles, they analysed the political confusions of the period, and each in his own enigmatic temperament plunged deeply into the mystery of the human condition: Swift the churchman with increasing pessimism; Defoe the dissenter also aware of the evil and violence that men and women create, yet optimistic with the determination to find 'Projects' for improvement.[1] Both Defoe and Swift wrote, among much else, on the religious question of whether it was right for dissenters to become acceptable for political office by attending a parish church once a year. Swift in his contribution to this furious and bitter pamphlet warfare between churchman and dissenter wrote of Defoe with contemptuous dismissal thus: 'one of these authors (the fellow that was pilloried I have forgot his name) is indeed so grave, sententious, dogmatical a rogue that there is no enduring him.'[2] 'The grave, sententious, dogmatical' character which Swift rightly saw in him no doubt had its origin in the fact that Defoe had been brought up in a

---

[1] *An Essay upon Projects*, 1697, written in hiding from debtors, shows this buoyant energy.

[2] Jonathan Swift, *A Letter from a Member of the House of Commons in Ireland to a Member of the House of Commons in England concerning the Sacramental Test*, *Swift's Miscellanies*, 1742, I, 135.

devout Presbyterian home under the ministry of Dr Samuel Annesley, an ejected minister in 1662, commemorated in one of the earliest writings of Defoe:

His native Candor, and familiar Stile,
Which did so oft his Hearers Hours beguile,
Charm'd us with Godliness, and while he spake
We lov'd the *Doctrine* for the *Teacher's* sake.[3]

Defoe had been intended by his parents to follow the example of Annesley by entering the Presbyterian ministry, but he wrote many years later in 1709: 'I acknowledge the pulpit is none of my office. It was my disaster to be set apart for, and then to be set apart from, the honour of that sacred employ.'[4] This statement is reticent and points to the ambivalence which many see in Defoe's character.

In spite of the surface impression in reading him that all is clear, direct, honest, indeed Christian good sense, and that morality and obedience to the dictates of Providence are the plain rules of life, Defoe's temperament was nevertheless marked by his experience of life including prison, resourceful in the talents of the secret agent for disguised identity and evasion, and he therefore gave the impression to many of his contemporaries of unscrupulousness and intrigue which he indignantly protested against though not with entire conviction to later readers.[5]

In his writings on the supernatural, the devil, second sight, and magic, there is ambiguity between his interest in paranormal phenomena and his journalistic desire to make his reader's flesh creep. This shows a curious insensitivity in one 'charm'd with the Godliness' of Annesley. Again, would the description of the 'conversion' of Moll Flanders have been satisfactory to those Presbyterian ministers whose integrity, learning and spiritual conduct Defoe admired?[6] Yet, setting aside as inappropriate Macaulay's description of *Roxana*, *Colonel Jack*, and *Moll Flanders* as 'utterly nauseous and wretched' and allowing Defoe his defence of himself against the abusive names to which he was subjected of, 'Villain, Rascal, Miscreant, Lyer,

[3] *The Character of the Late Dr. Samuel Annesley by Way of Elegy*, 1697, 6.
[4] *A Review of the State of the British Nation*, October 22, 1709, vol. XV, 341.
[5] *An Appeal to Honour and Justice Tho' it be of His Worst Enemies*, 1715. This is a sustained defence of his career and writings. Also see *Serious Reflections during the Life and Suprizing Adventures of Robinson Crusoe with his Vision of the Angelick World Written by Himself*, 1720, 25 ff., 64 ff., for casuistical arguments about 'credit' and 'trust' and 'relative honesty' in ch. 2. (1895, Dent, ed. C. A. Aitken).
[6] *The Fortunes and Misfortunes of the Famous Moll Flanders ... who was born in Newgate ... was Twelve Years a Whore ... Eight Years a Transported Felon in Virginia, at last grew Rich, liv'd Honest, and died a Penitent*, 1721, 280, 282, 333 (Bodley Head ed., 1929.)

Bankrupt, Fellow, Hireling, Turn-coat, etc.' the case can be made for showing that Defoe was a life-long, loyal and thorough Protestant and also a religious man devoted to the cause of Dissent, though eventually with personal variations from the dissenting norm, who especially admired the principles of the Presbyterians, and suffered in person and means for these causes. Further, precisely because of these convictions, Defoe had considerable zeal for and some influence upon the making of the union between England and Scotland amid all the difficulties and violence of its background. One of the fullest and most carefully prepared of his writings was his *The History of the Union*, a work neglected possibly because through his zeal to avoid offence and provide an objective historical record, it seems dull to those accustomed to his other writings with their crisp and lively style laced with vivid description and incident.[7]

This study of Defoe will seek to elucidate those two aspects of Defoe's work: his commitment to his Protestant religion, and his commitment to the Act of Union of 1707 which he saw as providing security for the continuation of Protestantism in Great Britain – if these commitments are ignored we will neither understand Defoe nor many of his writings. Inquiry into Defoe's character, personal convictions and activities in order to understand what Protestantism and Dissent meant for him begins with his father, liveryman of the Butchers' Company of St. Giles parish in Cripplegate, who followed Dr. Annesley into Dissent after the Ejection, for it was through this decision that James Defoe's son Daniel became a disparaged dissenter. This status he accepted with sufficient pride though it was accompanied by the psychological unease characteristic of the outsider (reinforced by his later misfortunes and his feeling of being misunderstood) which beset him through his life and which was probably a source of his ambiguity, his sense of being the secret agent observing human vagaries. He resented being called a 'hosier' by Gildon and wished to be thought of as a merchant, not a shopman but the resident of a country estate. Like Dickens he was concerned with being accepted as a gentleman. Defoe the outsider in his youth and early manhood experienced the resentment and persecution given to the dissenters; he was excluded from a university education; he was pilloried in reality for his ironic mockery of the High-Flying Churchmen in his *The Shortest Way with Dissenters*, and pilloried in verse in *The Dunciad* by Pope who held Defoe's efforts at poetry in

---

[7] *The History of the Union of Great Britain*, Edinburgh, 1709. 'Little more than a dry journal of what passed in the Scottish Parliament, yet he must have had an interesting tale to tell if he had chosen it.' Walter Scott, *Miscellaneous Prose Works*, Edinburgh, 1847, vol. 1, 403.

contempt; he was put in danger of his life from Jeffreys' instant executions after the failure of the Protestant rebellion of Monmouth at Sedgemoor, and later by the Edinburgh mob seeking out the 'English spy' during the violence preceding the Act of Union – in all these as well as in other ways, he must have felt the isolation of the solitary. For him later, *Robinson Crusoe* was more than a moralized tale of adventure, it was, as he wrote soon afterwards, the allegory of his own life.[8] Through his integrity of purpose he even found himself angrily resented by English dissenters, and later furiously condemned by Protestant Scots. As he wrote in his own *apologia pro vita sua, An Appeal to Honour and Justice*, he had lived at times like a 'grenadier on the counterscarp': an exposed position in which he was at the same time pleased with his own skill in getting clear, and angry that he should have to endure such isolation.[9]

Defoe had attended from about fourteen to nineteen years of age (1673–1678) the dissenting academy at Newington Green organised by the Presbyterian, Charles Morton, remarkable at the time for his educational aims and methods. One of these was later described by Defoe thus: 'the Master or tutor read all his lectures and gave all his systems, whether of Philosophy or Divinity, in English, and had all his declaimings and dissertations in the same tongue. And though the Scholars from that place were not destitute in the languages, yet it is observed of them, they were by this made masters of the English tongue, and more of them excelled in that particular than of any school at that time.'[10] In this academy Defoe had already begun to become 'a lord of language'. But he acquired there more than the beginning of his mastery of English; he also learned to debate on casuistry, that is, resolving individual cases in moral theology, developing this skill in practical divinity throughout his life.[11] With such an education under such a master and from a religious home, why did he not enter the dissenting ministry after 1678? A manuscript notebook survives containing, among other religious exercises, what he called *Meditations*, which are religious verses. In one of these he wrote of his desire to find peace in Christ and to escape:

---

[8] James Joyce noted this about Defoe in a lecture he gave in 1912 in Trieste (in which he referred to Defoe's 'practical and well-balanced religiousness'): 'Egli che immortale lo strano solitario Crusoe e tanti altri solitari perdute nel mare magno della miseria sociale come Crusoe nel mare dello acque sentiva forse coll' aviccanarsi della sua fine la nostalgia della solitudine.' Ed. from the Italian ms. by J Prescott, *Buffalo Studies*, vol. 1, No. 1, 1964, 14.

[9] *An Appeal*, 203, also the phrase is used in a letter to Robert Harley, Sept. 11th., 1707, G. H. Healey, *The Letters of Daniel Defoe*, 1955, 242.

[10] *The Present State of Parties in Great Britain: Particularly an Equiry into the State of the Dissenters in England*. . . . 1712, 319 ff. Morton became vice-president of Harvard.

[11] T. Wright *The Life of Daniel Defoe*, 1894, 8.

> From half convictions, which too harrassing prove . . .
> From all my feign'd humility
> My outward zeal, and my hypocrisy . . .
> From all my brain-begotten faith
> From all my doubt . . .'[12]

Many a future minister or priest has come to his ordination after spiritual anxieties and self-questioning, but 'brain-begotten faith' by its nature could cause 'doubt'; however, with Defoe we should not assume that this doubt may call in question his later assertions of religious faith – he is not to be imagined as following the course of those mournful fictional victims of 'doubt' which nineteenth century religious questioning projected, Mark Rutherford and Robert Elsmere. He put at the head of the religious verses in the notebook a grim sentence: 'If man were left to himself he would be a Judas to his Master, Cain to his brother, an Amnon to his sister, an Absalom to his Father, and a Saul to himself.'[13] If sometimes he may have brooded on this view in later life, it did not gain ground: his natural buoyancy upheld him. It is unlikely that the thought of his being heir, like the rest of mankind, to original sin, any more than the weakening of religious faith, prevented him from entering the ministry. What is more probable is that he questioned whether his energies and ambitions could be satisfied by it.

After leaving Morton's academy he became, as he described himself later, a merchant in hose. His state of mind at this period is indicated by his recollection of the so-called Popish Plot, promoted by Titus Oates, when it was essential to carry a weapon while walking in London streets. Defoe used what he called a 'Protestant flail' since 'a pistol is a fool to it, it laughs at the sword and the cane; for you know there's no fence against a flail. For my part I have frequently walked with one about me in the old Popish days, and tho' I never set up for a hero, yet, when armed with this scourge for a Papist, I remember I feared nothing.'[14] This bigotry was to change when after marrying and fathering children he became restless for adventures as well as for making a fortune in trade, travelled in Portugal and Spain and found that Spaniards though papists could be Christian, courteous, good-humoured and charitable – in *Robinson Crusoe* he demonstrated it.[15] Also either at home or abroad he fought

---

[12] MS Notebook of 1681 in Huntington Library, under title *Meditations*, a number of religious poems, 175 (Copy in microfilm of the complete works of Defoe, reel 1. University of Sussex Library).

[13] Ibid., 172.

[14] *Review*, vol. VIII, 614.

[15] *The Life and Strange Surprizing Adventures of Robinson Crusoe of York, Mariner, who lived*

a duel and then regretted this as a grave sin.[16]. These experiences must have helped him in his next and more serious adventure. He remembered in later life that in this period he was at a horse-race at Aylesbury where he saw 'the late Duke of Monmouth' amid a 'mighty confluence of noblemen and gentlemen': to see the Protestant hero and note his following was a more likely motive than to seek a doubtful gain among the jockeys.[17] Defoe soon followed the Protestant star in 1685, accompanied by old comrades from the Newington Academy, men, 'who had they lived would have been extraordinary men of their kind, viz., Kitt, Battersby, young Jenkyns, Hewling', names lost to us but elegiacally remembered by him as having ridden with him to Bridgwater to end their days with the Western Martyrs.[18] Defoe twice gave a brief and vivid account of the final events of Monmouth's venture, the skirmish near Bath, and the defeat at Sedgemoor; and, when it was safe to do so, claimed proudly his involvement as 'a Man that had been in Arms under the Duke of Monmouth against the cruelty and Arbitrary Government of his pretended Father.'[19] The Protestant flail had failed at Sedgemoor, nevertheless Defoe opposed Jacobitism in word and deed in any of its forms throughout his life. It was with the coming of the new Protestant star, William of Orange, that he found escape from frustration. Enraged by the pamphleteer Tutchin, who in *The Foreigners* had attacked the King and the Dutch, Defoe wrote the poem *The True-Born Englishman*, 1701, which brought him to the King's notice, approval and employment. He always kept William's memory with gratitude: 'I take all Occasions to do for the expressing the Honour I ever preserv'd for the Immortal and Glorious Memory of that greatest and Best of Princes, and Who it was my Honour and Advantage to call Master as well as Sovereign, whose Goodness to me I never forget; and whose Memory I never patiently heard abused, nor ever can do so.'[20] Defoe in his praise of King William had almost attained the words of the toast of the future Orange Lodges, 'the glorious, pious and immortal memory.' He affirmed with bitterness that had the King lived he, 'would never have suffered me to be treated as I have been in the world' – the pillory, Newgate,

---

Eight and Twenty Years all alone, on an uninhabited Island on the Coast of America . . . April, 1719, *The Farther Adventures of Robinson Crusoe* . . . *and of* . . . *his Travels Round three Parts of the Globe.* August, 1719, e.g. Section XXXVII.

[16] He refers evasively to this duel in the *Review*, vol. VII, 451.

[17] *A Tour Through the Whole Island of Great Britain.* (Everyman ed., 1974) vol. II, 14.

[18] Cited without reference in Morley, *The Earlier Life and the Chief Earlier Works of Daniel Defoe*, 1889, 17.

[19] The reference to being in arms is *An Appeal*, 195, 198.

[20] *An Appeal*, 195.

debt and long periods of living in hiding from his enemies. He can never be questioned on his loyalty to the Protestant cause. It was visible in his actions, and positively asserted throughout his life in speech and writing.

Defoe the dissenter, however, was difficult to identify as a sound dissenting Whig, and he was questioned by his fellows on the charge that he sometimes wrote for their political opponents and that his contributions to the dissenting cause were occasionally unhelpful to the point of creating serious damage. Again there is the teasing possibility in many readers' minds that his religion was on the surface, that he lacked conviction, or spirituality, and that he used his religion as an ornament, a weapon, or to make money. But Defoe the enigmatic should be allowed to appear as in the portrait showing him as a man reserved amid his apparent openness. Defoe the solitary kept concealed behind allegory and allusion his inner religious life; he worked out a religious structure half-hidden like that of Crusoe's sanctuary behind his concealing stockade. He was at times assertively positive about certain religious convictions, and at other times he became roundabout and allusive, writing as of another person, because he refused to be simplistic in his religion. Defoe the outsider, the grenadier on the counterscarp, who was to become the English agent in hostile Edinburgh, had learned to wear his masks and to use paradox at times. His masking irony and distracting allegory make it harder to try to demonstrate his religious sincerity than to show his Protestantism or his occasionally erratic career as a dissenter. Defoe's religion could often be shown as that of a man of hard determined practicality with little space for sentiment but it could also be seen expressed in irony and paradox. The theological position of Protestant Dissent if it ever fully gripped his heart and mind seems soon to have fallen into the background, but he retained his interest in its casuistic or moral theology with its analysis of motives and alternative possibilities of action.[21] Sometimes he echoes the old religious language, but it seems as if he intends no more than to show that he formally accepted its essential principles without allowing these to master his mind, emotions and grounds of action. However, his supreme efficiency in the sometimes unsavoury arts of journalism showed tastes and talents which confuse the impression he makes at other times of serious religious conviction. Defoe enjoyed his

---

[21] *Serious Reflections* particularly illustrates this, see also *Religious Courtship: Being Historical Discourses on the Necessity of Marrying Religious Husbands and Wives only . . .* 1722. *A Treatise Concerning the Use and Abuse of the Marriage Bed . . .* June, 1727 (Originally entitled *Conjugal Lewdness: or, Matrimonial Whoredom . . .* January, 1727).

pamphleteering and invented many of the techniques of modern journalism; the leading article, the role of special correspondent, the scandal column, and the making of bold assertions which by provoking angry denials brought otherwise concealed matters into public debate. He risked and received imprisonment and fines by exposing the behaviour of men in office and their scandalous politics; and in doing so he was not acting wholly out of honest indignation.[22] 'This, Sir, is an Age of Plot and Deceit of Contradiction and Paradox . . .' he wrote, and, 'It is very hard under all these Masks to see the true Countenance of any Man.'[23]

Defoe as a Presbyterian dissenter always held two positions. First that the difference between Church and Dissent was not so great as theological extremists on both sides asserted. Moreover he always repudiated the attempt to identify himself with Independents, Baptists or dissenting politically minded radicals whom he contemptuously called 'levellers.' He suggested that good sense and the rejection on the one side of Non-juring, Jacobite, High Flying churchmen who refused to accommodate the liturgy to the consciences of dissenters, and on the other side the reaction of what he called 'Fifth-Monarchists', could resolve the division; though as a pragmatist he may have been unconvinced at heart that this could finally happen. Secondly, he affirmed that dissenters, and especially Presbyterians, were unjustly persecuted, since they were good citizens and not rebels, who wished to live decently and in order according to their consciences. If opponents asked, What of Monmouth's rebellion? Defoe would quickly answer that churchmen had accepted the principles of 1689 with William of Orange, and therefore it is inconsistent of them to accuse dissenters of what they had done themselves. In developing these two positions, amid the intense passions aroused in both religious parties, Defoe was open to the charge of luke-warmness as a dissenter and untrustworthy in the view of a single-minded Whig bigot; even worse he could be seen as a traitor to the cause when he wrote for Tory ministers of state. Defoe's secretiveness did not help, for to simple partisans it looked like betrayal though for Defoe, who was not simply a party-man, it was necessary both for his personal survival and for allaying the destructive passions of the parties. His most famous pamphlet, *The Shortest Way with Dissenters*, 1702, brought him humiliation and

---

[22] *The Poor Man's Plea in Relation to all the Proclamations, Declarations, Acts of Parliament . . . for a Reformation of Manners and suppressing Immorality in the Nation* 1698. *The Freeholder's Plea against the Stockjobbing Elections of Parliament Men*, 1701, *Reformation of Manners, a Satyr*, 1702.
[23] *A Letter to Mr. Bisset*. 1709, 6, 10.

triumph, the acute anger of Tories, Whigs, churchmen and dissenters. By using his extraordinary force as a writer to support Dissent by the irony of writing as if he were an extremist churchman he was too successful:

> Alas for the Church of England! What with popery on the one Hand and Schismaticks on the other how has she been crucify'd between the two Thieves. Now let us crucify the Thieves ... The Posterity of the Sons of Error [should] be rooted out from the Face of this Land for ever.[24]

He had thought that from a dissenting point of view nothing could be better than mocking the extreme High-Flier, the no-nonsense-about-toleration churchman, but it misfired because Defoe got his timing wrong: his pamphlet was issued a few months after King William's death. The High-Church party had come into their own with Queen Anne: his enemies could destroy him. Six months earlier his trial, if it had taken place, would not have resulted so severely; he did not expect the ferocity which brought him to the pillory and Newgate which marked him for life.[25] 'You are an honest man you say! Pray, Sir, was you ever try'd?' This was a cry of pain. Though the pamphlet contained nothing that could clearly be construed as treason or libel, this did not prevent his arrest on the orders of the Tory High-Church minister Nottingham for 'high crimes and misdemeanours'. Defoe unfortunately took his counsel's advice, which might have succeeded in a different year, to confess that he had written the pamphlet and to appeal to the Queen directly for mercy.[26] Anne certainly had no share in his condemnation; she paid his fine, and sent money to his family after he was imprisoned. He never forgot his gratitude to her, as he never forgot gratitude to those who helped on other occasions; this is one of his virtues and should set aside the view that he was unscrupulous.[27] Why was he put on trial and so ruthlessly condemned to a fine and the pillory?

---

[24] *The Shortest Way*, 128, 133. Samuel Wesley, though formerly of the Newington Academy, called the dissenters 'villains, hypocrites, murderers'. See also Sacherevell, *Political Union*, 1702, 51. Not only Sacheverell used such expressions.

[25] *Review*. 21 March, 1705, vol. V, 'Violence, injury and barbarous treatment had destroyed him and his undertakings'. Also see his letter to Nottingham, 9 January, 1702/3, Healey, *The Letters of Daniel Defoe*, 1955, 2. 'As a Gentleman, Prisons, Pillorys and Such Like which are worse to me than Death ...'

[26] Defoe was betrayed by an anonymous informer to Nottingham for £50. William Colepepper his friend and counsel, was deceived by the prosecution into urging Defoe to confess his authorship and to ask for the Queen's mercy. Some of those on the Bench had been named in his bitter satires on moral reformation. See J. R. Moore, *Defoe in the Pillory and Other Studies*, New York, 1973.

[27] *An Appeal*, 200

Many of the members of the Bench or their friends were convinced Tories and high churchmen, (or Whig dissenters whom he had denounced for their Occasional Conformity) who had been humiliated by his attacks by name on their political corruption and vicious manners and who would also resent his insistence in the past on the legitimacy of Monmouth and his heirs. The consequence was inevitable and with a prepared jury they got their revenge.[28] Defoe was ruined in business, bankrupted as well as pilloried and gaoled, and received psychological damage which turned him inward on himself in spite of his bold front at the time and his energetic writing from prison. Even the dissenters were not amused by his ironic pamphlet; they were taken in as were their opponents, and they were also angry at the prospect of his endangering them since a bill to abolish Occasional Conformity was in progress and his attack would appear to justify its retention. Behind his irony, which some persons saw – and some see still – as religious indifference, there lies, however, deep religious conviction. Defoe held the doctrine of a personal Providence which directly ruled in human affairs, making known God's will through the promptings of spiritual powers. This can be seen in what for many a schoolboy, otherwise fascinated by Crusoe's adventures, were the *longueurs* of the story, the religious digressions which were for Defoe essential to understanding how life is lived. *Robinson Crusoe* is to be seen as a survey of, and reflections on, Defoe's experience of life, including the recent Scottish adventure, in which his account of Crusoe's disobedience to his father, his religious indifference, his hardening of heart in spite of warnings half-hidden in the words of, or in what happens to, the people he meets, culminates in his coming to the humility of self-knowledge – though this conversion is not described in the traditional evangelical language but has a pattern of its own.[29] Defoe wrote in the preface: 'The story is told . . . to the instruction of others by this example, and to justify and honour the wisdom of Providence. The editor believes the thing to be a just history of facts; neither is there any appearance of fiction in it.' The shipwrecks endured by Dampier and by Selkirk provided the factual basis, and the phrase about the absence of fiction is justified when we realise that Defoe is writing the moral interpretation of his own life. Not long after the publication of the book Defoe wrote in the persona of Crusoe *Serious Reflections during the Life of Robinson Crusoe* containing vigorous but discursive discussions on the workings

---

[28] See Moore, op. cit., for details.
[29] *Robinson Crusoe*. Section XXIII. 'The Great First Cause . . . a secret directing Providence.' While the phrasing is evangelical it lacks evangelical content.

of Providence; a curious and embarrassing section, presumably in self-justification, on the nature of honesty and deception; and a conclusion describing 'the Angelic World'. There is also self-justification at a deeper level since he states that *Robinson Crusoe* was '. . . one whole scheme of a real life of twenty-eight years . . . I have . . . suffered all manner of violence and oppressions, injurious reproaches . . . corrections from Heaven . . . There's not a circumstance in the imaginary story but has its just allusions to a real story . . .'[30] In *Serious Reflections* Defoe described the religious stance he has now achieved, and added:

> Divinity is not my talent, nor ever like to be my profession . . . [and] talking Scripture is out of fashion: but I must crave leave to tell my reader, that if there were no God or Providence, devil or future state, yet they ought not to be drunken and lewd, passionate, revengeful or immoral, 'tis so unnatural, so unruly, so ingenteel, so foolish and foppish, that no wise man as a man can justify it so much as to his own reason or the memory of his ancestors.[31]

Defoe makes Crusoe speak as an interested spectator of the human condition assuming a common sense attitude showing that religion, even for a worldly man has to be taken notice of; not to do so is to be unreasoning, ignorant or vicious. Rochester, sometimes cited by Defoe, had said 'in a lewd song' that 'Religion's a politick cheat', but be quotes this also from him:

> The secret trepidation racks the soul
> And while he says, 'No God, Nature replies, Thou Fool.'[32]

Behind 'reason' and 'ancestors' lies original sin, which God's overruling alone can alleviate.

Defoe believed in God and Providence, and *Robinson Crusoe* demonstrated it. Providence is not described in the form of predestination; it is Calvin without the awe before the majesty of God's purposes and without Calvin's repeated *prosternons nous*, it is later calvinism though without that dread commitment to covenanted election which drove the Cameronians whom Defoe wondered at in Scotland. Defoe's fellow English Presbyterians were now at least three removes from the theological structure of their presumptive, founder. Also, he himself had developed certain religious convictions in a way

---

[30] Wright, op. cit. 24. For example, twenty-eight years of Defoe's life were passed in silence with his family: he 'suddenly resolved to speak no more . . . he having married a fool' and 'living in a house with fools'.

[31] *Serious Reflections* (1895 ed.), 89.

[32] Ibid., 94.

unusual to them: in some ways he foreshadowed the coming of 'rational dissent' though he vigorously rejected the encroaching Socianism which was to destroy English Presbyterianism.

They would have agreed with his assertion that God guides by his Providence the whole world, and shows a particular care over and concern in the governing of mankind (though they would have hesitated over the implication of his belief in a personal guardian) for, 'Natural religion proves the first, reveal'd religion proves the last of these beyond contradiction'.[33] He wanted to show under Crusoe's persona and the island exile that what appear to be external accidents, or strange impulses from within, are the promptings of Providence. Providence yielded to as though urged by a personal Daemon; the framework of doctrine and morality which contemporary Presbyterianism worked within (which he accepted with his own modifications); the method of casuistry he was to show in *The Marriage Bed* and *The Family Instructor* and other religiously based works, which was to be an undertone to his novels and those other contributions to literature which he wrote after his breakdown in health in 1714; his experience of life in dangerous situations – all these when focused on his innate concern for Protestantism as the only guarantee of liberty, and as the necessary stimulant to the pragmatism which succeeds in 'Projects' for trade and the technical improvements which enhance it, urged Defoe to regard union with Protestant Scotland as essential to the future well-being of Protestant England. For Defoe, whatever else his complex character suggested, and however varied the great range of his writings, was an all-or-nothing dissenter. His Protestantism as it has been described here had led him to believe that it was fundamental to his own, and to his nation's, well-being. After the Revolution he consistently opposed Jacobitism and he was increasingly aware of the Presbyterian Church of Scotland as a bulwark against the danger from the Old Pretender. His *Review* had as a constant theme the need to persuade Scotland to unite with England to ensure a conclusive victory for Protestantism and the emasculation of Jacobitism. Defoe the Protestant flail, steeled by the hostility he had received from churchmen and even dissenters, from Whigs and Tories; strengthened by his belief in a personal Providence, armed with his skills of persuasion and his knowledge of Presbyterianism; his capacity for survival enlarged by his experience as an outsider with the ability to disguise his motives and live dangerously as a secret agent, was to become a major force in achieving that goal.

[33] Ibid., 194.

After his trial and its consequences when he had become more secretive, the years which followed showed him following a devious course as a secret agent of the government, though he claimed later he had been allowed to write according to his own judgement as a freelance, while not opposing the Queen or her ministers in person, using this as an opportunity to maintain a Whig-like viewpoint while writing at times in the Tory interest.[34] He became a leading, if not the leading, figure in Harley's intelligence network in England. He wrote to Harley twice in July 1704 urging on him a system of private intelligence, '. . . a Correspondence may be Efficiently Settled with Every Part of England, and all the World beside, and yet the Very Clarkes Employ'd Not kno' what They are a doeing.' He referred to Sir Francis Walsingham, secretary of state to Elizabeth I, as the 'Greatest Master of Intelligence of the Age' and advised Harley to 'keep a Sett of Faithfull Emissarys Selected by your Own Judgement. Let them be your Constant Intelligencers of Private affairs in the Court. . . . Intelligence is the Soul of all Public business.'[35]

This secretiveness and the clear apprehension of the theory and experience of the practice of intelligence work on behalf of the Queen's devious, subtle and able minister Harley must have brought Harley and then his successor Godolphin to see how important an agent Defoe could be in Scotland. Defoe had himself pointed out to Harley in his letter of July 1704:

A Settl'd Intelligence in Scotland, a Thing Strangely Neglected there, is without doubt the Principall Occasion of the present Misunderstanding between the Two kingdoms. In the last Reign it Caus'd the king to have Many ill things Put upon him, and worse are very likely to follow. I beg Leave to give a Longer Scheme of thoughts on that head, than is Proper here, and a Method how the Scotts may be brought to Reason.[36]

Harley could see him as uniquely matched for a unique service. Defoe had feared for the security of Protestantism in England (and in Scotland), and he had welcomed Monmouth and William to ensure it; he saw that the union of the nations, by securing the establishment of the Church of Scotland in its Presbyterian form, would be a bulwark for a Protestant succession in England. He saw that through

---

[34] This occasioned the view held of Defoe at the time, and since, that he was unscrupulous and time-serving. His most notorious activity was his writing for Nathaniel Mist's *Weekly Journal*, devoted to the Pretender. He undertook with some relish the dangerous work of 'disabling and enervating it' and other Tory journals, so that 'they could do no mischief to the government'. The role of double-agent appealed to his temperament but it seems to be inconsistent with his assertions of his own honesty.

[35] *Letters*, 28, 30, 32.

[36] Ibid., 38.

this union and its religious settlement the Pretender and Jacobitism would receive the severest political defeat, and all that would be left to them would be the double gamble of rebellion and the uncertain prospects of French military aid. He had welcomed Marlborough's bold conduct of the war since he hoped its successful conclusion would gravely weaken the military power of the French and their willingness to support Jacobite ventures. He was a Presbyterian, which would commend him to the Scots whose Church Assembly was a major political force: an Anglican agent from England to Scotland would have been defeated before he began. Yet he was not committed to the traditional dogmatic systems which still held their ground in Scotland; he could speak to various parties with a tolerant mind on theological issues, and even to Scottish Episcopalians, though it would have been difficult to find Episcopalians who were not, by force of political circumstances, Jacobite in sympathy. 'Prelatism' he had no use for and Protestant extreme sectarianism bored him. Other opinions he held, he kept to himself for fear of being thought lacking in zeal. A minister of the Church of Scotland could hardly accept unchallenged Defoe's view, in his *Advice to all Parties*, of 1705:

> The Church of England and the Dissenters have but one interest, one foundation and but one end. The moderate Churchmen and the charitable Dissenters are the same denomination of Christians, and all the difference which now, looked at near the eye, shows large, if viewed at the distance of Heaven, shows not itself.[37]

This minister, and much more so a fierce Cameronian, or indeed a plain Scottish Protestant, would have considered Defoe's view of popery in the same pamphlet to be an intolerable example of English frivolity:

> I believe there are a hundred thousand plain country fellows in England, who could spend their blood against Popery, that do not know whether it be a man or a horse.[38]

The theologically minded Scots knew better on that subject, but if challenged on this he could reply it was indignant irony. Further, Defoe was obviously a master of propaganda; his irony and sarcasm were well-tried and well-sharpened weapons which he could use with pungent force during the preparation of the union, and in defence of it after it was made. His ambiguous temperament allowed him to be open and direct in a coffee-house or merchant's home,

---

[37] *Advice to All Parties, By the Author of the True-Born Englishman*, 1705, 21.
[38] Ibid., 23.

showing himself as a no-nonsense businessman who knew about trade-figures and could be as ready as an accountant with estimates of tax-ratios between the two uniting countries, impressive in Edinburgh and the trading towns he would visit in Scotland.[39] On the other hand that ambiguity could show him as the solitary observer, by his isolation capable of seeing what another would not have noticed since he would allow himself no partisan emotions in this service, and would be able coolly to calculate where the centre of an issue lay amid the confusions created by conflicting Scottish passions. He possessed something of the temperament and talents which the English sometimes admire in, or concede to, the Scots; for example, hard-headed shrewdness, and, as one writer said of him, 'he could have founded a colony'; successful colonizing in the former English territories was going to be a Scottish export enterprise after the union.[40]

That Harley saw all these elements in Defoe as a potentially successful agent in Scotland where such a man could be so useful is a matter of reasonable conjecture: he knew Defoe well, he had used him already as an agent, he knew Defoe's powers, and to Defoe's uneasy surprise, in September 1706, he ordered Defoe to go to Scotland. That Defoe did well to be uneasy and write to Harley saying that he would go like Abraham not knowing whither he went, could be seen from his writing in the letter of July 1704, that Richelieu's success in part was due to the fact that he, 'Sacrifyz'd Many a faithfull Agent after he had Done his Duty, that he might be sure he should Not be betraid'.[41] The modern vogue for spy-stories has made us familiar with such a state of mind. Defoe could foresee what exposure on the counterscarp might involve. The dangers of the Edinburgh mob would be familiar to him. In his reply to Harley's order he asked, 'Under these Anxious Thoughts', for the terms of the treaty and the characters of those who had taken part at the meetings in London, and then he set down what he conceived to be duties: to inform himself of those parties and persons who were opposing the proposed union, and find ways to undermine their activities; in conversation to persuade people of influence on the virtues of the union; to write rejoinders to pamphlets attacking the union, the English and the Court; to remove apprehensions about the future status of the Church of Scotland.[42] Harley knew that the strongest

[39] *Letters*, 155 ff.
[40] *The Gentleman's Magazine*, vol LV, 882. 'Swift is superficial when compared with the details in Robinson Crusoe; Defoe might have founded a colony' – Walter Scott, *Miscellaneous Prose Works*, Edinburgh, 1847, I. 401.
[41] *Letters*, 39.
[42] Ibid., 126.

opposition would come from Scotland, and had decided that the proposed treaty should be put to the Scottish Parliament first.

The commissioners from both kingdoms had begun to meet in London to prepare the treaty in April, 1706, and Defoe was in print by May, 1706, with two pamphlets aimed at removing prejudices against it; he continued the series (with four more under the same title) into the following January after he had arrived in Scotland.[43] But it was in his *Review* that he hammered at the theme of the necessity of union, exposing the absurdities of the arguments against it, and pushing everything that could be said for it. From 26 September, 1706, onwards, the main line of his *Review* papers was mockery and cool indignation at the views of opponents of the union. His readers who may not have realised at first that he was in Scotland grumbled that he overworked the subject.[44] In the issue of 26 September, he wrote of enemies of the union in England who were trying to persuade the dissenters to reject it and then would put the blame on them if the union failed. Also he noted that English groups were intending to dissuade the Scots from accepting the treaty and then blame the Scots for the breakdown, while others were arguing that the English Church and English trade would be ruined by a union. He already was juxtaposing the contradictory positions of his opponents, namely, that it would destroy the dissenters and at the same time be hazardous to the established church; that it would be fatal to unite and yet an army should be sent to Scotland to enforce it.[45] In the same year he wrote a fanfare for his efforts to persuade the Scots to union in his full length poem *Caledonia* in honour of Scotland and the Scots nation.[46]

Scotland was not unknown territory to him: it will be remembered that Crusoe after visiting the north of his island was greatly attracted by it and Defoe as is well known said *Robinson Crusoe* was an allegory of his own life; from 1684 onward Defoe visited Scotland more than once, and had at one stage thought of removing his wife and family there either to avoid pressures from his creditors, or because he intended to set up in business and live there.[47] On 8 October he asserted that those who wanted a war with Scotland would, if it were

---

[43] *An Essay at Removing National Prejudices against a Union with Scotland*, Part 1, 1706, Parts II–IV, 1706, Part V, 1707.

[44] 'The fellow could talk of nothing but the Union and had grown mighty dull of late' – cited by T. Wright, *The Life of Daniel Defoe*, 1894, 140.

[45] *Review*, 6 October 1706, vol. III, 477, 478.

[46] *Caledonia*, 1706, a folio of 60 pages dedicated to the Duke of Queensbery.

[47] *Letters*, 188. C. E. Burch, 'Benjamin Defoe at Edinburgh University, 1710–11', *The Philological Quarterly*, vol. XIX, October 1940, 347, 348.

ever to happen, be the foremost among those to stay at home, and he presented them with what he called paradoxes, statements based on his knowledge of former wars between the two countries and the futility of hoping to achieve anything by war in 1706.[48] He pointed to the real possibility of war if efforts for union failed and, 'it will be bloody enough . . . every Victory you gain over them in the Field, you are beaten; the Scots are Conquerors by it and you Losers. . . . At the End of every War, they shall have the better of you, it shall cost you more to hold them, than to gain them, and more to lose them, than both.'[49] He appears to suggest that those in favour of a war are a section of the High Flying Tories who hold no hatred to the Scots as a nation but as a Presbyterian nation they detest them. He concluded with further telling paradoxes which by their irony and cogency must have been galling:

> How is it possible, they can propose a conquest of Scotland as the shortest Way to Peace and Union?
> Secondly, How a Union with England can endanger the Church of England; and the Kirk of Scotland both at the same time?
> Thirdly, How a Union of Scotland will endanger the Succession of the House of Hannover, and the House of Perkin, etc., both together? [presumably a mocking reference to the Pretender by inferring a status no higher for him than that of Perkin Warbeck].[50]

In the next issue on 10 October he stated that the advantages of union, 'are infinite unaccountable, and as Times go, incredible on both sides', and showed who would be the losers by it, essentially the French who would no longer be able by bribes and guile to weaken both kingdoms and turn, 'the Swords of two valiant People into the Bowels of one another'.[51] On 12 October he mocked at a pamphlet by what he called an 'English Jacobite', since only so stupid a person could entertain such a notion; who was apparently worried by the Act of Security in Scotland being a contrivance for recalling the Stuarts when the Act intended the very opposite and as to, 'Religion and Liberty, no Man can suppose so meanly of the Scots, as to imagine they could seek the safety of those two in a Frenchified Papist'.[52] Again and again he repeated in the *Review* in his period in Scotland that Scotland would increase in wealth, England in strength, both in tranquillity. He referred as frequently to the attitude of both

[48] *Review*, 8 October 1706, vol. III, 478.
[49] Ibid., 478.
[50] Ibid., 479.
[51] Ibid., 481.
[52] Ibid., 486.

the churches, each suspicious of the consequences of union, and demonstrated that it meant the establishing of the constitution and church-government of both churches; that English churchmen were foolish to fear a presbyterianising movement from Scotland since they outnumbered Presbyterians and dissenters by eight to one; that as things were the Church of Scotland was far from safe, and that nothing but miracle or union could make it so; and he urged that dissenters of both nations would be more secure. On this point if he meant they need not fear the return of popery he was right, but in the event, in Scotland, one consequence of the union was Presbyterian anger at the proposed English folly of toleration since for them Episcopalians were a dangerous sect for whom toleration meant increase, insolence and challenge.[53] He noted such oddities of emotion as the assertion in Scotland that the English dissenters were inclined to episcopacy and therefore not to be trusted by the Kirk; or the Scots nobleman who told dismal stories of Scots merchants with no trade, the poor with no salt, and the ladies no husbands; and also he bantered those who claimed he had been sent to Scotland in the pay of the English Prebyterians to bring about the union.[54] He cited a vigorous critic of his presence in Scotland and his writings there: he was accused of 'Lyes, Forgeries and Counterfeit', the intention being to ruin the church of God. He mocked at these criticisms, for he had to suppress the questioning and obey Harley's instruction.[55]

On 24 October, 1706, he wrote to Harley of the meeting of the Commission of Assembly and of his concern about some members claiming *jure divino* principles, but the more moderate majority had overruled them:

> I work incessantly with [the Commission]. They go from me seemingly satisfyed ... but are the Same Men when they Come Among Their parties ... in Generall They are the Wisest weak men, the Falsest honest men, and the steadyest Unsettled people Ever I met with. ...[56]

Defoe's paradox is typical both of his style and of his anxieties over the Presbyterian ministers; these men were important, their decisions in the church courts were more significant politically than activities in the Scots Parliament. Defoe added a vivid brief account of rioting in the streets, 'a Scots Rabble is the worst of its kind'. He told of how the mob sought him as 'One of the English dogs', and of his fear of being 'De Witted'; this reads like a passage from Scott's

---

[53] *Letters*, 302, 303; *Review*, vol. III, 539.
[54] *Review*, 18 March 1707, vol. IV, 61; *Letters*, 196.
[55] *Review*, 2 September 1707, vol. IV, 347.
[56] *Letters*, 133.

description of the Porteous riots, but with crisper force.[57] In his next letter he wrote of a country minister preaching before the Commission on the text, 'Let no man take thy Crown', pretending an allegory but reminding the impatient Defoe, who endured its length, of the mob's fury at the threatened loss of the Scots Crown.[58] Defoe used his skills as a casuist in trying to ease the conscience of those who consulted him on the problem of uniting with so sinful a nation as England. Addresses were coming in from all parts written in what he called the 'Cant of the Old Times' about a further reformation, and of the Lord's covenanted people.[59] He also noted the presence of a number of highlanders in Edinburgh: 'Formidable Fellows', fully armed, who, 'are all Gentlemen, will take affront from No Man, and Insolent to the Last Degree.'[60] He was worried that if a rising took place the army was not to be relied upon save for many of its officers; and there was real danger from the west where if the weather had not been excessively wet 15,000 Cameronians might apparently have marched on Edinburgh.[61] Harley seems to have been stirred enough to send some English regiments up to the Border to encourage the troops in Edinburgh who felt their weakness in numbers, since Defoe, anxiously excusing his presumption of offering advice, feared that 'if there is the least Violence here all will be in blood'.[62]

Defoe was not only working to alleviate ecclesiastical and party problems but also energetically advising the committee of Scots lords which dealt with the complex issues of how Scottish taxation and excise duties could be related to the English fiscal pattern, and of the 'equivalents' to be paid to Scotland, and 'drawbacks' paid to England.[63] He talked to merchants of conditions of trade, allaying their fears on the price of oatmeal, salt, and corn, which on one matter at least were justified; this was to cause trouble later, as he had foreseen and sought to forestall.[64] This he did in Edinburgh and

[57] Ibid., 135. Jan de Witt, Grand Pensionary, was killed by a Dutch mob, 1672. The hanging of Captain Porteous by an Edinburgh mob was described in Scott's *The Heart of Midlothian.*

[58] Ibid., 137.

[59] Ibid., 142. Defoe added in the *Review,* 26 November 1706, that these addresses were invented by Episcopalian Jacobites to confuse the people. This was denied by the Jacobite, George Lockhart, in *Memoirs concerning the Affairs of Scotland,* 1714, 229.

[60] *Letters,* 146.

[61] Ibid., The Rev. John Hepburn, the Cameronian leader, was opposing the union policy but privately betraying Cameronian proposals to the government: possibly he wanted to save his people from bloodshed. The Cameronians were extreme covenanters.

[62] Ibid., 150 and n. 7.

[63] Ibid., 143 and n. 2.

[64] Ibid., 165, 166. In 1725 riots broke out on the Malt Tax at Glasgow and Edinburgh; see P. H. Brown, *History of Scotland,* 1911, vol. III, 207–9.

through his agents elsewhere. He wrote complacently to Harley that he was all things to all men; to merchants he talked trade; to lawyers he said he would purchase land, though, 'God knows where the Money is to pay for it', a hint ignored by Harley; to men from Aberdeen, Glasgow, Perth and the rest he talked of identifying with their concerns as though he were a fish merchant, or a woollen or linen trader. 'I think I do my Country good service, and this Country no Injury', was, in the event, a reasonable comment.[65] But he described himself to Harley with blunt bravado as a spy with sums of money at his disposal. This must have been an attempt to quieten the embarrassment shown in the self-justifying passages in the *Serious Reflections of Robinson Crusoe*; he was the outsider free from other men's passions triumphing a little in his aloofness and yet uneasily aware that he was manipulating, for example, some of the ministers whom he regarded as honest men. Scots wrote of him with furious contempt, suspecting him at the time; and two hundred years later Scots, after the publication of his letters to Harley, have expressed as great a loathing – though perhaps they should take more note of how some Scots could be bought then.[66]

> In my Management here I am a perfect Emissary. I act the Old part of Cardinal Richlieu. I have my spyes and my Pensioners In Every place, and I Confess tis the Easyest thing in the World to hire people here to betray their friends. I have spies in the Commission, in the parliament, and in the assembly and Under pretence of writeing my history I have Every thing told me.[67]

The Duke of Hamilton, one of the powerful opponents of the union, who was cheered by the mob when he appeared in the streets of Edinburgh, and who was a constant cause of anxiety to Defoe and his Scots associates, was present at a private meeting where a bitter protest was made, with some point, saying that the Scots Parliament was imposed upon by English bribes, that Scotland was betrayed, bought and sold. Defoe learned of this and wrote to Harley that he had been promised a view of the document.

> In This Little scheme of their Affaires I have Acted a True Spy to you, for by an Unexpected success I have Obtained a Converse with Some Gentlemen belonging to the D of Gordon [a leading Jacobite] who are

[65] Ibid., 159, 163.
[66] Lockhart, op. cit., and *Memoirs of the Life of Sir John Clerk of Penicuick (1676–1755)*, Scot. Hist. Soc., 1892, 64. Also J. D. Cockburn, 'Daniel Defoe in Scotland', *Scottish Review*, 1900, 'a cool rascal . . . a liar . . . greedy . . . moral myopia . . . sordid qualities', 268, 269.
[67] *Letters*, 211.

Very Frank, and I Dare say the particulars Above are unknown to the Commissioner himself.[68]

His spying was, among other matters, seriously concerned to forestall risings by Jacobites or by Cameronians or by urban armed mobs, which could have escalated into serious bloodshed.

Defoe was accused at the time and since of making money out of his activities; therefore what he did with the money Harley had originally entrusted to him for use in Scotland requires a comment. Defoe was an enthusiastic if not always successful business man, though he blamed his losses on the malice of others or on his political misfortunes; but that he misappropriated money to his own use is at least unproven, to use the Scots law term, if not simply erroneous.

> I am lookt on as an English man that Designs to settle here and I think am perfectly Unsuspected and hope on that foot I do some service – Onely I spend you a great Deal of Money at which I am Concern'd but see no Remedy if I will go thro' with the work . . . tis the most Expensive place I was Ever in. But Indeed Sir that has not been my Expence. . . . I have had £75 and a Horse of Mr Bell [of Newcastle upon Tyne, Harley's man for keeping himself in touch with the north of England and Scotland] and I have just 13 guineas left, about 6 of which I propose to lay Out for the Effectual spreading this letter at Glasgow [*A Letter to the Glasgow Men*] and over all the West, and therefore propose to print about 2500 of them . . . the press Dreins me . . . I cannot relieve My Own Affairs Tho' My Wife wrott me last week she had been 10 dayes without Money. . . .[69]

There is no explicit reference in Defoe's letters to the passing on of money from Harley through Defoe and his agents to Scots in positions of influence, unless his words referring to the Assembly represent bribery: 'I have some Engines at work among the Ministers. In short, Money will do anything here'.[70] Much of the money went, as the passages quoted above show, in paying his agents, in printing his replies to attacks on the proposed union and less in providing for his daily living and that of his family. He had been made bankrupt in the summer of 1705 and his pleas for help from Harley mount anxiously: 'If you were to See Me Now . . . without Subsistence, almost grown shabby in Cloths . . . you would be Mov'd to hasten My Relief.'[71] In the event Defoe obtained neither an adequate government post, nor an adequate livelihood from his work on behalf

---

[68] Ibid., 189.
[69] Ibid., 143, 159, 169, 170 ('The grenadier on the counterscarp' again appears, 242).
[70] Ibid., 214.
[71] Ibid., 242.

of Harley and Godolphin during his periods of residence in Scotland. Except for the occasionally bantering tone about Scots affairs to suit Harley's taste there is nothing to indicate that he was other than strongly committed to the union, for religious and politically Protestant reasons. He genuinely admired the Scots, he told Harley: 'This people are a Sober, Religious and Gallant Nation, the country good, the Soil in most places capable of vast improvements and nothing wanting but English Stocks, English Art [agricultural and other skills] and English Trade to make us all one great people'. His powerful influence in the making of the union can be seen in Godolphin's letter to Harley: 'Defoe's letter is serious and deserves reflection. I believe it is true and it ought to guide us very much in what we are doing here. . . .'[72]

After the union was accomplished he stayed in Scotland again at least twice, the first time on government service. In 1708 he went at three days notice: 'My errand was such as was far from being unfit for a sovereign to direct or an honest man to perform.' His visit was caused by the threat of a Jacobite rising, the French having attempted to put ashore the Pretender with 5,000 men in the hope of rousing Jacobite support and wrecking the union.[73] Defoe was disturbed to find that there were a number of Scots now saying leave matters to the English and the French and 'let them fight it out'. What his activities were is apparently not now known. In 1709 his full and careful account of *The History of the Union* was published in which he used the records which he ironically described as being trustingly given to him by the Scots at the time of the union – but the book shows no hint of irony or disparagement, on the contrary it is fair to the Scots and still valuable for its historical content. From September, 1710, to February, 1711, he was again in Scotland but it is not clear that this time he was on government service. He had seriously thought of bringing his family to Scotland and setting up in business: his talking of trade to the Scots whom he had hoped to influence earlier was not merely a feigned political game. He entered his son Benjamin at the University of Edinburgh and Defoe strongly promoted the view that English and Irish dissenters should study there since they were excluded from other universities by tests and oaths imposed on them. He wrote a memorial to Principal Carstares on this subject, the man who had been especially helpful to him in the Assembly in winning support for the union: 'Mr Carstares in particular Merits

---

[72] Ibid., 187, for Defoe on Scotland. Godolphin's letter is in Hist. Mss. Commission Report, Appendix vol. IV, 382.
[73] Ibid., 257, n. 1.

Great Consideration' he had told Harley at the time.[74] Defoe had joined the Edinburgh Society for the Reformation of Manners in March, 1707, from which he withdrew with indignation in February, 1709, because the Society had failed to reprove one of its members, a barrister accused of adultery before the Edinburgh Presbytery: 'While you punish the poor, and the rich go free . . . you must expect to find no reformation in Scotland, any more than they have in England' – he had accused the English Society of the same weakness.[75] With journalistic enterprise he gained control of *The Edinburgh Courant* and *The Scots Postman*; further, he worked with the publisher John Moncur.[76] Defoe even began to use Scots words in his pamphlets of this period.

His concern for Scotland's economic strength and the sound establishment of the Church of Scotland can be seen in his memorandum of improvements for Scotland which contained a long description of the need for a naval base and dockyards in the Forth, anticipating by two hundred years the building of Rosyth, which would bring money, employment and increase of trade and provide against French naval attacks[77] Again with real and urgent seriousness he insisted to Harley in 1710 that the Church of Scotland should be maintained in 'its just Rights and Established privilege', and that 'Intrusions', 'the placing of ministers in parishes without the consent of the people,' should be discouraged and discontinued: Defoe foresaw what was coming. In 1712 the Toleration Act was passed allowing toleration to Scots Episcopalian dissenters which also restored the rights of patrons in appointing ministers to parishes. Defoe was justified in his anxiety: patronage was to be a continuing source of trouble and was a major cause of the Disruption of 1843.[78] In his *Memoirs of the Church of Scotland* of 1717, he wrote that since no full account of the glories and sufferings of the Church of Scotland had yet been given he, 'an officious stranger', set seriously about the work 'of ransoming things of such Consequence from the grave of forgetfulness' out of 'disinterested Zeal to do Justice and Service to the People of Scotland and to a Cause which he had too much at Heart to let lie neglected any longer. . . .'. He opposed the idea that

---

[74] Ibid., 193 and n. 3. Also see C. E. Burch, op. cit. 347, 348.

[75] *Review*, 7 April 1709, vol. VI, no. 4. See also C. E. Burch, 'Defoe and the Edinburgh Society for the Reformation of Manners', *Review of English Studies*, vol. XVI, 1940, 306 ff.

[76] In 1710. For Moncur see G. Chalmers, Collection on Scottish Printing, Laing Mss., 11, 452, Edinburgh University Library.

[77] *The Proposall*, in *Letters*, 280–4.

[78] Defoe described Scottish indignation at the proposed Act in the *Review*, 26 January, 2 and 5 February 1711–12. He wrote to Harley urgently opposing it 24 January, 1711–12, *Letters*, 367.

the superintendents of the sixteenth century had anything to do with episcopacy since they were subject to the Assembly of the Church, and he burst into capitals in stating that that Church was 'PRESBYTERIAN' in its origin. It is a highly partisan account; for example, the murder of Archbishop Sharp is glossed over, which is strange in view of Defoe's dislike of fanaticism. With dialogue and anecdotes which give colour and energy to his story he praises those who suffered persecution after 1689 including indiscriminately those whom Scott gently mocked in *Old Mortality*. His real goal was no doubt both to oppose Episcopalianism tarnished by its Jacobitism, and to protest against the 'Depradation' upon the Church through the restoratian of lay patronage: he cites in full a memorandum sent to him earlier by three ministers of whom his friend Carstares was one, seeking his aid to try and prevent the passing of the Act.[79]

His dedication of his *The History of the Union* to Queen Anne contains the following words which sum up his rejoicing at the union.

> The humble Author of these sheets, Madam, having amidst a throng of disasters and sorrows, been honoured by your Majesty, in being rendered servicable to this great transaction, and having pass'd throu' all the hazards tumults, and disorders of that critical time thinks himself doubly rewarded in having the honour to lay this account of these things at your Majesty's feet . . . It ought to be the comfort as it is the honour of the Church of Scotland, that her safety and your Majesty's authority, have the same establishment, are linked together by the indissolvable bonds of the same Union, have the same enemies, and the same friends, and in all probability must have the same duration.[80]

He had been pilloried for supporting the principles of Dissent through which he believed that the liberty of the people could be secured, for opposing the Anglican high church *jure divino* position and Jacobitism, and for seeking to ensure the Protestant succession. His humiliation was not entirely overcome by his having to become a government agent – though he spoke of this proudly as the service of the Queen – but the aspirations for which he had suffered were achieved as the words of his dedication to Anne show. His later years produced the period of creative power in the novels, and those other varied contributions to moral and historical literature, which express his

---

[79] *Memoirs of the Church of Scotland*, 8, 90. The *Memorandum*, which is a very able analysis of the historical background to and disadvantages of patronage was written by William Carstares, Thomas Blackwell and Robert Baillie. Defoe wrote to Harley 14 February 1711–12, 'I sincerely Lament the Case of Scotland' when the Act was before the Lords, *Letters*, 370.

[80] *History*, 1786, Dedication, XXVIII, XXVI.

paradoxical view of human nature combined with an intense realism rarely achieved by other writers. In the course of a life of labour amid difficult and dangerous circumstances Defoe wrote over five hundred titles in well-informed verse and prose in most literary forms on widely different matters, always presented in cogent and incisive style (indeed several potent styles) with latent within them, even under the sarcasm or the statistics, a moral purpose which could on occasion break out into the positive declaration of religious convictions. He saw his work in all its variety as a duty to be fulfilled and truth to be asserted even if it meant that he spoke as a solitary:

> He that opposes his own Judgment against the Current of the Times ought to be backed with unanswerable Truth; and he that has Truth on his side is a Fool as well as a Coward if he is afraid to own it, because of the Multitude of other men's Opinions. 'Tis hard for a man to say, all the World is mistaken but himself. But if it be so, who can help it?[81]

He died where he began in the parish of St. Giles, Cripplegate, described in the parish register as 'gentleman', an aspiration won. He was obscurely in hiding from the threat of a debtor's prison, from the threat of personal violence (he had already been assaulted by Mist), away from his family, a solitary, an outsider and enigmatic to the last, having achieved a life of remarkable variety, danger, obloquy, downfall and triumph. In his last known letter he added his last words to us:

> I am so near my Journey's end, and am hastening to the Place where the weary are at rest, and where the wicked cease to trouble; be it that the passage is rough, and the day stormy, by what way soever He pleases to bring me to the End of it, I desire to finish this Life with this Temper of Soul in all cases – *Te Deum Laudamus.*

Here is seen at the end his still continuing trust in the Providence which had given him like Socrates a Daemon to drive him onward.

---

[81] Cited in H. A. Taine, *History of English Literature* (Engl. trans.), The Colonial Press, New York, 1900, vol. 2, 403.

10

'An Inverted Hypocrite': Swift the Churchman

After *Gulliver's Travels* was published, Jonathan Swift wrote to Pope that: 'A Bishop here said, that Book was full of improbable lies, and for his part, he hardly believed a word of it'.[1] Remarks like this gave Swift, combined with his other talents, the character of a wit – most dangerous for a clergyman in search of a career, as he himself noted in his *Essay on the Fates of Clergymen*. '. . . the *Clergy*; to whose Preferment nothing is so fatal as the Character of Wit, Politeness in Reading, or Manners, or that Kind of Behaviour, which we contract by having too much conversed with Persons of high Station and Eminency; these Qualifications being reckoned by the *Vulgar* of *all Ranks* to be Marks of *Levity*, which is the last crime the world will pardon in a *Clergy-Man*.'[2] There are several matters on which Swift has been misunderstood but especially in his views on religion, for he has repeatedly from his own time to the present been condemned for being a 'divine who is hardly suspected of being a Christian'. It is

---

[1] *The Correspondence of Jonathan Swift*, ed. Harold Williams, 5 volumes, Oxford, 1963–1965, III, 189.

[2] *The Collected works of Jonathan Swift*, ed. Herbert Davis, 15 volumes, Oxford, 1939–64, XII, 40.

forgotten that he wrote to Archbishop King of Dublin (who, three years after *A Tale of a Tub* had appeared, attempted to reconcile the existence of moral evil with the omnipotence and goodness of God in a book soon to become famous):

> I very much applaud your Grace's sanguine Temper, as you call it, and your Comparison of Religion to paternal Affection; but the World is divided into two Sects, those that hope the best, and those that fear the worst; your Grace is of the former, which is the wiser, the nobler, and the most pious Principle; and although I endeavour to avoid being of the other, yet upon this Article I have sometimes strange Weaknesses. I compare true Religion to Learning and Civility which have ever been in the World, but very often shifted their Scenes; sometimes leaving whole Countries where they have long flourished, and removing to others that were before barbarous; which hath been the Case of Christianity itself, particularly in many parts of *Africa*, and how far the wickedness of a Nation may provoke God Almighty to inflict so great a Judgement, is terrible to think.[3]

Here is to be seen Swift's grim awareness of the basic sinfulness of humanity, a sinfulness which was a potential threat of barbarism, only held in check by the State maintaining religion seen in morality and obedience supported by learning. Swift also shows here his fear that if that religious grip were to slacken through men's pride and folly then God's Providence would judge the nation at fault by allowing it to revert to that barbarism which is man's natural condition unaided by Revelation. Failure to recognise these aspects of Swift's religious viewpoint can gravely distort our understanding of Swift's purposes as a satirist.

Nevertheless, the themes which Swift chooses in this analysis of his own religious views are not usually central in judgements of him as a man or as a writer. On the contrary, it is more usual to think that Swift was fundamentally irreligious; that he was using a career in the Church for personal ambition, since he lacked a political post; that he showed no respect for traditional Christian beliefs; that his religious writings are political tracts with pious titles; and that his handful of sermons are the chilled product of a rationalism without insight or conviction. In 1713 Robert Molesworth wrote to his wife: 'They have made Swift Dean of St. Patrick's. This vexes the godly party beyond expression'.[4] But not even the ungodly were delighted: Dean Smedley who shared with Swift little save his ecclesiastical title and ended as a refugee debtor in the Indies, claimed to have fixed this

---

[3] *Correspondence*, I, 117.
[4] *Correspondence*, I, 350, n.

poem to the door of St. Patrick's Cathedral on the day when Swift
was instituted as Dean:

> Today the Temple gets a Dean
> Of parts and fame uncommon
> Used both to pray and to prophane
> To serve both God and Mammon.
>
> This place he got by wit and rhyme
> And many ways more odd
> And might a bishop be in time
> Did he believe in God.
>
> Look down St. Patrick look we pray
> On thy own church and steeple
> Convert the Dean on this great day
> Or else God help the people.
>
> And now when'er his deanship dies
> Upon his tomb be graven
> A man of God here buried lies
> Who never thought of heaven.[5]

Swift well knew that so many men including his fellow clerics then as
now can forgive a clergyman almost anything save intelligence and
wit, and he vainly tried to correct the bad impression left by his *Tale of
a Tub* in an Apology prefaced to later editions. He was probably right
in believing that Sharp, Archbishop of York, had told Queen Anne,
no doubt with the approval of her companion the Duchess of Somerset,
that the author of *A Tale of a Tub* was unsuitable for preferment in
the Church.[6] Swift had the last word, caustic and contemptuous:

> By an old red-pate, murdering hag pursued,
> A crazy prelate, and a royal prude.
> By dull divines, who look with envious eyes,
> On every genius that attempts to rise. . . .[7]

thus demonstrating to those who might have promoted him to a
bishopric, the pungent articulate force which frightened them from
the solemn choice of doing so.

Leslie Stephen, though addressing a more discriminating audience

[5] *A Supplement to Dr. Swift's Works*, ed. J. Nichols, 1779, III, 226.

[6] For Swift's view that Archbishop Sharp told Queen Anne that the author of *A Tale of a
Tub* was unfit for appointment as a bishop see *Poems*, ed. Harold Williams, 3 vols., Oxford,
1958, I. Swift had referred to the Duchess of Somerset, formerly Baroness Percy, daughter of
the last Earl of Northumberland in his poen *The Windsor Prophecy* (1711), as 'Carrots from
Northumberland'.

[7] *The Complete Poems of Jonathan Swift*, ed. Pat Rogers, 1983, 163.

than that at the lecture where Thackeray had said of Swift, 'He puts his apostasy out to hire . . . and his sermons have scarce a Christian characteristic',[8] could still be no less obtuse: 'He felt the want of some religion and therefore scalped poor Collins' and '. . . the dogmas of theologians were mere matter for the Homeric laughter of the Tale of a Tub'. Stephen, who resigned his holy orders and was more concerned with 'honest doubt' than with 'earnest religion', shows his obtuseness fully in his final judgement on Swift – 'He had not the unselfish qualities or the indomitable belief in the potential excellence of human nature to become a reformer of manners, or the speculative power to endeavour to remould ancient creeds.'[9] This reflects as great a failure in understanding Swift as that of Thackeray (at a different level of intelligence), for Swift deliberately avoided and rejected from the first Odes to the final Legion Club those two purposes which Stephen assumes to be acceptable to his own contemporaries, that is, belief in the potential excellence of human nature and the speculative attempt to revise the Christian faith.

Nor does Swift escape misrepresentation in our own time, for the only book so far written comprehensively on the subject of Swift's religious thought, Canon Looten's La Pensée religieuse de Swift et ses Antinomies,[10] asserts that he not only undermined Christian doctrinal traditions but also the possibility of a natural theology – he pretended to defend Christianity and then stabbed it in the back.[11] F. R. Leavis in his essay on Swift's irony has received a far wider audience than Looten and his judgements are elsewhere often deservedly magisterial, but he can write thus: 'Of Jack we are told "nor could all the world persuade him, as the common phrase is, to eat his victuals like a Christian"; it is characteristic of Swift that he should put in these terms, showing a complete incapacity even to guess what religious feeling might be, a genuine conviction that Jack should be made to kneel when receiving the Sacrament', and: 'He showed the shallowest complacencies of Augustan good sense'.[12] However, the historian well-read in the sacramental controversy between Catholics and Protestants in the sixteenth and seventeenth centuries will realise that Swift's phrases can be matched from controversialists before him; while it does not excuse his coarse phrase it does provide it with a recognisable context. Again, who more

[8] The English Humourists of the Eighteenth Century: Swift. W. M. Thackeray, Works: The Biographical Edition, 1898, VII, 441.
[9] History of English Thought in the Eighteenth Century, 3rd edn., 1927, II, 373–4.
[10] Lille, 1935.
[11] Looten, 9.
[12] The Common Pursuit, Peregrine Books edition, 1962, 85 and 87.

bitterly than Swift opposed 'the shallow complacencies' of Bolingbroke and Shaftesbury, those arbiters of 'Augustan good sense', precisely because he knew them to be shallow? F. R. Leavis writes further: 'An outward show is, explicitly, all he contends for in the quite unironical *Project for the Advancement of Religion*, and the difference between the reality of religion and the show is, for the author of the *Tale of a Tub*, hardly substantial'.[13] To state that Swift's concerns in that pamphlet are surface matters, 'an outward show' is imperceptive, as will be shown later in this essay. The criticism that Swift's religion was superficial, since it had no essential ground in his life, is in itself a failure to get beneath the surface.

For a great number of contemporary writers the close relation of the Church and society has ceased to be conceivable today. They generally assume, when considering the Christianity of past times, that its faith and practices should be interpreted by our current views of what constitutes personal piety and loving kindness to others, and these views alone are considered to be the standards of Christian sincerity. This is no place to describe what is latent here, the over-simplification and sentimentalism about the person and work of Christ expressed by many of the literate and articulate in our time, aligned with naivety about the nature of the Church, its organisation, beliefs and practices, and indeed about the Bible upon which these are grounded. One consequence of this is that unction of the 'secular' Tartuffe, which is the hypocrisy of the religiously superficial or uncommitted. Swift, with passionate conviction, concealed the practice of his personal piety since it was nobody's business but his own; and with equally passionate conviction he rejected emotionalism in faith and practice as contemptible, erroneous and irreligious. We may think he overdid this; but at least we should examine impartially, and with patience, his reasons for doing so, which were complex and profound as well as rational and coherent, for they were one with other attempts to resolve the problem of the relation of a Church of convinced believers to a society of reluctant believers which has faced the Churches since the time of the Emperor Theodosius. That Swift inherited, and loyally struggled for, a traditional Anglican solution here can be seen demonstrably in his life. If Swift was a pretender to religion, and merely a professional writer who adopted Christian formulas and *mores* for the sake of earning a more secure income than Grub Street or politics provided, then this could be shown by investigation of the evidence. His enemies in his life-time provided abuse and innuendo but no evidence; too many of his detractors

[13] Leavis, 85.

today substitute for investigation an intuition (relying on uninformed conceptions) of what is appropriate to 'religion' and on their cultivated aesthetic response to his sharper ironies.

Swift's religion as country parson and as Dean of a cathedral contains no inner contradictions in the framing of his religious ideas, nor any break between his inner convictions and his outward pastoral activity: he is consistent throughout. A man's religion is tested by his prayers; consider these words from a prayer for the dying Stella, which began with an appeal for her need, and contains these phrases: 'O All-powerful Being, the least Motion of whose Will can create or destroy a World . . . Accept, O Lord, these Prayers poured from the very Bottom of our Hearts. . . . Forgive the Sorrow and Weakness of those among us, who sink under the Grief and Terror of losing so dear and useful a Friend.'[14] To the unaccustomed ear this may sound wholly formal, but even the *Sacra Privata*, a famous collection of private prayers and religious diary, by Swift's contemporary, Bishop Wilson (like Swift ordained by the Bishop of Kildare after graduating from Trinity College, Dublin), provides no more moving language. The all-powerful will that could create or destroy a world, and the grief and terror at the heart of life are themes central to Swift's religion. For him, when one contemplates the evil state of men and the latent chaos in the world, only an all-ruling Providence can save men from the vertigo of terror. He could find no lasting comfort in Archbishop King's attempt to resolve the problem of evil.[15] Two statements by Swift in letters to friends, when facing the death of the innocent and the young, may be added. To the Reverend James Stopford he wrote after the death of Stella, 'For my part, as I value life very little, so the poor casual remains of it, after such a loss, would be a burden that I must heartily beg God Almighty to enable me to bear', and after referring to the 'folly' of having too close friendships because the pain of loss is so great, added: 'Dear Jim, pardon me, I know not what I am saying; but believe me that violent friendship is much more lasting, and as much more engaging, as violent love. Adieu'.[16] When Lord Oxford's daughter died Swift wrote: 'To say the truth, my Lord, you began to be too happy for a mortal; much more happy than is usual with the dispensations of Providence long to continue', and then after the statement, harsh in our eyes, that God punished Oxford 'where he knew your heart

---

[14] Davis, IX, 253–5.
[15] Archbishop William King (1650–1729). *De Origine Mali*, 1702, trans. E. Law, 1929; an impressive attempt to reconcile moral evil with a beneficent Creator.
[16] *Correspondence*, III, 145.

was most exposed' and rewarded with a better life 'that excellent
creature he has taken from you', added '. . . I know not, my Lord,
why I write this to you, nor hardly what I am writing. I am sure
it is not from any compliance with form; it is not from thinking
that I can give your Lordship any ease. I think it was an impulse
upon me that I should say something: And whether I shall send
you what I have written, I am yet in doubt'.[17] There are, possibly,
those for whom these quotations show little beyond the fact that
Swift like other men felt melancholy in the face of death: but if
they catch no force of feeling and sincerity behind the religious
expression in them then they will indeed find no meaning in Swift's
writings on religion, nor could they detect the religious background
in his other more familiar work. The advice to Oxford to bow to
Providence was a commonplace of the time as *The Works of the
Learned and Pious Author of the Whole Duty of Man* clearly shows,
but Swift's framing of it and his addition is wholly from his own
heart.

For this was the private heart of Swift, which he least of all men
was willing to wear on his sleeve; but others could observe his pastoral
activities. Swift wrote to Stella once about a sermon he was to give
in London: 'I shall preach plain honest stuff'[18] – any of the fashionable
world who came to listen to the greatest wit in England would be
deservedly disappointed, and his surviving sermons are models of
plain direct Christian teaching set within the theological pattern of
his Church. No exception can be taken to his work as a parish priest
at Kilroot and later at Laracor. He used his income for restoring the
dilapidated church at Laracor, built a parsonage, and introduced
week-day services and regular preaching every Sunday. Bolingbroke
called him 'an inverted hypocrite' in pretending to the onlooking
world that he had little religion, preferring to conceal his faith and
practice from the eyes of others. Dr. Johnson may be the judge here,
not least because he was no admirer of Swift, a fact that puzzled
Boswell, who was: 'The suspicion of his irreligion proceeded in a
great measure from his dread of hypocrisy; instead of wishing to
seem better, he delighted in seeming worse than he was. He went in
London to early prayers, lest he should be seen at Church; he read
prayers to his servants every morning with such dexterous secrecy
that Dr. Delaney was six months in the house before he knew it. He
was not only careful to hide the good which he did, but willingly
incurred the suspicion of evil which he did not. He forgot what

[17] *Correspondence*, I, 405–6.
[18] *Swift's Journal to Stella*, ed. Harold Williams, 1948, I, 126.

himself had formerly asserted, that hypocrisy is less mischievous than open impiety.'[19]

Some biographers describe him as parsimonious and avaricious, but contemporaries witness to his charities (though many of these were so effectively concealed that they were unknown to outsiders) – 'to ask him for a pound was often to receive five' was a generous comment in his lifetime. A recently discovered letter shows his characteristic brusqueness masking a generous purpose: 'Sir: there is a Rascally Cousin of mine called John Swift, his Father is my Cousen German, called Mead Swift, as great a Rascal as his Son. He was a son of my Uncle Godwin as arrant an old Rascal as either. I was desired to be a trustee of the Marriage Settlement, along with a Rogue of an Attorney one Kit Swift another son of old Godwin.'[20] It is a matter of verifiable fact, and not mere opinion, that in spite of the scornful severity of language Swift used here, his dealings with John Swift were more than benevolent, they were generous and fatherly. Swift always emphasised 'the works of love'; for example, in writing to Pope: 'Pray God reward you for your kind Prayers. You are a good Man & a good Christian, & I believe your Prayers will do me more good than those of all the Prelates in . . . Europe, except the Bishop of Marseilles'.[21] Here he is writing to a Catholic, and behind his usual irony about bishops he makes exception for M. de Belsunce who remained to confess and comfort the sick and dying in the great plague at Marseilles in 1720. This was a practical demonstration of true religion that Swift, who usually had little good to say for 'Papists' but who approved them when they showed self-denying pity for others, was always ready to recognise.

Of his energy shown in supporting the rights of the Irish clergy in the matter of tithes and first-fruits, and in his administrative efficiency as Dean there can be no doubt, for the useful and able book by L. A. Landa has demonstrated it.[22] He could fight tenaciously with city and Archbishop for the rights of his cathedral, and for his rights as Dean with his chapter. Swift was a loyal supporter of the religious principles of the Revolution, but perhaps he carried this a little far in erecting a monument for the grave of the Duke of Schomberg, a hero of the Battle of the Boyne, which included words that challenged the meanness of the Duke's relations in Germany in

[19] Samuel Johnson, *Lives of the English Poets*, Everyman, 1958 edn., II, 268–9.
[20] *The Times Literary Supplement*, No. 3, 347, 356, April 21, 1966.
[21] *Correspondence*, IV, 335.
[22] L. A. Landa, *Swift and the Church of Ireland*, Oxford, 1954.

failing to provide enough money for the memorial. Most utterances of George II are of little worth, but his comment on this is memorable: 'God damn Mr. Swift, does he mean to make me quarrel with the King of Prussia?'[23]

All his life as a clergyman Swift struggled tenaciously for improvement in the status of the clergy, which meant improvement in their economic security. The purpose of this, as it had been for Archbishop Laud before him, was to ensure the authority of the Church throughout the country since this was in his eyes essential to the moral stability of society. He feared confusion, that 'Gothic barbarism' would return, and was certain that politicians alone, even the monarchy and Parliament alone, could not prevent collapse – the Church was the God-given instrument of order in society. Take away that support and confusion and terror would reign. He was far removed from the easy assumptions that used to be made about Augustan optimism.

Some literary critics tend to ignore a writer's declared intentions and seek to determine the structure and aims of his work by other routes. Even those who would shun this method nevertheless share with it all too often when they assume that Swift's assertion of his religious convictions and moral intention is camouflage for his real purpose. Modern literary criticism has produced many brilliant analyses of the surface of the satires, but is curiously silent about the assumptions behind them, and here a traditional literary-historical method, the analysis of the history of ideas, is more fruitful for real understanding of Swift's work. It should be clear from the start that he does not represent Augustan complacencies about man and society, for his view of the human situation and his private world mirror the confusion of purpose in England prior to the Revolution of 1689. Voltaire once said of Swift: 'pour le bien entendre, il faut faire un petit voyage dans son pays' – but Swift's country was more than England or Ireland, it was a private landscape in which dark shadows were cast. Swift reflects in his writings, beneath the surface force and clarity, the anxieties and doubt of the seventeenth century mind, and not the forward-looking optimism of his contemporary Shaftesbury – his Gulliver was not travelling to the 'Heavenly City of the Eighteenth Century Philosophers'.

Through the long gestation of the hidden years under Sir William Temple at Moor Park Swift was struggling to clarify for himself the problems posed for his generation by theologians, politicians, scientists

[23] R. W. Jackson, *Jonathan Swift: Dean and Pastor*, III.

and philosophers including those who represented both the old and
the new ways of thought. Some he rejected outright, some he came
to terms with – it is a measure of the force of his intelligence that
they were his own terms. That he should have chosen (after the
rebellious years at Trinity College, Dublin, and the years of service,
humiliating to his proud mind, as an ambiguous amanuensis to
Temple) to express his inward struggle through Odes modelled on
those of Cowley, may be surprising. But Cowley's *Odes* represent
precisely the form current at the time to express general ideas,
though these mostly lacked the content which Swift struggled to
articulate – that he failed to be lucid for the only time in his career
as a writer is largely a measure of the intellectual crisis he endured.
These few Odes have been studied more than once in accounts of
Swift's origins as a writer, but some further comment may still be
allowed. They refer to fears which were to be recognisable in Swift's
work throughout his life: 'The Tyranny of Years'. 'A Destroying
Angel stands (By all but Heaven and me unseen)'; 'Ignorance's
Universal North . . . with blind Rage break all this peaceful
Government'; '*The Wits* . . . own th' Effects of Providence, And yet
deny the Cause'; '. . . ev'n the Extravagance of Poetry Is at a loss
for Figures to express Men's Folly'.[24] To understand why the
disciple of the polished Temple, who arranged the beauty of his
formal gardens to celebrate calm and reasoned hopefulness, should
look aghast at:

> Disjointing shapes as in the fairy land of dreams. . . .
> No wonder, then, we talk amiss
> Of truth, and what, or where it is:[25]

requires a closer look at Swift's environment. It should never be
forgotten that Swift was born and partly bred in Ireland, an Ireland
weakened by the destructive force of Cromwell's policy of 'To Hell
or Connaught', by the mutual distrust of the English and Scottish
planters, by political corruption and religious divisions between
Anglican and Presbyterian and the consequence neglect of churches
and piety. He had to flee with others from Dublin when the invasion
came in the north, before the Battle of the Boyne made Ireland safe
for Protestants again. Ireland for him became an image of a brutalised
peasantry, half-dead religion, corrupt administration, and English
misgovernment. Not only this but he had a mixed political and
religious inheritance, shown in his comparative neglect of his sister

---

[24] *Poems*, 6, 7, 25, 19, 21.
[25] *Poems*, 61.

who sympathised with his mother's Puritan and nonconformist ancestry, whereas he himself preferred to rejoice in that clerical grandfather Thomas Swift who was, he wrote once with bitter exaggeration, 'persecuted and plundered two and fifty Times by the Barbarity of Cromwell's Hellish Crew'.[26] He had barely come of age when the Revolution took place, which (though he was after a fashion of his own a Tory Highchurchman) he always supported as the satisfactory and abiding answer to the unresolved problems left by the Civil War and only masked by the Stuart Restoration. He never lost his horror of the blind destructive force of Cromwell's army, nor his disgust with the frenzied religious 'enthusiasm' he associated with the 'toleration' of the sects under the Commonwealth. It is fundamental for understanding Swift to realise that he saw the generation preceding his birth as containing a religion which meant fanaticism, and politics which meant tyranny; and he saw the irrationality and intolerance of that time as breeding 'atheism' and moral collapse in his own day.

Amid these confusions, and faced by 'atheism and immorality' – '. . . men degenerate every day, merely by the folly, the perverseness, the avarice, the tyranny, the pride, the treachery, or inhumanity of their own kind'.[27] Swift found little help in earlier patterns of religion in that century. In view of the critical approach to Scripture shown in the London Polyglot Bible edited by Bishop Walton (accused by the Independent minister, John Owen, of leading men to doubt the authority of the Hebrew and Greek originals by putting out so many versions and variant readings), and explicit in the writings of the French Oratorian, Richard Simon;[28] and in view of the stalemate induced by the prolonged and exhausting controversy between Catholics and Protestants, each trying unsuccessfully to outflank the other by proving the finality of one system over the other, Swift could not propose *simpliciter* the authority of Scripture, or the authority of a Church based on a system of dogmas. His solution to this problem will be discussed later; it is sufficient to record here his recognition of the failure of Catholics, Puritans and Anglicans (both Laudian and merely Erastian), to give a final solution:

> For, sure, we want some guide from Heav'n to show
> The way which ev'ry wand'ring fool below

[26] *Correspondence*, V, 150.

[27] Davis, IX, 264.

[28] John Owen, an Independent, Vice Chancellor of Oxford, 1652–58. Appended to his *On the Divine Original, Authority . . . of the Scriptures*, was 'Considerations on the Prolegomena . . . of the Biblia Polyglotta' 1659. Richard Simon, Oratorian, *Histoire Critique du texte du Nouveau Testament*, 1689. *Histoire Critique du Vieux Testament*, 1678.

> Pretends so perfectly to know;
> And which for ought I see, and much I fear,
> The world has wholly miss'd;
>
> I mean, the way which leads to Christ:
> Mistaken Ideots! see how giddily they run ...
> Each fond of erring with his guide ...
> Others, ignorantly wise,
> Among proud Doctors and disputing Pharisees:[29]

Nor did the young Swift see any peculiar hope lie in the post-Revolutionary parties and their shifting alliances. He knew in Temple a distinguished servant of the State, a diplomatist wise in Courts and politics, and in the *Ode to Sir William Temple*, he could write:

> The wily shafts of state, those juggler's tricks
> Which we call deep design and politicks ...
> Methinks, when you expose the scene,
> Down the ill-organ'd engines fall; ...
> How plain I see thro' the deceit.[30]

As will be shown later his solution will not be to cry the shibboleth of a current political faction.

Why did not a mind as penetrating as Swift's concentrate on philosophy at a time when philosophical studies outstripped in quality and contemporary appeal the outmoded systems of theologians? His suspicion of the validity of speculative reasoning has already been mentioned, for it was early in life that he had seen the possibility of self-delusion in most of men's speculations, above all the delusion of making one's own thinking the standard for determining truth. His later appeal to reason was not to establish it as a self-justifying end, but to use it to explode illusions like burst balloons, and to support that balancing of religion and virtue under Providence which alone gave stability to men's purposes. Moreover, he had been taught and loathed at Trinity College, Dublin, the traditional systems of logic, still founded on Aristotle – Smeglesius, Keckermannus, and Burgersdicius – which he mocked to Temple:[31]

[29] *Poems*, 65.

[30] *Poems*, 57.

[31] These logical text-books were first referred to by Emile Pons, *La Jeunesse de Swift*, Strasbourg, 1925, 128, but have now been convincingly put into the context of Swift's satire by R. S. Crane *The Houyhnhms the Yahoos, and the History of Ideas*, in *Reason and the Imagination*, ed. J. A. Mazzeo, 1962, 213–253, and in R. S. Crane, *The Idea of the Humanities*, 2 vols. Chicago, 1957, II, 261–282.

> 'Tis you must put us in the way:
> Let us (for shame) no more be fed
> With antique reliques of the dead,
> The gleanings of philosophy,
> Philosophy! the lumber of the schools. . . .
> And we bubbled fools
> Spend all our present stock in hopes of golden rules.[32]

Since he came of age in the flowering of scientific method which had gone beyond Baconian induction to the precision of measurement established by the mathematics of Cartesianism, it might be assumed that so pragmatic, logical and lucid an intelligence as that of Swift would have turned to these studies for stability and hope. But his mockery at the pretensions and the methods of scientists is well-known and occurs not only in Gulliver's account of Laputa. There were two levels of hostility here. First, Swift had acquired from Temple an attitude to experimental science which appealed to his own temperament too, that enquiries into natural phenomena did not provide an adequate basis for establishing stability and values in human society private and political. Secondly, Swift suspected scientists of a total self-sufficiency which ignored the possibility that they also could be the victims of all too human folly, jealousy and egotism. Therefore, he both mocks and fears this new approach to the problems posed by the human situation, which demonstrated that natural phenomena are a better starting point than supernatural sanctions. While he could accept the attack by the Royal Society on the Aristotelian scholasticism of the universities, yet he could not accept the apologetic of Thomas Sprat (himself a clergyman) and others, that scientific method and the basic truths of Revelation were complementary – he foresaw the probability of unrestrained inquiry disturbing the delicate balance of stability in society. He believed, and showed it in his own fable of the bee and the spider in *The Battle of the Books* that 'sweetness and light' are the product of a balanced understanding of human nature, whereas the mechanical and mathematical arts produce imbalance and show neither sweetness nor light. The ironic contrasts of size in Lilliput and Brobdingnag are the product not so much of Rabelais as of pondering on the consequences of the improved techniques of microscopy.[33]

Swift could not believe that these inquiries listed among others by Sprat: 'Observations on the Bills of Mortality: on the leaves of Sage:

[32] *Poems*, 55.
[33] See the classic essays by Marjorie Nicolson, reprinted in *Science and the Imagination*, Ithaca, New York, 1956.

on small living Flies in the Powder of Cantharides: of insects bred in Dew: . . . of the teeth of Lupus Marinus, that they are the same thing with the Toad-Stones set in Rings: . . . of Bernacles: . . . of stones taken out of the Heart of Man',[34] would improve human relationships. Sprat had noted uneasily that experiments 'are inconstant' and that '. . . it is probable that the trials [experiments] of Future Ages will not agree with those of the present, but frequently thwart, and contradict them. . . .'[35] Swift was to use this argument forcefully in showing on Glubbdubdrib Aristotle confessing that he made many errors in natural philosophy; and on showing Gassendi and Descartes holding views of nature that are exploded because, '. . . new Systems of Nature were but new Fashions, which would vary in every Age; and even those who pretend to demonstrate them from Mathematical Principles, would flourish but a short Period of Time, and be out of Vogue when that was determined'.[36] Swift's pessimism about human nature set in a natural world resistant to human control, and subject to decay and death, denied to him the possibility of belief in a progress and improvement in the world, or the acceptance of the Cartesian method applied to scientific discovery, which would move masterfully from the known to the further knowable.

This much attention has been given to Swift's rejection of scientific methods because his rejection is total, and without this finality we might misread his aims, but, having been shown, it can be left aside; whereas, of religious, political and philosophical themes, while he rejects much that was offered to him from the past, he also accepts some things and modifies them for his own purposes. He rejected the scientists because they identified their work with the 'mechanical'. For Swift life could only be livable in terms not of mechanism but of the understanding of human nature itself, which was capable of being possessed by blind destructive forces only to be controlled by the harmonising of reason and Revelation, by 'virtue and religion', limited by the unquestioning acceptance of the authority of the constitution of the British State and of the canonical requirements of the established Church of England. The idea of limitation here is essential in Swift's thought. Man's irrepressible self-sufficiency riding on his ruthless egotism needs the strongest curb. Swift felt the vertigo arising from his horror of the destructive mindless energies of human folly, illusion and vice: he felt the terror of the incursion of barbarism,

[34] Thomas Sprat, *The History of the Royal Society of London for the Improving of Natural Knowledge*, 1667, 242.
[35] Sprat, 243.
[36] Davis, XI, 182.

of that wrath of God which would allow 'religion and civility' to depart from a nation as the penalty for its pride in itself and ignorance of Providence. Also he felt the slow disintegrative force of time; the loss of purpose, of innocence and of hope. In his account book, on the news of his mother's death he wrote: 'I have now lost my barrier between me and death'.[37] Again he wrote on another occasion: 'I was 47 Years old when I began to think of death; and the reflections upon it now begin when I wake in the Morning, and end when I am going to Sleep.'[38] He came to the conclusion that death must be intended by Providence as a blessing to men, and his Struldbruggs are a fearful demonstration of it. A poem that has been misunderstood as a cynicism more appropriate to Voltaire than to Swift the clergyman, *On the Day of Judgement*, shows him not dismissing the last judgement as a childish superstition, but as challenging the last pride of man: that he is worthy to stand before God for judgement. It is Swift's final condemnation of the vanity and complacent stupidity of men, he records God speaking:

> 'You who thro' frailty step'd aside,
> And you who never fell – *thro' pride*;
> You who in different sects have shamm'd,
> And come to see each other damn'd . . .
> The world's mad business now is o'er,
> And I resent these pranks no more.
> I to such blockheads set my wit!
> I damn such fools! – Go go, you're bit.'

But the poem began:

> With a whirl of thought oppress'd,
> I sink from reverie to rest.
> An horrid vision seiz'd my head. . . .[39]

Unlike Chesterfield who wrote of the poem to Voltaire as one worldly mocker at religious myths to another, Swift indeed was appalled by the 'horrid vision'. Further, he had written elsewhere, 'Miserable mortals! can we contribute to the *honour and Glory of God*? I could wish that expression were struck out of our Prayer-Books'.[40]

The self-sufficient energies of men, if they are not to become destructive, need to be subjected to limitation. What this meant and how it was to be achieved can be seen in considering how Swift faced the philosophies of his time.

[37] Davis, V, 196.
[38] *Correspondence*, III, 354.
[39] *Poems*, 507.
[40] Davis, IX, 263.

Swift addressed himself at Moor Park to the intellectual crisis of the late seventeenth century: *A Tale of a Tub*, long in his mind, when finally achieved is, for all its confidence and brilliance, still a summing up related to the stresses of the seventeenth-century situation and is not a prologue to the optimism of the works of Shaftesbury. Swift, seeking answers to that intellectual crisis, recognised the need to replace the traditional assumptions of pre-Cartesian philosophy and pre-Revolution churchmanship. He had seen how the Puritan theology of the covenants could destroy the stability of the State in the Civil War, and also had seen that the Laudian answer to the Puritans by insisting on *De iure divino* episcopacy, depending on absolutist monarchy, equally endangered stability. He was also aware of the route tried before him by well-informed laymen who found little assurance in clerical orthodoxies. Bacon could be cited as an influence of this type of thinking on the young Swift: but Bacon shared the religious-intellectual framework of later Calvinism, or Elizabethan Protestantism, as his own confession of religious belief shows.[41] This had little attraction for Swift. While Sir Thomas Browne could offer something to meet his needs, it was another more thoroughly critical layman, Thomas Hobbes, who opposed the religious extremisms of Puritanism and Laudianism and provided an alternative which attracted Swift's attention for a time. It is certain that he had studied Hobbes, for he had been Stella's Abelard and on the night of her funeral he wrote among reflections on her life: 'She understood the nature of government and could point out all the errors of Hobbes, both in that and religion'.[42] But Swift owed something to Hobbes, perhaps more than he realised, for he could echo Hobbes's summing up on morals: 'he deduced the manners of men from human nature; virtues and vices from a natural law; and the goodness and wickedness of actions from the laws of states'. Further, Swift knew from his wide reading of books of travels that morals tend to be relative and vary with climate and religion, and that one cannot accept *simpliciter* the traditional ethics of the Church. Hobbes in his chapter *Of the Natural Condition of Mankind, as concerning their Felicity, and Misery* ignores the traditional Christian doctrine of original sin, but is even more pessimistic than St. Augustine, for without external restraint there are '. . . no arts; no letters; no society; and which is worst of all, continual fear, and danger of violent death; and the life of man, solitary, poor, nasty, brutish, and short.'[43] Swift accepted the doctrine

---

[41] A.-M. Schmidt, *Calvin and the Calvinist Tradition*, trans. R. Wallace, 1960, 153–161.
[42] Davis, V. 231.
[43] *Leviathan*, ed. M. Oakeshott, Oxford, 1946, 82.

of original sin, and a more Christian answer to it than Hobbes proposed for the natural man, but Hobbes's pessimistic view of human nature unrestrained Swift could surely share – the Yahoo is part of a similar vision. Hobbes had written that man has the exclusive privilege of forming: 'general rules called *theorems* . . . But this privilege is allayed by another; and that is by the privilege of absurdity; to which no living creature is subject, but man only. And of men, those are of all most subject to it, that profess philosophy'.[44] The quotation calls to mind, first, Swift's early struggle to free himself from 'general theorems'; secondly, Gulliver's description of the Houyhnhnms who, puzzled by his shoes and stockings, neighed to each other and used 'various Gestures, not unlike those of a Philosopher, when he would attempt to solve some new and difficult Phaenomenon'.[45]

Yet Swift rejected Hobbes's system more than once as intolerable, however much he may have recognised the truth of some of his psychological insights, and there is more in common with Locke's ideas (though not with his philosophical system) in Swift's writings than with those of Hobbes. Locke wrote about metaphysical speculation in words which Swift would have approved, since it, 'let loose our Thoughts into the vast Ocean of *Being*. Thus men extend their inquiries beyond their capacity. . . .'[46] Locke also called Christian theology 'not a notional science, but a rule of righteousness'.[47] Both these general statements of Locke can be plainly found echoed in Swift's writings. How far Descartes disturbed or stimulated Swift would be difficult to determine, and the fact that Molyneux translated *Le Discours sur la Méthode* at Dublin when Swift was in his second year there at Trinity College may be one more fact without determinable consequences in the hidden life of a man of genius. But whether derived from him or not Swift reflects in his own work not Descartes' concern to demonstrate ultimate truth by mathematics but the view of Descartes that morality could be reduced to a few maxims: 'To obey the laws and customs of my country, constantly adhering to the religion in which God has given me the grace to be instructed from my childhood and governing myself in all other things by the wisest and least exaggerated opinions which were commonly received in practice by the most sensible of those with whom I had to live . . . to be as firm and resolute in my actions as I could be: . . . always to try to conquer myself rather

[44] *Leviathan*, 27.
[45] Davis, XI, 210.
[46] Locke's *Works*, 3rd edn., 1727, I, 2.
[47] *Works*, I, 3.

fortune.'[48] As Dean of St. Patrick's, for example, Swift was committed (as he once noted) to conquering himself rather than fortune.

A discipline of Montaigne who may have been one of the sources in which Swift found ideas common to Montaigne and his school, Pierre Charron, certainly wrote lines that Swift (whether he knew them directly, or mediated through Temple's conversation, or some other source) reflected in his own writings:

> Il faut estre simple, obéissant, et debonnaire pour estre propre a reçevoir religion, croire et se maintenir sous les loix, par réverence et obéissance, assujettir son jugement et se laisser mener et conduire à l'authorité publique. . . . La religion est en la connaissance de Dieu, et de soy-mesme; . . . son office est d'elever Dieu au plus haut de tout son effort, et baisser l'homme au plus bas, l'abatre comme perdu, et puis luy fournir des moyens de se relever, luy faire sentir la misère et son rien, afin qu'en Dieu seul, il mette son confiance et son tout. . . . La vraye science et le vray estude de l'homme, c'est l'homme.[49]

For some the question may arise whether these citations are necessary or fruitful in understanding Swift: but if the principle of interpretation proposed earlier in this essay is accepted (that Swift must be understood against the background of the thought of his time, especially of its 'laicised religion', or else we tend at least to misrepresent him), then Charron and the rest are relevant. Camille Looten, Philip Harth and John Traugott have produced discussions of influences upon Swift's religious views and the mould of his thought.[50] However, together with the reason already given for the citations above, it is difficult to accept Traugott's attempt to make Swift largely a disciple of Anglo-Catholic Laudianism, or his statement that Swift participated 'in the same intellectual, political and religious cause to which Sir Thomas More became a martyr':[51] the one is an anachronism, the other an oversimplification. This kind of situation arises by giving more attention to the writings of Swift than to their historical context and to the development of Swift's mind. Harth gives a useful and valid study of the 'Anglican rationalists' – his own phrase – from Chillingworth through Glanvill and the Cambridge Platonists to Stillingfleet: but that the range of Swift's balanced thought can usefully be discerned in their writings is

[48] Descartes, *Oeuvres*, Bibliotheque de la Pleiade Paris, 1953, 141.
[49] Pierre Charron, *Petit Traité de la Sagesse* Paris, 1646, 327 and 334. Swift owned a copy of *Charron of Wisdom, 2nd and 3rd. Books*, 1697. Sale Catalogue, 1745, item no. 648.
[50] Philip Harth, *Swift and Anglican Rationalism: The Religious Background to the Tale of a Tub*, Chicago, 1961; John Traugott, *A Voyage to Nowhere with Thomas More and Jonathan Swift*, reprinted in *Swift: A Collection of Critical Essays*, ed. E. Tuveson, New York, 1963.
[51] Traugott, 160.

not to me self-evident, for he would have regarded half of them with boredom (how could Cudworth's discursive platonising be reconciled with Swift's desire for reducing religious truths to the simplest principles?). Rather, Swift had to deal with the complications of Montaigne's 'Que sais-je?' and with Hobbes, Locke and Descartes, and by name and inference these recur more often in his writings than those other authors cited in Harth and elsewhere. Therefore too much attention should not be given to his statement that La Rochefoucauld was his favourite author, 'because I find my whole character in him'. The quotation from the *Maximes* given in Swift's *Thoughts on Various Subjects*, 'We have just enough Religion to make us hate, but not enough to make us love one another' is not a demonstration of his cynicism but of his sense of near despair.

Certain truths for Swift are the basic realities of the Christian faith: that Christ is God; that the Trinity is a mystery of faith to be affirmed and not subtly disputed; that man is corrupt in nature, and needs the bridle of moral law interpreted by the Church, not with elaborate casuistry but by plainly determined principles of virtue; that episcopacy is the only lawful authority for the ordination of the Christian ministry; that the sacraments of baptism and holy communion are mysteries of fundamental importance – a position to be accepted without arguing it either by the interminable regress of historical analysis or by the interminable logomachy of the metaphysical analysis of the nature of regeneration or of the Real Presence. He shows his lifelong loyalty to the High Church principle that the teaching authority of the Church is not subject to the State, not only in his frequent virulent attacks on Henry VIII as a lustful, godless tyrant who sought to be authority in the Church and despoiled her goods, but also in his early *Ode to Dr. William Sancroft*, the Non-juring martyr for the Church's independence, and in all his later writings.[52] 'The Church *of England* is no Creature of the Civil Power, either as to its Polity or Doctrines. The Fundamentals of both were deduced from Christ and his Apostles and the Instructions of the purest and earliest Ages'.[53] Again, 'although the Supreme Power can hinder the Clergy or Church from making any new Canons, or executing the old; from consecrating Bishops, or refusing those that they do consecrate: or, in short, from performing any Ecclesiastical Office, as they may from eating, drinking and sleeping; yet they

---

[52] Swift attacked Henry VIII in several places, for example, *Concerning the Universal Hatred which Prevails against the Clergy; Remarks upon a Book, The Rights of the Christian Church; Ode to Sancroft.*

[53] Davis, II, 69.

cannot themselves perform those Offices, which were assigned to the
Clergy by our Saviour and his Apostles; or, if they do, it is not
according to the Divine Institution, and consequently null and
void.'[54]

On the basis of this quotation some might consider Swift as a
representative of the old Laudian high-church theology, and that
therefore he would have supported the Non-Jurors who on the
ground of the Divine Right of Kings refused to take the Oath of
Allegiance to William and Mary out of loyalty to James II.
Nevertheless, Swift, always a supporter of the Revolution of 1689
and always opposed to excessive zeal in religion, wrote of the Non-
Juring schism: 'it seemeth to be a Complication of as much Folly,
Madness, Hypocrisy, and Mistake, as ever was offered to the
World'.[55] For him they had made the mistake of destroying balance
and proportion, of refusing to accept limitation, and thereby they
had opened the door to religion fanaticism. Decency, proportion,
restraint, he shared these attributes of Augustan classicism and required
them of the young cleric seeking advice: 'I should be glad to see you
the Instrument of introducing into our Style, that Simplicity which is
the best and truest Ornament of most Things in human Life, which
the politer Ages always aimed at in their Building and Dress, (*Simplex
munditiis*) as well as their Productions of Wit.'[56] This is not merely
the elegant posture of a Chesterfield, nor even the more informal
sympathetic and balanced 'politesse' of a Temple: these rules are the
closely-held bridle upon fanaticism. The complaint of Socinians and
Deists in his time was that the Christian's God was an arbitrary
tyrant, or an unintelligible mathematical surd of a three in one, who
should be thrust to a further distance from man and his rationalities;
so they slackened or ceased to grip the reins upon man's sinful energies
and rationalistic questionings. Swift, on the contrary, would find the
views of a Bolingbroke and of the Deists about God's tyranny in
omnipotence to be both psychologically and intellectually
contemptible. For him man needs powerful restraints to master the
weakness and passions in his flesh and in his reason. That there is no
solid firm foundation of virtue but in a conscience firmly directed by
the principles of religion is the theme not only of his sermon *On
Conscience*. If a Bolingbroke, a Collins or a Tindal should reply, from
one or other of their critical positions in regard to Revelation, 'how
do you explain or justify the grounds or mysteries of the Revelation

[54] Davis, II, 77.
[55] *Correspondence*, II, 222.
[56] Davis, II, 177.

you affirm to be the controlling principle behind the teaching of a decent limitation', Swift replies: 'There seems to be a manifest Dilemma in the Case: If you explain them [the Mysteries], they are Mysteries no longer; if you fail, you have laboured to no Purpose.'[57] The authority of the Church enduring through seventeen centuries suffices. Go beyond that limitation and you may emphasise piety until it becomes fanaticism and can end in the disgusting *Mechanical Operation of the Spirit*; or you may emphasise the 'free rights of the reason' and end in atheism leading to that condition described in Hobbes's *Leviathan*; or you may emphasise enthusiastic preaching and end in bawling from a tub; or you may give over to the State your need for an ideology and an ethic and you end in an intolerable tyranny. Like Goya's terrible painting of the Colossal Man striding destructive and unseeing through trampled screaming refugees against a black apocalyptic sky (*El Coloso o el Pánico*) Swift's mind pictured the horror basic in man if he were to be set free from all limitations – his own attacks of vertigo were not psychosomatic, but perhaps they had a horrible inevitability when seen in relation to his private vision of what could happen in the world.

This powerful emotion was not forced into his writings on religion: he preserved there the appearance of calm through intense self-discipline. Nor should we overlook his deep sense of responsibility, not only in his calling as a clergyman but as a writer, for the demonic power within him was continually subject to the mastery of his will; his feeling for form, his desire for serenity according to the 'simplicity of former ages' covers that inner depression and fear.

From the first collected editions of his works onwards Swift's writings on religious subjects have not been brought together, instead many of them are placed with tracts on political or Irish affairs. This has tended to leave the impression on those who begin the study of Swift that he had very little to say on religious matters from committed Christian convictions. For example, *An Argument to prove, That the Abolishing of Christianity in England, May, as Things now Stand, be attended with some Inconveniences, and perhaps, not produce those many good Effects proposed thereby*, is an ironical presentation of Swift's fundamental convictions about that faith of which he said elsewhere, 'in the capacity of a clergyman' he had been 'appointed by providence for defending a post assigned me, and for gaining over as many enemies' as he could.[58] This well-known phrasing of his conception of his calling, by it suppression of personal feeling

[57] Davis, IX, 77.
[58] Davis, IX, 268.

is frequently misunderstood as an example of his opportunism, and taken with the fierce intensity of *A Tale of a Tub* or the milder irony of *An Argument* . . . [*against*] *abolishing Christianity*, shows to superficial judges that his religious writings need not be taken seriously. Again, his self-depreciation as a preacher is taken at its face value by too many commentators. One would have to be well acquainted with Swift to understand his aside to a neighbouring parson: 'Those sermons You have thought fitt to transcribe . . . were what I was firmly resolved to burn and especially some of them the idlest trifling stuff that ever was writt',[59] and the reluctant agreement that Dr. Sheridan could have some of them: 'they may be of use to you, they have never been of any to me.'[60] Landa has shown that Swift paid careful attention to sermon preparation and provided evidence that Swift at St. Patrick's Cathedral listened carefully to the sermons of visiting preachers and offered criticisms of them afterwards.[61]

In an age when the writing and publishing of sermons was a major and lucrative part of publishing, it is characteristic of Swift that he sought to keep his preaching for those whom it concerned. Those eleven sermons that survive emphasise Swift's own expression of themes he thought central to the needs of his people at that time. That more of Swift's sermons have not survived is probably in part due to his realistic clear judgement which recognised that possibly sermons in general, but certainly his own, should be kept out of the hands of Curll – or the Duchess of Somerset. While Swift deals with the great doctrinal and moral truths of the Christian faith as did other preachers before and after him, yet we can also, in certain of the sermons, see summarised his characteristic views, which have been discussed here: the balance between Church and State, against fanatical deviations to left or right; and the need for accepting without unnecessary argument the authority of the fundamental truths of Revelation. The sermons show beyond doubt that Swift fulfilled his own statement: 'I believe that thousands of men would be orthodox enough in certain points, if divines had not been too curious, or too narrow, in reducing orthodoxy within the compass of subtleties, niceties, and distinctions, with little warrant from Scripture, and less from reason or good policy.'[62]

His sermon on the commemoration of the Martyrdom of King

[59] *Correspondence*, I, 31.
[60] Davis, IX, 98.
[61] Introduction to the *Sermons*, IX, 97–137, and *Swift and the Church of Ireland*, 193.
[62] Davis, IX, 262.

Charles I sets forth in simple terms that careful balance which he
regarded as the only barrier against the return to barbarism. His
intense feeling here marks his concern with what were fundamentals
for him. It is significant that unlike most High Churchmen Swift
does not merely praise Charles as a religious martyr, a non-pareil, for
he had too much realism to fail to see how far Charles and Laud had
endangered the stability of the Church by *de iure divino* principles. He
also points out that Charles introduced 'a practice, no way justifiable,
of raising money; for which, however, he had the opinion of the
judges on his side: For, wicked judges there were in those times as
well as in ours'.[63] He then accuses the Long Parliament of having
claimed all authority to itself and so destroying the balance of the
constitution. The Irish rebellion and massacre of Protestants, the
factious schisms and heresies in England, and the beginning and
progress of Atheism, he blames on the Puritan parliament, and even
the turning to Catholicism of James II is also derived from its
intransigence. In simple terms there lies behind this sermon as in his
other writings where these themes occur the view that Puritan
fanaticism in religion led to the destruction of the necessary, the
fundamental, relation of Prince, Lords, Commons and Church, with
interrelated powers and responsibilities – here is the basic political
religious answer of Swift to the needs of the English nation. Over
against this he saw dissenters demanding toleration, and indeed more
than this, even comprehension within a Church establishment
modified to suit them; for Swift this would be the return to the very
position Charles I had faced before the Civil War broke out.
Therefore, said Swift, it is an intolerable demand: dissenters will not
be persecuted, but the settlement of the Church of England made in
1662 must not be altered to suit them. They cannot expect the
comprehension within the established Church which some of them
sought, particularly the Presbyterians, since their views and practices
would destroy the proper balance between Church and State in their
weakening, if not overturning, of the traditional worship, mysteries
of the faith, and canonical practice of the Church of England, and in
their constantly threatening to use the 'right of conscience' to oppose
the State, or the Church settlement, after the manner of the Catholics.
Dissenters must accept the limitations of their position, and be
thankful for the measure of toleration they receive without
demanding more. Behind his political philosophy and those varied
writings which express it, lie the fundamental convictions of Swift
about the right relation of Church and State (for him the State

63 Davis, IX, 221.

would disintegrate without the support of the Church and what, under God, it represented); and about the nature of man, foolish, proud and rebellious, which needs restraint, or limitation, by a moral order grounded not on speculative reason, always volatile, but on Revelation.

The vigorous, indeed harsh, rejection of what Puritanism and its heir, Dissent, stood for, which Swift urged succinctly in the *Sermon upon the Martyrdom of Charles I*, is expanded and applied in his straightforward tracts: *A letter from a Member of the House of Commons in Ireland concerning the Sacramental Test*; *The Sentiments of a Church-of-England Man*; *A Preface to Bishop Burnet's Introduction*; *The Presbyterians' Plea of Merit*; *The Advantages proposed by repealing the Sacramental Test*; and, by the method of ironical inversion, in the tract, *Reasons . . . for Repealing the Sacramental Test in Favour of the Catholicks*. In his discussion of the grounds for maintaining the Sacramental Test Swift shows that the dissenters have liberty to own their property and to practise their religion undisturbed – what more can they want or deserve in view of their past rebellious disposition? Elsewhere Swift, for example, describes them as '*Puritans*, and other Schismaticks, [who] without the least Pretence to any such Authority, by an open Rebellion, destroyed that legal Reformation . . . murdered their King and changed the Monarchy into a Republick.'[64] For him the Presbyterians, especially the Scottish planters of Ulster, need to be kept under the tightest rein, for the Scots of Ulster are 'an industrious People, extreamly devoted to their Religion, and full of an *undisturbed* Affection towards each other', who by 'Parsimony, wonderful *Dexterity in Dealing*' and their solidarity advance their own power and reject anything to do with the Church of Ireland.[65] They complain like other dissenters that it is unconscionable that holy communion should be made the test of political loyalty for those wishing to serve the State; no doubt, says Swift, but if they were offered instead an oath to be loyal to the constitution of Church and State they would claim it to be against conscience, and 'this is no sincerity in arguing', for the circle comes round again. The argument of these tracts is forceful, showing his inevitable stylistic vigour, and lighting up the facets of his fundamental position on the Church's function under God and in the State. He gives no place to Bishop Burnet's plea for leniency to Dissent, for such authors treat this subject *tamquam in republica Platonis, et non in faece Romuli* – here again his realism, without illusions, is as apparent as the force in the quotation.

[64] Davis, XII, 290.
[65] Davis, II, 116.

Since Burnet was a former Presbyterian, a Scot and the kind of Whig whose views Swift loathed, he described him as one who 'was absolute party-mad, and fancied he saw Popery under every bush'.[66] For Swift 'toleration' is of little use, since when it once was tried (that is, under the Commonwealth) it corrupted the essentials of religion by the unlimited liberty of professing all opinions.

The mind that prepared the sermon *On the Martyrdom of Charles I* and the following sentences from the sermon *On Brotherly Love*: 'This Nation of ours hath for an Hundred Years past, been infested by two Enemies, the Papists and Fanaticks, who each, in their Turns, filled it with Blood and Slaughter, and for a Time destroyed both the Church and Government'; 'There are too many People indifferent enough to all Religion; there are many others who dislike the Clergy; and would have them live in Poverty and Dependence: Both these Sorts are much commended by the Fanaticks [that is, Dissenters] for moderate Men, ready to put an End to our Divisions, and to make a General Union among Protestants'.[67] This mind also prepared consistently these Tracts dealing with the problems posed by Dissent. We fail to do Swift justice if we do not recognise too that these writings are all of a piece with one of his major purposes in *A Tale of a Tub*: to attack the turbulence of Jack and his followers which is Dissent in action, and the fantasies of the Aeolists which represent the irrationality and emotional fanaticism of Dissent.

But Dissent was not the only focus of Swift's smaller writings on religious matters. Matthew Tindal, a leading Deist, had written *The Rights of the Christian Church* on which Swift wrote *Remarks* which were not finished and were published posthumously, but which should not be overlooked. For Tindal wanted to make the Church wholly subject to the State, a view which Swift is often accused of holding. But Swift in fact opposed this: establishment does not give being to the Church by Act of Parliament, any more than the existence of God can be demonstrated by being conferred, as it is, by Act of Parliament. 'But the Church of *England* is no Creature of the Civil Power, either as to its Polity or Doctrines. The Fundamentals of both were deduced from Christ and his Apostles, and the Instructions of the purest and earliest Ages, and were received as such by those Princes or States who embraced Christianity, whatever prudential Additions have been made to the former by human Laws, which alone can be justly altered or annulled by them.'[68] Authority

---

[66] Davis, V, 184.
[67] Davis, IX, 172, 175.
[68] Davis, II, 79.

in the clergy comes from Christ, but the right to exercise it lies in civil governments: once again Swift is demonstrating man's tendency to confuse cause and appearances. We today may reject Swift's argument in the *Remarks* and oversimplify our criticism of him here, but if we do then we are overlooking the fact that Swift was reproducing a doctrine of classical Protestantism. His argument on this theme is neither improbable nor inconsistent, rather it is the central doctrine of Anglicanism from Richard Hooker onwards.

In his *Sentiments of a Church-of-England Man* he insisted without qualification that a member of that Church, 'ought to believe a God, and his Providence, together with revealed Religion, and the Divinity of *Christ*'[69] and that he must accept episcopacy as most agreeable to the primitive institution of the Church and most suited for preserving order and purity. Morality and religion may be miscalled the prejudices of education by freethinkers, but in doing so they demonstrate their wish to have liberty for their vices and self-sufficient opinions. Confusion between the executive and legislative power (a confusion which Swift says Hobbes himself made and was the foundation of the political mistakes in his books) is the basis for unintelligent attack on Church and State relations by those who wish to alter them. 'The Freedom of a Nation in fact consists in an absolute *unlimited legislative* Power, wherein the whole Body of the People are *fairly* represented; and in an *executive* duly *limited*.'[70] Here is one ground for understanding how Swift could combine Whig and Tory principles in a period when a man must be one or the other undiluted – like the Whig bishop Burnet or the Tory bishop Atterbury, 'party-mad'. Swift did not apostatise in changing from the new style of Whigs to the Tories, he held to his integrity of judgement on what would best serve the State and the Church, Revelation and morality. He did not change his views: with the political developments of the early eighteenth century it was the party lines which changed. Swift was a Tory churchman of 1662, and a Whig of 1689 – and in essentials remained so. His failure to achieve a bishopric lay partly in his holding to these convictions when such appointments largely went by party. In 1708 he wrote, at the end of *The Sentiments of a Church-of-England Man*, 'I should think that, in order to preserve the Constitution entire in Church and State; whoever hath a true Value for both, would be sure to avoid the Extreams of *Whig*, for the Sake of the former, and the Extreams of *Tory* on Account of the latter.'[71]

[69] Davis, II, 4.
[70] Davis, II, 23.
[71] Davis, II, 25.

Swift plainly thought of the Church not only as having its own divine origin, although since it was established in law it was subject in its canons and practices of government to the executive and legislative powers of the State, but also as being essential to society, intended by God's providence for this purpose, among others, to demonstrate, encourage, and give pastoral care to the moral well-being of the members of the community. We can find these beliefs recommended as capable of being advanced even at the lowest level of princely example and encouragement in *A Project for the Advancement of Religion, and the Reformation of Manners*; shown in *Gulliver's Travels* in the views of the King of Brobdingnag; and the sermons *On the Testimony of a good Conscience* and *The Duty of Mutal Subjection*. Johnson thought that *A Project for the Advancement of Religion*, while showing great purity of intention, was 'if not generally impracticable, yet evidently hopeless': but something like it was successfully advocated and realised under Victoria the Good, at least to the extent that it allowed the 'hypocrisy which is the tribute that vice pays to virtue'.

Near the end of *A Project* Swift quotes Machiavelli on the value of reducing things to their first principles: therefore, he urges, we should clarify where the roots of abuses in religion and morality lie, and attack them at those roots. This piece has been described by F. R. Leavis as a call for 'outward show in religion'; for Johnson, however, it urged more 'zeal, concord and perseverance' in religion than men are capable of. Swift himself agreed that on the method he advocated there might arise nineteen hypocrites for one good man: but that ratio would be worth it, from the quality of the good men. What he had condemned in *A Project*, he condemned more forthrightly in similar terms in his sermon *On the Testimony of Conscience*: 'So, that upon the Whole, there is hardly one Vice which a meer Moral man [that is, 'those Men who set up for Morality without regard to Religion'] may not upon some Occasions allow himself to practise. . . . And the Reason we find so many Frauds, Abuses, and Corruptions where any Trust is conferred, can be no other, than that there is so little Conscience and Religion left in the World, or at least that Men in their Choice of Instruments have private Ends in view, which are very different from the Service of the Publick.'[72] Without recourse to his stylistic brilliance on the one hand, nor to the exhortatory tone and appeal to emotion too common in the pulpit on the other, Swift states plainly in this sermon his view of the human condition and some of the basic principles which lie behind all his writings.

[72] Davis, IX, 153, 157.

Swift's pamphlet *A Letter to a Young Gentleman lately entered into Holy Orders* is used most frequently by those concerned with his analysis of a good prose style and how it should be formed, but his purpose here was focused on giving advice on the professional equipment of a clergyman – advice which achieves more good sense in short space than many similar efforts on the pastoral training of the clergy. 'As I take it, the two principal Branches of Preaching are first to tell the people what is their Duty; and then to convince them that it is so. The Topicks for both of these we know are brought from Scripture and Reason'. Once again he is seen reducing the complex and contradictory to first principles, and then advising that these should be directed with the greatest concentration of force to the appropriate targets. Among other sound points Swift, approving for once of a dissenter, claims that he had been 'more informed by a Chapter in the *Pilgrim's Progress*, than by a long Discourse upon the *Will* and the *Intellect*, and *simple* or *complex Ideas*'.[73] In his own sermon *On Sleeping in Church* he provides an irony and an indignation lacking in *A Letter* which forcefully exemplify part of its intention – the two should be read together for to some degree they complement each other. In *A Letter* he writes: 'For a Divine hath nothing to say to the wisest Congregation of any Parish in this Kingdom, which he may not express in a Manner to be understood by the meanest among them': in *On Sleeping in Church* he writes more pungently that 'Refinements of Stile, and Flights of Wit, as they are not properly the Business of any Preacher, so they cannot possibly be the Talents of all. In most other Discourses, Men are satisfied with sober Sense and plain Reason; and, as Understandings go, even that is not over frequent'.[74]

Swift the ironist of *An Argument [against] Abolishing Christianity* shares something of the Erasmian tradition of the *Praise of Folly*, for the humanist element in Swift's early reading is not only to be found in Montaigne, but the method and the style of *An Argument* are peculiarly Swiftian and have made it a frequent choice for representative selections from his writings. He tells us of the sad fate of two young gentlemen who, 'by meer Force of natural Abilities, without the least Tincture of Learning; having made a Discovery, that there was no God, and generously communicating their thoughts for the Good of the Publick; were some Time ago, by an unparalleled Severity, and upon I know not what *obsolete* Law, broke *only* for *Blasphemy*'. But how many of those to whom *An Argument* is familiar

---

[73] Davis, IX, 66, 67.
[74] Davis, IX, 66, 217.

know the following, from a sermon, *On Sleeping in Church*, which shows Swift's method of turning the enemy's weapon against him, his contempt for the 'tritical', and his concern for plain but forceful discourse: 'these Men, whose Ears are so delicate as not to endure a plain Discourse of Religion, who expect a constant Supply of Wit and Eloquence on a Subject handled so many thousand Times; what will they say when we turn the Objection upon themselves, who with all the lewd and profane Liberty of Discourse they take, upon so many thousand Subjects, are so dull as to furnish nothing but tedious Repetitions, and little paultry, nauseous Commonplaces, so vulgar, so worn, or so obvious, as upon any other Occasion, but that of advancing Vice, would be hooted off the stage.'[75] The main theme of *An Argument* is seen where Swift ironically affirms that he has no intention of defending the real Christianity of the apostolic age, for to restore it is a wild project; he is only defending nominal Christianity on such grounds as that it would be useful to have one man who could read and write in a parish, and that the abolition of the Christian religion might bring in popery, though he admits that parsons could provide useful recruits for the army and the fleet since they are a tiresome set of men whose only duty it is to bawl one day in seven. The complementary form of *An Argument* can be found in the sermon *On the Excellency of Christianity* where we can compare the assertion in the former, 'to offer at the Restoration of *real* Christianity would indeed be a wild Project', with this: 'Why doth not Christianity still produce the same effects? [as among the primitive Christians] it is easy to answer, First, That although the number of pretended Christians be great, yet that of true believers, in proportion to the other, was never so small; and it is a true lively faith alone, that by the assistance of God's grace, can influence our practice. Secondly, we may answer, That Christianity itself hath very much suffered by being blended up with Gentile philosophy'.[76] Behind all this, however, there is the constant theme with Swift, the need for maintaining an educated, well-ordered, well-provided for and respected body of clergy: he recurs again and again to the damage caused to the Church and, therefore, to society, through the poverty and disrespect accorded to the clergy. For example, in the unfinished piece *Concerning that universal Hatred which prevails against the Clergy*, the ground is never mere professional assertion, but is that moralism basic to Swift's world-view, that the clergy are the God-given agents for maintaining moral stability in society.

[75] Davis, IX, 214.
[76] Davis, IX, 249.

It has been shown how certain of his sermons interpret briefly and underline his other writings on religious themes, but the sermons can also be shown as reinforcing the purposes of the great satires and indeed the whole of his writings. Eleven sermons were published out of the many Swift preached as parish priest and later as Dean, and it is an open question whether even these came to be published through his intention that they should survive. They are usually neglected in considering his literary achievement because of failure to find in them his stylistic brilliance, the assumption that sermons are insignificant for literary criticism, and the frequent but erroneous belief that Swift must have found preaching a tiresome distraction from his real interests as a writer, and therefore that what he preached would hardly relate to his major works. Nevertheless, here in the sermons Swift states plainly without masks, inversions, or stylistic devices the point of view and the beliefs which lie behind the great satires and the political and religious essays. His judgement on human nature, so often described as pessimistic, negative or even cynical, is repeated in the sermons, where he shows that he inherits and believes profoundly in the moral realism of the traditional Christian doctrine of original sin. On man's desperately sinful condition Swift has no doubt: man left to himself is a creature of pride, vanity, lust, stupidity, and folly. It is significant that John Wesley could quote with approval *Gulliver's Travels* on man's depravity in his tract on *The Doctrine of Original Sin*. Swift's positive conclusion to his sermon *On the Testimony of Conscience* should be pondered by those who fail to see any connection between Swift the Dean and Swift the satirist: 'It plainly appears, that unless Men are guided by the Advice and Judgment of a Conscience founded on Religion, they can give no Security that they will be either good Subjects, faithful Servants of the Publick, or honest in their mutual Dealings; since there is no other Tie thro' which the Pride, or Lust, or Avarice, or Ambition of Mankind will not certainly break one Time or other.'[77] That a stable society cannot be created by man's own resources without reference to the Church, the guardian of Revelation, is not only the implication of the satires, and the affirmation of the religious essays, it is the blunt purpose, as has already been shown, of the sermon *On the Martyrdom of Charles I*, and is energetically expressed in the sermon *On Brotherly Love*:

> A Moderate Man, in the new Meaning of the Word, is one to whom all Religion is indifferent, who, although he denominateth himself of the Church, regardeth it no more than a Conventicle. He perpetually raileth

[77] Davis, IX, 158.

at the Body of the Clergy, with Exceptions only to a very few, whom he hopeth and probably upon false Grounds, are as ready to betray their Rights and Properties, as himself. He thinks the Power of the People can never be too great, nor that of the Prince too little; and yet this very Notion he publisheth, as his best Argument, to prove him a most loyal Subject. Every Opinion in Government, that differeth in the least from his, tendeth directly to Popery, Slavery and Rebellion. . . . Lastly, his Devotion consisteth in drinking Gibbets, Confusion, and Damnation; in profanely idolizing the Memory of one Prince [William III] and ungratefully trampling upon the Ashes of another [Queen Anne].[78]

Here we have in fact the character of a new Whig, for Swift, the very ground of instability in the State. That Swift thought this kind of writing proper for a sermon shows his realism, and his contempt for the platitude that judgements on politics should not reach the pulpit.

A useful introduction to Swift's Irish tracts and to the *Drapier's Letters* is provided by the sermon *Causes of the Wretched Condition of Ireland*, for it contains a clear and forceful summary of the Irish problem in which the endemic troubles of, for example, absentee landlords, and numbers of starving beggars, are set down. Another sermon *Doing Good* is subtitled *On the Occasion of Wood's Project* where Swift strikes at 'the meanest instrument' who 'by the concurrence of accidents, may have it in his power to bring a whole kingdom to the very brink of destruction, and is at this present endeavouring to finish his work'. He adds:

Perhaps it may be thought by some, that this way of discoursing is not so proper from the pulpit. But surely, when an open attempt is made, and far carried on, to make a great kingdom one large poor-house, to deprive us of all means to exercise hospitality and charity, to turn our cities and churches into ruins, to make the country a desert for wild beasts and robbers, to destroy all arts and sciences, all trades and manufactures, and the very tillage of the ground, only to enrich one obscure, ill-designing projector, and his followers; it is time for the pastor to cry out, that the wolf is getting into his flock, to warn them to stand together, and all to consult the common safety.[79]

Again, the sermon *On False Witness* is about much more than the evil of malicious gossip, for in faction-ridden Ireland Swift notes the scandal of another feature of Irish politics, the Informer, 'evil Instruments who . . . are always ready . . . to offer their Service to the prevailing Side and become Accusers of their Brethren. . . .'[80] He

---

[78] Davis, IX, 178.
[79] Davis, IX, 235–6.
[80] Davis, IX, 180.

points his congregation to the way to defend themselves against false accusation and the activities of the *agent-provocateur*, showing that innocence is always the best protection for those who are to be as harmless as doves, but adds pointedly that they should be as wise as serpents in keeping to loyalty.

In his sermon *On the Excellency of Christianity* Swift challenges the contemporary assumptions made by the Deists, and by Bolingbroke and Shaftesbury, that the virtues of the Greeks and Romans were the highest examples of the good life and accessible without the need of the Christian Revelation. He argues that even the best philosophers of Greece and Rome showed defects in morals which were, 'purely the flagging and fainting of the mind for want of a support by Revelation from God'.[81] And that Plato with all his refinements left, 'the wise and the good man wholly at the mercy of uncertain chance, and to be miserable without resource'.[82] This is complemented by his sermon *On the Trinity* where – with some theological astuteness – he gives a positive answer to the Deists' criticism of Trinitarian orthodoxy, and a statement of the essential themes of the orthodox reply to the Anti-Trinitarians, and also the characteristic challenge to man's rationality: '*Reason* itself is true and just, but the *Reason* of every particular Man is weak and wavering, perpetually swayed and turned by his Interests, his Passions, and his Vices.'[83]

A final group of three sermons shows Swift fully committed to pastoral concern about the obligations of love and service which men owe to each other. In two of them he emphasises a theme unacceptable to our unitary view of society but which was fundamental to the political outlook of his time. In *The Duty of Mutual Subjection* by taking literally the words, 'Be subject to one another' (though he recognised as do modern commentators that the intention here is to emphasise humility) Swift affirms that, since society is hierarchical, each man has his station and his obligations; and in *The Poor Man's Contentment* he consoles the poor by pointing out that vices and miseries beset the rich and powerful, that wealth is not a blessing, and that the poor man is free from its insistent temptations. Swift is saved from smugness here by the forthrightness of his demand that the poor man should be helped and cared for by the richer, by reminding the poor that Christ was born among them, and by sharply affirming that virtue does not reside with rank and wealth. The sermon *On Conscience* demonstrates clearly Swift's grim

[81] Davis, IX, 247.
[82] Davis, IX, 246.
[83] Davis, IX, 166.

view of the sinful condition of men, not least of those who appear to live with virtue before the world but who are in reality hypocrites and self-seekers, and he allows no place to those who substitute Honour for virtue, mocking 'The Catechism of Honour, which contains but two Precepts, the punctual Payment of Debts contracted at Play, and the right understanding the several Degrees of an Affront, in order to revenge it in the Death of an Adversary'.[84] Here Swift the preacher agrees with Swift the political observer and the satirist, in saying: 'There is no way of judging how far we may depend upon the Actions of Men, otherwise than by knowing the Motives, and Grounds, and Causes of them; and, if the Motives of our Actions be not resolved and determined into the Law of God, they will be precarious and uncertain, and liable to perpetual Changes ... a Religious Conscience is the only true Foundation upon which Virtue can be built.'[85]

In these eleven sermons can be found in little space the focal points of Swift's view of man, society, the Church and the State, Ireland, Christian faith and virtue, together with his repudiation of those who will not accept a decent limitation for the sake of order – the religious extremist, the self-confident rationalist, and the factious party-man, in all their ramifying activities disturbing that balance without which life would become intolerable. In his sermon *On the Excellence of Christianity* he said: '[The Christian religion] is *without hypocrisy*; it appears to be what it really is; it is all of a piece. By the doctrines of the gospel we are so far from being allowed to publish to the world those virtues we have not, that we are commanded to hide, even from ourselves, those we really have, and not to let our right hand know what our left hand doth'.[86] Here in his own words to his congregation at St. Patrick's is the key to Swift's 'inverted hypocrisy'. It points to what 'really is' and was 'all of a piece' with his religion. The Swift of the satires concealed from being obvious the religious motivation of his thought, not through indifference nor merely as the stylistic necessity of avoiding 'tritical' moralising, but through conviction: 'we are so far from being allowed to publish to the world those virtues we have not, that we are commanded to hide, even from ourselves, those we really have.'

[84] Davis, IX, 153.
[85] Davis, IX, 154, 156.
[86] Davis, IX, 248.

11

Alessandro Gavazzi: A Barnabite Friar and the Risorgimento

Think now
History has many cunning passages, contrived corridors
And issues, deceives with whispering ambitions,
Guides us by vanities. Think now
She gives when our attention is distracted
And what she gives, gives with such supple confusions
That the giving famishes the craving. Gives too late
What's not believed in, or if still believed,
In memory only, reconsidered passion.[1]

Historians no doubt have problems enough without setting before themselves that 'memento mori' from Eliot, who, though he was describing an old man seeking to understand his own past, leaves nevertheless an echo in the mind disturbing to those who practise the historian's craft. We assume a confidence which in our heart of hearts we do not always, or should not always, possess. Eliot's words not

---

[1] *The Complete Poems and Plays of T. S. Eliot*, London, 1969. *Gerontion*, 38.

only demonstrate the difficulty of one man understanding his own past, but also the historian's difficulty in understanding those whom they select for questioning from among the vast multitudes of the silent dead, whose deeds, artifacts, ideas, passions, hopes and memories have died with them. We dig into the past, obtain data from archives, brush off the objects found, collect statistics, annotate, arrange, describe, establish a chronology – but do we effectively understand the dead, especially since we are affected by our own beliefs, customs and ideologies? We are, of course, all aware of this: we silently scorn the lecturer who raises these diffident hesitations. For we know our duty: we examine all that we can, we describe our findings, we annotate them, we draw conclusions, or leave our demonstrations to speak for themselves. There are reasons, as I shall hope to show, that these considerations – Eliot's ominous words and our determination not to be disquieted by them – bear upon the subject of this paper, Alessandro Gavazzi, almost unknown to English speakers.

To find materials for an account of the life and work of Alessandro Gavazzi is not difficult, (with the exception of his manuscript autobiography);[2] for example, there are the close-printed newspaper cuttings from British newspapers of his speeches, though many of

---

[2] A full description of this manuscript *Autobiografia* is given by Robert Sylvain, 517–18 in the second volume of his biography of Gavazzi, *Alessandro Gavazzi, Garabaldien, Clerc, Predicant des Deux Mondes*, Québec, 1962. Armando Lodolini had described the manuscript earlier in his *Contributo alla biografia del Padre Alessandro Gavazzi Rassegna storico del Risorgimento*, 43, Rome, 1956, 434–48. Extracts have been published by Giorgio Cencetti, *Alcune pagine dell'autobiografia del P. Alessandro Gavazzi, Atti e Memorie della Deputazione di Storia patria per le Provincie di Romagna*, Nuova Serie 1, Rome, 1948, 153–73. These extracts, the only original text available, as well as occasional and translated paragraphs in Sylvain's biography of Gavazzi have been used in this paper. My visit to Rome in 1974 in order to see this manuscript autobiography and other materials concerning Gavazzi, which since 1950 had been in a permanent exhibition *Mostra didascalia* at the Archivio di Stato di Roma, Palazzo della Sapienza, proved fruitless because a process of centralising all archives was being undertaken by the city authorities. An inquiry about a copy of the manuscript in the possession of G. Conti, a close relation of the Conti who had known and written the last and uncritical biography of Gavazzi was made but was also unavailing since the negative answer was made that it was impossible to read the handwriting and admission to Sig. Conti was refused. Judging by the extracts given by Cencetti, and Sylvain's translated citations, the autobiography should be a work of considerable importance for the history of the Risorgimento, for the religious history of the nineteenth century in England and elsewhere as well as in Italy. Sylvain rightly describes it as strange that it remains unpublished, refers to it as 'ce précieux manuscrit', and states that 'les faits sont-ils indiqués avec suffisamment de précision et d'honnêteté: on n'y surprend jamais Gavazzi falsifiant une circonstance biografique ou historique. Nous avons vérifiée, toutes les fois que nous l'avons pu, l'exactitude de son récit par la comparaison avec des renseignements venant d'autres sources. Or ces recoupements ont toujours confirmé la véracité du mémorialiste'. This is the more significant since it is the judgement of a Roman Catholic historian, who is justifiably distressed by Gavazzi's 'excès de plume . . . par tirades d'injures à l'adresse de ses anciens confrères et de ces coreligionnaires de jadis . . .'

them do not show their source or date.[3] Moreover, these cuttings could reduce him to the level of that anti-papal oratory popular in English-speaking Victorian Protestantism, and therefore to being not worth much more than a footnote in a volume of Dessain's edition of Newman's letters and journals – and he may not even attain that memorial. But those newspaper records do not show what Eliot called 'reconsidered passion', that passionate intensity with which Gavazzi was involved in the Risorgimento in the period leading to the brief Roman republic and its downfall. What they show is his talent for noisy and gesticulatory declamation. They do not demonstrate why he was adored by Catholic crowds as the 'Savonarola of the piazzas' in the forties, and why he was still a useful supporter of Garibaldi's renewed attacks in Italy in the sixties when Gavazzi's vigorous speeches as a returned exile roused enthusiastic *vivas* from Naples to Venice.

If the historiography of the Italian Risorgimento is full of 'cunning passages' and 'contrived corridors' and 'supple confusions' not least it is because the literature is vast (autobiographies, diaries, letters, as well as materials in military, municipal and ecclesiastical archives) and discussion of it still arouses deep and bitter controversy in Italy.[4] Walter Maturi's book *Interpretazioni del Risorgimento* gives brief extracts and analyses from over fifty works from Denina's *Rivoluzioni d'Italia*, 1770 (and it is significant that the understanding of the Risorgimento has to begin with eighteenth century roots) to those writings of the English historian Denis Mack Smith which were published by 1960. Even in the 692 pages of his book Maturi has not covered all historians but has selected certain writers to show varying interpretations and emphases. Given these varieties of interpretation listed by Maturi, against what clearly defined framework in the Risorgimento can Gavazzi be placed? For some no doubt the politics of the left should suffice (whether anarchist–socialist, as shown in *Gesu Socialista* by Arnoldo Nesti, or in the work of the marxist Antonio Gramsci who called the reunification of Italy 'a passive revolution') but as Nesti notes Italy lacked an experience like the Paris commune.[5] There was too much utopian talk, together

[3] These are in eight octavo volumes: there is also a quarto volume of cuttings called *Memorie* (as well as published works by Gavazzi in Italian, in the library of the Facoltà Valdese di Teologia, Roma. These collections appear to have been made by Gavazzi himself, or those who acted from time to time as his secretaries. The closely printed cuttings are trying to read, and are accompanied often by not much more than a date.

[4] The publicist, Indro Montanelli, in his *L'Italia del Risorgimento* (1831–1861), Milan, 1972, at 685 under *Bibliografia* wrote: 'Una completa bibliografia di opere sul Risorgimento è impossibile da redigere perché richiederebbe un volume a parte.' This would be a conservative estimate.

[5] Arnaldo Nesti, *Gesu Socialista*, Turin, 1974, 10.

with the powerful influence of the strongminded toughness of Garibaldi, so stubbornly concerned for 'liberty', in the Risorgimento to make marxist analysis fruitful. In fact any purely political analysis of the Risorgimento would leave out too much: there were so many non-political factors within the movement. In English terms the Risorgimento was simply a struggle for liberal ideals and institutions as can be seen across the spectrum from Swinburne's lush poeticising *Songs before Sunrise* to Trevelyan's traditionally whig trilogy of praise for Garibaldi, of whom he wrote in his autobiography – 'Garibaldi attracted me because his life seemed to be the most poetic of all true stories'.[6] But Mack Smith disillusioned after the war with Mussolini's Italy and Hitler's Germany, finds a fascist lurking behind many a Risorgimento figure.[7] Perhaps Gavazzi was popular with the English in his exile here because, in spite of his oratorical gifts and anti-papalism, he showed no interest in political partisanship – his popularity, in certain areas, with working-class audiences does not imply that he raised political issues; rather it implies his diffused social concern for the Italian poor and the probably latent 'orangeism' of those audiences.

Political analysis will not explain Gavazzi: for him religiously suffused patriotism was the essential matter. He had no use for Mazzini's republicanism, and no declared understanding of what might come of the Piedmontese conservative state. Politically he was no more than a noise in the street – even though his oratory stirred like a trumpet. When he walked with an arm linked with Garibaldi in Rome in 1848 he was not demonstrating a political choice, he thought he was walking towards a nation and a Church revived anew in Italy. Sociological analysis would not help. At the touch of a sociologist's finger Gavazzi would collapse like a pricked balloon, but the same could almost be said of Mazzini. If we turn to the history of the institutions created by the Risorgimento, they seem to have been as bureaucratically ramshackle as those of modern Italy, before the new industrial technology began there. The only institution created by Gavazzi faded away in a generation, though he could be an

---

[6] George Macaulay Trevelyan, *An Autobiography and Other Essays*, (London, 1949) 13.

[7] Denis Mack Smith, *Cavour and Garibaldi: 1860*, Cambridge, 1945; *Garibaldi, A Great Life in Brief*, London, 1957; *Italy, A Modern History*, Michigan, 1959. W. Maturi, *Interpretazioni del Risorgimento*, Turin, 1962, 688: 'Mack Smith è ossessionato dal problema del fascismo: nella storia d'Italia dal 1861 in poi tutto conduce al fascismo', and, 'garibaldinismo e fascismo', 689. Maturi's judgement is not unique to himself, but is also noticed by recent historians. It is part of the purpose of this paper to suggest that Mack Smith's view is illiberal and does not do justice to the idealism and religious convictions of many of those who took part in the Risorgimento, though not calling in question the thoroughness of his scholarship nor, for example, his conception of the rôle of Cavour.

excellent organiser.[8] In the history of ideas Gavazzi would make little showing. He had a remarkable talent for oratory, and a ready pen: but he spoke too often and wrote too much amid an active daily life, for him to produce significant original ideas, or sustain a close analysis of themes requiring intellectual force and disciplined scholarship. His importance lay in his quickness in assimilating views current in his time and, through his own varied experience of life, providing these views with potency and an original exposition of them in speeches, pamphlets, journalism, and full-scale books. Gavazzi had a powerful personality sustained by great physical strength and energy, which assisted that flood of words which poured from him in speech and writing, and gave these their peculiar flavour and power. The style and the manner are now badly dated, but we can still see why he moved both Italians and English speakers on the platform and in print.

In view of these limitations the only option open in historical method is the biographical. It will be by narration, especially of two remarkable periods of his life, combined with an attempt to discover what his views were in those two distinctive stages, that this study of Gavazzi will be attempted. For him the Risorgimento was more a religious passion than a political programme. Unfortunately, we are not helped in understanding him because too little attention has been given by historians (although Italian writers are aware of the need) to the religious passions within the Risorgimento.[9] Amidst the multitude of books on the subject of Italian renewal a full-scale analysis of the religious energies behind the movement for Italian unity has yet to be written. Pius IX spent half a life-time anathematising the Risorgimento and his excommunications fell all over Italy like autumn leaves in Vallombrosa. Yet Catholic historians, even if they are not dedicated to the attitudes of the Jesuit journal famous in those years, *Civiltà Cattolica*, are hardly likely to be interested in compiling embarrassingly long lists of names of priests, secular and religious, who supported the Piedmontese or Garibaldi, and even less likely perhaps to write with sympathetic understanding the history of the renegade priests, who found the strain of being at once loyal to Pius IX and to the aims of a united Italy too great to bear and left the

---

[8] That is, the *Chiesa Libera d'Italia*, eventually renamed *Chiesa Evangelica d'Italia*, v. n. 149 below.

[9] For example: Georgio Spini, *Risorgimento e Protestanti*, Naples, 1956. Arnaldo della Torre, *Cristianesimo in Italia dai filosofisti ai moderni*, Milan, no date. Valdo Vinay, *Evangelici Italiani esuli a Londra durante il Risorgimento*, Turin, 1961. The London City Mission Magazine and the minutes of the meetings at the Mission's headquarters in London contain much information on Italian ex-priests employed by the Mission.

Church, while they still claimed to be Christians.[10] Alessandro Gavazzi was one of these and they were no small company. Some came as exiles to England, the home of liberalism and anti-papal Protestantism. But he must not be confused with hypocritical confidence tricksters like Achilli, whose morals and intrigues seemed to English Catholics to be typical of Risorgimento renegade priests, and a public warning of the consequences of religious disobedience.[11]

Gavazzi's life-span from 1809 to 1889 had three crucial stages: 1847–9 which in his manuscript autobiography he called *Patria*, the years of exile 1849–59 entitled *Esiglio*, and the years of renewal in the attempt to re-unite Italy 1859–68 which he called *Ritorno*.[12] His life up to the age of thirty-eight he seems to have regarded as commonplace; its significance paled for him compared with the years of *Patria, Esiglio* and *Ritorno*.[13] He did not live to complete his autobiography, no doubt he felt he could leave to others who shared his final years with him an account of his life when in those last years 1868–89 he worked hard but ineffectively to build up his Free Church of Italy.[14] A few brief extracts from his autobiography have been published and what is apparently the introduction appears under the ambiguous title, 'The Beginning of the End' in which Gavazzi states that he will not concern himself with the philosophy of history, nor with 'theatrical

---

[10] V. n. 103 for these priests.

[11] Dr Giacinto Achilli, a former Dominican friar described by Wilfred Ward in his *Life of Cardinal Newman*, London, 1912, I, 276, as 'an unfrocked priest, not only without a character of any kind, but one who might without exaggeration be described as a portent of immorality'. Ward, 279, quotes Cardinal Wiseman's detailed though florid indictment of Achilli's career as a seducer of women 'and worse'. However, *Bell's Messenger*, a sporting magazine – an unusual place for the review of a religious work – wrote of Achilli's *Dealings with the Inquisition, or Papal Rome, her priests and her Jesuits with important disclosures*, London, 1851: 'Dr Achilli's most valuable book which, independently of the most important information it contains, breathes a spirit of fervent piety and devotion which no one but a man thoroughly convinced of the truths of Christianity as set forth in the only infallible Word of Truth, could have used.' (I derive this citation from the second edition which contains extracts from reviews of the first edition.) It was this sort of acceptance by Protestants of Achilli which helped him to bluff his way as an honest convert, and made Newman's task at the famous libel trial so difficult. Achilli's book has a thoroughly offensive self-righteous tone. His manuscript autobiography is in the British Museum.

[12] Cencetti, op. cit., 155.

[13] See Cencetti, n. 2 above. Sylvain, however, states that the first two parts are entitled: *La Famiglia* and *Il Chiostro*, 517. This is not indicated by Cencetti in his introduction to the *Alcune pagine*, but Sylvain who knew the manuscript well must be correct. In the 'Introduzione' Gavazzi wrote . . . 'mi ritrarrò quale fui nella famiglia, nel chiostro, nella crociata, nell'esiglio e nel rimpatrio . . .'

[14] The autobiography apparently ceases at 1870 ('*Ritorno*, va de 1859 à 1870': Sylvain, 517). A pastor of Gavazzi's *Chiesa Libera d'Italia* who knew him well in his later years, Ludovico Conti, wrote *In occasione del centenario della nascita di Alessandro Gavazzi: cenno biografico* (Rome, 1909). Unfortunately, his account of this period has nothing of the force and interest of Gavazzi's own writing, and contains more of pious adulation than of useful analysis.

situations', nor with the temptation to what he calls *romanzo* – but that he will follow the simple chronology of events as they happened beginning with his family, moving on to his claustral life, to the 'crusade' (1847–9), to the period of exile, and his return to see Italy at last united.[15] He adds with an old man's resignation and with some restrained pathos that he wrote not out of vanity or ambition, but to give the portrait of a man who had nothing other in his heart than to see his Italy crowned queen in the Campidoglio. This comes at the end of a long passage in which he begins by stating that he wishes to leave to posterity some memory of one who belonged to the elect company of those who during the period of the Italian revolutions sacrificed all for the motherland with no other compensation than insults and persecutions – and to claim to have attained in this company a modest niche.[16]

He added with some bitterness that he had an original sin which no baptism could cancel, namely that he belonged to no party. He had accepted only the liberalism of progress (this phrase has a mazzinian ring). He had followed one flag, that of Italy, but on it was the name of no sect or party. Gavazzi went on to deny that he was a legitimist monarchist believing in divine right for that would have been to restore medieval vassalage. He wrote that he had not remained as 'the priests *botteganti di sagrestia* [shopkeepers of the sacristy] those who dreamed only of prestige when their throne and dominion were lost'.[17] After he was 'no longer a priest and papist he had been first among those who fought . . . obscurantism, superstition, the Syllabus and vaticanism'.[18] He was not a moderate other than in the sense of not going to extremes, but if moderate meant conservative then that implied a *camorra* of inept, ambitious, thieves and he was then no moderate.[19] (Conrad's *garibaldino* in *Nostromo* used to invoke Cavour's name as a curse, for he was 'the arch-intriguer sold to kings and tyrants'.)[20] Gavazzi added that he was not a republican: nor was he a *rosso* like so many *garibaldini* even if he had marched with them with the good will of their *gran Capitano*. He wrote that when he was challenged at Leghorn by those who said 'born Catholics should die Catholics', he replied that he was a

[15] Cencetti, 160.

[16] Ibid., 157–60.

[17] Ibid., 158.

[18] Ibid., . . . i traffici, l'oscurantismo, la superstizione, il sillabo, ed il vaticanismo . . . cordialmente mi odiano.

[19] Ibid., 158: Non sono moderato. Se il nome in Italia non fosse stato, sconsacrato da una camorra d'inetti, d'ambiziosi, di egoisti, di broglioni, di ladri; vorrei anch'io essere dei moderati nel vero senso del liberalismo progressivo, conscio che gli estremi non durano.

[20] Joseph Conrad, *Nostromo*, London, 1923, 24.

Catholic without Catholicism, rather he had returned to the true religion of the Italian Fathers from whom these very Catholics had apostatised.[21] Finally to those who said that 'his poor name would go down in dishonour to the grave', he would offer no defence but he would relate his actions which could speak for themselves.[22] The style of the autobiography is that of an ageing weakening mind, discursive with digressions, though it is not without flashes of the colourful pungent phrases which had made him the formidable orator who had thundered to vast receptive crowds in the great squares of Venice, Rome and Naples. Those generalisations of Gavazzi's introduction to his own account of his life need the framework of factual details to justify them. Since his autobiography is unpublished his other writings must be the basis for relating and understanding his life – this however would be a large undertaking. Robert Sylvain provides a most useful bibliography of books, pamphlets and fly-sheets by Gavazzi numbering 138, and more could be added to that number.[23] Further, there are in the library of the Facoltà Valdese at Rome eight volumes of newspaper cuttings of Gavazzi's speeches in England, the United States, and Canada, a volume of cuttings from L'Eco d'Italia, and another volume of newspaper cuttings called Memorie which contains further materials and a collection of Orations in England.[24] Again there are four accounts of Gavazzi's life, three published in the mid-nineteenth century, and the last in 1909, all written by men who knew him intimately and who used his personal anecdotes and letters.[25]

Well, ' 'tis sufficient to say according to the proverb that here is God's plenty'. However, Sylvain's full-scale work, and the shorter but excellent life by Luigi Santini do not cover all the ground and

21 Cencetti, 158: . . . che chi è nato cattolico deve morire cattolico . . . perchè io tornai alla religione vera dei Padri Italiani, di cui essi cattolici non sono che antifrati di apostasia . . .

22 Ibid., 159.

23 Although Sylvain worked at the library of the Facoltà Valdese at Rome, he seems to have overlooked some of Gavazzi's pamphlets that are available there.

24 L'Eco d'Italia was an Italian newspaper for immigrants to New York, edited by Gavazzi's friend Secchi de Casali.

25 Two are short admiring accounts – G. B. Nicolini (not to be confused with the neo-ghibelline writer G. B. Niccolini): The Life of Father A. Gavazzi, Chief Chaplain to the Roman Army of Independence, Edinburgh, 1851. This was reissued at New York 'continued to the time of his visit to America', 1854. This bibliographical point is not noticed by Sylvain, in his admirable bibliography, 526. G. M. Campanella, Life of Father Gavazzi, London, 1851: Campanella was also a friar who had left Catholicism for exile and Protestantism and who also wrote and published an interesting autobiography cited below, n. 60. The other two lives by men who knew Gavazzi are that of Conti in Italian already mentioned above, and the Life of Alessandro Gavazzi by J. W. King, London, 1857, which contains first-hand reports of Gavazzi's recollections of his life before he came to England as well as extracts from letters of Gavazzi and King used below.

leave a number of questions unanswered.[26] Usefully, Sylvain pointed out in his preface that in his work he intended to fill an obvious gap in Canadian and American historiography; further he apparently felt it necessary to analyse once again the myth that Pius IX could be seen as a potential head of the movement for Italian unification, and that the explanation must be made once again that Pius IX was the spiritual head of all Catholics, whether they were Italian or not without analysing the religious background of the Risorgimento. Sylvain rightly gave considerable space to the American and Canadian visits of Gavazzi for this had not been done before. He set these visits against the background of the appearance of the American 'know-nothing' anti-Catholic movement, and he described in detail the background of Catholic history in Canada against which he set the meetings of Gavazzi in Quebec and Montreal which caused serious riots, and also showed how Gavazzi, on returning to the United States, helped to cause the ignominious flight of the pontifical delegate Msgr. Gaetano Bedini.[27] He also gave in full the argument, traditional even to the extent of being well-worn, in defence of *Pio Nono* and his stand against the Risorgimento. By comparison Sylvain gave little space to Gavazzi's exile in England, and since he wrote more in sorrow than in anger about Gavazzi's apostasy, he still left open unanswered questions about the crisis of conscience created by the Pope's opposition to yielding an inch of his temporal power. Santini's life is half the length of Sylvain's, since he wrote to a shorter perspective, and is generously sympathetic, but the period of the English exile of Gavazzi is written more factually than analytically, a statement which would also cover his account of Gavazzi's activities in the Roman period 1847–9. Both authors omit matters of importance. Why did Sylvain, who had studied at the British Museum and also examined the volumes of British newspaper cuttings in the library of the Facoltà Valdese at Rome, not inquire into the impact of Gavazzi's lectures in Britain? Why did he not ask who sponsored them, who supported him by their presence on his platforms, why did Gavazzi revisit certain towns more frequently than others, and were there riots there as in Ireland and in Canada? Why do both Sylvain and Santini almost ignore Gavazzi's attitude to

[26] Luigi Santini, *Alessandro Gavazzi (Aspetti del problema religioso del Risorgimento)*, Collezione storica del Risorgimento Italiano, 2, serie 3, Modena, 1955.

[27] Volume 2 of Sylvain's work, the pages of which are numbered consecutively from volume 1, contains from 287 to 442 (the remainder of the volume of text is completed by 511) very detailed accounts of Gavazzi's visits to the USA and Canada, with much useful material on the history of Roman Catholicism in those countries. Sylvain, while objective and fair, writes in the manner of Catholic historians before the second Vatican Council – this insistently apologetic stance is occasionally wearing on the reader.

Mazzini and his ideas and make hardly any reference to the possible influence on him of Rossini, Gioberti and others? On the question why Gavazzi became a Barnabite friar the answer may not be known, but Sylvain concluded that he made his vows at sixteen without a true religious vocation because Gavazzi said in 1858 that, 'claustral vows are a sacrilegious attack on individual liberty and amount to moral suicide'.[28] On this basis one could argue, and scholars both Protestant and Catholic have done so, that Luther, who also denounced monastic vows later in life, never had a true vocation for it. This unjustly poses a doubt on a man's integrity from the beginning.

Giacomo Leopardi in one of his *Pensieri* wrote, 'the years of childhood are in the memory of every man, the fabulous years of his life; as in a nation's memories the fabulous years are those of that nation's youth'.[29] Surely, Gavazzi became a Barnabite friar after education in one of the schools of the Order in his native city of Bologna (which was in the papal states) because like his friend and fellow-Barnabite Ugo Bassi who was to be a poet and martyr for Italian unity, he had deep religious feeling 'in the fabulous years' of his youth.[30] This is still true even if we allow that the friars saw in the boy Alessandro, described later by a contemporary as being a precocious boy both in his physical and intellectual development, talents which would be useful to their order. Again the influence of his mother must not be overlooked: he was her second son, she had twenty children by his father and four more from a second marriage and she survived to a healthy and indomitable old age, proud of her sons – all this argues that she was a woman of powerful character. The family were devout Catholics, and the fact that Gavazzi dedicated one book to his mother, using her name in the title, and also caused another book of his, in praise of a saint noted for almsgiving, to be

[28] Sylvain, I, 18, n. 23, quoting Gavazzi's *My Recollections of the Lives of the Last Four Popes*, London, 1858, 8–9.

[29] Iris Origo and John Heath-Stubbs, *Giacomo Leopardi* – selected prose and poetry – London, 1966, 195.

[30] Ugo Bassi (1801–59), Barnabite friar, poet, martyr in the struggle for Italian unity. In common with other men of the Risorgimento his career is the subject of controversy between anti-clerical writers and Catholics. He shared Gavazzi's religious background and training, and took part with him in the forties in impassioned speeches for the reunification of Italy. He had a more sensitive and reserved character than Gavazzi. He was executed by the Austrians and died a Catholic, though expelled from his Order shortly before his death. It was bitter reflection in exile on Bassi's treatment by the Pope and the Austrians, which led Gavazzi to deliver a funeral oration for his dead friend in London after which he began to turn from Catholicism. Information on the career in the Order of Barnabites of both Bassi and Gavazzi can be found in Giuseppe Boffito, *Scrittori barnabiti, o della Congregazione dei Chierici Regolari di San Paolo, 1533–1933, Biografia, Bibliografia, Iconografia*, 4 vols., Florence, 1933–37. An excellent Catholic account of Bassi's life is: G. F. de Ruggiero, *Il Padre Ugo Bassi*, Rome, 1936.

tastefully bound in leather with a label on the front cover: *Se io viva ancor eccone O Madre il segno*, then there must have been a close link between mother and son.[31] Again, on the subject of his becoming a Barnabite friar it is worth remembering that after he left the Order and became what he called a Catholic Christian – he always refused to call himself a Protestant which caused him some serious misunderstandings in exile – he maintained all his life two of his religious vows, namely, chastity (and though they tried hard enough no opponent could bring any calumny against him on this) and also poverty: in the first year of exile he came near to starvation, and all his life he gave to charities, and showed little worldly calculation in money matters.

When the congregation of clerks regular of St Paul named Barnabites were founded in 1533 (a small Order mostly confined to Italy), one of its declared aims was 'reform of the clergy and other social groups', though there is no evidence that Gavazzi obtained the basis of his later social conscience from his early Barnabite training.[32] What he would have to undertake as part of his rule was study of the Pauline epistles, education and mission work. In 1825 he travelled to the house of his Order in Naples, a journey which impressed itself on his adolescent memory which revived again in 1858 when he described his horror on entering the beggar-ridden misery of the region outside of Rome.[33] On his early studies his later comment in 1864 was that the papacy required seminarists, 'to be deep in the legends of the saints and in blaspheming liberty'.[34] How this word 'liberty' recurs among the men of the Risorgimento! Conrad's *garibaldino* in far South America looked at the portrait of Garibaldi and muttered: 'this was your liberty: it gave you not only life but immortality as well.'[35] Obviously Gavazzi's phrase is an inadequate

[31] *Il beato Giacomo Elemosinario Panegirico del P. Alessandro Gavazzi, Barnabita di Bologna*, Orvieto, 1844. This book was well-printed on fine paper. The copy in the library of the Facoltà Valdese is bound in leather and the words cited are on the front cover printed on a leather label. Presumably after his mother's death Gavazzi placed it in his own libary. For some time after the second world war, many books of Gavazzi's libary were in the possession of the Methodist church which took over Gavazzi's house and church (v. below, 363). A Methodist minister the Reverend R. Kissack who for a period lived in Gavazzi's former house at Rome, told me that among books given to Gavazzi, was one from W. S. Landor. That Gavazzi attracted the attention of Victorian English men of letters should not be overlooked in assessing his achievements, v. n. 111 below.

[32] Boffito 1 and 2.

[33] *My Recollections*, 10; again, on the squalor of the poorer districts of Rome, 232.

[34] Gavazzi, *A mio padre Angelico, lettera*, Pistoia, 1864, 22, cited in Santini, 17, who states that Gavazzi was not alone in this protest. Rosmini and others made similar though less pungent criticisms.

[35] Conrad, op. cit. 21.

description of seminary training among the Barnabites. For example, the Barnabite friar Luigi Lambruschini at the age of twenty-three taught classical literature, philosophy, mathematics, dogmatic and moral theology, Greek and Hebrew. He was either another *doctor mirabilis* or the depth and originality of his courses were rather shallow; nevertheless the subjects went beyond Gavazzi's minimising, and Lambruschini became distinguished as a cardinal and secretary of state at Rome.[36] The year after Gavazzi entered the Barnabite house at Naples his father, who had been a professor of law at the university of Bologna, died. Gavazzi, perhaps to be near his widowed mother and her other children, was moved to the Barnabite house at Marsa near Bologna, from which he frequently visited his family. He now began to study oratory in the frigid and florid style of the period. In 1829 on his way back to Naples he passed though Rome where Leo XII had just died and, as Gavazzi wrote later, like a 'fanatical papist' (although at the time it was an act of a devout friar) he kissed the slippered foot of the corpse with veneration.[37]

At Naples where he taught in the Barnabite college he published some poems in 1830, which show a young man's desire to burst into print rather than any taste or talent. He was ordained priest in 1832 and moved to various houses of the Order, and in Alessandria in Piedmont in 1833 he founded the friendship with Ugo Bassi which lasted until Bassi was shot by Austrian troops after the 'crusade'. In 1836 Gavazzi was becoming known as a preacher of talent, as was Bassi a little later. Both men were innovators as preachers; they imitated the new style of preaching that was introduced in France in Lamennais' time, popular in appeal in the attempt to restore Catholicism after the revolutionary destruction of so much in French Catholic life. This new style involved using loud and soft changes of voice, and strenuous gestures, and here too possibly lay the origin of Gavazzi's later theatrical style of oratory though his temperament would draw him strongly to theatricality. Further, this change suggests that Bassi and Gavazzi may have known something of the views of Lamennais and his followers.

Gavazzi was invited to preach the lenten course of sermons in the great Frari church in Venice. However, the Austrian police refused him permission to enter their territory. This is the first indication that Gavazzi might be something more than a devout Barnabite whose

[36] He should not be confused with Raffaele Lambruschini one of the strongest supporters of the movement for reform in the Catholic Church. For Luigi Lambruschini's lecturing programme, see Santini, 17 n. 6.
[37] *My Recollections*, 81.

sole concern was piety. Protestants are accused of seeing Jesuit intrigues everywhere, but Catholics have not been averse to this either: it must be stated, nevertheless, that jealousy existed between the Jesuits and the Barnabites and that the Jesuits were particularly supporters of political legitimism, opponents of liberalism, and became increasingly powerful at Rome in the reign of Gregory XVI (1831–46) and in the reign of Pius IX, especially after his return to Rome in 1850. The strongest supporter of the Jesuits in Piedmont was the foreign minister, Count Solaro della Margarita, and he had caused the police to prevent Bassi from preaching a lenten course in Turin: perhaps the Count had passed a hint about Gavazzi to the Austrian police at Venice.[38] The king of Piedmont grumbled incidentally that his life was poised between the daggers of the *carbonari* and the chocolate of the Jesuits.

Of this period Gavazzi left no recollections later save to complain of the bad Latinity of the Order whose 'stupid systems' he said, 'absorbed the best years of our youth.'[39] In 1839 and 1840 he published a few small works of piety and some more tedious poetry – it is unfortunate that it is so easy to string verses together in Italian. However, it was a poem which brought him his first real challenge from governmental authority. It was a sententious effort on the unpoetic subject of a steam-boat setting forth to steam from Turin to Venice; and it was issued during the second Italian scientific congress which happened to be meeting in Turin.[40] Consciously or unconsciously the ebullient Gavazzi by issuing this poem at the time was in effect taking a nationalist attitude, for the members of the scientific congress were hostile to the repressive governments in Italy. That Metternich of Italian conservatives, Count Solaro della Margarita, had stated that, 'science and art were only the apparent pretext of the Congresses; their true aim was an Italian revolution'.[41] This hostile judgement was shared by Lambruschini and also the contemporary pope, Gregory XVI, who refused to allow railways and gas lighting into the

[38] Count Solaro della Margarita wished to write a history of Italy to defend his position, which was that of leader of the Piedmontese clericals opposed to all liberalism. See Maturi, 228, 229. Against Gioberti's *Gesuito moderno* he believed that opposition to the Jesuits was 'war on governments, religion and God'. Sylvain, 42.

[39] Gavazzi's comment appeared in *L'Eco d'Italia* (New York, 7 January 1854). Santini, 17, notes that Adolfo Omedeo in his *Le Missioni di riconquista cattolica nella Francia nella restaurazione, (Aspetti del cattolicesimo della restaurazione)* (Turin, 1946) points to the poor training of the clergy at this period.

[40] *Cenni sul battello a vapore che per primo partirà da Torino per Venezia, coll'aggiunta di una poesia sullo stesso soggetto*, Turin, 1840.

[41] Solaro della Margarita, *Memorandum storico-politico*, Turin, 1930, 138: 'Io avversai fin dall'alba queste congreghe tanto applaudite' because he knew that 'scienza e arte non essere che il pretesto apparente, il vero fine la rivoluzione italiana'.

papal states on the grounds that revolutionary views travelled by rail and, presumably, they could be more clearly illuminated by gas-light.[42] Moreover Gregory, wiser than the Piedmontese, refused to allow the Italian scientific congress to meet in any town of the papal states. Gavazzi made more trouble for himself in Piedmont by preaching powerfully in favour of orphanages for the lost children of the streets. This gave offence to the Jesuits who disapproved of these orphanages because they had been invented by foreigners who were probably Protestants. So Gavazzi was moved to Parma, somewhat under a cloud.

Since his preaching seemed too stirring he was appointed as chaplain to the male and female prisons in Parma (which would confine his oratory to the narrow limits of prison walls), where he found the conditions to be appalling. His attention was fully focused now on social questions and he published a booklet *Le Carceri* which showed compassionate sympathy for the harsh lives of he prisoners, their inability to find work after their sentences expired, and the tragic destitution of their families. Further, he published a book of devotions for prisoners, *L'Amico dei carceri* in 1844, which among other things stressed that prisoners could better endure their lot by living in the grace and fear of God, and that sanctification could be achieved by viewing the life of a prisoner as a life similar to that of a Christian martyr of the first centuries of the Church. There is no question that the Barnabite Gavazzi was a fully committed priest of apostolic life and conviction. He crowned this period by writing a book on the recorded sayings of the founder of the Barnabite Order, Zaccaria, accompanied by a brief life of him. He even offered himself for missionary work in Burmah but this was not taken up, and a memoir on the necessity of foreign missions which he prepared for the chapter general of his Order still survives in their archives.[43] At

---

[42] Fredrik Nielsen, *The History of the Papacy in the nineteenth century*, London, 1906, 2, 75: 'The moderate Liberalism which desired that the papacy should accommodate itself to modern times, was in his eyes [Cardinal Lambruschini] as dangerous as the revolutionary ideas of Mazzini; and the new Secretary of State [Lambruschini] regarded lighting by gas, railways and scientific congresses with as much suspicion as Liberalism.' However, it was Gregory XVI himself who opposed gas and railways. See *Gregorio XVI: Miscellanea Commemorativa*, part 2, Roma, 1948, 343. Also G. Gioacchino Belli, in his *Sonnetti Romaneschi*, dialect verses which show the dislike of the Romans for Gregory's administration (v. below, 361 and n. 140), has a poem on the subject of Gregory after death wanting to go to heaven; eventually he arrives there and meets St. Peter who asks him: 'How long was the journey?' 'A month' replied Gregory. 'Why so long?' asks St Peter. Gregory replies: 'Ben ti sta' gli soggiunse, poteri fare la strada ferrata e a quest'ora saresti già arrivato.'

[43] *Sulle missioni straniere*, submitted for the consideration of the chapter general in 1844. It consists of twelve quarto sheets, and is now in the archives of the Barnabites at Rome. To the credit of Gregory XVI it should be stated that he 'dedico viva attenzione alle missioni', for

Orvieto in papal territory, he preached a panegyric on the local saint and almsgiver *Il Beato Giacomo Elemosinario* which he published in 1844. Perhaps Gavazzi intended to show the innocuousness of his preaching: it is certainly a dull exercise in that traditional Italian rhetorical style which was carried over from the eighteenth century.[44] It was a copy of this book which Gavazzi caused to be bound and provided with the inscription to his mother, referred to above, which can now be seen in the library of the Facoltà Valdese at Rome. In 1845 at Perugia he showed a rapid change of style for he preached a lenten course which aroused such admiration that a pamphlet was published cordially entitled *Omaggio di publica ammirazione e gratitudine all'esimio sacro oratore padre Alessandro Gavazzi*.[45] From this it appears that Gavazzi had preached on Christian matrimony, denounced the growth of luxury and effeminacy of manners and even rebuked the use of tobacco. Police spies were everywhere in Italy and the police chief, Nardoni, reported to the governor of Rome that Gavazzi had said some imprudent things. Gavazzi knew nothing of this report and, carried away by the popular enthusiasm he was creating, he turned a sermon intended in praise of the miraculous madonna at Ancona into an impassioned attack on the sorrows of Italy and Italians, divided and oppressed by foreigners. The fact that the miracle of the madonna of Ancona had consisted in her moving her eyes to warn people of the approach of French troops in the Napoleonic period, while it gave the ground for Gavazzi's observations, did not prevent the anger of the consuls of Austria and Naples.[46] Gavazzi was slipping even nearer to speaking out for the Risorgimento. Before long he was called to Rome by the order of Pope Gregory XVI, *ad audiendum verbum*. He went to Rome to the house of his Order, and from there, being forbidden to preach, he was sent to the novice

example, he increased the number of vicars apostolic in China – see K. Bihlmeyer and H. Tuechle, *Storia della Chiesa*, Italian translation by Igino Rogger, Brescia, 1962, 4, 149, and also section 206 – though 'viva attenzione' is overstated.
[44] This book has been described above, n. 31. A characteristic passge is: E insiemente che ei possa ascoltato esaudito perorare in pro vostro, ve lo accertino le sue ferite sostenute per amor di giustizia, e che in lui sono come meriti messi d'altri maggiori privilegi; sicurando Agostino che esse sono nel martire altrettanto valevoli bocche a chieder grazie, ad ottenere favori. E non vorrà proteggervi? Troppo vorrà. Giacchè chi meglio di esso si può conoscere di voi? Al vostro Giacomo è cognita l'aura di questo cielo, l'aspetto di questa natura, il suono di questa favella: i consapevoli colli della sua infanzia, il dolce loco che lo raccolse bambino, il focolare di sua paterna casa a lui sono noti: palpita in quel suo caldissimo petto un cuore pievese: egli è il naturale patrono della sua patria. (28–9).
[45] Perugia, 1845. Lodolini, gives illustrative materials from the *Archivio di Stato di Roma*, Direzione Generale di Polizia, anno 1847, Padre Alessandro Gavazzi, Busta 266. The chief of papal police, Nardoni, when reporting Gavazzi's attacks considered his sermon nevertheless to be 'sublime preaching'. v. Lodolini, 436.
[46] Lodolini, 437.

house at San Severino Marche in Umbria, a region *malonconiche e sinistre*.[47] So he took up his pen again and wrote a book of religious exercises, 1846, and no doubt brooded over his dislike for Gregory XVI on whom he was to make a most embittered attack in England in 1858.[48]

The death of Gregory and the election of Cardinal Mastai-Ferretti as the new Pope, came some months later; both events were met with enthusiasm by liberals – Gregory had at first refused to make Giovanni Mastai-Ferretti a cardinal, because he said 'in the house of Mastai even the cats were liberal'.[49] Gavazzi benefited from the new Pope's amnesty, wrote an enthusiastic set of verses to Pius IX and published them at Parma.[50] Gavazzi began preaching again, this occasion was at the funeral of the gloomy and reactionary Count Maldonado Leopardi, who had contemptuously dismissed the writings of his son Giacomo, today regarded as one of the finest of Italian poets. The family were scandalised as Gavazzi held forth on the bad education of the nobles of the count's generation. If Giacomo Leopardi had survived he would have been sardonically amused at the denunciation given to that political bigotry of his father which had darkened his youth.[51] Unstoppable now that he had found his stride, Gavazzi, in the cathedral of Senigaglia (the town where the new Pope's family had long resided, and where Pius's father was a count and gonfaloniere) preached an impassioned address to commemorate the birthday of Pius IX which was published about the same time as a new edition of the poems to Pius he had written earlier.[52] The volume, luxuriously bound, was presented to Pius by his younger brother Count Giuseppe Mastai who knew

---

[47] See L. Gualtieri, *Memorie di Ugo Bassi, Apostolo del Vangelo, Martire del'independenza Italiana*, Bologna, 1861, 49, for a description of this grim remote monastery in Umbria where in 'solitude and silence' both Bassi and Gavazzi at different periods were confined as a penance for politically dangerous preaching.

[48] *My Recollections*, 273 ff.

[49] Nielsen, 2, 114.

[50] *Pio IX Pontifice Massimo. Tributo di affetti di A. Gavazzi, Bolognese*, Florence, 1846. Two specially bound copies were presented in turn to count Mastai and later the Pope. Among other emotional declarations in these poems is the following: 'Io amo Pio l'amo dell'amore onde si ama Dio senza limiti, senza misure, senza ragioni, tutto virilità e caldezza ...' Santini, 39.

[51] 'Paternal power, in every law-abiding country, brings about a kind of children's slavery, more stringent, because it is more domestic, and more oppressive than any law, and which ... can never fail to produce a most damaging effect ...' Giacomo Leopardi, II. Gavazzi's sermon at the Count's funeral was published, *Nel funere del Conte Monaldo Leopardi, parole del p. Alessandro Gavazzi, Barnabita bolognese*, Loreto, 1847.

[52] *Il genetliaco di Pio IX Pontefice Massimo. Discorso del P. Alessandro Gavazzi, Barnabita bolognese, recitato nel Duomo di Senigaglia, il 13 maggio 1847*, Senigaglia, 1847. *Il busto di Pio Nono donata dai Romani ai Bolognese, Epigrafia e sonnetti di Alessandro Gavazzi*, Rome, 1847.

Gavazzi. Gavazzi had not finished with the praises of Pius yet; for in the church of the virgins at Macerata he preached with immense verve a sermon on the subject of 'Mary and Pius IX', but Gavazzi quickly dismissed the needs of the Virgin, 'since she was so well-beloved she needed no special sermon, whereas there was real need to praise unreservedly Pius IX who was bringing in a new life to the Church', a fact Gavazzi helped forward by denouncing once again Gregory, the new Pope's predecessor. The crowd in the packed church verged on the sacrilegious by applauding with wild enthusiasm. The papal legate, overwhelmed as much by the obvious political appeal of the sermon as by the thunderous applause it occasioned, wrote to the Barnabite cardinal who was Bishop of Ancona, who in turn wrote to the General of the Order at Rome, stating that Gavazzi's democratic eloquence passed all limits and even censured governments: he admitted it was true that Gavazzi was a man of talent, well-informed, and of ardent temperament, but in need of restraint – so it would be better if Gavazzi could be called back to Rome.

He arrived in Rome in May 1847 and now began what he wrote of later as the first great period of his life. He found the people in a state of intense excitement, and after seeking through Count Giuseppe Mastai an audience with the Pope, obtained it. His heart, 'bursting with joy', he was about to kneel and kiss the Pope's slippered foot, but with gracious condescension Pius gestured him to leave this and offered Gavazzi the fisherman's ring to kiss. They spoke to each other for about half an hour with great cordiality and probably complete mutual misunderstanding. Gavazzi was carried away by the well-known charm of Pius and saw before him the Pope who would renew the Church and set himself at the head of a league of Italian states if not a united Italy. Pius saw an over-enthusiastic friar who had a great popular following, and who, if his oratory could be tamed, would be a useful instrument of papal support. Pius smiled and asked Gavazzi whether he had been applauded in a church. The reply was quick-minded, and parried an implicit reprimand: 'No, they did not applaud me most holy Father, they applauded what was said of you'. Pius laughed and the audience continued in which the Pope admired the talents of Gavazzi's fellow Barnabite, Ugo Bassi, and ended apparently with the command that Gavazzi was not to preach again on nationalism or political subjects.[53]

---

[53] Gavazzi related this interview in his *Autobiografia*, according to Sylvain who translated some sentences from this conversation. Gavazzi also related the interview in *The Lectures Complete of Father Gavazzi as Delivered in New York*, ed. G. B. Nicolini, New York, 1854, 259–60.

Gavazzi had not, however, suffered a severe check for he was appointed as assistant priest in a Barnabite church in Rome. When the first anniversary of Pius arrived, a crowd of fifty thousand with banners waving and bands playing marched to the Quirinal palace to receive the papal benediction. On that evening Gavazzi preached to a vast crowd in the baths of Diocletian, a panegyric on Pius which lasted for an hour and a half and was followed by the *Te Deum* and enthusiastic applause.

Events in Rome were moving fast towards political confrontation between the papal government and popular democratic groups. Gavazzi indiscreetly chose at this point to preach a politically based sermon denouncing once more the evils of Gregory's pontificate and calling for liberal leadership from Pius IX. Because of this, and the extreme political tension at this time his superiors once again forbade him to preach. Later, during his exile, Gavazzi claimed that it was Pius himself who had put him under this interdiction. In January 1848 soldiers of the Austrian general, Radetsky, killed a number of citizens in Milan and elsewhere in Lombardy during the risings that year.[54] In spite of the interdiction, Gavazzi took the pulpit in the former Pantheon and with deep emotion urged the Romans to avenge the Lombards who had died for Italy under the accursed Austrians, and he repeated a similar outburst to the students in the chapel of the university. For this he was confined to a monastery near Rome, but the students found out where he had been placed, came out in force, serenaded him,and drew him in a carriage back to Rome. Once again Gavazzi passionately exhorted the Romans to go to the aid of the Lombards, speaking from the carriage; and his fiery oratory continued to its peak at the Colosseum with an appeal for volunteers for a 'holy war', indeed a new crusade.[55] On that day large numbers of Roman citizens began to take action in the drama of the regeneration of Italy. Pio Nono, reluctant but smiling, gave his blessing to the newly enrolled troops who gathered in the Vatican gardens in March 1848. He made Gavazzi chaplain general and he even had to endure the sight of the tri-coloured badge on Gavazzi's Barnabite habit, excused on the dubious ground that it represented the colours of an Italian religious Order. Once again the Pope and Gavazzi were at cross-purposes: Gavazzi wanted to take part in a

---

[54] G. F-H. and J. Berkeley, *Italy in the Making January 1st 1848 to November 16th 1848*, Cambridge, 1940. The troubles began on 3 January in Milan, known as 'I Lutti di Lombardia'.

[55] This was called afterwards the opening of *il dramma della regenerazione d'Italia*; Gavazzi addressed a crowd of 40,000 calling for a *guerra santa*. Cardinal Manning was present and described the impression this vast passionate crowd made on him. E. S. Purcell, *Life of Cardinal Manning*, I, 374–5.

crusade to throw the Austrians out of Italy, whereas the Pope ordered Durando, the general of the papal troops, not to cross the Po but merely to defend papal territory if it were attacked.[56] The papal army marched northwards and four of Gavazzi's brothers marched with its chaplain general. At each stage of the march Gavazzi preached encouragingly to the troops and was heard with special enthusiasm in his native Bologna. At Parma he addressed huge crowds and brought in numbers of new recruits. From now on he began to be known as 'the new Peter the Hermit'. One who heard him preach said, 'He who did not hear Gavazzi that day failed to hear eloquence never heard before'.[57] Gavazzi's themes were not only nationalist but also were concerned with the indifference of the rich to the poor, and attacked those whom he regarded as reactionary nobles and the conservative-minded clergy.

The Pope feared that he was losing control of the situation, that there might be revolt in the papal states, that his troops might be involved in war with Austria, and that the international character of

[56] This was the agonising dilemma for Pius IX – he had not intended attack by his troops on the Austrians, but he must have known that once the enflamed patriotic youth of his states had marched, they could not sit down at the frontier and do nothing to help the Piedmontese. In any event he had placed the command of his army ultimately under orders from the king of Piedmont. But Pius had not formally declared war, and there was the possibility of his troops, if an attack commenced, being captured and shot out of hand as *franc-tireurs* by the Austrians. The Piedmontese and their supporters elsewhere in Italy including those in the papal states were determined to draw Pius into supporting the war on Austria. Massimo d'Azeglio, the Piedmontese writer and politician, who had been appointed adjutant general to Durando, had a clear eye for the position and issued an order of the day on 5 April in the name of Pius which showed papal and Piedmontese troops as conducting a crusade against the barbarous Radetsky: Durando approved of this attitude and intended to carry out its implications. See chap. 9 *The papal difficulties*, in Berkeley, 153 ff. Nevertheless the difficulties which Pius IX felt did not turn him aside from the fundamental conviction that the papal states were inviolably his province as ruler. The Belgian ambassador at Rome, Van de Weyer, wrote to Leopold I, on 6 February 1859, (though this is a decade later, other evidence would bear out that the views of Pius had always been consistent on this point) citing a remark made by Pius IX to Odo Russell the British representative in Rome, who corresponded on Roman affairs with the Foreign Office (v. below n. 58): 'Quoiqu'il arrive ajoute le S. Père, je serai toujours pape; mais plutôt que de séculariser le gouvernement, je suis prêt à descendre aux catacombes, nouveau martyr de l'Eglise.' Archives Generales Royaume Bruxelles, Van de Weyer Papers, no. 124: cited in Aloïs Simon, *Palmerston et les Etats Pontificaux en 1849, Rassegna Storica del Risorgimento*, 43, Rome, 1956, 542. Simon added: 'En maintenant les Etats Pontificaux le Saint Siège voulait certes conserver certains droits acquis par l'histoire et surtout sauvegarder l'indépendence spirituelle du souverain pontife mais il avait aussi une nostalgie de la théocratie.' Ibid., 543.

[57] Luigi Gualtieri, *Memorie de Ugo Bassi, apostolo del Vangelo, martire della Indipendenza Italiana*, Bologna, 1861, 68–9. Sylvain regards Gualtieri as too much biased in favour of Gavazzi and Bassi, and states that he was responsible for some accepting too readily exaggerations about the circumstances of the death of Bassi which embittered Gavazzi and Garibaldi when these were reported to them verbally, and adds that Gualtieri's book was accepted too uncritically by G. M. Trevelyan in his *Garibaldi's Defence of the Roman Republic*, London, 1907, 308. Nevertheless, no effective help was given by Catholic prelates and clerical diplomats on Bassi's behalf, who it should be remembered was still a priest and had not carried arms.

the papacy would be lost if he could be seen as supporting a war to unite Italy. On the 29 April he delivered his allocution in which he declared that he abhorred war, had an equal affection for all peoples, that Austrians and Italians were fellow-Catholics, and that he had no intention of presiding over an Italian republic, rather, Italians must remain loyal and faithful to their respective legitimate sovereigns in Italy.[58] This open challenge caused great popular resentment against his government, and the allocution was seen by those who until then had looked to Pius to lead the movement for the regeneration of the nation and of the Church as turning his back on them and siding with anti-nationalist conservatism. It would be difficult to exaggerate the effect of what Pius had said. It conclusively showed that Pius was opposed to the Risorgimento.[59] Gavazzi was badly shaken by the allocution, and fell back on the view that the Pope had been

[58] The bitterness aroused by this allocution among Italian patriots is understandable because the papal declaration helped in the defeat of the Italians in 1848. It was in any case, as the events showed, fatal to the intention of Pius to preserve the temporal power. Patriots now saw that unity could only be achieved by challenging and overcoming papal rule in the papal states. Whether the danger of schism was as immediate and probable as Pius claimed is an open question. That his dilemma, however, was extremely difficult is plain: that his resolution of it and the way he became increasingly obstinate later in trying to repress the Risorgimento were wise is less plain. For the allocution see the Italian translation in L. C. Farini, *Lo stato romano dal anno 1815 al 1850*, 4 vols., Florence, 1853, 2, 92. The Pope in addressing German language Catholics claimed that considerable measures of reform had been under way in the papal states, therefore, since he was carrying out the advice of European governments, how could he be regarded as a revolutionary? How far Pius was effecting reforms can be seen from Odo Russell's despatches from Rome, *The Roman Question*, ed. N. Blakiston, London, 1962, which show how often Russell repeated the advice of the British government for the Pope to reform his administration, to the irritation of Pius, in the years 1858–70. Reform obviously meant different things to Palmerston, and his successors, and to Pius. Russell's report of the opinion of Pius on Italians is interesting: 'The Italians are a dissatisfied, interfering, turbulent, and intriguing race, they can never learn to govern themselves. It is impossible ... A hotheaded people like the Italians require a firm and just government to guide and take care of them ...' Russell's reply, exemplifying the lack of justice, led Pius only to smile and take snuff, 37.

The second part of the allocution was addressed to Italians stating that Pius could not prevent volunteers from among his subjects fighting for Italy, but he had not declared war since he represented on earth the author of peace, and that his duty as sovereign pontiff was to show equal paternal love to all peoples. In the third part of his allocution he vigorously rejected the idea that he could preside over an Italian republic, rather Italians should remain loyal to their legitimate sovereigns – these included the Austrians: the point that embittered Gavazzi and Italian patriots generally.

[59] 'Thus vanished the dream of Gioberti.' A. M. Ghisalberti published the letters of Count de Liederkerke de Beaufort to the Belgian government in two differently titled books: from the second, *Rapporti delli cose di Roma (1848–1849)*, Rome, 1949, Sylvain cites this quotation I p. 327. For Gioberti v. below, 340–4. The count's letters, like those of other despatches from foreign ambassadors or government representatives at Rome, including those of Odo Russell, give more objective reports on the events and attitudes of the time than those of the participants. The violent emotional reaction of the patriots of the papal states helped to plunge Rome into revolution against the Pope. Within a few days of the allocution the papal government was losing control: the political clubs (*Circoli*) and the civic guard began to take over, Berkeley 3, 185.

manipulated by the curia and the Jesuits. The papal army pushed on to Venice and its chaplain-general Gavazzi made heroic speeches in the piazza San Marco, though his views on the needs of the poor alienated the Venetian leader Daniele Manin. The papal troops marched back to Treviso and formed the right wing of the Piedmontese army in an unavailing attack on the Austrians. Gavazzi, using his great physical strength, was prominent in rescuing wounded soldiers while under heavy fire.[60] The Neapolitan troops withdrew to Naples, and the joint Italian army thus weakened was defeated at Vicenza.

The impact of these experiences turned Gavazzi into a political orator. He felt a bitter sense of betrayal – the betrayal of the ideal of 'the crusade', betrayal by the Neapolitans, and betrayal by the Pope. He became a man 'for the people' (here he meant the supporters of an orderly liberal progress to unite Italy, not revolutionaries), and for 'Italians of faithful hearts': these could be trusted, but not princes, not politicians, not the Pope.[61] The police of the papal states were ordered to arrest him, but they feared to do so in his native Bologna to which he had now returned. He moved on to Tuscany and then to Milan. In July the general of the Barnabite Order sent out rescripts of secularisation for both Gavazzi and Bassi. Insubordination and immorality would have been grounds for this but the latter was untrue, so presumably the charge essentially was that they had gone beyond their office as religious in taking part in political demonstrations. Gavazzi never received the rescript in person, and by now had come to believe that the Barnabite general had been pushed into issuing it by Pius who wished to conciliate the Austrians at any price. Cardinal Oppizoni, the Archbishop of Bologna, was

---

[60] Santini reports, 63 n. 30, a letter sent from Venice to Gavazzi's mother by three of her sons, Giovanni (a colonel of volunteers), Paolo (a sergeant-major) and Alessandro, describing their safety after the battle of Treviso, to be found in the appendix to G. Zaccagnini, *Pistoia durante il Risorgimento nazionale*, Pistoia, 1940. G. B. Nicolini in his *Lectures Completes*, who was present at the battle describes Carlo, another brother of Gavazzi, shouting to Alessandro not to expose himself to the storm of Austrian bullets but to shelter with him behind a tree: but Gavazzi ignored him and carried wounded men under fire to the ambulances. In his *Autobiografia*, in the section on the battle of Treviso, printed by Cencetti, Gavazzi does not refer to himself but he describes with pride how a troop of *miei Voluntarii* charged up a steep valley against the Austrian guns which was a *preludio gloriossimo di quella di Balaklava in Crimea sotto la guida di Lord Cardigan*, 167. Another brother of Gavazzi, Pietro, a doctor served in this campaign as an army surgeon. G. M. Campanella, *Life in the cloiser in the Papal court and in Exile: an Autobiography*, London, 1877, see above n. 25, wrote in the appendix (p. 9) that he visited Gavazzi's mother in Bologna in 1848 – she 'was truly one of the strong women of ancient times . . . inflamed with the love of country. She told us how all her five sons had exposed themselves bravely against the foreigner . . . the mother was truly worthy of such sons'.

[61] Sylvain, I, 174, 175, translates a passage from Gavazzi's, *L'Italia inerme e accattona*, p. 45, demonstrating this.

embarrassed when he interviewed Gavazzi, who had returned to Bologna to quieten the wilder citizens, and did not show him the rescript. Gavazzi wrote later: 'It was not that we had betrayed our vows [when Bassi and he were ejected from their Order] it was because of the apostasy of the pontiff to the cause of Italy.'[62] Increasingly now Gavazzi was concerned with the rights of the people, not as a demagogue of revolution, but as a man deeply offended by the neglect of the poor, and the failure to provide pensions for those disabled in the struggle to free Italy from foreign rule. Garibaldi had now landed at Nice and was poised ready with his gathering legion to commence the struggle. He came to Bologna and Gavazzi and Garibaldi addressed in turn, from the hotel balcony of the most impressive hotel in the city, a great crowd which had gathered to welcome the guerrilla leader.[63] It had been assumed with some probability that Gavazzi persuaded Garibaldi not to march with his legion against the Austrians who were gathered around Venice, but to remain in the papal states since significant changes might occur there.[64] The Pope's response to Gavazzi's welcome to Garibaldi was to write to Cardinal Amat, the papal legate at Bologna, that Gavazzi should be arrested forthwith and placed in a lunatic asylum.[65] The problem was to find someone who could effectively fulfil this order. Not for the first or last time in his life, Gavazzi when presented by a hostile attack was prepared to defend himself by force. He snatched up a large knife from the refectory table of the Barnabite house when the police came at night to take him, until the Barnabite superior, his former teacher, persuaded the police to withdraw from their sacrilegious assault in a conventual building. 'Death before prison', Gavazzi had shouted when the police pursued him into the refectory.[66] It can easily be seen why Garibaldi, always suspicious of priests, made Gavazzi chaplain to his forces: he accepted and doubtless preferred not Gavazzi's too ready rhetoric on the piazzas, but the bold fortitude (which his legionaries would respect) of a priest who

[62] Sylvain I, 175.

[63] Cencetti, 169. Also see *Un Esperimento*, number 8, *Garibaldi a Bologna*, an enthusiastic article by Gavazzi describing the scene at the hotel. This journal by Gavazzi ran for eight numbers, 17 October to 11 November 1848, Bologna. (Library of Facoltà Valdese, Rome.)

[64] Ermana Loevinson, *Garibaldi e la sua legione nello Statto Romano*, 3 vols., Rome, 1902–7, I, II. Holding back Garibaldi and his legion near to Rome was of fundamental importance, and Gavazzi was the most probable influence in this. Also v. T. Casini, *Garibaldi nell'Emilia, Archivio Emiliano*, Modena, 1907, 182.

[65] *Epistolario di Luigi Carlo Farini*, ed Luigi Rava, 4 vols, Bologna 1911–35, 2, 668, for the Pope's demand to Cardinal Amat; also see M. Minghetti, *Miei Ricordi*, 3 vols, Turin, 1889–90, 2, 398. These references are cited by Sylvain, who is better on the literature favourable to the clerical interpretation of these events than with that of the men of the Risorgimento.

[66] Cencetti, 171, '. . . che morte si, ma giammai mi avrebbero avuto prigione.'

had shown that he really meant what for romantic revolutionaries was no more than a melodramatic slogan: 'Give me liberty or give me death'.[67] Now the Pope authorised general Zucchi at Bologna to take Gavazzi by force even from a sacred conventual building in contravention of canon law. Zucchi arrested Gavazzi with a troop of solders and gave orders for him to be removed to the prison for immoral priests at Corneto. But the armed troop, while eating at an inn at Viterbo the following night, with Gavazzi under guard, were challenged by the civic guard there, some of whom had served in 'the crusade' and recognised not a shame-faced broken priest but their former chaplain general. The civic guard took him from Zucchi's men and Gavazzi celebrated his release at a public banquet in Viterbo – and, inevitably, made a lengthy after dinner speech.[68]

What he had apparently foreseen and warned Garibaldi to expect had now taken place. Papal authority was challenged at Rome: the moderate Rossi, who was trying to introduce a form of representative government at Rome, was murdered. Faced by revolution Pius fled disguised to Gaeta in the Neapolitan kingdom. Garibaldi came with his legion and Gavazzi also entered Rome, and his arm in Garibaldi's walked through cheering crowds who, like himself, expected a brave new world to be born.[69] Garibaldi, more down to earth, wary of Mazzini's dreams of a *Respublica Romana* restored, and aware of the dangers of foreign intervention especially that of a French army, prepared for the attack. Gavazzi was appointed chaplain and organiser of ambulances for the Roman troops of the recently proclaimed republic. He was now, while still a priest, fully committed as a

[67] Garibaldi in his *Memorie Autobiografiche* Florence, 1888, does not write directly of Gavazzi – there are many omissions of persons in this collection of not over-articulate reflections – but various contemporary writers and journalists show that Garibaldi respected Gavazzi's courage and appointed him more than once as chaplain and organiser of ambulances. Moreover, he was glad of Gavazzi's aid in Naples and elsewhere as one who could enhearten his soldiers and obtain popular support by his irresistible oratory. The slogan originated with the American, Patrick Henry: it had a more literal meaning for many young Italians who died believing it, than for Henry's more cautious hearers.

[68] The Bishop of Montefiascone and Corneto was deeply alarmed at the prospect of Gavazzi being incarcerated in the 'Ergastulum' for immoral priests, since he was sure distubances would occur, but the papal administration was now in disarray after the murder of Rossi. A. Zappoli, *L'arresto di Padre Gavazzi*, an article in *La Constituente*, 25 November 1848. Sylvain cites here G. Natali, *Il padre Gavazzi e l'entrata di Garibaldi nello Stato Pontifico* in *Il Commune di Bologna*, 21 (1934).

[69] The prominence of Gavazzi at this stage is shown by the fact that it was he who after assisting at mass on easter Sunday in St Peter's, blessed the crowd with the blessed sacrament from the vatican loggia. He wrote: 'Io feci benedire il popolo dalla gran loggia Vaticana nel giorno di Pasqua col Santissimo Sacramento.' (*Eco d'Italia*, 1 October 1853.) The mass at St Peter's was sung by a Piedmontese priest who had been inhibited for supporting the Risorgimento. To usurp thus the privileged papal altar was a sacrilege which seems not to have worried Spola, the celebrant, nor Gavazzi, the assistant, nor the vast crowd who gathered there.

revolutionary, a servant of the triumvirate ruling the republic, and rejoicing to be a comrade of Garibaldi's legionaries. An incident from this period was to form a colourful part of his later anti-papal oratory, the breaking open of the prison of the holy office; Gavazzi was among the first to explore its dark chambers and look horrified on heaps of human bones, and the concealed trap of an underground pit containing human hair and putrefying remains. The prison was ordered to be cleaned out and turned into a lodging house for the poor.[70]

It was stated above that in writing on Gavazzi 'few options are open apart from biographical narrative': however, it was added, that Gavazzi can be seen as exemplifying the religious crisis created by the Risorgimento for many Catholics. The narrative of what happened to him from his entry into the Barnabite Order at sixteen to his becoming a chaplain and organiser of ambulances under Garibaldi during the Roman revolution at thirty-nine, has been given. The question must now be asked, what forces were at work in the Italian church which transformed the innocent novice, the loyal Catholic, the devout writer of works of piety, the admirer of Pius IX, into the impassioned orator of the crusade against the Austrians (for him, a conservative revolution) chaplain to the troops of the anti-clerical Garibaldi, and soon after into a vigorous denouncer of the papacy and of Roman Catholicism? Leopardi had written: '. . . in a nation's memories the fabulous years are those of that nation's youth', and though he did not live to see them the fabulous years of Italy's youth were those of the Risorgimento: but here we enter a confusing maze of interpretations, as was suggested above, when we seek to study that movement. To understand Gavazzi, and many other priests or laymen who were pulled between conflicting loyalties, we must consider the force of religious energies in the Risorgimento. If we ignore this religious force then Gavazzi becomes at worst no more than a renegade, a ranting second-rate actor in a demagogic

---

[70] Luigi Bianchi, *Incidents in the Life of an Italian*, London, 1859. Bianchi describes himself as present, and saw a chamber high in the roof with heaps of bones. He added (146) that an aged bishop and two nuns were set free. This matter has long been a disputed difficulty. Gavazzi recounted these horrors later in Britain and north America when the Inquisition was one of his most successful anti-papal subjects. Clerical writers affirm the bones, furnace and instruments of torture were hastily set up in the prison of the holy office – there was a cemetery nearby – as an exhibition of papal cruelty. Anti-clerical writers deny this, Gavazzi claimed to have been the first to enter the prison and his horrified description points to visible evidence. I have found no instance of calculated lying on matters of fact by Gavazzi elsewhere, but this, of course, does not preclude his being the victim of a theatrical display by republican anti-clericals who had worked hard as scene-shifters in the hours before he entered the prison on 1 April 1849.

melodrama; at best, a self-willed friar who lost his vocation and betrayed his Church.

The Risorgimento is commonly understood to have begun in Italy in 1831, when Gavazzi was twenty-two. Five years before this Lamennais had written prophetically: 'Society awaits, in order to be reborn, a new activity in Christianity, a great deed noble in itself: henceforth it will not be with diplomacy that the world will be saved.'[71] It was by diplomacy and war, with Cavour and Garibaldi as significant exemplars, that Italy was united; but diplomacy and war must have ideas and emotions behind them to rouse men to support or endure them. There had to be ideas and purpose to justify the Italian dead at Treviso and many later battlegrounds. Lampedusa in *Il Gattopardo* describes a Sicilian, the prince of Salina, reflecting in 1860 on the corpse of a young soldier of the fifth regiment who had crawled into his gardens to die. 'Soldiers become soldiers in order . . . to die in defence of their king. . . . The image of that gutted corpse often reappeared as if crying to be given peace . . . for to die for someone or something is to do well and is in order, provided that he who does so knows or feels sure for whom or for what he is dying . . . "He died for the King [of Naples] it is clear, who represents order, continuity, decency, right, honour . . . who alone defends the Church" . . . but kings should not fall below a certain level for generations, for if they do the idea they represent suffers also.'[72] The kings referred to had been the product of Metternich's reaction, restored by the congress of Vienna, but incompetent in their absolutism; on the principle of throne and altar such men were supported by Gregory XVI for whom conservative repression was the truth of God and liberalism in any form the instrument of the devil. That conservative intention gave the Austrian empire the chief control not only immediately in Lombardy and Venetia but mediately elsewhere in Italy – and in the south was that kingdom where Lampedusa's prince saw the idea of kingship and honour degraded by repression and corruption. Italians, however regional their traditional loyalty, felt that change must come, and that change could only come by new principles, by new aspirations and ideas. In searching for these ideas and emotions more attention should be given to religious writers and also clergy and devout laymen active in the Risorgimento; and, in doing so, the later effort by members of the

---

[71] Translated from Paul Dudon, *Letters inédites de Lammennais à Ventura*, *Etudes*, 1 (March 1910), 612. The date of this letter to Ventura was 14 May, 1826.
[72] Tomasi di Lampedusa, *Il Gattopardo*, Milan, 1958. Translated here from the 1963 Feltrinelli edition, 13–14.

Catholic Church in Italy to minimise or distort the history of that movement should not be overlooked.[73] That Catholics should be indignant at the vulgar and violent anticlericalism of many partisans of Italian unity is obviously acceptable, but that should not carry with it indifference to the agony of conscience of religious men who sought what they believed to be for their country's good. 'History has many cunning passages, contrived corridors . . . deceives with whispering ambitions . . .' Eliot's words echo in the memory when one remembers that the Christian Democratic Party, dominant in Italy since 1945, has sought consistently to undermine Garibaldi's prestige, neglected his house and documents, and blamed him for the fiasco of fascism.[74] But it was beyond irony when that party pushed Garibaldi into the background and supported the Touring Club of Italy in publishing a volume honouring Pius IX as the real hero of the occasion when the events of 1860 were celebrated in 1961.[75] This and other examples from recent times eliminate the crisis of conscience of Gavazzi and many others like him, and convey the impression that whatever was religiously valid in the Risorgimento must be seen through a distorting hindsight.

What was 'religiously valid' goes back further than 1831. There were two strong influences, both originating in France, Jansenism and the Catholic renewal begun by Lamennais and his followers. The kingdom of Piedmont, the heartland for the reunification of Italy, was neighbour to France and therefore it had been open to Jansenist influences. Italian Jansenism showed its power at the synod of Pistoia, 1786, held in Tuscany under Bishop Scipione Ricci.[76] Among the fifty-seven points for reform made at the synod were reform of the liturgy, including the encouragement of reading the Bible in Italian; the revision of disciplinary procedure including reform of the religious Orders; the introduction of synodical government; the obligatory residence of parish priests; the closing of the Holy Office. The synod, which established a comprehensive statement of Italian Jansenism,

[73] Anthony P. Campanella, *Guiseppe Garibaldi e la Tradizione Garibaldina una bibliografia dal 1807 al 1970*, Comitato dell'Instituto Internazionale di Studi Garibaldini, 2 vols, Geneva, 1971. 'The Roman Catholic church, the perennial enemy of liberal Garibaldian principles . . . has, through its vast network of churches, schools and propoganda media . . . precluded any dissemination of the true facts concerning him.' To this church 'Garibaldi represents the anti-Christ par excellence'. The phrase 'true facts' show Campanella as too emotionally committed, but the basis of his criticism is sound.

[74] Campanella *Bibliographia*. The citations are from his introduction.

[75] Ibid. He adds, 'thus honouring the great enemy of Italian independence'.

[76] Maturi, 602–3, refers to three historians who have discussed the influence of Jansenism in northern Italy. For brief statements on Ricci and the synod of Pistoia, Bihlmeyer-Tuechle, 4, 57, 103, with accompanying references to the literature of the subject.

showed through their decisions a decentralised anti-papal tendency.
The memory of the work of Bishop Ricci remained long after the
synod had been condemned by a papal bull in 1798, including his
hostility to 'Scholastic inventions', and, particularly, the idea that
ecclesiastical reform was necessary and possible. Jansenism's power
lay in its moralistic drive, its strong appeal to the conscience, which
impelled to action for religious renewal. If ecclesiastical reform was
blocked by repressive conservative governments supporting the
throne and altar principle backed by the papacy, then anxious
consciences could ask, Was the Church not of greater importance
than the civil power? In northern Italy the university of Turin had
been a Jansenist powerhouse until the Jesuits obtained control of it
after 1821 – a fact, though comparatively small in itself, which had,
no doubt, some bearing on Charles Albert's reference to the Jesuits'
chocolate and to Cavour's attitude to religious Orders later. The
conflict concerning the synod of Pistoia, pursued through books and
pamphlets, lasted for years. Here were ideas Catholic, moral,
reforming and practical which lingered on in northern Italy. Mazzini
had in his youth known the moral purposiveness of Jansenism.

Again, the proximity of France led to the influence of Lamennais
whose work increasingly emphasised loyalty to the papal principle
against that of the union of throne and altar, the absolutist
anachronism which he found so exasperating either under the restored
Bourbon or the 'citizen king' in France.[77] For him a renewed
Catholicism in which the essence of Christianity was freedom, and in
which the rights of the poor must be claimed, turned for support not
to kings but to the papacy. When Lamennais countered the
condemnation of his views by Gregory XVI in *Mirari vos*, 1832, with
his *Paroles d'un croyant* in 1834, he showed that it was possible for
Catholics to be loyal to the faith of the Church while rejecting the
Church's contemporary rôle in politics including the important
stumbling-block of the temporal power of the Pope in the papal
states. This had considerable influence on Catholic intellectuals which
the encyclical *Singulari nos*, 1834, failed to overcome. Manzoni – the
devout author of that historical novel *I Promessi Sposi* which presented
the ideal of Catholicism at its best – accepted the reformist and
liberalising views of the neo-guelfs, and wrote of Lamennais that he
was the sole voice in France for justice, truth and liberty. The neo-

---

[77] For a brief view of the later views of Lamennais see *Catholicisme*, publ. Centre
Interdiscplinaire des Facultés catholiques de Lille, Tome 6, Paris, 1967, cols 1721, 1722. A. R.
Vidler, *Prophecy and Papacy*, London, 1954, unfortunately ends before examining the later years
of Lamennais in which his social and political views were so widely influential.

guelfs, whatever they owed to Catholic writers elsewhere in Europe, were inspired by the Italian problems and Italian ideas to resolve them. The Catholic intellectual and religious elements in the Risorgimento were born among the neo-guelfs, those liberal Catholics who questioned the traditional assumptions of the rôle of the Church in society in relation to the state.

Liberal Catholic views would owe something to the cultural renewal in the eighteenth century in Italy shown in the work of the historians Giannone and Muratori, and the philosophy of Vico which is still seminal today.[78] But the tracing of the genealogical descent of ideas is difficult and it is dangerous to be too positive about lines of descent and influence. Republicanism and the 'principles of eighty nine' were brought into Italy following on the French revolution and the Napoleonic invasion: the *carbonari* were part of the consequence. Mazzini took the republicanism of the revolution as a weapon against the nexus of throne and altar, and used the nationalism which was part of the reaction to the revolution to urge an association of free european nations inspired by the vague theistic overtones of 'God and the People' in which Italy would be free, united, and helping to renew humanity.[79] But the neo-guelfs opposed to these vaguely defined aspirations, a Catholicism renewed, politically liberal, and looking to guidance from the papacy disentangled from the net of the temporal power and giving leadership to an Italy freed and reborn. The intellectual force of this liberal Catholic movement, which opposed the views of Mazzini's party of 'young Italy' and the methods of their network of secret societies, was provided by two priests and philosophers, Vincenzo Gioberti and Antonio Rosmini.[80] They started from the same basis as the Christian romanticism shown

[78] Maturi also cites a chain of those who demonstrated ideas of national independence for Italy: Machiavelli – Vico – Cuoco – Mazzini – Gioberti, 526. P. Giannone (d 1748) was a historian who wrote on his native Naples with a strong anti-papal bias and who believed in minimising hierarchial control of the church. A. Muratori (d 1750) is a name famous among ecclesiastical historians for his integrity, diligence and objectivity as a scholar, whose ecclesiastical position can be seen reflected in the dislike shown to him and his works by the Jesuits. G. B. Vico (d 1744) wrote the remarkable *Scienza Nuova*, Naples, 1725, showing the history of civilisation as a spiral, though Vico's view of history as guided by God's providence has little interest to historians in our time. His interest in language influenced James Joyce, 'a lord of language'.

[79] Luigi Salvatorelli, *Il problema religioso nel Risorgimento*, [*Rasegna Storica*], anno 43, fasc 1 (1956), 213: '. . . il Mazzini fece del Risorgimento italiano, e anzi della sistemazione europea in associazione di nazioni libere, una esigenza della religione "Dio e Popolo".' – this excluded the papacy. Also see Mazzini, *Opere* 4, 1: 5, 42, 43 (Salvatorelli's reference) – (v. n. 89 below).

[80] Torre, 111, Torre claims that Gioberti affirmed that Italy contained in itself, above all through its religion, all the conditions required for its material and political renewal. For a list of Gioberti's major writings see Maturi, 721, and for the historiography on Gioberti see Maturi's index.

by Manzoni – a romanticism which, however fruitful in ideas, had lacked political realism. Gioberti was a Piedmontese who became a priest, was attracted to the movement for a united Italy, and was banished at the same time as Mazzini in 1833 because of his vigorous liberal political views. From his exile in Brussels in the following years he wrote various works which gripped a younger generation of laymen and priests, not so much by his philosophical works, anti-Scholastic in form and grounded on the assertion of the intuitive vision of God, as by his writings on the recovery of national independence combined with religious renewal which were so influential. His *Prolegomini Primato morale e civile degli Italiani*, 1845, affirmed the idealised vision of the papacy as guiding an Italian confederation of states and as the moral arbiter of the nations. He took a view wholly opposed to that of Mazzini on the papacy, since Gioberti showed that the papacy was necessary for Italy, because through it national unity could be blessed by unity of faith. What Lamennais found helpful in France in Chateaubriand's *Génie du Christianisme*, Gioberti's Italian disciples found in Manzoni's idealised view of Italian Catholicism in the seventeenth century, and in Gioberti's own eloquent prose. Manzoni's remarkable novel *I Promessi Sposi* which first began to appear in 1825 and achieved its final form in 1840–2, emphasised tolerance, freedom, human brotherhood purified by a religion of peace and love in a Catholicism that ignored 'curialism' and Jesuit triumphalism.[81] Here was the rallying point for new ideas on combining political liberalism, Catholic belief, social improvement, church renewal under a Pope with the vision to guide the nation forward, while avoiding the anti-clericalism and violence of the republican groups. Gioberti's *Prolegomini* turned against Austria, the oppressor nation carefully unnamed in his previous book, and also attacked the Jesuits whom he had come to dislike in his Turin years for he regarded them as pro-Austrian and the fuglemen of reaction and oppression in the name of curial necessity – moreover they had vigorously attacked his earlier work. He crowned his anti-Jesuit polemic with a study in five volumes published in 1846 *Il Gesuito moderno*. Powerful propaganda for the neo-guelfs can also be found in count Cesare Balbo's *Delle Speranze d'Italia* of 1844 exhorting patriots to defy the Austrians, and the book by the

---

[81] Manzoni's novel still attracts a number of readers, and has had a renewal of life in a new English version. The viewpoint of Manzoni has been described in Maturi (p. 40) as *una formula felice*, namely 'nel considerare come ideale dello storico la fusione del Vico e del Muratori, della filosofia e della filologia, dal gusto di vedere le cose dall'alto con genialità di pensiero e del gusto del particolare preciso appurato dopo pazienti indagini archivistiche'. It is a moving story, and owes something to the powerful influence of Walter Scott on the continent.

moderate but determined statesman Massimo d'Azeglio, the son-in-law of Manzoni, *Degli ultimi casi di Romagna*, 1846, making clear to Europe at large the miserable condition of the people immediately under papal government.[82] But Gioberti and others, it is now increasingly clear, were equalled and surpassed by another priest, Antonio Rosmini, who in 1830 had published an invigorating study of the origin of ideas, and in 1842 issued his *Filosofia di diritto della politica*. The following year, together with count Balbo, he produced a pamphlet on a new constitution, especially concerned with the papal states – this was the feverish period of constitution-making in the various Italian states.[83] Pope Pius IX, whose attempts at change led the elderly Metternich to his ironical comment, 'I had foreseen everything but a liberal pope', was interested in Rosmini's views, including the publication, which had been in manuscript since 1832, of his *Delle cinque piaghe della Santa Chiesa* which set down ways of reform and renewal in the Church in which Rosmini took for starting point the principles of men of the sixteenth-century Oratory of Divine Love, Sadoleto, Contarini, Caraffa and Pole. He emphasised better education for ordinary laity, and also for the priests, pointing out the poor quality of seminary training. His constitutional programme, which interested Pius IX, proposed that the states of Italy should be free of foreign rule, united and meeting together in a government body at Rome under papal protection.

Reform or liberal Catholicism in Italy, with or without political concerns, from Jansenism through Lamennais to Rosmini and Manzoni, is known ground to historians of the period to whom the previous paragraphs should be a familiar summary. But this summary is the necessary setting for discussing the change of Gavazzi from a pious young friar with a talent for preaching, to the orator ejected from his Order who shared in the Roman revolution which led to the flight of the Pope and Garibaldi's first major conflict for Italian unity. Unfortunately, citations by Sylvain, and the extracts in an Italian journal, from Gavazzi's autobiography show an old man reviewing distant memories of action: he apparently was uninterested in explaining his development by recalling his intellectual progress in describing what books he read in his youth and young manhood, or

---

[82] Massimo d'Azeglio was a potent figure, his *I miei ricordi* – best edition edited by Ghisalberti, Milan, 1963, – is one of the better autobiographies of the first half of the nineteenth century – he was an artist, a professional soldier and politician, and author. His observations and judgements are shrewd and forceful.

[83] Rosmini is attracting attention among Catholic writers today because his views are more acceptable to their contemporary theological needs that those of the ultimately antagonistic Gioberti and Lamennais. But it is significant that references to him are few in Maturi's index.

what men he talked to who were familiar with the ideas of reformed Catholicism and of the neo-guelfs. Gavazzi remembers the fires of old passions, of heroic adventures, and of courageous oratory – intellectual analysis, the origin and significance of particular ideas, did not interest him. This was to be a major weakness of his platform addresses in England and north America, and it also accounts for the ephemeral quality of many of his writings in which he makes no effective mention of the thought of the makers of the liberal Catholic tradition. Nor, when he had ceased to be a Catholic, do his writings and speeches show the intellectual's concern with depth, and the scholar's concern with precision, in the use of history and theology.

Gavazzi was a man who did not originate ideas or put together with original intellectual labour a continuous analysis of social, political or religious matters. His mind was quick to assimilate by hearing others talk, and to skim through an article or a book, grasping here and there a telling phrase or an idea which could be given an emotional colouring: from this assimilation he derived the content of his oratory, his books and pamphlets. What emerges from his sermons and books before 1845 are, first, that he had accepted in his early years as a Barnabite the excellent if somewhat routine religious emphases of his Order, which enabled him to express traditional piety dressed in the conventional rhetoric of the period; secondly, we can see that these traditional and worthy pieties were increasingly energised with ideas on social matters (the needs of the poor, the prisoners, the dispossessed, the indifference and selfishness of the rich and the nobles), and on religious reform (the concern for improvements in the training of priests, the questioning of the superficial quality in the lives of many monks and nuns, the search for something fresh and quickening, the increase of piety, and irritation with the creaking bureaucratic machinery of the Church). However, the phrases and themes he began to use increasingly in the years 1838–45, so far as they can be obtained from his comparatively few publications of this period, are difficult to identify as showing the influence of specific authors or movements. He may well not have known, or attached importance to, the names of liberal or reform Catholics, and in any event if he knew the names or was aware of the sources and aims of a movement, since his knowledge probably came not so much from careful and systematic reading as from listening to others, he would not have been able to give a considered and cogent presentation of, or judgement on, the work of particular authors. Since the Gavazzi family were Bolognese (though of Venetian origin) they would share in Bologna's concern as the lay-capital of the papal states to be forward-looking and resentful of ecclesiastical conservatism in politics, although his father appears to have been conservative in outlook.[84] Giuseppe Patuzzi, a maternal uncle of Gavazzi, took part in the revolution at Bologna in 1831 and emigrated to France in 1836; he was to be praised for his patriotism later by his nephew.[85] Gavazzi felt other influences showing zeal for liberty besides that of his mother's family (and his mother, especially dear to Gavazzi, showed pride in the patriotism of her sons), his father's successor in the chair of civil law at the university of Bologna, Antonio Silvani, who had been briefly exiled after 1831 because of his liberal views, became a close friend of the young Barnabite. Silvani was much concerned with constitutional changes and his conversation must have affected Gavazzi.[86] In preaching in San Petronio at Bologna on the immaculate conception Gavazzi contrived to exalt the historical greatness of Bologna and its future political rôle. It was about this period that he had become a close friend of Ugo Bassi, who had become an advocate of 'liberty' and social reform. Again, Gavazzi's various travels included Turin more than once, where liberal views were discussed. These visits together with the friendship of Silvani who was concerned with political reform, and of Bassi an older man than Gavazzi and burning with zeal for Italy – all these are influences on an impressionable young preacher of strong character. From these may come some elements of remembered Jansenism and its moral earnestness, which could reinforce ideas on the Church as aiding social justice derived from Lamennais and his followers, for example Raffaele Lambruschini in Italy. Beyond this it would be speculation: but by the late thirties it is certain that Gavazzi, while ignoring the methods and propaganda of the secret societies, had available for his sermons themes which showed concern for political and social reform, and patriotic zeal for Italy, and which echo those of the contemporary writers on reformed Catholicism.[87]

Whether he owed anything to Mazzini, and the movement of 'young Italy', is worth investigation but difficult to determine:

[84] Sylvain cites the manuscript of Gavazzi's *Autobiografia* for Gavazzi's view of his father as a conservative if not a reactionary.
[85] *My Recollections*, 196–7: '. . . my only uncle, the general of the civic guard [at Bologna] who afterwards merited the honour of being exiled for the cause of Italy, and died in exile. The reader will, I trust, pardon my honest family pride.'
[86] Santini, 31. Silvani again renewed relationship with Gavazzi in 1847.
[87] King, 96, quotes Gavazzi; 'During my seven years' exile I have never seen Mazzini nor have I corresponded with him . . . I am the last to approve him as a political leader.' Mazzini instituted secret societies. There is no evidence to connect Gavazzi with Freemasonry, in Italy a politically oriented and anti-clerical body – moreover his brusque common sense would have no taste for its rituals.

Mazzini's phrase 'God and the people' could find an echo in Gavazzi's sermons and writings, but this would not tie him to Mazzini's views. Gavazzi always opposed republicanism as a valid political future for Italy, although in his patriotic zeal to help Garibaldi to defend Rome against the French army in 1849 he could not help working under the Roman republic's brief triumvirate. The idea of an analogy between the experiences and aspirations of Italians and those of the Jews of scripture was not uncommon at that time: both were a martyr people overwhelmed by domestic and foreign tyranny, and as the Jews hoped that after Babylon there would come a restoration of land and people, so Italians yearned for unity and freedom from foreign domination.[88] Mazzini believed that Italy could only be freed from foreign rule and united with the aid of religion. Gavazzi could readily accept this. When Mazzini said: 'We need a new religion, a religion of duty', Gavazzi might well agree about duty but he could not have accepted Mazzini's vague theism as an adequate religion.[89] Gavazzi's reform principles were closer to those of the neo-guelfs than to Mazzini and his republicanism. Gioberti's *Prolegomini del Primato morale e civile degli Italiani* which appeared in 1843 stole Mazzini's thunder. It is reasonable to believe that the books of Balbo and Gioberti's book influenced the eager young Barnabites Bassi and Gavazzi, who at the same period were aware of the views associated with the disciples of Lamennais. Again, Pius VII, for Gavazzi's generation, had been the Pope who had endured insults and oppression by the French and could be idealised (and was idealised with purpose by Rosmini in a panegyric on the death of Pius VII) as a heroic figure opposing foreign oppression of Italians, and a symbol of neo-guelf aspirations for a 'liberal' Pope.[90] Perhaps here lies the enthusiasm of Gavazzi when Pius IX was enthroned. But whether Rosmini's later works were studied and assimilated by Gavazzi is an open question, and is probably doubtful. He had found sufficient fuel after 1845 to feed the furnace of his oratory, without needing Rosmini's patient study of philosophical constitution-making which envisaged a new Italy of federal states under the guidance of Pius IX.

A stronger possibility of influence on Gavazzi is that which could be called neo-ghibellinism whose basic principle differed from that of the neo-guelfs (who saw the papacy as taking the lead in purifying

[88] Spini, 76.

[89] Torre, 101, quotes Mazzini as demanding a new religion, a religion of duty in which there would be three dogmas, the existence of God, the law of progress, and the general co-operation of men (cited from Mazzini's *Fide e Avenire*).

[90] Santini, 5, 'Pio VII che, spogliato dal regno e condotto prigioniero a Savona, assorgeva a simbolo della nazionalità oppressa'.

society and the Church) in declaring that the papacy was incapable of such leadership since it had become too corrupt to reform itself much less Italy. The neo-ghibelline group, less easy to describe because it was less homogeneous than the neo-guelfs, held to the same view as the latter that religion must be maintained as the necessary source of moral energy and as the formative principle by which the reunification of Italy should be attained. But unlike the neo-guelfs, the neo-ghibellines had differing views on how this religion should be expressed. Mazzini believed that, 'religious thought purifies the individual and to try to act without religion is false'.[91] Gabriele Rossetti stated a central theme of this group: *il cristianismo in se stesso e virtu morale che si trasforme in forza politica è vigor privato da cui deriva il pubblico; è nobilita individuale da cui proviene la nazionale.*[92] The heroic figures of the Christian past in Italy for the neo-ghibellines were Dante, Petrarch, Tasso, Machiavelli and Sarpi, and they viewed the papacy, in the light of the writings of these men of a former age, as still the source of corruption in contemporary Italy. Niccolo Tommaseo who was to become one of the heroes of the 'five days of Milan' which caused the Austrian reprisals leading to 'the crusade' of 1847–9, wrote that Italy would not be made a nation again until it first reacquired the purity of the religion of its ancestors before there had been brought in the dogma of purgatory and the practice of the confessional which was 'the school of corruption'. Tommaseo knew Gavazzi, and attacking the confessional as a source of moral corruption was to become one of Gavazzi's standard lecture subjects. Further, Gavazzi later published a little book in England called *The Priest in Absolution* attacking the revival of confession in the Church of England by Father Knox Little at St Albans, Cheetwood, Manchester, and Father A. H. Mackonochie in Holborn, London.[93] When Mazzini wrote to Lamennais in 1834, the year in which Lamennais was condemned by the Pope: 'The papacy has killed faith under a materialism more dangerous and abject than that of the

[91] Torre, 96, citing Mazzini *Opere* 4, 1.

[92] Torre, 118, citing Rossetti's *Roma verso la meta del secolo XIX*, London, 1840. Gabriele Rossetti was to make a famous name for himself in exile in England not so much by his writings or by his becoming a professor of Italian at the newly founded King's College, London, but by becoming the father of a remarkable literary family – Christina, Dante Gabriel, and William Michael. He adopted strong anti-Catholic polemical views and, in later life, some degree of Protestant evangelicalism. Vinay, op. cit., 123.

[93] *The Priest in Absolution: an Exposure*, 'by Alessandro Gavazzi, Minister of the Free Christian Church in Italy' London, 1877. The following sentence (p. 31) has a period flavour: 'And yet, after the experience of centuries, Dr Pusey dares to assert in one of his letters to the *Daily Express* that a great injustice has been committed towards "a large body of well-educated English clergymen, in thinking that any clergy of ours would ask anything, or English wives and daughters listen to, what it would be unfit for father or husband to hear".'

eighteenth century . . . papal materialism proceeds from the mantle of Jesuitism . . . the papacy has suffocated love in a sea of blood . . .'[94] Gavazzi would find an echo for his own later thinking – not that he derived such judgements necessarily from Mazzini but from those who held such views among the people he knew in the forties. The tragedy, *Arnoldo da Brescia*, (who had been executed at Rome for opposing the temporal power of the Popes in 1155) by G. B. Niccolini is a significant document of the ideals of this group of which he was a leading member.[95] Gavazzi was to lecture later in exile on Dante as a heroic symbol of purer religion and defiance of papal political activity. From various echoes in his later speeches and writings Gavazzi showed he was more influenced by the neo-ghibelline attitude after his exile in 1849. But one other source of influence on Gavazzi at a later stage was that of the political leadership of Piedmont, especially that of Cavour.

Gavazzi's career up to the fall of the brief Roman republic has been outlined, the period of his exile in Britain will be considered later; in his autobiography he called the years 1859–68 *Ritorno*, and at this point his relationship as an opponent of the Catholic Church, as well as the papacy, to Cavour's political views will conclude this examination of the interconnection of his religious convictions and the political environment of this second and different experience of the stages taken towards Italian unity.

By now Gavazzi was wholly opposed to the Roman Catholic Church, as well as anti-papal, and had adopted most of the principles of evangelical Protestantism, though with strong reservations on the doctrine of grace, and moulded this Protestantism to his own pattern. (He was obnoxious to the Plymouth Brethren, who had made some powerful Italian converts, and to the strongly evangelical Presbyterian congregations in Italy, because of his modifications of traditional Protestant evangelical orthodoxy.)[96] Not long after his return to

---

[94] Torre cites Mazzini writing these words to Lamennais, and gives *Opere* 5, 42, 44, as the reference.

[95] 'Niccolini non era democratico, ma liberale laico.' Maturi, 403.

[96] Gavazzi wrote *Che sia il plimuttismo: Studio storico-polemico*, Florence, 1876, in order to counteract their infiltration of his free churches. His sources were: *The Errors of Darby and the Plymouth Sect*, *The Record* (1862); *Plymouth Brethrenism: its ecclesiastical and doctrinal teachings*, *British Quarterly Review* [*October 1873*]; *The Heresies of the Plymouth Brethren*, J. L. Carson, Coleraine, 1862; *Brethrenism or the special teachings ecclesiastical and doctorinal of the Brethren, or Plymouth Brethen*, Duncan Macintosh, London, 1872 *A Catechism of the doctrine of the Plymouth Brethren* London, 1866. There were several Scottish Presbyterian ministers working in Italy – R. Stewart of Leghorn who worked with the *Valdesi*, and J. MacDougall whose work was among English-speaking Presbyterians in Italy, were among these. The latter showed sympathy to Gavazzi, but Stewart strongly opposed him in Italy and in Scotland. Gavazzi found Stewart a constant thorn in the flesh.

Italy he prepared a pamphlet *Sulla necessitá d'una religione per gl'Italiani* which shows he was not only negatively anti-papal but he was also searching for a way of relating the patriotic desire for unity and reform to a new way of religion. His problem was that he was unattracted by the forms of Protestantism already developed in Italy, Waldensians, Plymouth Brethren, Presbyterians or other evangelical groups. In 1860 he also challenged the view, propagated by Napoleon III, that Italy needed a French alliance and also now took a positive stand against Mazzini's republicanism in favour of an Italy strong under the Piedmontese monarchy. It would be most useful to know what was Gavazzi's attitude to Cavour, and especially to Cavour's initiative in breaking the deadlock between the Piedmontese creation of Italian unity and that papal intransigence seen in Pio Nono's *non possumus* to the suggestion that he should give up the papal states. In October 1860 Cavour spoke for all Italians seeking reunification when he said in Parliament: *La nostra stella e di fare che la città eterna . . . diventi la splendida capitale del regno italico.*[97] 8176 secular priests and 767 religious, especially men from the south, signed a petition to the Pope in favour of Cavour's utterance: 'two voices cry aloud *Viva il Papa e Viva Roma Metropoli del Nuovo Regno* – it will be your blessed destiny to harmonise them.'[98] Pius replied with his by now usual and immediate threat to excommunicate all the signatories unless they immediately withdrew. This shows both the feeling among Catholic clergy, and the obstinate difficulty in solving the problem. Cavour's other and even better-known way to break the deadlock was his declaration: *Libera chiesa in libero stato*[99] – 'moral forces overcome moral obstacles.' He was attempting to persuade Pius that by giving up the temporal power the Pope would acquire greater not less freedom.

Gavazzi's concern for a new religion for Italians could fit this pattern; he was later to institute a Free Church in Italy, claiming to be uncommitted to traditional Protestantism, expressing the religion of the early church at Rome, and dissociated from the curialism and

---

[97] Torre, 167.

[98] Ibid., 167.

[99] There has long been discussion on the origin of this famous phrase. E. Passerin d'Entrèves, *Rassegna Storica* 41 (1954)., 494–506 argued that Cavour adopted it from Montalembert the French liberal Catholic associated with the famous journal *L'Avenir* and the historian of the monks of the West. Montalembert claimed this himself. But Cavour wished Rome to be the captial of Italy and Montalembert did not; moreover he was an ardent ultramonist which Cavour was certainly not. It is more likely that Cavour, who knew French-speaking Switzerland well, derived it from Alexandre Vinet the distinguished theologian of Lausanne, who broke away from the cantonal state church to found *une église libre*. What is not in doubt is that Cavour opposed any authority being given to the Catholic church in temporal affairs.

triumphalism of the Catholic Church.[100] Unfortunately so many of Gavazzi's writings are expressed in terms of personal experiences and recollections that once again one cannot be sure how much he knew of Cavour's views on religious matters. He begins frequently from personal griefs, observations and hopes and expresses these in rhetorical terms which can in certain phrases resemble Cavour's statements at this period, but this is not sufficient proof. Moreover, his concern not to be identified with one political party or party leader may have led to his generalising his assertions, and also he may have been aware of the Protestant origins of Cavour's famous phrase and was wary of using it. In any case the Piedmontese government regarded Gavazzi as a trouble maker.

A more powerful and sympathetic figure for Gavazzi was Garibaldi, to whom he wrote offering his services in 1860, and whom he followed to Sicily and shared in his successes there, once again acting as organiser of ambulances, and encouraging the 'Thousand' with his inspiring oratory – while Pio Nono wrote desperately in a private letter of the *pirati e predoni* who formed that 'pernicious band of desperate men'.[101]

It was stated above that Gavazzi was far from being alone in being a priest who helped the cause of Italian unity, even though his own character and experiences and eventual Protestantism were very different from that of the others. Many of the lower clergy, especially in the south, were devoted to Garibaldi's campaign: a large number of them even formed a *legione ecclesiastica* which was attached to the XVI Cosenz division, commanded by a Sicilian priest, Paolo Sardo.[102] A number of articles and monographs have been written about priests who took part in the Risorgimento. There were three distinguished priests in Salerno, for example, who left their posts to follow the 'Thousand', an abbot Sacchi, Vincenzo Padula, and Ovidio Filippo Patella, who were men of learning detesting the social evils and religious corruption deriving from Bourbon absolutism in the kingdom of Naples – they found prison, exile and the horrors of battlefields. Two of these men eventually took up again their priestly functions after the reunification of Italy.[103] Men like these, including Gavazzi, could no longer accept Cavour's utterance in the chamber of deputies: 'The Roman Question cannot be solved by the sword: only moral forces overcome moral obstacles.' Better known was one

[100] v. 362 below.
[101] A. Monti, *Pio IX e il Risorgimento italiano*, Bari, 1928 cites this from a letter of Pius to monsignor Papardo, 9 June 1860.
[102] Santini, 143.
[103] Beniamino Palumbo, *Preti del Risorgimento*, *Rassegna Storica* 43 (1956), 511 ff.

of the remarkable priests of the Risorgimento, Gregorio Ugdulena, erudite, devout, patriotic and a lover of liberty; his contribution was political, from being a former university teacher he became a strong influence in the parliament of united Italy.[104] These men differed from Gavazzi in believing that *il gran rifiuto* of Pius IX did not cancel out the principles of the neo-guelfs: they showed that many Catholics, including priests, believed that the movement for Italian unity, freedom from foreign occupation and constitutional liberty could be reconciled with Catholicism. But between these priests, who remained in Italy and sought that reconciliation between church and nation, and Gavazzi lay his bitter years of exile in which he had become a Protestant, though a peculiarly Gavazzian Protestant. To understand the cause of that separation his activities in exile must be examined.

After the discussion of the ideas and politics of the Risorgimento, and the brief references to Gavazzi's activity after returning to Italy in 1859, a more extended account of his exile in England must be given. Since Gavazzi had taken part in the defence of Rome against the French and supported therefore the revolution, he was declared a rebel and sought by the police in 1849. He was fortunate to get a passport from the American consul, and with better chance than Bassi, who was caught and shot by the Austrians in the north, he escaped with Garibaldi, and, after separating from him, reached Leghorn and sailed for London.[105] He reached unknown England, penniless, heart-broken, ignorant of the language, and drifted into that mixed, sometimes raffish, group of Italian exiles already gathered in Soho. He survived on ten shillings a week he earned by giving Italian lessons: once he was saved from extreme hunger by meeting another exile, a former colonel of the pontifical volunteers.[106] He still felt strongly his priestly vocation and, shocked by the irreligion of many of the exiles, he tried to minister to them. He interrupted an anti-Catholic meeting of Italians and others by shouting aloud his allegiance to the Catholic faith and his priesthood.[107] When he received news of the execution near Bologna, by orders of the Austrian general Gorzkowski, of his friend Ugo Bassi, whom monsignor Bedini (appointed as the papal representative in the legations) had done nothing to aid, Gavazzi, mourning his friend – and bitterly remembering Bedini whom he was to attack in the

[104] Ibid., 513, 514.
[105] King, 40 – Freeman, the American consul, had attended the celebrations after the flight of Pius from Rome, and American opinion supported the republican ideal, and opposed the temporal power of the Pope.
[106] Campanella, 137.
[107] Santini, 103: 'era frate e frate sarebbe rimasto per sempre.'

United States later – delivered a funeral address which he published at his own expense.

Cardinal Wiseman inhibited him from continuing his activities as a priest, even though Gavazzi claimed in an interview with Wiseman that he had a special commission from the Pope.[108] Gavazzi might have drifted downwards into obscure semi-starvation if he had not been taken up at this stage by another inhibited priest, the Irishman Francis Mahony, who had trained for the Jesuit Order, but had not continued in it, became a priest in Italy, returned to his native Cork but, 'instead of observing the modesty which adorns and the deference which promotes a young chaplain, he indulged his talent for caricature at the expense of personages whom prudence at least might have counselled him to let alone' . . . 'He became a half-pay soldier of the church minus the half-pay'.[109] Mahony used his brilliant gift for languages, especially Latin and Greek, and his equally remarkable gift of English prose style, to become one of the circle of writers for *Fraser's Magazine* in 1834, and sit with Thackeray, Southey, Carlyle and other supporters of the 'Queen of the Monthlies' in 'their tavern-in-the-town-conviviality', singing their favourite *All Round my Hat I wear a Green Willow*, which Mahony could turn into Greek or Latin, French or Italian verse with remarkable speed. Mahony wrote under the pen-name of 'Father Prout', famous once though now forgotten.[110]

He heard Gavazzi deliver his oration for Bassi, found it impressive, and, himself fervently opposed to ultramontanism, offered Gavazzi help. Mahony obtained for him the Princess Theatre lecture room, off Oxford Street, where Gavazzi gave twelve lectures on the character of Pius IX, the influence of the Jesuits, and related subjects, beginning 5 January 1851, one of which was attended by Palmerston who wrote: 'I went one day to hear Gavazzi's harangue against the abuses of the Catholic Church. He spoke for an hour and a half to several hundred hearers with much eloquence and effect.'[111] Mahony

---

[108] King, 47. Wiseman inhibited him as soon as Gavazzi's sermons in Italian were announced at a small chapel near Soho Square: Gavazzi refused to recognise the inhibition after an interview with Wiseman who said Gavazzi needed a licence from the pope.

[109] Ethel Mannin, *Two Studies in Integrity: Gerald Griffin and the Rev. Francis Mahony*, London, 1954, 147. The first quotation is from the reverend George O'Neill, SJ, who wrote a centenary study of Mahony for the National Literary Society in 1905. The second quotation is from a writer in the *North British Review* (December 1866).

[110] Mannin, 152, 153.

[111] Campanella, 135: 'A numerous attendance of persons of every social position filled the large rooms in which these lectures were given. I remember to have seen Earl Russell, and Lord Palmerston several times at the lectures given by the generous patriot'. The quotation from Palmerston is in E. Ashley, *The Life of H. J. Temple, Viscount Palmerston*, London, 1876, 1, 257. In 1850 Ruskin broke an engagement to hear Gavazzi lecture, and Carlyle told his wife

translated these lectures for the *Daily News*, and they were collected as a booklet, *Orations by Father Gavazzi*, later in 1851. Gavazzi's attacks, since they were based on first-hand experience and that useful addiction to autobiographical illustration so frequent in his speeches and writings, were bound to be popular when given soon after the establishment of the Catholic hierarchy in July 1850 by Pius IX. Palmerston's support and that of other distinguished men, together with Mahony's brilliant and precise English rendering of Gavazzi's oratory, brought Gavazzi out into the foreground where various groups of Protestants could provide him with audiences. But they were puzzled, and since they were all too familiar with heresy-hunting they frequently wanted to know whether Gavazzi was an orthodox Protestant. His biographer, J. W. King, in his book published in 1857, put their questions thus:

> What is your friend Gavazzi? Yes, yes, the uttering of great truths, the aspirations of a nobly patriotic and truly Christian heart are all very well. But there is no profession. Of what peculiar creed is he now? To what section of the Protestant faith does he belong? When did light first break in upon him? Was there no terrible wrestling with the Man of Sin? . . . Evangelical Christianity is not a straw's worth if he does not cast aside that suspicious toga [Gavazzi's Barnabite habit], preach from the pulpit and yield himself up to the Faith as it is in the Church.[112]

King's rendering of these doubts shows the narrow mind and raucous voice of Victorian Protestantism. Newspaper reporters, more worldly, wrote: 'He is the Shakespeare of actors and has no living rival . . . magnificent voice and physical strength . . . He speaks English with wonderful accuracy but with a foreign accent . . . He pours denunciation [upon the Church of Rome], not from the Protestant but from the Catholic point of view.'[113] It is true that Gavazzi had set himself earnestly to learn English and in time gained a sound grip of the language and fluency in it; but exact reporting of his addresses and his few surviving letters in English show some oddities and Italianate phrasing – his accent, moreover, was stronger than the report quoted suggests.

Gavazzi's reply to British Protestant doubts about his Protestant views is given by King, who quotes a letter from Gavazzi to himself:

Gavazzi was a blockhead – but somebody had enthusiastically claimed that Gavazzi reminded him of Carlyle. W. H. Rudman, *Italian Nationalism and English Letters*, London, 1940, 229.

[112] King, 49. In his *The Evangelization of Italy* (1855), Gavazzi showed Protestant orthodoxy in writing, 'We are saved by faith and by the will of God not by our own works – the Fundamental principle of our religion is justification by faith and grace, not by works.' 4.

[113] King, 53.

When and how and why I came out of Rome I need not discuss here, for I detest all public exhibitions of conversion, as smelling of business and hypocrisy . . . As a lecturer and expounder of my principles, as you well know, I never forget to declare solemnly that I am no Protestant for I have nothing to Protest against. My aim . . . is not to protest against Rome, but to destroy the whole system, root and branch. There is nothing to reform in the Church of Rome, which is nothing but an abuse from beginning to end . . . As an Italian, however, there are still further and grave reasons for declining to embrace any Protestant denomination. It could entirely destroy my hopes of the future evangelisation of Italy. It may be wrong but so strong are the prejudices of Italians against Protestantism at large that, to go to them in a Protestant name would be like driving from my platforms the very people I look for . . . I take the opportunity to exclaim against those societies that spend their money, in sending and maintaining missionaries in Italy. I say publicly that this is the way to strengthen Romanism . . . Let the work be left to the Italians themselves aided by Protestant advice and prayers only . . . There was a Christianity in Rome before there was any catholicity . . . It is to that primitive, apostolic, evangelical Christian church that I anxiously look for a return . . . let everyone know that I am an unsectarian, independent, evangelical Christian.[114]

This shows why so many British Protestants were uneasy about him: he would not conform to their pattern. Either because of his seminary training, or from simple conviction, he detested what was thought of as essential to evangelical Protestantism in English Dissent, and emphasised in the non-established Presbyterianism of Scotland, the doctrine of grace focusing on original sin and predestination, denying free-will and emphasising personal assurance and final perseverance. In his last years in Italy when he formed his Free Church he was harassed by strongly evangelical groups supported by British funds especially the *plimuttisi*, and he turned aside from the Waldensians because he regarded them not as Italians but as half-French, and infected with calvinistic predestinarian doctrines.[115] This extract also shows Gavazzi's concern to prevent another kind of foreign intervention in Italy than that which had made him proclaim 'the crusade' against Austria, the religious divisions of foreign Protestantism – the problems of Italian unification were bad enough without adding to them. Further, Gavazzi's conception of what a true church should be is briefly mentioned: essentially he wanted to pass by all the problems posed by Catholicism and Protestantism, and take as his model a

---

[114] King, 63.
[115] Spini, 192 ff. and also Paolo Sanfilippo, *Il Protestantismo Italiano nel Risorgimento*, Rome, no date, 31 ff.

simplified view of the Christian community shown in the New Testament. His hostility to historical forces, and his emphasis on Paul as the apostle of the Romans show the influences he derived from his Italian nationalism. This refusal to face historical facts was a characteristic of the *littérateurs* of the Risorgimento – and who now would consult Chateaubriand's *Génie du Christianisme* for its historical analysis however great its value as a document of romanticism?

Soon after getting established in London, Gavazzi like many another political exile before and after him obtained a reader's ticket for the British Museum, and read widely in questions concerning the Protestant controversy with Rome, early church history, and the authority of the Bible. He would hardly be concerned with the painstaking analyses of the scholar, but he would be reading omnivorously, pursuing questions he had not asked himself before. Somewhere in these first two years in England but, for the reason he himself gave to King we do not know when, he decided against the Catholic Church. G. M. Campanella a fellow exile who published in 1877 his *Life in the Cloister, in the Papal Court and in Exile –An Autobiography*, and dedicated it to Gavazzi, wrote of the poorest of the Italian refugees being on the slippery slope to crime from despair: 'In this unfortunate position Gavazzi was as if both materially and morally sent by Providence to the rescue, for he not only gave succour in money [derived from collections at his lectures] to those most near falling on the slippery way, but he also gave them persuasive and useful advice and counsel of morality and patriotism.'[116] Gavazzi never forgot the patriotism – but in justice to him we should remember Massimo d'Azeglio's words, and he had an astute and cool judgement and wide experience as a politician and diplomatist: 'We must create Italians if we would have an Italy.'[117]

Gavazzi was now established as a public lecturer on the 'evils of the papacy' and travelled to the major towns of the British Isles to set forth his denunciations. It would be a useful study to establish who were the various sponsors of these occasions, why he returned several times to certain towns, who were the clergy or prominent laymen appearing on his platforms, since something more could be learned in closer detail about Victorian Protestantism in the fifties and

---

[116] Campanella, 150

[117] Massimo d'Azeglio, *Things I Remember*, trans E. R. Vincent, London, 1966, 311. Gavazzi, *The Evangelization of Italy*, 19, 'When the trumpet of war sounds for my dear Italy I shall be there, not with rifle and sword, but with Bible in one hand and the Italian national banner in the other, to annihilate the capital enemy of my country – Pope and popery, and to plant the standard of universal freedom upon the ruins of the Vatican.' There is more here of the *garabaldino* than the evangelist.

in the return visits he made in later years. From the volumes of
newspaper cuttings which survive on these addresses (unfortunately
cut so close that names and dates and sometimes places are not given)
his standard subjects were: the Bible and the papal system; the Pope
and his double-headed supremacy; monks and nuns;
transubstantiation; popedom, and the temporal power of the Pope;
worship of the virgin Mary and the saints; auricular confession;
the Inquisition; the present state and future hope of Italy; the
Jesuits.[118] His oratory even reverberated as far as holy Russia
since N. A. Dobroliubov published some of them in his *Sobranie
Socineniy* at Petersburg, 1862, now housed in the Lenin state library
at Moscow – the translator was something of a political demagogue,
and Russia would welcome, in any case, an attack on Roman
Catholicism.[119]

Dr Spence Watson of Newcastle-upon-Tyne, wrote to G. M.
Trevelyan, who had asked for information about Gavazzi, that in his
youth nearly half a century before he had been present at some of his
meetings:

> He was far too eloquent not to be verbose, and he certainly was violent. I
> remember little of what he said in his lectures. His description of the
> prisons of the Inquisition and of the immorality of the priesthood were
> exceedingly vivid; but he struck me, after all, as being a genuine man
> with the faults which one would expect to find in a clergyman who had
> certainly a strong love of his country and had gone through much for it,
> but who had become so used to stirring great audiences that that which
> was a means to excite interest in the matters in which he absolutely
> believed, in the first instance, had become in itself an end. He lectured in
> a long black gown, and the great action that he used, and the way in
> which he threw his gown about him and off again was very theatrical,
> but it had a certain effectiveness.[120]

Other witnesses, unnamed reporters for provincial newspapers, give a
similar description though lacking in Spence Watson's insight on 'the
means' and 'the end'. In his first two years in England Gavazzi used
an interpreter; but before long he dispensed with this aid and from
the Woolwich Athenaeum to the Carlisle Athenaeum (with 'the very
Rev. the Dean and his lady present') and the Free Trade Hall in

[118] All of these topics recur frequently in newspaper reports of his meetings in the volume of
newspaper cuttings and printed ephemera, *Memorie*, and also in the volumes of newspaper
cuttings *Orations*, in the Facoltà Valdese at Rome. These topics are also to be found in *Lectures
of Gavazzi at New York*, New York, 1854.

[119] Campanella *Bibliografia*, no. 7819. Nikolai Aleksandrovic Dobrolinbov, *Otez Aleksandr
Gavazzi, i ego propovedi*, in *Sobranie Socineniy*, Petersburg, 1862.

[120] Trevelyan, *Defence* 76, n. 2.

Manchester he exposed the errors of Rome. Questions were asked about him in the House of Commons, for example by Mr Moore attacking Peel, who said in the prose style Dickens had had to endure in his youth as a press reporter: 'The low Jacobins of the continent were said to see the Gamaliels at whose feet the honourable baronet loved to sit, and the expressions he had used were worthy of his tutelage, for he recognised in them the philosophy of Mazzini and the apostasy of Gavazzi.' (Peel had been one of Gavazzi's audience at the Princess Theatre lecture room: and Moore was pro-Austrian). Gavazzi challenged him with the vigour if not the language of a *garibaldino* in *The Globe*: '. . . I need not suggest to you that your own name ὤμωρε signifies in that language, especially as one Erasmus (an apostate of the same extent as myself) has written a *Moriae Encomium*. If you know as much Italian as Greek, I invite you to hear me tomorrow at Wallis Rooms on the whole subject' – did Mahony suggest that gambit?[121]

In the *Memorie*, a quarto volume of newspaper cuttings in the Facoltà Valdese library at Rome, Gavazzi's public addresses are reported, those which he made in the later sixties and early seventies when visiting Britain to seek funds for his new Free Church of Italy which he had founded after his return to Italy, and which was fully organised by 1870. There is a typical hand-bill: 'Workmen's Hall, Birkenhead, Father [sic] Gavazzi will deliver his farewell lecture previous to his departure for Rome, on the New Dogma of Papal Infallibility and its startling consequences. Rev. Dr. Blakeney in the chair. Tickets – Body 1s, Gallery 6d.'[122] These prices suggest that by comparatively expensive tickets Irish labourers might be kept out. The question of where, and with what consequences and how often, Gavazzi was attacked in towns where a large Irish population existed also needs investigation.[123] The cuttings in the *Memorie*, like those volumes of newspaper cuttings dealing with his visits to Quebec and Montreal in the late fifties detailed at length by Sylvain, barely mention trouble – Gavazzi or his secretary preferred to collect for posterity his own words to additional news reports of rioting before or after meetings.

In 1854 the *Manchester Guardian* reported a lecture by Gavazzi when the chairman for the occasion, an energetic 'no popery' man, was the evangelical churchman canon Hugh Stowell of Christ

---

[121] *Orations of Fr. Gavazzi (Decade the Second)*, London, 1851, 69. (Mahony had helped with the translations of Gavazzi's first lectures.) Gavazzi, *The Globe*, 18 March.

[122] *Memorie*, 3, 4.

[123] S. W. Gilley, *The Garibaldi Riots of 1862, The Historical Journal*, vol. XVI, 1973, has brief references to Gavazzi and also a reference to anti-Italian Irish riots in 1855.

Church, Salford, who informed the audience that Gavazzi wanted a real king in Italy and 'not a wretched drivelling old woman'.[124] In 1856 Gavazzi toured South Wales, and he appeared there again on a visit from Italy in 1863. But a correspondent to *Y Faner ac Amserau y Cymru* who reported hearing him in Siloh Calvinist Methodist chapel, Aberystwyth, described the sermon as 'containing more philosophical ingenuity than practical substance' – a guarded way of saying that though Gavazzi was an impressive anti-papal orator yet he did not satisfy Calvinist Methodist standards for the content of a sermon.[125]

A small attendance at Glasgow in 1865 for a lecture on the French in Rome was blamed by Gavazzi on one of the self-appointed watchdogs against his heresies, Stewart, an ardent predestinarian – but perhaps a cold November night to hear about the French had no compelling power for Glaswegians.[126] At the Music Hall, Newcastle-upon-Tyne, the reverend Wildon Carr who presided presumably led the applause after Gavazzi's comparison of cloister life to 'a little lady in a large crinoline – a very small quantity of substance in a very large envelope'.[127] *The Scotsman* for 1865, shows him denouncing the Davenport brothers for hearing voices from the dead; elsewhere we learn the young men's improvement society at the Liverpool Institute under the chairmanship of the reverend M. Clegg was edified by him.

These brief allusions to his tours on the anti-papal circuits may be brought to the following climax given in an address at St George's Presbyterian church, Southport, where he refers to a new house and church built for his Free Church 'on the bank of the Tiber at the feet [*sic*] of the castle of S. Angelo. Turning to his left on his balcony he could see the Vatican a few hundred yards away, and some beautiful morning he and the Pope would open their respective windows and if they caught each other's eyes he would bid his holiness good morning because he could preach the Gospel freely and the Pope less cheerful would be looking impotently over Rome'.[128] By this period in the late seventies in Italy Gavazzi had apparently mellowed – but one essential goal of his life had been achieved, a united Italy and the abolition of papal civil government over Italians.

---

[124] *Orations*, 82.
[125] I owe this information to a member of the staff on the National Library of Wales, Aberystwyth; another member provided the translation of the reporter's Welsh phrase in *Y Faner*.
[126] *Memorie*, cutting from *Daily Review* of Glasgow for 7 November 1865.
[127] *Memorie*, 43.
[128] *Memorie*, 210, *Southport Daily News* (the newspaper cutting is cut too close to give the date, but it must have been on a visit to England by Gavazzi after 1870).

Something should be said about a few at least of his writings: many were ephemeral, consisting of journalism, as well as sermons and lectures, but some were set pieces. His early attempt at the traditional rhetorical style of pulpit oratory is tedious, and its interest lies in showing how greatly he changed later in theme, style and manner. His nearest approach to a full-scale work of scholarship was his book on St. Peter, *La Favola del Viaggio di S. Pietro a Roma*, 1868, where in three parts forming 320 pages he sought to prove that Peter had never been to Rome nor was he martyred there, nor, thereafter, was he the first bishop of Rome, nor were the papal claims for special authority justified. In all this his aim would be to challenge in advance the rumours of the coming Vatican Council I and the probability of a declaration of papal infallibility. In the preface Gavazzi contemptuously wrote of the *vanità puerile* and *religione da teatro* of Pius, and the famous *non possumus* was dismissed as mere 'feminine obstinacy'. The book is built up on negations derived from wide but superficial reading, and in the light of modern scholarship displays some eccentricities; but at the time most convinced Protestant controversialists in England as elsewhere would have agreed with his main themes. Gavazzi asserts that it is clear from the Bible that Peter's commission was not to be in Rome but in Babylon – and he adds that 'Hebrews were numerous in Assyria'.[129] He continues that historical tradition is against it: Eusebius was simply wrong and there is no proven episcopal descent from Peter; Ignatius was rhetorical; Papias was credulous; Hegesippus was spurious as were also the *Apostolic Constitutions* and the *Clementine Recognitions*; and he cuts down the erroneous assumptions in Tertullian, Origen and Cyprian. He concludes by showing that archaeology is no help; the cathedral of St. Peter is in no sense his.[130] For a good knock-down method of argument Humpty Dumpty could not have done better, but he would have been less verbose.

Among his writings in English two are worth mention and quotation: *My Recollections of the Last Four Popes, and of Rome in their Times*, 1858, and *No Union with Rome: An Anti-Eirenicon*, 1866. Cardinal Wiseman, for Gavazzi a fanatic on three counts – he had an Irish father, he was born in Spain, and he was educated at Rome – had addressed a large gathering at Myddleton Hall, Islington, on Pius VII, Leo XII, Pius VIII, Gregory XVI and Pius IX praising their virtues and achievements.[131] A few days later Gavazzi furiously

129 These arguments are from the first section.
130 These arguments are from sections 2 and 3.
131 Cardinal N. P. Wiseman, *Recollections of the Last Four Popes and of Rome in their times*,

rebutted Wiseman's eulogies in the same auditorium. He then produced, extended into a book, the substance of his attack on Cardinal Wiseman's bland and graceful periods. In the preface he warms up with this judgement of Wiseman: 'The author, to spare his readers all intellectual fatigue has, with a charity which deserves to be transmitted to posterity, taken care to say nothing.'[132] Later in the book a memory of his youth when he first visited Rome and crossed the frontier at Radicofani into the papal states came back to him: 'What is the sign by which the traveller perceives that he has entered the dominions of the priests? The appearance of squalor, poverty and wretchedness, which surrounds him on every hand ... a heap of dirty cottages ironically called the town of Radicofani ... The Roman States ... the desert of Italy, and more than the desert, the opprobrium of the peninsula.'[133] The Jesuits received a dismissive sentence: '... the fatal order ... its own confession, which I have many times heard boldly repeated by Jesuits, [is] that its sole aim is to push back our age to feudalism, to ignorance, and the state of Catholic servility anterior to the French Revolution.'[134] Wiseman incautiously had said of Gregory XVI: 'I am not aware that there was a single political execution in his pontificate.' Gavazzi's response was blunt: 'May God pardon all liars! ... in 1843 alone ... in Bologna ... six were condemned to death for political crimes, and the sentence was executed ...'[135] Gavazzi's intense patriotism overcame what little tact he possessed when he even attacked one of England's heroes by exploding into these words: '... history, so long as the world shall last, will bear witness to the ineffaceable infamy of Nelson.'[136] Gavazzi must have startled even hardened Protestants, when referring to his 'imprisonment' under Gregory XVI at San Severino monastery, by stating that friends at Rome, including a Roman colonel in the pontifical army, sent him a list of concubines of the prelates, cardinals and even of Gregory himself, 'with the exception of Lambruschini', so that by seeking this feminine aid he could obtain release – 'I

London, 1858. Gavazzi, *My Recollections* in the preface, v, wrote: 'In answer to his lecture on the Four Popes I delivered one after in the same place. How did they resemble each other? As much as Italy and Ireland.'

[132] Gavazzi, *My Recollections of the last Four Popes*, vi.

[133] Ibid., 10.

[134] Ibid., 38.

[135] Ibid., 200.

[136] Ibid., 255. *The Encylopaedia Britannica* (11 ed, New York, 1911) 19, 355, pompously stated: 'The story of Nelson's visit to Naples in the June of 1799 will probably remain a subject for perpetual discussion' – this means he acted in a discreditable manner. Emma Hamilton persuaded Nelson to support the queen of Naples and the feeble Bourbon king, and he acted entirely arbitrarily in quelling republicans and hanging their leaders. Gavazzi was one of those Italians who evidently neither forgot nor forgave this.

scorned [this] method but preferred to remain in captivity rather than obtain my freedom by such vile instrumentality'.[137] However, Gavazzi's height of scorn for Gregory XVI, his *bête noire*, is found in this astonishing sentence: 'Meanwhile, let the admirers of the succession of St. Peter delight themselves in their holy Pope, "the virtuous Gregory", who, on his part, stretched upon the couches of the beauteous Gaetanina, and surrounded by a coronet of youthful satellites, exclaims from his apostolic heart, *Deus nobis haec otia fecit.*'[138] Sylvain understandably loses his calm control, in describing Gavazzi's career, at this point: '. . . la masse d'anecdotes dont ces pages regorgent, suffisent, pensons-nous, à demonstrer *ab absurdo* que l'on ne peut ajouter foi aux assertions d'un pamphlétaire qui n'hésite pas à confier au papier les ragots les plus infects avec une absence désarmante d'esprit critique.'[139] Two points are worth making about Gavazzi's violent polemic: first, he believed the truth of what he was saying, he was no sly inventive Achilli, nor was it his intention to be merely scurrilous; the second point is that his anecdotes about Gregory were based on well-known popular assumptions in Rome which were wittily put in dialect verses by Guiseppi Belli and passed about as flysheets. Mazzini quoted one when in exile in England; the Italian political exiles would have known these and the Romans among them would know how popular opinion supported these wry judgments.[140] Members of Gregory's own Order published two commemorative volumes in honour of him in 1948, and one of the contributors, Ghisalberti, dealt fully with Belli's verses on that Pope which are freely quoted without the indignation of Sylvain, rather they are used as helping to build up a portrait of that period.[141] The

---

[137] *My Recollections*, 274 The violence of Roman anti-papalism can be seen here.

[138] Ibid., 277, v. also n. 140 below. This coarse sentence is as regrettable as its appreciation by a large section of Victorian Protestantism.

[139] Sylvain, 2, 459.

[140] Mazzini copied a sonnet of Belli's in his London exile in a letter to a friend, see A. M. Ghisalberti, at *Gregorio XVI*, Toma 2, 350 (see n. 141 below).

[141] 'Il carabiniere A. Bianchi Giovini', wrote *Il Papa e la sua Corte*, Rome, 1860 *Miscellanea Commemorativa*, according to A. M. Ghisalberti, 'Gregorio XVI e il Risorgimento', in *Gregorio XVI*, Toma 2, 1948, and described the 'fig-like' nose of Gregory and his *abuso del vino*. Ghisalberti also refers to Gaetano Moroni's beautiful wife, and quotes Belli's poem of 1835, *Er Papa Omo*, in his *Sonnetti Romaneschi* no 1533 (see n. 42 above):

> A Palazzo der Papa c'è un giardino
> Co un boschetto e in ner bosco un padijone
> Pien de sofà a la turca e de potrone
> E de bottije de rosojo e vino,
> C'eppoi ne le su' stanzie un cammerino
> Co 'una porta de dietro a un credenzone
> Che mette a una scaletta, e in concrusione
> Corisponne ar quartier di Ghitanino
> Ghitanino è ammojato: la su' moje

real thrust of Gavazzi's argument is to discredit the Popes praised in Cardinal Wiseman's book and to draw the attention of English-speaking readers to the evils of papal government in Italy: 'The evil government of the priests went to such lengths, that it became a proverb in the Roman States, "Better be under the Turks than under the priests". Can Wiseman deny these facts?'[142] Gavazzi also shows his neo-ghibelline allegiance: '– if the substitution of the Orleans for the Bourbon branch was legitimate in France [this is aimed at the legitimist principle of Metternich supported by the Jesuits and Pius IX], it can but be legitimate in the Roman States to substitute a popular and Italian government for the cruel anomaly of the Papacy'.[143] If nothing else the passion of the writer, and the autobiographical basis of his attack, give interest to this forgotten book. The style has energy and pungent phrasing. Gavazzi can hardly have achieved this without some help, even if this was limited to proof-reading. 'Father Prout' was in Paris during this period, and perhaps had no hand in the preparation of the text but the sentence quoted above about Gregory XVI has a twist and a Latin tag which echo his style. King and others of Gavazzi's English friends lacked this sarcastic stylistic force.

Gavazzi's *No union with Rome* is an indignant onslaught on Tractarian respect for Roman Catholicism; it is an odd chance that his preface is dated from Newman Street. Gavazzi was indignant at Pusey's reunion scheme, and had been profoundly suspicious of the Oxford movement since his first visit to England.[144] 'You, Doctor [Pusey], with utter want of charity and logic, assert that rationalism was given us by Lutheranism, as Socinianism was given us by Calvinism . . . where is the English Church? In the homeopathic fraction of Oxford, a Tom Thumb of Anglicanism . . . I shall advise him [Pusey] to go to Rome to study Romanism better than he has

---

É una donna de garbo, assai divota
Der vicario de Dio che lega e scioje
Oh, nun vojo dì antro: e ho-ffatto male
Anzi a pparla cusì, dove se nota
Oggni pelo e se pensa ar criminale.

See *Tuttii Sonnetti Romaneschi*, ed. Bruno Cagli, 5 vols, Rome, 1964–5), 4, 361. These pieces of Belli's were not immediately printed but passed around in manuscript, Gavazzi's use of this material shows that touch of vulgarity referred to below, 363. In any event Wiseman had already gracefully dealt with Gregory's large nose in his *Recollections*.

[142] *My Recollections*, 51.

[143] Ibid., 185, 186.

[144] H. P. Liddon, Life of *E. B. Pusey*, London, 1898, 4, 107. Pusey wrote to Keble a letter which he called his 'First Eirenicon' – this was a defence of the catholicity of the Church of England against an attack on it by Archbishop Manning in 1864. But it also contains suggestions on how re-union could be achieved between Rome and Canterbury.

done from his books or in the company of Newman, who strives to
retain in his new faith a portion of the liberty he enjoyed in the
English Church.'[145] When Gavazzi explained to readers his own
religious views – this book is an interesting *apologia* for them, since it
contains an exposition of his unusual religious position – Pusey, if he
had troubled to read it would have been shocked by Gavazzi's
dismissal of the Athanasian creed as 'the apocryphal composition of a
half-crazy monk, [which] reduces itself to the riddle of a sphynx,
while, in its condemnatory clauses, it belongs to the religion of Belial
or Juggernaut.'[146] But for Pusey there would be nothing to choose
between a Gavazzi and an Achilli – false and renegade priests both.
Gavazzi's religious position is seen in these sentences: 'As I belong
neither to the English Church nor to any other Protestant
denomination, my sole aim in Italy being the revival of the Church
of Rome as it was in the glorious days of the Apostle Paul, so I feel
myself called upon only to defend the great principles of Christianity
common to all . . . in all the confessions of the reformed Churches
there is what I call human and theological doctrine in open questions
and in the mode of explaining dogma . . . I have in my favour . . .
the patristic axiom of the great Augustine, *in dubiis libertas* . . . I am
an Evangelical Christian of the Italian Church, as established in Rome
by the Apostle St. Paul, without Pope and without Popery.'[147] He
had a valid and prophetic criticism of Protestant proselytising in
Italy: '. . . sad experience has taught me that the sects which send
agents and missionaries to evangelize Italy have nothing in view but the
glorification of their own denomination, by the transplanting of which
to Italy we shall end miserably with religious strife and divisions . . .'[148]

The archons of ecumenism in our day since they appear to regard
the study of church history as unfruitful, or indeed as 'irrelevant',
may not know that Gavazzi wrote in 1866: '. . . the reader may see
how logical I am in that while I strive to promote the unity and
brotherhood of the Churches of Italy . . . it is but natural that I
should desire to see the reunion of the different denominations of
England'; nor may they know of the failure of his great efforts in
setting up a Free Church of Italy uncommitted to dogmatic niceties,
and free of the mortmain of past history which he had hoped,
therefore, could be the basis for uniting Protestants.[149] In his last aim

[145] *No Union with Rome: an Anti-Eirenicon*, London, 1866, 50, 51.
[146] Ibid., 96.
[147] Ibid., 299.
[148] Ibid., 299. See Santini, 185 ff. chapter unnumbered, entitled 'Problemi delle giovani
Chiese protestanti italiane (1877–1883'.
[149] *Sixteenth Evangelization Report of the Free Christian Church in Italy*, Glasgow, 1887.

– a church which would draw to it the diverse and divided Protestant bodies of Italy – he achieved no success. His indefatigable tours abroad to raise funds made possible the establishing of a number of congregations, a theological college and central church 'at the foot of S. Angelo', but after 1896 there was no future. The *plimuttisi* he had feared found places in his congregation and divided them; his pastors wanted more 'order'; and the *Chiesa Christiana Libera d'Italia* disappeared largely into the Wesleyan and Episcopal Methodist churches in Italy after 1905.[150]

Eliot's words that history 'gives too late what's not believed in' echo again in the mind: the religious passion of the Risorgimento (for it began, in spite of the secret societies, or Mazzini's well-intentioned intrigues, as a religious crisis) had faltered by 1870. Gavazzi had found a new birth of religious conviction and aims through 'the crusade', and then had had to readjust painfully, and ultimately unsuccessfully, to a new religious position. History has left him as a shadow 'in memory only reconsidered passion'. Is reconsideration of Gavazzi worth the trouble? Neither Pusey nor Eliot in their respective generations would have thought so. My own implied judgements that politically he was a noise in the street, and religiously not much more than rhetoric on public platforms, are perhaps too harsh. We may remember Jowett's no doubt justified criticism of an essay by Cosmo Gordon Lang when the future archbishop was an undergraduate at Balliol: 'Words are not always ideas, nor are ideas always realities' – this dictum could apply to Gavazzi.[151] For all his theatricality, and the vulgar streak that irritated the young poet Mameli[152] to aversion when dying, Gavazzi deserves to be remembered as a brave, patriotic and religious man, who took far-ranging decisions on principle, and not for self-advancement, who shows us that great movements in the past are misunderstood by historians if they ignore or reject the significance of the religious convictions of those who participated in them. An epigraph for Gavazzi could be the words he placed on his book which he had dedicated to his mother: *Se io viva ancor eccone O Madre il segno* – he still lives when we see *il segno* of religious aspirations in the Risorgimento.

---

[150] J. R. McDougall prepared the report, and after 1896 he stated that this church had no independent future.

[151] J. G. Lockhart, *The Life of Cosmo Gordon Lang*, London, 1949, 27.

[152] Trevelyan, *Defence*, 308.

Index of Modern Authors

Aitken, C. A. 256
Allen, H. M. 130
Allen, P. S. 2, 19, 21, 53–8, 62–4, 66–9, 71–2, 75–6, 78, 115, 130, 175–6, 180
Anrich, Gustav 127
Armstrong, Elizabeth 35
Asensio, Eugenio 22
Ashley, E. 351
Azcona, Tarsicio de 6

Baer, Yitzhak 5, 28
Baron, Hans 87, 96, 104–5, 118
Bartel, O. 172, 184
Bartels, Petrus 177
Barth, Karl ix, 127–8
Barth, P. 126
Bataillon, Marcel 8, 10, 11, 13, 43–6, 81
Baum, W. 146
Baum, J. W. 129–31
Bell, A. F. G. 49
Béné, Charles 55
Bentley, J. H. 21, 38–9, 66, 77
Berkeley, G. F. -H. and J. 330–2
Bianchi, Luigi 336

Bihlmeyer, K. 327, 338
Bizer, E. 153
Blakiston, L. 332
Bludau, A. 77
Boffito, Giuseppe 322–3
Bonilla, A. 11
Boyle, M. O'R. 82
Brady, jr., T. A. 115
Brandi, Karl 162
Brandt, A. von 104
Bretschneider, E. G. 162
Brewer, J. S. 244
Broadhead, Philip 105
Brooks, P. N. 105
Brown, P. H. 273
Brown Patterson, W. 234
Bruce, John 234
Buck, L. P. 105, 107
Buisson, F. 195
Burch, C. E. 270, 277
Burton, Edward 224
Butterworth, C. C. 218–19

Cagli, Bruno 361
Campanella, Anthony P. 338, 350–1, 355
Campanella, G. M. 320, 333, 354

Casini, T. 334
Castro, Americo 15, 28
Castro, J. Villa-Amil y 14, 41
Cencetti, Giorgio 314, 318–20, 333–4
Chabas, Roque 16, 25
Chalmers, G. 277
Chrisman, M. V. 115, 119
Cirot, G. 50
Clair, C. 43
Clebsch, W. A. 210, 215
Clemen, O. 155
Cockburn, J. D. 274
Collinson, Patrick 242–3, 252–3
Conrad, Joseph 319, 323
Conti, Ludovico 318, 320
Cornelius, C. A. 107, 112–13
Crane, R. S. 291
Cross, Claire 233
Cuming, G. J. 225
Cunitz, E. 146
Cytowska, Maria 175

Dacheux, L. 117
Dalton, Hermann 174, 176, 179, 183, 191
Darlow, T. H. 43
Davis, Herbert 280, 285, 290, 293–6,
    298–312
D'Azeglio, Massimo 354
Delgado, Muñoz 20
Dénuce, J. 44
De Ruggiero, G. F. 322
Dessain, C. S. 315
De Voght, Henry 44
Dickens, A. G. 87, 212–13
Diéz Merino, L. 37
Dittrich, F. 161
Dixon, R. W. 171–2, 185
Doernberg, Erwin 209
Dorey, T. A. ix
Dowden, J. 225–8
Dudon, Paul 337
Dugmore, C. W. 202

Eberhardt Hans 100
Eckert, W. P. 149
Eells, Hastings 157–8, 167
Eliot, T. S. 313-15, 338, 363
Ellis, Henry 218, 224, 226
Elton G. R. 217, 223
Enders, E. L. 129
Erichson, A. 131
Eschenhagen, Edith 98

Espinosa, Benito Hernando y 8–10

Farini, L. C. 332
Ferguson, W. K. 59–61
Fernández Marcos, Natalio 38
Fernández-Sevilla, Julio 17
Fernández Vallina, F. J. 41
Frere, W. H. 202, 225–7
Fuente, D. Vicente de la 8, 10

Gabler, Ulrich 102
Gairdner, J. 209
Galindo, Paschalis 25
Gams, P. B. 180
Garcia Oro, José 3–4
Gardiner, S. R. 254
George, C. H. 242
Ghisalberti, A. M. 332, 342, 360–1
Gil, Luis 12, 17
Gil Fernández, Juan 22
Gilley, S. W. 356
Ginsburg, C. D. 35
Gioacchino Belli, G. 326
González Carvajal, T. 43, 49
Gramsci, Antonio 315
Greaves, Richard 215, 250
Green, Lowell C. 82
Gualtieri, Luigi 328, 331
Gulik, Wilhelm van 159, 163

Hadot, J. 66
Hall, Basil 32, 44, 205, 253
Hanbury, B. 247
Hardwick, C. 222
Hare, Julius 235
Harth, Philip 297
Healey, G. H. 258, 263
Heath-Stubbs, John 322
Hefele, Carl Joseph 6, 12
Hein, K. 182
Heredia, Beltrán de 8, 10, 17
Herford, C. H. 249
Herminjard, A. L. 166
Hess, A. C. 6
Heylyn, P. 235
Hildebrandt, F. 227
Hill, Christopher 239–40
Hipler, F. 181
Hirschberg, A. 173
Holborn, H. 95
Hopf, C. 135, 227
Huerga, Alvaro 44

Hughes, P. 235
Hume, M. A. S. 232
Hussey, M. 248

Iserloh, E. 164

Jackson, R. W. 288
Jacobs, H. E. 209, 220–1, 223, 225, 229
Janelle, P. 213
Jedin, H. 48, 84, 143, 147–9, 155, 167, 169–70
Johnson, A. F. 42
Jonghe, H. J. de 77
Jørgensen, E. J. 181–2, 194
Joyce, James 258, 340

Kahle, Paul 35, 37
Kamen, Henry 4, 6
Kawerau, D. G. 183–4
Kidd, B. J. 124
King, G. G. 18
King, J. W. 320, 344, 350–4
Kipling, Rudyard 252
Kitson Clark, G. 242–3
Knox, R. B. ix
Koenigsberger, H. G. 87
Kolde, T. 143, 159
Kowalska, Halina 206
Krahn, Cornelius 109–111, 114, 187
Krodel, Gottfried G. 100
Kropf, Lewis L. 180
Kruske, K. A. R. 182, 192, 202–3, 205
Kuyper, A. 173, 183–4, 187–9, 192–205

Lampedusa, Giuseppe Tomasi di 337
Landa, L. A. 287, 301
Laski, H. 88
Latham, R. C. 248
Lau, F. 153
Law, E. 285
Lea, H. C. 4, 6
Leavis, F. R. 283–4, 306
Leff, Gordon 101
Lefranc, A. 12
Lemus y Rubio, Pedro 17
Lenz, Max 156–8
Liddon, H. P. 361
Lipgens, W. 155
Llamas, José 29, 31, 36
Llorca, Bernardino 2–4, 7, 9, 11, 15–16
Llorente, Miguel de la Pinta 5, 45–7
Lloyd Thomas, J. 245

Lockhart, J. G. 363
Lodolini, Armando 314, 327
Loevinson, Ermanda 334
Looten, Camille 283, 297
López Rueda, Jose 18
Lortz, J. 84, 147, 155

Mack Smith, Denis 315, 316
Mackensen, H. 159–61, 163
McConica, J. K. 217
McCord, J. I. ix
Mannin, Ethel 351
Maravall, J. A. 27, 29
Margarita, Solaro della 325
Margolin, J. -C. 149
Márquez, A. 44
Martínez de Velasco, Eusebio 10
Matheson, Peter 143, 152, 157, 161
Maturi, Walter 314, 316, 338, 340–2
Mazzeo, J. A. 291
Menéndez Pelayo, Marcelino 2
Metzger, B. M. 39
Meyer, Carl S. 209–11, 223
Miller, Perry 242
Minghetti, M. 334
Moeller, Bernd ix, 87–8, 121
Mönckeberg, R. 203
Montanelli, Indro 315
Monti, A. 349
Moore, J. R. 263–4
Morley, H. 260
Mosse, George L. 87
Moule, H. F. 43
Müller, Nikolaus 98

Nader, Helen 19
Naef, Henri 94, 121–4
Natali, G. 335
Nesti, Arnaldo 315
Nettleship, H. 52
Nicolini, G. B. 320, 329, 333
Nicolson, Marjorie 292
Nielson, Fredrik 326, 328
Norton, F. J. 18, 20, 41–3
Nuttall, Geoffrey 250

Oakeshott, M. 296
Odriozota, Antonio 17
Olmedo, Felix G. 17, 22, 24
Omedeo, Adolfo 325
O'Neill, George 351
Origo, Iris 322

Ortega Monasterio, Teresa 36
Ortiz, Aloysius 25
Ortiz, Antonio Domínguez 5, 28
Ozment, Steven E. 87, 104

Palumbo, Beniamino 349
Parker, T. H. L. ix
Pascal, G. 181, 183–4
Passerin d'Entrèves, E. 348
Pastor, Ludwig 143, 149, 152, 154, 159–
    60, 165
Pattison, Mark 52
Payne, J. B. 82
Pelikan, J. 145
Pérez, Joseph 27
Pérez Castro, Federico 21, 26–7, 29–30,
    33, 41
Pflugk-Hartung, J. von 106
Pierce, W. 246
Pineau, J. -B. 130
Pinta Llorente, Miguel de la see Llorente,
    Miguel de la Pinta
Pollet, J. V. 182, 199
Pons, Emile 291
Porreño, Baltasar 6, 13
Porter, H. C. 241
Potter, G. R. 101
Pozo, C. 47
Pratt, Josiah 70, 208, 218
Prescott, J. 258
Preus, J. S. 98
Procter, F. 202, 225–7
Purcell, E. S. 330

Quentin, H. 41

Ranke, Leopold von 142, 150, 160,
    166
Rava, Luigi 334
Reicke, Bo 66
Rekers, B. 44, 47, 49
Reuss, E. 146
Rico, Mariano Revilla 20, 39
Robinson, G. C. 235
Rogers, Pat 282
Rooses, M. 44
Roth, F. 105
Rückert, Hans 160
Rudman, W. H. 352
Rummel, V. E. 76
Rupp, E. G. 82, 87, 103, 108, 210
Rupprich, H. 97

Saénz-Badillos Angel 12, 17, 19–21, 23,
    38–9
Sainz de Zúñiga, C. M. Ajo G. y 7,
    9–10
Sainz Rodríguez, Pedro 3, 6, 14
Salvatorelli, Luigi 340
Sanfilippo, Paolo 353
Santini, Luigi 320–1, 323–5, 333, 344–5,
    349–50, 362
Sanz, Manuel Serrano y 45
Scheuner, D. 126
Schickler, F. de 192
Schildauer, J. 104
Schlecht, H. 100
Schmidt, A. -M. 295
Scholderer, V. 42
Schubert, Hans von 106
Schwiebert, E. G. 97
Scott, Sir Walter 257, 269, 272–3, 278
Scrivener, F. H. A. 69
Sicroff, A. 15
Simon, Alois 331
Simpson, P. and E. M. 249
Smith, H. M. 209
Spini, Georgio 317, 345, 353
Sprunger, K. L. 252
Stephen, Leslie 282
Stoughton, J. 218
Strauss, Gerald 93, 100–1, 105
Stupperich, Robert 107, 162
Sylvain, Robert 314, 318, 320–2, 329,
    331–5, 342, 344, 356, 360

Taine, H. A. 279
Tarelli, C. C. 66
Tarsicio de Azcona, see Azcona, Tarsicio
    de
Tawney, R. H. 88, 238
Tjernagel, N. S. 209, 210, 215
Torre, A. de la (A. de la Torre y del
    Cero) 5, 9, 11, 17
Torre, Arnaldo della 317, 340, 345–8
Traugott, John 297
Trevelyan, G. M. 238, 316, 331, 355,
    363
Trinkaus, Charles 56, 82
Trinterud, L. J. 210, 241
Tuechle, H. 327, 338
Tuveson, E. 297

Van Gulik, Wilhelm see Gulik,
    Wilhelm van

Vegas Montaner, L. 41
Vercellone, C. 37
Vickers, Brian ix
Vidler, A. R. 339
Villoslada, Ricardo García 9
Vinay, Valdo 317, 346
Voet, L. 43
Von Brandt, A. see Brandt, A. von
Von Pflugk-Hartung, J. see Pflugk-
    Hartung, J. von
Von Ranke, Leopold see Ranke, Leopold
    von
Von Schubert, Hans see Schubert, Hans
    von

Waetzwoldt, W. 107
Walton, Robert C. 121
Ward, Wilfred 318
Watson, P. S. 231
Weber, Max 88

Wendel, F. 120, 133–5
Williams, Harold 280–2, 285–7, 290,
    294, 299, 301
Wincklemann, O 93
Woodhouse, A. S. P. 237–8
Wright, D. F. 199
Wright, L. P. 18
Wright, T. 258, 265, 270

Yule, G. 170, 205, 252

Zaccagnini, G. 333
Zakrzewski, V. 181
Zantuan, Konstantin 173, 175–6, 181
Zappoli, A. 335
Zeissberg, H. 173
Zophy, J. W. 105, 107
Zúñiga, Sainz de see Sainz de Zúñiga
Zweig, Stefan 195

General Index

Ab Ulmis 191
Achilli, Giacinto 318, 362
Adrian of Utrecht
  (Cardinal) 27, 43
  (Pope Adrian VI) 106
Agricola, Johann 230
Alba, Duke of 44
Albert, Charles 339
Albrecht of Prussia 205
Aleandro, Cardinal 58, 60, 78, 149
Alexander VI, Pope 3, 4, 8
Amat, Cardinal 334
Amerbach, Bonifacius 58, 64, 176–7,
  170–80, 184
Ames, William 252
Amsdorf, Nikolaus von 154, 157
Anabaptism 86–7, 101–4, 109–10,
  119–20, 132–3, 135, 182, 184–7,
  197, 243
Angoulême, Marguerite of 233
Angulo, Juan de 11
Anna of Opdenburg, Countess 184–5, 191
Anne, Queen 242, 263, 278, 282
Annesley, Samuel 256
Aquila, Greek version of Old Testament
  38
Aquinas, Thomas, St. 61, 73

Arias Montano, Benito 21, 43–4, 47, 49–
  51
Aristotle 48, 63, 291–3
Askew, Anne 208
Atterbury, Francis, Bishop 305
Augsburg Confession 146–7, 153, 161,
  165, 204–5, 220–2, 229–30, 233
Augustine of Hippo, St. 23, 32, 45, 54–6,
  60, 362

Bacon, Francis 292, 295
Badius, Ascensius 58
Baillie, Robert 278
Balbo, Cesare 341, 345
Bale, John 208–9
Barbosa, Arias 20
Bar Hanina 59
Barnes, Robert 209–10, 215–16, 218
Baronius, Cesare 145
Barrow, Henry 247
Bassi, Ugo 322, 324, 328–9, 331, 333,
  344–5, 350–1
Batt, James 55, 62
Baxter, Richard 245–6, 250–1, 253–4
Bayley, Lewis 254
Beaufort, Countess de Liederkerke de
  332

Bedini, Gaetano 321, 350
Bell, Henry 235
Belli, Giuseppi 360–1
Belsunce, M. de, Bishop 287
Bembo, Cardinal 54
Beninga, Eggerik 192
Beroaldo, Filippo 61
Bertram (Bertramus), J. F. B. 177
Bessarion, Cardinal 14, 37
Beza (Bèze), Theodore de 66
Bible
    Antwerp Polyglot (Biblia Regia)
        43–4, 49–50
    Complutensian Polyglot 13–42
    English 219–20
    New Testament (Erasmus) 43, 53, 57,
        64, 67–78
Bilney, Thomas 70–1
Blackwell, Thomas 278
Blaurer, Ambrosius 154
Bolingbroke, Henry St. John, 1st
    Viscount 284, 286, 299, 311
Bolzani, Urban 62
Bonamino, Lazarus 181
Booth, William, General 238
Boswell, James 286
Botzheim, Johann 62, 175
Bradford, John 214, 231
Bradshaw, William 247
Brandenburg, Elector of 144, 150, 155,
    159, 169
Brandt, Sebastian 117
Braniczki, Jan 174
Brenz, Johannes 154, 226, 228–31
Brethren of the Common Life 54, 79,
    109, 181, 195
Brocar, Guillén de 14, 18, 41, 43–4
Browne, Robert 251
Browne, Sir Thomas 295
Browning, Robert 85
Bucer, Martin vii, 84, 88, 213, 215, 225,
    230
    and Laski 172, 187, 190–1, 199,
        201
    ministry, doctrine of 127–41
    and Regensburg Colloquy 143–4,
        146–7, 150, 153–4, 156–62,
        167–70
    and Strasbourg 86, 90, 118–20
    works
        Commentary on Ephesians 132,
            137, 139

Commentary on the Gospels 129,
    132–3
Das ym Selbs niemant . . . 119, 131,
    141
De Ordinatione 137
De Regno Christi 120, 128, 132–3,
    135–7, 139–41
De Vera Animarum Cura 136–9
Defensio de Christiana Reformatione
    136–9
Ein summarischer Vergriff der
    Christlichen Lehre und
    Religion 133, 136, 138
Getrewe Warnung gegen Jakob
    Kautz 132–3.
Pia Deliberatio 140
Budé, Guillaume 12, 62–3, 126
Bullinger, Heinrich 173, 180, 189, 191,
    193–5, 198–9, 201, 204, 215, 224,
    226
Bunyan, John 238–9, 246, 251, 253
Burcher, John 224
Burkhardt, Chancellor of Saxony 161
Burnet, Gilbert, Bishop 303–5

Cajetan, Cardinal 45, 146
Calixt (Georg Calixtus) 231
Calov (Abraham Calovius) 231
Calvin, Jean 48, 84, 88, 90, 238
    and Bucer 120, 135
    and Defoe 265
    and English Reformation 81
    and Erasmus 65, 84–5
    and Farel 123, 186
    and Geneva 86, 90, 123–8, 135
    and Laski 187–90, 194–5, 197–200,
        202, 204
    and Luther 125–6, 215
    and Puritan theology 253
    and Regensburg Colloquy 146, 154–7,
        162, 164–5
    Institutio Religionis Christianae 123,
        125, 126
Camden, Sir William 234
Campeggio, Cardinal 107
Campeggio, Tommaso, Bishop 154, 159
Cano, Melchor 47
Capito, Wolfgang 19, 117–19, 132, 135,
    154, 157–8
Caraffa, Cardinal 342
Carillo, Alonso, Archbishop of Toledo
    7

Carlstadt (Andreas Bodenstein) 98, 103, 108, 184, 189
Carlyle, Thomas 351
Caronselet, John 130
Carstares, William 276, 278
Cartagena, Antonio 11
Cartwright, Thomas 211, 247, 250–1
Casimir, Prince 100
Cassel, Liturgy of 225
Castelar, Luis Pérez de 11
Castellio, Sebastian 32, 71, 195
Castile, King of 9
Castillo, Juan de 46
Castro, Bartolomé de 19–20
Castro, León de 47–50
Catherine of Siena, St. 14
Catholic Kings, the 3–6, 15
Cavour, Count Camillo Benso di 316, 319, 337, 339, 347–9
Cecil, William 191, 193
Cellarius, Jean 64
Celtis, Conrad 173
Cervantes 15
Cervini, Cardinal 152
Charles I 302–4
Charles V, Emperor vii, 10, 45, 81, 91, 95–6, 105, 119–20, 133, 144, 150–2, 156, 159, 161, 169, 185, 190–1
Charles of Ghent 5 see also Charles V, Emperor
Charron, Pierre 297
Chateaubriand, Vicomte de 341, 354
Cheke, Sir John 191
Cheney, Richard, Bishop 234
Chesterfield, Philip Dormer Stanhope, 4th Earl of 294, 299
Chillingworth, William 297
Christian III, of Denmark and Norway 203
Chrysolaras, Manuel 18
Chrysostom, John, St. 189
Cicero 83
Ciruelo, Pedro 9, 29, 31
Cisneros, Francisco Ximenez de see Jiménez de Cisneros, Cardinal
Cisneros, Garcia Ximenez de 6–7
Clarendon, Edward Hyde, 1st Earl of 245
Clement VII, Pope 150
Cochlaeus, Johannes 97, 146, 153–4, 156–7
Colepepper, William 263

Colet, John 58, 61, 63, 67, 79, 81
Colines, Simon de 65–6
Collins, Anthony 299
Cologne, Elector of 155, 169
Conde de la Coruña 9
Contarini, Cardinal 46, 79, 84, 144, 148, 152, 157, 159–69, 342
Coronel, Pablo de 11, 13, 21
Coverdale, Miles 219–20, 228
Cowley, Abraham 289
Cox, Richard, Bishop 233
Cranmer, Thomas, Archbishop viii, 147, 171, 190–1, 201–2, 213, 217, 220–9
Crofton, Zachary 248
Cromwell, Henry 254
Cromwell, Oliver 126, 238, 243, 251, 289, 290
Cromwell, Thomas 223
Cruciger, Felix 206
Cuoco, Vincenzo 340
Curll, Edmund 301
Cyprian, St. 198

Dante 346–7
Davenant, John 253
D'Azeglio, Massimo 331, 342
De Dominis, Archbishop of Spalato 244
Defoe, Benjamin 276
Defoe, Daniel viii, 254, 255–79
    Act of Union (1707), commitment to 257, 266–78
    death 279
    early life and education 255–6, 258–9
    'Protestant Flail' 259–60, 266
    Protestantism, commitment to 257, 260–5
    in Scotland 269–78
    secret agent of Harley and Godolphin 267–9, 272–6
    and Swift 255
    works
        Advice to all Parties 268
        An Appeal to Honour and Justice 256, 258, 260, 263
        Caledonia 270
        Colonel Jack 256
        An Essay at removing National Prejudices against a Union with Scotland 270
        An Essay upon Projects 255

The Family Instructor 266
The History of the Union of Great Britain 257, 276, 278
The Marriage Bed 261, 266
Meditations 258–9
Memoirs of the Church of Scotland 277–8
Moll Flanders 256
The Present State of the Parties 258
Religious Courtship 261
Review 263, 266, 270–3, 277
Robinson Crusoe 258–9, 261, 264–6, 270
Roxana 256
Serious Reflections during the life of Robinson Crusoe 256, 261, 264–5, 274
The Shortest Way with Dissenters 257, 262–3
A Tour through the whole Island of Great Britain 260
The True-Born Englishman 260
Defoe, James 257
Delaney, Dr. 286
Denck, Hans 81
Denina, Carlo 315
Descartes, René 293, 296, 298
Dickens, Charles 257
Diego de Deza 13
Divara, widow of Jan Matthys 113–14
Dobroliubov, Nikolai Aleksandrovich 355
Drummond of Hawthornden, William 249
Ducas, Demetrius 17–18
Duns Scotus 19, 60
Duque del Infantado 9
Durando, General 331
Dürer, Albrecht 84, 89, 106–7

Eck, Johann 54, 99, 143, 145–6, 150, 153–6, 161, 165–9
Edward VI 133, 140, 192–3, 197, 200, 202, 213, 220, 222–3
Egmond, Nicholas 78
El Cid 5
Elizabeth I 210, 212, 220, 227, 232–4
'Elsmere, Robert' 259
Enno, Count 182, 184
Erasmus, Desiderius vii–viii, 2, 11–12, 17, 19, 32, 45, 52–85
and Augustine, St. 54

and Bucer 129–30, 134
and Calvin 65, 84–5
and Catholic historians 84, 147–9
and Complutensian Polyglot Bible 39, 65–7, 76
and Henry VIII 216–17
humanism of, *see philosophia Christi*
and Jerome, St. 53–8, 63–4, *see also* publications
and Laski, Jan 173, 175–8, 180–1, 183, 188–90, 194–5, 198
and Laski, Jaroslav 174–5
and Luther 65–6, 73, 78–80, 84–5
philosophia Christi 46, 52, 54, 79–83
publications
    Adagia 67, 72, 78, 80
    Annotations see *New Testament*
    Annotations of Valla 38, 56, 63, 66
    Ciceronianus 53–4
    Colloquia 80
    De Libero Arbitrio 56, 73, 84
    De Recta Pronuntiatone Dialogus 64
    Enchiridion 65, 80, 194
    Hyperaspites 78
    Jerome, Life of 58–61, *Works* 61, 64
    Moriae Encomium 65, 80, 356
    New Testament (1516) 43, 53, 57, 64, 67–77
        Annotations to 53–57, 67–79
        criticisms of 75–8
        Latin text 66–7, 70–72
        Greek text 56–7, 67–9
        Paraclesis 58, 71, 82–3
        prefaces 71
        Ratio seu Methodus 53, 71–3, 82
    New Testament (1519) 74, 77–8
    New Testament *Paraphrases* 77, 80, 84
    Querela Pacis 80, 82
and Strasbourg 90, 115–17
and trilingual studies 53, 61–3
and Valla 56–7, 66
and Vergara 21, 45
and Vulgate 70–2, 74–5
and Zúñiga (Stunica) 20, 23, 76–7
Estienne, Robert 35, 66

Farel, Guillaume 123, 155, 186
Feize, Chancellor of Hesse 157, 161
Felipe de la Torre 29
Ferdinand I of Austria and Hungary 149,
    153, 179, 181
Ferdinand V of Castile 3–6, 12, 28
Feyken, Hille 114
Field, Richard 253
Fisher, Christopher 57
Fleetwood, General 254
Foligno, Angela de 14
Fonseca I, Alonso de, Archbishop of
    Seville 22
Fonseca III, Alfonso de, Archbishop of
    Toledo 29, 31
Fox, George 238–9, 249
Foxe, John 70, 208, 215, 218, 230, 235
Foxe, Richard, Bishop 53
Francis of Assisi, St. 3
Francis I 10, 12, 81, 151, 166, 168, 170–1,
    175, 180
Franck, Sebastian 119
Frederick the Wise, Elector of Saxony
    97, 103, 146
Freeman (US Consul) 350
Froben, John 57, 58, 64, 67–8, 177
Fuller, Thomas 244–6

Galeoto, Marcio 22
Gardiner, Stephen, Bishop 208, 213, 218,
    223–4
Garibaldi, Giuseppe 316–17, 331, 334–8,
    342, 345, 349–50
Gavazzi, Alessandro viii, 313–63
    anti-Catholicism of
        in England 350–7
        in Italy 347–9
    Barnabite friar 323–8
    and Bassi, Ugo 322, 324, 328–9, 331,
        333, 344–5, 350–1
    biographies of 314, 320–2
    brothers 333
    and Free Church of Italy 318, 348–9,
        353, 357, 362–3
    and Garibaldi 331, 334–6, 342, 345,
        349–50
    and Gregory XVI, Pope 325–8, 337,
        339, 358–61
    life
        in England 350–7
        in Italy, 1847–9 329–36
        influences on, pre-1847 343–6

and Pius IX, Pope 317, 321, 325,
    328–36, 338, 342, 345, 348–52,
    358
and Risorgimento 337–46
and Wiseman, Cardinal 351, 358–60
writings
    Autobiografia 314, 318–20
    La Favola del Viaggio di S. Pietro a
        Roma 358
    My Recollections of the Last Four
        Popes 358–61
    No Union with Rome 358, 361–2
    Orations 352
    other works 324, 326–8, 348
Geiler, Johann 116–17
George II 288
Gerard, Cornelius 54–6
Gerbel, Nicholas 69, 117, 131
Geree, John 248
Giannone, Pietro 340
Gildon, Charles E. 257
Gilles, Peter 67
Gioberti, Vincenzo 325, 332, 340–2,
    345
Giustiniani, Paolo 160
Glapion, John 217
Glarean (Glareanus), Heinrich 177
Glanvill, Joseph 297
Godolphin, Sidney Godolphin, 1st
    Earl of 267, 276
Gomez de Castro, Alvar 1, 5, 10,
    12, 24–5, 45
Gonzalo, Gil 9
Gorca, Lukas de 182
Goya 300
Grajal, Gaspar de 46
Granvelle, Bishop 143–4, 154–6,
    158–9, 161, 167
Grafton, Richard 243–4
Gray, Thomas 92
Greenham, Richard 253
Greenwood, John 247
Gregory XIII, Pope 49–50
Gregory XVI, Pope 325–8, 337,
    339, 358–61
Greverade (person unknown) 55–6
Grimani, Cardinal Domenico 68
Grindal, Edmund 234
Gropper, Johann 144, 154, 156–63,
    165–6, 168, 170
Grotius, Hugo 85, 231
Gualter, Rudolph 234

Gustavus Vasa (Gustavus I of
  Sweden) 216
Guzmán, Hernán Núñez de (*El
  Comendador Griego,
  Fernandi Puntiani or El
  Pinciano*) 11, 18–20, 23, 26,
  40

Hamilton, Duke of 274
Hamilton, Patrick 215
'Hans the Drummer' 98
Hardenberg, Albert 181–4, 188, 192,
  195, 201, 203
Harley, Robert 258, 267, 269, 272–8
Hastings, Sir Francis 241
Hedio, Caspar 117
Helwys, Thomas 247–8, 253
Henry VIII 81, 208, 212–13, 215–17,
  220–2, 225, 231, 234, 298
Henry, Patrick 335
Hepburn, John 273
Hermann, Archbishop of Cologne 136,
  140, 158, 225
Hermonymous of Sparta, George 62
Hernández, Francisca 45
Herrera, Hernando Alonso de 11
Hesse, Landgrave Philip of 144, 150, 153,
  156, 158–9
Heylin, Peter 252
Hilles, Richard 226
Hobbes, Thomas 295–6, 298, 300
Hofmann, Melchior 108–11, 119, 184,
  187
Hooker, Richard 122, 211–12, 305
Hooper, John, Bishop 172, 176, 201,
  213–14, 235
Horne, Robert 234
Hosius, Stanislas, Bishop 180–1
Hugh of St. Clair 35
Humanism, biblical vii–viii, 117 *see also*
  Erasmus, *philosophia Christi*
  Jiménez de Cisneros, Cardinal
Humphrey, Laurence 241
Huss, John 116, 211
Hutten, Ulrich von 58

Ignatius Loyola, St. 15
Ildefonso, San 8
Illyricus, Flacius 145
Inquisition 5, 15, 16, 17, 27–9, 44–6,
  48, 50
Isabella, Queen 3–4, 6, 22

James II 299, 302
James VI and I 234, 239, 248
Jan of Leiden (Jan Beukels *or*
  Bockelzoon) 109–14
Jeffreys, Judge 258
Jerome, St. 23, 31–2, 39, 41–2, 45, 53–61,
  63–4, 68, 72, 76, 78, 82
Jiménez de Cisneros, Cardinal vii–viii,
  1–51
  and biblical humanism 8, declines
    after his death 44–51
  church reformer 3–4
  and Complutensian Polyglot Bible
    biblical studies for 13
    editing 14–15, 32–35
    editors *see* Guzmán, Hernán
      Núñez de; Nebrija,
      Antonio de; Vergara, Juan
      de; Zamora, Alfonso de;
      Zúñiga, Diego López de
    project origin 12
    publication 42 *see also* Antwerp,
      Polyglot Bible of
    texts used 35–41
    typography 41–2
    and Vulgate 14, 20, 31–3, 39–41
  early life 2–3
  death 43
  Inquisitor General 5–6, 19
  and Moors 5–6
  personal character 6–7
  Regent of Spain 4–5
  and university of Alcalá de Henares
    (Complutum) 1, 7–11
Jiménez, Juan 11
Joachim of Fiore 113
John, Count 185
John, Elector of Saxony 233
John a Lasco *see* Laski, Jan
John Frederick I, Elector of Saxony
  153–4, 170, 216
John of the Cross, St. 15
John Paul II, Pope 170
Johnson, Samuel 286–7, 306
Jonas, Justus 147, 223–4, 226
Jonson, Ben 249
Jowett, Benjamin 363
Joris, David 187
Joye, George 218–19
Jud, Leo 219

Kautz, Jakob 132

Keble, John 361
Kimhi, David 30
King, William, Archbishop 281, 285
Kissack, R. 323
Knipperdolling, Bernard 110–11, 113–14
Knox, John 126, 194, 201, 205, 215, 234
Krzycki, Andrzej 175, 181

Lambert, François 230
Lambert, John 209
Lambruschini, Cardinal Luigi 324–6, 359
Lambruschini, Raffaele 324, 344
Lamennais, H. F. R de 324, 337–9, 341–2, 344–7
Landor, Walter Savage 323
Lang, Cosmo Gordon 363
La Rochefoucauld, François, 6th Duc de 298
Lascaris, Joannes 61–2
Laski, Jan, Archbishop of Gniezno 172–4, 176, 178–80
Laski, Jan (John a Lasco), Protestant Reformer vii, 171–207
  brothers see Laski, Jaroslav and Laski, Stanislas
  church, doctrine of 185–90, 193–201 see also works
  and church in Emden 182, 184–90, 195–201, 203 see also works, Epitome
  and church in Poland 204–7
  and Church of the Strangers, London 192–3, 200, 202 see also works, Forma ac Ratio
  early life 172–3
  and English Reformation 190–1
  Iuramentum, oath affirming Catholic beliefs 183–4
  marriages 182, 202
  ordination 174
  and Reformers
    Calvin 187–90, 194–5, 197–200, 202, 204
    Erasmus 173, 175–8, 180–3, 188–90, 194–5, 198
    Luther 175, 187–9, 194, 204
    Melanchthon 181–2, 187, 189, 194, 197, 204
    Zwingli 171, 178, 185, 187, 189, 198–9

  uncle see Laski, Jan, Archbishop of Gniezno
  works
    Catechism 189, 193
    Confession 193
    Epitome 188–9, 193–4, 196
    Forma ac Ratio 193, 198, 201, 203, 205
Laski, Jaroslav, father of Jan Laski 173
Laski, Jaroslav (Jerome), brother of Jan Laski 173–6, 179–80, 182
Laski, Stanislas, brother of Jan Laski 173, 179, 190
Latimer, Hugh, Bishop 213
Latomus, Bartholomew 146
Laud, William, Archbishop 231–2, 245, 252, 288, 302
Leder, Lucas 100
Lee, Edward 75–6
Lefèvre d'Etaples, Jacques 20, 63, 68, 175
Leo X, Pope 13, 32–3, 37, 42–3, 58, 62, 68, 71, 76, 81, 106
Leo XII, Pope 324
León, Luis de 16, 46, 48
Leopardi, Giacomo 322, 328
Leopardi, Count Maldonado 328
Leopold I 331
Lerma, Pedro de 9, 46
Link, Wenzeslaus 105
Little, Fr. Knox 346
Llull, Raymond 14
Locke, John 296, 298
Lockhart, George 273–4
López de Toro, José 45
Lorena, Nicolas de 51
Lucena, Juan de 17
Lund, Archbishop of 152
Luther, Martin vii, 88, 96–100, 103–4, 106, 108, 144–8, 238
  and Bucer 118–19, 127, 129–30
  and Calvin 125–6, 215
  and Contarini 148, 160
  and English Reformation 208, 210–16, 218–21, 223, 225–8, 230–1, 233, 235
  and Erasmus 65–6, 73, 78–80, 84–5
  and Laski 175, 187–9, 194, 204
  and Regensburg Colloquy 158–60, 163, 168

and Wittenberg 86, 96–7
and Zwingli 89, 121

Macaulay, Lord, 237, 256
MacDougall, J. 347
McDougall, J. R. 363
Machiavelli, Niccolo 101, 306, 340, 346
Mackonochie, Alexander Heriot, Fr. 346
Mahony, Francis ('Father Prout') 351–2, 356
Mameli, Goffredo 363
Manin, Daniele 333
Manning, Cardinal 330, 361
Manríquez, Rodríguez 44
Mansfeld, Count 191
Manutius, Aldus 61, 67
Manzoni, Alessandro 339, 341–2
Margarita, Count Solaro della 325
Mariana, Juan de, S.J. 50
Marlborough, John Churchill, 1st Duke of 268
Marpeck, Pilgram 119
'Marprelate, Martin' 241, 246
Marshall, William 219, 225
Martínez de Cantalapiedra, Martin 46–7
Martyr, Peter (Pietro Martire Vermigli) 190–1, 202, 211–12
Mary, Queen 202, 231, 234
Masius, Andreas 49
Mastai, Count Giuseppe 328–9
Matamoros, Alfonso García 45
Mather, Cotton 242
Matthys, Jan 109–11
Maximilian I, Emperor 43, 54, 95
Mazzini, Giuseppe 316, 335, 339–41, 344–7, 356, 360
Medina, Bartolomé de 47–8
Meghen, Peter 67
Melanchthon, Philipp 63, 98, 144, 146–8
see also Augsburg Confession
and Cranmer 147, 191, 229
and English Reformation 210–11, 220, 223, 225, 229–32
and Laski 181–2, 187, 189, 194, 197, 204
and Regensburg Colloquy 147–8, 153–6, 166–8
Mena, Juan de 18
Metternich, Prince Clemens Lothar Wendel 337, 342
Micronius, Martin 193, 203
Milton, John 239, 243, 251

Miranda, Sancho Carranza de 11
Mist, Nathaniel 267, 279
Molesworth, Robert 281
Molyneux, William 296
Moncur, John 277
Monmouth, Duke of 260, 262
Monmouth, Humphry 230
Montaigne 297–8, 307
Montalembert, C. R. F 348
Morales, Antonio de 11
More, St. Thomas 53, 58, 81, 84, 134, 217, 297
Morone, Giovanni, Bishop 152, 154–5, 159, 161, 164–5
Morton, Charles 258–9
Mountague, Richard, Bishop 231
Müntzer, Thomas 103
Muratori, Lodovico Antonio 340
Murner, Thomas 146
Myconius, Friedrich 97

Napoleon III 348
Nausea, Friedrich, Bishop 156
Neal, Daniel 242
Nebrija, Antonio de 2, 7–8, 11–14, 16–26, 40–1, 44
Nelson, Horatio, Viscount 359
Niccolini, G. B. 320, 347
Nicholas of Lyra 31, 33, 80
Nichols, J. 282
Nottingham, Daniel, 2nd Earl of 263
Noviomagus (Lutheran) 203

Oates, Titus 259
Oecolampadius, John 64, 69, 84, 86, 90, 177–8, 181, 183, 185, 195, 214, 230
Oliván, Pérez de 11
Oppizoni, Cardinal 333
Orange, William of 260, 262–3
Origen 80, 82
Orosius, Paulus 59
Osiander, Andreas 154, 226, 228, 231
Owen, John 290
Oxford, Robert Harley, 1st Earl of 285–6

Pablo Parisio, Pedro 27
Padula, Vincenzo 349
Pagnini, Santi 29, 47–8, 50
Palermo, Archbishop of 130
Palmerston, Henry John Temple, 3rd Viscount 332, 351–2

Palmerston, Henry John Temple, 3rd
    Viscount 332, 351–2
Pardo, Miguel 11
Parker, Henry 240, 242, 251
Parker, Archbishop Matthew 229
Patella, Ovidio Filippo 349
Patuzzi, Giuseppe 344
Paul III, Pope 27, 144, 149–50, 153, 159,
    166, 169
Peel, Sir Robert 356
Pellican, Conrad 64, 177, 219, 230
Penry, John 247, 251
Pepys, Samuel 248–9
Perkins, William 250–1, 253
Petrarch 346
Philip II 43–4, 49–50
Pflug, Julius 154, 161, 168
Pirckheimer, Willibald 77
Pistorius (Pistoris), Simon 161, 167
Pius II, Pope 7
Pius VII, Pope 345
Pius IX, Pope 317, 321, 325, 328–36,
    338, 342, 345, 348–52, 358
Pius XII, Pope 10
Plantin, Christopher 43–4
Plato 63, 134–5, 311
Platonists, Cambridge 297
Poggio, Giovanni, Bishop 153–4
Pole, Cardinal 152, 166, 342
Pope, Alexander 257, 280, 287
Porteous, Captain John 273
Preston, John 251
Prosper of Aquitaine 59
Pucci, Antony 71
Puritanism viii, 237–54, 290, 295, 302–4
Pusey, Edward Bouverie 346, 361–3

Quevedo 15
Quiñones 227
Quirini, Cardinal 166

Rabelais, François 292
Radetsky, Count Johann Joseph 330–1
Radziwill, Nicholas 204
Rainaldus, Odoric 166
Ramée, Pierre de la (Ramus) 48
Ramírez, Clemente 11
Ramírez, Miguel 27
Reál, Alfonso de Alcalá de 21
Regensburg, Colloquy of 142–70
Regensburg Book 161–9
Remigius (Remi of Auxerre) 25

Reuchlin, Johannes 30, 33, 64, 67, 69,
    181
Ribera, Francisco 51
Rhegius, Urbanus 230–1
Rhenanus, Beatus 19, 67, 117, 129,
    177
Ricci, Scipione, Bishop 338–9
Richelieu, Cardinal 269
Ridley, Nicholas 172, 191–3, 198
Rinçón, Antonio 180
Robinson, John 249, 251–2
Rochester, John Wilmot, Earl of 265
Rogerius, Servatius 67
Rogers, John 220
Rosmini, Antonio 340, 342, 345
Rosners, Antoinette van 182
Rossetti, Gabriele 346
Rossi, Pellegrino, Count 335
Rothmann, Bernhard 109–14
Rous, Francis 250
Rufinus, Tyrannius 59–60
Ruskin, John 351
Russell, Odo 331–2
'Rutherford, Mark' 259
Rutherford, Samuel 214
Rymer, Thomas 192

Sacheverell, Henry 263
Sacchi, Abbot of Salerno 349
Sachs, Hans 106
Sadoleto, Jacopo 54, 144, 342
Salmerón, Alfonso 51
Sanfelice, Bishop of Cava 48
Sarcerius, Erasmus 223, 231
Sardo, Paolo 349
Sarpi, Paolo 143, 346
Savonarola, Girolamo 14, 98
Saxony, Duke George of 97, 100, 150
Saxony, Duke Henry of 150
Saxony, Electors of
    Frederick the Wise 97, 103, 146
    John 233
    John Frederick I 153–4, 170, 216
Scheurl, Christoph 107
Schomberg, Duke of 287
Schwenkfeld, Caspar 119
Schwebel, J. 131
Seckendorf, Veit Ludwig von 143
Seripando, Gerolamo 48
Severus 59
Seymour, Edward, Lord Protector 208
    see also Somerset, Duke of

Shaftesbury, Anthony Ashley Cooper,
    3rd Earl of 284, 295, 311
Shakespeare, William 237, 241
Sharp, Archbishop James 278, 282
Sickingen, Franz von 118, 131
Sículo, Lucio Marineo 16–17
Sigismund I, of Poland 173, 180–1
Sigismund II, of Poland 203–4
Sigüenza, José de 21
Silvani, Antonio 344
Simon, Richard 290
Simons, Menno 187, 190
Sleidan, John (Johannes Sleidanus) 143,
    156
Smedley, Dean 281–2
Somerset, Duchess of 282, 301
Somerset, Duke of 191
Soto, Dominic de 47
Southey, Robert 351
Speier, Archbishop of 131
Spence Watson, Dr. 355
Spengler, Lazarus 86, 106
Spenser, Edmund 241
Sprat, Thomas 292–3
Spurgeon, Charles Haddon 237
Standish, Henry 75
Standish, Miles (Myles) 242
Stankar, Franciszek 206
Staupitz, Johann 106, 146
Stella (Esther Johnson) 285–6, 295
Stewart, R. 347
Stillingfleet, Edward 297
Stopford, James 285
Stow, John 243–4
Stunica see Zúñiga, Diego López de
Sturm, Jacob 117, 155, 157–8
Sturm, Johann 161
Strype, John 230, 234–5
Swift, John 287
Swift, Jonathan viii, 255, 280–312
    Dean of St. Patrick's, Dublin 281–2,
        287
    not irreligious 280–1, 283–4
    as parish priest 286
    and philosophy 291, 295–6, 298
    and politics 289–91
    and science 292–4
    and Stella (Esther Johnson) 285–6, 295
    works
        An Argument against Abolishing
            Christianity 300–1, 307–8
        The Battle of the Books 292

Concerning the Universal Hatred
    which Prevails against the
    Clergy 298, 308
The Drapier's Letters 310
An Essay on the Fates of Clergyman
    280
Gulliver's Travels 280, 292–3, 296,
    306, 309
Legion Club 283
A Letter to a Young Gentleman
    lately entered into Holy
    Orders 307
Odes 283
    Ode to Dr. William Sancroft
        298
    Ode to Sir William Temple
        291
    On the Day of Judgement 294
A Project for the Advancement of
    Religion 284, 306
Reformation of Manners 306
Remarks upon a Book 298, 304–5
The Sentiments of a Church of
    England Man 305
Sermons 286, 301–4, 308–12
    Causes of the Wretched
        Condition of Ireland 310
    Doing Good 310
    The Duty of Mutual Subjection
        306, 311
    On Brotherly Love 304, 309–10
    On the Excellency of Christianity
        308, 311–12
    On False Witness 310
    On the Martyrdom of Charles I
        303–4, 309
    On Sleeping in Church 307–8
    On the Testimony of a Good
        Conscience 306, 309,
        311–12
    On the Trinity 311
    The Poor Man's Contentment
        311
The Tale of a Tub 281–4, 295, 301,
    304
Thoughts on Various Subjects 298
Tracts 303
Swift, Kit 287
Swift, Mead 287
Swift, Thomas 290
Swinburne, Algernon Charles 316
Symmachus 38

Talavera, Hernando de 3–4, 6
Tasso 346
Tauler, John 116–17
Tavera, Juan, Inquisitor General 27
Taverner, Richard 223, 230
Temple, Sir William 288–9, 291–2, 299
Teresa of Avila, St. 15–16
Thackeray, William Makepeace 283, 351
Theodosius, Emperor 284
Theodotion 38
Theophylact of Bulgaria 75
Thomas à Kempis, 79, 117
Tindal, Matthew 299, 304
Toledo, Archbishop of 2, 9
Tomiczki, Piotr, Bishop 174–5
Tommaseo, Niccolo 346
Toro, Alonso de 7
Traheron, Bartholomew 191
Travers, Walter 251
Troeltsch, Ernst 238
Truytje, wife of Hardenberg 188, 190
Tunstall, Cuthbert, Bishop 70
Tutchin, John 260
Turner, William 191
Tyndale, William 209–10, 213, 215, 218–19, 230

Ugdulena, Gregorio 350
Ussher, Archbishop James 141
Utenhove, Charles 176, 179
Utenhove, John 179, 202–3

Valla, Lorenzo 23, 38, 56–7, 63, 66, 68
Vallejo, Juan de 5, 7, 12
Vatable, François 48
Veltwyk 157–8, 161, 168
Ventura 337
Vergara, Francisco de 21
Vergara, Juan de 20–1, 40, 45
Vergerio, Pietro Paolo, Bishop 154
Vico, Giovanni Battista 340
Villacreces, Pedro de 3
Villar del Say y Loranca 11
Vincent Ferrer, St. 14
Vinet, Alexandre 348
Viret, Pierre 123
Virués, Alonso de 45
Vitoria, Francisco de 47
Vives, Luis 44
Volprecht, Wolfgang 226
Voltaire 288, 294

Waldeck, Franz von 108–9, 112
Walsingham, Sir Francis 267
Walton, Brian, Bishop 37, 290
Warham, William, Archbishop of Canterbury 56, 58, 71, 175, 218
Watson, John 72
Wauchope 156
Wesley, John 235, 309
Wesley, Samuel 263
Westphal, Joachim 192, 195, 202
Wettstein, Johann Jakob 38
Weyer, Van de 331
Widdowes, Giles 242
Whitgift, Archbishop John 211, 253
Wigginton, Giles 247
Williams, Roger 126
Wilson, Thomas, Bishop 285
Wimpfeling, Jacob 68, 117
Wiseman, Cardinal 318, 351, 358–61
Witt, Jan de 273
Wittenberg, Elector of 98, 144
Wolsey, Cardinal 218
Wullenwever, Jürgen 104

Ximenes de Cisneros, Francisco see Jiménez de Cisneros, Cardinal
Ximenes de Cisneros, García 6–7

Zaccaria, Antonio 326
Zamora, Alfonso de 11, 21, 25–7, 29–33, 36–7, 40, 42, 44
Zamora, Juan de 26
Zapolya, John 179–80
Zasius, Ulrich 72
Zayas, Gabriel de 50
Zell, Matthew 117
Ziegler, Clement 119
Zucchi, General 335
Zúñiga, Diego López de (Stunica) 14, 20, 23, 38, 40, 65–6, 76–7
Zúñiga, Juan de 22
Zwingli, Ulrich 118, 123, 214–15, 230
and Erasmus 81, 84
and Laski 171, 178, 185, 187, 189, 198–9
and Luther 89, 121
and Ulm 102–3
and Zürich 86, 90–1, 102, 120